13th Edition

Keeping Your School Safe & Secure:

A Practical Guide

- Bullying
- Crisis Management
- Weapons
- Intruders
- Drugs & Alcohol
- Student Searches

CEEL
Center for
Education & Employment Law

Center for Education & Employment Law
P.O. Box 3008
Malvern, Pennsylvania 19355

First edition 2007
Thirteenth edition 2019
Printed in the United States of America.

ISBN 978-1-944331-23-8

Published 2019 by: Center for Education & Employment Law

Library of Congress Control Number: 2008937927

Cover Design by Jen Erb

Other Titles Published By
Center for Education & Employment Law:

K-12 Education Law in America
Higher Education Law in America
Private School Law in America
Students with Disabilities and Special Education Law
Deskbook Encyclopedia of Public Employment Law
Deskbook Encyclopedia of Employment Law

TABLE OF CONTENTS

CHAPTER TWO

Emergency Preparedness and Response

CHAPTER THREE

School Safety and Liability

CHAPTER FOUR

Campus Law Enforcement

CHAPTER FIVE

Employment

CHAPTER SIX

Extracurricular Activities

TABLE OF CONTENTS

CHAPTER SEVEN

Health Issues

INTRODUCTION

We are excited to introduce this updated edition of ***Keeping Your School Safe & Secure: A Practical Guide***. Designed for the busy education professional, this easy-to-use resource presents a unique combination of materials designed to help administrative professionals formulate and implement a comprehensive plan to keep schools a safe place to learn. Case summaries, source materials, forms, checklists and practical guidance are organized into chapters by subject area for easy reference. A comprehensive index and case tables make it easy to quickly find the information you need.

We are now providing all forms in an easily accessible online format to make them more customizable and convenient than ever.

School security and related issues continue to predominate the education landscape. Rely on ***Keeping Your School Safe & Secure: A Practical Guide*** with confidence as a valuable tool to avoid legal liability and protect the health and safety of your students.

ABOUT THE EDITORS

Curt J. Brown is the editorial director of the Center for Education & Employment Law. Prior to assuming his present position, he gained extensive experience in business-to-business publishing, including management of well-known publications such as *What's Working in Human Resources, What's New in Benefits & Compensation, Keep Up to Date with Payroll, Supervisors Legal Update,* and *Facility Manager's Alert.* Mr. Brown graduated from Villanova School of Law and graduated magna cum laude from Bloomsburg University with a B.S. in Business Administration. He is admitted to the Pennsylvania bar.

James A. Roth is the editor of *K-12 Legal Notes for Education* and *Special Education Law Update*. He is a co-author of *Students with Disabilities and Special Education Law* and an adjunct program assistant professor at St. Mary's University in Minnesota. Mr. Roth is a graduate of the University of Minnesota and William Mitchell College of Law. He is admitted to the Minnesota bar.

Thomas D'Agostino is a managing editor at the Center for Education & Employment Law and is the editor of the *Higher Education Legal Alert* newsletter. He graduated from the Duquesne University School of Law and received his undergraduate degree from Ramapo College of New Jersey. He is a past member of the American Bar Association's Section of Individual Rights and Responsibilities as well as the Pennsylvania Bar Association's Legal Services to Persons with Disabilities Committee. Mr. D'Agostino is admitted to the Pennsylvania bar.

Elizabeth A. Wheeler is editor of the monthly newsletter *Private Education Law Report* and the *Private School Law in America* deskbook. She's also a contributing editor for the *Higher Education Legal Alert* newsletter. A graduate of Macalester College and Capital University Law School, she's a member of the Massachusetts bar. Before joining the Center for Education and Employment Law, she was a legal editor for a South Boston publisher, where she edited employment law and education law newsletters.

Carol Warner is the editor of *School Safety & Security Alert* and *Higher Education Law in America.* She's also a contributing editor for *Higher Education Legal Update* and *K-12 Legal Notes for Education.* Before joining the Center for Education & Employment Law, she was an editor for two employment law newsletters: *What's Working in Human Resources* and *What's New in Benefits & Compensation.* Ms. Warner is a graduate of The New York Institute of Technology and holds a Bachelor of Arts in English with an emphasis in professional writing.

HOW TO USE YOUR GUIDE BOOK

We have designed ***Keeping Your School Safe & Secure: A Practical Guide*** in an accessible format for both attorneys and non-attorneys to use as a research and reference tool toward prevention of legal problems.

Research Tool

As a research tool, our guide book allows you to conduct your research on two different levels – by topics or cases.

Topic Research

- If you have a general interest in a particular **topic** area, our **table of contents** provides descriptive chapter headings containing detailed subheadings from each chapter.
  - For your convenience, we also include the chapter table of contents at the beginning of each chapter.

Example:

For information on Autism, the table of contents indicates that a discussion of this topic begins in Chapter Seven on page 347:

CHAPTER SEVEN
Health Issues

♦ If you have a specific interest in a particular **issue**, our comprehensive **index** collects all of the relevant page references to particular issues.

Example:

For information on entranceway security, the index provides references to all of the text dealing with building security instead of only the text dealing with entranceways:

Case Research

♦ If you know the **name** of a particular case, our **table of cases** will allow you to quickly reference the location of the case.

Example:

If someone mentioned a case named *Fennell v. Marion Independent School Dist.,* looking in the table of cases, which has been arranged alphabetically, the case would be located under the "F" section.

✓ Each of the cases summarized in the guide book also contains the case citation, which will allow you to access the full text of the case if you would like to learn more about it. *See How to Read a Case Citation, p. 413.*

- If your interest lies in cases from a **particular state**, our **table of cases by state** will identify the cases from your state and direct you to their page numbers.

Example:

If cases from California are of interest, the table of cases by state, arranged alphabetically, lists all of the case summaries contained in the guide book from California.

→ **CALIFORNIA**

American Nurses Ass'n v. Torlakson, 335
Broney v. California Comm'n on Teacher Credentialing, 317
C.A. v Los Angeles Unified School Dist., 245
C.B. v. City of Sonora, 204
C.G. v. Glendale Unified School Dist., 238
Camfield v. Board of Trustees of Redondo Beach Unified School Dist., 39, 118
Chavez v. Martinez, 199
Corales v. Bennett, 370

✓ Remember, the judicial system has two court systems – state and federal court – which generally function independently from each other. *See The Judicial System, p. 409.* We have included the federal court cases in the table of cases by state according to the state in which the court resides. However, federal court decisions often impact other federal courts within that particular circuit. Therefore, it may be helpful to review cases from all of the states contained in a particular circuit.

We hope you benefit from the use of ***Keeping Your School Safe & Secure: A Practical Guide***. If you have any questions about how to use the guide book, please contact Thomas D'Agostino at tdagostino@pbp.com.

TABLE OF CASES

A

B

C

D

TABLE OF CASES

I

J

K

S

TABLE OF CASES BY STATE

CONNECTICUT

DELAWARE

DISTRICT OF COLUMBIA

FLORIDA

GEORGIA

HAWAII

IDAHO

ILLINOIS

INDIANA

IOWA

KANSAS

KENTUCKY

LOUISIANA

MAINE

MARYLAND

MASSACHUSETTS

MICHIGAN

MINNESOTA

MISSISSIPPI

MISSOURI

MONTANA

NEBRASKA

NEVADA

NEW HAMPSHIRE

NEW JERSEY

NEW MEXICO

NEW YORK

NORTH CAROLINA

NORTH DAKOTA

OHIO

OKLAHOMA

OREGON

PENNSYLVANIA

SOUTH CAROLINA

TENNESSEE

TEXAS

UTAH

VERMONT

VIRGINIA

WASHINGTON

WEST VIRGINIA

WISCONSIN

WYOMING

CHAPTER ONE

Access and Building Security

Page

I. INTRODUCTION

An important key to maintaining school safety and security is controlling access to school facilities. A variety of tools are available to help schools ensure that access to school facilities is gained only by authorized personnel. A one-size-fits-all approach to controlling school access is inappropriate. Although some issues relating to school access are common to most schools, an individualized assessment must be undertaken to determine which specific security steps are best-suited for your particular facility.

Several factors should be taken into consideration when determining how best to ensure safe access to school facilities. These include:

- the grades that the school serves
- the layout of the school campus
- the enrollment level
- the location of the school (e.g., urban vs. suburban or rural), and
- the crime level in the neighborhood where the school is located.

Access control should be viewed as an important component of a comprehensive security program that makes schools a less attractive target to intruders and safer overall. This can be referred to as "hardening" of your school. An effective way to harden your school is to layer security measures, including the following, courtesy of Brad Spicer, the CEO of SafePlans in Missouri:

- Build strong relationships with local police and fire departments. Have a contact person you can call for help with questions.
- Bring in a fresh set of eyes to take a look at your security plans. Doing so may help you spot an overlooked hazard.
- Know who is in your building by controlling access. Systems can alert officials when doors are left propped open or unlocked.
- Provide training on situational awareness to staffers.

II. ENVIRONMENTAL DESIGN

It is important to note the value of incorporating environmental design elements that ensure school safety and security to the maximum extent possible. While this is a benefit that can be most fully utilized by incorporating environmental design principles into new facilities at the design stage, some of these design elements can also be incorporated into existing school campuses. In addition, expansion and reconstruction plans create a valuable opportunity to increase school safety by incorporating environmental design elements that take school safety into account. In all of these cases, the likelihood of crime can be reduced via an effective use of the school's physical environment.

A. Crime Prevention Through Environmental Design

An approach to increasing safety called Crime Prevention Through Environmental Design (CPTED) recognizes the important role that the design of the built environment can play in reducing the risk of criminal activity. CPTED is not intended to replace traditional crime prevention approaches. Instead, it should be thought of as a complementary tool that can be incorporated into an overall comprehensive plan to make schools safer.

The CPTED approach incorporates several concepts that are applied to increase the security level of the studied facility. The approach has been used to provide an increased measure of security at facilities such as government buildings, commercial complexes and parks. Although not originally developed specifically with schools in mind, the approach is particularly useful in school settings, partly because application of its principles can substantially increase the safety of school premises while preserving a welcoming environment and avoiding a prison-like atmosphere. CPTED is also relatively cost-effective.

CPTED has a strong record of success. The Broward County, Florida school district experienced a dramatic reduction in crime after implementing CPTED, and some state legislatures have mandated its use in schools.

The CPTED approach involves several discrete components, including natural surveillance, natural access control, and territoriality.

1. Natural Surveillance

The natural surveillance component of CPTED seeks to maximize the safety advantage that is gained when the environment's physical features keep obstacles to surveillance to a minimum and enable authorities to observe the facility's entire physical environment without undue interference and without a need to resort to advanced technological measures. Essentially, this component seeks to maximize the ability of authorities to observe the environment, in general, and especially higher-risk areas, such as parking lots and building entrances. Several potential barriers impede the ability to maximize surveillance capabilities, such as solid walls, overgrown shrubbery, and inadequate lighting.

2. Natural Access Control

Natural access control, a second important component of CPTED, refers to the benefit obtained by taking steps to design the facility's physical environment in a way that deters criminal activity by creating a perception of risk to potential offenders. This is accomplished, for example, by constructing the physical environment so that visitors are guided through the physical space of the facility by means of clear routing, signage, and other steering features.

3. Territorial Reinforcement

A third component of CPTED is territorial reinforcement. This component seeks to create an environment that encourages authorized users of the space to develop a sense of territoriality or ownership over the space. When users develop this sense of territoriality, potential offenders are discouraged from engaging in criminal activity. An example of a design feature that encourages territoriality is clear border definition.

Professional resources are available to aid schools in conducting a CPTED analysis. School personnel also can perform a CPTED analysis by undertaking a comprehensive study of criminal behavior and other misconduct that occurs on campus. Such a study can identify and categorize the types of problems that take place and ascertain whether patterns exist with respect to time and/or location. Ideally a comprehensive study will yield information that can be used to change the physical environment in a way that reduces the incidence of criminal behavior or other improper conduct.

4. Case Study: Effective Use of CPTED

The Broward County, Florida school district was one of the first in the country to effectively utilize CPTED concepts in the school environment. After completing an evaluation, the district applied a number of CPTED strategies. Based on the assessment, the district considered changes relating to vehicle access and border definition. It also considered relocating parking lots and replacing restroom entrance doors with open mazes. In addition, it evaluated strategies relating to the maintenance of landscaping and the effective use of lighting and color in and around school facilities. The district's use of CPTED techniques resulted in a significant reduction in school-related crime.

B. Specific Environmental Elements

The following are examples of ways in which schools can help prevent crime in the school environment by controlling specific environmental elements in ways that increase the security of entrance areas.

1. Entrances

A basic key to maintaining a safe school environment is controlling access to the school campus. The school campus should be designed (or redesigned) so that students and visitors must pass through a particular designated entrance or entrances. The school's main entrance should be the school entrance that is closest to the school's main parking lot. It should be clearly marked and in the front of the school near the administrative areas of the building. By locating the main entrance in this manner, visitors will be steered toward it and not to another less prominent entry point. In addition, main entry points should be located in areas of high visibility so people entering and exiting can be observed easily by school personnel. Glazing of windows and doors enhances the ability to conduct effective surveillance. Windows should be kept free of announcements and other postings that impede the ability to conduct effective surveillance of the entrance area. It is preferable for both the entrance area and the parking area to be observable from the school's administrative area. The entrance should be wide enough to minimize pedestrian traffic congestion during peak periods. For many schools, an opening of at least 20 feet will be required to enable smooth ingress and egress.

Minimizing the number of entry points is a critical key to maintaining building security. Providing just one entry point is not a feasible option for most schools and, in fact, can be counterproductive to the overall effort to maintain safety. Decisions relating to the number of entrance points that should be provided in addition to the main entrance must be made with reference to each school's particular characteristics, keeping in mind that it is desirable to maintain a number of entry points that allows for manageable ingress and egress without unnecessarily creating the added risk that each additional entrance point potentially represents. Secondary entrances are an area of particular concern, and they require special attention because they are often a problem area. Secondary entrances should be placed in visible locations and should be monitored. They should be subject to all the security controls that apply at the main entrance point.

☑ CHECKLIST – *Entrances*

- ☐ The main entrance is located close to the school's main parking lot.
- ☐ The main entrance is marked by clear and adequate signage.
- ☐ The main entrance and parking lot can be easily monitored by administrative personnel from inside the school building.
- ☐ Windows and doors near the main entrance include glazing.
- ☐ Windows are kept free of postings and other impediments to visibility.
- ☐ The entrance is wide enough to accommodate pedestrian traffic at peak times.
- ☐ The number of entrances is kept to a minimum.

- ☐ Signage steers visitors to a particular entrance.
- ☐ Secondary entrances are monitored.

2. Traffic Control/Parking

School parking areas require extra attention because they frequently are locations where vandalism and other crimes take place.

Access to the school and its parking areas should be controlled by limiting the number of entrance and exit points to campus. The number of access points to parking areas should be limited. This reduces the likelihood that the parking area will be perceived as a public space. Vandal-proof lighting in parking areas should be provided, and the use of gates to limit or prevent access to parking areas during low-use times should be considered.

Gates must be kept in good working order, and special care must be taken if students are in any way involved with their operation. In New York, an eighth-grader had his fingertips severed as he closed a parking lot gate. The student had been assigned to close the gate each day. A jury awarded him $600,000 after evidence showed three other students had suffered hand injuries involving the gate.

Controlling the flow of both vehicular and pedestrian traffic is of critical importance. Vehicular and pedestrian traffic should be routed in a manner that separates the two and minimizes congestion while also enabling easy observation. Where feasible, traffic lanes of ingress and egress should be separated by a landscaped median. In addition, automobile traffic should be separated from bus traffic once entry to the school campus is gained. Bus parking should be configured so that buses can maneuver the lot without needing to back up to park or turn. It is preferable to avoid long and straight stretches of roadway on the campus. Avoiding long straight stretches helps to keep down the speed of vehicles and reduce the risk of injury to pedestrians. Where appropriate, traffic-control devices, such as speed bumps, can help reduce the probability of vehicles traveling at excessive speeds on the school campus.

Visitor parking should be designated as such via proper signage, and signage should further define authorized uses within the parking area. The ability of students to gain access to parking areas at times other than arrival time and dismissal time should be restricted. In addition, parking areas and vehicular routes should be observable from a point or points within the building's interior that include administrative areas and/or classrooms.

It is necessary to maintain proper access routes for emergency service personnel. Service and delivery routes should be separated from other traffic routes.

☑ CHECKLIST – *Traffic Control/Parking*

- ☐ Vehicular routes and parking areas can be observed from administrative areas and/or classrooms inside the school.

- ☐ Access to parking areas is restricted to a limited number of entrances.
- ☐ Automobile traffic is separated from bus traffic by barriers and/or routing.
- ☐ Pedestrian traffic is separated from motor vehicle traffic by barriers and/or routing.
- ☐ Undesignated spaces within parking areas are minimized.
- ☐ Traffic control devices are used to control speeds as needed.
- ☐ Long, straight stretches of roadway are minimized.
- ☐ The parking area includes signage that sets out the authorized use of the assigned space.
- ☐ The parking area has vandal-resistant lighting.

3. Signage and Sightlines

Signage serves the dual role of helping to control access and providing notice of prohibited behavior.

The campus should include clear signage that directs all visitors to the school's main office, where they can be screened to make sure they have a legitimate reason to be on the campus. Preferably, the main entrance should be visible from both the administration area and main point of vehicular access.

Maintaining open sightlines is another important key to campus security. Building placement, landscaping, the placement of signage and lighting should all take into account the need to maintain open sightlines. This is especially true in higher-risk areas of the school campus, such as parking lots, pickup/drop-off points, bus stops, hallways and stairwells. These higher-risk areas can be identified by analyzing the school's incident history.

Borders within the school's campus should be clearly defined.

☑ CHECKLIST – *Signage*

- ☐ There is a sign or marquee that identifies the school by name and is visible from a point beyond the school's physical borders.
- ☐ Signs include large lettering.
- ☐ Signs are well lit.
- ☐ Directional signage is used as needed to control traffic flow.
- ☐ Signage directs visitors to a main point of entry.
- ☐ Signage does not create a place to hide.
- ☐ Signage does not block lines of sight.
- ☐ Signage indicates restricted areas.
- ☐ Signage indicates bus-loading and drop-off zones.

4. Preventing Roof Access

A number of steps can be taken to reduce the likelihood of unauthorized access to the roof of a campus building. Access to rooftop areas should be available only from inside the building, preferably from a locked point. Placement of landscaping and trees should not enable access to the roof of any building.

Covered walkways should be designed in a manner that does not create opportunities for unauthorized access to a building's roof or other upper-level area. In addition, if the campus includes columns that potentially could be scaled to gain unauthorized access to a roof or upper-level area, the columns should be made from smooth building materials. Alternatively, a slippery finish or coating should be applied to the columns. Campus walls and other architectural features should be designed in a manner that does not allow for footholds or handholds to create an ability to gain unauthorized roof access. Niches in exterior walls should be avoided or eliminated, as these can create hiding places for unauthorized and dangerous materials.

A failure to take proper steps to prevent unauthorized rooftop access can prove fatal. In Colorado, a teenager fell to his death while playing "Capture the Flag" with friends. The group went to a school on the weekend and climbed onto its roof. The boy tripped over a ledge and fell to his death.

5. Landscaping

As previously noted, landscaping should take into account the need to maintain open sightlines and to deny unauthorized access to rooftop areas. There are additional important points to keep in mind regarding the important role that landscaping can play in maintaining building security. It generally is advantageous to delineate space throughout the school campus both internally and externally. Delineating space as a defined area with a particular purpose helps to remove any perception that the space is available and open. It also makes it easier to assign security responsibilities for specific areas within a school's campus. One way to delineate space in the outside areas of a school campus is through the effective use of landscaping.

Landscaping can be used to define the outer boundaries of school property without the use of fences. Where fences are used, landscaping can be added to help create a more welcoming look while maintaining the security that the fences provide.

It is important to make sure landscaping is maintained so that it does not create hiding places. Shrubbery should be trimmed to a height of less than two feet. Tree canopies should be kept at a minimum height of eight feet, and hedges should be kept low enough to avoid serving as a hiding space. Controlling the growth of landscaping plants is also important to enabling clear lines of sight. Landscaping also can serve as a way to direct and control traffic, giving direction to vehicles and pedestrians, or limiting access to particular areas.

☑ CHECKLIST – *Landscaping*

- ☐ The school's landscape design does not create hiding places.
- ☐ The school's landscape design maintains open sightlines.
- ☐ The school's landscaping is well maintained and is not overgrown.
- ☐ The school's landscaping does not block lighting.
- ☐ Shrubbery is kept at a maximum height of less than two feet.
- ☐ Tree canopies are trimmed to a minimum height of eight feet.

For an additional, more general checklist addressing the assessment of grounds and buildings, see form 92.

III. TRAINING AND EDUCATION

School staff, students and parents all play an important role in preventing criminal activity that results from unauthorized access. Staff should be trained to intercept strangers and to report them to administration if they do not feel safe approaching a stranger on campus. Students should be instructed not to open doors or otherwise enable access by strangers. Students also should be instructed that they are not to assist other students in circumventing prescribed access procedures or routes. Parents should be provided with detailed information regarding the access control strategies the school utilizes. Parents need to understand the importance of following the school's rules and procedures governing access to school facilities.

It is helpful to take inventory of particular skills or expertise staff members possess that would be useful in the event of an emergency, such as experience in firefighting, or search and rescue. Such individuals can be added to the school's crisis team. For examples of forms that can be used to conduct a staff skills inventory and to create a crisis team member list, log on to our website at *www.SchoolSafetyAndSecurityAlert.com.*

The Pennsylvania Department of Education has set out school safety recommendations that encourage school staff and students to be watchful for and to report suspicious activities, including the following:

- an unusual interest in entry points, security points and/or access controls
- an interest in gaining site plans, bus routes, attendance lists or other sensitive information
- an unusual degree of interest in personnel or vehicles approaching or leaving facilities or parking areas
- observation of security drills and procedures
- prolonged surveillance by people appearing to be vendors or others not usually seen in the area, and
- an unexplained presence of people in areas where they should not be.

While safety drills certainly play an important role in employee training, a lack of adequate communication in this regard can lead to a variety of unforeseen problems. For example, a former elementary school teacher in Oregon sued her school district, claiming that an unannounced active shooter safety drill caused her to develop an anxiety disorder. The former teacher claimed that she was not warned in advance about the drill, during which a school resource officer allegedly burst into her classroom and pointed a gun at her head.

Having staffers assume roles other than the ones they normally play can be an effective training tool. One Nevada school district had principals act as teachers and teachers act as students during security drills. The drills were recorded and reviewed. Participants reported benefiting from seeing the crisis from a different viewpoint.

IV. DOORS AND WINDOWS

A. Doors

Exterior doors should be designed to prevent unauthorized building access. The National Clearinghouse for Educational Facilities offers a checklist that lists a number of desirable attributes for exterior school doors, including the following:

- Doors should have a minimal degree of exposed hardware and should be installed using non-removable pins.
- Although exit-only doors do not need outside locks and handles, access should be possible in some manner in an emergency, such as by using a proximity card.
- Doors should be made from steel, aluminum alloy, or solid-core hardwood. If constructed of glass, doors should be fully framed and equipped with tempered glass that is breakage-resistant.
- To prevent doors from being pried open, door frames should be installed without excess flexibility.
- Exterior locks should be mounted flush to the door surface and should not rely on protruding lock devices such as a key-in-knob device.
- Exterior swinging doors should be equipped with a deadbolt lock that is at least one inch with a one-inch throw bolt and hardened steel insert, as well as a free-turning glass or steel-tempered guard, and double-cylinder locks if glass is located within 40 inches of the locking mechanism.
- Panic bar latches should be protected by pick plates.
- Panic push bars should be equipped with tamper-proof deadbolt locks and a metal plate covering the gap between the doors.
- Strike plates should be securely fastened to door frames.
- If the door is key-controlled, it can be equipped with contacts so it can be tied into a central monitoring and control system.

- Double doors should be equipped with heavy-duty, multiple-point long flush bolts.
- If a door is particularly vulnerable to unauthorized use, consider installing door alarms or delayed opening devices, or using sensors or cameras to monitor it from a central location.

Exterior doors should permit a view of the outside via narrow windows, sidelights, fish-eye viewers or cameras, while preventing intruders from opening any door from the inside by breaking a window or sidelight.

If schools fail to implement the listed safety measures, injuries can occur. Here's an example: An Oregon middle school student was walking into school on a rainy day when she suddenly slipped. Her foot slammed into and shattered the glass door. The broken glass severed her Achilles tendon and left her permanently injured.

A common and potentially devastating problem is that of students who open locked doors for outsiders seeking entry to the interior of a school building. Oftentimes, students do so thinking they are being helpful and polite. School administrators need to make students understand how important it is to follow the strict rule against opening outside doors for people seeking entry. But how? Mark Baker, a school superintendent in Indiana, developed a plan to get the message across to students without scaring them. Baker ensured that students received frequent reminders about the rule, including during assemblies, in homeroom, by way of morning announcements, and from special advisers such as guidance counselors.

Even the most secure exterior doors won't be very effective if staffers or others on the inside open them for unauthorized visitors. To address this danger, the principal of a New Jersey school aimed a school surveillance camera at a locked door and had two outsiders – a college-age man and a young mother – knock on the door every 10 minutes for an hour. The camera caught images of students and faculty opening the door. The principal then used the video as "teachable moments," thus reducing the frequency with which the doors were opened to outsiders.

In response to the tragic mass shooting at Sandy Hook Elementary School in December of 2012, Connecticut Gov. Dannel Malloy created a 16-member public safety panel called the Sandy Hook Advisory Commission. In March of 2013, the commission issued an interim report that included a number of specific recommendations relating to school doors. The panel recommended that all K-12 classrooms be equipped with doors that can be locked from the inside by the teacher. It also recommended that all exterior doors in K-12 schools be equipped with hardware that can implement a full perimeter lockdown.

Some devices are designed to create an additional layer of security by making it more difficult for an intruder to breach a locked interior door. One such tool is called a "Bearacade." The Bearacade is a door control system that creates another layer of protection between students and would-be attackers. The device can be installed on doors without leaving the classroom. It slides on the bottom of the door and secures the classroom with a 1/4" stainless steel pin. Reflective markings on the outer portion of the device let authorities know that the device is in use, and its makers say it can withstand up to 4,000 pounds of external pressure.

A similar device is called "The Sleeve." The Sleeve is a 12-gauge steel case that fits around an interior door's closer arm, securing it from the inside. The closer arm is installed at the top, in the inside of classroom doors. The device covers the closer arm, preventing it from being opened from the outside. It can withstand more that 550 foot-pounds of pressure.

Devices of this type must be used only after it is clear that they comply with all applicable fire codes. The National Fire Protection Association has created a guide that answers questions about fire codes, including how these devices can create some unanticipated challenges. To view the guide, go to *bit.lyFireCode419.*

An Illinois high school with 65 doors on its main floor decided to improve security by reducing the number of those doors used during the school day. It locked many of the exterior doors and restricted access to them with key controls. The school explained to staffers that keys had to be limited to make sure the security team knew exactly when normally locked doors were opened.

Also in Illinois, two school districts began using a system that installs safety magnets in door frames. When the magnet is removed, a locking mechanism is engaged. Use of the magnets allows teachers to secure classrooms without having to go outside into hallways to lock the doors with keys.

It is clear that schools have steadily placed increased importance on keeping entrance and exit doors locked during the school day. According to Indicators of School Crime and Safety: 2016, a report compiled by the National Center for Education Statistics, the percentage of students who reported locked entrance or exit doors during the day increased from 38% in 1999 to 78% in 2015.

B. Windows

School administrators who want to provide staff and students with the advantages afforded by natural lighting should do so with an awareness of the security risks that windows can create, especially with respect to unauthorized entry.

Placement of windows plays a key role in minimizing unauthorized entry. Ideally windows are placed where they enable easy surveillance of school grounds, and especially higher-risk areas. For example, it is important to include windows that enable staff to monitor the school's main entrance. These windows should be kept free of announcements or other postings that create an obstacle to effective surveillance.

Windows that are operable (that is, ones that can be opened and closed) should have locks that can secure them in a closed position. Window film can be used to reinforce window glass and hold it in place should it be subjected to impact. Second-floor windows should be inaccessible from the outside. Ideally, each room should include at least one designated window that can be used to escape in the event of an emergency.

Basement windows are an area of particular concern and should be protected by window well covers or grills.

V. SPECIFIC MEASURES AT ENTRANCEWAYS

Specific security measures implemented at entrance areas will depend on factors such as budget and incidence history. These measures are not undertaken singly but are part of a comprehensive overall security plan.

A. Metal Detectors

The use of metal detectors at school entrance points is an extreme measure that can help prevent unauthorized access but is often subject to criticism. Walk-through metal detectors can be utilized in conjunction with handheld detectors, which can be used to investigate further when an individual triggers the walk-through detector. Use of a walk-through detector requires a significant investment of space. The detector itself will typically fill a space approximately three-feet wide and two-feet deep. Of course, the staging area is much larger. It must allow enough room to provide a comfortable environment for those waiting to pass through. Space also is needed for people who are being scanned to place items in a pass-through container and to turn around and pass through a second time, if needed. Care must be taken to locate the system in an area where it will not be subjected to potential sources of interference, such as nearby electromagnetic equipment or even plumbing in the walls.

Opponents say metal detector use is overly intrusive and creates an atmosphere of fear. Because metal detectors cannot distinguish between items that are prohibited (such as a knife) and items that are not (such as a set of keys), trained personnel are needed to operate and monitor them. This need, in combination with the cost of the detectors, the cost of hiring trained personnel to man them, and the fact that the layout of many schools makes it difficult to efficiently implement a metal-detection system, makes the use of metal detectors impractical for many schools.

School safety expert Curt Lavarello urges school administrators to think very carefully about the logistics of effectively utilizing a metal detector before taking the leap to acquire one. Think about how long it would take to filter every single student through a single line, he advises, and consider whether there is enough room for all students to line up inside in case of bad weather. Lavarello also points out that the use of a metal detector will not be very effective unless all other school entry points are cut off.

Despite these challenges, metal detectors can in some cases be an efficient tool for reducing the likelihood of an unauthorized intrusion. Many people believe the presence of metal detectors can create a sense of security and act as a deterrent.

According to Indicators of School Crime and Safety: 2016, a report compiled by the National Center for Education Statistics, the percentage of students who reported the presence of metal detectors at their schools rose only slightly between 1999 and 2015, from 9% to 12%.

B. Closed-Circuit Television (CCTV)

Closed-circuit television technology can deter unauthorized access and help prevent crime throughout the school campus. A CCTV system intended to prevent access by intruders must be designed with reference to, and in coordination with, conditions that exist at the school with respect to external lighting and landscaping conditions. When cameras are placed at external locations, steps should be taken to minimize the likelihood of compromises to performance that can arise due to vandalism and exposure to outdoor elements. These systems typically monitor entrance points and parking areas, recording images that can be preserved electronically. Decisions relating to placement are made with reference to the level of risk associated with particular areas. Although full-time monitoring of CCTV cameras is not financially feasible for many schools, CCTV creates a record of any suspicious or illegal activity and can serve as an effective deterrent.

Case in point: In Wisconsin, a school's CCTV system recorded a student spraying a sticky substance on the steps of his high school as a senior prank. But the prank stopped being funny after two people were hurt after slipping and falling on the steps. The student was charged with two counts of recklessly endangering safety and was subjected to up to 20 years in jail and a $50,000 fine.

Many school administrators have seen the benefits of security cameras, and in a November 2010 release the National Center for Education Statistics and Bureau of Justice Statistics reported that the percentage of public schools using security cameras increased from 19% to 55% between the 1999-2000 school year and the 2007-08 school year. But despite the benefits, some students and parents express concerns that surveillance cameras may violate students' privacy rights. Calming concerns is a crucial step. One of the most effective ways to get parents and students on board is to develop a written policy outlining how and where security cameras will be used. Consider including the following information in the policy:

- list specific areas in school that will be monitored by the cameras
- list areas of the school where cameras will not be used, such as bathroom stalls and locker rooms, and
- say whether recordings from cameras will be produced as well as how long they will be kept and who has access to the recordings.

The use of security cameras in schools has increased dramatically since the start of the century. According to Indicators of School Crime and Safety: 2016, a report compiled by the National Center for Education Statistics, the percentage of students who reported the use of security cameras at their schools skyrocketed from 39% in 2001 to 83% in 2015.

C. Security Personnel/Greeters

The use of security guards and/or greeters is a low-tech but effective tool for preventing unauthorized access to a school's campus. Located at entrance points, security guards can check identifications and respond immediately to suspicious activities. Greeters, who are often parent volunteers, can serve a similar function at entrance points. Grandparents, caregivers, and retired community members also serve as good sources of greeters. The greeter's role is not to directly intervene to stop criminal activity. Instead, greeters can determine whether a visitor has a legitimate reason to be on the school's grounds and can direct the visitor to a specific location where he can complete applicable sign-in procedures. Ideally, greeters should also receive training relating to the school's evacuation plans and emergency procedures. Students should not be used as greeters.

D. Card Readers

Access-control card systems can be used to help keep track of who is entering a school facility. When this technology is used, an identification card is encoded and recognized by a card reader. When the reader recognizes the card, access is gained, such as by lifting a mechanical arm to permit access to a parking area. This system carries the advantage of not requiring live personnel to operate. But there are drawbacks. Cards can be passed from one person to another person, and more than one individual or vehicle may be able to enter at the same time using just one authorized card.

1. Case Study: Use of 'Smart Cards'

Cards can also be used to regulate the movement of students inside the school. At New Jersey's Dumont High School, for example, students are given "smart cards" that allow administrators to control specific areas the students can access. For example, access to a gym can be limited to sports team members. The cards also permit administrators to track the use of bathrooms and computers. In addition, they can be used to pay for meals and to take books from the school's library.

E. Use of PIN Codes

Access can also be limited by requiring individuals to enter a personal identification number (PIN) code into a keypad in order to gain entrance to a designated area of the school. The use of PIN codes is more effective as a security measure when it is combined with the use of identification cards and card readers. Their use includes potential drawbacks, including a vulnerability to vandalism and the ability of authorized users to permit entry by unauthorized personnel.

F. Biometrics

Biometric devices permit access only upon identification of a particular physical trait associated uniquely with the authorized user. Examples include fingerprint readers, systems that verify identity by measuring the size and shape of the entering individual's hand, and technology that reads retinal impressions. This technology works in essence by collecting data relating to a specific individual's physical or behavioral characteristics and comparing it to data that already is on file. These devices carry the advantage of allowing authorized users to enter without having to remember any type of identification card. Because they rely on unique individual characteristics, they also carry the advantage of being more reliable than identifiers such as identification cards. Although biometric devices are more commonly used in applications that require the highest level of security, such as prisons and international border points, they may become more prevalent in school applications as technologies improve.

1. Case Study: Eye-Scanning System

A 2006 evaluative study of an eye-scanning system used in three New Jersey elementary schools highlighted the advantages and shortcomings of relying on this particular type of biometric technology as an access security measure in the school setting. Teachers and staff, and more than 700 school parents had their eye images scanned into a computer system. To gain access to the school, they were required to have a camera on school grounds scan images of their irises. Five cameras were placed in exterior locations, and another six were placed in interior locations. The study found that the system provided an accurate identification and unlocked the door 78% of the time. Another 6% of attempted entries were properly denied because the individuals' eye scans were not in the computer. But 16% of the time, there were problems with scanning due to outdoor lighting conditions or a failure of the individual to line up his eyes properly with the camera. Despite the shortcomings, parents and staff indicated a perceived increase in school security.

2. Case Study: Fingerprinting

One of the nation's largest providers of child care and early educational services has installed biometric security systems at all of its corporate locations. Tutor Time, which has more than 100 locations nationwide and serves more than 28,000 students, began requiring fingerprint information and a PIN number from individuals seeking access to its facilities. The organization does not maintain a database of actual fingerprints. Instead, fingerprints are scanned into a system and converted into a series of numbers to produce something similar to a bar code. The "bar code" is then matched with a specific authorized user.

VI. LIGHTING

Proper illumination of entry areas and parking areas is a key to preventing unauthorized access to facilities. Because light fixtures are vulnerable to vandalism, they should be mounted as high as possible and covered with a material or housing that prevents breakage of lenses. Lighting fixtures can be controlled by clocks or by photocells that turn them off at dawn and on at dusk, although a manual override feature should be included. Lighting controls and switches must be protected, and the accessibility of electrical panels must be restricted.

Lights should be placed so as to minimize glare and the creation of shadows. Ideally, the lighting near entrance points should cast a pattern of light horizontally rather than vertically. Flush-mounted or recessed light fixtures should be used when possible. Because light-colored surfaces reflect light more efficiently than dark-colored surfaces, the presence of light-colored surfaces at entry points will increase the overall level of entry-point security. Maintaining a fixed schedule for maintenance of all outdoor lighting, including lighting at entrance points, is another important safety key. Decisions relating to the provision of lighting must be made with reference to the need of lighting to work effectively with other security measures that may be in place, such as the use of closed-circuit television.

☑ CHECKLIST – *Lighting*

- ☐ There is a regular schedule of maintenance for outside lights.
- ☐ Special attention is paid to adequacy of lighting at entrance points and other high-risk points of potential intrusion.
- ☐ Light lenses are protected by an impact-resistant material.
- ☐ Lighting fixtures do not provide handholds that can be used to climb into the building.
- ☐ Exterior lighting minimizes glare and shadows.

VII. CONTROLLING ACCESS BY VISITORS

A detailed procedure for controlling access to the school by authorized visitors is essential. Visitors should be steered to a main entrance by clear appropriate signage and by the layout of the school's exterior. Ideally, they will be intercepted by a greeter or security officer outside the school building before they can proceed to sign in at a main office, where school personnel can verify that they are at the school for a legitimate purpose. A similar measure was implemented in the Burke County School District in Waynesboro, Georgia. School visitors there are identified and cleared with the help of a camera outside of the building. Once inside, visitors complete the check-in process and receive an identification badge.

Schools should strongly consider implementing a requirement that visitors produce photo identification to verify identity. Visitor badges, which must be located outside the reach of visitors in a secure area, should be dated and issued once authorization for the visit is confirmed. The date, time, name, purpose, and intended destination of the visitor should be recorded in a log that each visitor should sign. School personnel should accompany visitors to the specific area of the visit. An important but sometimes overlooked feature of a visitor access policy is the incorporation of a "checkout" procedure whereby the visitor surrenders his pass or badge before leaving and the time of the visitor's departure is noted in the school's log. The log should be checked periodically during the day to determine whether any visitor appears to be remaining at the school for an inordinate amount of time.

A relatively extreme measure is to ban unannounced parent visits. The step was taken by Nathan Parker, the superintendent of the Summit Public Schools in New Jersey. Saying the move would improve safety, Parker told parents that unannounced school visits were being banned, regardless of the reason for the visit. For a sample authorization to release a student, log on to *www.SchoolSafetyAndSecurityAlert.com.*

A check-in policy that relies simply on a visitor typing in a name is vulnerable to exploitation. Brad Kent, an assistant principal at a middle school in Arkansas, was faced with the task of improving this system. With his assistance, the school upgraded to a system called "KeepnTrack." Using this system, visitors had to give their IDs to the school receptionist, who scanned their ID cards. The system works with any state driver's license. It prints a photo scan on a yellow sticker, which creates a photo ID for visitors to wear while on campus. The scan also runs visitors' licenses through the national registry of sex offenders. In addition, the system can be used to run criminal background checks. For more information on the program, go to *www.keepntrack.com.*

It is important for all staffers to be trained on how to approach people who look like they do not belong in the building. School resource officer Michael Rudinski of the Hyattsville (Maryland) Police Department explained a universal greeting staffers use. Staffers say, "Hi, I am [name and title] at [school]. I see that you [circumstances]. How can I help you with that?" Having this plan in place beforehand helps staff approach people with confidence, and faculty and staff are more likely to speak up rather than look the other way.

Following court-ordered custody agreements is sometimes easier said than done. Mike Cowsert, a school resource officer at Timber Ridge Schools in Arlington Heights, Illinois, described the problem of having non-custodial parents trying to sign out their children without the custodial parent's consent. To combat the problem, the school issued identification badges to parents at student orientation and explained that the badges would have to be shown to sign children out of school. Where custody was an issue, badges were provided to custodial parents only. The use of the badges enabled office staffers to determine whether the parent had the authority to pick up the student.

Of course, investing in relatively sophisticated visitor management systems is a step that should be taken only after careful consideration. Kevin Allen, president of visitor management system vendor LobbyGuard in Raleigh, North Carolina, says many administrators are not confident enough in their tech knowledge to feel good about making the best decision on which vendor to go with. He advises schools to make sure the contract allows them to reevaluate after a period of no more than three years. He also tells them to insist on a 90-day, no-questions-asked full refund provision before signing a purchase order.

Additional advice regarding vendors of school security technology more generally comes from Singlewire Software, leaders in security software. Singlewire urges schools to ask vendors whether their system is compatible with other systems and devices; whether it can be configured for panic button triggers; and what kind of support the vendor provides.

A. Case Study: Visitor Screening

More and more schools are adding another layer of protection to visitor screening policies by checking the identities of visitors against lists of sexual predators. Typically, the prospective visitor's driver's license is swiped through a computer that searches for a match against lists of offenders. Some systems also allow administrators to search for a match against lists of court orders that restrict parental custody of students. The Charter School for Applied Technologies, located in Tonawanda, New York, has utilized the tool. When a license does not show a match against the lists, the school issues a pass that includes the visitor's photograph. In the event of a match, school officials are notified immediately by phone and email.

Schools considering implementation of a background check system should be aware of a new associated threat: lawsuits challenging the legality of the systems under the Constitution.

A couple filed a suit against a Texas school district, claiming its background check system violated their rights to freely associate with their children. They also added a claim of unreasonable search and seizure.

The couple cited concerns about identity theft. They didn't like the idea of a private company collecting their personal information. One of the plaintiffs asked the school to check her status against a database maintained by the Justice Department. She said the school denied her request. The school district's director of police and public safety said before the suit was filed, there had been no complaints about the system.

Schools must be extremely vigilant to ensure students are picked up only by authorized individuals. Sandra White, principal at a Mississippi school, explained how a simple procedure effectively met this goal in a specific case. When a teacher did not recognize a man who tried to pick up a student, the teacher kindly but firmly explained that she needed to check his identification and confirm it on a pickup sheet. At the office, the man's name was not on the list. The teacher called the child's mother to confirm that the man had authority to pick up the child. The mother confirmed the man's authority to do so. The next day, the mother went to the school to add the man's name to the list.

☑ CHECKLIST – *Visitor Policy*

- ☐ School entrance points include signage that steers visitors to an office location.
- ☐ Sign-in areas are adequately staffed.
- ☐ Visitors must produce photo identification.
- ☐ Visitors are required to wear dated visitor passes or badges once authorization is confirmed.
- ☐ Visitors are escorted to their specific visit location.
- ☐ Visitor identification passes and badges are kept in a secure area.
- ☐ Visitors are required to sign a log indicating date, time, and intended destination.
- ☐ Visitor identification passes and badges are collected from visitors upon exit.
- ☐ Time of building exit is recorded in a log.

For steps key personnel should take in response to a school intruder, log on to *www.SchoolSafetyAndSecurityAlert.com*. Information about specific steps to take in situations involving a weapon, and in potentially violent situations in general, can also be found on the same website. For resources for victims and families in child abduction cases, go to the federal Office of Juvenile Justice and Delinquency Prevention's Web page, located at *http://www.ojjdp.gov*.

VIII. COORDINATING WITH FIRST RESPONDERS

Coordinating with first responders, such as police, fire and EMS personnel, is key to maintaining building security. In September 2007, the Attorney General of Pennsylvania introduced a tool schools can use to improve coordination between schools and first responders in the event that security at a school's entrance is breached and an emergency response is required. The Attorney General's Office created a School Safety Project CD-ROM. Based on a program that was developed by a local school district within the state, the CD-ROM helps schools create building safety plans that first responders can access on websites in an emergency. The CD-ROM helps districts create a secure website that includes information relating to many aspects of the facility, such as floor plans, photographs of school grounds, and a contact list of school administrators. The program on which the Attorney General's guide is based was developed by the Susquenita School District at a cost of approximately $1,000. First responders can access a password-protected website and view floor plans, school access roads, and photographs of classrooms and corridors. They can even access a real-time view of classrooms and offices, as the website includes images taken from school security cameras. This feature enables first responders to gain an inside view of the school building before entering.

IX. EFFECTIVE LOW-TECHNOLOGY ALTERNATIVES

Ideally, technological measures designed to protect entry points should be combined with less technical, but effective strategies and techniques to decrease the risk of criminal behavior. The U.S. Department of Justice's Office of Justice Programs has compiled the following list of low-technology but effective tools for deterring unauthorized entry to school facilities. Some of these measures are discussed elsewhere in this chapter. Utilizing the combination of them that best fits a particular school's needs can have the effect of increasing entry-point security.

- Post signs warning that unauthorized trespassers are subject to arrest.
- Post signs indicating that all vehicles on campus are subject to search.
- Provide a guard to check identifications at the main entrance to the school.
- Provide authorized vehicles with parking stickers so that unauthorized vehicles can be more easily identified and removed.
- Require student uniforms so that outsiders can be easily identified.
- Implement a school policy that bars hats, shirts that include messages related to alcohol, drugs, violence or gangs and exposed tattoos.
- Provide greeters at all open entrances.
- Provide a minimal number of entrances.
- Implement a policy under which students walking around the school campus during class time are challenged for a pass and are potentially subjected to search.
- Close off the main student parking lot during the day.
- Provide fencing that defines school property and discourages casual intruders.
- Confiscate the student ID of students who are suspended or expelled and make their photographs available to security staff.

Here's an instance that proves low-tech preventive measures are effective ways to keep students safe: A swift, coordinated response to warning signs enabled school officials and law enforcement authorities to thwart a shooting plot at a Pennsylvania high school. Local police had been informed that guns had been stolen from the home of a 15-year-old student. When school officials realized the student fit the profile of a potential shooter – a white teenage loner with few friends – they took action quickly.

School officials began to check students' backpacks and lockers. They also talked to students who knew the possible suspect. The superintendent notified school board members about what was going on, and the faculty met with its emergency response team.

The student's plan to go on a shooting rampage near the start of the new year unraveled when one of his friends told a teacher that he knew the location of the missing guns. The teacher immediately reported the information to school officials, and police recovered the guns. The student was arrested – before causing any harm.

X. CASE STUDY: INSTALLATION OF FACILITY MANAGEMENT SYSTEMS

The Harrison County School District Two, located near Colorado Springs, Colorado, serves more than 11,000 students and has 23 schools. In 2002, the district decided to upgrade its security systems at all of its schools, which included elementary schools, middle schools, high schools, alternative schools and charter schools. After soliciting several proposals, the district decided to install a security system that included closed-caption television, digital video recording, and card access control.

A vendor installed card readers on perimeter doors of schools, and all staff members were issued combination identification badges and access cards. All exterior building locks were re-keyed, and key distribution was limited. A digital video recording unit was installed at every district school. All front lobbies were outfitted with cameras. Surveillance was added for exteriors and some interior areas. Digital video recorders replaced VCRs, and some secondary buildings were outfitted with pan-tilt-zoom cameras.

A policy was implemented whereby all perimeter school doors, except the ones at front lobby entrances, remained locked at all times. Cameras began recording all activity at lobby entrances at all times, with monitors enabling school staff to observe those areas. Each school's security system was linked to a central location, where monitors at all the school facilities could be viewed at all times. The installed system also enabled administrators and security personnel to view video from a remote location by using a Web browser.

The system was installed in a way that enabled it to interface with the district's pre-existing burglar alarm system. This alarm system alerted the district's private security company whenever an alarm was triggered after hours.

In cases of a security breach, the system enables personnel to export video clips to a CD-ROM for delivery to local law enforcement authorities. The system includes an authentication process which verifies that stored video has not been altered.

A lockdown capability is also included. Staff can activate a button in the front office that locks perimeter doors and deactivates card readers. When a school is placed in lockdown, entry can occur only via the front door after staff has had the opportunity to view the person or persons seeking access, and chooses to permit access by manually unlocking the door.

The system also provides wireless personal panic control devices that are distributed to key personnel. These devices can be activated to signal a need for assistance from any location on the school grounds. When activated, the devices cause a white strobe light to turn on in the school's front office and send emails and pages to members of a designated response team.

The district reported great success with the new system. Soon after installation was completed, an individual who entered three different school buildings during a lunch hour, and stole cash and credit cards from teachers' purses, was caught on tape. The system also reduced fighting and vandalism.

XI. LEGAL DECISIONS

A. Intruders

◆ A 17-year-old non-student intruder sexually assaulted an elementary school student in a school bathroom. About 14 years later, the student sued the school district and claimed a violation of her equal protection rights. **The court rejected her claim because she did not show that the district discriminated against her** and that the district treated her worse than students who were not in her protected group. *McGuire v. Northwest Area School Dist.*, No. 3:11-CV-1022, 2011 WL 5444084 (M.D. Pa. 11/8/11).

◆ An intruder entered an elementary school through its main entrance. A teacher asked him if he needed help, but he ignored her. She then went to the office to see if he had signed in. Two other teachers also saw the intruder in the hallway. When one of them questioned him, he said he needed to use a restroom. The teacher pointed out a restroom and told the intruder he needed to return to the office after using it. The teachers then lost sight of the intruder, who entered another restroom and sexually assaulted a five-year-old student. The student's mother filed a negligence claim against the school district. A trial court ruled against her on the basis that the assault was not foreseeable. An appeals court reversed, finding **reasonable minds could differ as to whether the district's response to the presence of the intruder constituted a breach of its duty of care** and as to whether the assault was a foreseeable consequence of the district's failure to initially note the intruder's entry and monitor the situation more closely. *A.W. v. Lancaster County School Dist. 0001*, 784 N.W.2d 907 (Neb. 2010).

◆ A non-student entered a high school and requested a visitor's pass. When his request was denied, he became angry. School employees escorted him from the school building, but they did not make sure he left the premises. The man then re-entered and stabbed a former schoolmate in a hallway. The schoolmate and her parents sued the school, its principal and others, claiming they were negligent. A trial court granted a defense motion for summary judgment, and an appeals court upheld the trial court's ruling. The appeals court explained that the defendants owed a duty of reasonable supervision to the student who was attacked. However, **they could not be liable for negligence because the attack was not reasonably foreseeable and preventable**. The attacker did not go to the school looking for the student he attacked, and he did not even know she was a student there. There was no evidence that the defendants had any warning indicating the attacker would come into the building and stab a student. The stabbing occurred suddenly and without warning, and the defendants' failure to prevent it was not negligent. *Boudreaux v. St. Tammany Parish School Board*, No. 2007 CA 0889, 2007 WL 4480703 (La. Ct. App. 12/21/07).

◆ While teaching a volleyball class, a teacher noticed two young men come into the gym. She recognized one as a student at the school, but she did not recognize the other. When the teacher walked toward the men and blew her whistle, the unknown man struck her in the left temple. The man left but returned a short time later and punched her in the back of the head, causing her to lose consciousness. She suffered serious injuries. **The teacher sued the city, claiming it was negligent as a landlord of the school when it allowed the attacker to gain unauthorized access.** She also claimed the city breached a special duty to protect her from harm and breached a contract with a teachers' union by failing to properly implement a school safety plan. The court granted the city's motion for summary judgment. Because the city was acting as a public government entity and not as a landlord when it undertook efforts to provide security, it was immune to the teacher's negligence claim. The court also rejected the teacher's claim that the city breached a special duty it owed to her by failing to implement a school safety plan and protect its teachers. Neither the maintenance of a comprehensive security system nor school officials' representations that they "take security seriously" created a special duty. Finally, the court rejected the contract claim because the city could not be held liable to individual teachers for any alleged contract breach between it and the teacher's union. *Daniels v. City of New York*, No. 04-CV-7612 (CM), 2007 WL 2040581 (S.D.N.Y. 6/26/07).

◆ A deranged convicted felon entered a school building holding a picture of a young girl. The school principal confronted the intruder, who then left. The school subsequently instituted a new access control policy. An individual was stationed in the school's lobby to screen people entering the school, and visitors were instructed to sign in at the principal's office. The policy further required staff to monitor visitors through a floor-to-ceiling window in the principal's office. About a year after the incident involving the intruder, a different intruder gained unauthorized access to the school and attacked a 10-year-old student with a hammer. The attack caused serious injury. The student's parents sued the school's principal, the county school superintendent, the board of education and others, alleging they were negligent in failing to develop a school safety plan as required by state law and allowing the attack to occur. A trial court granted the defendants' motion for summary judgment, and an appeals court affirmed. **The school had prepared and put into place a school safety plan** before the attack. Because the plan was in place before the attack occurred, the defendants were entitled to immunity on the negligence claims. The ruling of the trial court was affirmed. *Leake v. Murphy*, 644 S.E.2d 328 (Ga. Ct. App. 2007).

◆ A father drove his 12-year-old son to a high school that the boy and his brother attended. The father waited outside while the boy entered the school to find his brother, who was participating in a school event. The 12-year-old was sexually assaulted in the school by a convicted sex felon who had gained unauthorized access. The incident took place on a Saturday, when school was not in session. The parent sued the school, its president and its principal, **claiming they were negligent in leaving the school doors unlocked and unattended during school-sponsored activities**. The court upheld a ruling against the parent, finding that he failed to show the defendants owed him a duty of care. There is generally no duty to protect others from the criminal acts of third parties. Although a duty may exist when there is a special relationship between the defendant and the plaintiff, a special relationship giving rise to a duty did not exist in this case. School was not in session, and the 12-year-old was not participating in any school-sponsored event at the time of the assault. In addition, the parent did not show the assault was foreseeable. *Roe v. Univ. of Detroit Jesuit High School and Academy*, No. 264269, 2006 WL 475285 (Mich. Ct. App. 2/28/06).

◆ A high school student sued a board of education, a high school and others after she was raped in a school bathroom by a non-student intruder. **The student alleged that the defendants wrongfully failed to provide security guards in the area of the alleged attack and near exterior doors.** She said students frequently opened exterior doors to allow other students to enter. The board of education, high school and private security firm appealed a trial court's decision to deny their motions for summary judgment. The appeals court reversed the trial court's ruling. The alleged security deficiencies arose from the allocation of security resources, which was a governmental function. Because such decisions are in the nature of a governmental function, the district and high school could not be held liable unless they had a special relationship with the student that created a special duty to protect her. No special duty existed, as there was no direct contact between the student and the school defendants before the alleged attack. Also, the school defendants did not have notice of prior sexual assaults at the school and had no reason to anticipate an intruder would enter and commit a violent crime against a student. Finally, the claim against the private security firm failed because the school defendants controlled the security guards at the school. The lower court's ruling was reversed. *Doe v. Town of Hempstead Board of Educ.*, 795 N.Y.S.2d 322 (N.Y. App. Div. 2005).

◆ A substitute teacher sued a board of education after she was attacked by a school intruder, claiming the board negligently failed to provide adequate security. The court reversed a trial court's decision to deny summary judgment to the board. **Because the provision of security against attacks by school intruders is a governmental function, there is no liability unless there is a special duty to protect.** In this case, there was no special duty to protect the substitute teacher. The implementation of security measures did not create a special duty, and the board made no special promise of protection to the substitute teacher. *Bain v. New York City Board of Educ.*, 702 N.Y.S.2d 334 (N.Y. App. Div. 2000).

◆ A high school secretary noticed a neatly dressed man carrying what appeared to be flower boxes near a school entrance. The secretary asked the man if she could help him. He uttered an incoherent response, thanked her, and moved along. A short time later, the man was observed by an individual who worked at the school as a water safety instructor. At the time, the man was standing between a swimming pool and bleachers. **The layout of the school building made it easy to become disoriented, and it was not unusual for male visitors to become disoriented and walk through the girls' locker room.** The water safety instructor, who also believed the man was delivering flowers, concluded that he had reached the area by walking through the girls' locker room. She began to walk toward him to ask why he was in the building. While doing so, she met a school custodian who had also seen the man exit from the girls' locker room into a lobby area. When the custodian saw the man, he commented that it was odd to see someone coming out of the girls' locker room. The man again uttered an incoherent remark and moved on. About an hour after the secretary first saw the man, she observed him again near a school entrance. This time, the man was talking to a student. She did not confront him, even though she later admitted that he did not belong in that location because it was not the school's main entrance. A short time later, the man sexually assaulted a student in the locker room. The student's parents sued the school district, claiming it failed to provide adequate supervision and security. A lower court granted immunity to the individual school employees but not to the school district, and the school district appealed. The appeals court affirmed, finding that the school district was not entitled to immunity. **The employees engaged in discretionary acts that deserved the protection of official immunity. However, this immunity did not extend to the school district. If it did, the district would be rewarded for failing to develop and implement a basic security policy.** *S.W. v. Spring Lake Park School Dist. No. 16*, 592 N.W.2d 870 (Minn. Ct. App. 1999).

◆ A teacher was killed when a local resident with a history of mental illness entered her daycare center through an unlocked rear entrance and shot her. The center was operated out of a wing of a local high school. The rear entrance was open because it was being used by construction contractors. The teacher's husband sued the school district and owner of the daycare center, claiming they created the danger that resulted in the teacher's death by unlocking the back entrance. A trial court ruled against him, and he appealed. The appeals court affirmed the ruling against the teacher's husband. The state generally has no obligation to protect citizens from the violent acts of private individuals. Although an exception applies when the state creates a danger that causes harm, the exception was not applicable. **The district could not have foreseen that allowing construction workers to use the back entrance would result in the shooting, and it did not willfully or deliberately disregard a foreseeable danger.** *Morse v. Lower Merion School Dist.*, 132 F.3d 902 (3d Cir. 1997).

◆ While providing instruction in her classroom, a teacher was confronted by four intruders. One of the intruders accused the teacher of having physically abused a student. The intruder then assaulted the teacher with a metal chair, causing back injuries. **The teacher sued the board of education, claiming it was negligent because it failed to monitor and control the people who entered the school.** The teacher also claimed that the school negligently failed to provide proper security and created a dangerous condition. In addition, she claimed the board breached a union contract that required school principals to develop safety plans. The court granted the board's motion for summary judgment. The board was immune to the negligence claim because the provision of security was a governmental function rather than a proprietary function. The court rejected the teacher's claim that the school assumed a special duty to protect her and thus was not immune to the negligence claims against it. The teacher alleged that this special duty arose when the school's principal told her not to worry because she was "in a good school." She also alleged that a special duty arose based on the collective bargaining agreement between the teachers' union and the board. The court held that neither the principal's statement nor a collective bargaining agreement provision requiring principals to develop safety plans created a special duty. Therefore, the teacher's negligence claims failed and summary judgment was awarded to the board. *Genao v. Board of Educ. of the City of New York*, 888 F.Supp. 501 (S.D.N.Y. 1995).

◆ While leaving her high school following her last class for the day, a student inadvertently bumped shoulders with another student. The second student told the first that "she was going to kill her." The first student then met her sister, who also attended the school, in another area of the school. She attempted to report the incident at a security office, but she received no response when she knocked at the door. She and her sister were then assaulted as they tried to leave the school. **The second student struck one**

of the sisters in the head and elbow with a hammer, and the second student's brother, who was not a student at the school, stabbed the other. The sisters sued the city's board of education and others, claiming negligent supervision. A jury returned a verdict of $50,000 for one of the sisters and $750,000 for the other. A lower court set aside the verdict and dismissed the complaint, finding the evidence did not prove negligent supervision. On appeal, the court reinstated the verdict, finding the jury could permissibly find that the board failed to provide adequate supervision. *Mirand v. City of New York*, 190 A.D.2d 282 (N.Y. App. Div. 1993).

◆ A teacher selected a fourth-grade student to supervise a classroom of second-graders while their teacher went to retrieve supplies from another part of the building. While the teacher was away, the fourth-grader was lured from the classroom by an intruder. The intruder exited the school with the student by proceeding through an unlocked rear door and through an open gate of a security fence. He then forced her into a wooded area and raped her. The student's mother sued the school district, claiming negligence. A jury found in her favor and awarded nearly $251,000. The district appealed, arguing that it could not be held liable because the actions of the intruder were not foreseeable. The appeals court rejected the argument and upheld the jury's verdict. There was enough evidence for the jury to find that school officials were on notice that students were in danger of being assaulted by intruders. The school was located in a statistically high crime area, and there had been sexual assaults and other violent crime in the surrounding area. Also, school security was deficient. **The gate on a security fence at the rear of the school was left open and unlocked, and a set of doors at the back of the school did not close and lock properly due to an alignment problem. Doors at the front of the school did not close properly, and an intercom system was not functioning properly at the time of the assault.** Further, unaccompanied and unknown adult males were permitted to roam school hallways. All of these things raised a factual issue of foreseeability that was properly submitted to the jury. The trial court's judgment was affirmed. *District of Columbia v. Doe*, 524 A.2d 30 (D.C. Ct. App. 1987).

B. Search and Seizure

◆ Pursuant to a high school's policy, a student who left school and returned during the same day was searched. When he was told to empty his pockets, he pulled out a bag containing 44 tablets of ecstasy. He later claimed that the search violated his Fourth Amendment rights. He asked the judge in a juvenile proceeding to suppress the evidence uncovered by the search. The judge denied the request, and the student appealed. The appeals court upheld the judge's ruling. It decided that the school did not violate the student's Fourth Amendment rights. The search was conducted pursuant to a written policy, and the policy applied to all students. Also, **the policy was**

justified by legitimate safety concerns, and the search was not overly intrusive. *People v. Sean A.*, 120 Cal.Rptr.3d 72 (Cal. Ct. App. 2010).

◆ An alternative learning center, which was attended by students who had been removed from other school campuses due to disciplinary problems, subjected all entering students to a search. The daily search required students to pass through a metal detector, be patted down, remove their shoes for inspection and empty their pockets. All students and parents attended an orientation session that included a description of the search policy. During a search, an examining officer found a marijuana cigarette inside the shoe of a student. At a trial held to determine whether he should be adjudicated delinquent, the student filed a motion to suppress the evidence. The motion was denied, and the student was adjudicated delinquent. He appealed, renewing his argument that the evidence should have been suppressed because it was discovered as a result of an unlawful search. The court rejected the student's argument and affirmed the lower court's decision. **Even though the search was not conducted based on individualized suspicion, it was justified by the school's need to maintain a safe learning environment in a high-risk setting.** Public school students are subject to a greater degree of supervision than adults, and the state had a compelling interest in maintaining safe schools. In addition, the uniform nature of the searches guarded against an abuse of discretion by administrators. The search was an administrative search that intruded on the privacy of students only to the extent necessary to satisfy the state's interest in maintaining safety. The lower court's ruling was affirmed. *In re O.E.*, No. 03-02-00516-CV, 2003 WL 22669014 (Tex. Ct. App. 11/13/03).

◆ A public high school in Philadelphia periodically subjected all students to a point-of-entry search for weapons. When the searches were conducted, students were required to stand in line and empty their pockets while their backpacks, coats and other personal effects were searched. Students were also scanned by a handheld metal detector. During one such search, a student removed a Swiss army-type knife from his pocket. He was arrested for bringing a weapon onto school property and was adjudicated delinquent after a juvenile hearing. After a court affirmed the disposition, the student appealed again. On appeal, he renewed his argument that the evidence should have been suppressed because the search was made without any individualized reasonable suspicion. The court rejected the argument and affirmed the lower court's decision. **The search was justified because it affected a limited privacy interest and was minimally intrusive.** In addition, the student population and parents were notified of the purpose of the search and the manner in which it was conducted via a school policy and procedure manual, mailings, and notices that were posted throughout the school. The purpose of the search – to keep weapons out of public schools – was compelling. Therefore, the search did not violate the student's constitutional rights. *Ex rel. F.B.*, 726 A.2d 361 (Pa. 1999).

◆ A high school subjected students to random searches for weapons using a handheld metal detector. It provided students and their parents with notice of this practice before it was instituted. On one day, the school decided to search all students who entered the attendance office without hall passes or who were late. A knife was found in the pocket of one of the students who was searched, and she was charged with the crime of bringing a knife onto school grounds. The trial court denied her motion to suppress the evidence and sustained the petition against her. She appealed, challenging the denial of her motion to suppress the evidence. The appeals court affirmed the lower court's decision. **Special needs administrative searches can be conducted without individualized suspicion so long as the government need is great, the privacy intrusion is limited in nature, and it would be unworkable to require a more rigorous standard of suspicion.** In this case, the searches were minimally intrusive, and it would be unworkable to institute a system that relied more on suspicion. Therefore, the search did not violate the student's rights under the Fourth Amendment. *People v. Latasha W.*, 70 Cal.Rptr.2d 886 (Cal. Ct. App. 1998).

◆ To keep weapons out, a public high school set up metal detectors that students passed through shortly after they entered. A student turned around to leave when he saw other students lined up to pass through a metal detector. When he was stopped by a police officer and told he would be required to go through the detector, he raised his shirt to reveal a pistol and said "someone put this gun on me." The student was arrested, and he filed a motion to suppress the evidence. The trial court sustained the motion, finding that **the student could have turned around for innocent reasons that were unrelated to the metal detector**. The state appealed, but the reviewing court affirmed. A person is seized when his freedom of movement is restrained, and the student's detention constituted an illegal seizure. Although the state argued that the officer was performing an administrative search, the cases it relied on to support its argument did not prevent people from choosing not to pass through a checkpoint. In addition, the officer did not have a reasonable suspicion to believe the search would turn up incriminating evidence. Instead, the decision to order the student to pass through the detector was based on a hunch. *People v. Parker*, 672 N.E.2d 813 (Ill. App. Ct. 1996).

◆ The parent of a student who was fatally shot at his high school sued the city, the board of education and others. The parent claimed the city and board negligently allowed people who were armed and dangerous to gain unauthorized access to the school and failed to use metal detectors on the day of the shooting. The parent further claimed that by placing metal detectors at the school, the city and board voluntarily assumed a duty to provide special protection against criminal acts by third persons. She separately claimed that the city and board owed a special duty to the student because he was in their control and because they were uniquely aware that he was at risk. A lower court ruled against the parent, and she appealed. The appeals court affirmed. The city's decision to use metal detectors did not negate the immunity it enjoyed under a tort immunity statute. Nor did a special duty exception to immunity apply, because the parent did not show that a special relationship existed between the city and the student. For similar reasons, the decision favoring the board was affirmed. **The decision to use metal detectors did not make the board an insurer against all criminal activity.** In addition, there was no showing that the decision not to use the metal detectors every day increased the incidence of crime at the school. *Lawson v. City of Chicago*, 662 N.E.2d 1377 (Ill. App. Ct. 1996).

◆ As he entered his public high school in Philadelphia, a student was instructed by a school employee to remove his coat and place his book bag on a table to be searched. The employee then scanned the student with a metal detector and patted him down. All entering students were subjected to the same scan and pat-down procedure that day. When the employee felt a bulge resembling a knife in the student's coat, he searched the coat and found a box cutter in one of its pockets. The student was later arrested and charged with possession of a weapon on school property. At the criminal trial, his motion to suppress the physical evidence was denied, and he was convicted and placed on probation. He appealed, claiming the physical evidence should have been suppressed because he had been subjected to an unlawful search and seizure. **The student claimed the search and seizure were unlawful because there was no reasonable suspicion or probable cause to believe he had violated any law or school regulation.** The court held that the search did not violate the student's constitutional rights. Administrative searches are permitted even in the absence of individualized suspicion when they are conducted as part of a general regulatory scheme to ensure public safety. The search was reasonably related to the school's interest in promoting student safety, and it was justified because of the high rate of violence that was present in the Philadelphia public schools. All students were subjected to the search, and the uniform procedure that was followed assured that officials would not improperly exercise discretion with respect to the searches. The order adjudicating the student delinquent was affirmed. *Ex rel. S.S.*, 680 A.2d 1172 (Pa. Super. Ct. 1996).

◆ A school chancellor adopted guidelines for searching students as they entered public high schools, and several schools were selected for periodic scanning. At the start of the school year, students at the selected schools were told they would be subjected to a search at some point. The students were not told ahead of time when the searches would take place. Although all entering students could be searched, the guidelines allowed personnel to limit the search, such as by searching every second or third student. Any student chosen to be searched was asked to place bags and parcels on a table, and to remove any metal objects from pockets. Students were then scanned with a metal detector. When a bag or parcel activated the detector, students were asked to open it. If a body scan activated the detector, students were again asked to remove metal objects. Students were taken to a private area if a second body scan activated the detector again. They were then asked a third time to remove metal objects before being subjected to a pat-down search. A student who was subjected to a search under the guidelines was arrested after a metal detector activated on her bag and a knife was discovered inside. She filed a motion to suppress, arguing it was discovered in violation of the Fourth Amendment. The court denied the motion. **The search was permissible because the need to maintain school safety outweighed the minimally intrusive nature of the searches.** In addition, the searches were permissible even though the guidelines did not include any provision requiring administrators to gain the consent of students before conducting a search. Children are required to attend school, and a consent element "would be all but impossible to administer." *People v. Dukes*, 580 N.Y.S.2d 850 (N.Y. Crim. Ct. 1992).

C. Release of Students

◆ A family acquaintance changed the emergency contact form at a child's school to indicate he was the child's stepfather. He then signed her out of school 10 times over a three-month period. The child's mother learned about the change and told the school not to release the child to anyone but her. The child was not released to the acquaintance again. **About a month later, the acquaintance picked up the child at her bus stop in the morning and took her to Mexico.** The school did not tell the mother that her daughter was absent. The mother sued the school, alleging deprivation of her due process rights and negligent infliction of emotional distress. The court dismissed the case. The harm was too attenuated from the school's actions to create liability, and the mother did not allege facts that would demonstrate deliberate indifference on the school's part. *Luu v. Esterly*, 367 F.Supp.3d 335 (E.D. Pa. 2019).

◆ A seventh-grade student with autism was assigned by his new school district to be a "walker" because he lived only about a half mile from school. This meant he was not provided transportation services. He usually walked to and from school with his older sister. However, he tried to walk home alone one day when his sister had to stay after school. He was struck and killed by a car while crossing a busy street. His parents sued the district and several individual defendants, alleging substantive due process claims. **The court denied a defense motion for dismissal, finding that the complaint stated a valid state-created danger claim.** Specifically, it alleged that the harm was foreseeable; that school administrators' actions "shocked the conscience"; that the child was a foreseeable victim or member of a discrete class subject to potential harm; and that the school acted affirmatively to create the danger that resulted in the child's death. *Weiser v. Elizabethtown Area School Dist.*, No. 17-625, 2018 WL 1071929 (E.D. Pa. 2/27/18).

◆ A Tennessee elementary school adopted a new policy that required parents to stay in their cars during student pickup times. Instead of getting out of their cars, parents were to hold up a sign. A school staffer would then bring their student to the car. A father arrived at school and walked up to the building to pick up his children. He had a heated discussion with the school resource officer. Two days later, the father again walked up to the building. The school resource officer arrested him. **The father sued, claiming the policy violated his constitutional right to "family unity."** The court rejected his claim, finding that the school's policy only minimally interfered with his access to his children and fell far short of a constitutional violation. *Howe v. Aytes*, No. 2:14-cv-000077, 2016 WL 3262600 (M.D. Tenn. 6/10/16).

◆ A student's father had custody, and his mother had visitation rights. His mother was allowed to pick him up from school on certain days. The mother and his stepfather tried to sign the boy out on a non-allowed day. While a school office employee tried to call the father, the mother and stepfather became angry and the stepfather threatened to kill everyone at the school with an AK-47. The stepfather was later arrested and convicted of attempted terrorism. But an appeals court reversed the conviction on the basis that **the stepfather's statement did not create an imminent danger**. *State v. Watts*, No. M2013-02750-CCA-R3-CD, 2015 WL 3863242 (Tenn. Ct. Crim. App. 6/23/15).

◆ A mother said a teacher at her daughter's elementary school released the daughter to a person who was not authorized to pick her up. The person then allegedly sexually assaulted the child, who was later found on a playground. The mother sued the school district and others, asserting a due process violation. The defendants filed a motion to dismiss, but the court denied it. **The allegations of the complaint were sufficient to plead that the alleged sexual assault was a foreseeable result of the teacher's actions** and were also sufficient to plead that the teacher took affirmative steps to place the child in danger. *L.R. v. School Dist. of Philadelphia*, 60 F.Supp.3d 584 (E.D. Pa. 2014).

◆ A father dropped his son off at school. Later that day, a woman identifying herself as the boy's mother called the school. She claimed that the boy had an appointment and that her boyfriend would pick him up. The boyfriend was not on a list of people who could pick up the child, and the school allowed the man to leave with the child. The child was then taken to Mexico, where his mother lived. The father sued, alleging violation of his substantive due process rights, negligence and intentional infliction of emotional distress. A jury found in his favor on all claims, but the trial court granted a defense motion for judgment as a matter of law as to the emotional distress claim. On further review, a federal appeals court decided that the defendants were entitled to qualified immunity as to the due process claim. However, **it upheld the jury's finding of negligence**. *Ramirez v. Escondido Unified School Dist.*, 648 Fed.Appx. 669 (9th Cir. 2016).

◆ The guardians of a nine-year-old female student filled out a school form that listed the adults who had permission to remove the child from the school. Six times, the school released the child to a man who said he was the student's father. **The school did not ask the man for identification, and on several occasions he sexually abused her and then returned her to school.** The student's parents sued the school district and other defendants, claiming a violation of the student's due process rights under the federal Constitution. A district court granted a defense motion to dismiss, and a federal appeals court affirmed. The district did not create or knowingly increase the danger to the student, so there was no constitutional violation. *Doe v. Covington County School Dist.*, 675 F.3d 849 (5th Cir. 2012).

◆ A man entered a high school and told a front-office employee that he was the uncle of a student at the school. The man told the employee he was at the school to pick up the student and take her to an appointment. School policy called for the staffer to ask the man for picture identification and to verify that the adult was listed in the student's file as a person who was authorized to remove her from school. However, **the staffer did not ask for picture identification or check the student's file, which would have revealed that only the student's parents were authorized to remove her from school**. The student was released to the man, who took her to a house and molested her. When the student's mother sued the staffer for negligence, a trial judge ruled for the staffer. However, an appeals court reversed. It said that although public school employees in the state can't be sued for negligently performing discretionary acts, the student-checkout policy made her acts "ministerial." Therefore, the staffer could be sued. However, a jury was needed to decide whether the molestation of the student was a reasonably foreseeable consequence of the staffer's failure to adhere to the policy. *Cotton v. Smith*, 714 S.E.2d 55 (Ga. Ct. App. 2011).

◆ A high school custodian repeatedly sexually molested a student. The custodian would remove the student from class with written permission he obtained from the school's main office. Then, the custodian would proceed to sexually abuse the student. The abuse was discovered when school surveillance video showed the custodian taking the student into a custodial closet. The custodian was criminally charged, and he was incarcerated. The student's parents sued the local board of education, alleging claims under the federal Constitution based on the board's alleged failure to ensure students were free from sexual assaults, its alleged deprivation of educational services and its alleged failure to supervise a safe and open environment for educational services. **The parents claimed their son was sexually molested as a result of the board's policy of granting permission to the**

custodian to repeatedly remove the student from class. The complaint also asserted a federal statutory claim and state tort and constitutional claims. The board of education filed a motion to dismiss. The court refused to dismiss the claims the parents raised under the Fourteenth Amendment. The law recognizes liability for sexual molestation, and it also recognizes a property interest in educational benefits that are temporarily denied. Further, the law recognizes that in some circumstances the state has an affirmative duty to care for and protect particular individuals. In this case, it would be premature to dismiss the parents' claim that the board failed in its duty to protect the student. The state law tort claims were barred by immunity, and the claim under the state constitution was dismissed because there was an adequate state remedy. Finally, the court dismissed claims of breach of contract and violation of the Americans with Disabilities Act. *Cooper v. Brunswick County Board of Educ.*, No. 7:08-CV-48-BO, 2009 WL 1491447 (E.D.N.C. 5/26/09).

◆ A mother enrolled her six-year-old daughter at a school and informed the school secretary that her estranged husband had abducted the child in the past and was not to have contact with her. The secretary did not note the warning on the child's registration form, and it was not entered into the school's computer system. School procedures required the receptionist to check a student's registration card before releasing any child to make sure the person picking up the child was authorized to do so. If a particular child's registration card did not list the person attempting to pick up the child from school, the receptionist was to consult a school administrative official. During school one day, the receptionist received a call and a fax from someone who posed as the child's mother. The impostor instructed the receptionist to release the child to the estranged husband. The receptionist looked for the child's registration card but could not locate it. She then released the child to the estranged husband. The school reprimanded the receptionist for failing to consult with an administrator before releasing the child. The child's mother sued the principal and receptionist. The trial court concluded that the principal and receptionist were immune from liability under state law. The mother appealed, but only as to the ruling regarding the receptionist. The appeals court explained that public officials are generally immune from damages caused by their performance of discretionary functions. However, they are not entitled to immunity if harm is caused by their negligent performance of ministerial acts. In this case, the receptionist was performing a ministerial act when she released the student. **The policy regarding the release of students did not allow for the exercise of any discretion on her part.** She had been specifically told that she was to consult an administrator if she received a fax request to release a child from school. Because the receptionist's conduct did not involve discretion, she was not entitled to immunity. The lower court's ruling in favor of the receptionist was reversed. *Smith v. McDowell*, 666 S.E.2d 94 (Ga. 2008).

◆ A high school teacher brought a 14-year-old special education student to the assistant principal's office, stating that she had found the student walking in the hallways. The student provided the telephone number of a man she said was her uncle. **School policy barred the release of students to anyone other than a parent, legal guardian, police authority, or a person designated in writing by a parent. Nonetheless, the assistant principal allowed the student to call the man to arrange for her to be picked up from school.** He then left the student alone in the lobby of the school's main office. The man picked her up from school and allegedly sexually abused her at his home. The student's mother sued the vice principal and the school district, asserting due process and state-law claims. A magistrate judge granted summary judgment in favor of the assistant principal, finding that he was immune from suit. The mother appealed. The appeals court affirmed the decision in favor of the assistant principal. The assistant principal was entitled to qualified immunity on the student's federal claims because the student did not adequately allege a violation of substantive due process. The assistant principal was not obligated to protect the student due to a special relationship. The student could not prove her claim that the assistant principal had a duty to protect her because he created the danger that led to her alleged harm. The assistant principal did not restrain the student in a way that created a constitutional obligation to protect her. In addition, he did not act with deliberate indifference. The student's state-law claims failed as well, because the assistant principal's actions did not result in the student's alleged injury. The decision of the lower court was affirmed. *Doe v. San Antonio Independent School Dist.*, 197 Fed.Appx. 296 (5th Cir. 2006).

◆ The father of two children sought a divorce from his wife. The wife obtained a temporary restraining order splitting custody of the children. A school policy allowed students to leave with their parents if the approval of the principal was first obtained. The date and time of student departure and return was to be recorded with the reason for leaving school. The father became upset when he came to school and learned his mother-in-law had taken the children to their mother. The mother told staff not to release the children to their father, but a staff member said that would require a court order. The next day, the father came to the school for both children. The reasons he gave for signing them out were "keeping promise by mother" for the daughter and "pay back" for the son. Police later arrived at the father's house to find it ablaze. The father brandished a knife, and the police killed him. The children's bodies were found inside the house. The mother sued the school board in a state court for negligence.

The court held for the board, and the mother appealed. The state court of appeals held that schools, teachers, and school administrators have a duty to exercise ordinary care for student safety. The board was not liable for negligently violating its own sign-out policy. There was no evidence that staff knew about a dispute until the mother called the day before the murders.

Without a court order, a school has no legal duty to follow the instruction of one parent not to release a child to the other parent. The court affirmed judgment on a claim based on the father's violent nature. However, failure to read his reasons for signing out the children was evidence of breach of the duty to exercise ordinary care. **The court rejected the board's claim that it had no legal duty to examine a parent's reason for signing out a child.** The reasons the father gave for signing out the children might cause a reasonable person to suspect he intended to cause them harm. The state Governmental Tort Liability Act did not protect the board, since the decision to release the children did not involve planning. The decision was reversed, and the case was remanded. *Haney v. Bradley County Board of Educ.*, 160 S.W.3d 886 (Tenn. Ct. App. 2004).

D. Other Cases

◆ A parent claimed that a school coach bullied and harassed his older daughter for three years before she graduated. He had his younger daughter transfer to a neighboring district. His younger daughter played sports, including on the grounds of the former district. After a heated meeting attended by the parent, the coach and the superintendent of the former district, the superintendent told the parent he could enter that district's property only if he provided one day advance notice and only during his daughter's games. The parent sued the district and the superintendent, alleging violation of his right to free speech, assembly and association as well as his right to due process and equal protection. He sought a preliminary injunction that would allow him to attend events on district property that were otherwise open to the public. **The court granted the injunction.** The loss of First Amendment freedoms constituted irreparable harm to the parent, and any alleged harm to the district was "largely illusory and speculative." Further, the public interest favoring the protection of constitutional rights outweighed the district's interests, and the parent was likely to succeed on the merits. *Coffelt v. Omaha School Dist.*, 309 F.Supp.3d 629 (W.D. Ark. 2018).

◆ A parent whose daughter had been molested by a teacher protested outside her school with a licensed gun in plain view. The school district's superintendent filed a petition for an order of protection against the parent. A court ordered the parent to stay away from the school. The parent appealed, alleging violations of his rights under the First Amendment and the Second Amendment. The appeals court affirmed the lower court's decision. The evidence showed that **the parent engaged in a course of conduct that involved continuing harassment**, and the superintendent and parents were threatened by his conduct. The order for protection did not violate the parent's rights under the First Amendment or the Second Amendment. *S.B. v. Seymour Community Schools*, 97 N.E.3d 288 (Ind. Ct. App. 2018).

◆ When a man learned there had been a shooting at his younger sister's school, he rushed to the school to check on her. When he arrived, he had a concealed handgun tucked into the waistband of his pants. An officer on scene believed the man was acting suspiciously. He patted him down and found the gun. The man was arrested on an unlawful possession of a firearm charge. He appealed his conviction, arguing that the warrantless search was illegal. A state appeals court agreed. **An officer safety exception to the warrant requirement did not apply** because the man followed the officer's directions and did not pose an immediate threat. Also, a school safety exception to the warrant requirement did not apply because the officer's general concern that the man may have been involved in the shooting did not create a reasonable suspicion that he posed an immediate threat of serious harm. The lower court's decision was reversed. *State of Oregon v. Powell*, 406 P.3d 1111 (Or. Ct. App. 2017).

◆ A student's parent had a history of angry, aggressive and disruptive interactions with staff at his child's school. He raised his voice when speaking with school employees, yelled at school employees, and acted aggressively toward them. He said his conduct was caused by a disability. The school's principal decided to require the parent to gain prior permission before coming to the school, and the parent did so several times. He nonetheless sued the principal and others, claiming the restriction violated the Americans with Disabilities Act. A court granted summary judgment against him, finding that **the restriction was imposed based on his history of aggressive behavior and not by reason of his disability**. *Lagervall v. Missoula County Public Schools*, No. CV 16-57-M-DLC-JCL, 2017 WL 3610549 (D. Mont. 8/22/17).

◆ A student's father repeatedly approached his daughter's school basketball coach to ask how she could get more playing time. The father then engaged in heated discussions with school administrators about the situation. The school responded by banning the father from the school and from school-related events both on and off campus. When the father was subsequently denied access to school sporting events, **he filed a lawsuit against the principal alleging violation of his First Amendment right to free assembly**. An appeals court said the principal was entitled to immunity on claims arising from the ban from school premises. But it denied immunity as to claims premised on the bans from on-campus sporting events and off-campus events. *Johnson v. Perry*, 859 F.3d 156 (2d Cir. 2017).

◆ Parents enrolled their three children in the same elementary school. One of the children had a disability and was eligible for special education. After the mother complained that she heard a teacher at the school had a drinking problem, the principal threatened to bar her from campus if she did not stop. Then, the father had an altercation with another parent at the school. The school told the father he could not come to campus without prior approval. It later placed the same restriction on the mother after she intimidated staffers by using profanity, monitoring them and expressing dissatisfaction with their performance. **The parents sued, accusing the school of violating the Americans with Disabilities Act** by barring them from coming to school to advocate for the child who was eligible for special education. The court dismissed their claim, noting that the school restricted access but did not altogether bar them from school facilities. *Camfield v. Board of Trustees of Redondo Beach Unified School Dist.*, No. 2:16-cv-02367-ODW(FFM), 2016 WL 7046594 (C.D. Cal. 12/2/16).

◆ An elementary school had concerns about a father volunteering at the school after the father engaged in threatening behavior that included verbally threatening the principal, disrupting a parent-teacher meeting and pounding on car windows to get the attention of other parents. The school's district sought a restraining order that would bar the father from the school's campus. The father responded by alleging in his own lawsuit that the suit against him was motivated by racism and violated his speech rights. **The court granted the restraining order** because some of the father's speech contained credible threats. It also dismissed the father's claim. *Poway Unified School Dist. v. Garnier*, No. D067571, 2016 WL 6247683 (Cal. Ct. App. 10/26/16).

◆ An attorney visited a private school to interview witnesses on behalf of clients he was representing. He entered by a road leading to a parking lot, neither of which had "no trespassing" signs. The attorney interviewed two student witnesses inside a campus building. When school staff learned of the his presence, they called police. The next day, a local police officer called the attorney and said he was not to return to the school. He also told him he would be receiving a citation for trespass. **The citation was issued, and the attorney sued the officer for malicious prosecution and violation of his rights under the First Amendment.** The court rejected the malicious prosecution claim because the attorney was not subjected to a seizure and there was probable cause to issue the citation. It also rejected the First Amendment claim because the attorney did not engage in constitutionally protected conduct when he interviewed the witnesses. He did not have a First Amendment right to interview witnesses wherever he chose. *Considine v. Jagodinski*, No. 13-7263, 2015 WL 1573391 (E.D. Pa. 4/9/15).

◆ A mother arrived at a high school to pick up her son from Saturday detention. They walked through interior double doors directly onto the school's baseball facility, and the doors locked behind them. The entrance/exit gates to the baseball facility were locked, and the pair tried to exit by climbing a six-foot-high fence. The student did so successfully, but the mother was injured. She sued the school for negligence, but she lost. Although there were no signs near the double doors indicating that they were for exit only, the school did not breach any duty to the mother. **It was**

not foreseeable that she would exit the double doors and get trapped in the baseball facility. She also had other options: She could have used her son's cell phone to get help, and she could have had him re-enter the building and let her out. *Gutchewsky v. Westside Community Schools*, No. A-14-446, 2015 WL 1243207 (Neb. Ct. App. 3/17/15).

◆ A school's entrance doors had glass panes. A seventh-grader pushed on the glass and it shattered, cutting him. He and his mother sued, claiming the school had maintained a dangerous and defective condition. The court denied the school district's motion for judgment without a trial. Though safety glass wasn't required when the school was built and no current law required retrofitting, the district was in the habit of replacing broken glass with Plexiglass. Therefore, **a question existed as to whether the district knew it was dangerous to leave glass in the doors**. A trial was needed. *Karathanasis v. Union Free School Dist.*, No. 56217/2011, 2013 WL 3828389 (N.Y. Sup. Ct. 7/24/13).

◆ A high school student's father objected to a school's plan to have students use "Smart IDs," which include a radio frequency chip to track students. The father rejected the district's offer to let the child use an ID without the chip. **The student and her father sued, claiming a violation of their religious rights.** They alleged that they would be "condemn[ed] to hell" if they allowed tracking of the girl at school. The court rejected the father's request to order the district to let the girl stay at school without the ID while the case proceeded. It said the father was not likely to win, as the offer of a chip-free ID was sufficient. *A.H. v. Northside Independent School Dist.*, No. SA-12-CA-113-OG, 2013 WL 85604 (W.D. Tex. 1/8/13).

◆ A high school student's mother said she told school officials that a schoolmate was getting violent with her son. The student said that while he was standing outside a school office, the schoolmate and the schoolmate's father physically attacked him. He sued the school district officials, alleging a violation of his substantive due process right to be free from harm. The court ruled against him, finding that "the failure to create greater security barriers for entry to a public school" did not support a substantive due process claim. **School officials generally do not have a constitutional duty to protect students from attacks by third parties.** Though an exception to this rule would apply if the district created the danger that caused the injury, the district did not create the danger in this case. *Campbell v. Brentwood Union Free School Dist.*, 904 F.Supp.2d 275 (E.D.N.Y. 2012).

◆ A high school student was seriously injured in her school's parking lot when the car she was sitting in was rear-ended by a student who was driving another vehicle. The injured student's parents sued the school district for negligence, claiming it was liable for failing to ensure safe driving conditions in the lot. **The court ruled for the district, finding it was immune to the claim raised against it** because an element of judgment was involved with respect to regulation of school parking lot traffic and because the judgment involved economic concerns and public policy. *J.S. v. Lamar County School Dist.*, No. 2011-CA-00260-COA, 2012 WL 2895914 (Miss. Ct. App. 7/17/12).

◆ A ninth-grader was expelled for having a knife at school. He was allowed back on the condition that he would not again violate any major rule, but he subsequently threatened one student and punched another. He also wrote a threatening message on his backpack. His readmission was finally rescinded after he became irate at a meeting and the principal concluded he had violated a rule barring intimidation and harassment. After his expulsion, he continued visiting the school to pick up friends and use the weight room. When a teacher told him to leave, he punched a locker and was banned from campus. He was cited for trespassing after he ignored the ban. He sued, claiming the district wrongfully failed to provide him with notice and a hearing before instituting the ban. He lost, because once he was expelled from the school he had the same right as any other member of the general public to access it. At that point, **he had no constitutional right to access the campus**. *Hannemann v. Southern Door County School Dist.*, 673 F.3d 746 (7th Cir. 2012).

◆ Parents of students divorced, and the father was granted physical custody. Following the divorce, the mother needed the father's permission to see the children. The father informed the children's school that he did not want the mother to visit the children at school. When the school denied the mother access, she sued and claimed a violation of her constitutional right to control the education of her children. The court rejected her claim. **Parents do not have a constitutional right to make decisions relating to how a school is run.** The school's actions did not prevent the mother from raising her children as she saw fit. *Schmidt v. Des Moines Public Schools*, 655 F.3d 811 (8th Cir. 2011).

◆ A woman drove to a high school to drop off her son at a field house that was located on the high school's grounds. As she was leaving, she drove her vehicle into a free-swinging metal gate. The gate penetrated the vehicle and injured the woman. She and her husband sued a school resource officer, alleging he violated a duty to secure the gate, report its broken latch to authorities, and have the gate equipped with a working latch. Under state law, the school resource officer could be sued if the acts of inspecting the gate and reporting/repairing any damage to it were discretionary. If the acts were ministerial and did not involve the exercise of discretion, the school resource officer was entitled to immunity unless he acted with malice or intent to injure. **The court ruled that the school resource officer was**

entitled to immunity. The parties agreed that he did not act with malice or intent to injure, and there was no formal policy or procedure that created a ministerial duty on the part of the school resource officer to inspect the gate. *Scott v. Waits*, 703 S.E.2d 419 (Ga. Ct. App. 2010).

◆ A school district regulation required all visitors to present state-issued photo identification before entering secure areas of the school where students were present. Information on the visitor's identification document was photographed and checked against lists of registered sex offenders. The parent of elementary school students visited their school but refused to allow school officials to scan her driver's license or input her information manually. As a result, the parent was not permitted to access areas of the school that she wished to visit. Instead, she met with her children's teachers in a conference room. The parent subsequently was similarly blocked from accessing particular areas of the school when she visited to attend a musical, a volleyball game and a Thanksgiving lunch. The parent sued the district, claiming violations of her constitutional rights to speech, assembly, association, freedom from unreasonable search of seizure, privacy, procedural due process and substantive due process. She also asserted claims under state law. A trial court ruled against her, and a federal appeals court affirmed. **The parent did not have a fundamental right to access the secure areas of the school, and she was not denied the ability to make fundamental decisions about her children's education.** Further, the regulation was narrowly tailored to achieve the compelling state interest in determining whether a potential visitor was a registered sex offender. *Meadows v. Lake Travis Independent School Dist.*, 397 Fed. Appx. 1 (5th Cir. 2010).

◆ A high school student was suspended for three days for packing snow into the gas cap of a schoolmate's car. The student's father went to the school and acted in a loud and threatening manner. The father left at the request of the vice principal, but he said he planned to complain to the superintendent and local media. He also reportedly told the vice principal he "better look for another job." The father was later arrested for creating a disturbance at the school, but the charge against him was eventually dismissed. The father and student filed a lawsuit. The student claimed he was suspended without due process, and the father accused the police of malicious prosecution. The court rejected the claims. The student's due process rights were not violated because the vice principal spoke to the student about the incident three times and allowed him to tell his side of the story. And **the father's claim of malicious prosecution failed because witness reports supported the conclusion that the police had ample cause to arrest him for creating a disturbance at school**. *Scrocca v. Alton Police Dep't*, No. 1:08-cv-0042-JL, 2009 WL 2246753 (D.N.H. 7/28/09).

◆ A 17-year-old high school student was killed in his school's parking lot when a vehicle driven by another student struck him. The administrator of the student's estate sued the school district and a security company employed by the district, claiming negligent supervision of the parking lot where the accident happened. **The court held that the district was not liable because it did not have specific notice or knowledge of a particular danger at a particular time.** Therefore, the district could not have reasonably anticipated the accident. The security company could not be held liable because there was no evidence it failed to perform its duties under its contract with the district. Even if it failed to supervise its security guards at the school, such a breach could not be deemed a proximate cause of the accident. *Ravner v. Autun*, 876 N.Y.S.2d 453 (N.Y. App. Div. 2009).

◆ A parent entered a school gymnasium to pick up his stepson. He left the gymnasium by going through double doors that led to a commons area. One of the doors came off a closing mechanism and fell on the parent's head. He sued for negligence, and a trial court ruled for the district. It found a state tort claims act recreational use exception to liability was applicable. Under the exception, a claim could not be brought if injury occurred while the property was being used for recreational purposes. After a state appeals court affirmed the trial court's decision, appeal reached the state's highest court. The parent argued that the recreational use exception was inapplicable because the injury occurred in a commons area and not in the gymnasium. The lower court had found the school commons was a "transitional area" from outside the school into the gymnasium. The lower court found the commons was an appendage to the gymnasium and was therefore a part of a "recognized recreational use area." **The state's high court explained that the legislative purpose of the tort claims act was to immunize government entities so as to encourage them to build recreational facilities without fear of lawsuits.** To be immune, the school district had to show the parent was claiming only ordinary negligence and that the injuries resulted from the use of a "qualifying property," meaning a property that was "public" and was intended to be used for recreational purposes. Although the commons was not used exclusively for recreation, the court found it was "an integral part of the use of the gymnasium." The commons was used to sell tickets and concessions during events, and it was not "incidentally connected" to the gymnasium. The commons was necessarily connected to the gymnasium as a principal means of access and for purchasing tickets and concessions. The parent's use of the commons at the time of the injury was consistent with the plan of the building. **Extending immunity was consistent with legislative intent. A school would be discouraged from opening a gymnasium for recreational use if liability was permitted in an area that was integral to its recreational usage.** The school district was immune from liability under the recreational use exception. *Poston v. Unified School Dist. No. 387, Altoona-Midway, Wilson County*, 189 P.3d 517 (Kan. 2008).

◆ After a fire alarm sounded at a high school, a guidance counselor was severely injured when a student pushed open a door. The guidance counselor sued several defendants, including the city where the school was located. He relied on the theory that the swinging double doors were negligently designed. A jury issued a verdict in his favor, and the defendants appealed. The appeals court negated the jury's verdict and issued a ruling in favor of the defendants. It explained that the issue in the case was whether the building design complied with safety standards that were in place when the school was constructed. The guidance counselor's expert testified that the design of the double doors was unsafe because it placed people going through the left door into the path of the door on the right. The expert also testified that the lack of a restricting mechanism allowed the doors to be opened too quickly. The court explained that the expert's testimony did not establish that the design of the doors violated the building code that was applicable when the school was built in 1970. **Rather, expert testimony offered by the defense showed that the doors complied with the building code that was in effect at the time of construction. In addition, the guidance counselor did not show the design of the doors was unsafe in light of the design standards that applied when the school was built.** The guidance counselor did not prove his claim of negligent design. Therefore, the judgment entered on the jury's verdict was reversed. *Hotaling v. City of New York*, 866 N.Y.S.2d 117 (N.Y. App. Div. 2008).

◆ A parent volunteer was asked by another parent to check on the other parent's child at the school. The volunteer parent said she signed a volunteer sign-in sheet and then went to the classroom of the other parent's daughter. She said a teacher's aide nodded her approval to enter the classroom, and the volunteer parent visited with the girl and a paraprofessional for about two minutes. The volunteer parent then left the building before returning at lunch time to perform volunteer duties. During lunch, the other parent asked the volunteer parent to check on the other parent's daughter again. On her way out of the building that day, the volunteer parent looked in the window of the girl's class but did not go in because the door was closed. **The same day, the school sent the volunteer parent a letter banning her from the school for five weeks.** It claimed the volunteer parent had violated a state law that banned "interfering with peaceful conduct of activities." The volunteer parent objected. After a hearing, the length of the ban was reduced. The volunteer parent sued the school district, claiming a violation of her due process interest in the care, custody and control of her children. She also asserted other claims, including a claim of emotional distress. The court granted the school's dismissal motion. It noted that **public education is committed to the control of school authorities, and parents do not have a right to total control over every aspect of their children's education**. Instead, school authorities have broad discretion when it comes to operating their schools, and the school permissibly limited the volunteer parent's access to its premises. *Mayberry v. Independent School Dist. No. 1 of Tulsa County, Oklahoma,* No. 08-CV-416-GKF-PJC, 2008 WL 5070703 (N.D. Okla. 11/21/08).

◆ A school parent, who was the president of the Parent Teacher Student Organization (PTSO) at her son's elementary school, criticized the school's performance and safety policies. The school's principal said the parent threatened administrators and teachers and violated visitation policies. He banned her from school, prevented her from distributing flyers and cancelled a PTSO meeting. The parent sued the principal and other school officials, **claiming the actions taken against her violated the First Amendment because they were designed to prevent her from criticizing the school**. She claimed the defendants' actions were a retaliatory response to her criticisms. The court denied cross-motions for summary judgment, finding factual issues were present. There was conflicting evidence about whether the principal took adverse action against the parent for a permissible reason. Also, it was not clear whether the school had created a public forum for speech. Therefore, it was too soon to issue a definitive ruling on the First Amendment claim. *Williamson v. Newark Public Schools*, No. 05-CV-4008 (WJM), 2008 WL 1944849 (D.N.J. 5/1/08).

◆ A parent who was visiting a school got into a confrontation with a school employee. A school safety agent witnessed the confrontation and attempted to separate the parent and the school employee. The school safety agent advised the school employee to walk away from the confrontation. The school employee walked to a staircase to return to her classroom. Moments later, the parent followed her into the stairwell and attacked her. The school employee sued the board of education to recover for her injuries. A trial court denied the board's motion for summary judgment, but the appeals court reversed. **The appeals court held that the school employee did not show that the school safety agent had assumed an affirmative duty to act to prevent the attack.** The school employee did not show that the school agent was aware that the parent posed a threat of violence. Therefore, the board was not liable for the school employee's injuries. *France v. New York City Board of Educ.*, 834 N.Y.S.2d 193 (N.Y. App. Div. 2007).

◆ The parent of a high school student complained to the school's principal after the student broke his leg during a school football practice. The parent claimed that the student received no medical attention from any of the coaches present at the practice. Two years later, the parent complained to the principal again after the student was inserted into a football game even though he was feeling ill. A short time after he made the complaint, the principal barred the parent from entering any school district property except to drop off and pick up his son. The principal also circulated a memo stating that he physically feared the parent and that the parent was "the most out-of-control parent [the principal] had witnessed in 31 years of education." The parent later sued the school district, claiming it violated his constitutional rights by barring him from school property. The court granted the district's motion to dismiss the claim. The court was unable to locate any authority for the proposition that the parent had a constitutional right to enter school property. To the contrary, **school officials have a right to assure that parents conduct themselves properly while they are on school property**. The parent did not show that the decision to bar him from school property violated his constitutional rights. *Van Deelen v. Shawnee Mission Unified School Dist. #512*, 316 F.Supp.2d 1052 (D. Kan. 2004).

CHAPTER TWO

Emergency Preparedness and Response

I. INTRODUCTION

From active shooters to weather emergencies, schools have to plan for a whole variety of worst-case scenarios. Many states make school emergency plans a legal requirement. But even when it isn't, it's a best practice for schools to have a plan to address every viable threat staff can think of as well as those that staff uncover by research – the biohazards we address later in this chapter might be a good example of that.

Once a plan is in place, it should be updated at least annually, but ideally as often as someone comes up with a way to improve it.

It's also important to have regular training sessions on the plan's procedures so people know what to do in a crisis *before* one happens. If a dangerous situation is occurring or impending, you want everyone to already know what to do next.

That's the common sense side of emergency planning. What about your legal duties?

The requirement to have school emergency plans is governed by state and local laws and regulations – but the federal government takes the matter so seriously that it issued guidance to schools and districts: the *Guide for Developing High-Quality School Emergency Operations Plan*, a collaboration by the departments of Education, Health and Human Services, Homeland Security and Justice along with the Federal Bureau of Investigation and the Federal Emergency Management Agency.

The guide is available online at *rems.ed.gov* – as is info on free training opportunities and "EOP Interactive Tools"; "a suite of emergency management planning tools" – software, apps and an offline interactive workbook – to help educators create and assess emergency operations plans.

In this chapter we'll touch on the federal guidance as well as other best practices before concluding with court decisions connected to school crisis planning or a school's response to an emergency.

II. SCHOOL EMERGENCY OPERATIONS PLANS

A. Federal Guidance

1. Overview

The developers of the *Guide for Developing High-Quality School Emergency Operations Plan* understand your school likely already has an emergency operations plan in place.

The way they envision you using the guidance is to perform needed tweaks by comparing your existing M.O. to the info and procedures suggested in the guide.

The main focus of the guidance is on planning, but that's intended to be seen in the context of these five mission areas:

- **Prevention** of threatened or actual school emergencies

- **Protection** of students, teachers, visitors, school networks and property
- **Mitigation** of threatened or actual harm at school
- **Response** that establishes a safe and secure school environment, saves life and property, and facilitates the transition to:
- **Recovery**, which means a restoration of the learning environment

2. Your Planning Team

Having set the example by having six federal agencies team up to produce the *Guide*, the guidance emphasizes the importance of collaboration in school safety planning.

It suggests your "core planning team" should include not only administrators but also:

- teachers
- school psychologists and nurses
- facilities and transportation managers
- food personnel
- representatives of students, parents, persons with disabilities, racial minorities, and religious minorities, and
- first responders, such as: police officers, SROs, fire officials, EMTs, and also public health and mental health practitioners.

And don't forget students. You can find and download the "Involving Students in Prevention Checklist" at *www.SchoolSafetyAndSecurityAlert.*

3. The Feds' Standard for 'High Quality'

The guidance also contains benchmarks to help you assess the quality of your plan.

As a basic matter, your plan has to comply with the state laws and local requirements that pertain to school emergency operations plans.

Beyond that, the guidance says plans are:

- **adequate** if they effectively address critical courses of action
- **feasible** if tasks can be accomplished with the available resources, and
- **acceptable** if they get tasks done on time and within budget and the plan complies with the law.

The guide calls a plan **complete** if it:

- "Incorporates all courses of action to be accomplished for all selected threats and hazards and identified functions"
- "Integrates the needs of the whole school community"
- "Provides a complete picture of what should happen, when, and at whose direction"
- "Estimates time for achieving objectives, with safety remaining as the utmost priority"
- "Identifies success criteria and a desired end state" – and

- "Conforms with planning principles outlined in this guide."

EOP EVALUATE is available at *rems.ed.gov* to help you determine how your existing plan measures up to federal guidance. Check out it and related emergency planning resources by clicking on "EOP Interactive Tools" under the "Technical Assistance" drop-down menu.

4. Useful Features

The guidance also has helpful info on complying with federal law in the context of a school crisis.

It contains an overview of the Family Educational Rights and Privacy Act (FERPA) to address concerns schools have found confusing in the past.

The guide also contains info on the Health Insurance Portability and Accountability Act of 1966 to help you with matters of confidential health records.

There is also information about how to make sure your plan complies with the Americans with Disabilities Act.

As we discuss later in this chapter, it also contains a helpful "Active School Shooters" section.

Now let's move on to best practices.

B. Plan Considerations

1. Basic Plan Elements

There is no one-size-fits-all approach to crisis management plans.

Each school has a unique school community with unique needs, and schools in different parts of the country face different risks. For example, if your school is in an earthquake-prone area, you'll want to check out FEMA's Earthquake Preparedness Checklist, available from the Forms Library at *www.SchoolSafetyAndSecurityAlert.com.* You'll also want to see the info on earthquake drills at *shakeout.org*, the product of multiple partners including FEMA.

But even schools in the same general area of the country and facing the same general risks are going to have different challenges depending on whether the school is, for example, in a big city or a quiet little town.

Importantly, each state has different laws that its schools must follow.

The bottom line: For a crisis management plan to be truly effective, it must be tailored to your school's specific needs.

That said, some things are true of all plans. For example, each one has to comply with the law.

Also, every crisis management plan should be considered a work in progress. That's because the day-to-day realities at school are constantly changing. For example, one important preparedness step is to assign crisis duties to personnel – but staff come and go. You may lose (or gain) a CPR expert, someone fluent in sign language, a person with a first aid certificate, etc. It's important to keep staff members' areas of expertise in mind because a pregnancy leave, a resignation, or a new hire may mean you need to reassign duties under your plan.

Students also come and go, shifting the established needs of your community. That can mean making sure different disabilities are accommodated or new languages are covered to make effective communication with students and their parents possible.

Also, lessons learned from a previous incident can mean that the plan should be tweaked to take advantage of real-life experience.

☑ CHECKLIST – *Basic Plan Elements*

- ☐ complies with the law
- ☐ is periodically reviewed and updated as needed
- ☐ includes provisions relating to students with disabilities
- ☐ addresses potential language barriers, and
- ☐ is updated based on real-life experiences when appropriate.

See the Forms Library at *www.SchoolSafetyAndSecurityAlert.com* for two "Vulnerability/Hazard Assessment" checklists: one for emergency operations plans, the other for instructional facilities.

2. Students Not on Campus

Have you planned for the possibility that a crisis may occur when students and staff are away from campus under circumstances that mean the school still has responsibility for them? For example, what if a class is on a field trip or a team is in transit to an away game when an emergency strikes? If possible, having at least one school transportation specialist on your planning team could make sense. Concerns to address here include:

- establishing communication protocols ahead of time – not just between the school and the away-group, but also between the school and the students' parents
- making sure staff always have emergency supplies before they leave campus – which might include water, energy bars, first aid supplies, a flashlight and a reliable communication device, and
- anything else that seems appropriate given the circumstances.

It's also important to remember to plan for events at school before and after the school day. Do you and your staff know what to do if an event occurs while after-school clubs are meeting or when there's a packed house in the auditorium for the annual talent show?

3. Communicating With Parents

Are you sure you can access contact info as needed in an emergency? It's a good idea to keep contact info in multiple places – both online and in hard copies that are laminated or kept in reliably waterproof containers.

Also, having compiled this info in the first place, you'll want to make sure to make it someone's responsibility to update it regularly.

Another important consideration is letting parents know where and how to get information about an ongoing incident. For a sample letter to parents on how your emergency planning affects them, search the Forms Library at *www.SchoolSafetyAndSecurityAlert.com* for "Sample Parent Letter: Pre-Incident."

One thing you may want to let families know in advance is that they should not come to campus during an emergency as they and their cars could physically block ambulances, fire trucks and emergency personnel.

Does it make sense to use social media to communicate with parents during an emergency? If so, you'll want to consider how to go about that, whose responsibility to make it, and how best to get the word out to families.

Even if you're planning to be all over social media, you'll probably want to provide as many other sources as you realistically can. Many parents have smartphones and access to the Internet, but it's not 100%. Also, service disruptions could be an issue in some emergencies.

Alternative ways for parents to get information about an incident in progress include calling a pre-arranged phone number to hear a recorded message that will be updated as often as possible under the circumstances. You may also be able to direct them to a local TV or radio station that has agreed to broadcast info about your school in case of an emergency.

Don't forget to plan for communicating with parents in as many languages as it takes.

And see the Forms Library at *www.SchoolSafetyAndSecurityAlert.com* for a "Reunification After a Crisis" checklist.

4. Emergency Supplies

Do you store emergency supplies at school in case of an emergency?

There are many approaches for schools that do, but they all tend to fall under two categories: either the school gathers all the emergency supplies, or the school gathers some of the supplies while parents and students, or some other party, supplies the rest.

Under one model plan, for example, parents are instructed to pack up specified drinks and snacks and a few other items (such as a laminated copy of the student's emergency card, a reassuring message and photo from the family, pocket-sized tissues and a small book or game) in a gallon zip-lock bag placed inside a 50-gallon plastic snap-top container and then bring it to school for storage.

The American Red Cross has reported that some schools have made it a practice to donate their emergency stockpiles of food to a charity at the end of each school year.

In addition to food and water, emergency supplies typically include first aid gear, radios and flashlights.

5. Evacuation and Lockdown

Evacuation and lockdown plans are basic – but that's because they're so important. It's never a bad idea to take another look at yours.

Evacuation requires predetermined routes, on-campus assembly sites (to evacuate from) and off-campus assembly sites (to evacuate to). You need several of each as the first choices might be unreachable or unusable due to the emergency.

For example, schools generally expect to evacuate staff and students by using school buses, but the roads may be impassable or buses may be unavailable. That's why alternate ways to remove students from danger should be made a part of your plan.

The evacuation provisions in model plans stress the importance of making sure students remain accounted for by:

- keeping classes together during the evacuation so that teachers can continue to keep track of their own students, and
- having teachers take roll both immediately before the evacuation and as soon as they arrive at the evacuation destination.

Keep in mind that authorities may ask that a school be evacuated for unforeseen reasons during a broader crisis. On 9/11, for example, Stuyvesant High School was near ground zero, but that was not why it was evacuated – the FBI wanted to use the school building as a command center.

Lockdowns are used to keep students safe inside from a danger outside. Your school will have its own procedures based on building features and other unique considerations, but one procedure many schools follow is to train staff in soft and hard lockdowns. The difference depends on the threat level. A mild threat may only require a soft lockdown – perhaps locked doors only. A serious and immediate threat calls for a hard lockdown: locked doors, lights and computers off, everyone silent, blinds closed (or everyone otherwise kept out of an intruder's line of sight). In a hard lockdown, it's possible every one is hiding while poised to run or fight.

Go to *www.SchoolSafetyAndSecurityAlert.com* for a "Sample Notice to Parents Regarding Lockdown Drill" to download and use at your own school.

6. Sheltering-in-Place

Sheltering-in-place is a response to the more specific danger of needing to minimize students' exposure to contaminants in the environment – a chemical accident, for example. The chosen rooms should have as few windows as possible. Basic necessities, such as food, water and bedding, should be stored there in advance, along with emergency supplies, such as flashlights, radios, first aid supplies and medicine.

For sheltering-in-place, the American Red Cross suggests an interior room that's located above the ground floor and has no windows. This is because some dangerous chemicals are heavier than air. Even with precautions, heavy chemicals could seep into basement rooms. As an extra safety measure, provide people a wet cloth to keep over their noses and mouths.

The Red Cross also says all HVAC and fans should be turned off and all vents and cracks around doors should be sealed with duct tape. If only a room with windows is available, it should be covered with plastic and sealed over completely with duct tape.

See the Forms Library at *www.SchoolSafetyAndSecurityAlert.com* for checklists showing steps to take in such circumstances. Search for "Gas Leak Response" and "Hazardous Spill Response."

7. Planning for Your Staff in a Crisis

Virtually every crisis presents twists no one could have imagined – and therefore no one could have planned for. That's one reason training staff on the plan is so important. Having the basics down makes it a lot likelier staff will be able to intelligently adapt the original plan to cover unexpected events.

Sometimes the unexpected element is people's reactions. No one knows what they'll be like under pressure until they actually experience it. Also, people are different – and so are their responses to a crisis. Some people may find themselves cool-headed and decisive, while others might have to fight the tendency to panic or freeze. Training can help tilt the scale toward cool-headed decisiveness.

Another thing that can help is having easy-to-read-and-understand checklists on hand. Many plans call for them – and some call for them to be laminated to make them not only more durable but also more legible, since you can wipe off a laminated surface.

Simple, straightforward checklists that contain basic action plans and also relevant contact info can help get frozen people up and going again and on to the next step.

Even if you trust everyone to stay calm, focused and move quickly, it's a good idea to have simple reminders that can be easily scanned and followed.

Here's something else to keep in mind and possibly include in the plan: One common mistake experts have cited is schools waiting too long to call in emergency services and alert its own crisis team.

The best bet is to go ahead and call for help and alert the team even if there's a chance the situation might be resolved by the time help arrives. If that turns out to be the case, that's actually a good thing. And if there's any risk of injury or loss of life or property, it's best to err on the side of safety.

For templates you can download and fill in with the names and numbers you'll need in an emergency, search for "Crisis Team Member List" and "Emergency Telephone Numbers" in the Forms Library at *www.SchoolSafetyAndSecurityAlert.com.*

8. Planning for After the Crisis

Experience has shown that there are several predictable recovery needs that many schools experience after an emergency is over.

Because they're predictable, they can be planned for and addressed in the crisis plan. They include:

- helping students, families and staff cope with trauma
- repairing any physical damage to the facility
- addressing insurance requirements, and
- dealing with the media.

Perhaps the most predictable recovery need in the wake of a crisis at school is that students, families and school staff are likely to need help coping with the emotional fallout that accompanies living through a disaster. One way to support staff is by utilizing a thank you letter such as the one provided in our Forms Library at *www.SchoolSafetyAndSecurityAlert.com.*

You may want to get advice from experts in whatever field is needed. And don't forget in planning for the after-effects of trauma that you may have your own onsite experts. School counselors have the added advantage of already having a relationship with many of the people who might need help.

Schools that go to off-campus professionals for preliminary advice for the plan might use the advice-gathering process as a kind of audition to determine if the expert might also be a good person to bring back to help the school if the worst happens.

Another predictable recovery need concerns the school building. Even apart from additional safety considerations – such as leaking roofs that could lead to slip-and-fall accidents or falling rubble that could cause injuries – the physical damage left after a disaster can be a potent reminder of traumatic experiences. Among other pressing reasons, making repairs can be an important way to psychologically help your community move beyond the event.

One thing you can do to prepare for property damage is make sure you have plenty of "before" pictures. Still images work, and so do videos. If you can manage it, aerial photos are also a good idea if FEMA is likely to be involved. You'll probably also want to make sure some kind of camera is on hand to take "after" photos of property damage as well.

It can also be a good idea to find out in advance exactly what other kind of insurance requirements the school is likely to have to comply with in case it has to make claims on any policies.

Another predictable recovery-stage need is for a spokesperson or spokespeople to deal with the media. Many schools already have staff and established procedures in place for this.

For a "Sample Statement to the Media: School Violence," see the Forms Library at *www.SchoolSafetyAndSecurityAlert.com.*

Finally, the plan should call for debriefing sessions with school staff and emergency personnel after any actual crisis so the school can incorporate lessons learned from the incident into the plan.

C. Special Considerations

The Governmental Accountability Office (GAO) is the agency that acts as the investigative arm of Congress.

The GAO made a 2007 study of school planning and preparedness and then issued a follow-up report in 2016.

Its 2007 report found that virtually all plans addressed bombs or bomb threats, hostage situations, and the natural disasters likely for the locality. Go to *www.SchoolSafetyAndSecurityAlert.com* for a "Bomb Threat Report Form" and the checklist, "Bomb Threat Procedures."

Schools should also be prepared to follow up on environmental risks, such as chemical spills. Also available at *www.SchoolSafetyAndSecurityAlert.com* is a "Parental Consent Form for Mercury Testing."

The GAO also found in 2007 that city-based school districts were more likely than rural school districts to plan crisis responses for terrorism (86% as opposed to 70%) and much more likely to plan for incidents involving radiation (60% compared to 29%) or anthrax (57% of urban districts versus 26% or rural districts).

In addition to those findings, the GAO's 2007 study also identified areas in which many plans weren't following recommended practices. In 2016 it found improvements, but continued to stress the importance of:

- including procedures to ensure the safety of special needs students
- including a plan to continue teaching students in case the school closed due to a pandemic or other emergency
- conducting school drills and exercises, and
- training with first responders and community partners.

This section will focus on topics that many schools and districts may still need information to address.

1. Special Needs Students' Safety

Just as a good crisis management plan is tailored to address the crises a school is likely to face, a good plan for students with disabilities is drafted to take into account the special needs of the students the school actually has in its own community.

The GAO's 2016 update found around 69% of school districts had plans that took the needs of school community members with disabilities into account.

Recommended practices include:

- keeping track of where special needs students are located throughout the school day
- identifying the staff assigned to evacuate or shelter with these students, and
- providing any devices needed to transport them to evacuation areas.

Educators told the GAO in 2007 that districts devise their own procedures for keeping special needs students safe in a crisis because disability groups don't agree on the best practices.

One reason for this might be that while all students are unique, students with disabilities tend to be the most unique of all. Some need motorized wheelchairs to cross a room, while others need specialized laptops to communicate. Still others – Down syndrome or autistic children, for example – have cognitive limitations that may require a teacher with real experience of what works with a particular student to get him or her on the evacuation bus or to keep the child from panicking during lockdown or sheltering-in. And while first responders can tell at a glance if a student has Down syndrome, the same isn't true if a student is autistic.

A study of 2014 data led the CDC to estimate one in 59 eight-year-olds had an autism spectrum disorder – and indications that this population is increasing emphasize the importance of crisis planning to specifically address the needs of these students.

Info provided by The Autism Society for paramedics and ER staff warns of typical reactions that could be especially problematic in a crisis.

Children with autism may over-react to loud noise and bright lights – running away or turning aggressive if confronted by a siren accompanied by flashing lights, for example. The 2016 GAO report cites one district that provides noise-reducing headphones for students less able to tolerate loud noises like fire alarm sirens.

Other issues concerning autistic students can include: not understanding the significance of first responders' badges or uniforms; not following directions; refusing to make eye contact; getting inappropriately close; responding in confusing ways (or not at all) to requests for information; answering every question with "Yes!" or using gestures instead of language.

The unique problems posed by autistic children during emergencies have led several groups to create specialized training for first responders in dealing with this population – something you may want to discuss when you liaise with your own first responders for planning or practice drills.

For more on first responder training on dealing with individuals with autism, go to *autismalert.org*.

Autistic students and other special needs students often need extra help under normal circumstances. This need for extra help can greatly increase in a crisis. As the National Organization on Disability has said, perhaps the most effective tactic for special needs individuals to survive an emergency is to have strong relationships with nondisabled people.

Disabilities are categorized differently by different groups, but there are some special needs experiences that may be common enough to take account of for crisis management planning. For example:

- People who use wheelchairs, crutches or other mobility devices are going to need special help if an emergency disables elevators or leaves piles of rubble blocking paths – especially if a speedy exit is required.
- Individuals who are blind are likely to be badly disoriented by loud, overwhelming noises – like sirens. Extremely loud noises drown out the ambient sounds that normally give blind people cues

about who and what is in their immediate environment and what is happening there.

- People with cognitive or developmental disabilities like ADHD, Down syndrome and Tourette's are likely to have trouble following instructions.

☑ CHECKLIST – *Special Needs Planning*

- ☐ Establish a pre-set location to which special needs students can be escorted so they can be rescued.
- ☐ Consult with emergency responders about their own protocols for dealing with special needs individuals – and adopt them, if appropriate.
- ☐ Alert emergency responders to the presence of any special needs students likely to need additional help, such as the mobility-impaired.
- ☐ Obtain devices – such as specialized, light-weight chairs – to help evacuate students with severe mobility problems.
- ☐ Train staff to use any specialized devices deemed necessary to evacuate these students, and play it safe by assigning more people to operate them than are actually needed.
- ☐ Provide (or train) a sign-language interpreter, if needed.
- ☐ Provide written instructions in Braille, if needed.
- ☐ Make sheltering-in arrangements for service animals. Although pets aren't permitted in shelters, federal regulations allow service animals – although they can be excluded if they threaten others' lives or safety or if they become a nuisance. That said, anyone with known allergies to animals should be assigned to a different room.
- ☐ Store pet foods, medicines, plastic bags and disposable gloves for service animals along with other emergency supplies – and earmark water for them.
- ☐ Store backup devices of any vital special-needs device.
- ☐ Store spare or alternative power sources for the devices.
- ☐ Store needed medication along with emergency supplies.
- ☐ Provide cards for special needs students to wear to alert first responders of their condition and the limitations it causes them. For example, a card for a person with a cognitive disability might state that this person has trouble understanding language, so patience and a simple vocabulary are needed.

Go to *www.SchoolSafetyAndSecurityAlert.com* and search the Forms Library for "Students/Staff Needing Special Assistance for Evacuation" for a template to help you build a list of those needing this help at your school.

2. Planning for Disease Outbreaks – and Delivery of Education

The recurrence of vaccine-preventable diseases like the measles and chickenpox has been getting the headlines lately – and you should plan accordingly – but never underestimate the flu.

A flu pandemic isn't the only crisis that could shut down schools and require you to find viable means to deliver education to students in their homes – but it's one of the likeliest.

Flu pandemics are caused by a highly contagious flu virus so new (or so long since it last circulated) that many people have little or no immunity to it. With a virus-specific vaccine possibly not available for at least six months, the chance of serious illness or fatality goes way up.

But the risks posed by the flu are significant even without a pandemic. Pneumonia and the flu are eighth on the Centers for Disease Control and Prevention's (CDC's) most recent list of leading causes of death.

The 1918 flu pandemic killed 500,000 Americans. Pandemic numbers aren't always that dramatic. The 1957-58 pandemic caused 70,000 fatalities. The 1968-69 pandemic caused only 34,000.

Researchers estimate the 2009-10 H1N1 pandemic killed 2,634 more people than would have died if it had been a regular flu season.

Thanks to widespread public outreach associated with H1N1, most schools have taken onboard the recommendations from the U.S. Department of Health and Human Services (HHS) and the CDC.

They suggested pandemic flu planning could include education campaigns to prevent spread of the virus by:

- frequent hand washing
- sneezing and coughing only into either a tissue, which is then immediately disposed of, or against the upper arm if a tissue isn't available, and
- encouraging everyone in the school community to stay home at the first sign of illness.

For the latest on the flu in the U.S., see *cdc.gov/flu*.

☑ CHECKLIST – *Flu Virus Avoidance*

- ☐ Focus on protecting high-risk students and staff, such as anyone who's pregnant or has asthma or diabetes
- ☐ Establish a plan to cover key personnel if they're out sick
- ☐ Work out ways to make it harder for the virus to spread – such as by holding class outside when feasible, regularly washing much-handled surfaces (like door knobs and computer equipment) with the usual cleaning supplies and moving student desks farther apart
- ☐ Cut any program that might encourage staff or students to come to school when sick – for example, prizes for good attendance

- ☐ Set up a special room to care for anyone who's sick until they can be sent home
- ☐ Have a supply of gloves and masks on hand for those who care for them

Based on experiences schools had with the H1N1 virus, it also might be a good idea to get a supply of disposable thermometers. A fever is associated with the flu, and some schools dealing with H1N1 outbreaks had several students displaying flu symptoms at once.

You should also be aware that some students displaying flu symptoms may be in your care longer than you expect. In fact, some schools had a serious problem with parents sending sick children to school during the spring 2009 outbreak. That's probably not too surprising, given the economic pressures many parents face plus the difficulty of finding child-care. In any event, realities being what they are, this may be something you want to anticipate and plan for.

The CDC also advises schools to contact and work with local health authorities in anticipation of a pandemic.

The 2007 GAO report identified these procedures for educating students when the school is closed:

- electronic or human telephone trees to convey academic information
- web-based instruction
- mailed lessons and assignments, and
- classes broadcast over local TV or radio stations.

Depending on the availability of electricity during a crisis and the level of Internet access among your school community, you may want to consider some kind of web-based delivery of education.

Alternative-education plans are extremely important because experts can anticipate circumstances in which schools could be closed for longer than a year – although a more conservative estimate is that pandemic-related school closures could last from a few weeks up to three months.

The spring of 2009 saw schools closed to protect public health by limiting the spread of the virus. These closures weren't long, but future closures could be – not just to limit spread of a virus but because there might be so few teachers available due to illness that there aren't enough to supervise the students.

For more on school planning, see *cdc.gov/flu/school/index.htm.*

3. Training

Based on a GAO survey for its 2016 report, it estimated about half of districts hold emergency exercises with fire department and law enforcement personnel annually – but that about a quarter have never trained with emergency medical services personnel and about a third have never done so with public health officials.

The danger of not conducting this participatory training is that it can lead to confusion over who's doing what during an actual event.

Training, on the other hand, can provide responders basic and necessary information, such as how to get into the school, where to turn on (or off) utilities, and how to find their way around. It can speed up response time and may save lives if, for example, the medics told to report to the gym already know where the gym is.

For a template to download and fill in with the contact info you'll need, search for "Emergency Telephone Numbers" in the Forms Library at *www.SchoolSafetyAndSecurityAlert.com.*

a. Training With First Responders

It is important to keep in mind that law enforcement, firefighters and emergency medical services have their own protocols. By training with them, schools can learn whether any protocols conflict or are otherwise counterproductive. Also, first responders have a level of training and experience that most school staffs lack. This is a valuable resource. Schools should take advantage of it.

Training with first responders can also clarify whether you're likely to have communication problems. FEMA suggests always using plain language to make sure everyone understands what is needed. It may be obvious to someone very familiar with the campus that "Ken-one" is short for No. 1 Kendall Street and means the auditorium, but it won't be obvious to Officer Rodriguez who just moved here from two states away.

Plain language is a good idea even when it comes to communicating effectively with staff inside the school. A first-time substitute teacher will have no idea that the "Code Purple" announcement over the intercom means he's supposed to lock the classroom door and tell students to lie flat on the floor.

Training with first responders can also help schools make sure in advance that their technology will work with emergency responders' equipment so that they can communicate in a crisis. Incompatible equipment can lead to the school and responders failing to connect or even jamming each other's gear and shutting down communication entirely.

Eight of the 27 districts that the GAO interviewed in researching its 2007 study said that their one-way radios and other equipment didn't work with the first responders' equipment. School officials in Iowa told the GAO that their district had a special problem in that it shared a radio frequency with only some of the first responders, not all of them.

It's vital to fix such disconnects *before* an emergency.

b. Training With Community Partners

While the police, the fire department and emergency medical services spring immediately to most school staffs' minds, not as many think of working with public health professionals and benefiting from the training and expertise they can provide. These community partners can be especially helpful in the event of a biological and radiation emergency.

In addition to other help, public health professionals can help schools plan the best response to biological and radiation events. They can provide expert guidance on specific hazards as well as such info as when sheltering-in-place is called for and how to care for children who may have been outside when an event occurred.

Biological weapons ultimately make people very ill, but the initial symptoms can fall within the normal range of everyday complaints. Therefore, one of the greatest risks of a biological attack is that it will not be recognized as such until after there has been a significant loss of life. The more quickly a biological attack is recognized, the more casualties can be prevented by distributing the available vaccines and antidotes.

In the case of anthrax, for example, the initial signs of the gastrointestinal form of the disease look a lot like food poisoning. The preliminary symptoms of the inhalation form of anthrax could easily be mistaken for a cold or the flu. Symptoms could appear within a month after contact with the bacterium, but they can take longer than a month to appear.

There is a vaccine to prevent anthrax. Even after it's contracted, a 60-day course of antibiotics can sometimes provide a cure.

Schools can help reduce the lag time between seeing symptoms and recognizing a biological attack – and thus save lives – by assigning a staff member to monitor diseases at school and look for patterns. It also helps to have staff who:

- can distinguish between normal illnesses and anomalies caused by biological weapons
- keep in close touch with the public health department, and
- know how and where to report unusual symptoms.

In terms of crisis management planning for an actual incident, a supplement to the Report of the National Advisory Committee on Children and Terrorism suggests:

- training staff in Blood Borne Pathogen Standards
- training staff to use personal protective gear and respirators and conduct a decontamination
- having one accessible switch to perform an emergency shutdown of the HVAC system in order to keep anything airborne from spreading, and
- having a procedure in place to let parents know about the illness and the best way to treat it.

As with pandemics, a biological attack might require schools to close – with all that this implies – in order to avoid the spread of disease.

The CDC's website has an A-Z listing of bioterrorism agents posted at *emergency.cdc.gov/bioterrorism*. This listing includes information about how the diseases are contracted, the symptoms, and if vaccines or cures are available.

With respect to radiation, ideally schools would be prepared to administer potassium iodide in case of radiation exposure within two hours of a "dirty bomb" explosion or a catastrophic incident at a nuclear plant.

A radiation event could require either sheltering-in-place or an evacuation. Public health professionals can help schools to determine when each of these options is the most appropriate choice.

D. Issues Raised by Real-Life Crises

1. School Shootings

As this book went to press in 2019, at least 22 gun incidents had been reported at U.S. schools, with at least two of them – in Highlands Ranch, Colorado, and Prescott, Arkanas – believed to have been premeditated attacks. To state the obvious, each such incident is a tragedy and even one life negatively impacted by it is one too many. That said, it's the especially shocking school shootings that have led to the prevention and planning efforts and resources we discuss in this section.

The Columbine High School shooting on April 20, 1999, was carefully planned by two extremely disturbed students. Including their suicides, 15 people died. Significantly, it was realized after the fact that the perpetrators had been broadcasting big clues about the massacre they were planning.

According to facts alleged in just one of the many personal injury cases brought in the wake of the tragedy, the perpetrators' videos for a video production class featured them "carrying guns, presumably fake, down the school hallways, computer graphics of the school exploding, and a collage of violent shooting scenes from commercial movies. In these videos and in class discussion, [they] spoke of killing, of their ownership of guns, and of their bombmaking abilities."

This lawsuit further alleged that the perpetrators "wrote and spoke of their hatred, anger, possession of firearms, and desire and intent to kill and injure others, including Columbine students" in psychology and creative writing classes. *Castaldo v. Stone*, 192 F.Supp.2d 1124 (D. Colo. 2001).

Among the lessons learned from Columbine is that schools need to take such red flags seriously and respond accordingly. Though suspensions and expulsions based on students' depictions of violence have led to multiple First Amendment suits by parents, courts typically uphold a school's need to take such measures to ensure school safety.

Another lesson learned from Columbine: Students there were aware of warning signs they didn't pass along to teachers or administrators. This helped put it on schools' radars that they need to have "if you see something, say something" efforts at school.

On December 14, 2012, 20 first-graders and six school staff members were killed by an armed intruder, a disturbed 20-year-old, at the Sandy Hook Elementary School in Newtown, Connecticut.

The Sandy Hook tragedy prompted a national discussion about whether school personnel should be armed and whether schools should be required to have active shooter drills. States went on to pass laws saying yes to each.

The feds' *Guide for Developing High-Quality School Emergency Operations Plans* comes out in favor of active shooter drills but urges schools to tailor them to the students' ages. The guide includes an "Active

Shooter Situations" section that provides a lot of useful information. Again, the guide is available online at *rems.ed.gov.*

Most recently, a student expelled from Marjory Stoneman Douglas High School in Parkland, Florida, came on campus on February 14, 2018, with a semi-automatic rifle. He killed 17 members of the school community.

In July 2018, the U.S. Department of Homeland Security and the U.S. Secret Service released *Enhancing School Safety Using a Threat Assessment Model; An Operational Guide for Preventing Targeted School Violence*. It sets out an eight-part prevention plan for schools to put in place: establishing a threat-assessment team; defining the behavior to watch for or prohibit; creating a central reporting mechanism; deciding the point to involve law enforcement; establishing assessment procedures; developing risk management options; creating and promoting a safe school climate; and training.

The guidance provides especially helpful details concerning student behavior to watch for – behavior that might indicate a student is planning to commit a violent attack.

You can download the guide from *dhs.gov* or *secretservice.gov*. Search for "Enhancing School Safety" to access the PDF.

Also in 2018, the Department of Homeland security issued the second edition of *K-12 School Security*. As it explains, "This resource guide was developed to address only one of the specific threats that schools face – gun violence." Among other things, it provides guidance on including this topic in your emergency operations plan, provides information on technology you may want to consider (door blockers and gunshot detection systems, to name two), and provides directions on accessing and taking a school security survey for gun violence that will help you assess any vulnerabilities and then recommend ways to address them.

The guide and the survey are available at *dhs.gov/publication/k-12-school-security-guide*.

And for steps key personnel should take in the event that an intruder gains unauthorized access, search for "Intruder Response" in the Forms Library at *www.SchoolSafetyAndSecurityAlert.com.*

2. School Walkout Protests

In the aftermath of the 2018 Parkland shooting, national school walkouts were planned – including for April 20, 2018, the 19th anniversary of Columbine – to protest gun violence in schools and the failure to stop it.

Walkout protests may not have been on your radar to plan for before – but they are now, and the government's Readiness and Emergency Management for Schools Technical Assistance Center has issued guidance on how to incorporate such protests into your emergency operations plan.

Among the issues it flags for you to consider are: whether to have school police officers accompany students who leave campus, how to handle lost instructional time and whether to discipline students for walking out of school.

Responding to Student Demonstrations and Protests in Schools and School Districts is available online at *rems.ed.gov/docs/RespondingtoStudentProtests.pdf*.

3. Tornado Safe Rooms

In May 2013, a massive tornado in Moore, Oklahoma, destroyed two elementary schools and killed seven second- and third-graders.

This opened up widespread debate on whether tornado safe rooms should be required in schools.

According to info provided by FEMA: “A safe room is a hardened structure specifically designed to meet FEMA criteria and provide ‘near absolute protection’ in extreme weather events, including tornadoes and hurricanes.”

On the pro side of the debate, requiring safe rooms in schools – especially in states where severe storms are common – could save lives. On the con side, the cost would be astronomical. One school safe room can cost as much as $1 million.

Currently, there are few mandates requiring schools to have safe rooms. Alabama law requires new schools to have safe rooms, and a few school districts have also decided to find a way to make safe rooms happen – but those are the exceptions.

For more info, check out FEMA’s Safe Room Funding page at *fema.gov/safe-room-funding*.

4. Wildfires

In November 2018, wildfires ravaged Paradise, California The many, severe losses to the community included two elementary schools and a high school. Rebuilding could cost as much as $50 million.

School was back in session in fall 2019, but many students had been shifted to a different school, with grade school students in what used to be the middle school, and grades 7-12 in the high school.

Importantly, toxic conditions in the wake of the fire meant new water systems were needed in the schools.

While the 2018 Paradise-area wildfires were unusually devastating, wildfires have become increasingly damaging in recent years. To address this, the Readiness and Emergency Management for Schools Technical Assistance Center has released guidance to help schools address this risk in emergency operations plans.

Set out as step-by-step guidance that starts with planning and ends with recovery, the guidance includes examples of experts to have on board (such as state foresters); important planning steps (like determining how vulnerable your school is to wildfires); and mitigation steps (that might include a new filtration system to improve indoor air quality when smoke from nearby fires is an issue).

Access this guidance at: *rems.ed.gov/docs/WildfireFactSheet_508C.pdf*.

III. LEGAL DECISIONS

A. Intruder- and Student-Attack Cases

Students and teachers have tried to hold schools responsible for injuries caused by students or school intruders by arguing that the school's crisis planning somehow created a duty to ensure their safety.

When the claim is brought as an alleged constitutional violation, courts virtually never find "the state" (here, a public school or the police) legally responsible for the violent acts of private individuals.

There are two very narrow exceptions, not recognized by every jurisdiction. The first is the state-created danger (or enhanced danger) doctrine. The second is the special relationship doctrine.

Under the **state-created danger doctrine**, the state can be held responsible for a person's injury if the state did something that either created the danger that caused the injury or significantly increased it.

Under the second exception, the **special relationship doctrine**, an injured party can prevail by showing that the government took actions that created a legal duty to protect him or her. (The special relationship doctrine can also create liability under states' personal injury laws.)

The decision in a case filed after the Columbine shootings clearly illustrates the operation of the legal framework described above.

The Colorado federal court dismissed most of the injury lawsuits brought by students and teachers in the wake of the Columbine shootings, finding the state was not legally responsible for private individuals' violent acts. But the court refused to dismiss the following case, finding both the state-created danger and special-relationship exceptions applied.

◆ The police created a legal duty to protect a Columbine teacher who bled to death after medical attention was delayed for four hours. **The police interfered with the teacher's ability to save himself and took actions that increased his danger of bleeding to death.**

A teacher was standing outside a cafeteria packed with early lunch period students when he saw two students approaching with guns. The teacher went into the cafeteria and shouted for the other students to run. He lagged behind until the last of the students escaped up a stairway. As he was urging the last ones up the stairs, one of the gunmen shot him twice in the back. The teacher managed to shepherd approximately 50 students into an upstairs classroom before he collapsed.

The teacher had spotted the gunmen at approximately 11:35 a.m. and was shot about five minutes later. Perhaps half an hour after that, rooftop police sharpshooters with high-powered binoculars saw the gunmen commit suicide in the library.

Although the officers in command knew about the suicides almost immediately, they incorrectly characterized the state of affairs inside the school as a "hostage situation" and followed "hostage situation" procedure by allowing no one in or out of the building – including the firefighters and

SWAT team that wanted to rescue the teacher and the emergency medical staff that wanted to provide him onsite care.

Inside the classroom, another teacher and several students applied makeshift compresses to staunch the injured teacher's bleeding. By 12:30 p.m., at least two people had made 911 calls – which were relayed to the responding officers – to report how seriously the teacher had been injured and to tell emergency responders exactly where to find him. They also hung a large sign in the window reading: "1 BLEEDING TO DEATH."

An uninjured teacher spent the afternoon keeping 911 operators informed of the deterioration of the injured teacher's condition. Starting at around noon and continuing for more than three hours, the 911 operators kept relaying the police's message that help was "on the way" and would arrive soon, and that no one should leave the classroom to seek medical help.

At around 2:00 p.m., a 911 operator alerted the police that the people in the classroom were threatening to throw chairs through the windows to attract help for the injured teacher. Although the police knew the gunmen were dead, they told the operator to say this plan was more likely to draw the gunmen than medical help. About half an hour later, an uninjured teacher tried to leave the school to find a medic, but a SWAT team member, acting under police orders, forcibly pushed him back inside.

Once rescue personnel did enter the building, the injured teacher was the last wounded person they reached – even though he was the only person identified as someone who could be saved by emergency medical treatment and they had been told exactly where to find him. A SWAT team finally reached him at 4:00 p.m. By that time, his originally survivable injuries had become fatal. He died.

The deceased teacher's personal representative sued the board of county commissioners, the sheriff's department and several individual officials, alleging deprivation of life in violation of the deceased teacher's right to due process. The United States District Court for the District of Colorado denied the government defendants' request to dismiss the suit.

The district court explained that the U.S. Supreme Court held in 1989 that the Fourteenth Amendment's Due Process Clause does not impose a duty on a state to protect individuals from private acts of violence. Its purpose is "to protect the people from the State, not to ensure that the State protects them from each other." *DeShaney v. Winnebago County Dep't of Social Services*, 489 U.S. 189, 109 S.Ct. 998, 103 L.Ed.2d 249 (1989).

However, the district court continued, the Tenth U.S. Circuit Court of Appeals – which has jurisdiction over Colorado – had adopted two exceptions to this rule, both of which applied here. The special relationship doctrine applied because the government created a duty to protect this teacher by interfering with his ability to save himself, falsely assuring those caring for him that help was coming soon and ordering them not to seek other aid. **The state-created danger exception also applied because the police took actions that increased the teacher's danger of bleeding to death** by keeping him from the medical treatment that could have saved his life. Because these exceptions applied, the court refused to dismiss the case. *Sanders v. Board of County Commissioners of County of Jefferson, Colorado*, 192 F.Supp.2d 1094 (D. Colo. 2001).

As the following cases show, courts have not been persuaded by arguments that schools should be held legally responsible for injuries caused by a student or a school intruder because the schools had – or didn't have – a crisis plan.

It's also worth noting that the federal *Guide for Developing High-Quality School Emergency Operations Plans* makes a point of specifying up front that it is meant as "informal guidance" and doesn't create legal duties or rights.

Instead, to hold the schools liable, courts have insisted the injured parties must establish that either the special relationship doctrine or the state-created danger exception applies.

In one recent decision, New York City's education department decided to settle a lawsuit that challenged its oversight and enforcement of its regulations concerning school bullying.

◆ A New York federal court approved the terms to settle a suit against New York City's education department by students. The suit claimed city schools routinely failed to comply with the department's violence and bullying regulations – and education department staff didn't adequately address complaints about the lack of compliance.

The suit alleged that the schools' alleged failure to follow the rules violated the Fourteenth Amendment's guarantees of equal protection and both procedural and substantive due process; New York law and its constitution; and the Individuals with Disabilities Education Act.

Under the settlement, the department agreed, among other things, to introduce an electronic reporting system, available in multiple languages, that would let parents report bullying electronically and learn when their complaints were substantiated or resolved.

It also agreed to **require principals to complete bullying investigations within 10 days unless they could document extenuating circumstances**. The department also designated two new teams. One's task was to generate monthly reports on schools' compliance with the regulations, analyze trends across the city and provide targeted support to schools that needed extra help. The other team's job was to take over bullying investigations from schools under certain circumstances.

The court approved the agreement, finding the negotiation process to arrive at it was procedurally fair and that its substantive terms met the standard required by Rule 23 of the Federal Rules of Civil Procedure as they were "fair, reasonable and adequate." *Doe #1 v. New York City Dep't of Educ.*, No. 16-CV-1684 (NGG (RLM), 2018 WL 3637962 (E.D.N.Y. 7/31/18).

◆ A student injured in a gang-related attack claimed administrators increased the risk of his attack by covering up past attacks on others instead of entering them in a record and reporting them to the police. A Pennsylvania federal judge granted the school district judgment, finding the facts didn't bear out his claim.

Onesimus Gayemen had been at his new high school only a few days when four students asked for his black, red and white bead necklace. They said it was connected to a gang. He didn't know what they meant. They attacked him, leaving him with a fractured jaw and a concussion.

One assailant was incarcerated for the assault. The other three were prosecuted through the juvenile justice system. A detective later explained the necklace had made them think Onesimus was in a gang.

Onesimus sued the school district under a state-created danger theory, alleging it had violated his Fourteenth Amendment right to bodily integrity.

To state a valid claim, he had to show the district did something that made him more vulnerable to danger than if it hadn't acted at all. He didn't.

Under the school's Positive Behavioral Support System, assaults and violations of the district's gang policy called for suspension or expulsion. **School administrators were supposed to use an online system to document student discipline – and use it to track students who flashed gang signs, wore gang colors or otherwise signaled gang membership.** They were also supposed to report crimes to the police.

Onesimus claimed the district concealed gang-related fights and attacks instead of recording them in the online system and reporting crimes to the police – but produced no valid evidence to back his claim that the district failed to appropriately address gang-related violence and that this made him more vulnerable to suffering a gang-related attack. *Gayemen v. School Dist. of the City of Allentown*, No. 14-CV-1518, 2016 WL 3014896 (E.D. Pa. 5/26/16).

◆ A gym teacher hospitalized after an intruder's attack couldn't sue the city for her injuries. **The city didn't create a special relationship with her by putting safety measures in place or breach a duty of protection to her by not complying with its own school safety plan.**

A strange man appeared in the gym during class. He struck the teacher and then left. The teacher sent a student to alert a security guard about the intruder, but the student came back to say he couldn't find a guard. The intruder returned unnoticed and hit the teacher from behind, knocking her unconscious. Her injuries included a fractured skull, a fractured rib and hemorrhaging around her left temple.

The teacher sued the city for personal injury, but the court granted the city summary judgment.

New York law almost always found the city immune to personal injury suits based on the operation of a school's security system. The only exception was if the injured party could prove a special relationship that created a duty of protection. The teacher couldn't.

She claimed the school assumed a special duty to protect her because it implemented safety measures, such as metal detectors, door locks, panic bars, video surveillance, patrols by school aides and safety agents, and security telephones in the classrooms.

But the rule in New York was that police protection was owed to the community at large, not to specific individuals.

The teacher needed to show someone with the authority to make promises on the city's behalf created a special relationship with her by promising the city would keep her safe. Instead, she admitted the safety training she received from city employees was for all teachers, not just her. *Daniels v. City of New York*, No. 04-CV-7612(CM), 2007 WL 2040581 (S.D.N.Y. 2007).

◆ A student at a high school with escalating violence and chronic security shortages couldn't hold the school district responsible for injuries he suffered in another student's attack.

A tenth-grader was punched in the eye by a student in a school stairwell. The other student was aiming at someone else, who ducked. The injured student had a fractured facial bone and traumatic hyphema of the eye. He spent six days in the hospital.

Violence at the high school had gotten worse over the previous four years. The principal described the school as "out of control" with fights, fires and other serious issues.

The student said there should have been a surveillance camera in the stairwell. Also, the school was short four security officers and had not had full security staffing in 83 of the 85 previous days.

The student sued the school district, alleging it violated his Fourteenth Amendment right to bodily integrity and safety. The court granted the school district summary judgment. The student appealed to the Third U.S. Circuit Court of Appeals, but it affirmed judgment for the school district.

The student couldn't hold the school district responsible for his injury because the district didn't create the danger he faced.

The general atmosphere of violence at the school made it foreseeable any student might be attacked by another student, but the court didn't find the attack was a direct result of the district's actions.

The student also didn't show a surveillance camera in the stairwell would have prevented the attack or that security staff shortages increased the danger he'd be injured. Even if all the guards had been there that day, there was no guarantee one would have been in the stairwell at the time of the attack. *Mohammed v. School Dist. of Philadelphia*, 196 Fed.Appx. 79 (3d Cir. 2006).

◆ A teachers' union contract and an official circular creating a school security plan didn't create a special relationship that let a teacher hold the state responsible for his injuries from an attack in a school hallway.

A teacher was assaulted in the hall outside his classroom. He sued the school board, alleging his union contract and the state's official circular adopting and implementing a school security plan created a duty for the school to protect him.

A jury found in the teacher's favor, but the trial court set the verdict aside, finding the teacher's union contract and **the state's adoption of a school security plan didn't create a special relationship** between school authorities and the teacher. Without a special relationship, he couldn't hold them liable for not protecting him from third-party violence on school property. The teacher appealed, but the appellate court affirmed. *Krakower v. City of New York*, 217 A.D.2d 441 (N.Y. App. Div. 1995).

B. Negligence Claims

In the cases below, students and parents had mixed success in convincing a court to find their schools were negligent for not establishing or following a security plan.

◆ A Connecticut appeals court ruled that the town of Newtown and its board of education had immunity to negligence claims based on creating, enforcing and following Sandy Hook Elementary School's safety guidelines.

On December 14, 2012, Adam Lanza shot his way into Sandy Hook Elementary School. He killed 20 first-graders and six staff members, wounded two other staffers and then killed himself.

Two Sandy Hook students' parents sued the town and its school board for negligence. Under Connecticut law, a municipality can be liable for negligence in performing ministerial acts (which must be done in a specified way) but not in performing discretionary acts (for which actors can use their own judgment).

The parents argued that creating, enforcing and abiding by school security guidelines were ministerial acts. But the trial court found they were discretionary – so the defendants had immunity to the claims.

The appeals court agreed, finding school administrators' act of adopting school security guidelines was "an act of discretion encompassed within their general duty to manage and supervise" employees and students. It also found the guidelines "contained qualifying language such as *may* or *should*" that indicated employees "had discretion to exercise judgment in following them" rather than setting out exactly how employees "should respond to a shooting." It thus agreed the town and school board had immunity to the parents' suit. *Lewis v. Town of Newtown*, 191 Conn.App. 213 (Conn. App. Ct. 2019).

◆ A New Mexico charter high school that had written safety policies – but none for parking lots – was entitled to state-law immunity from a suit by a student who was attacked by another student in a school parking lot.

The student was walking to her car after school when a classmate emerged from another car, knocked her down and beat her so severely she suffered a torn ligament that required surgery and a painful rehabilitation.

The classmate later said the girl she beat up had bumped her in the hall that day and laughed at her on an earlier occasion.

The injured student and her mother sued the school for negligence, arguing charter schools weren't entitled to public school's state immunity to negligence claims but, even if they were, this claim should be allowed under an exception to state immunity. The trial court disagreed. It granted the school judgment without a trial. An appeals court affirmed.

The exception – for an injury caused by public employees' negligence in operating or maintaining equipment or premises – had been applied to public employees' failure to have or follow safety policies. But while the school had no *written* policy on supervising the parking lot, it did assign a teacher to monitor it after school. She made a bathroom stop on her way to the parking lot that day. When she got there, the fight was already over and there was no sign it had happened. **The court held, "New Mexico law does not require that a public high school have a written policy concerning parking lot safety."**

The appeals court agreed, finding the mother and daughter had pointed to "no statute, regulation, or case requiring New Mexico public schools to have such written policies." They also couldn't show that not having a written policy created a dangerous situation for students. Concluding that the claim here was for negligent supervision, which fell under the state's immunity, it affirmed judgment for the school. *Kreutzer v. Aldo Leopold High School*, 409 P.3d 930 (N.M. Ct. App. 2017).

◆ A negligence claim could go forward against a Kentucky principal who didn't submit a board-required plan for supervising students.

Dewitt Elementary School, its PTA and its afterschool program rented inflatable playground equipment for an event to reward children in the afterschool program. At it, student Christopher Brock fell off the back of an inflatable slide. He suffered a fractured skull.

Christopher's family sued school officials. The officials asked for judgment without a trial. The court granted it – apart from deciding that Principal Marcie Walker was not entitled to immunity on a charge of negligence *per se*. She admitted she hadn't submitted a supervision plan required by board policy. On appeal, the appeals court affirmed.

The **board policy required principals to submit a plan before the start of the school year to address student supervision** during bus loading and unloading, at meals, in halls, in restrooms, on playgrounds, before and after school, on field trips and at other school activities.

Kentucky public school employees have governmental immunity to negligence claims for discretionary acts but not for "ministerial" acts. The state's supreme court defined a ministerial act as one "the employee has no choice but to do" – and Walker's task to submit a supervision plan was specific and mandatory. As such, she was not entitled to immunity from a negligence suit based on her failure to do so. *Walker v. Brock*, Nos. 2014-CA-000868-MR & No. 2014-CA-000953-MR, 2016 WL 4410706 (Ky. Ct. App. 8/19/16) (Unpublished).

◆ The mother of a charter school student raped at an off-campus end-of-year party claimed the school board was negligent in not ensuring the school crisis plan was implemented – but a Louisiana appeals court held the claim failed. The board had no duty to supervise students off campus after the end of the school year.

Freshman Unique Hayes went to an end-of-year party hosted by a classmate's mother at a hotel. There, a boy Unique had never met before raped her in a stairwell. Unique's mother sued multiple defendants, including the school board – but the trial court dismissed the school board from the case. The mother appealed, but the appeals court affirmed.

State law gave the board immunity to this suit unless its negligence breached a legal duty it owed Unique. The board had no legal duty to protect Unique here as it was well established under Louisiana law that **a board's duty to exercise reasonable supervision over a student was limited to situations where the student was under its supervision or control**. Unique wasn't under the school board's supervision or control at an off-campus party that occurred after the end of the school year and where no school official was present. The school board was properly dismissed from the suit. *Hayes v. Sheraton Operating Corp.*, 156 So.3d 1193 (La. Ct. App. 2014).

◆ Finding state education department regulations had "the force and effect of law," the Delaware Supreme Court OK'd a negligence per se claim based on an alleged breach of rules concerning suicidal students.

The Delaware Department of Education's (DOE's) Regulation 621 required school districts to have written emergency plans that followed the DOE's Emergency Preparedness Guidelines.

A "Quick Referral Reference" posted on the DOE's website said schools with a suicidal student should contact the student's parents or guardian immediately.

To comply with the guidelines. the school district adopted the policy: "Crisis Intervention Procedures for Suicide Threats." Third on its list of six protocols was: "Contact Parent[.]"

After 16-year-old Roger Ellerbe's friend told a teacher and then a school counselor that Ellerbe was suicidal and had attempted suicide two days earlier, the counselor called Ellerbe into the office.

The counselor was working under a contract with the district. She didn't know the district had a protocol for dealing with suicidal students.

She spent four hours with Ellerbe and sent him back to class when she decided his crisis had ended. She sent an email to teachers, counselors and an assistant principal to tell them about the incident. She didn't call the boy's grandmother, his guardian.

That night, Ellerbe hanged himself at home.

Ellerbe's family sued the district for wrongful death. This claim required them to show the district was negligent. Finding they couldn't, the trial court granted the district judgment without a trial.

The family appealed to the state's highest court. It reversed, finding the case could go forward because the family stated a valid claim of negligence per se.

In Delaware, violating a statute or ordinance enacted for the safety of others constituted negligence per se. **The family claimed the district violated a school policy, but the court found it had "the force and effect of law."** As the family could make a valid negligence claim, their wrongful death claim could go forward. *Rogers v. Christina School Dist.*, 73 A.3d 1 (Del. 2013).

◆ A trial was needed for a student's personal injury suit because factors – including the school's failure to follow its security plan – indicated a New York district may have breached its duty to supervise students.

The district was aware of escalating aggression between two students.

First, a teacher had to restrain seventh-grader Ashley Bivens from physically attacking ninth-grader Tajoura Walley. A week later, the students got into a physical fight on a school bus, and a volleyball coach had to break it up. The next day, Bivens and Walley started a fight as soon as they got to school. Teachers had to separate them, and both girls were suspended.

The day their suspensions ended, Bivens went straight from the school bus to Walley's locker and stabbed Walley in the leg with a knife.

Walley sued the district, alleging it breached its duty to supervise them. She argued their escalating dispute put the district on notice that another incident could occur when they returned to school from their suspensions for fighting. She also **argued the school had failed to follow its security plan** by not:

- providing counseling, and
- having teachers stand outside their classrooms at the start of the school day to prevent problems.

The district agreed it breached its duty to supervise, but asked for judgment without a trial as its negligence wasn't the proximate cause of Walley's injury. It argued Bivens' attack was so sudden and spontaneous no amount of supervision could have prevented it.

The judge agreed and granted the district judgment. But Walley appealed, and the appellate court reversed.

As a prior New York decision held, the test for proximate cause was "whether under all the circumstances the chain of events that followed the negligent act or omission was a normal or foreseeable consequence of the situation created by the school's negligence." If it wasn't foreseeable, the school couldn't be held liable for it. But if that wasn't clear, a jury was needed – and that was the case here. *Walley v. Bivens*, 81 A.D.3d 1286 (N.Y. App. Div. 2011).

◆ The Nebraska Supreme Court rejected a mother's argument that the state education department's regulations for school safety plans created a legal duty that could be violated if a school district didn't follow the regs.

An intruder entered an elementary school's unlocked door and ignored a sign telling all visitors to check in at the office.

Two teachers spotted him and reported him to the office.

Meanwhile, five-year-old C.B. came back from the bathroom to tell his teacher "a bad man" was in there. C.B. later said the man pulled down his pants and performed oral sex on him.

The district's "Safety and Security Plan" and the school's "Emergency Procedures and Security" guidelines called for dealing with an intruder by talking to the person and then deciding whether to lock down the school and call 911.

The administrator went inside the restroom and found the man sitting in a stall. After C.B.'s teacher told the administrator what C.B. said, the administrator locked down the school and called 911. Police arrived and arrested the intruder.

C.B.'s mother sued, alleging the district was negligent because its security system was ineffective. The trial court granted the district summary judgment. It found the assault on C.B. wasn't foreseeable and the district had made a *prima facie* showing that its security plan was adequate.

On appeal, the Nebraska Supreme Court sent the case back for a trial to decide if the attack was foreseeable – but **rejected the mother's argument the school should be held liable because its safety plan allegedly didn't follow the state education department's regulations**.

The regulations set the standard for school security plans but didn't create an extra legal duty that went beyond the district's existing duty to act with reasonable care to protect students from a sexual assault. *A.W. v. Lancaster County School Dist. 0001*, 280 Neb. 205 (Neb. 2010).

C. Claims Based on State Requirements

◆ A Michigan appeals court found the state's concealed carry law did not preempt a school policy banning guns at schools and school events.

Ulysses Wong had a concealed-pistol license. Wong's son attended a school in the Ann Arbor Public Schools system. After the system passed policies to ban the possession of guns on school property and at school events, Wong and Michigan Gun Owners, Inc., sued to allege that state law allowing concealed carry of firearms preempted the system's policies banning guns at school. If that was true, the state had sole authority to regulate firearms, so the system couldn't pass rules concerning guns.

Michigan courts ask four questions to determine if state law preempts an area of law: Does state law say it does? Does the legislative history imply it does? Has the state pervasively regulated this area of law? Does the nature of the area of law demand exclusive state regulation? The trial court found the answer to each question was no – so found for the school system.

The plaintiffs appealed, arguing one state rule was needed because a "patchwork" of different school policies would cause "confusion" and "burden" the police and the public.

The appeals court disagreed. It affirmed the lower court's decision, adding the system's policy "ensures that the learning environment remains uninterrupted by the invocation of emergency procedures that would surely be required each and every time a weapon is openly carried by citizens into a school building." *Michigan Gun Owners, Inc. v. Ann Arbor Public Schools*, 318 Mich.App. 338 (Mich. Ct. App. 2016).

◆ California laws require public schools to have school safety plans. The plans must include anti-harassment and anti-discrimination policies.

An appeals court found the father of a boy who was allegedly bullied for being disabled and Hispanic could seek to enforce those laws against a school district his son no longer attended.

Hector F.'s seventh-grade son Brian was eligible for special education based on emotional disabilities, including bipolar disorder. English wasn't Brian's first language, and he was in the school's only bilingual classroom.

Hector went to administrators after seeing Brian had large bruises and scratches. Brian went on to file reports with the school to say other students were physically and verbally abusing him, including with ethnic slurs.

The principal's proposed solution was to move Brian out of the bilingual classroom. His parents rejected this proposal.

Hector and Brian sued the school district. **The father claimed the district hadn't adopted state-required safety plans.** He also alleged the district wasted taxpayer money by responding to harassment complaints in a way that discriminated against Hispanics and the disabled. He wanted a "writ of mandate" to enforce the laws. After Brian moved on to a high school in another school district, a trial court decided Hector couldn't seek this remedy – but an appeals court found he could.

Generally, the state allows writs of mandate only to "beneficially interested" persons, but Hector fell within a public interest exception. The appeals court wrote that the laws "articulate a well identified public interest in maintaining a system of taxpayer funded public education which is free of the destructive influence of discrimination, harassment and bullying." Here, the writ was intended to enforce a public duty. The court found Hector had a right to seek enforcement of the law both as a taxpayer and a member of the public. *Hector F. v. El Centro Elementary School Dist.*, 227 Cal.App.4th 331 (Cal. Ct. App. 2014).

In 2007, Georgia courts heard three appeals involving the interplay between the state's requirement that schools have crisis management plans and lawsuits brought by students who were seriously injured at school. In two cases, the school was sued because it didn't have a plan in place. In the third, the school was sued, although it did have a plan in place. In each case, the court found the school was immune to the student's lawsuit.

◆ A student who was nearly raped at school couldn't sue the members of the school board for negligence based on the board's failure to implement a school safety plan at her school because the board had state immunity to this claim.

A female student was sexually molested at school by a male student who also tried to rape her. Despite a state law requiring schools to have safety plans, there was no such plan in place at her school.

The student brought a Title IX claim against the school board. She also sued the individual board members, alleging they were negligent for failing to implement a school safety plan. The board members objected to her lawsuit, arguing they couldn't be held negligent because they had no individual legal duty to create the safety plan.

In Georgia, state employees were immune to lawsuits alleging negligence only if the duty they allegedly failed to perform was discretionary rather than ministerial. Discretionary duties called for greater personal authority and judgment, whereas ministerial duties were more like those performed pursuant to orders.

Because the *Murphy v. Bajjani* case (reported below) had determined Georgia school boards and superintendents had a discretionary duty when it came to preparing school safety plans, this court agreed with the board members that the student could not sue them for negligence based on their failure to develop a school safety plan. As a result, the court invited the board members to ask the court to grant it summary judgment. *Snethen v. Board of Public Educ. for the City of Savannah*, No. 406CV259, 2007 WL 2345247 (S.D. Ga. 2007).

◆ The Georgia Supreme Court held that a student severely injured by another student at school couldn't sue school administrators or members of the school board for negligence based on their failure to create a school safety plan as required by state law. Georgia law granted them immunity to negligence claims unless they acted with actual malice or intent to cause injury – which they did not.

In June 2007, the Supreme Court of Georgia reversed a lower court's judgment in favor of a high school student who was seriously injured at school by another student. The lower court determined the individuals sued by the student – including his principal, vice principal and members of the school board – were responsible for the student's injuries because the school hadn't created a school safety plan as required by Georgia state law. The law called for schools to devise a plan to respond to the following potential emergencies: natural disasters, hazardous material or radiological accidents, terrorism and violence.

The state supreme court reversed the judgment for the student and dismissed the case against the school defendants because it determined **these public employees had qualified immunity under the state's constitution with respect to safety plans**. This meant that they could not be sued for negligence unless they had acted maliciously or with intent to injure.

This decision hinged on which kind of duty the safety-plan law created: ministerial or discretionary. The court determined that drafting safety plans was a discretionary act (an exercise of educated, personal judgment) as opposed to a ministerial act (something more akin to following established procedures). Ministerial acts weren't covered by qualified immunity for negligence, but discretionary acts were.

The court dismissed the case against the school defendants because it found that creating a school safety plan was a discretionary act and the school defendants hadn't acted with actual malice or intent to cause injury. This meant they were immune to the student's claims. *Murphy v. Bajjani*, 647 S.E.2d 54 (Ga. 2007). A Georgia appellate court adopted the supreme court's judgment in another proceeding based on the same incident. *Bajjani v. Gwinnett County School Dist.*, 651 S.E.2d 366 (Ga. Ct. App. 2007).

◆ A county board of education, its individual members, the superintendent and **a school's principal and staff were entitled to official immunity because there was a valid safety plan in place at the school when a psychologically disturbed stranger gained unauthorized entry to it and attacked a 10-year-old with a hammer**.

Georgia law requires schools to create safety plans. This school provided evidence that it did have a safety plan in place before the intruder attacked the 10-year-old, but the child's parents argued that the plan wasn't valid because it had been developed by the Georgia Emergency Management Agency (GEMA) and other third parties instead of the school itself. But the Georgia Court of Appeals found that the law specifically sanctioned input from approved third parties and that it required GEMA to provide public schools training and technical assistance, which included safe school planning and model school safety plans.

This case pre-dated the state's supreme court decision that settled the law by finding creation of a school safety plan was a discretionary duty instead of a ministerial duty. But it also held the duty was discretionary and therefore shielded school officials from negligence charges. *Leake v. Murphy*, 644 S.E.2d 328 (Ga. Ct. App. 2007).

D. Evacuating Students With Disabilities

◆ The mother of a student in a wheelchair sued a school board for violating federal disability bias laws by not providing an aide to, among other things, help evacuate him in an emergency. A Florida federal court found she must instead bring her suit under the Individuals with Disabilities Education Act (IDEA) – but can't until she completes all hearings required by that law.

A 14-year-old needed a wheelchair due to a degenerative muscular condition. His wheelchair wasn't motorized, and he couldn't operate it himself. He also needed help with tasks like emptying and packing his backpack. Also, the school had three stories, but **only school staff was allowed to operate the elevator. That created safety concerns as the school had no plan to assist him in an emergency.**

His IEP team decided he'd benefit from a paraprofessional to perform the tasks he couldn't and to ensure his physical safety. The team later told his mother the board had agreed to appoint a full-time paraprofessional to help support his needs, but not in a one-to-one capacity.

She sued the board, alleging it violated the Americans with Disabilities Act and Section 504, but a federal court dismissed her suit. It found the suit actually alleged a failure to provide the free appropriate public education required under the IDEA – so the mother had to comply with the IDEA's requirement to fully complete the required administrative hearings before she could file a lawsuit in federal court. *Moragas v. School Board of Miami-Dade County*, No. 19-21517-Civ-Scola, 2019 WL 3252229 (S.D. Fla. 7/19/19).

◆ Finding no constitutional violations in the case of a 14-year-old disabled student who was injured during a school bus evacuation drill, an Alabama federal judge dismissed her family's lawsuit.

C.M.'s disabilities include cerebral palsy, osteopenia and arthritis. She's mainly nonverbal and uses a wheelchair. She can walk only short distances. After C.M. had swollen ankles following a fire drill, her mother told the principal and C.M.'s teacher that C.M. shouldn't walk in such situations unless it was absolutely necessary.

About three months later, the Talladega City Schools' transportation director told the special-needs students' bus driver to have a bus evacuation drill and include a wheelchair student. The driver decided to include C.M. even though C.M. took a different bus.

The Alabama School **Bus Driver Handbook said special-needs buses had to have evacuation blankets on board and use them to "drag students who are non-ambulatory towards the available exit"** so as to remove them from the bus and then "drag or carry them to a safe location."

During the drill, the driver didn't use a blanket to drag C.M. Instead, she was helping C.M. walk to the exit when C.M. lost her balance and fell. X-rays showed C.M. broke her wrist in three places, fractured a bone in her neck and chipped a bone in her back.

C.M. and her mother sued the school board, C.M.'s teacher and the bus driver in federal court, alleging constitutional violations and negligence. But the court found C.M.'s equal protection rights weren't violated as she was never deprived of access to a free, appropriate public education. It also found the facts the family alleged "though unfortunate and lamentable, do not rise to the level of conscience-shocking conduct necessary to support a substantive due process claim."

As the federal claims couldn't succeed, the court dismissed the suit, adding that the family was free to refile the negligence claims in state court. *McKenzie v. Talladega City Board of Educ.*, 242 F.Supp.3d 1244 (N.D. Ala. 2017).

◆ A disabled student couldn't sue the school board for disability bias based on staffs' failure to properly execute an emergency evacuation plan for children with disabilities.

A middle school student had a form of dwarfism that limited her strength and mobility. She had a computer with voice recognition software, a motorized wheelchair and a full-time aide.

In 1996, her school was evacuated for a bomb threat. She and another student with disabilities were left alone in the building under adult supervision for about an hour. No bomb was discovered.

Her parents filed a complaint with the state department of education, alleging the school board discriminated against her based on her disability by not evacuating her during the bomb threat. After mediation, the parents agreed to drop their complaint in exchange for the school board's agreement to adopt a new emergency preparedness plan.

In case of an emergency, students with disabilities would be in a "safe room" with an adult monitor, a dedicated cell phone and a special flag to alert emergency responders. If evacuation was necessary, emergency personnel would rescue the disabled students from the safe rooms.

The school instituted the plan based on advice from local fire and police officials and then explained it to staff and students. It also held a successful practice drill. But two months later, the school had an unscheduled fire drill and the student was left alone for two minutes until the student's math teacher – not assigned as the safe-room monitor – stopped by to check on her and then stayed with her for the rest of the fire drill.

The student's parents sued the school board, alleging disability discrimination in violation of Section 504 of the Rehabilitation Act and Title II of the Americans with Disabilities Act based on the bomb-threat and fire-drill incidents. The court granted the school board summary judgment. The parents appealed, but the Fourth U.S. Circuit Court of Appeals affirmed judgment for the school.

The parents couldn't sue over the bomb-threat incident because the parents had definitively resolved that dispute by agreeing to drop the complaint in return for institution of the new safety plan.

Based on only the fire-drill incident, the parents couldn't show the school board excluded the student from safe evacuation procedures during an emergency. The school had developed a plan, based on expert advice, specifically aimed at safely evacuating children with disabilities. It had equipped its safe rooms and run a successful drill. **Although the student was left alone for two minutes in a safe room, the imperfect execution of an otherwise reasonable evacuation plan did not constitute disability discrimination.** *Shirey ex rel. Kyger v. City of Alexandria School Board*, 229 F.3d 1143 (4th Cir. 2000).

E. Cases Involving Staff

◆ A federal magistrate judge in Georgia found a teacher who quit, partly because she was concerned her legal blindness was a safety risk for students, can't successfully sue the district for disability bias – but can allege that the district's refusal to grant her the reasonable accommodation of an available, non-teaching job resulted in her "constructive discharge" (that is, that she was as good as fired because she was basically forced to quit).

The teacher repeatedly told her school that **her sight limitations meant**

she couldn't fulfill the key functions of her position – including ensuring student safety in the classroom and during emergency evacuations. She ultimately quit and then sued the school system under the Americans with Disabilities Act (ADA).

To bring a successful ADA bias claim, she had to show she was a "qualified individual" under the act – meaning she could perform the essential functions of her job with or without reasonable accommodation. As the teacher repeatedly admitted she couldn't perform the essential functions of her job, this claim couldn't go forward.

But her failure-to-accommodate claim could, as her request to be reassigned to one of three available alternative positions was denied – and this refusal to grant her this requested accommodation arguably ultimately resulted in her constructive discharge. *Gaynor v. Atlanta Public Schools*, No. 1:17-cv-03562-TWT-AJB, 2018 WL 3849871 (N.D. Ga. 4/27/18).

◆ A New Jersey court upheld the state's Public Employment Relations Commission's (PERC's) decisions that a school board: 1) breached the state's Employer-Employee Relations Act (EERA) by not bargaining with the teachers union before implementing school-safety technology that impacted teachers' privacy and union rights at work, and 2) retaliated against the union president by suspending him a month without pay for advocating against the measures.

Under the board's new safety policy, cameras were placed in virtually all areas of the schools, leaving teachers no private area to discuss job concerns with union leaders. The policy also **required staff to wear radio frequency identification cards that enabled a reader to locate them on school grounds or in a school bus**.

The teachers union accused the board of committing an unfair labor practice and of retaliatory discipline of the union president. PERC found for the union on both charges.

The EERA required public employers to bargain with employees' unions over changes at work that directly affected employees' work and welfare (and hadn't already been decided by law and wouldn't interfere with the government's right to set policy). PERC found the school-safety policy met this standard. Among other things, PERC said the board hadn't identified a need to monitor faculty lounges.

The EERA also prohibited government employers from interfering with employees' exercise of their rights under the act. PERC found the union president engaged in activity the EERA protects from retaliation when he met with the school superintendent to express concerns about the new policy and provided info about the policy to union members and encouraged them to attend a board meeting.

The board said the unpaid suspension was for, among other things, discussing the security system with students. But PERC found the discipline too harsh for the alleged offenses, especially given his clean employment record. This coupled with the timing of the suspension made PERC conclude the board had retaliated against the president.

The board appealed, but the court upheld PERC's decision. *In re Belleville Educ. Ass'n v. Belleville Board of Educ.*, 455 N.J.Super. 387 (N.J. Super. Ct. App. Div. 2018).

◆ An Oregon federal judge refused to dismiss emotional distress and assault claims against a school district and members of its safety committee that sprang an unannounced live shooter drill on unsuspecting teachers.

The 2012 Sandy Hook school shooting prompted a rural school district in Oregon to plan for a similar event. It was of special concern that emergency response time to these schools could take more than an hour.

The school board formed a safety committee to plan a response to a school intruder or active shooter.

Committee members, the superintendent and teachers attended "Run, Hide, Fight" presentations on the recommended response to active shooter incidents. After it, the elementary school principal told teachers to develop "Run, Hide, Fight" plans for their classrooms.

Unbeknownst to teachers, members of the safety committee decided to hold an unannounced active shooter drill during the teachers' in-service day. Their classroom "Run, Hide, Fight" plans were due that day and no students were expected to be at school.

For the drill, two of the committee members covered their faces with paintball mask goggles. One wore military pants and boots. The other wore a hoodie. They carried firecrackers and starter guns loaded with blanks.

The principal told the teachers to work on their safety plans in their classrooms. Teacher Linda McLean was in her classroom when she heard a loud bang (a firecracker). Then a masked man burst into her room, pointed a gun at her and pulled the trigger. It sounded like a real gun and McLean thought she was going to die. The man said, "You're dead" and ran out.

The drill took about 90 seconds total. Two teachers collided while running for the exit. One fell, hitting her knee. Another wet herself.

McLean sued the district and members of the safety committee on multiple claims. Her constitutional claims failed, but the court refused to dismiss her intentional infliction of emotional distress and civil assault claims. A reasonable jury could find the defendants intended to cause the teachers severe emotional distress and that their actions were outrageous – and that the civil assault requirements were met in that the defendants intended McLean to believe the "shooter" was going to harm her. *McLean v. Pine Eagle School Dist., No. 61*, 194 F.Supp.3d 1102 (D. Or. 2016).

◆ A New York appellate court affirmed a ruling that a board of education acted in bad faith by replacing a union position with a virtually identical – but nonunion – position.

After a school district abolished its Director of Emergency Planning position, the union of the person who lost the job sued the district's board of education.

The union accused the board of acting in bad faith, claiming it replaced the emergency planning position with a nearly identical one called Homeland Security Coordinator – which union members couldn't hold because it was civil-service exempt.

Both positions required a comprehensive understanding of emergency management and involved responsibilities relating to emergency preparedness, including implementing safety plans and organizing training programs.

The board argued it was entitled to abolish a position at any time – but prior New York decisions had held "a position may not be abolished as a subterfuge to avoid the statutory protection afforded to civil servants." The court found that was the case here and held the board acted in bad faith. The board appealed, but the appellate court affirmed. *In re Gallagher v. Board of Educ. for Buffalo City School Dist.*, 81 A.D.3d 1408 (N.Y. App. Div. 2011).

CHAPTER THREE

School Safety and Liability

Page

I. BULLYING AND HAZING

In *D.B. v. Jersey City Board of Educ.*, No. A-2095-17T2, 2018 WL 6424126 (N.J. Super. Ct. App. Div. 12/7/18), a New Jersey court held the state's Anti-Bullying Act does not create a private right of action to enforce in a court. Legislators vested the state education commissioner with authority to enforce the act, with the intent of preventing student suicides and peer bullying through student disciplinary processes.

In *Eskenazi-McGibney v. Connetquot Central School Dist.*, 89 N.Y.S.3d 295 (N.Y. App. Div. 2018), the court held New York's anti-bullying law focuses on preventing misconduct rather than after-the-fact punishment. It held the act relies on proactive techniques such as training and intervention.

◆ According to a New York student and his family, school officials allowed a classmate to repeatedly bully the student. In a state court, the family claimed the classmate committed multiple physical assaults and made death threats at his school, on the school bus and on a school field trip. In the complaint, the student said officials and teachers assured him the classmate would be dealt with, but that he was never disciplined and that the bullying continued. In pretrial activity, school officials sought dismissal, arguing the state Dignity for All Students Act (DASA) creates no private right of action to enforce in a court. The court refused to dismiss the case, and school officials appealed. A New York Appellate Division Court found the DASA prohibits discrimination, harassment and bullying by public school employees and students on school grounds or at school functions.

The act requires schools to create policies, procedures and guidelines for environments free from harassment, bullying and discrimination. **As no DASA provision authorized civil damages, a victim of harassment, bullying or discrimination could not pursue damages in a private DASA lawsuit.** In the court's view, civil liability would be inconsistent with the act's legislative scheme, which calls for balanced, age-appropriate responses for creating school environments free of harassment, discrimination and bullying. The DASA employs proactive techniques such as training and early intervention to prevent discrimination and harassment. While the court affirmed the decision on the DASA claim, it held the student could pursue other claims against the school district. In the court's view, the complaint asserted enough facts to continue with the claims for negligent supervision, negligent retention and negligent performance of a government function. *Eskenazi-McGibney v. Connetquot Central School Dist.*, 169 A.D.3d 8, 89 N.Y.S.3d 295 (N.Y. App. Div. 2018).

◆ A New Jersey parent claimed third-grade teachers repeatedly subjected her son to bullying, harassment and discrimination. Among other things, she claimed a school security guard removed her son from his classroom and shoved him. She said her son was assigned to detention and deprived of his lunch for failing to complete assignments. The parent said her son was ostracized during an oral hygiene demonstration and that a teacher took a picture of him when he fell asleep at his desk. Based on these and many other incidents, the mother reported school employees to the state Division of Child Protection and Permanency. She transferred her son to another school, where he made the honor roll. In a state-court action, the parent sued the district's board under the New Jersey Law Against Discrimination (NJLAD) and the state Anti-Bullying Act. The court dismissed the case, finding the state Anti-Bullying Act creates no private cause of action.

Further, no case law supported the student's age discrimination claim. The parent moved the court to reconsider its ruling and for permission to add negligence claims. The court found the requests untimely and denied her motion. A state appellate court upheld the lower court's finding that age alone did not support an NJLAD claim. Next, **the court found the state Anti-Bullying Act was enacted to reduce the risk of suicide among students, not to create school liability**. Legislators intended to strengthen standards and procedures for preventing, reporting, investigating and responding to bullying and harassment. The law utilized an extensive enforcement scheme over which the state education commissioner had jurisdiction. As a result, the court upheld the dismissal of the Anti-Bullying Act claim. While NJLAD peer harassment claims against school districts were viable, there was no support for the age discrimination claim. No facts indicated the student was mistreated based on his young age. But the case was returned to the trial court with instructions to allow the parent to add negligence claims. *D.B. v. Jersey City Board of Educ.*, No. A-2095-17T2, 2018 WL 6424126 (N.J. Super. Ct. App. Div. 12/7/18).

A. Bullying Claims

1. Negligence

◆ Liability in bullying cases is typically determined under traditional negligence and constitutional law principles. In negligence cases, a school district or board of education may be held liable for student-on-student violence only if it had "specific, prior knowledge of the danger that caused the injury." An exception was made by the Court of Appeal of California in *Hector F. v. El Centro Elementary School Dist.*, 227 Cal.App.4th 331,173 Cal.Rptr.3d 413 (Cal. Ct. App. 2014). The court held a parent had standing as both a citizen and taxpayer to enforce a comprehensive law requiring safety plans in all schools. It found a "manifest public interest in enforcing the antibullying statutes" and no countervailing reasons not to enforce them.

In contrast to *Hector F. v. El Centro Elementary School Dist.*, a Connecticut court held there is **no private cause of action** to enforce the state's anti-bullying statute. *Mazzo v. Town of Fairfield Board of Educ.*, No. CV 126031781S, 2013 WL 4872203 (Conn. Super. Ct. 8/20/13).

◆ Courts have found no liability for harm that is "sudden" or "without warning" and have held that schools and staff members are not liable for injuries that are unforeseeable. Schools are not considered the "insurers of student safety," and state immunity laws offer school districts and their employees immunity unless there is some intentional misconduct, deliberate indifference or other gross departure from professional standards.

New York courts have held there is no school liability for injuries caused by sudden, impulsive acts that are not preceded by prior misconduct. A school district is liable for student-on-student violence only if it had "specific, prior knowledge of the danger that caused the injury." A student's acts must have been foreseeable by the district to impose liability. If an assault occurs so suddenly that it could not be prevented by any amount of supervision, there is no school liability. Many courts have held prior unrelated incidents of student discipline do not put a school on notice of a specific threat of danger requiring supervision. While schools have a duty to supervise students, "this duty does not make schools insurers of the safety of their students, for they cannot be reasonably expected to continuously supervise and control all movements and activities of students." *Mirand v. City of New York*, 84 N.Y. 44, 637 N.E.2d 263 (N.Y. 1994).

◆ A first-year Indiana vocational education program student said he seriously injured his leg when he fought with a second-year student who was regarded as a hothead and a bully with anger issues. In a state court, the first-year student sued the second-year student and school district. The district argued he contributed to his own injuries, barring any recovery. During pretrial activity, the student sought to introduce a sworn statement by an expert on bullying culture that listed 15 ways the school district could have avoided the incident. The court found the expert's opinion stated improper legal conclusions and held for the district. On appeal, the state court of appeals stated that the outcome depended upon whether the school provided its students appropriate supervision. It found the expert's statement was directly relevant to this question as it discussed 15 things the school could have done to provide adequate supervision and possibly prevent injury. **The court held the student should have a chance to show the school breached its duty of proper supervision.** It rejected the district's argument that contributory negligence operated as a complete bar to the case. *Severance v. New Castle Community School Corp.*, 75 N.E.3d 541 (Ind. Ct. App. 2017).

◆ The mother of a Tennessee high school student who committed suicide was unable to prove school officials knew of bullying and harassment at school that she claimed was the cause of his suicide. She said the school failed to enforce its anti-bullying policy and overlooked evidence that the bullying students had histories of abusiveness and harassment while at the school. The Sixth Circuit affirmed a lower court's judgment that held the suicide was not foreseeable. **The mother did not claim school employees knew of the bullying or that her son ever reported it.** *Tumminello v. Father Ryan High School*, 678 Fed.Appx. 281 (6th Cir. 2017).

◆ A New York student said classmates called him names, urinated on him, took or damaged his belongings and fought with him. Several times, the school received reports of this bullying. While the student said some remedial action was taken, he claimed the bullying continued. He said the misconduct hurt his academic performance, requiring him to repeat grade nine. Because the student fought with his classmates, the school suspended him and eventually transferred him to a program operated by a Board of

Cooperative Educational Services. The student and his parent sued the school district in a state court for physical, mental and emotional injuries.

The family added a claim under the state Dignity for All Students Act (DASA), which requires all school boards in the state to create policies and guidelines to create a school environment free from bias and harassment. A state court found the district was not deliberately indifferent to the incidents reported by the student. Finding the DASA does not create a private right of action to enforce in a court, the court dismissed the case. A New York Appellate Division Court did not disturb the finding that the DASA creates no private cause of action. The court found the negligent supervision claim was to be analyzed under *Mirand v. City of New York*, this chapter. The court found the school district knew of the conflicts between the student and his classmates. **But there was evidence that not all incidents were reported, and many of his complaints indicated he also engaged in harassing and violent conduct.** Since many facts were still in dispute and had to be resolved by the trial court, the court held the district's motion for judgment on the negligence claims should have been denied. *Motta v. Eldred Cent. School Dist.*, 141 A.D.3d 819 (N.Y. App. Div. 2016).

◆ A federal court held a New York student did not support claims for $750,000 in damages under federal laws or the state's Dignity for All Students Act (DASA). In pretrial activity, the court held a due process claim had to be dismissed. State and local governments are not liable for the failure to protect an individual from harm inflicted by private parties. In addition, the court held no exception to this general rule applied. Next, the court found no evidence that similarly situated students at the student's school were treated more favorably than she was. It held obesity is not recognized as a suspect (legally protected) classification. Although the student initially sought Title IX damages, she no longer pursued them.

The court dismissed her claim for punitive damages, finding the school district had immunity from such claims. **As for the DASA claims, the court reviewed the legislative history and found support for the view that the law creates no private right of action for damages.** In sum, the court found the student did not produce evidence that the district discriminated against her due to a medical disability and/or weight. Nor did she point to anyone similarly situated who was treated differently. *Terrill v. Windham-Ashland-Jewett Cent. School Dist.*, 176 F.Supp.3d 101 (N.D.N.Y. 2016).

◆ A Mississippi student reported bullying and intimidation by a group of students. Her mother reported the bullying and asked administrators at the school for their help. The school suspended one of the bullies from riding the school bus for five days. Despite the bus suspension, the principal placed the suspended bully on the same bus the next day. While on the bus, the bully and others attacked the student and beat her into unconsciousness with a metal belt buckle. Later, the bully was expelled from school. The student's family sued the school district in a state court for negligence under the Mississippi Torts Claims Act (MTCA). The court held the school district was entitled to discretionary immunity, and the student appealed to the Supreme Court of Mississippi. On appeal, the court explained that the MTCA is the exclusive civil remedy in the state for acts or omissions by a governmental entity. Sovereign immunity protects entities such as school districts (and their employees who act within the course and scope of their duties) in specific situations described in the MTCA. Under state case law precedent, the court held the school district had a duty to hold the bully and her accomplices to a strict account for their conduct. State antibullying laws place a ministerial duty on schools to prevent bullying. But the lower court did not address either Section 37-9-69 or the state's antibullying laws.

The court held these laws did not convert the school's duty to prevent bullying into a discretionary one. In returning the case to the lower court, the supreme court ordered a trial to determine whether the school district used ordinary care under a state law provision regarding discretionary function immunity. Finding the school district had a ministerial state law duty to provide a safe environment, the court reversed the judgment. *Smith v. Leake County School Dist.*, 195 So.3d 771 (Miss. 2016).

◆ A Kansas seventh-grader reported students made fun of his "lazy eye" and his height. A classmate pushed him, put him in a headlock and threw him to the ground. After the classmate threatened the student with a knife, police were called. The school district suspended the classmate out-of-school and required him to report to the office upon arrival at school. He was also sent to a classroom at lunch time. But another classmate then began threatening the student. As the two were in a bus-loading area after school, the classmate hit the student and fractured his jaw. The student was removed from the school by his mother, and she filed a state court lawsuit against the school district, bullies and their parents. In pretrial activity, the family settled the claims against the bullies and their parents. The principal sought judgment based on the Paul D. Coverdell Teacher Protection Act of 2001.

The court explained that the Coverdell Act is a No Child Left Behind Act provision immunizing teachers from liability for taking "reasonable actions to maintain order, discipline, and an appropriate educational environment." The family conceded the principal was entitled to Coverdell Act immunity, and the court awarded him judgment. It also held for the school district, and appeal reached the state court of appeals. In assessing the lower court judgment, the court noted the district had received immunity based on *respondeat superior* principles. *Respondeat superior* allows employers to be held liable for harm caused by employee negligence within the scope of employment. **But the Coverdell Act only immunizes teachers, administrators and other school employees. No language in the act immunizes a school district as an entity.** Moreover, the court held the district could not claim immunity under the doctrine of *respondeat superior*. As the principal received judgment on Coverdell Act grounds, there had been no determination regarding negligence. Since the district had an independent duty to reasonably protect students from harm, liability was not imputed to it based on employee negligence. *Sanchez v. Unified School Dist. 469*, 50 Kan.App.2d 1185, 339 P.3d 399 (Kan. Ct. App. 2014), (Kan. Review Denied, 7/22/15).

◆ A New Hampshire student was punched in the face during a fight on her school bus. The driver reported the fight, and the principal met with the student the next day. She asked the principal not to report the incident to her mother, but the principal said he would have to do so. Despite a school policy requiring notification to parents of any student involved in a reported bullying incident, the principal did not tell the parent about the fight. Later, the student reported receiving threats on social media from a classmate. When the principal learned of this, he went to the cafeteria and told the classmate to see him. A fight broke out, resulting in injuries to the student and an emergency room visit. When the principal met her mother in the emergency room, he told her for the first time about the bus incident and threats. In a state court, the student's parent sued the school district. The court dismissed the case, finding the negligence claim based on the failure to notify the parent of alleged bullying was barred by state law immunity.

On appeal, the Supreme Court of New Hampshire rejected the parent's claim that the principal had a common law duty to protect and supervise her child. In addition, the state law declared that it created no private right of action. Another provision of state law provided for immunity from suit from any civil liability for good-faith conduct arising from the reporting, investigation, findings, recommended response or implementation of a response under state law. No law imposed on schools an "overarching duty to protect and supervise in all instances and against all harms." Any duty of schools to exercise supervisory responsibility over students was limited. **The court declined the parent's invitation to extend the duty of reasonable supervision over students to create a new duty to report bullying.** There was no statutory duty to inform parents of generalized threats at school and no common-law duty to notify parents of third-party threats. As a result, the court held for the district. It also declined the parent's invitation to find a constitutional violation. *Gauthier v. Manchester School Dist., SAU #37*, 168 N.H. 143, 123 A.3d 1016 (N.H. 2015).

◆ Soon after a student's family moved from Georgia to New Jersey, she encountered problems in her classroom. During her fourth-grade year, her mother reported that classmates had spit on the student, hit her, kicked her and confronted her physically. The school called meetings at which the parents and students discussed the reports and appropriate behavior.

More incidents were reported the next year. Most reports came from the mother, and the school could not verify many of them. The student said she felt the misconduct was directed toward her mother's obesity and her aunt's disability. She was placed in a new school but had difficulty with her peers there. An escort plan was formulated to ensure the student's safety and to separate her from girls who were making her feel uncomfortable. Sh was diagnosed with adjustment disorder, enuresis and trichotillomania. Her mother sued the school board, superintendent and others in a federal court for violations of the Constitution and the New Jersey Law Against Discrimination (LAD). In pretrial activity, the court explained that the state Anti-Bullying Act required each school district to adopt a policy prohibiting harassment, intimidation or bullying. **Although the act required schools to have procedures for investigating such reports, the law created no private cause of action** and did not create or alter any state law tort liability. A number of incidents were investigated by a school anti-bullying specialist, but no evidence or witnesses were found. As for the LAD claim, the court found no reasonable jury could find there had been bullying based on gender. Although the mother asserted discrimination on the basis of being from the South, the court held this did not support a claim for national origin discrimination. The court held for the board and officials. *Thomas v. East Orange Board of Educ.*, 998 F.Supp.2d 338 (D.N.J. 2014).

◆ An Illinois student said peers subjected him to verbal and physical abuse at school for an extended time. He said he was punched and pushed by other students and that he told school officials many times about bullying. After the student claimed to have been beaten up outside his classroom by peers, he sued the school district in a state court for negligence, asserting it failed to provide him with a safe environment. The court dismissed the case, finding the district had immunity under the Illinois Local Governmental and Governmental Tort Immunity Act. Appeal went before the Appellate Court of Illinois. It noted the trial court's finding that dealing with student bullying was a discretionary decision for which the Tort Immunity Act provided absolute immunity. The court explained that the act protected local entities and employees from liability arising from government operations.

A public employee in a policy-making position or exercising discretion could not be held liable for any injury resulting from an act or omission in determining policy. Under prior state cases, a principal had broad discretion in handling bullying cases and was entitled to discretionary immunity under the Tort Immunity Act. **A bullying policy could provide a school district with discretion to determine whether bullying had occurred, what consequences would result and any remedial actions.** Since a school's handling of bullying incidents fit within the definition of a "discretionary act" under the Tort Immunity Act, the court held for the school district. *Malinksi v. Grayslake Community High School Dist. 127*, No. 2012-CA-002178-MR, 2014 IL App. (2d) 130685-U (Ill. Ct. App. 2/14/14).

◆ A 14-year-old Iowa student was considered vulnerable and functioned at a third-grade level. She was rarely without direct supervision, and her teachers usually took precautions beyond what school policy required. A special education teacher saw her spending time with a 19-year-old special education student. Although she saw them touching and kissing, she assumed they had an age-appropriate relationship. On a day when the student's mother allowed the student to ride the bus home from school with a friend, the student skipped her last class. She then left school with the friend, met the 19-year-old student and went to still another student's house.

The 19-year-old then took the student to the garage and raped her. After the mother learned of the rape, she sued the school district in a state court for negligence. After a jury trial, the court denied motions by the district. The jury returned a verdict of $500,000 for the student, reducing it by 30% based on her own fault. When the case reached the Supreme Court of Iowa, it held the scope of liability was for a jury to decide. Generally, tort law limits liability to the physical harm resulting from the risks that make an actor's conduct a tort in the first place. The court held the issue was left to the judgment and common sense of the jury. The court rejected the school district's argument that **the off-campus location of the assault and the fact that it took place after school hours disposed of the case**. As a result, the court affirmed the judgment for the student. *Mitchell v. Cedar Rapids Community School Dist.*, 832 N.W.2d 689 (Iowa 2013).

2. Constitutional Claims

Federal constitutional liability for school entities based on peer bullying is limited by precedents such as *DeShaney v. Winnebago County Dep't of Social Services*, 489 U.S. 189 (1989). In *DeShaney*, the U.S. Supreme Court held there must be a "special relationship" between a state agency and a victim of private violence for a constitutional duty to exist. A "Dear Colleague" letter by the U.S. Department of Education's Office for Civil Rights details federal expectations for confronting bullies in schools. See *http://www2.ed.gov/about/offices/list/ocr/letters/colleague-201010.html.*

◆ A Virginia high school student admitted improperly touching three classmates in violation of the school code. After she provided a statement to the school principal, she was suspended for 10 days and referred for a hearing to consider longer-term discipline or reassignment to an alternative setting. The principal's referral letter stated that the reason for suspension and referral was that the student had "engaged in the sexual battery of other students while on school grounds." At her hearing, she appeared with an attorney and acknowledged she was accused of sexual assault. Her attorney sought to establish that her conduct was not "sexual battery" as defined by state criminal law. At her hearing, the student admitted touching a classmate's vagina, but stated that this had been consensual. The student also stated she "accidentally" touched another classmate's breast and touched one classmate's "inner thigh" and not her vagina. During the course of questioning, the student admitted she violated the school disciplinary policy. Following the student's admission, the hearing officers found she committed multiple acts of willful, offensive touching. While the hearing officers were unable to determine whether the student's inappropriate touching rose to the level of sexual battery, they found this was irrelevant, since improper touching violated the board's rules and regulations. The discipline included reassignment to an alternative learning center (ALC) for at least one year.

After losing her appeal to the board, the student petitioned a state court, which held the discipline violated her due process rights. When the case reached the Supreme Court of Virginia, it explained that decisions regarding student safety and welfare are generally granted to school boards under the Virginia Constitution. In this case, the student was provided notice and opportunity to be heard about her suspension. **The court noted many decisions finding a disciplinary transfer to an alternative school does not deprive a student of due process rights, unless the education available at the ALC is significantly different than that provided at a regular public school.** The court found the classmates provided detailed statements describing sexual assault. It found the hearing officers were justified in finding the student committed nonconsensual touching that was "willful, deliberate, and far outside the bounds of acceptable student conduct." In upholding the findings that the student violated the school board's policy against improper touching, the court held the notice she received was constitutionally sufficient. *Fairfax County School Board v. S.C.*, 827 S.E.2d 592 (Va. 2019).

◆ The U.S. Court of Appeals, Ninth Circuit, affirmed a lower court decision dismissing claims by the family of a Nevada seventh-grader who committed suicide after months of bullying at her school. According to the family, school officials knew about the bullying but failed to respond. In the court's opinion, the complaint did not assert any affirmative misconduct, only inaction. It was not asserted that the district exposed the student to a danger she did not already face. **As constitutional liability for a state-created danger may only be imposed for affirmative misconduct, the court held for the school district.** *Lamberth v. Clark County School Dist.*, 698 Fed.Appx. 387 (9th Cir. 2017).

◆ A federal court held a Texas school district should not be held liable for injuries to a student with disabilities arising from a sexual assault in an elementary school lavatory. On appeal, the U.S. Court of Appeals, Fifth Circuit, held liability under the U.S. Constitution through 42 U.S.C. § 1983 requires proof of a deprivation of rights by a person acting under color of state law. **The Due Process Clause does not require states to protect citizens from private actors such as the assailant in this case.** The student did not assert abuse by a state actor or a specific deficiency by the district that allowed abuse to occur. The claims were not based on private conduct by the assailant but on the district's shortcomings in monitoring students, training teachers and reporting sexual assault. As a result, the court held the constitutional claims were properly dismissed. Title IX liability requires actual knowledge by a school district of sexual harassment by a harasser who is under the district's control, among other things. Yet the student admitted he did not tell his teacher about the incident and he begged his mother not to reveal it. Since ADA and Section 504 liability depended upon proof of actual knowledge by the district, these claims failed. Rejecting all the claims, the court held for the school district. *Doe v. Columbia-Brazoria Independent School Dist.*, 855 F.3d 681 (5th Cir. 2017).

◆ An Indiana student said she was relentlessly bullied by classmates as early as grade three. She said the bullying became more physical and vicious when she entered grade six. The student said other girls threw basketballs at her head, tripped her and ignored her during practice. She said this conduct escalated even further during her seventh- and eighth-grade school years. The student claimed school officials intervened only twice and that some staff members joined the bullying or were complicit in misconduct. During the student's eighth-grade school year, she said other basketball team members taunted her and called her names. Her mother yelled at the bullies. Later, the student's father and grandfather confronted the bullies, leading to a call to police. Eventually, the principal banned the father and grandfather from the school. The family sued the school district in a federal court.

Appeal reached the U.S. Court of Appeals, Seventh Circuit, which explained that **the Due Process Clause of the Fourteenth Amendment does not impose an affirmative obligation on states to ensure those interests are not harmed through other means**. The court held the clause does not guarantee minimal levels of safety and security. In this case, it was not shown that teachers and coaches instigated, created or increased bullying of the student at school. Nor did the record support the student's contention that inaction or ineffective responses to her reports increased the danger. While she claimed school staff participated in bullying incidents, the court found the actions were not sufficiently egregious to create liability. An equal protection claim failed due to a similar lack of evidence. Since the student could not demonstrate any violation of her constitutional rights, the court held she could not proceed with the case. *D.S. v. East Porter County School Corp.*, 799 F.3d 793 (7th Cir. 2015).

◆ A Texas parent said her child experienced many years of bullying at his school and that school officials did not respond to repeated complaints. She said her child was shoved into walls, pushed, kicked and spat upon and that school officials increased the danger by punishing him for defending himself and not imposing any punishment on the perpetrators. In a federal court, the mother sued the school district and principal, asserting constitutional violations and state tort claims. The court dismissed the tort claims with permission for the family to refile them in a state court. It then held the federal claims were not viable. Appeal reached the Fifth Circuit.

The court explained that to state a constitutional claim against a Texas agency, a party must show an official policymaker has violated a constitutional right and was the moving force behind the violation. Texas law was clear that a school district's board was the final policymaker in school liability cases. But the mother did not mention an official policy, arguing only that there was a widespread district custom of tolerating bullying. She claimed the majority of the district's board of trustees knew of or approved of their employees' actions in a way that established an official district custom or policy. But the court held the mother did not assert sufficient facts to show an official policy. Moreover, the Fifth Circuit has repeatedly refused to recognize a "state-created danger" theory as a basis for constitutional rights protection. As the complaint did not assert enough facts to show a policy or custom of tolerating bullying, the court held for the district and principal. *G.M. v. Shelton*, 595 Fed.Appx. 262 (5th Cir. 2014).

The U.S. Supreme Court later denied the parent's request to review the Fifth Circuit's decision. *G.M. v. Aledo Independent School Dist.*, No. 14-1070, 135 S.Ct. 2830 (cert. denied, 2015).

◆ Pennsylvania parents said their children were bullied and injured at their middle school. They said that despite notice, the school district did not respond. In fact, the parents claimed school officials criticized and belittled them to deflect their responsibility to stop the misconduct. The parents sued the school district and officials in a federal court, asserting constitutional violations and a number of state law claims. The court dismissed the case, and appeal reached the Third Circuit. First, the court dispensed with a claim that officials had retaliated against the families. The court held allegations of inaction were insufficient to maintain a constitutional claim.

As the parents did not plead any retaliatory action by the school district, the court held the trial court had correctly dismissed the First Amendment claim. Their claims based on violation of due process rights were also properly dismissed. The families did not assert any affirmative acts by the district but only argued that it did not act to prevent bullying by the classmates. To recover for a constitutional violation, **any deprivation of rights must be attributable to a state actor and not a private actor such as a bully**. As the actions at issue were attributed to students and not the district, there was no due process violation. *Monn v. Gettysburg Area School Dist.*, 553 Fed.Appx. 120 (3d Cir. 2014).

◆ A North Carolina high school senior attacked a freshman with a box cutter in a school hallway, injuring her face, neck and scalp. A teacher/coach intervened almost immediately. After the attack, the senior pled guilty to assault and no contest to a weapons possession charge. She received a suspended sentence and was placed on supervised probation.

After an investigation, the principal suspended the freshman for 10 days. She attended a half-day school schedule for the rest of the school year. Meanwhile, the senior was suspended for the rest of the school year. In a state court lawsuit, the freshman's parent claimed the school board violated her child's right to the opportunity for an education free from psychological abuse and harm. After a hearing, the court dismissed both the negligence and constitutional claims on the basis of state law immunity. On appeal, the Court of Appeals of North Carolina noted the state supreme court has held that no state constitutional claim could be made other than for matters directly related to public school educational opportunities. **Public school students had no constitutional right to recover damages from an education board for injuries resulting from a negligent failure to supervise public school employees.** Similarly, the court held there was no right under the state constitution for a student to recover damages from a board of education for injuries resulting from a negligent failure to remain aware of and supervise the conduct of other public school students. While the court held the student was permitted to raise a constitutional claim, it held for the board, finding no actions by the board affecting the nature, extent and quality of the educational opportunities made available to public school students. *Mack v. Board of Educ. of Public Schools of Robeson County*, 748 S.E.2d 774 (N.C. Ct. App. 2013, N.C. review den, 10/3/13).

B. Threatening and Bullying Speech

In *Shen v. Albany Unified School Dist.*, this chapter, the court considered federal cases that have cited *Tinker v. Des Moines Independent Community School Dist.*, 393 U.S. 503 (1969), in approving discipline for off-campus speech. The court found "these cases establish that **students have the right to be free of online posts that denigrate their race, ethnicity or physical appearance, or threaten violence**. They have an equivalent right to enjoy an education in a civil, secure, and safe school environment."

◆ An Oregon seventh-grader was disciplined for bullying and sexually harassing two disabled students near their school, shortly after a school day. The student first denied but later admitted participating in the incident and making inappropriate comments. After investigating, school administrators determined the incident came within the school district's definition of sexual harassment. They found the student participated in harassment, lied to them and disobeyed their request not to discuss the incident with his friends. The student's parents sued the school district in a federal court, asserting due process and speech rights violations. The court held for the district, and the parents appealed to the U.S. Court of Appeals, Ninth Circuit.

The court reviewed the school's disciplinary findings and found there was verbal conduct of a sexual nature. Prior Ninth Circuit cases have found schools may regulate off-campus speech. In this case, the court found the offensive comments by the student and his friends were made as school was letting out, just a few hundred feet from school property. There was no clear line between the school's property and the adjoining city park where the incident took place. The court found the area was closely tied to the school. All of the relevant factors indicated the student's speech was susceptible to school discipline. **The harassment in this case implicated the right of students to be safe and secure.** The court held schools must have authority to discipline students for engaging in sexually inappropriate and harassing speech. **The court found it was a reasonable exercise of the school's authority to be concerned with the well-being of its students as they**

walked home from school. Since the harassment took place so close to the school, administrators could have reasonably expected the effect of the harassment to spill over into the school environment. *C.R. v. Eugene School Dist. 4J*, 835 F.3d 1142 (9th Cir. 2016).

◆ While off campus and without using any school resources, a Mississippi student posted a recording containing profanity and threatening language regarding two teacher/coaches on his publicly accessible Facebook profile page. He later posted it on YouTube. When school officials were told of the posted recording, the student was removed from school pending a disciplinary committee hearing. At his hearing, the student said he did not report any conduct by the coaches because he felt any reports would have been ignored. He claimed the "students all have Facebook" and would hear his voice. Finding the recordings constituted harassment and intimidation of the teachers in violation of the school's policy and state law, the committee recommended a seven-day suspension from school and a six-week placement in the county's alternative school. By the time his case reached a federal court, the alternative placement had nearly ended and the request for an order was denied as moot. Three months later, the court granted the board's request for judgment. In 2014, a three-judge panel of the Fifth Circuit Court of Appeals held the board violated the student's rights.

A majority of the judges of the Fifth Circuit agreed to rehear the case and issued a new order for the board. This time, the court found "this incredibly profane and vulgar rap recording had at least four instances of threatening, harassing and intimidating language against the two coaches." While students do not forfeit their rights under *Tinker v. Des Moines Independent Community School Dist.*, this chapter, **the court held the First Amendment "does not provide students absolute rights to such freedoms."** After reviewing many post-*Tinker* cases, the court rejected the argument that *Tinker* is limited to speech within the confines of a school. The internet, cell phones, smartphones and social media did not exist when *Tinker* was decided. Off-campus communications might reference events at a school or involve members of the school community, yet can be accessed anywhere by anyone at any time. The court held school officials need to react quickly and efficiently when threats, intimidation and harassment are directed to the school community. In this case, the conduct could be forecast to cause a substantial disruption. Threats, harassment and intimidation of teachers disrupted the school's mission and could not be permitted. *Bell v. Itawamba County School Board*, 799 F.3d 379 (5th Cir. 2015).

◆ An Ohio student said peers at her schools harassed and bullied her throughout her middle and high school career. She reported routine abusive statements by peers who called her a "dirty Jew" and said she would "rot in Hell" because she did not believe in Christ. She was hit, tripped and shoved in school halls. On one occasion, the student was stabbed in the leg with a pencil. The family reported daily harassment on a school bus, but the bus driver never disciplined the harassers or filed a report. The student reported being assaulted in a school choir room. She was taken to a hospital and had to use crutches for several weeks. But verbal and online harassment continued. After four years of harassment, the student's mother removed her from her school and sued the district and school officials in a federal court.

Appeal reached the U.S. Court of Appeals, Sixth Circuit, which found the complaint adequately stated school officials had knowledge of the misconduct. **While the officials were entitled to immunity for a federal due process claim based on a state-created danger theory, the court held they did not have immunity regarding the equal protection and state law claims.** In the court's view, the conduct described by the family would have emboldened bullies by giving them "license to act with impunity." Officials could not be "shielded from liability where they took meager steps they knew to be ineffective to address severe and pervasive harassment that went on for years." As a result, the court held the equal protection and state law claims would go forward in further court proceedings. *Shively v. Green Local School Dist. Board of Educ.*, 579 Fed.Appx. 348 (6th Cir. 2014).

◆ An Oregon student was assigned a C grade, which prompted his mother to ground him for part of the upcoming summer break. The student made a series of Facebook comments about the teacher, saying she was "the worst teacher ever" and calling her names. In response to a friend's comment, the student wrote "Ya haha she needs to be shot." Within 24 hours, the student's mother instructed him to delete the entire post, which he did. The postings were made with a home computer on a day when school was not in session. Six weeks after the postings, the parent of another student placed a printout of the Facebook postings in the principal's mail. After the principal questioned the student, she suspended him in school for three and one-half days. The parent objected and sued the school district in a federal court for First Amendment and due process violations. The court referred the case to a federal magistrate judge, who recommended dismissing the due process claim but ruling for the student on the First Amendment claim. In considering the recommendation, the court found Ninth Circuit authority declaring that **schools may take disciplinary action in response to off-campus speech that presents "an identifiable threat of school violence."**

The court agreed with the magistrate judge that the student's postings did not meet the "material and substantial" impact rule from *Tinker v. Des Moines Independent Community School Dist.,* 393 U.S. 503 (1969). While the teacher reported feeling "scared, nervous and upset," the court found there was no threat to her safety in this case. In the court's view, there was no showing that the student's postings materially and substantially interfered with school discipline. In fact, the student did not intend the comments to reach school. No students missed school, and the teacher did not miss work. Significantly, the court found the school took no action indicating that it considered the postings to be a threat. The principal simply had the student sit in the office for over three school days. As a result, the court adopted the magistrate judge's report to find a speech rights violation. It agreed with the school district that there had been no due process violation. The student was later awarded over $66,000 in attorneys' fees and costs. *Burge v. Colton School Dist. 53*, 100 F.Supp.3d 1057 (D. Or. 2015).

◆ Pennsylvania sisters claimed they were repeatedly threatened, assaulted and racially intimidated by another student and her friend at their high school, by phone and the Internet. Eventually, the other student was put on probation and ordered to have no contact with one sister. She was adjudicated delinquent, and no-contact orders from the juvenile court were provided to the school. Despite the court orders, the other student boarded the sisters' bus and threatened one sister. That evening, she elbowed the other sister in the throat at a school football game. After the incidents were reported, officials told the sisters they could not guarantee their safety. Officials asked the parents to consider moving the sisters to another school, and they soon did so. In a federal court, the sisters sued the school district and assistant principal, claiming due process violations. It dismissed the case, and the sisters appealed to the U.S. Court of Appeals, Third Circuit.

On appeal, the court held the Due Process Clause did not create an affirmative duty by a state to protect a person from other persons. A narrow exception applied if a "special relationship" existed between a state and a person who is taken into custody against his or her will. But this exception had only been applied to prisoners or involuntarily committed individuals. A school's authority over a child during the school day did not implicate the type of physical custody to create a "special relationship." Nor did knowledge of the risks created by the other student's presence create a duty. While the school's response might have been as "inadequate as it was unfair," the court held the school did not authorize the other student to bully the sisters. There was also no reason to apply the "state-created danger" theory of constitutional liability, as there was no affirmative act by the school district. **Finding no constitutional duty to prevent bullying, the court held for the district.** *Morrow v. Balaski*, 719 F.3d 160 (3d Cir. 2013).

◆ From off-campus locations, a Nevada student sent friends a series of increasingly violent and threatening instant messages. He invoked the image of the Virginia Tech massacre, boasting he could "get 50+ people / and not one bullet would be wasted." Friends grew concerned when he sent messages about a school shooting to take place on April 20. This is Hitler's date of birth and the date of the Columbine shootings. Some of the student's friends told a coach about the threats, and the principal was notified. Police interviewed the friends and viewed the online messages. They questioned the student in the principal's office. After a hearing, the school board voted to expel the student for 90 days. He sued the board for constitutional rights violations. A federal court held for the board, and the student appealed.

The U.S. Court of Appeals, Ninth Circuit, held that courts had to balance the speech rights of students against the need to provide a safe school environment. In doing so, the courts were "not to react in favor of either." The idea was to strike an appropriate balance between safety and speech rights. In this case, the court held school officials did not violate the student's rights. The nature of the threats was "alarming and explosive." For this reason, the court held **officials did not have to wait for an actual disruption to materialize before acting**. As it was reasonable for the officials to interpret the student's messages as a safety risk and a substantial disruption, there was no speech rights violation. The court held the student had adequate warning from a student handbook that he faced discipline for making threatening statements. There was no due process violation, and the judgment for the school district was affirmed. *Wynar v. Jefferson County Board of School Commissioners*, 728 F.3d 1062 (9th Cir. 2013).

C. Hazing and Locker Room Incidents

◆ A Texas sixth-grade student was disciplined for bullying, horseplay and not following directions. For each incident, the AP investigated and assigned the student disciplinary consequences. A day after the student was placed on a behavior contract for misconduct, a teacher found a sexually explicit note on his desk. The note was addressed to a classmate and requested sexual acts in graphic language. During the AP's investigation, the classmate denied reading the note. Because of this, the AP did not contact her mother. The AP and a school police officer met with the student to discuss the resulting discipline. Less than two weeks later, another graphic note detailing various sexual acts was found in the student's desk. This note suggested that sexual acts take place that day, but it did not specify the classmate by name. When the AP questioned the student, he again denied writing a note. The AP assigned him a day of in-school suspension and two days of out-of-school suspension. Soon after being allowed to return to school, the student sexually assaulted the classmate in a school lavatory.

Following a school investigation, it was determined that the student forced the classmate to perform oral sex. The student was suspended and placed in an extended alternative placement. In a federal court, the classmate sued the school district for sex discrimination in violation of Title IX of the Education Amendments of 1972. **The court explained that to impose liability on a school district, the recipient must act with deliberate indifference to known harassment in its programs or activities.** In this case, the court found nothing put school administrators on notice that the student presented a risk of sexually assaulting the classmate. Administrators were unaware of any contact or relationship between the two. The court held it was not reasonable to expect the school to conclude there was a risk of sexual assault based on what the administrators knew. In the court's opinion, the administrators did not act with deliberate indifference, as they did not act in a manner that was clearly unreasonable. In a memorandum opinion, the U.S. Court of Appeals, Fifth Circuit, held for the school district. *Gray v. Crowley Independent School Dist.*, 723 Fed.Appx. 254 (5th Cir. 2018).

◆ A Connecticut student said his football coach "witnessed, participated in, encouraged and condoned" harassment and vulgar name-calling by peers. He said he was assaulted by peers nearly every school day and was sexually assaulted by a classmate while peers looked on. Over two years later, the classmate was convicted of sexual assault. By the student's account, teachers did not discipline his harassers, despite knowing about their conduct. He said a paraprofessional in his special education resource room taunted him and that classmates joined in. After the student said he was cornered and punched repeatedly during a practice, his mother reported the incident. She said a school track coach responded that the student was "embellishing his complaints" and said the incident was "horseplay." The track coach then removed the student from the team, citing his grades. The student's mother removed her son from school and the student sued the school board, football coach and other officials in a federal court.

Although the court dismissed the complaint as insufficient, it granted a motion for reconsideration. The court found the student presented newly discovered evidence to support a due process claim against the coach and school athletic director. He claimed the school had "a culture of harassment and violence." For example, the student said the team's "quarterback initiation" ritual called for the quarterback to hold down a freshman player and put an eraser in his rectum. He said the school did not remove players from the team despite severe hazing, harassment and physical assault. The student claimed a coach knew of a locker room assault but said "just don't mount each other." **The court held the student presented enough facts to support a due process claim against the coach under a state-created danger theory.** It found the new evidence was sufficient to show the coach transmitted a message to students that their misconduct was permissible. Next, the court denied a motion for immunity on three negligence claims. It also held the student could pursue a claim for intentional infliction of emotional distress against the coach. *Doe v. Torrington Board of Educ.*, No. 3:15-cv-00452 (MPS), 2017 WL 3392734 (D. Conn. 8/7/17).

A plaintiff in a hazing case must show that the school was aware of the hazing before liability may be imposed on the school. Ordinary negligence principles may apply, but school liability may also depend on state law definitions. Kathleen Conn, Ph.D., J.D., LL.M., who is of counsel with King, Spry, Herman, Freund & Faul, LLC of Bethlehem, Pennsylvania, says schools should take the following steps to address athletic team hazing:

- Increase bus and locker room supervision
- Have a district anti-hazing policy at the high school and middle school levels
- Recognize sexualized hazing as sexual violence and address it as such, and
- Ensure coaches do not approve, participate in or turn a blind eye to hazing.

◆ A Michigan student had a sexual relationship with a teacher at his school. When this was revealed, the teacher pleaded guilty to two sex crimes and was sentenced to at least 23 months in prison. After cooperating with the police investigation, the student claimed he was harassed by his school peers, shunned by athletic coaches and subjected to retaliation by school administrators because the teacher lost her job and ended up in jail. In general, the student claimed the "entire school turned on him," and "everybody hated him for it," causing him severe anxiety. He said he contemplated suicide. He declined to try out for the school baseball team, saying coaches considered him "a cancer." After the sexual assault, the school offered the student several educational accommodations. But after being disciplined for misconduct, he left the school. The student sued the school district in a federal court, claiming he was punished for the teacher's arrest and that the school did not protect him from peer harassment.

After the court held for the school district, the student appealed to the U.S. Court of Appeals, Sixth Circuit. It found he relied on assumptions and produced insufficient evidence to pursue his retaliation claims. No reasonable jury would find actions such as placing the student in a different school group or denying him entry into particular classes was evidence of retaliation. The court found legitimate educational reasons for each of the matters the student complained about. Undisputed evidence showed the district made informed decisions to discipline him for misconduct. The court found the school took other steps to make him feel more comfortable and provide him a fresh start. As for the student's Title IX claim, the court held he did not show he was harassed because of his sex. **The school district responded to each report of harassment in a manner that was not clearly unreasonable.** *Gordon v. Traverse City Area Public Schools*, 686 Fed.Appx. 315 (6th Cir. 2017).

◆ While off campus, a New Jersey student posted a YouTube video and tweeted about other students at his high school. The video criticized a school football teammate. After school officials learned about it, they suspended the student for two days. He first denied any involvement but later admitted making the tweets. Officials determined the student violated the state's Anti-Bullying Bill of Rights Act and district policies. The postings contained racial epithets and harsh commentary about particular students at the school. Officials imposed a nine-day suspension on the student. He sued the school district in a federal court, claiming the suspensions violated the state civil rights act and state constitution, in addition to violating his First Amendment rights. During pretrial activity, the student argued the postings were "innocuous and not disruptive to the school." School officials argued the postings bullied, harassed and intimidated others at the school, causing substantial disruption. They also noted his initial denial created disruption.

The court found Third Circuit cases supporting the ability of schools to punish expression outside a school, if officials "can point to a well-founded expectation of disruption." New Jersey's Anti-Bullying Bill of Rights Act intends to strengthen standards and procedures for preventing, reporting, investigating and responding to incidents of harassment, intimidation and bullying on and off school grounds. New Jersey school districts must have procedures to report bullying and provide consequences and remedial action for those who cause harassment, intimidation or bullying. The court found the law covers any electronic communication that is reasonably seen as motivated by distinguishing characteristics. **An off-campus communication may be subject to the law, if a reasonable person should know it will substantially disrupt or interfere with the orderly operation of a school or the rights of other students.** The student's tweets were held to be insulting to students and were motivated by race, gender or other distinguishing characteristics as contemplated by the law. School administrators were required by the law to investigate complaints about his Twitter account. Complaints from parents and students about the tweets constituted material and substantial disruption to the work and discipline of the school. In ruling for the board, the court noted the student had admitted making the offensive postings. *Dunkley v. Board of Educ. of Greater Egg Harbor Regional High School Dist.*, 216 F.Supp.3d 485 (D.N.J. 2016).

◆ An Ohio student said teammates on his high school baseball team sexually assaulted him after a coach tacitly approved of it. Two of the assaulting students were arrested and charged with rape. All four students who either perpetrated the incident or stood by and watched were suspended from school. A juvenile court later found the two primary perpetrators guilty of assault and barred them from playing baseball for the rest of the year. In a federal court, the victim's parent sued the school board, claiming the board knew of an environment of physical abuse and bullying at the high school. In pretrial activity, there was evidence that sexualized touching was very common at the school. But school officials insisted they did not know of any unwanted sexualized touching and did not know about a "culture of hazing" or other aggressive conduct described by the victim.

After considering the parties' submissions, the court held for the board on the claims arising under Title IX of the Education Amendments of 1972, state law tort claims and constitutional rights violations. On appeal, the U.S. Court of Appeals, Sixth Circuit, observed that the family's case hinged on a theory of state-created danger. **Case law established that (with rare exceptions) the Due Process Clause of the U.S. Constitution does not impose a duty on schools to protect students from harm inflicted by private actors, such as classmates.** The court found a reasonable jury could believe the victim's description of a comment by a coach as evidence that the perpetrators had tacit permission to use hazing. But the court found no evidence that the school board knew of a culture of violence or had an official policy or custom leading to, causing or resulting in the deprivation of constitutionally protected student rights. Even assuming a jury would accept his theory of an environment of abuse and bullying at the school, the court held he did not show the board had any notice of it. In fact, once the victim reported the incident, the perpetrators were swiftly punished. Since the victim could not meet the standard of liability for federal constitutional claims filed against a municipal entity, the court affirmed the judgment for the board of education. *Richardson v. Huber Heights City Schools Board of Educ.*, 651 Fed.Appx. 362 (6th Cir. 2016).

◆ A high school senior who was disciplined for severely hazing and sexually harassing a teammate on an overnight wrestling trip had no viable due process claims against his school district, according to the U.S. Court of Appeals, Ninth Circuit. The student admitted hazing and degrading the teammate by taping him to a table, exposing his genitals, spanking him, placing him in a hotel hallway while still taped to the table, taking pictures of him and urinating on him. **A lower court had found the student received adequate notice and a hearing regarding his exclusion from school.** A semester suspension for this "vile" conduct was upheld. *Borovac v. Churchill County School Dist.*, 621 Fed.Appx. 479 (9th Cir. 2015).

◆ Texas parents said their 13-year-old son committed suicide after being repeatedly bullied at school. They said much of the misconduct took place in the school locker room. Among their claims was that members of the football team stripped the student, tied him up and put him in a trash can. Students called him "fag," "queer" and "homo," and one student videotaped the attack. The parents said the video was then put on YouTube. Shortly after this incident, the student committed suicide. According to the parents, school officials knew of the bullying but were deliberately indifferent to it.

In a federal court, the parents asserted the school had policies against bullying, but officials ignored them. The court dismissed the case. On appeal, the Fifth Circuit Court of Appeals held the complaint asserted widespread harassment by peers. In addition to the videotaped incident, it was alleged that football players accosted the student in the locker room many times. There were charges that boys took off his underwear while a teacher observed them. As a result, the court reversed the judgment on a Title IX claim and returned it to the district court. **The court held the removal of a person's underwear without consent on numerous occasions would constitute pervasive sexual harassment.** But the parents could not pursue their equal protection claim, which had been properly dismissed. *Carmichael v. Galbraith*, 574 Fed.Appx. 286 (5th Cir. 2014).

◆ An Indiana high school basketball team manager said four senior team members harassed him constantly in the school locker room. He said the seniors taunted him with sexual comments, "flashed" him and grabbed his genitals. He said they "gooched him," a term used for anal penetration with fingers, either directly or through clothing. During a school bus trip, the student claimed some seniors called him to the back of the bus, held him down and anally penetrated him. A parent reported the incident a few weeks later, and some of the seniors were expelled. In a federal court, the student asserted Title IX violations and other claims. The court found a same-sex harassment claim may survive under Title IX based on gender stereotyping.

Although the court held there had been severe and objectively offensive harassment that denied the student educational opportunities, it found the school acted almost immediately upon learning about the bus incident. Actual notice of harassment is required for school liability to exist under Title IX. The student claimed that the coaches and school must have known about the sexual assaults because they had been occurring in the basketball program for years. But the court dismissed the Title IX claim as unsupported by admissible evidence. While the court found no merit to the student's constitutional claims, it agreed to consider his state tort law claims in further proceedings. When the student appealed the federal claims to the Seventh Circuit, it affirmed the judgment. In the court's view, **the school district could not have violated Title IX or other federal laws because there was no evidence it actually knew about the misconduct until it had ended**. *Davis v. Carmel Clay Schools*, 570 Fed.Appx. 602 (7th Cir. 2014).

D. Legislative Responses

Maryland law requires county education boards to have policies stating that the primary purpose of student discipline is rehabilitative, restorative, and educational. The state board of education must establish school discipline guidelines that define standards of conduct and consequences for violations. **"Restorative approach" is defined by the law as a relationship-focused student discipline model that is preventive and proactive, emphasizes building strong relationships and setting clear behavioral expectations that contribute to the school community's well-being.**

Restorative approaches respond to behavior that violates the clear behavioral expectations that contribute to the well-being of the school community, focusing on accountability for any harm done by the problem behavior and addressing ways to repair relationships affected by the problem behavior with the voluntary participation of an individual who was harmed. Regulations adopted by a county board must provide for educational and behavioral interventions, restorative approaches, counseling, and student and parent conferencing. County boards must provide alternative programs, including in-school suspension, suspension, expulsion or other appropriate disciplinary measures. Maryland Session Laws, 2019 Regular Session Ch. 691 (H.B. 725). Maryland Educ. Code § 7–306.

The "**Tennessee** Educators Protection Act" intends to deter meritless litigation and to sanction deliberately false reports against educators. School employees are not civilly liable for taking actions related to the control, grading, suspension, expulsion or discipline of a student on school grounds or under supervision of an educational entity, unless the action violates a law, rule or clearly articulated policy. School employees are not liable for making reports to appropriate law enforcement authorities or school officials based on reasonable grounds to suspect a student is under the influence of alcohol or a controlled substance that was not lawfully prescribed to the student, or is involved in an illegal activity. A student who makes a false accusation of criminal activity against a school employee is subject to school discipline and other sanctions. One-Hundred-Tenth Tennessee General Assembly, Ch. 407, S.B. 729. Tennessee Code Annotated §§ 49–1–1201 - 49–1–1208.

A 2016 **Kentucky** amendment clarifies that the term "bullying" is not to be interpreted to "prohibit civil exchange of opinions or debate or cultural practices protected under the state or federal Constitution where the opinion expressed does not otherwise materially or substantially disrupt the education process." As used in the law, "bullying" means unwanted verbal, physical, or social behavior among students that involves a real or perceived power imbalance and is repeated or has the potential to be repeated. The conduct must occur on school grounds, school transportation or a school event and disrupt the education process. Kentucky 2016 Regular Session, Ch. 81. S.B. 228. Kentucky Revised Statutes § 158.148.

Wyoming law states that electronic communications solely between students attending a school in the state are not a public record of that school. In addition, electronic communications solely between students attending a school in the state and a sender or recipient using a nonschool user address are not a public record of that school. The law covers the University of Wyoming, community colleges and public schools in the state. Sixty-Third Wyoming Legislature, Ch. 48, H.B. No. 13. Wyoming Statutes § 16–4–201.

An **Oklahoma** amendment allows out-of-school suspensions of students for electronic communications in violation of the state School Safety and Bullying Prevention Act. No public school is required to provide education in a regular school to a student who has been removed from a public or private school in Oklahoma or another state for an electronic communication made with the intent to terrify, intimidate, harass or threaten to injure or physically harm faculty or other students. Schools may elect not to provide education services in a regular school setting to a student who has committed electronic threats, until they determine a student no longer poses a threat to self, other students or school district faculty and employees. Fifty-Fifth Oklahoma Legislature, 2016 Second Regular Session, Ch. 90, H.B. 2614, Oklahoma Statutes § 24-101.3.

A **Montana** law promotes safe schools by prohibiting bullying of students and clarifying means of redress for victims. "Bullying" means harassment, intimidation, hazing, or threatening, insulting, or demeaning gestures or physical contact, including any intentional written, verbal, or electronic communication or threat directed against a student that is persistent, severe, or repeated. To meet the statutory definition of bullying, conduct must cause a student physical harm, damage a student's property, or place a student in reasonable fear of harm. In addition, bullying is conduct that creates a hostile environment by interfering with or denying a student's access to an educational opportunity or benefit; or that substantially and materially disrupts the orderly operation of a school. "Bullying" includes retaliation against a victim or witness who reports information about an act of bullying and includes athletic hazing. Montana 2015 Session Laws, Regular Session, Ch. 253 H.B. No. 284.

II. THREATS AND VIOLENCE

A. Students

In *Parmertor v. Chardon Local Schools*, 47 N.E.3d 942 (Ohio Ct. App. 2016), the court rejected claims that an Ohio school board's failure to add building security measures could be deemed a "physical defect" of a school for purposes of immunity. Log on to *www.SchoolSafetyAndSecurityAlert.com* and search "School Violence Prevention" for a customizable "School Violence Prevention and Intervention Checklist."

◆ An Oregon parent discovered a "hit list" in her son's diary while cleaning his room. The list named 22 students at his high school and a former employee and stated: "I am God" and "All These People Must Die." The parent brought copies of the diary entries to a therapist. Believing the entries triggered her mandatory reporter duty, the therapist informed the police. Police searched the family home and confiscated several weapons and 525 rounds of ammunition belonging to the student. The parents brought the student to a police station, bringing a copy of the hit list. He admitted he created the hit list but said "he would never carry out" such thoughts. Police did not bring criminal charges, but they advised the school about the hit list, guns and the graphic depictions of school violence. In compliance with an Oregon notification law and a district policy, administrators called the parents of the students named on the hit list, informed all parents in the district about the incident and assured them their children were safe. After a hearing, the district expelled the student for one year based on a threat of violence that caused a significant disruption. He sued the school district and officials in a federal court. The court held the district could regulate the off-campus speech because it had a sufficient connection to the school.

The student appealed to the Ninth Circuit, which held **a school district may take disciplinary action in response to off-campus speech when it reasonably determines that it faces an identifiable and credible threat of violence**. The court held the school district reasonably found the student presented a credible threat. A decision by the police not to prosecute him did not prevent the district from addressing threats of violence at school. In sum, the court found "**schools must be permitted to act preventatively, taking into account other students' interest in a safe school environment**." While schools cannot ordinarily discipline students for the contents of off-campus diaries, the court held they have a right to address credible threats of violence involving the school. Targeting students for a school shooting "represented the quintessential harm to the rights of other students to be secure." *McNeil v. Sherwood School Dist. 88J*, 918 F.3d 700 (9th Cir. 2019).

◆ Families of the victims of a shooting rampage at a school in Chardon, Ohio sued school officials in a state court, claiming there should be school liability. The families said the shooter attended an alternative school for at-risk students with serious academic or behavioral problems and was known to be mentally unstable and at high risk for committing more violent acts. In pretrial activity, the court granted state law immunity regarding negligence claims against the school district, board of education, board members, the alternative school where the shooter was a student, a county educational service center, and school officials. But immunity was denied for claims asserting the officials acted recklessly and with conscious disregard for safety, and for claims for malice and willful and wanton misconduct.

When the case reached the state court of appeals, it explained that state law immunizes political subdivisions and their employees unless an exception applies. **The court found no evidence of unreasonable board policies.** Since the shooter caused the attack and was the sole, direct cause of the injuries, the court held the board and employees could not be denied immunity for creating a "physical defect" at the school. In 2016, the court of appeals denied immunity to the administrators and employees on claims that they acted willfully, wantonly and with malice. In 2018, the trial court held for the administrators and employees on these claims. After the court of appeals affirmed the judgment, the state supreme court denied appeal. *Parmertor v. Chardon Local Schools*, 47 N.E.3d 942 (Ohio Ct. App. 2016; (Ohio appeal not allowed, 156 Ohio St.3d 1405, 2019 -Ohio- 2261 6/12/19).

◆ A Connecticut elementary school teacher claimed administrators had a policy of not involving themselves in any issues related to student discipline. She said two students assaulted her in her classroom, causing a severe sprain of her left knee and ankle. Claiming the administrators acted willfully and maliciously by failing to send security, call 911 or respond to her calls for help in any way, the teacher sued the school board in a state court. Although she argued administrators acted intentionally and with knowledge that the no-discipline policy would cause her harm, the court held her claims were barred by the exclusivity provisions of the state workers' compensation act.

The teacher appealed to the Connecticut Appellate Court, which found her case did not fall within an exception to the exclusivity provisions of the workers' compensation act. **Typically, employees may only resort to the workers' compensation system when they are injured at work, even if a co-worker causes the injury.** An exception exists when an employer intended to injure the employee, or intentionally created a dangerous condition that made the employee's injuries a substantial certainty. In this case, the court found the teacher did not show any intentional conduct by the administrators. As she did not show the administrators directed or authorized an assault, the court held for the board. *Binkowski v. Board of Educ. of City of New Haven*, 180 Conn.App. 580 (Conn. App. Ct. 2018).

◆ An Oregon student was injured when she tried to break up a fight between classmates. The incident took place across the street from her high school, in an area she claimed was well known as a location for fights. The student claimed the school district was on notice that a fight was likely to occur. According to the student, she joined other students who tried to break up the fight. She said one of the classmates assaulted her, causing facial fractures, a concussion and other traumatic injuries. No school staff members were present. The court dismissed the case, agreeing with the school district that its supervisory decisions were protected by discretionary immunity. Appeal reached the Court of Appeals of Oregon, where the student claimed the school had knowledge of an impending fight between the classmates, and failed to act. She argued the school made the choice not to offer any supervision at the off-campus location, amounting to a failure to act that did not deserve immunity. A school security employee testified that the location was one of several off-campus areas he patrolled each day.

The court agreed with the school district that it exercised its discretion in providing supervision of students both on and off campus. **Decisions regarding the number and location of security personnel within a high school amounted to discretionary policy choices that were entitled to immunity under state law.** No admissible evidence indicated to the court that school staff members knew (or should have known) there was an impending fight brewing between the two classmates. Since a school district "has wide policy discretion" in the carrying out of its duty to care for students, the court held the district was entitled to immunity. *Rush v. Corvallis School Dist. 509J*, 292 Or.App. 252 (Or. Ct. App. 2018).

◆ A Georgia high school student with disabilities claimed she was gang-raped by male students in a school lavatory. Campus police investigated the incident and found probable cause to arrest the males. Later, school board members questioned the propriety of an investigation by campus police. A few days later, the campus police turned the case over to the county police department. During the county investigation, the student was interviewed by two male officers and retracted her account. The criminal charges were dropped. After the student withdrew her initial story of the incident, school officials prepared a disciplinary letter against her for sexual misconduct.

A school committee determined the conduct was a manifestation of the student's disability, an no discipline was brought against her. The student and her parent sued the school district in a federal court for violating Title IX. The court held for the district and the case reached the U.S. Court of Appeals, Eleventh Circuit. It upheld the lower court's findings that the district response was not deliberately indifferent to the rights of the student. **The court deemed the campus police investigation adequate and thorough, finding no merit to the claim that the county investigation**

was improper. Finding the school district's response was not clearly unreasonable, the court held the district was entitled to judgment. *Doe, I v. Bibb County School Dist.*, 688 Fed.Appx. 791 (11th Cir. 2017).

◆ A New Hampshire student with autism and an emotional disturbance underwent a series of psychiatric hospitalizations after engaging in aggressive, sexualized behavior. After being placed in a residential education center, he entered a day program where a girl began interacting with him in a sexual manner. The student expressed fears to school employees about the girl's behavior. A school IEP team met three times during this period but did not discuss the girl's conduct. The parents were not told about it.

A decision was made to change the student's placement. Several months after he left the center, he sexually assaulted his younger sister. When the parents requested his records, they learned about the girl's misconduct and placed their son in a residential school. They sued the school district, education center and various officials for negligence and violations of Title IX of the Education Amendments of 1972. **A federal court rejected the parents' claim that schools owe a duty to students to inform their parents of events occurring when the student is in school custody.** Such a duty would be grounded in a special relationship that is not recognized by New Hampshire courts. While the court dismissed most of the negligence claims, it refused to dismiss claims against a district director and federal claims against the center. *Ashley M. and Kevin M. v. Spaulding Youth Center*, Civil No. 16-cv-37-JL, 2016 WL 5477574 (D.N.H. 9/29/16).

◆ A Florida student reported being attacked by another student with a history of school discipline, bullying, fighting and class disruption. She said the attacker was in possession of a blade prior to the attack and should have been serving an in-school suspension (ISS) on the day of the attack. As a result of the incident, the student suffered a broken leg. In a state court action against the board, the family of the injured student submitted four theories of negligence. One was the theory that the board was negligent for not placing the attacking student in ISS on the scheduled day. A jury agreed with this theory and with the theory that the board negligently supervised the attacker just before the assault took place. On appeal, the board argued the trial court committed an error by excluding testimony by a third party that a racial slur may have prompted the incident. But the court noted no student, administrator, teacher or other student heard a slur. It found any such evidence "amounted to no more than improperly stacked inferences."

Next, the court held the board was foreclosed from arguing that the jury should not have been able to hold it liable for failing to place the attacker in ISS under sovereign immunity principles. The board could not challenge the jury's alternative basis for liability – that negligent supervision of the attacker resulted in harm to the student. The court found the board's current argument was different from its initial defenses that it had no duty to the student and enjoyed sovereign immunity. As **negligent supervision was an**

accepted basis for school liability, and the court found "plentiful evidence" to support the verdict, it held for the student. *Duval County School Board v. Buchanan*, 131 So.3d 821 (Fla. Dist. Ct. App. 2014).

◆ A Mississippi student with a mental disability was placed in a regular classroom for part of each school day. According to a classmate, the student had a "documented history of emotional outbursts and misbehavior." She said that on two occasions, the student threatened her. The classmate said that on the second occasion, the student grabbed her, held her head against a wall and rubbed a cleaning wipe into her eye. In a federal court, the classmate's mother said school officials violated her child's due process rights by failing to immediately remove the student from the classroom when they learned of his violent propensities. The court held for the school district, and appeal reached the U.S. Court of Appeals, Fifth Circuit.

In *Doe v. Covington County School Dist.*, 675 F.3d 849 (5th Cir. 2012), the Fifth Circuit refused to adopt the state-created danger theory in a case involving a school's failure to protect a child from being signed out from her school by an unauthorized adult. The court noted language from *Doe* declaring that **to create any opportunity for school liability, "the school must be aware of an immediate danger to a specific and identifiable student."** The court found the classmate was only one of many who "faced a generalized risk resulting from the school's attempt to integrate a mentally disabled child into a normal school environment." As as result, the court affirmed the judgment for the school officials. *Dixon v. Alcorn County School Dist.*, 499 Fed.Appx. 364 (5th Cir. 2012).

◆ While in his high school's student center, a New York student told some of his classmates and a teacher that he was "going to just blow this place up." After discussing the statements, school administrators were unsure about the seriousness of the risk, and they called the student's parents and the police. The student was suspended for five days and charged with insubordinate, disorderly, violent, disruptive conduct and violation of the school code. Following a manifestation determination at which no connection was found between the student's behavior and his disability, the school board held a hearing and recommended suspension for 25 more days.

After the district superintendent and board adopted the recommended discipline, the student appealed. The state commissioner of education approved the board's action, and appeal reached the New York Supreme Court, Appellate Division. The court explained that the relevant inquiry was whether his conduct might reasonably have led school authorities to forecast substantial disruption of or material interference with school activities. In this case, the student had declared to several others that he was going to blow up the school. In the court's opinion, these **statements on school property made it reasonably foreseeable that there would be a substantial disruption**. Since school officials could reasonably conclude that the student's statements would substantially disrupt the school, their decision to suspend him did not violate his speech rights. The commissioner's decision upholding the suspension was affirmed. *Saad-El-Din v. Steiner*, 953 N.Y.S.2d 326 (N.Y. App. Div. 2012).

◆ After being expelled from their high school for fighting two other students, two South Carolina brothers appealed to the district superintendent and the school board. When the decisions were upheld, they did not appeal to a court. Nearly two years later, the family sued the school district in the state court system, claiming due process violations. The court held for the district, finding the students' decision not to appeal their expulsions to a court was a failure to exhaust administrative remedies. The state court of appeals reversed the decision. Appeal reached the Supreme Court of South Carolina, which found the students received all the process they were due.

Under *Goss v. Lopez*, 419 U.S. 565 (1975), **a public school student facing a short-term suspension only needs to receive notice of the charges being brought and an opportunity to explain his or her side of the story**. As expulsion is a more serious disciplinary action than a short-term suspension, the South Carolina court found an accused student deserves greater procedures and protections when facing expulsion. Section 59-63-240 of the state code specifies that parents must be notified in writing of the time and place for a hearing in expulsion cases. At a hearing, parents have statutory rights to have counsel present and to present evidence and question witnesses. In this case, the family chose not to have counsel at the initial hearing and did not exercise the right to present evidence or question witnesses. Finding the state law protections were constitutionally sufficient, the court reinstated the trial court's decision. *Stinney v. Sumter School Dist. 17*, 391 S.C. 547, 707 S.E.2d 397 (S.C. 2011).

B. School Employees

◆ A New York court upheld the dismissal of a teacher who violated a school protocol by leaving a student who was having a crisis and then taunted her by sending get-well cards and a home-school application to her home. In employment termination proceedings, a hearing officer found the teacher used poor judgment and failed to take responsibility or demonstrate remorse for her conduct. **On appeal, a state appellate division court found the board could reasonably find the teacher abdicated her responsibilities.** Her poor judgment, failure to take responsibility for her actions and lack of remorse indicated her behavior was unlikely to change. *Denicolo v. Board of Educ. of City of New York*, 171 A.D. 565 (N.Y. App. Div. 2019).

◆ A Kansas student claimed a teacher/coach routinely spoke to females in sexualized terms. She said this went on for years and that school employees knew he had once been involved in an inappropriate sexual relationship with an underage student. Further, the student claimed the teacher/coach called her "dumb" in a class, asked what sex acts she did with her boyfriend, made sexual comments during classes and bragged about his own sexual acts. She said he discouraged her from attending school events. Eventually, the student withdrew from school and sued the teacher/coach and school district. She claimed she suffered retaliation and bullying from classmates after the coach told them he might be fired. After the student sued under Title IX of the Education Amendments of 1972 and the Due Process and Equal Protection Clauses of the Fourteenth Amendment, a federal court dismissed the due process claim. But it denied the coach's request for qualified immunity on her equal protection claim. On appeal, the Tenth Circuit held **incidents of sexual harassment directed at other students could be used as proof of the student's hostile environment claim**.

Prior cases have established that sexually charged comments, even if not directly about gender, qualify as "gender-related." The court found the complaint sufficiently alleged that a pervasively hostile environment existed. In particular, the coach was alleged to have routinely and openly spoken to and about female students in sexualized terms. The student said he asked another female gym student to engage in a sexually suggestive dance and boasted about convincing girls to remove their shirts and engage in activities wearing only sports bras. Next, the court found the law regarding sexual harassment is actionable as an equal protection violation, and that this has long been clearly established. It held a reasonable official would know the conduct of which the coach was accused would create a hostile environment. *Doe v. Hutchinson*, 728 Fed.Appx. 829 (10th Cir. 2018).

◆ An Alabama band teacher was fired for leaving a pistol in his locked office. He admitted it was his gun and said he had accidentally left it in the band room office while he accompanied the band to a competition in Georgia. At a board hearing, the teacher argued his excellent record justified a lesser penalty. But the board voted for termination based on violation of its weapons policy. A hearing officer later found the teacher violated the board's policy and that the board had authority to discharge him. While finding the teacher's exemplary service record justified a lesser penalty than termination, the hearing officer declined to reduce the sanction. He felt the Alabama Students First Act of 2011 did not authorize him to modify a school board's decision. After a state appeals court upheld the decision, the case reached the Supreme Court of Alabama. According to the court, the Students First Act removed fact-finding duties from hearing officers and vested education boards with this role. But the standard of review was the same as under prior laws governing teacher discipline and dismissal.

Unlike the appeals court, **the state supreme court held the arbitrary-and-capricious standard permitted a hearing officer to impose a lesser penalty than a board of education**, if the hearing officer found the board's sanction arbitrary and capricious. As a result, the court held the case should return to the hearing officer with instructions to review the sanction imposed by the board under the arbitrary-and-capricious standard of review. *Lambert v. Escambia County Board of Educ.*, 199 So.3d 761 (Ala. 2015).

When the case returned to the hearing officer, he found the board did not consider (or insufficiently considered) the evidence in deciding to dismiss the teacher instead of suspending him. The board appealed to the court of civil appeals. It found the supreme court has held that review of a board's decision must be extremely deferential. **The Students First Act expressed an intent to restore the primary authority and responsibility for maintaining a competent educational workforce with school boards.** Finding the hearing officer did not properly defer to the board under the arbitrary and capricious standard, the court held for the board. *Lambert v. Escambia County Board of Educ.*, No. 2150548, 2016 WL 5338669 (Ala. Ct. Civ. App. 9/23/16, Ala. certiorari denied, 11/18/16).

◆ An Arkansas student claimed that over a 10-month period, her bus driver bullied her on a regular basis. She said the driver called her an "ignorant bitch" and repeatedly said "go home and kill yourself" and "nobody loves you." The student said the driver threatened to paddle her if she reported the bullying and enlisted a coworker to help keep the abuse under wraps.

According to the student, a teacher witnessed the co-worker threatening her but did nothing. When the student's parent learned of the bullying, she complained to school officials. She said they ignored her complaints and did not address the bullying. The parent filed a criminal complaint against the driver and sued the school district in a federal court for constitutional violations. In addition to suing the district superintendent, school board members and other officials, she sued the driver. The court deemed the conduct "unfortunate" but found no constitutional violation. Appeal reached the U.S. Court of Appeals, Eighth Circuit. It noted the argument that the driver's harassment was "conscious-shocking behavior" because she encouraged the child to commit suicide in a manner "tantamount to attempted manslaughter." **The court found that while the driver's conduct was "reprehensible," it did not meet the standard of liability for violation of due process rights by a school official or school entity.** *Moore v. Lusks*, 667 Fed.Appx. 592 (8th Cir. 2016).

◆ A 42-year-old Indiana teacher began exchanging personal emails with a 17-year-old student via his school email. Soon, he texted the student naked pictures of himself and began sending her graphic, sexual propositions. The two kissed in the teacher's classroom, but she declined his invitation to go to his house. When the school learned of the relationship, it reviewed the teacher's school emails. On the same day, he was pulled out of class and suspended. The school called the police and child protective services. The teacher was forced to resign. Due to gossiping by other students, the student finished the school year at an alternative school. She sued the school district and teacher in a federal court. In pretrial activity, the court found **the school responded promptly when it learned of the inappropriate relationship**.

The court found the student pointed to no authority that the school had a duty (or that it was even a best practice) to read every email going through its server. As a result, her claim under Title IX of the 1972

Education Amendments was dismissed. Next, the court held the student failed to describe any unconstitutional system-wide policy or practice. Her constitutional claims were subject to dismissal because the district lacked notice of the teacher's actions. There was no evidence that the school did not adequately train staff members. Due to the failure by the parties to present arguments on an equal protection claim against the teacher, the claim would be resolved at a trial. There was also insufficient information before the court to dismiss an invasion of privacy/illegal seizure claim at this stage of the case. As for the state law claims against the teacher, the court found a jury might find for the student. He had sent her nude pictures of himself, arranged private time during which she would be required to be with him, and knew of her vulnerability based on her emails and knowledge of her parents' divorce. While the school was no longer a party, the remaining claims against the teacher would go forward. *Doe v. Crown Point School Corp.*, No. 2:12-cv-00264-PPS, 2015 WL 5038093 (N.D. Ind. 8/26/15).

◆ Maryland's highest court agreed with criminal prosecutors that intimate (but not sexually explicit) letters from a paraeducator to an eight-year-old student supported the paraeducator's sexual abuse conviction. The Court of Appeals of Maryland held there was sexual abuse despite the lack of sexual contact. In a prior case, the court had held **child sexual abuse includes failure to act to prevent molestation or exploitation when it is reasonably possible to do so**. Based on the totality of the letters and evidence that the two had hugged and held hands, the court found the child was exploited under the Maryland Child Sexual Abuse Statute. In affirming a prison sentence of 13 years, the court found sufficient evidence to support the conviction. It held "sexual abuse" was not limited to specified acts of incest, rape, sexual offense, sodomy and other practices listed in the statute. The court found the statute was not impermissibly vague and held the broad statutory language struck a careful compromise between the need for specificity and the desire of legislators to craft a law to "target the ever-shifting manner in which some people will target and abuse children." *Walker v. State of Maryland*, 432 Md. 587, 69 A.3d 1066 (Md. 2013).

◆ Three Colorado students who were subjected to inappropriate conduct by a former teacher at their high school lost their appeal against their school district and administration. The students claimed the teacher sent them explicit texts, sought nude pictures and solicited sexual relations with them. While the court allowed claims against the teacher to proceed, it held the case could not proceed against the district or administrators who did not know of the teacher's conduct. **A single state law claim for failure to report child abuse was allowed to proceed against a school security guard and coach who knew of an incident of sexual conduct between the teacher and one student.** In a brief order, the U.S. Court of Appeals, Tenth Circuit, affirmed the judgment. *Doe v. Boulder Valley School Dist. No. RE-2*, 523 Fed.Appx. 514 (10th Cir. 2013).

C. Parents

◆ Georgia school administrators investigated rumors that a twelfth-grader was making fun of a classmate who did not make the volleyball team. When she denied the rumor, an investigator took her phone and began looking for bullying messages. After determining the student did not do anything wrong, the investigator returned her phone to her. When her parent learned of the phone search, he repeatedly called district administrators, threatening legal action. The superintendent stated that the parent could not address the board of education because he had threatened litigation against the school district. After reviewing video footage of a meeting between the parent and school volleyball coaches, the superintendent and a school resource officer (SRO) determined the parent "posed a threat to the safety of the school's employees and students" and instructed him to direct all communications to a school attorney. When the parent returned to the school, the superintendent advised him he was not allowed there and directed the SRO to remove or arrest him if he returned. A letter was sent to the parent, barring him from unauthorized appearances on school grounds or at school events, except to bring his daughter to or from school. He was also allowed to attend school volleyball games but had to stay in a designated parents' section. Unaware of the letter, the SRO removed the parent from a school volleyball game.

The parent sued the superintendent, SRO and other school officials for constitutional violations. A federal court found the officials were entitled to qualified immunity because the parent identified no violation of clearly established law. He appealed to the Eleventh Circuit Court of Appeals. **Addressing the search of the cell phone first, the court found no clear precedent showing the search in this case was unlawful.** While *New Jersey v. T.L.O.*, 469 U.S. 325 (1985), set the parameters for school searches, the court found the decision did not clearly establish any principle of law that would mandate a conclusion that the phone search in this case was unlawful. A school policy against bullying and disrespectful behavior arguably gave the officials grounds to believe the search would turn up evidence of a rules violation. Next, the court found *Riley v. California*, 573 U.S. 373 (2014), a criminal case involving searches of the phones of adult suspects, did not establish that the phone search was unlawful. In the court's view, **the superintendent did not violate any clearly established law by limiting the parent's access to school. The few decisions on this issue have not established a parental right of access to schools.** The court found it was permissible to prevent the parent from addressing the board, given his statements that he would sue the district. Last, the court agreed with the lower court that the SRO and other officials did not violate the parent's clearly established constitutional rights by removing him from the school volleyball game. This was simply a mistake. Finding no merit to the parent's arguments, the court held for the school officials. *Jackson v. McCurry*, 762 Fed.Appx. 919 (11th Cir. 2019).

◆ An Indiana parent came to his daughter's school with a holstered handgun. He stood on a sidewalk and held a sign that read "we protect pedophiles." Parents questioned officials about the parent and one was upset about his presence. After the parent said he was protesting the treatment of his daughter, the superintendent asked him to put his gun in his car, stating a gun near students was "a major threat." The parent asked the superintendent how he would feel if he "brought his AK-47." He then said he would return to the high school at dismissal time that afternoon. The superintendent obtained a state court for an order for protection. The court found "stalking has occurred," and the parent "represents a credible threat of safety."

On appeal, the Indiana Court of Appeals held the state Civil Protection Order Act allowed "another representative" of a child to seek an order for protection on behalf of the child. According to the parent, a single act could not constitute "stalking." The court held the term "stalking" requires "repeated or continuing harassment" that would cause a reasonable person to feel threatened." This described "not just current, but future activity." When asked to put the gun away, the parent refused, became upset, suggested he might have a concealed weapon, and threatened to use an AK-47. This supported a finding of continuing harassment. No infringement upon the parent's First and Second Amendment rights was found. **Guns may be prohibited at school without violating the Second Amendment.** *S.B. v. Seymour Community Schools*, 97 N.E.3d 288 (Ind. Ct. App. 2018).

◆ California parents were involved in incidents with other parents and school staff. The father had an altercation with another parent and the mother raised her voice and used profanity when meeting with the principal. The parents did not send their younger child to school based on their displeasure with a certain teacher, prompting the principal to threaten a truancy report. The mother then came to the school and used profane language and epithets against the principal. After further incidents, the mother's access to school was restricted. The parents sued the district in a federal court. It held their state-law claims had to be dismissed, since **school officials cannot be held individually liable when acting within their judgment or discretion**.

The retaliation claims failed because the school district had legitimate, non-retaliatory reasons for restricting the parents' access to campus. Nothing indicated to the court that there must be a substantial and material threat before restricting campus access to parents. Next, the court found no merit to the constitutional rights claims. The parents' speech rights claims failed because public schools are not considered "public forums" for First Amendment purposes. Last, the court found no merit to the parents' due process claims. They had no constitutionally protected right to access a school campus, and the restrictions placed on them were ultimately lifted. *Camfield v. Board of Trustees of Redondo Beach Unified School Dist.*, No. 2:16-cv-02367-ODW-FFM, 2017 WL 3037780 (C.D. Cal. 7/17/17).

◆ An Idaho parent tried to pick up his nine-year-old daughter from school in violation of a child custody order. Police arrived and reviewed a copy of his divorce decree. After determining the parent was not exercising visitation rights as specified in the decree, the police ordered the parent out of the school. According to the school district, the parent "yelled all the way out of the school," then got into a verbal altercation with the child's stepfather outside the building. The district superintendent sent the parent a letter prohibiting him from entering school property. The letter also barred the parent from attending school-related activities without further notice.

During the next school year, the parent went to a district high school to pick up his eldest daughter from a school football stadium after she had a panic attack. He also persisted in communicating with school district staff. The school district reissued its letter barring him from school property. In a federal court, the parent sued the school district and its superintendent for speech rights, due process and state law violations. **The court found there is no parental right to physically access a child's school. In fact, many courts have held parents have no constitutional rights to be on school premises.** But the court held a jury would have to consider the parent's claim to access school property to vote, attend school board meetings and attend events such as basketball and football games. Last, the court declined an attempt to strip the superintendent of immunity for claims brought against her in an individual capacity. *Zeyen v. Pocatello/Chubbuck School Dist. #25*, No. 4:16-cv-00458-DCN, 2018 WL 2224053 (D. Idaho 5/15/18).

◆ A Georgia parent became frustrated at an event at her daughter's high school. She told a faculty member repeatedly that the event's organizer "needs to be shot in the head." A school resource officer investigated and obtained statements by witnesses who said the parent was upset, yelling and repeatedly declared that the organizer should be shot. The resource officer obtained an arrest warrant for disrupting a public school, and the parent was arrested. State prosecutors later declined to prosecute the case after she agreed to write a letter of apology and undergo an anger management evaluation. Months later, an assistant principal incorrectly told the parent that a criminal trespass warrant prohibited her from entering school property. The parent sued the school district and officials, in a federal court.

The court held for the district and officials, and the parent appealed to the U.S. Court of Appeals, Eleventh Circuit. The court held the school officials were entitled to qualified immunity. It found no case in which the Supreme Court, the Georgia Supreme Court or the Eleventh Circuit had addressed the extent to which school officials may address a parent's speech at a school event. As a result, the parent failed to show any clearly established First Amendment right that could have been violated. Next, the court held a reasonable officer could have found probable cause for an arrest warrant. **Evidence indicated the parent persisted until an employee took out her phone to call the police.** Finding the resource officer could have believed there was probable cause to arrest the parent for violating a Georgia law prohibiting the disruption of a public school, the court held for the school resource officer. As a one-time incident did not implicate a school district custom or policy, the court held there could be no claim against the district. *Yates v. Cobb County School Dist.*, 687 Fed.Appx. 866 (11th Cir. 2017).

◆ A California parent had previously worked for a school district as a student teacher, impact teacher for struggling students and assistant football coach. While still employed by the district, he testified at an expulsion hearing on behalf of a student. Like the parent, the student was of African-American heritage. A school official claimed the parent became disruptive and made some intimidating comments, such as "he had served his country as a Marine for 10 years and had 12 certified kills." Early in the next school year, the parent was accused of threatening behavior in the school parking lot. An official claimed the parent interrupted presenters at a board meeting and became aggressive. He made Facebook postings accusing the principal of racist comments. Claiming student and staff safety concerns, the district posted a deputy outside the school. The parent came to the district office and told an official that the principal "should stay away from his children because [she] had made racist slurs to them." According to the official, the parent then said if the principal did not stay away from his children "it will be a bad day." The school district obtained a temporary restraining order from a state court that required the parent to stay at least 100 yards away from the principal and her two daughters. He continued emailing district officials, accusing them of racism. The court denied the parent's motion to assert First Amendment protections, and he appealed.

The Court of Appeal of California noted that state law authorizes employers to seek restraining orders on behalf of their employees to prevent threats or violent acts in the workplace by employees or others. An employer may obtain a workplace restraining order for an employee who has "suffered unlawful violence or a credible threat of violence from any individual, that can reasonably be construed to be carried out or to have been carried out at the workplace." In the court's view, evidence supported the workplace violence restraining order. *Poway Unified School Dist. v. Garnier*, No. D067571, 2016 WL 6247683 (Cal. Ct. App. 10/26/16).

◆ Based on safety concerns, a Tennessee elementary school changed its after-school pickup policy by disallowing parents from entering the building. Early checkouts were prohibited except for emergencies. A parent who was unaware of the new policy walked to the school to pick up his child. He was encountered by a school resource officer (SRO), and the two had a heated discussion. Two days later, the parent again walked up to the school to pick up his child. This time, the SRO arrested him and took him to jail. The parent sued the county, the principal, the SRO and the school board in a federal court. He asserted a right to pick up his child from the school as he saw fit. In pretrial activity, the parent settled his claims with the SRO and the county. The principal and the school board then sought dismissal of the remaining claims. The court held the minimal interference with parental access to their children presented by the school's pickup policy fell "far short of a constitutional deprivation." As the Sixth Circuit has held, **parents lack rights to direct how public schools instruct children, set their curriculums, determine the hours of the school day, hire teachers, offer extracurriculars and decide many other issues of public education**. *Howe v. Aytes*, No. 2:14-cv-00077, 2016 WL 3262600 (M.D. Tenn. 6/10/16).

◆ A parent claimed his son's school district repeatedly denied services to his son and retaliated against him by filing a false report with the state department of human services. The parent claimed the false report by school authorities led to a juvenile proceeding against his son based upon a fabricated incident. In a federal court, the parent sued the school district and two school officials for constitutional rights violations. He did so without the assistance of an attorney. In his complaint, the parent stated his son was suspended from school for about half of a school year. He stated that after he requested a hearing to challenge the suspension, school officials lied under oath at the hearing. As for specific relief, the parent sought a declaration that school officials had violated his First Amendment speech rights. In response, the district noted the complaint did not declare any action was motivated by retaliation against the parent for exercising his speech rights. After explaining that the parent was entitled to pursue claims on his own behalf, the court held he could not pursue claims on behalf of his son without first hiring an attorney. It dismissed the claims on behalf of the student, which could be revived with the assistance of counsel.

Although the court found the complaint adequately stated that the parent engaged in protected activity by speaking on behalf of his son at an administrative hearing, it held **his statements could not be plausibly construed to show the district retaliated against him**. None of the actions attributed to school officials could be linked to any constitutionally protected activity. *Wright v. Tanner*, No. 16-CV-117-CVE-PJC, 2016 WL 4991619 (N.D. Okla. 9/16/2016).

D. Others

◆ A federal court upheld significant parts of New York's SAFE Act, which was enacted in response to the 2012 Sandy Hook Elementary School mass shootings. It upheld the act's regulation of "assault weapons" and large-capacity gun magazines, finding it furthered the interest in public safety and did not violate the Second Amendment. The court upheld a requirement for ammunition sales to take place "face-to-face" to prevent Internet sales. It also upheld the act's ban on military-style gun features. But the state did not justify a prohibition on the possession of gun magazines with more than seven rounds of ammunition. Also struck down was the act's reference to muzzle "breaks" and the regulation of semiautomatic pistols that were a "version of an automatic rifle, shotgun or firearm."

On appeal, the U.S. Court of Appeals, Second Circuit, consolidated the case with a challenge to similar legislation enacted by the Connecticut legislature in response to the 2012 Sandy Hook Elementary School mass shootings. **The court held core provisions of the laws prohibiting possession of semiautomatic assault weapons and large-capacity magazines did not violate the Second Amendment**, and that the challenged provisions were not void for vagueness. But a New York provision regulating load limits and Connecticut's prohibition on one particular Remington non-semiautomatic weapon infringed upon Second Amendment rights. The court upheld the prohibition of semiautomatic assault weapons and large-capacity magazines and invalidated a limit on load capacity of seven rounds. *New York State Rifle and Pistol Ass'n, Inc. v. Cuomo*, 804 F.3d 242 (2d Cir. 2015).

◆ A 2007 legislative amendment placed private contractor employees under the scope of Florida Statutes Section 1012.467. This required criminal background screening for non-instructional contractors. Those who were found to have been convicted of child abuse and certain other charges were disqualified from access to public school grounds when students were present. The statute defined the term "convicted" to include a no contest plea. An employee of a private contractor underwent a level-two criminal background screen as required by the new law and was notified that he would no longer have access to school property due to a 1996 no contest plea to a child abuse charge. As he had to work on school property when students were present in order to perform his job duties, the contractor fired him. A state court enjoined the board from barring him from school property. The board appealed to a state district court of appeal.

On appeal, the court held the statute changed the nature of a no contest plea. It held a "substantive, vested right" is in turn an "immediate right of present enjoyment, or a fixed right of future enjoyment," and not a mere expectation. In this case, the trial court had improperly referred to the employee's loss of a job and his "right" to come on school property. **The school board never terminated the relationship or demanded that the contractor fire him, and he had no vested right to go on school grounds.** Since the employee failed to show the school board had divested him of any right of present enjoyment or a present fixed right of future enjoyment, the court reversed the judgment of the trial court. *School Board of Miami-Dade County, Florida v. Carralero*, 992 So.2d 353 (Fla. Dist. Ct. App. 2008).

◆ A Virginia court convicted a man of taking indecent liberties with a child in his custody. Upon his release from a brief period of imprisonment, he registered as a sex offender and completed his term of probation. After a hearing, a state court considered the man's application to go onto school property to observe his stepson's activities, and to pick him up, drop him off and go to school conferences. The court granted him conditional rights to be on school property and terminated his duty to re-register every 90 days as a sex offender. The Commonwealth of Virginia, city school board and its superintendent of schools appealed to the Supreme Court of Virginia.

According to the Commonwealth, Virginia Code Section 18.2-370(B) granted school boards authority to determine whether to allow a convicted sex offender to enter onto school property. After noting that Section 18.2-370.5 prohibited convicted violent sex offenders from entering public school grounds in most circumstances, the court held the law gave circuit, juvenile and domestic relations courts the authority to remove this statutory ban. It held "decisions regarding the safety and welfare of students are manifestly a part of the supervisory authority granted the school boards under Article VIII." Allowing the offender a right to enter school property related to the education of his stepson, and not the public safety. Instead, the Commonwealth correctly argued that a court had supervision over a violent sex offender on probation or a suspended sentence. **Once a court lifted the statutory ban on sex offenders from entering school property, the school board would be permitted to exercise its supervisory authority under the state constitution.** The court reversed the judgment and returned the case to the circuit court for it to decide whether and under what circumstances the statutory ban from school property on the offender might be lifted. *Comwlth. v. Doe*, 278 Va. 223, 682 S.E.2d 906 (Va. 2009).

III. HARASSMENT

A. Gender

1. Harassment

In the mid-1980s, courts began recognizing sexual harassment as a form of sex discrimination that violates federal law. See, for example, *Meritor Savings Bank v. Vinson*, 477 U.S. 57, 106 S.Ct. 2399, 91 L.Ed.2d 49 (1986). Sexual harassment and assault may create school liability under Title IX of the Education Amendments of 1972, the Equal Protection Clause of the Fourteenth Amendment, and other federal laws. See *Fitzgerald v. Barnstable School Committee*, 555 U.S. 246 (2009), and *Davis v. Monroe County Board of Educ.*, 526 U.S. 629 (1999). Failure to prevent sexual harassment and assault also gives rise to state law tort claims.

To avoid liability under Title IX, educators must comply with the basic regulatory requirements of federal law. Schools must publish a notice of non-discrimination and name the particular laws involved. They should explain what kind of conduct these laws prohibit, state that the school will enforce them and describe what the penalty will be.

Legal commentators have observed that many victims of peer bullying and harassment do not know how or where to report such misconduct. Schools must appoint a Title IX coordinator and conspicuously post information on how and where to report sexual harassment and misconduct.

The nationally known law firm of Hogan Lovells has devised the following checklist to help prevent student harassment claims.

☑ CHECKLIST – *Harassment Prevention*

- ☐ Foster an atmosphere of mutual respect among faculty, staff and students.
- ☐ Have clear policies on prohibited conduct.
- ☐ Set clear boundaries of acceptable behavior for students and employees.
- ☐ Make sure teachers, staff, students and parents are aware of policies and expectations.
- ☐ Make clear who is available to **welcome** concerns and complaints about such issues.
- ☐ Encourage staff and students to speak up about inappropriate behavior whenever it occurs.
- ☐ Intervene early to monitor and correct potentially problematic behaviors: sexual or gender-based teasing; inappropriate jokes about sex; "casual" comments of a sexual nature; or any unwelcome touching.

Thorough investigation of harassment reports is another key to avoiding school liability in Title IX cases. Here are Hogan Lovells' suggestions:

☑ CHECKLIST – *Harassment Investigation*

- ☐ Develop a timeline for the investigation to ensure that it is completed properly.
- ☐ Develop a plan for the investigation.
- ☐ Determine the type of harassment that may be present.
- ☐ Determine what facts are necessary to show the type of harassment.
- ☐ Determine potential witnesses that need to be interviewed.
- ☐ Determine what, if any, documents need to be reviewed.
- ☐ Draft possible questions for each interview.
- ☐ Conduct interview of complainant and witnesses.
- ☐ Consider using a team approach.
- ☐ Use open-ended questions.
- ☐ Ask the complainant and/or parents what they would like done.
- ☐ Ask questions that establish a foundation for the incidents, such as who was there, where each incident took place and when each incident took place.
- ☐ Tell the witness that the investigation is ongoing and that no decision will be made until all witnesses and relevant information have been considered.
- ☐ Ask questions that elicit facts – not perceptions.
- ☐ Ask if there are any other witnesses.
- ☐ Take notes.

☐ Analyze all relevant information.

☐ Communicate the results, but be careful of privacy rights.

The checklist information above is copyrighted by Hogan Lovells (formerly Hogan & Hartson) and the National School Boards Association (NSBA). See *http://www.nsba.org/* and *http://www.hoganlovells.com/*.

2. Peer Harassment Case Law

Davis v. Monroe County Board of Educ., 526 U.S. 629 (1999), is the leading school case on peer sexual harassment claims arising under Title IX of the Education Amendments of 1972. Title IX prohibits sex discrimination by recipients of federal funding. In *Davis*, the Supreme Court held schools could be liable under Title IX for student-on-student harassment. To prevail in a Title IX case, students must show (1) sexual harassment by peers; (2) deliberate indifference by school officials with "actual knowledge" of the harassment; and (3) harassment so severe, pervasive and objectively offensive it deprived the student of access to educational opportunities. **In order for school liability to exist, there must have been deliberate indifference by school officials to known acts of peer sexual harassment, where the school's response is clearly unreasonable under the circumstances.** A teacher's knowledge of peer harassment may create "actual knowledge" that may trigger school liability.

In *Fitzgerald v. Barnstable School Committee*, 555 U.S. 246, 129 S.Ct. 788, 172 L.Ed.2d 582 (2009), the Supreme Court held Title IX does not bar gender discrimination claims against schools under 42 U.S.C. § 1983. Section 1983 is a post-Civil War statute that creates no rights, but is a vehicle to enforce rights created by other federal laws and the Constitution. Because the *Fitzgerald* case has the potential to expand school liability in peer sexual harassment cases, educators must be willing to investigate all harassment claims and intervene promptly in a manner that is reasonably calculated to remedy misconduct.

◆ According to a Texas high school student's federal court complaint, a male classmate was upset that she was rejecting his frequent romantic advances. She said he engaged in repeated conduct that made her feel very uncomfortable and unsafe at school. The classmate jumped over a railing on the second floor of the school in an apparent suicide attempt as the student looked on. A teacher broke the classmate's fall, and he was not seriously injured. The student was distraught over the suicide attempt and told a school counselor that the classmate was obsessed with her. The school responded by adopting a safety plan to provide her a security guard escort and a schedule that minimized her encounters with the classmate while they were at school. A specific plan was created for a choir activity they both participated in. Despite these proactive measures, the student sued the school district in a federal court, alleging deliberate indifference to sexual harassment in violation of Title IX of the Education Amendments of 1972.

The court held for the school district, and the student appealed to the Fifth Circuit. The court explained that a school district is liable for student-on-student harassment only if it has knowledge about severe harassment and is deliberately indifferent to it. For a district to be deemed to have "knowledge" of peer harassment, a school employee with the authority to institute corrective measures on the school's behalf must have notice of the harassment. The court found that in this case, no school employee knew of any harassment until the classmate's apparent suicide attempt. **When the school learned of the situation, it took corrective measures that – even if not ideal or preferred by the student – did not show deliberate indifference to known harassment.** In the court's view, the district took proactive measures in response to her report. It would be inappropriate to second-guess the school's choices because officials were not only dealing with the classmate's reported harassment but with his mental health issues. Finding no Title IX violation, the court held for the school district. *E.M. v. Austin Independent School Dist.*, 770 Fed.Appx. 712 (5th Cir. 2019).

◆ A Missouri kindergartner claimed she was sexually harassed and assaulted by other students at her school. Her parent claimed discrimination in public accommodations in violation of state law as well as liability for negligence. In a state court, the family sued the school district and several individual employees. The school district sought pretrial judgment on the state-law discrimination claim, arguing it was not a "person" as defined by the Missouri Human Rights Act (MHRA). It further argued it did not waive sovereign immunity for common-law torts claim by purchasing liability insurance. The court denied the district's motion and the district responded by petitioning the state court of appeals for a special order called a writ of prohibition. In 2018, the court of appeals held for the district. In a 2019 lawsuit by a transgender student against the same district, the state supreme court rejected the district's argument that it was not a "person" as contemplated by the MHRA. See *R.M.A. v. Blue Springs R-IV School Dist.*, 568 S.W.3d 420 (Mo. banc 2019). The state supreme court then returned the case filed on behalf of the kindergartner to the court of appeals for reconsideration in light of *R.M.A*. The court held the kindergartner's MHRA claim was viable and its prior order to the contrary had to be quashed. Next, the court found that when a public entity purchases liability insurance, state law generally provides that immunity is waived to the extent of (and for the specific purposes covered by) the insurance policy.

The court explained that *respondeat superior* is not a legal cause of action (such as negligence) but is rather a doctrine by which an employer may be held liable for the misconduct of employees acting within the course and scope of their employment. Sovereign immunity protects states and their political subdivisions from liability, including *respondeat superior* liability, unless sovereign immunity for the political subdivision is expressly waived. **But the court held the coverage extended by the policy in this**

case to school employees for personal liability did not expressly extend coverage for the district's *respondeat superior* liability. Finding the policy did not waive the district's sovereign immunity for the common-law tort claims based on *respondeat superior* liability, the court returned the case to the trial court for further proceedings. *State ex rel. Blue Springs School Dist. v. Grate*, 576 S.W.3d 262 (Mo. Ct. App. 2019).

◆ A Kentucky school district suspended a student after he sexually assaulted a fellow cheerleader. He was assigned to an alternative school for the rest of the semester, where he had no further disciplinary incidents. The district superintendent twice rejected recommendations that he return to the high school before allowing him to return for his senior year. As a condition for his return, he was to have no contact with the cheerleader. Building administrators monitored the student's compliance and reviewed schedules to assure he did not share any classes with the cheerleader. Administrators were unable to prevent every encounter between them. They saw each other in the cafeteria and on the way to their sixth-period classes. These sightings made the cheerleader uncomfortable and caused her anxiety. But the two never interacted. The cheerleader's father claimed the student's presence at school created a hostile environment for his daughter. He said her grades suffered and that coaches treated her unfairly in retaliation for reporting the sexual assault. In a federal court, the cheerleader's parents sued the school district for violating Title IX. A federal court held for the district, and the parents appealed to the U.S. Court of Appeals, Sixth Circuit. It found they had to show the district was deliberately indifferent to an environment of sexual harassment in order to impose Title IX liability.

In the court's view, the cheerleader did not show deliberate indifference by the district. Upon learning of the sexual assault, the district acted immediately. When the student confessed, he was suspended and transferred to an alternative school. Upon his readmission to the high school, the school district imposed strict conditions on him that worked as intended. **The court found administrators formulated a remedial policy that prevented the student from further harassment in a manner that was not unreasonable.** There was no merit to a claim that coaches retaliated against the cheerleader. Since she did not claim the student harassed her after his return to school, the court held for the district. *M.D. v. Bowling Green Independent School Dist.*, 709 Fed.Appx. 775 (6th Cir. 2017).

◆ A 14-year-old Washington middle school girl met an 18-year-old high school boy at a school track practice. They began exchanging texts and later left campus together. The boy drove the girl to his house and raped her. He was charged with crimes and eventually pleaded guilty to second-degree assault. In a state court, the student sued the school district for negligence. In pretrial activity, it was revealed that a county sheriff had notified the high school principal that the boy was a registered sex offender. Evidence suggested the principal failed to develop a safety plan and violated a district policy requiring him to inform teachers of the offender's registered status.

The court granted the district's dismissal motion, noting the student was not in the district's custody at the time of the rape. It was found that her decision to skip practice and leave campus with the offender broke any chain of causation. The case reached the state supreme court which held **Washington courts recognize "an enhanced and solemn duty" of reasonable care to protect students.** This includes a duty to protect them from foreseeable risks of harm that students may inflict on each other. School districts have a duty to protect students in their custody from foreseeable dangers. It is foreseeable that one student might rape another. In this case, the court found the district's duty arose while the student was still on school grounds. It held she did not have to be in the school's custody at the time of injury for a duty to arise. Maryland and California courts have held a school district cannot escape liability for failure to properly supervise a student on school grounds, simply because the injury takes place off school property. **The court held schools have a duty of reasonable care to protect students from foreseeable dangers.** An intervening criminal act did not exonerate the district. The court found enough evidence for a jury trial. *N.L. v. Bethel School Dist.*, 378 P.3d 162 (Wash. 2016).

◆ A Maryland student said he was bullied and teased by a classmate and other students. Despite several reported incidents, the two students were placed in the same classroom the next school year. The student continued to report harassment, including an incident in which the classmate tried to climb into his lavatory stall while his pants were down. In response, the student was offered a lavatory escort. During the school year, the classmate was told that further complaints would be grounds for a suspension. Meanwhile, the student's mother discovered text messages from her son to the classmate and found explicit photos sent by the classmate. She reported this to the police. When questioned by a detective, the student revealed that the classmate had forced him into sexual activity in the school library and a school lavatory. He had not previously told his parents of these incidents.

The classmate said the contact was consensual, and the student also told the detective he had consented to it. In a federal court, the student's family sued the board for violating Title IX. The court held for the board, and the family appealed to the U.S. Court of Appeals, Fourth Circuit. As the lower court had found, the school district had responded to all of the incidents once they were reported. **The students were separated to the extent possible in class, and procedures to protect the student were implemented for lavatory use.** These measures were held sufficient under Title IX. As the Fourth Circuit found the school's response to the reports was not clearly unreasonable, the board prevailed on the Title IX claim. Liability for negligence and gross negligence could not be based on a theory that the classmate's behavior should have been seen as an escalating pattern. As a result, the board of education prevailed on all the claims. *Doe v. Board of Educ. of Prince George's County*, 605 Fed.Appx. 159 (4th Cir. 2015).

◆ A Mississippi high school student was sexually assaulted by a male student who pushed her into a vacant school bus and forced her to perform oral sex. Later, her father sued the school district for negligence claims including inadequate school security and failure to warn his daughter of the male's history of sexual misconduct. The parties engaged in the pretrial information-gathering process known as "discovery" for a period of over a year and a half. During discovery, the male's history of criminal and delinquent misconduct was revealed. Prior to his transfer to the student's school, he had committed five instances of inappropriate touching of females and sexual battery against a 12-year-old girl. He had been arrested and placed under a no-contact order. Asserting discretionary-function immunity, the district moved for pretrial judgment. The court granted the district's motion, and the case reached the Supreme Court of Mississippi.

In *Brantley v. City of Horne Lake*, 152 So.3d 1106 (Miss. 2014), the court held state law immunity was no longer limited to decisions involving policy considerations. Under *Brantley*, courts were to first determine whether the governmental function at issue was considered "discretionary" or "ministerial." Next, a court was to examine any narrower duty associated with the activity at issue to determine whether a statute, regulation or binding directive rendered a duty "ministerial." To defeat discretionary-function immunity, the student would have to show an act done in furtherance of a broad discretionary function "also furthered a more narrow function or duty which is made ministerial by another specific statute, ordinance, or regulation promulgated pursuant to lawful authority." Since the court's rules for assessing discretionary-function immunity had changed greatly during the pretrial stages of this case, the court returned the case to the trial court for review under *Brantley*. **In returning the case to the lower court, the supreme court held the school district did not waive its immunity.** *Doe v. Rankin County School Dist.*, 189 So.3d 616 (Miss. 2015).

◆ Parents of a bilingual special education child who was sexually assaulted in a school lavatory could pursue negligence claims against Connecticut school officials for allowing students to go to the lavatory unsupervised. According to a state court complaint filed by the student's parents, a teacher repeatedly chose a certain classmate to accompany the student during non-lunchtime lavatory breaks. They claimed the classmate sexually assaulted their child on more than one occasion. Further, the parents claimed that allowing special education students to leave a classroom unattended was unsafe and that the teacher ignored their child's request that the classmate not be permitted to go with him. The school officials sought a judgment based on immunity for discretionary conduct. The court explained that for a negligence action to survive pretrial dismissal, there must be evidence that a legal duty was breached. Next, the injured party must have suffered an injury that was caused by an allegedly negligent party. If a duty is found to exist, the injured party must show the defending party did not exercise reasonable care under the circumstances and caused the injury.

In order to impose tort liability, it must be shown that without the defendant's negligence, the injury would not have occurred and that the negligence more likely than not caused the injury. Concluding that a fair and reasonable mind could find the sexual assaults would not have taken place if the teacher had refused to allow the classmate to accompany the student to the lavatory, the court refused to dismiss the case. Evidence was presented that the student did not want to go to the lavatory with the classmate. Although the teacher claimed state law immunity because her decisions involved discretion and judgment, the court found a factual issue existed regarding whether there was a school policy or directive in place creating a ministerial duty in this case. As a result, the court denied the officials' claim to immunity. *Doe v. New Haven Board of Educ.*, No. NNHCV105033148S, 2015 WL 6144099 (Conn. Super. Ct. 9/18/15).

3. Harassment by School Employees

◆ According to a state-court complaint filed by a West Virginia student, a teacher engaged in grooming behaviors, said she was "sexy" and sent her pictures of his genitalia while asking her to send him nude photos of herself. The complaint further alleged that the teacher followed the student into a lavatory and forced her to perform oral sex on him. The student claimed that during an incident in the classroom, the teacher touched her vagina while holding his hand over her mouth. She stated that when she tried to stop his sexual advances, he threatened her with violence. In her lawsuit, the student tried to hold the board of education liable for the teacher' misconduct under two negligence theories. She first sought to hold the board vicariously liable. Second, she sought to hold the board directly liable for the negligent hiring, retention, supervision, monitoring and/or training of the teacher. The court agreed with the board that it could not be held vicariously liable for the teacher's criminal misconduct as he acted intentionally and outside the scope of his employment. The board had immunity from this claim. In the court's view, the board was also not liable for negligent supervision.

After the court dismissed all the claims, the student appealed. When the case reached the Supreme Court of Appeals of West Virginia, it noted the student claimed other board employees knew of the teacher's misconduct but did not intervene, report the misconduct or take other action. The court found the lower court had several options besides dismissal in a negligence case where a government entity raised the defense of immunity. **Instead of dismissing the case, the lower court should have let the student respond to the board's immunity defense.** Further, the court found the student could request that the case enter the pretrial fact-finding process known as discovery in opposition to the board's dismissal motion. The court held the trial court committed error by failing to allow the student any opportunity to develop her case and instructed it to conduct further proceedings. *Doe v. Logan County Board of Educ.*, 829 S.E.2d 45 (W.Va. 2019).

◆ A Pennsylvania student said she had sex with her band teacher while she was still in high school, but did not disclose the relationship until she went to college. When she did so, the teacher was charged with criminal conduct. He pleaded guilty to one count of corruption of minors and sentenced to jail time. In a federal court, the student sued the teacher, her school district and several administrators for civil rights violations. She added claims against the teacher's prior employer and two of its administrators. After the student settled her claims against the teacher, the court granted pretrial judgment to the school districts and officials. The student appealed to the U.S. Court of Appeals, Third Circuit, which noted the lower court's finding that while the teacher's conduct "was deliberate and reprehensible," it was not attributable to the school districts or their administrators. **As the lower court held, the student did not show the prior employer had any actual, contemporaneous knowledge of abuse.** When administrators at the teacher's previous school district heard rumors of a possible sexual relationship, both the student and her parent denied it. Under established law, a government entity is not liable for a constitutional violation based on simple negligence. While the court found the previous district could have done more to learn the truth by confronting the teacher, it could not be held liable as it did not know about any past sexual abuse by the teacher. **Rumors of abuse were found insufficient to show the school district had been deliberately indifferent to a risk of abuse.** As for the student's school district, each of her liability theories failed. Neither the school principal nor the assistant principal knew of any misconduct until after she graduated. They could not be liable for a constitutional violation simply because they knew the student was spending a lot of time in the band room. Next, the court held the school district was not liable for failing to train staff members to recognize and report grooming behavior by the teacher. Last, the court found no merit to a claim that the district had deficient hiring practices that were directly responsible for the sexual abuse. In fact, the teacher had three favorable letters of recommendation, a clear criminal record and no record of child abuse. Simple negligence did not support any of the student's theories, and the court affirmed the judgment against her. *Kobrick v. Stevens*, 763 Fed.Appx. 216 (3d Cir. 2019).

◆ A Virginia teacher texted suggestive remarks to an 11-year-old student. Among her messages was that the student was "cute" and she "wished he was 18 years old so they could be together." When the student's parents learned of the messages, they contacted the police. Using the student's cell phone, a detective texted the teacher, posing as the student. She replied with five pictures. One was taken in a bathtub and partially showed her breasts. During the teacher's prosecution, prosecutors introduced the pictures at trial along with a five-page transcript of the text-message conversation between her and the detective who posed as the student. At her trial, the teacher argued that one of the laws she was charged with violating – pertaining to communications to obtain a child or promote a child for various prohibited sexual offenses – required a communication with a third party. She also argued none of the pictures she sent showed sexual parts as proscribed by law. The court rejected all the teacher's arguments and found her guilty of exposing herself and using an electronic device to procure or promote illegal activity.

The case reached the Supreme Court of Virginia, which found the teacher violated a Virginia law by using an electronic device to procure or promote illegal activity involving the student. **It was sufficient for the Commonwealth to show she communicated with the student with the purpose of procuring or promoting him to engage in unlawful acts.** Since a rational jury could have found beyond a reasonable doubt that the teacher communicated with the student with the purpose of a scheme to take indecent liberties with him, and she unlawfully exposed herself to him, the court upheld her conviction. *Dietz v. Commonwealth of Virginia*, 294 Va. 123, 804 S.E.2d 309 (Va. 2017).

◆ In *Gebser v. Lago Vista Independent School Dist.*, 524 U.S. 274, 118 S.Ct. 1989, 141 L.Ed.2d 277 (1998), the U.S. Supreme Court set the liability standard for school districts in sexual harassment cases filed by students asserting harassment by employees under Title IX. The case involved a Texas student who had a sexual relationship with a teacher.

When the case reached the Supreme Court, it rejected the liability standard advocated by the student and U.S. government, which resembled *respondeat superior* liability under Title VII. Title IX contains an administrative enforcement mechanism that assumes actual notice has been provided to school officials prior to the imposition of enforcement remedies. **An award of damages would be inappropriate in a Title IX case unless an official with the authority to address the discrimination failed to act despite actual knowledge of it, in a manner amounting to deliberate indifference to discrimination.** Here, there was insufficient evidence that any school official should have known about the relationship between the student and teacher to impose Title IX liability. Accordingly, the school district could not be held liable for the teacher's misconduct.

◆ A Michigan high school freshman began exchanging explicit texts and photos with a teacher. Eventually, the teacher sexually assaulted the student. Later, she pleaded guilty to assault with intent to commit sexual penetration and was sentenced to at least 23 months in prison. After cooperating with the police investigation, the student claimed he was harassed by his school peers, shunned by athletic coaches and subjected to retaliation by school administrators because the teacher lost her job and went to jail. He claimed the "entire school turned on him," and "everybody hated him for it," causing him severe anxiety. He said he contemplated suicide and decided not to try out for the school baseball team. The student left school and enrolled in online courses. He sued the school district in a federal court, which held for the district. On appeal, the U.S. Court of Appeals, Sixth Circuit, found no reasonable jury would find evidence of retaliation.

Legitimate educational reasons were stated for each of the matters the student complained about, including suspensions for tobacco use and making inappropriate comments. The school appointed a tutor to improve his school work, not to retaliate against him. Undisputed evidence showed the district made reasonable decisions to discipline the student for misconduct. Witnesses confirmed he viewed an explicit picture of a classmate. The court found the school took steps to make him feel more comfortable and provide him a fresh start. As for the student's harassment claim under Title IX, the court held he did not show he was harassed based on his sex. **The court found the school responded to each report of harassment in a manner that was not unreasonable.** *Gordon v. Traverse City Area Public Schools*, 686 Fed.Appx. 315 (6th Cir. 2017).

◆ Ohio school district officials convinced the state court of appeals that their school district's board of education was entitled to the benefit of immunity in an action that was instituted by two female school students who presented the allegation that their assistant high school basketball coach sexually assaulted them. The state court of appeals explained in its decision that a school district sheds its state-law immunity under a state-law exception for any negligence of employees with respect to proprietary functions. As the board argued, prior cases indicate the provision of a system of public education is a governmental function. In addition, state law declares that a governmental function may include something performed by a political subdivision pursuant to a legislative requirement or voluntarily for the common good of all, or that promotes or preserves the public health, safety or welfare. A governmental function is one that involves activities not engaged in or not customarily engaged in by non-government persons.

As the board argued, sports and extracurricular activities are intimately related with the school experience and are a part of the public education described in state law. The hiring, retention and supervision of the assistant girls' basketball coach was inherently a part of the provision of public education by the board, the court said. For that reason, the hiring, retention and supervision of the coach was a governmental function for the purpose of evaluating whether the board of education was entitled to immunity on the claims raised. **As the board enjoyed immunity in connection with the provision of a girls' basketball team, the court issued a ruling in favor of the board of education and against the plaintiffs.** *Wilson v. McCormack*, 93 N.E.3d 102 (Ohio Ct. App. 2017).

◆ An Oklahoma teacher had a sexual relationship with a 14-year-old student. The father claimed the student suffered depression, isolation and self-blame for the relationship. In addition, the father said members of the community publicly chastised him and questioned him about the scandal. The student transferred to another school, where he was unable to play basketball. The student was described as bullied, socially withdrawn and suffering from anxiety. In a federal court, he sued the school district for violating his constitutional rights and Title IX of the Education Amendments of 1972. He asserted negligence claims and claims against the teacher for battery and infliction of emotional distress. The father also sought damages for her conduct. In pretrial activity, **the court held the student could proceed with several of his claims against the school district**.

According to the court, the student was entitled to damages from the teacher based on the battery and intentional infliction of emotional distress claims. Based on his loss of companionship of friends, his lost basketball dreams and the stigma of the teacher's conduct, the student won $1 million in damages. But the court denied any damage award for the father, as he was unable to prove any direct damages. In fact, the father did not show he was aware that the student had left his custody at the relevant time. *M.C. v. Hollis Independent School Dist. No. 66 of Harmon County, Oklahoma*, No. CIV-15-343-C, 2017 WL 3446031 (W.D. Okla. 8/10/17).

◆ A Minnesota middle school coach lent his cell phone to a 14-year-old girl to call her parents for a ride home. She later retrieved his number from her home phone caller ID and began texting him explicit messages on her cell phone. Eventually, they had sexual contact in the school weight room. Another student's parent learned of the explicit text messages and called the student's mother. The day the school learned of the relationship, the police were called and the coach was arrested. The district fired him, and he pled guilty to criminal charges. The parents sued the coach and school district in a state court for vicarious liability, negligence, negligent supervision and other claims. The court held for the district, and the student appealed.

On appeal, the state court of appeals held the school district was entitled to immunity. It agreed with the school district that state law creates a general rule of immunity from vicarious liability for torts committed by state employees, unless committed within the scope of office or employment. Next, the court rejected the student's claim that the district should be held liable because "red flags" made sexual abuse by the coach foreseeable. To succeed on a negligence or negligent supervision claim, the student had to show there was some risk of foreseeable harm. The incidents cited by the student did not include any sexual conduct. She said she yelled at the coach during a football practice and shouted "Chris, I love you" at another. The court found none of the incidents similar to (or indicative of) sexual abuse in a way that put the district on notice of any inappropriate relationship. **Finding the red flags gave no objectively reasonable indication of a specific danger of sexual abuse, the court held the abuse was not foreseeable** and ruled for the district. *Doe 175 v. Columbia Heights School Dist., ISD No. 13*, 873 N.W.2d 352 (Minn. Ct. App. 2016).

◆ The Court of Appeals of Iowa refused to dismiss a student's Title IX claim, basing its decision on *Gebser v. Lago Vista Independent School Dist*. The student was involved in sexual relationships with two high school coaches. The court held Title IX claimants may recover damages from a school if the student was subjected to sexual harassment and abuse by a teacher. **Recovery is limited to situations where an official with**

authority to address the misconduct with corrective measures has actual knowledge of the misconduct but fails to adequately respond. Since the school's response was not clearly unreasonable, the Title IX claim failed. The court rejected claims asserting the school district should have a heightened duty of care. The student's participation in sports created no duty to protect her from the employees. Since "a relationship that is actively concealed is not foreseeable," the court held for the school district. *Lindemulder v. Davis County Community School Dist.*, No. 15-0067, 2016 WL 1679835, 884 N.W.2d 222 (Table) (Iowa Ct. App. 4/27/16).

◆ The Supreme Court of Washington denied a school district's appeal from a lower court decision allowing a parent to pursue claims for negligent hiring, retention, supervision and training of a school security guard who raped and impregnated her daughter. **The parent claimed the guard sexually groomed her daughter and that many school employees knew of the relationship but failed to act.** While the state court of appeals affirmed the dismissal of many of the parent's claims, it allowed her to pursue her negligence-based claims against the district. *Evans v. Tacoma School Dist. No. 10*, 186 Wash.2d 1028, 385 P.3d 124 (Wash. 2016).

◆ A 14-year-old California student gained a second chance to hold the Los Angeles Unified School District (LAUSD) liable for negligence based on sexual abuse by a former teacher who invited her to be friends on a social networking site. After she turned 14, the two had sex many times. A friend of the student reported the relationship to another employee at the school, who made a report. As a result, the teacher was arrested. He pled no contest to one of the charges and served prison time. In a state court, the student sued LAUSD for several negligence-based claims. After a two-week trial, a jury returned a verdict for LAUSD. The student then appealed to the state court of appeal, which held the trial court's instructions had improperly required the student to show the teacher had a "dangerous propensity to sexually abuse minors." California Civil Jury Instructions only required the student to prove the teacher had the potential to sexually abuse minors in order to establish a claim for negligent hiring, supervision or retention.

Next, the court held the student was not required to show the teacher was unfit because he had committed prior acts of misconduct. He hugged female students, talked to them about his personal life, rearranged his classroom and laid on a table near two female students. Next, the court agreed with the student that the lower court had erroneously allowed LAUSD to admit evidence of her prior sexual history in order to measure the damages she was claiming for emotional distress. While this evidence was only supposed to shed light on her damages, the court found it had been discussed throughout the trial. It had also been improper for the lower court to instruct the jury to apply comparative fault principles. Since the teacher had acted in a criminal manner, the student could not have consented to sexual misconduct and could not be apportioned any part of the damages. The court explained that

"the law puts the burden on the adult to avoid the sexual relationship." Since the jury instructions harmed the student, the court returned the case to the trial court for a new trial. *S.M. v. Los Angeles Unified School Dist.*, 250 Cal.App.4th 543 (Cal. Ct. App. 2015).

4. Non-Student Harassment and Assault Cases

◆ A Mississippi adult was able to sign a young child out of school by falsely indicating he was her parent six different times. He then sexually molested her and returned her to school. After the child's parents learned of this, they sued the school district in a federal court. Among their claims was that the school's check-out policy violated the Constitution by allowing employees to release a child without first verifying the signer's identity or authority to sign out the child. A federal court held constitutional liability was foreclosed under the U.S. Supreme Court's decision in *DeShaney v. Winnebago County Dep't of Social Services*, 489 U.S. 189 (1989).

Appeal reached the Fifth Circuit, where a three-judge panel held for the family. But a majority of judges of the Fifth Circuit voted to rehear the case and found a constitutional claim could proceed only if the district had a duty to protect the student from a private party. This required a special relationship between the student and district. But state compulsory attendance laws did not create a special relationship between schools and their students. The court held **public schools have no special relationship with students that would require protection from harm by private actors such as the adult in this case**. The parents raised other arguments, but the court rejected them. It held the student's young age was not a relevant factor under the special relationship analysis. Carelessness by school employees did not mean they knew that the adult was unauthorized to sign out the child. And the parents did not claim the district was deliberately indifferent to a known danger. The court held for the district. *Doe v. Covington County School Dist.*, 675 F.3d 849 (5th Cir. 2012).

◆ A Nebraska elementary school policy required visitors to check in at the main office. An intruder entered and was confronted by a teacher. She asked him if she could help him, but he ignored her. Two other teachers also noticed him, and one directed him to a restroom. Although she told him to report to the office after he was finished, he instead went to another restroom where he sexually assaulted a five-year-old student. The student's mother sued the school district in a state court for negligence. After finding the district's security plan was adequate, the court held for the district. Appeal reached the Supreme Court of Nebraska, which stated that under prior law, the foreseeability of a particular injury was part of the inquiry into whether an entity had a legal duty to the injured party. But the court found that approach required a court to decide legal questions "uniquely rooted in the facts and circumstances of a particular case." In any negligence case, the legal duty of a party was to conform to the standard of conduct. By contrast, foreseeability questions depended upon the unique facts of each case.

The court held foreseeability is not part of the analysis of duty, as this transforms a factual inquiry into a legal issue. It also expands the authority of judges at the expense of juries. The court found this improper, as **foreseeability questions involve common sense, common experience, and the application of community standards and behavioral norms**. These areas have long been understood to be within the province of a jury, and not a judge. Under the court's decision, a jury would have to determine, based on the facts of each case, whether or not the evidence established a breach of duty. **School districts owe their students a duty of reasonable care, as the duty of teachers to supervise and protect their students is well-established.** But the question of whether the assault in this case was reasonably foreseeable involved a fact-specific inquiry for a jury to determine. It had thus been improper for the lower court to award pretrial judgment to the district. The case was returned to the lower court. *A.W. v. Lancaster County School Dist. 0001*, 784 N.W.2d 907 (Neb. 2010).

B. Sexual Orientation and Gender Identity

Search "Gender Support Plan" and "Gender Transition Plan" at *www.SchoolSafetyAndSecurityAlert.com* to download authoritative guidance from our Forms Library.

◆ A North Carolina student who identified as gay said peers bullied him at school and subjected him to slurs, threats and violence. He said four students pursued him for months and sometimes followed through on threats of violence. The student said he was chased through the school, pushed into lockers, punched, harassed and assaulted. He said a school coach did not intervene despite knowledge that the four students were "looking to beat him up." He said he and his parents spoke with administrators, to no avail.

The student said he attempted suicide three times in a 16-month period and was hospitalized each time. In a federal court, he sued the board of education, district superintendent, the high school principal, teachers, a school resource officer and others. After a hearing, the court dismissed claims for constitutional violations, sexual harassment and emotional distress. In a separate opinion, the court addressed a negligent supervision and training claim against the board. **North Carolina law requires a party alleging negligent supervision and training to show specific acts of negligence and incompetency based on an employee's inherent unfitness or prior acts.** Further, the student had to show his injuries resulted from incompetency or unfitness and that the board knew (or had reason to know of) an employee's incompetency. Although the student claimed there was a reasonable inference that the board should have known of staff incompetence in handling harassment complaints, the court held he did not show the board knew of employee incompetence that might allow him to pursue the negligent supervision and training claim. *Nance v. Rowan-Salisbury Board of Educ.*, 336 F.Supp.3d 593 (M.D.N.C. 2018).

◆ Although born female, a Virginia student felt a deep sense of being male from a young age. By the end of his freshman year of high school, the student experienced such distress that he could not attend class. The next year, he legally changed his name, began using male pronouns, dressed as a male and wore a male hairstyle. The student presented his school with medical information confirming he was receiving treatment for gender dysphoria and was to be treated as a male in all respects. With the principal's support, the student used male restrooms at school without incident for seven weeks. Parents learned that the student was using boys' lavatories at school, and they complained. The board of education issued a policy limiting the use of restroom and locker room facilities according to biological gender. The board prevented the student from using boys' lavatories and installed three single-user lavatories. He sued the board in a federal court, asserting the policy of assigning students to lavatories based on biological sex violated both Title IX and the Equal Protection Clause of the Fourteenth Amendment. The court denied the student's request for relief, but the Fourth Circuit Court of Appeals later held for the student. *Gloucester County School Board v. G.G.*, 822 F.3d 709 (4th Cir. 2017).

On appeal, the U.S. Supreme Court stayed an order that would have allowed the student to use male lavatories. It returned the case to a lower court for reconsideration in view of the Trump administration's decision to withdraw Obama-era guidance that deemed discrimination based on gender identity to be a violation of Title IX and its regulations. *Gloucester County School Board v. G.G.*, 137 S.Ct. 1239, 197 L.Ed.2d 460 (U.S. 2017).

The case returned to the district court, which noted that 34 C.F.R. Part 106.33 – a Title IX regulation – permits the use of separate toilets, locker rooms and showers on the basis of sex. The court reviewed employment cases arising under Title VII of the Civil Rights Act of 1964, focusing on *Price Waterhouse v. Hopkins*, 490 U.S. 228 (1989). In *Price Waterhouse*, the Supreme Court held Title VII bars discrimination based on "sex stereotyping." In this case, the court held the expansive view of the forms of sex discrimination from *Price Waterhouse* should also apply in this Title IX case. Applying the Title VII cases, the court held the student stated valid preliminary claims. Last, the court rejected the board's claim that the policy was necessary to protect privacy. **The student used the boys' lavatory without incident for seven weeks before parents complained about it.** The court denied the board's motion to dismiss the case. *Grimm v. Gloucester County School Board*, 302 F.Supp.3d 730 (E.D. Va. 2018).

◆ A male-born Ohio student began to identify as a female at age four, and her parents followed the advice of medical professionals to socially transition her in conformity with her gender identity. They began treating her as a girl and legally changed her name. An elementary principal enforced a district policy requiring students to use lavatories corresponding to their biological sex. A request to change school records to reflect the student's name change was denied. After the student was limited to use of a lavatory in the school office, the parents complained about harm to her mental health. They said her anxiety and depression led to hospitalization for suicidal ideation and depressed mood. A federal investigation concluded that the school district was in violation of Title IX of the Education Amendments of 1972. The U.S. government issued a letter of impending enforcement action, threatening to suspend, terminate or deny federal financial assistance to the district. As the student's fourth-grade school year approached, she attempted suicide.

The school district sued the U.S. government in a federal court to block its enforcement of Title IX. The court denied the request. It held the student was to be treated and referred to as a girl, and could use a girls' lavatory. In so ruling, the court held transgender status is protected by the Equal Protection Clause. The district appealed to the Sixth Circuit, which distinguished the case from *Gloucester County School Board v. G.G.*, this chapter. **The court held sex stereotyping based on a gender nonconformity is prohibited by federal law.** The court found the student is a vulnerable 11-year-old with special needs who will suffer irreparable harm if she is excluded from girls' restrooms. Since exclusion from girls' restrooms had caused "substantial and immediate adverse effects" on her daily life, the district's request to stay the lower court order pending review was denied. *Dodds v. U.S. Dep't of Educ.*, 845 F.3d 217 (6th Cir. 2016).

◆ In *L.W. v. Toms River Regional Schools Board of Educ.*, 189 N.J. 381, 915 A.2d 535 (N.J. 2007), **the Supreme Court of New Jersey recognized a cause of action against school districts for student-on-student harassment based on perceived sexual orientation**. Liability would be imposed for peer harassment only if a district failed to reasonably address harassment and the district knew or should have known about it.

◆ In *Romer v. Evans*, 517 U.S. 620 (1996), the U.S. Supreme Court held that sexual orientation discrimination violates the Establishment Clause. In *Oncale v. Sundowner Offshore Services, Inc.*, 523 U.S. 75 (1998), the Court held same-sex harassment may violate Title VII of the Civil Rights Act of 1964. In addition, many state human rights acts establish sexual orientation as a protected class of persons. But the U.S. Court of Appeals, Eighth Circuit, has held that bullying or harassment that is not based on a student's gender does not create liability under Title IX. Instead, it held that under Title IX, the "acts of discrimination" must be "on the basis of sex."

◆ In *Donovan v. Poway Unified School Dist.*, 167 Cal.App.4th 567, 84 Cal.Rptr.3d 285 (Cal. Ct. App. 2008), a California court observed that school administrators are better situated than courts to address peer sexual harassment. Administrators can take affirmative steps to combat racism, sexism and other forms of bias which courts cannot. And administrative actions are typically resolved more quickly than lawsuits.

◆ A Maine child who was born male was later diagnosed with gender dysphoria. An educational plan, modeled after a Section 504 plan, was devised to address the student's gender identity. The team agreed the student would be called "Susan." A counselor emphasized the need for Susan to use the girls' lavatory starting in grade five, and the team agreed. A male student followed Susan into the girls' lavatory to show he also had this right. After a controversy and media coverage, the school discontinued Susan's use of the girls' lavatory. For the rest of grade five, Susan used a unisex faculty lavatory. The family filed a complaint with the state human rights commission. The commission found there had been discrimination and joined the family in a suit against the school district. The case reached the Supreme Judicial Court of Maine. It noted the state Human Rights Act made it unlawful to discriminate against individuals, or to withhold or deny equal enjoyment of public accommodations based on sexual orientation.

While the state Sanitary Facilities Law required schools to offer clean toilets that were separated by sex, the court found the law did not offer any guidance about gender identity. By contrast, the Human Rights Act had the intent of ensuring access to opportunities and public accommodation. Schools had to maintain separate lavatories for each sex, but the court found the Sanitary Facilities Law did not dictate a discriminatory result. Each school was responsible for creating its policies concerning the use of public accommodations. School policies had to comply with the human rights act. **The court held treating the student differently from others based on transgender status was discrimination forbidden by the Human Rights Act.** *Doe v. Regional School Unit 26*, 86 A.3d 600 (Me. 2014).

C. Race and National Origin

Title VI of the Civil Rights Act of 1964 prohibits race discrimination in any program that receives federal funds. Many discrimination complaints allege violations of Title VI, the Equal Protection Clause, and analogous state law provisions. Courts require proof of intentional discrimination in Title VI cases. School officials may be held liable for violating Title VI if they are deliberately indifferent to clearly established student rights. Courts frequently analyze race-based peer harassment cases under the liability standard described in *Davis v. Monroe County Board of Educ.*, this chapter.

◆ A Texas student came to school with a homemade device in a pencil box with a circuit board, 9-volt battery, wires, transformer and button board that he described as an alarm clock. A teacher confiscated it and later in the day, police escorted the student to a room where he was questioned by several officers. After over an hour of questioning, the student was brought to a police station where he was handcuffed, fingerprinted, questioned and charged with bringing a "hoax bomb" to school in violation of state law.

Although the criminal charges were dropped, the school suspended him for three school days for violating the student code. The student's father later sued municipal and school officials and entities, asserting a variety of civil rights violations. During pretrial activity, a federal court held the student could not pursue civil rights violations claims against the district and city. He did not show any of the violations he asserted were the result of an official policy statement, ordinance, regulation or decision. Although the student claimed the school district violated his equal protection rights and Title VI of the Civil Rights Act of 1964, the court held he did not allege that the district's board had an unconstitutional policy of discriminatory discipline based on race or religion. In the court's opinion, **he did not support a claim that the board ratified anti-Muslim bias in the community in the form of its disciplinary policy. He did not state enough facts to support an inference of unequal disciplinary treatment based on race or religion.** As the court found nothing indicated intentional discrimination or different treatment of the student based on race or religion, all of the officials were entitled to qualified immunity. *Mohamed v. Irving Independent School Dist.*, 300 F.Supp.3d 857 (N.D. Tex. 2018).

◆ A Minnesota student with ADHD, a major depressive disorder and post-traumatic stress disorder had a Section 504 accommodation plan. Another student discovered racist graffiti written in whiteout in a school lavatory stall. Students publicized this through social media, "causing significant tension." School staff members reported being "fully occupied responding to distraught and concerned students." They described receiving "an avalanche of calls" about the graffiti, including at least 20 media inquiries. Due to the large number of black students enrolled at the school, an assistant principal felt student safety was implicated. After reviewing security camera footage, she identified the student as the probable graffiti writer. A search of the student's backpack yielded a whiteout pen and other items supporting this suspicion. After he was suspended based on the security footage and backpack items, the school continued investigating.

The school initiated expulsion proceedings but determined the student's behavior was not a manifestation of his disabilities. After an expulsion hearing, a hearing officer recommended expelling the student for 12 months. The school board upheld the recommendation, and the parents sued the school district in a federal court. According to the parents, the district improperly considered only whether the student's behavior was "caused by his disability, instead of whether it was related to or connected to his disability." But the court disagreed, noting that federal guidance and case law supported use of the "caused by" a disability standard. The court stated that **special education laws allow schools to discipline students with disabilities in the same way as non-disabled students, if the behavior at issue is not a manifestation of a disability**. Ruling that the school district properly found the student's misconduct was unrelated to his disability, the court held there was no need to fully reevaluate him. *Doe v. Osseo Area School Dist., ISD No. 279*, 296 F.Supp.3d 1090 (D. Minn. 2017).

◆ A Maryland student was bullied by classmates based on his disabilities. His parents said classmates also insulted him with homophobic slurs. The student said that classmates sexually harassed or physically threatened him. He used a racial epithet in response to three African-American students who had been calling him names. The student or his parents reported most of the harassment to the school. In most cases, the offending students were disciplined. Later, the school assigned a paraeducator to accompany the student to monitor his safety and serve as a witness. The student's mother and stepfather both worked for the school district. They began to publicly criticize and question the school's efforts to prevent harassment. After the parents attended a hearing to consider discipline of the student for using a racial epithet, the stepfather claimed the school took retaliatory actions against him. He was not hired to teach a summer P.E. class he had taught the prior three summers. Later, the parents sued the school board in a federal court, asserting bullying of the student and retaliatory action against the stepfather in response to his advocacy. But the court found "absolutely no evidence" that the board discriminated against the student.

After the court dismissed the case, the family appealed to the U.S. Court of Appeals, Fourth Circuit. It held there could be no school liability, as it was not proven that any bullying was based on a disability. In fact, the evidence strongly suggested the student was both a victim and perpetrator of race-based bullying. There was evidence that the school responded to every reported instance of bullying. **In ruling for the board, the court noted federal law does not require schools to eradicate each instance of harassment.** Instead, schools are held liable for known student-on-student harassment only when their response (or lack of a response) is clearly unreasonable. The Fourth Circuit found no merit to the stepfather's claim that he was not hired for summer work based on his advocacy. In fact, he was hired to teach P.E. the following summer. Finding no merit to the appeal, the court held for the board. *S.B. v. Board of Educ. of Harford County*, 819 F.3d 69 (4th Cir. 2016).

◆ An African-American student attended a private Illinois high school. He was diagnosed with attention deficit hyperactivity disorder (ADHD) and classified as a student with a disability. During his freshman year, the school provided accommodations based on his disability. According to the student, two teacher/coaches at the school began to harass and threaten him before his senior year, saying he would fail and have to repeat grade 12. He also claimed the teacher/coaches said he had no talent and was not a good football player. Near the end of his senior year, the student said he was involved in a disciplinary incident with other students. He said that each student was suspended for three days but that, unlike others, he had to finish the semester at home. The student claimed the school denied his request to review the suspension and excluded him from his graduation ceremony and prom. A federal court denied his request for an order allowing him to attend the graduation ceremony. Later, the school sought to dismiss the case.

The court found the student made only vague and conclusory allegations of discrimination. He did not state facts allowing a causal inference between the school's action and race or disability discrimination. His claim "that non-black students received substantially better treatment" was insufficient to proceed. The court found the student's disability discrimination claim provided very little detail that could support an inference of intentional discrimination. **There were no allegations that his accommodation plan was not followed or that the coaches retaliated against him for requesting accommodations.** In ruling for the school, the court found that numerous courts have held Section 504 does not create a private cause of action to enforce due process rights. *Thurmon v. Mount Carmel High School*, 191 F.Supp.3d 894 (N.D. Ill. 2016).

◆ Three African-American sisters reported repeated racial harassment by classmates at their Texas schools, including frequent use of the "N-word." One of the sisters found a noose near her car in a school parking lot with a note disparaging African-Americans. When she reported this to the school, police were called and an investigation was begun. All three sisters reported being targeted for racial slurs and epithets. They were sometimes drawn into fights with white students, which resulted in discipline for students of both races. One sister reported that the school athletic director admonished her for violating a school rule by wearing streaks of burgundy in her hair.

One of the sisters became involved in a bullying incident with white students. Based on these and other incidents, the family filed a grievance with the district's board of trustees. School employees were then required to attend trainings on discrimination, harassment and bullying, and students had to attend a special school assembly. Ultimately, two sisters withdrew from the school district. The family sued the district, softball coach and athletic director in a federal court for civil rights violations. The court held for the district and officials, and the family appealed to the Fifth Circuit. In the court's view, the repeated use of the N-word and the noose incident demonstrated severe, pervasive and objectively offensive peer harassment. Moreover, the harassment deprived the sisters of access to educational opportunities or benefits. But the court held the family did not show the school was deliberately indifferent to the harassment. **Some action was taken in response to almost all the reported incidents.** Training was provided, and the sisters were allowed safety accommodations. School officials cooperated with police and FBI investigations, and students who called the sisters names were suspended for misconduct. The court held the school district did not commit an equal protection violation. School officials did not violate the sisters' rights by enforcing district hair color and school team rules. As a result, the court held for the district and officials. *Fennell v. Marion Independent School Dist.*, 804 F.3d 398 (5th Cir. 2015).

◆ Washington parents withdrew their consent to their child's special education program shortly after moving into a new school district. During his first two months in the new district, the parents said his teacher and a co-principal blamed him for classroom incidents in which a classmate made cruel and racial remarks. The parents said the school blamed their child for other incidents and improperly decided not to question important student witnesses. When the child wrote two "disturbing essays" describing incidents in which the classmate was violently harmed, nobody told the parents. After the district investigated, information about one of the essays appeared in the report. As soon as the parents saw it, they asked for an immediate transfer of their son. They filed a complaint against the school district, and their case reached the state court of appeals. It held the district did not follow proper investigation procedures by neglecting to interview all the students in the work group. The essays were not shared with the parents, and the school did not take into account the discrepancy between his grades in social studies class and his other classes. The court found the school refused to consider any scenario in which the child was not to blame for conflicts with the classmate. The school district did not appropriately discipline the classmate, despite his history of serious behavior problems.

The court found the parents showed the harassment was severe, pervasive and objectively offensive and deprived their child of access to educational opportunities or benefits. He was repeatedly humiliated and reduced to tears in front of his peers. In ruling for the student, **the court held school districts have a duty to promptly investigate harassment and take prompt and effective steps calculated to end it**. Finding the district acted with deliberate indifference to the reports of harassment, the court held there was a violation of state law. *Mercer Island School Dist. v. Office of Superintendent of Public Instruction*, 186 Wash.App. 939, 347 P.3d 924 (Wash. Ct. App. 2015). Washington review denied 12/2/15.

◆ A high school in northern California had a history of gang and race-related violence. In 2009, the school recognized Cinco de Mayo in a "spirit of cultural appreciation." But the event prompted threats among students of different ethnic backgrounds. Some students hung a makeshift U.S. flag and chanted "USA." During the 2009 incident, a school assistant principal (AP) had to intervene when a student threatened others who had raised the U.S. flag. A student who had worn U.S. flag clothing to school on Cinco de Mayo in 2009 was among several students who again sought to display the flag on Cinco de Mayo 2010. In response to rumors of a confrontation between students of different ethnic backgrounds, the AP told the student he should turn the shirt inside out or risk his own safety. The student and another student who went home with an excused absence joined their parents in a federal court case against the school district, principal and AP.

The case reached the Ninth Circuit Court of Appeals, which found other recent federal appeals court cases have held that schools may prohibit speech that might reasonably lead school officials to forecast substantial disruption of (or material interference with) school activities. **Many federal cases have held school officials need not wait for actual disruption**

before acting. "In fact, they have a duty to prevent the occurrence of disturbances." The administrators in this case were faced with a threat of school disruption and impending violence, and the court found the AP was entitled to judgment on the speech rights claim. Since the lower court had correctly held for the AP, the court affirmed the judgment. *Dariano v. Morgan Hill Unified School Dist.*, 745 F.3d 354 (9th Cir. 2014).

◆ According to the parent of a six-year-old Virginia student, peers targeted him for threats and theft. She said he was mocked for not fighting back and repeatedly called "gay" "nigger," "bitch" and "motherfucker." She reported this to the vice principal, who spoke with one offending student. The mother said that a few weeks later, the same student again called her son names in front of other classmates. She said the school administration then failed to act. Within a week, the parent withdrew her son from the school. Only then did a school bullying specialist call her. She filed a federal lawsuit, but the court dismissed it. On appeal, the Fourth Circuit held a claim filed under Title IX required additional consideration. But the Title VI claim failed. In a 1992 case, the U.S. Supreme Court held no private action for damages is authorized by Title VI unless intentional discrimination is alleged. **The parent's failure to allege intentional conduct by the school was fatal to the Title VI claim.** She only sought to hold the school board liable for the response of administrators to peer harassment based on race. Although the parent claimed the school's response was dilatory and inadequate, the court found the school had only days to respond to her complaint just before a spring break. Since the Title VI claim failed, that part of the judgment was affirmed. *M.D. v. School Board of City of Richmond*, 560 Fed.Appx. 199 (4th Cir. 2014).

◆ A part-white, part-Latino student moved to an overwhelmingly white New York school district. Students began threatening him and repeatedly calling him "nigger." During the rest of the student's high school career, he continued to report incidents of racial harassment and taunting, some of which involved physical contact, death threats and a reference to lynching. The family attorney, and later the local human rights commission and the local NAACP affiliate, suggested a "shadow" to accompany the student while he was at school. These entities also sought to implement racial sensitivity programs in the district. Although these services were offered for free, the district declined them. A district compliance officer, who was supposed to investigate Title IX violations, did not respond to complaints. The student's mother made the choice to allow him to accept a special education diploma rather than to attend school further.

The student sued the school district in a federal court for race discrimination. A jury found the district violated Title VI and awarded the student $1.25 million. After the court reduced the damages to $1 million, appeal went to the U.S. Court of Appeals, Second Circuit. Applying *Davis v. Monroe County Board of Educ.*, this chapter, the court held **official**

action was "deliberately indifferent" under either Title IX or Title VI if it was "clearly unreasonable in light of the known circumstances." A reasonable juror could find the harassment met Title VI liability standards, as it was "severe, pervasive, and objectively offensive." Peers "taunted, harassed, menaced and physically assaulted" the student, called him "nigger" nearly every day, and threatened him with death. Staff members reported many incidents to the principal, and the mother contacted school administrators 30 to 50 times. Other reports were lodged by the human rights commission, the NAACP, and the police. While the school district was not required to eliminate all the harassment, it ignored many signals that more action was necessary. The decision for the student was affirmed. *Zeno v. Pine Plains Cent. School Dist.*, 702 F.3d 655 (2d Cir. 2012).

D. Disability

◆ The Supreme Court of Mississippi declined to review lower court judgments finding a school district not liable for the sexual assault of a 16-year-old student with Down syndrome by a 19-year-old male student with disabilities in a school lavatory. A trial court found the district did not breach a general ministerial duty to supervise students and had no specific duty to escort the student under her IEP. Later, the state court of appeals agreed with the trial court that the school took reasonable steps to minimize any foreseeable risks. **While the student's guardians claimed the school promised to escort the student, the court of appeals held they sought to add a term to the IEP that did not exist.** *J.E. Jackson Public School Dist.*, 265 So.3d 180 (Table) (Miss. petition for cert. denied 3/7/19).

◆ An Arkansas student with autism committed suicide at home on the same day a classmate told him he should go home and kill himself. Although his mother said he did not mention the incident and seemed fine when she left the house, the student took his life. The parents met with the principal to encourage him to investigate the death. But the mother said he "was not interested in the names of the students he was told might have information about events prior to [her son's] death, and he denied that bullying occurred in his school." Further, the parent claimed the principal told his staff not to talk about the death and prevented a student who had written a poem inspired by the student from performing the poem at a school talent show.

The parents sued the superintendent in a federal court for violations of Section 504 of the Rehabilitation Act. Finding insufficient evidence to support the claim, the court held for the superintendent. On appeal, the U.S. Court of Appeals, Eighth Circuit, explained that in the context of education, **a Section 504 claim requires parents to show school officials acted in bad faith or with gross misjudgment by departing substantially from accepted professional judgment, practice or standards**. The court found no evidence that school officials knew of specific bullying incidents before the student's death. It held the school's immediate response to the disciplinary incident in which he fought with a classmate did not indicate bad faith or gross misjudgment. While there was some delay in allowing the student to pass more easily between classes, there were no specific reports of bullying or who was doing it. There was no evidence that the student was the target of anything more than the kind of teasing and name-calling that the Supreme Court has held is not actionable. Last, the family cited no authority holding that a school district can discriminate against a student after his death by failing to investigate harassment that might have occurred before he died. *Estate of Barnwell v. Watson*, 880 F.3d 998 (8th Cir. 2018).

◆ The parents of a New York student with a learning disability complained to her school that bullying of the child occurred almost every day of a school year. When the committee on special education (CSE) met to discuss her placement for the next school year, the parents claimed the principal said a CSE meeting was an inappropriate place to discuss bullying. When the case reached a federal court, it held schools are required to investigate promptly and respond appropriately when they learn that disability harassment may have occurred. It also held free appropriate public education protections apply to bullying cases. The court applied the "deliberate indifference" approach from sexual harassment cases under Title IX of the 1972 Education Amendments and *Davis v. Monroe County Board of Educ.*, 526 U.S. 629 (1999). It held **"a school must take prompt and appropriate action" in response to bullying incidents, and take appropriate steps to prevent future incidents**. This duty existed regardless of whether the conduct was covered in an anti-bullying policy and regardless of whether a student had complained. *T.K. and S.K. v. New York City Dep't of Educ.*, 779 F.Supp.2d 289 (E.D.N.Y. 2011).

When the case returned to administrative levels, a hearing officer found bullying had occurred but the child was not significantly restricted in her educational opportunities. The case returned to the federal court, which held that when a school responds to bullying, its actions must be prompt and appropriate. **Evidence of past bullying and prior implementation of IEPs was important in determining if the student was provided a free appropriate public education (FAPE).** In this case, the court found the bullying of the child created a substantial probability that it would severely restrict her educational opportunities if left unaddressed. **The court found a school should convene an IEP team as part of its response to peer bullying.** Since the child was not offered a FAPE, the parents were entitled to be reimbursed for their private placement costs. *T.K. v. New York City Dep't of Educ.,* 32 F.Supp.3d 405 (E.D.N.Y. 2014).

On appeal, the U.S. Court of Appeals, Second Circuit Court, held bullying may substantially interfere with a child's learning opportunities. The court held **the school department denied the student a FAPE by refusing to discuss bullying at IEP meetings, despite reasonable concerns by the parents**. Since the persistent refusal to discuss bullying in the IEP process significantly impeded the parents' participation rights, the court upheld a decision to award them their private school tuition costs. *T.K. and S.K. v. New York City Dep't of Educ.*, 810 F.3d 869 (2d Cir. 2016).

◆ Washington's Supreme Court upheld a decision ordering a new trial in a case filed by a student who sought to hold his school district liable for being punched by a disabled student. The injured student claimed he suffered a broken jaw when he fell to the floor after the disabled student hit him. **After a jury found the school district was not negligent, the state appeals court sent the case back for a new trial.** When the case returns to the trial court, it will have to decide whether to instruct jurors that state and federal laws require schools to educate disabled students in general education settings, to the maximum extent appropriate. *Hopkins v. Seattle Public School Dist. No. 1*, 186 Wash.2d 1029, 385 P.3d 123 (Table) (Wash. Review Denied, 12/7/16).

◆ The parents of a North Carolina student with disabilities filed an action for negligent supervision against her board of education arising from repeated bullying and harassment on the basis of her gender and disability. According to the family, the school failed to take corrective action or discipline peers who harassed the student, and there was no investigation by the school. The court held there is a high standard of proof in negligent supervision cases. North Carolina recognizes employer liability only in "those cases involving notoriously unsuitable employees or allegations of misconduct repeatedly ignored by an employer." **To prevail, the student had to show the board either knew of (or had reason to know) school administrators were incompetent.** But the court found the family did not make this showing. The family did not claim any complaints were made to the board or that it had even heard of the harassment. The court rejected a claim that the duration, severity and volume of the complaints put the board on notice of a need to train and further supervise employees about responding to harassment and bullying. Since no facts suggested the board should have known administrators were ill-prepared to handle harassment and bullying, the claim failed. In addition to dismissing the negligent supervision claim, the court dismissed a state constitutional claim. *M.H. v. Onslow County Board of Educ.*, No. 7:16-CV-00069-FL, 2016 WL 5678402 (E.D.N.C. 9/30/16).

◆ A 12-year-old student with severe Attention Deficit Hyperactivity Disorder (ADHD) took a picture of another student sitting on a toilet at school. During the school year, he had many other behavior incidents including disobedience, running into a teacher, roughhousing in classes, belching in a student's face, insulting classmates with vulgar language and asking a girl "if she was making porn." The student's parents claimed the vice principal encouraged the parent of the student who had been photographed to file a criminal charge. The school held a manifestation determination review (MDR) to determine whether the student's conduct was a manifestation of his ADHD. An MDR committee found the incident did not result from the student's ADHD, and he was placed in a disciplinary alternative educational placement (DAEP) for 60 days. After the criminal charges were dismissed, the MDR did not revoke the DAEP placement. A hearing officer held for the district, finding a legitimate reason for the discipline. Next, the family filed a due process hearing request.

A hearing officer dismissed the case, upholding the disciplinary decision. When appealing the due process decision to a federal court, the parents added claims under Section 504 of the Rehabilitation Act and asserted constitutional violations. The court held for the school district, and the parents appealed. The U.S. Court of Appeals, Fifth Circuit, found they asserted the district created a hostile educational environment. According to the parents, school officials improperly encouraged parents and a teacher to file criminal complaints against their child. The court held their statements were conclusory and did not plead a case for discrimination. The parents charged school officials with a conspiracy based on their child's disability. But they did not attribute any misconduct to the school district that was based on his disability. In fact, the student was not placed in a DAEP setting until after the MDR determination found his behavior was not the result of a disability. **Since the parents did not sufficiently plead that any actions were taken on the basis of a disability, their Section 504 claim was properly dismissed.** *C.C. v. Hurst-Euless-Bedford Independent School Dist.*, 641 Fed.Appx. 423 (5th Cir. 2016).

◆ A California student with disabilities said his teachers did not stop bullying by a classmate that escalated over a five-month period leading to his withdrawal from school. His parents asserted that peer harassment took place on a daily basis and in plain sight of teachers and an aide assigned to the student. They claimed bullying continued after he complained to teachers and mentioned it in his writing projects. When the parents reported the bullying, they said teachers and administrators admitted the misconduct but downplayed its seriousness. The school said the student was being properly supervised and said the classmate was assigned to detention for bullying. But the classmate later cornered the student in a lavatory, sat on him and tried to force him to eat soap. The student said he suffered a concussion and later had post-traumatic stress and seizures as a result.

After removing their child from school, the parents sued the school district in a federal court. Applying the standard from *Davis v. Monroe County Board of Educ.*, 526 U.S. 629 (1999), the court found the student could proceed with a state law disability discrimination claim based on peer harassment. **State law did not provide blanket immunity for the claims brought against school officials based on peer bullying.** While punitive damages were unavailable against the district, the court held the student could pursue punitive damages claims against the employees. *J.E.L. v. San Francisco Unified School Dist.*, 185 F.Supp.3d 1196 (N.D. Cal. 2016).

◆ A Texas parent became concerned that a student with a disability who had sexually assaulted a girl and spent time in an alternative education program would be returned to his child's middle school. He insisted the returning student be moved to another school, but officials reassured him that others would be protected. In December of the school year, the disabled student and another male were accused of "T-bagging everybody." The child of the complaining parent said the boys "hung their crotches in students' faces and humped them." He also reported that the disabled student teased and taunted his child many other times. A school assistant principal and the principal investigated the charges and put the disabled student and his friend on in-school suspension. After interviewing over 50 students, administrators recommended sending the disabled student and his friend to a disciplinary alternative educational placement. The complaining child's parent withdrew his son from the school and sued the school district for harassment in violation of Title IX of the 1972 Education Amendments.

After a federal district court dismissed the case, the parent appealed to the Fifth Circuit Court of Appeals. The court held that school liability for peer sexual harassment under Title IX requires proof that the school district had actual knowledge of the harassment. It must be shown that the harassment was "so severe, pervasive, and objectively offensive" that it barred a victim's access to an educational opportunity, and that the school district remained deliberately indifferent to the harassment. In this case, the lower court had found the school district had no knowledge of the harassment until the "T-bagging" was reported. Student witnesses said the conduct took place when teachers were not looking. **When administrators learned of the problem, they took prompt investigative and remedial action.** After confirming the misconduct, the offending students were disciplined and eventually transferred. **Since the court found the district had no actual knowledge of harassment, it found no Title IX violation.** *Kelly v. Allen Independent School Dist.*, 602 Fed.Appx. 949 (5th Cir. 2015).

◆ Alabama parents of a student with disabilities who committed suicide sought to impose liability for her death on school officials. They claimed officials knew about peer harassment and bullying but failed to address it. A federal court rejected the parents' theory that any school employee named in the lawsuit had authority to take corrective action to end peer harassment. While the bullying alleged in this case was severe, the court rejected the family's claim that the bullying was so open and obvious that anyone at the school would know about it. Only actual knowledge of peer harassment could trigger school liability under Title IX of the 1972 Education Amendments. Of the three identified school employees who might have some knowledge of misconduct, only the assistant principal had the ability to take corrective measures in response to bullying complaints. But the parents did not prove he knew of the bullying or had even heard about it. **Since the parents could not show an "appropriate person" with the authority to act to end the bullying had actual knowledge of any**

misconduct, the court held for the board of education. *Moore v. Chilton County Board of Educ.*, 1 F.Supp.3d 1281 (M.D. Ala. 2014).

◆ A California parent claimed his son was repeatedly abused, beaten and kicked by peers because of his disabilities and his non-native English speaker status. The parents made two written incident reports detailing attacks on their son and identifying the assailants. But they claimed school officials did not act and suggested only that he change classrooms to avoid the perpetrators. In a California superior court, the father sought a special order against the school district. The court dismissed the case, holding the parent did not have standing to pursue it. On appeal, the state court of appeal held **the case involved a well-identified public interest in maintaining a school system that was free of the destructive influence of discrimination, harassment and bullying**. State legislators enacted interrelated statutes to protect students from discrimination and harassment based on race, gender, sexual orientation or disability. California public schools had an affirmative duty to combat racism, sexism and other forms of bias. A code provision required school districts to have comprehensive safety plans. The court held the father had standing to pursue the case both as a parent and a taxpayer. *Hector F. v. El Centro Elementary School Dist.*, 227 Cal.App.4th 331,173 Cal.Rptr.3d 413 (Cal. Ct. App. 2014).

IV. USE OF TECHNOLOGY

A. Internet and Cyberbullying

In *Dunkley v. Board of Educ. of Greater Egg Harbor Regional High School Dist.*, 216 F.Supp.3d 485 (D.N.J. 2016), this chapter, a federal court found Third Circuit cases supporting the ability of schools to punish off-campus expression based on a well-founded expectation of disruption. It also held off-campus speech may be subject to New Jersey's Anti-Bullying Bill of Rights Act, if a reasonable person should know it will substantially disrupt or interfere with school operations or the rights of other students.

◆ Ten days after a gunman killed 17 students at Marjory Stoneman Douglas High School in Parkland Florida with an AR-15 assault rifle, an Arkansas student posted a picture of himself on Instagram wearing a trench coat and holding an AR-15 assault rifle. Other students commented on his post, with remarks including "school shooter meme," and "when I drop my pencil, start shooting." Parents communicated with the high school principal and other officials about the Instagram activity. Police officers searched the home of the student's father. After a discussion with the police, the student offered to turn over three guns he had in his possession. No criminal charges were brought against him. When school resumed on the Monday after the posting, the police and the FBI asked school officials to pull students out of classes to attend assemblies where officers discussed appropriate media postings. The school later expelled the student for one year for violating two school district policies. He took an alternative online program that allowed him to remain on track to graduate with his class.

In a federal court, the student sought to block his expulsion and remove any reference to the discipline from his transcript. In denying his request, the court held **the "substantial disruption" test from *Tinker v. Des Moines Independent Community School Dist.*, 393 U.S. 503 (1969), applies to off-campus student speech**. Eighth Circuit authority made clear that school districts may punish speech which either caused a substantial disruption or where it was reasonably foreseeable that such speech would reach the school community and cause a substantial disruption. In the court's view, it was reasonably foreseeable that the posts would reach the school community and they caused substantial disruption there. The student was not denied a public education, as he had access to an alternative education program. The court denied his request for injunctive relief. *McKinney v. Huntsville School Dist.*, 350 F.Supp.3d 757 (W.D. Ark. 2018).

◆ A Wisconsin high school freshman began wearing T-shirts to school depicting weapons. One depicted a variety of firearms and bore the slogan "Celebrate Diversity." Another depicted the word "LOVE" written in letters made up of images of various weapons. Although the school principal told the student he could not wear clothing to school that depicted weapons, he continued wearing them. At the time, the school district had no policy prohibiting clothing with gun depictions. But the board amended its dress code to prohibit wearing gun attire at school. In a federal court, the student sought an order to prevent the principal from disciplining him for wearing the gun T-shirts. According to the court, the T-shirts stated an opinion about gun ownership. As the student expressed his belief on a matter of public concern, the court found his speech was protected by the First Amendment.

In analyzing the case, the court considered the "substantial disruption" standard from *Tinker* in a "somewhat softened form" suggested by the Seventh Circuit in *Nuxoll v. Indian Prairie School Dist. # 204*, 523 F.3d 668 (7th Cir. 2008), and *Zamecnik v. Indian Prairie School Dist. # 204*, 636 F.3d 874 (7th Cir. 2011). Under the "somewhat softened" *Tinker* standard, **the court found the principal did not have to prove that the speech at issue would actually cause "forbidden serious consequences**." It was "enough for the school to present facts which might reasonably lead school officials to forecast substantial disruption." In this case, the school presented evidence that staff members felt uncomfortable about the shirts, especially in view of the Parkland, Florida, shootings and then-recent school walkouts to protest school violence. Other evidence of disruption included declarations that class instruction was disrupted on multiple occasions due to student discussions and arguments about the T-shirts. Students also became distracted by news crews who came to the school to interview the student. But the court found no students felt threatened by the shirts. It also held the school did not show teachers were prevented from doing their jobs. Finding the school could not satisfy the "somewhat softened" *Tinker* standard, the court held for the student. *Schoenecker v. Koopman*, 349 F.Supp.3d 745 (E.D. Wis. 2018, 7th Cir. appeal filed 11/20/18).

◆ A California student was expelled for making racist social media postings about students at his school. Among his posts were images of a "Ku klux starter pack, featuring a noose, a burning torch, a black doll, and a white hood." The student posted a screenshot of an African-American student with the caption "i wanna go back to the old way," and an image of a white man beating a black slave hung by his hands. One post showed a student and her basketball coach, both African-Americans, with nooses around their necks. The postings compared African-Americans to gorillas. When the student's Instagram account became known on the school campus, he was permanently expelled and some of his followers were disciplined. At least six lawsuits were filed by the student and his followers.

A federal court found 10 school students were depicted on the account. Several photos were taken on school property. When the Instagram account became known at the school, a number of the targeted students reported becoming distraught and agitated. With the exception of one student, the others who were subject to discipline liked or commented on the Instagram posts. Five students who expressed approval or liked postings that targeted the students were properly disciplined. In finding they were properly disciplined, **the court found school officials do not have to wait for disruption to take place**. It held the school's authority to discipline the student who made the postings "is not open to serious question." The police had been called since some posts could be construed as threats. But four students who did not approve any content on the Instagram account targeting individuals at the school created no substantial risk of disruption and were entitled to pretrial judgment. The court held for the district regarding the student and followers who approved or liked his postings. *Shen v. Albany Unified School Dist.*, Nos. 3:117-cv-02478-JD, 3:17-cd-02767-JD; 3:17-cv-03418-JD; 3:17-cv-03657 JD; 3:17-cv-02478-JD, 2017 WL 5890089 (N.D. Cal. 11/29/17).

◆ A Nebraska student made an off-campus social media comment that was interpreted as a threat and caused disruption at school. Her anonymous post stated "Tomorrow gonna be hella fire, be there." She included a fire emoji in the posting. An anonymous response said "Don't show up to school tomorrow" and included a gun emoji. The school posted extra security and searched the school for safety threats. After an investigation, the student admitted making the post. She was suspended for 15 days. At her hearing, the board rejected the student's claim that "hella fire" was a harmless and sarcastic comment. **A state trial court upheld the suspension, finding the post could be considered a threat.** The state supreme court later rejected the student's appeal on procedural grounds because she did not serve the board with a petition as required by the Nebraska Student Discipline Act. *J.S. v. Grand Island Public Schools*, 297 Neb. 347 (Neb. 2017).

◆ A Michigan student tweeted threats to stab a classmate. The classmate reported this to a school counselor and assistant vice principal (AVP). The AVP then questioned the classmate and learned that the student had been bullying her. The AVP called the student's mother and asked to meet with her. Later, the mother claimed the AVP issued a suspension by phone. The next day, the AVP met with the student, her mother and brother. She told them some students had told her the student brought a knife to school, and she suspended the student. Family members met with the superintendent. He advised them of the evidence, then stated he would recommend expulsion. The board refused to allow the student's brother to attend the hearing, as she had asked for a closed meeting. After a hearing, the board voted to expel the student. She sued the school district, board members and administrators in a federal court. The court held for the district and officials. On appeal, the U.S. Court of Appeals, Sixth Circuit, held there was no due process violation. **Students who are a continuing danger may be immediately removed from school.** The student received enough explanation of the charges to prepare her defense. As for the expulsion hearing, the court found she had three opportunities to tell her story. At the hearing, the student's father read the prepared statement which the brother intended to read. There was no evidence that the brother had anything more to add. Rejecting the student's arguments, the court held for the district. *C.Y. v. Lakeview Public Schools*, 557 Fed.Appx. 426 (6th Cir. 2014).

◆ A Texas student claimed classmates were bullying her and school officials did nothing when she reported it. An assistant principal (AP) called her into his office to discuss the circulation of lewd pictures of the student and a friend off campus. After the meeting with the AP, the student was transferred to a district alternative learning academy for 30 days. A provision in the district student code of conduct prohibited "sexting" and cyberbullying by students either on or off school property. In a federal court, the student sought to stop the transfer. She added claims related to the bullying. First, the court rejected her claim that relevant terms in the student code of conduct were too vague to satisfy constitutional requirements. It held terms such as "abusive," "obscene," "sexually oriented," "sexting" and "substantial disruption" were sufficiently clear that a student of ordinary intelligence would know what conduct was prohibited. Schools do not have to spell out in detail what is meant by "obscene" or "sexually oriented."

There was no merit to the due process claims. Fifth Circuit authority held students had no constitutionally protected interest in halting a disciplinary transfer to an alternative school. Next, the court found the student's negligence claims against the district, AP and the school principal were barred by state law immunity. **Nor could liability be imposed on school officials for failing to report bullying to child protection authorities or not developing a policy governing reports of child abuse or neglect.** A speech rights violation claim against the AP and principal failed, and the court held for the school district on all of the student's other claims. *S.N.B. v. Pearland Independent School Dist.*, 120 F.Supp.3d 620 (S.D. Tex. 2014).

◆ Three Colorado students who were subjected to inappropriate conduct by a former teacher at their high school were denied an appeal to review their claims against their school district and administration. According to their complaint, the teacher sent the students explicit texts, sought nude pictures and tried to solicit sexual relations with them. **While the court allowed claims against the teacher to proceed, it held the case could not proceed against the district or administrators**, who did not know about his conduct. A claim for failure to report child abuse would proceed against a school security guard and coach who knew about an incident of sexual conduct between the teacher and a student. In a brief order, the U.S. Court of Appeals, Tenth Circuit, affirmed the judgment. *Doe v. Boulder Valley School Dist. No. RE-2*, 523 Fed.Appx. 514 (10th Cir. 2013).

B. Cell Phones and Other Electronic Communication

◆ An Illinois student said his principal searched his phone applications and files and located an Instagram account with "negative memes of a student reported to have been bullied." The student was issued an in-school suspension of two days. In a federal court, he alleged the principal had a custom of searching and seizing phones without reasonable suspicion of a crime or school rules violation. In pretrial activity, the court refused to dismiss the claims against the principal, finding the evidence about what he knew prior to searching the phone was unclear. It found no support for the search based on a letter sent (after the fact) by the superintendent to the student's father indicating that other students had implicated the student in cyberbullying. **In the court's opinion, the complaint supported a claim for an unlawful search.** As the complaint indicated the superintendent knew of the principal's custom of unlawful phone searches, he faced potential liability for approving of, condoning or ignoring the custom. But as he was not personally involved in the search, he could not be held individually liable for it. Last, the court held the school district had no liability, as the principal and superintendent lacked district policymaking authority. *Simpson v. Tri Valley Community Unit School Dist. No. 3*, No. 1:17-cv-01340-JES-JEH, 2018 WL 3354878 (C.D. Ill. 6/1/18).

◆ While teaching at a middle school, a Texas teacher developed a close relationship with an eighth-grader. Despite a school policy against texting between teachers and students, the two began texting about sexual topics. When the student's mother learned of this, she called the police and the school principal. After being arrested and charged with online solicitation of a minor and engaging in an improper relationship with a student, the teacher made a plea agreement with prosecutors. In return for dismissal of the online solicitation charge, he pleaded guilty to the improper relationship charge. The teacher also agreed to forfeit his teaching license and to refrain from applying for teaching licenses anywhere in the U.S. Later, the teacher applied for an order – called a writ of habeas corpus – claiming that the improper relationship statute was unconstitutional. At the time of his offense, the statute prohibited a school employee from engaging in online solicitation of a minor student enrolled in the school at which the employee works. According to the teacher, the improper relationship statute referenced a provision of the online solicitation of minors statute which had been declared unconstitutional in 2013. He argued this ruling invalidated the improper relationship statute. The court disagreed, finding the improper relationship statute had elements that were not found in the other statute.

After the Court of Appeals of Texas affirmed the judgment, the teacher appealed to the Court of Criminal Appeals of Texas. It rejected his claim that he was "seeking relief for a conviction of a non-crime under a statute that has already been held to be invalid." While the improper relationship statute referred to some of the same conduct described by the online solicitation provision, it required that a perpetrator be a school employee and the victim be a student. **Since the two laws were found materially different, the teacher's arguments failed and the court denied his request for relief from the improper relationship charge.** *Ex Parte Beck*, 541 S.W.3d 846 (Tex. Ct. Crim. App. 2017).

◆ A Louisiana student said school officials interrogated him and forced him to unlock his parent's cell phone without notice to the parent. His parent filed a federal court complaint against the school board. In pretrial activity, the court held punitive damages were unavailable in a case arising under 42 U.S.C. § 1983. A government entity such as a school board is not subject to Section 1983 liability unless there is a violation of a federally protected right that can be attributable to the enforcement of a municipal policy, practice or decision of a final municipal policymaker. In this case, the court found the student did not identify a specific board policy. Although he attempted to bring a state-law claim against the board for violation of the state's pupil discipline law, the court found he did not identify which provision of law the board was charged with violating. **Based on the student's failure to make specific charges against the school officials, the court dismissed all the claims.** *Decossas v. St. Tammany Parish School Board*, No. 16-3786, 2017 WL 1133114 (E.D. La. 3/27/17).

◆ A Texas high school counselor learned of explicit texts between her daughter – a freshman at the school – and a paraprofessional who worked in the daughter's after-school music program. The counselor and her husband met with the paraprofessional and his wife. But the counselor and a colleague did not report the texts to law enforcement officers, child protective services or school administrators. Another staff member reported the texts. The counselor and her colleague were placed on leave for failing to report the texts. The colleague was reprimanded, but the district proposed terminating the counselor. A hearing examiner found the counselor violated a school policy requiring her to report child abuse in accordance with state law. But the hearing examiner found she did not feel abuse occurred, and he held the board lacked good cause to dismiss her. The board decided to terminate the counselor's contract. After the state commissioner of education affirmed the decision, appeal reached the Court of Appeals of Texas. It found failure to make a required report subjected an employee to discipline, including employment termination. The court disagreed with the hearing officer's finding that the counselor did not have to report the texts.

Neither the district policy nor state law limited the reporting requirement to situations when a teacher actually believed abuse or neglect had occurred. As the board found, a report must be made if there is sufficient reason to believe future abuse may occur. The counselor's actions indicated she feared future abuse. The paraprofessional continued working at the school, and the delay in reporting his conduct endangered other students. **A school board had the power to decide whether a violation was good cause for employment termination.** The court rejected the counselor's claim that her discipline was arbitrary and capricious, despite the slight discipline issued to her colleague. When child safety was at risk, a court would not overturn discipline due to such a disparity. *Judson Independent School Dist. v. Ruiz*, No. 04-13-00706-CV, 2015 WL 1501758 (Tex. Ct. App. 3/31/15; Tex. review denied, 3/27/16).

◆ An investigation of sexting by students was begun in Tunkhannock, Pennsylvania schools after officials found photos of nude and semi-nude female students on cell phones. Officials learned that male students had been trading the images over their cell phones. The district attorney investigated and made a public statement to the media that possession of inappropriate images of minors could justify criminal prosecution for possession or distribution of child pornography. Teens suspected of "sexting" were then presented with a choice of either attending an education program or facing child pornography charges. As part of the education program, female students were asked to write a report explaining "why you are here," "what you did," "why it was wrong," and related issues.

Several parents brought a federal court action to halt the proceeding. They said the threat of prosecution came in retaliation for their refusal to attend the education program. The court granted them preliminary relief, and appeal went before the U.S. Court of Appeals, Third Circuit. The court explained that parents have well-recognized due process rights to raise their children without undue state interference. **The government cannot coerce parents to accept official ideas of morality and gender roles.** While the district attorney could offer the education program voluntarily, he could not coerce attendance by threatening prosecution. It appeared to the court that the school district attorney's motive in bringing the prosecution was retaliatory and was not a good-faith effort to enforce the law. *Miller v. Mitchell*, 598 F.3d 139 (3d Cir. 2010).

C. Surveillance

☑ CHECKLIST – *Practice Tips For School Video Surveillance*

Sara C. Clark, Deputy Director of Legal Services for the Ohio School Boards Association, has the following suggestions for school surveillance:

- ☐ Install surveillance cameras only in locations where people would not have a reasonable expectation of privacy, such as hallways, lunch rooms and parking lots.
- ☐ Notify staff, parents, students and others in the community that surveillance cameras are present and in use.
- ☐ Post signs in the areas where cameras are in use. Include a notice in staff and student handbooks.
- ☐ Narrowly limit the time and scope of taping.
- ☐ Establish procedures for maintaining and viewing records.

◆ Pennsylvania's Supreme Court agreed to review a lower court decision finding surveillance video depicting students was not exempt from disclosure under the Family Educational Rights and Privacy Act (FERPA). The video depicted an incident on a school bus in which a teacher was accused of disciplining an elementary student. **A lower court ordered school officials to disclose the video to a media entity, finding video images of students on the bus were "not directly relevant to those students."** It held the images were directly relevant to the teacher's performance and thus not "education records" under FERPA. The supreme court announced that it would consider whether the footage may be disclosed under FERPA. *Easton Area School Dist. v. Miller*, No. 530 MAL 2018, 2019 WL 42256, 201 A.3d 721 (Table) (Pa. petition allowed 2/4/19).

◆ An Arkansas school district investigated reports of fights between a student with disabilities and his teachers. His parent sought disclosure of related records under the Arkansas Freedom of Information Act (FOIA). The superintendent denied the request, saying the records related to job performance. In a state court, the parent claimed a right to view the records. As the district did not discipline the first teacher and the second resigned, she argued the records were not the result of an investigative report that was exempt from disclosure. But the court held they were exempt. On appeal, the Court of Appeals of Arkansas explained that a state FOIA exception cited by the parent opened employee evaluation or job-performance records for public inspection in specific cases where there was a final administrative resolution. "Final administrative resolution" included an employee suspension or termination proceeding at which the records formed a basis for the disciplinary decision. Further, the exception required that there be a "compelling interest" in disclosure.

In this case, the court found insufficient evidence to show the records had to be disclosed under the relevant FOIA exemption. Prior decisions and opinions of the state attorney general stated that employee recommendation or termination letters, reprimands and other disciplinary records are classified as "job-performance records." Neither employee had been disciplined with the use of the records at issue. The court found there was no merit to the parent's argument that the second teacher's resignation "amounted to a constructive termination." His resignation did not result from any negotiations with the school district and took place before any hearing. **As the records requested by the parent were not used as a basis for employee discipline and there was no compelling reason for disclosure, the court held for the school district.** *Davis v. Van Buren School Dist.*, 572 S.W.3d 466, 2019 Ark. App. 157 (Ark. Ct. App. 2019).

◆ A Utah student became involved in a fight with other students outside a classroom at their middle school. His parent asked the school for all digital video of the area during the relevant time. His request was made under the state Government Records Access and Management Act (GRAMA). The district responded that disclosure of the video was governed by the Family Educational Rights and Privacy Act (FERPA). The school district explained that since FERPA governed the video, the parent would have to obtain the written consent of the parents of all students depicted in order to see it. The parent filed a state court action against the district. After reviewing the video records, the court found other students were clearly identifiable. It found FERPA governed the request and held the district had properly denied the parent's request for unrestricted access to the records.

After learning the images of the other students could be blocked out for about $120, the court held the parent could have a copy of the video records with the images of other students blocked out at his expense. He instead appealed to the Court of Appeals of Utah, which held **a surveillance recording is an "education record" under FERPA. Unless there is written consent by parents, FERPA prohibits the release of education records that are maintained by an educational agency.** The court held the FERPA term "education record" applied to all records, files, documents and other materials containing information directly related to a student that were maintained by an educational agency. As FERPA applied, the court held the school district had correctly insisted that the parent obtain consent from all other parents before disclosing anything. Next, the court found the GRAMA was applicable to the extent consistent with FERPA. The state law allowed the district to provide the parent with a copy of the video record, with the images of students other than his own son blocked. State law provided that a government entity could charge a fee for providing a record in a requested form. As a result, it was appropriate to require the parent to pay the district for the cost of blocking out student identities. *Bryner v. Canyons School Dist.*, 351 P.3d 852 (Utah Ct. App. 2015).

◆ A West Virginia student said he was hurt by another student in what he called a "choking game" intended to restrict blood flow and experience a high. Administrators investigated and deemed the incident "horseplay." The student sued the school district in the state court system for negligent supervision. After a state circuit court held for the school board, the student appealed to the Supreme Court of Appeals of West Virginia. Among his claims was that the board failed to provide enough supervision in the cafeteria. The court found evidence that two or three teachers were in the cafeteria at the time of the incident. While the student claimed a "choking game" had been going on in the school for decades and was well known, the court instead looked to the student accused of doing the choking. It found he had no history of violence and had no known issues with the student. No evidence indicated school employees had actual knowledge of a "choking game." **The court rejected a claim that an employee should have been constantly monitoring the 16 cameras positioned in the high school throughout the school day.** It was not feasible for school employees to see what every student was doing in the cafeteria or hallways at every moment of the school day. In the court's view, the student did not show the hallways were inadequately supervised. *Glaspell v. Taylor County Board of Educ.*, No. 14-0175, 2014 WL 5546480 (W.Va. 11/3/14).

V. TRANSPORTATION

For checklists regarding school buses, parking and other transportation risks, log on to our website at *www.SchoolSafetyAndSecurityAlert.com* and search "School Bus Vulnerability/Hazard Assessment."

◆ After the regular Minnesota cross-country season ended, a high school head coach urged all team members to participate in the Nike Cross Nationals Heartland Regional cross-country meet in South Dakota. Some team members agreed to ride to the meet with the team's assistant coach. Others went with a student whose parents had emailed the team's head coach that they were comfortable with their son's driving skills and would let him use their car. After the students gathered at their assistant coach's house, they began driving to the meet. But once on the road, the student lost control of his vehicle, which collided with another vehicle. There was evidence that he was distracted by cell devices used by his teammates. One of the occupants of the other vehicle was killed. The occupant's spouse was injured, but she survived. In a state court, she sued the school, head coach, assistant coach and student for negligence. After the spouse settled with the student, the court dismissed her claims against the school and coaches. She appealed to the state court of appeals, which held the school had no duty to the general public to prevent harm caused by the student.

On appeal, the state supreme court stated that generally, a person has no duty of care to another person if the harm is caused by a third party's conduct. **But schools may be held liable as third parties when the school has a "special relationship" with the injured person and harm to the person is held foreseeable.** In this case, the court held an exception to the general rule would exist if the school's conduct created a reasonable risk of injury to a foreseeable plaintiff. The school's conduct went beyond passive inaction because the coach assumed supervision and control of the team trip. As there was evidence that the school was negligent and that the assistant coach acted on the team's behalf, the court found pretrial judgment had been inappropriate. Further, the court of appeals should not have found the risk was unforeseeable. In close cases such as this one, the issue of foreseeability should be submitted to a jury and not resolved by a court. The case would return to the trial court for resolution of issues such as foreseeability and whether the spouse had proved each element of a negligence claim. *Fenrich v. The Blake School*, 920 N.W.2d 195 (Minn. 2018).

◆ A New Jersey student was placed in an out-of-district program operated by a county special services board. According to her parents, she felt stigmatized by having to ride a "small and distinctive minibus." After becoming agitated, the student exited through the emergency door of the moving bus and was fatally injured. In a federal action against the school district, bus company, county board and various individuals, the parents claimed a teacher and others acted in reckless disregard for their child's health, safety and welfare by transporting her on the minibus. The court noted the complaint asserted that the county board had recommended separate transportation, and that the student had previously engaged in dangerous behavior such as leaving the school and walking in traffic.

Evidence was also presented that the student had expressed her dislike for riding the minibus and had refused to board it. While any duty of care most directly belonged to the bus staff, the court found the exercise of that duty "required input from the educational professionals most familiar with [the student's] disability and the precautions that it would require." Since the claims and facts were closely intertwined into "a single case or controversy," the court held the county board should remain a part of the case. In the court's view, **the complaint stated the existence of a duty of care, breach of that duty, actual and legal causation, and damages**. Rejecting a claim to immunity under the state Tort Claims Act, the court refused to dismiss the case. *Williams v. Board of Educ. of Paterson*, No. 15-0765 (KM), 2017 WL 3131974 (D.N.J. 7/21/17).

◆ A Connecticut student said up to 15 students assaulted her shortly after she and her attackers got off the bus in front of her home. She claimed that before the incident, the assaulting students momentarily exited the bus at a previous stop. But the driver allowed them to re-enter, despite knowing about physical and verbal threats during the bus ride. During pretrial activity, the driver and her employer argued they did not owe any duty of care to the student. The driver stated "there was no fight" and that "there was nothing accumulating to this for me to even know there was going to be a fight" on the day of the incident. The court found evidence that a recording made during the bus ride indicated a fight was taking place.

The driver was recorded saying "Hey you guys. Can't you guys wait till you go outside?" Some 15-20 seconds later, the driver was recorded yelling "Do it outside!" The court found this evidence sufficient to create a jury question regarding whether the driver knew or should have known about the potential danger to the student following her exit from the school bus. In addition, the court found school bus companies are held to a high standard of care. **A state law required "taking reasonable precautions to protect the children from dangerous conditions immediately outside the bus.** The court held a fact question existed on the student's claim for breach of a duty of ordinary care. Additional derivative claims could not yet be resolved. As further development of the facts was needed, the court denied the motions for pretrial judgment. *Acevedo v. Durham School Services*, No. CV 146025831S, 64 Conn. L. Rptr. 210 (Conn. Super. Ct. 4/4/17).

◆ A Texas parent said her kindergartner was put on the wrong school bus and then dropped off alone alongside a busy highway. Although she said her son tried to tell the bus driver that he was supposed to go to daycare and should not be on a school bus, she said the driver did not call the school. In the parent's state court action, the school district sought immunity under the Texas Tort Claim Act. Appeal went before the Court of Appeals of Texas, which explained that under the Tort Claims Act, school districts are liable for injuries and deaths caused by wrongful acts or omissions of employees, if their negligence "arises from the operation or use of" a motor vehicle, where the employee would be personally liable under state law. The court found the "arises from" language of state law meant there must be a connection between the injury and the operation or use of a motor vehicle.

Prior Texas cases have held the operation or use of a motor vehicle must have actually caused the injury, and not simply furnished the condition that makes an injury possible. The court found that boarding a student on a bus and then leaving him at an incorrect location related to the supervision or control of the student, not the operation or use of a motor vehicle. When injuries arise from the supervision or control of the student, the court found immunity is not waived, even if the injury took place on a bus. Further, the court found the Tort Claims Act makes clear that immunity is not waived for claims arising out of intentional torts. Since the court found the complaint only showed the bus furnished the conditions that made the student's injuries possible, the judgment against the school district was reversed. *Dallas County Schools v. Vallet*, No. 05-16-00385-CV, 2016 WL 7163824 (Tex. Ct. App. 12/8/16).

◆ An Illinois high school freshman left an after-school event called the International Fair and walked to a McDonald's a block from campus on the other side of a 12-lane road. While trying to return to school, the student was struck and injured by a moving vehicle. In a state court, the student's parent sued the school district for willful and wanton failure to supervise her child. She sought damages and charged the district with voluntarily undertaking the responsibility to supervise the streets and intersections near the high school by hiring crossing guards, traffic control officers and police during certain after-school events at the high school. After the court dismissed the complaint, appeal went before the Appellate Court of Illinois.

On appeal, the court held the state Tort Immunity Act bars liability unless there is a duty to provide supervision imposed by common law or statute. Liability cannot be imposed against a local public entity unless the entity or an employee fails to provide supervision in a manner that is found "willful and wanton." Under the parent's theory, the school district was liable for failing to use due care in performing a voluntary undertaking. But the court held she did not show which intersections around the school were assigned crossing guards or how frequently they were used at after-school events. As she did not support her claim that the school used crossing guards for after-school events, her voluntary undertaking theory failed. **After-school events are optional, and without facts showing the school had a closed-campus policy for after-school events, the parent could not proceed with her case.** *Renkiewicz v. Township High School Dist. 211*, No. 1-15-0989, 2016 IL App (1st) 150989-U (Ill. App. Ct. 1/22/16).

◆ A Maryland student died after being hit by a car as she crossed a busy highway to try to catch a school bus. Her family later sued the school board for negligence. The case came before a jury, where the family produced evidence that the school board was supposed to have bus stops on both sides of the busy highway where the accident took place, but did not. A jury found the board was negligent and awarded over $90 million to the family.

The court granted the board's motion notwithstanding the verdict, and the family appealed to the state court of special appeals. It found a state regulation required the board to have a bus stop on both sides of the four-lane highway. For this reason, the board owed the student a duty of care. Next, the court held the student's failure to use a crosswalk did not make her contributorily negligent as a matter of law. The lower court should have let the jury decide this matter. The board had to show the existence and nature of its insurance coverage, and its coverage limits. If the board was self-insured or part of a pool, it had immunity for damages over $100,000. If the board had private insurance with limits above $100,000, the verdict was to be reduced to the amount of the policy limit. If the board had no insurance at all, the verdict could not be reduced. Last, **the court rejected the lower court's findings that the verdict was shocking to the conscience and had to be reduced by $20,000 received by the family in a settlement from the driver**. There could be no reduction based on the settlement, because the driver did not admit negligence. The court returned the case to the lower court. *Davis v. Board of Educ. for Prince George's County*, 222 Md.App. 246, 112 A.3d 1035 (Md. Ct. Spec. App. 2015).

◆ A Pennsylvania student suffered a crushed pelvis and amputation of one leg when a school district-owned bus accelerated out of control onto a sidewalk and struck her. In a state court action for negligence, the district admitted the bus driver caused the accident and that it was liable. Although the district had $11 million in insurance coverage, it argued recovery was limited to $500,000 by the state Political Subdivision Tort Claims Act.

After a four-day trial, a jury returned a verdict of over $14 million against the school district. The court granted the district's motion to reduce the verdict to $500,000. Arguing that the statutory cap on damages was unconstitutional on several grounds, the family appealed. Before the state high court, the family argued the damage cap violated equal protection principles and unfairly reduced the verdict by over 96%. The court held **Pennsylvania's decision to allow tort recovery and then subject it to a liability cap involved questions of policy best addressed by the state General Assembly**. In addition, the court found the family did not show any state classification violated the principles of equal protection. Next, the court rejected claims based on three state constitutional provisions. It found the General Assembly acted within its constitutional authority when providing for limits to tort claims. Despite the tragic facts of the case, the court refused to overturn its prior decisions and held for the school district. *Zauflik v. Pennsbury School Dist.*, 104 A.3d 1096 (Pa. 2014).

◆ A Georgia student was hit by a car when trying to cross a road at his usual bus stop. Visibility was reduced by heavy fog, and the car failed to yield for the stopped bus. In a state court negligence action, the parties made a pretrial stipulation that the bus driver was immune from personal liability for performing a discretionary function in the scope of her employment and acting without malice. It was further stipulated that the district had waived immunity to the extent of its $1 million commercial liability insurance coverage. The district then hired a new attorney and argued for immunity. The court instead found the district waived sovereign immunity to the extent of the insurance it had purchased. The school district appealed to the Court of Appeals of Georgia. It held the state legislature created a two-tier scheme by which local governments were deemed to have waived immunity. Under tier one, school districts waived immunity up to prescribed limits for incidents involving motor vehicles, regardless of insurance. Tier two provided for a waiver to the extent a local entity purchased liability insurance that was greater than the prescribed limits set forth in tier one. Since the school district in this case had purchased liability insurance greater than the amount prescribed in tier one, it had waived sovereign immunity to the extent of the insurance coverage it purchased.

The court rejected the district's argument that the General Assembly intended to exclude school districts from the waiver provision. **Immunity was waived to the extent of the district's insurance coverage.** As the parent did not appeal the part of the trial court order pertaining to the bus driver, the driver was relieved of any personal liability. *Tift County School Dist. v. Martinez*, 331 Ga.App. 423, 717 S.E.2d 117 (Ga. Ct. App. 2015).

◆ Nebraska's highest court held a county could not be held liable for a school bus accident based on its failure to have a traffic sign inspection policy. The case involved a collision between a pickup truck and a school bus at a rural blind intersection. At the intersection, a stop sign facing the truck was missing. An injured motorist sued the county and a property owner in a state district court, which found both of the drivers negligent. But the court also found the county liable, finding it would have discovered the sign was missing if it had regularly inspected signs. **Appeal reached the state supreme court, which held the trial court was wrong to find the lack of an inspection policy was a legal cause of the accident.** The court reversed the part of the judgment finding the county liable and returned the case to the trial court for a reallocation of liability between the pickup driver and the school district. *Hall v. County of Lancaster*, 287 Neb. 969, 846 N.W.2d 107 (Neb. 2014).

◆ A New York sixth-grader had attention deficit disorder, attention deficit hyperactivity disorder and a mild mental disability. She crossed a busy road to try to catch her bus after the driver missed her stop. The student was then struck by another vehicle and seriously injured. In a state court negligence action, the court held the student's status as a special needs child imposed an expanded duty on the district. Appeal reached the New York Court of Appeals, which held **a school had no duty to prevent injury to a student released from a bus in a safe and anticipated manner**. But it held a school breached a duty if it released a child without supervision into a foreseeably hazardous setting it helped to create. Evidence showed the student had walked onto the highway and was not in the district's custody when she was struck. Finally, the court found no special duty was owed to the student by virtue of her IEP or "the special busing services" afforded her in the IEP. In fact, the IEP only directed the district to transport her to and from school. Rejecting the parent's other arguments, the court held for the school district. *Williams v. Weatherstone*, 22 N.Y.3d 384 (N.Y. 2014).

◆ An 11-year-old Arizona charter school student was struck and injured by a truck in the crosswalk of a busy intersection as she rode her bicycle home from school. The intersection had traffic lights and crosswalks but no crossing guards. The student's parents sued the school for negligence in a state court. In pretrial activity, the court held the school had no duty to protect the student as she traveled to or from its campus. The parents appealed to the Court of Appeals of Arizona, which stated that **as a general rule, an educational institution had no duty to supervise students going to or from their homes**. Arizona law recognized that if a school voluntarily offered protection at a street crossing, a duty of care was then imposed on that conduct. Although a school may create a duty for itself by an affirmative act, the court found no such act in this case. It held the school did not owe the student any duty of care to protect her while she went home.

Instead, the court found the student had left the school's custody at the relevant time. Since the charter school did not have custody of the student at the time, the court held it had no protective obligation to her and lacked any student-school relationship when she was hit. Rejecting all the parents' other arguments, the court held for the charter school. *Monroe v. Basis School, Inc.*, 234 Ariz. 155, 318 P.3d 871 (Ariz. Ct. App. 2014).

◆ West Virginia's Supreme Court upheld the dismissal of a school bus driver who left her bus running to use the lavatory while students were on board. In a brief memorandum decision, the court noted **the bus driver had violated a state law against leaving a bus while it was still running**. The driver admitted she did not have to leave the bus running despite her urgent need to use the lavatory. As a result, employment termination was appropriate. *Hale v. Board of Educ. of Lewis County, West Virginia*, No. 13–0469, 2014 WL 350892 (W.Va. 1/31/14).

◆ A Washington middle school student was hurt when a car hit her as she crossed a street in front of a neighboring elementary school. A supervising adult traffic monitor had dismissed the crosswalk patrol seven minutes before the accident. In a state court, the student's guardian filed a personal injury action against the driver and school district. The court held the school district had no duty at the time of the incident. On appeal to the Washington Court of Appeals, the court found schools have a duty to protect students in their custody from reasonably foreseeable harm. While the guardian argued the school district had a common law duty to station patrols or monitors at designated crosswalks, the court found no support for this theory in a case involving a middle-school student crossing the street in front of an elementary school. **State laws and rules about school patrols set forth only "suggested procedures," not the times a patrol should be on duty.** As the lower court had correctly held for the district, the judgment was affirmed. *Brady v. Reinert*, 175 Wash.App. 1074 (Wash. Ct. App. 2013).

◆ An Indiana high school student was struck and injured by a school bus as he bicycled to school. According to records of the bus transportation service that served the student's school district, the driver left the bus terminal about 10 minutes late on the morning of the collision. In a state court, the student's family sued the driver and transportation service for negligence. The student argued the contract between the school district and transportation service "called for money back guarantees when a driver is late," making the contract relevant to his theory that the driver was running late and was negligent. At the close of the trial, the student's attorneys asked the jury to return a $35 million verdict. Instead, the jury awarded the student $5.2 million, reduced by the amount of his own negligence, which was found to be 25%. On appeal, the state court of appeals found no merit to the bus service's claim that there had been an unfair trial. The court also rejected arguments that the trial court made incorrect rulings of evidence. The driver admitted that she could be penalized for lateness. The court rejected a claim that there was a "runaway jury." **The reduction for comparative negligence indicated the jury had exercised discretion.** Since there was evidence to support the $3.9 million damage award, the court left it intact. *Reed v. Bethel*, 2 N.E.3d 98 (Ind. Ct. App. 2014).

VI. STUDENT SAFETY

For a customizable playground safety checklist, log on to our website at *www.SchoolSafetyAndSecurityAlert.com* and search "Playground Safety."

◆ An armed intruder broke into the Sandy Hook Elementary school in Newtown Connecticut, killing 20 first-graders and four adults before taking his own life. The parents of two children who died in the massacre later sued the town and school board in a state court for negligence. The court held the officials were entitled to immunity and held no reasonable jury could find the response by faculty and staff to the invasion was the cause of the students' deaths. The parents then appealed to the Appellate Court of Connecticut, which explained the general rule that a municipal entity is immune from liability for negligence or other torts unless a state law abrogates immunity. Under state law, municipal officials are immune from liability for negligence arising out of discretionary acts. The court said this reflected a value judgment that the interest in allowing government officials the freedom to exercise discretion outweighed the benefits of imposing liability for injuries resulting from the use of judgment. By contrast, immunity does not extend to "ministerial acts," which are acts involving no exercise of judgment. Contrary to the parents' claims, the court held **the school's safety guidelines left officials and staff members with discretion concerning school safety, including the execution of lockdown procedures and a school evacuation plan**.

As the state supreme court has held, supervision of public school employees is a discretionary function that is entitled to immunity. A 2018 state supreme court case declared the supervision of students to be a discretionary act. The parents did not identify any state law or rule imposing a ministerial duty on school officials to create or implement security guidelines. School security guidelines adopted by the board did not create a ministerial duty prescribing the manner of action during the shooting. The court noted the guidelines refrained from mandatory terms such as "shall," instead using qualifying terms such as "may" and "should" in describing responses to emergencies. In sum, the court affirmed the trial court's decision that no reasonably jury could find the security guidelines in this case prescribed a ministerial duty on school employees. *Lewis v. Town of Newtown*, 191 Conn.App. 213 (Conn. App. Ct. 2019).

◆ Nevada's Supreme Court held a student who suffered an eye injury during a floor hockey game in a P.E. class could not pursue negligence claims against his school district. As participation in the P.E. class was mandatory, the court did not find the student "voluntarily exposed himself" to the risk, which is an element of the assumption of risk doctrine. The court found its conclusion consistent with New York and California cases rejecting the implied assumption of risk doctrine for compulsory P.E. classes. Next, the court agreed with the district that some of the claims were barred by discretionary-function immunity. Discretionary-function immunity does not bar claims alleging inadequate supervision and instruction. While discretionary, these decisions are not "policy-based" and do not qualify for immunity. On the other hand, **the district's decisions to include floor hockey in the P.E. curriculum and to not provide students any safety equipment were "policy-based and discretionary," and fully protected by immunity**. Although discretionary-function immunity did not bar all the student's negligence claims, the court found he was not due judgment based on insufficient evidence that the district caused his injury.

The student did not show his injuries could have been prevented by intense supervision. While he said nonstandard equipment was used and that the teacher used larger team sizes than those specified in the rules, he did not show this contributed to his injury. Since the student could not say whether more or different measures could have prevented injury, the court held reasonable jurors could not have found the school district caused his injury. *Clark County School Dist. v. Payo*, 403 P.3d 1270 (Nev. 2017).

◆ A Pennsylvania school board resolved to hire armed school police officers as permitted by 24 P.S. § 7-778. It then petitioned a state court for an order approving of armed school police officers with extensive training and the power to arrest, issue citations and/or detain students until the arrival of local law enforcement officers. After reviewing the petition, a trial court judge denied it, finding "more thought was needed as to whether a school police force should be created, as well as what type of training is needed for school police officers who would be armed." The school district appealed to the Commonwealth Court of Pennsylvania, which held the lower court lacked authority to approve of a school police force. It agreed with the school district that the lower court abused its discretion by adding new standards and requirements to the law. Schools may apply to a local judge to appoint persons designated to act as school police. Upon receiving an application, the judge can make appointments and grant the powers to arrest, issue citations for summary offenses or the authority to detain students until local officers arrived. In the court's opinion, the law did not authorize a trial court judge to approve the creation of a school police force. Instead, **the law only allowed for the approval of appointments for individual police officers**. Judges could approve the powers which a district sought to confer on officers. The law provided that if a school district authorized an officer to carry a firearm, he/she must have the training described in the law.

As courts did not have the discretion to approve or disapprove of a school police force, the court held for the district. *In re: Petition of the Gateway School Dist. to Approve the Arming of School Police Officers Pursuant to 24 P.S. Section 7-778*, 154 A.3d 886 (Pa. Commw. Ct. 2017).

◆ A California student flicked a cigarette at a classmate in front of their school before entering in the morning, prompting a fight. Claiming he was injured in the fight, the student sued the school district and principal in a state court for negligence. The court held the district had immunity under state Education Code Section 44808. On appeal, the state court of appeal found that, **absent a specific undertaking by a school district, board, school officer or employee, there is no liability for the conduct or safety of students who are not on school property**. The court found the concern of the legislature in enacting Section 44808 was to limit school liability before or after school hours while students were going to school or coming home. Immunity applies to a student who is off school property, unless (1) the school is providing transportation, (2) has sponsored an activity off campus or (3) has "otherwise specifically assumed responsibility." A fourth Section 44808 provision states that a school must fail to exercise reasonable care under the circumstances in order to impose liability. The court held the failure to exercise reasonable care mentioned in Section 44808 is not a separate duty, but instead refers to any failure to exercise reasonable care in one of the three enumerated off-campus exceptions to immunity.

Prior state court decisions have found school districts have Section 44808 immunity from liability for accidents involving students who are on their way to their schools. In this case, the students were off campus and on their way to school at the time of their fight. Moreover, the court found no undertaking to supervise the student. No on-campus negligence led to the fight. Both students were on their way to school and had yet to come under the supervision and care of the school. Finding there had been no undertaking by the school district to supervise the area in front of the school, the court held for the district. *Riedl v. Western Placer Unified School Dist.*, No. C076641, 2017 WL 1422593 (Cal. Ct. App. 4/21/17).

◆ After the fatal shootings at Sandy Hook Elementary School in Newtown, Connecticut, a rural Oregon school board discussed its emergency response capability. Teachers attended a presentation called "Run, Hide, Fight," which suggested responses to active shooter incidents. At a board meeting, the board considered the costs of improving school security. Shortly thereafter, a private security company owned by the board's chair sent the board a cost estimate for upgrading the district's security system. The board decided against the upgrade. A few weeks later, the board chair, school principal, a school safety officer and another board member held an active shooter drill at a district school. Teachers were not told of the drill. The board chair and security officer entered the school wearing disguises and paintball goggles. They lit fire crackers and used starter pistols to simulate gunfire. The security officer entered a teacher's classroom, pointed a starter pistol at her and fired. He said, "You're dead," and then ran out. The teacher did not realize it was a drill and said she thought she would die.

Fifteen months later, the board chair's security company received a contract to upgrade the school's alarm system. In a federal court, the teacher sued the board chair, principal, security officer, district and others. First, the court denied four constitutional claims, finding no protected interest in freedom from assault and terror. But the court held the teacher could pursue her intentional infliction of emotional distress and assault claims. A reasonable jury could find school officials intended to cause severe emotional distress and could find their actions were "outrageous." Since the teacher stated a case for civil assault, she could proceed with this claim. She could also sue the board chair's security company. A jury could infer he was at least partly motivated to encourage the board to upgrade its security system by demonstrating a need for it. A jury would have to decide whether the officials acted intentionally and whether other claims were exempt from workers' compensation exclusivity provisions. *McLean v. Pine Eagle School Dist. No. 61*, 194 F.Supp.3d 1102 (D. Or. 2016).

◆ A 17-year-old Washington student died in a motor vehicle crash shortly after leaving the house of her 22-year-old basketball coach. Witnesses said the student and her boyfriend arrived at the coach's house just after midnight and that he provided them liquor. Later, the student and her boyfriend were killed when a vehicle driven by the boyfriend crashed at a high speed. In a state court, the student's estate sought damages for wrongful death from the school district, county sheriff's department and several others. Many of the claims were dropped or settled, and the court awarded pre-trial judgment to the district. On appeal, the state court of appeals explained that Washington courts recognize a special relationship between school districts and students that creates a duty to protect students from harms committed within the district's scope of authority. School districts have a duty to reasonably anticipate dangers, and to take precautions to protect students in their custody from such dangers. Moreover, school districts have a duty of reasonable supervision over students while they are in school or engaged in school activities, when it is in a school's power to control them.

But a school district does not owe a duty to students when the link between the harm and negligence is too remote. In this case, the court agreed with the district that a gathering at a coach's house after midnight on a Friday was outside school authority. There is no duty if the event causing injury is distant in time and place from normal school activity. The presence of the coach did not transfer authority over the party to the school district. This precluded any district liability. Last, the court found no evidence of negligent hiring, supervision or training. *Anderson v. Soap Lake School Dist.*, 2016 WL 6883283, 196 Wash.App. 1071 (Wash. Ct. App. 2016).

◆ A Louisiana student attended a party at a hotel that was hosted by the mother of a classmate at her charter school. She said she was raped in a stairwell at the hotel by a student who had repeatedly bullied and harassed her at school. She said school administrators did not respond to her complaints. In a state court action against the school board, the student claimed the rape would never have occurred had the board taken necessary steps to stop in-school harassment. After a hearing, the case was dismissed.

The student appealed to the Court of Appeal of Louisiana, which noted the school's argument that it did not rely on a state law immunity provision in trial court proceedings. Instead, the school argued it had no knowledge that an off-campus rape was likely to occur. In the court's view, the student had to prove the incident was foreseeable and that the school was somehow responsible for a student who was not in its control or custody. There was no evidence that the school had such a responsibility in this case. Further, constant supervision of all students is not possible and is not required for educators to discharge their duty to provide adequate supervision. **To impose liability upon a school board, the court held there must be proof of a causal connection between a lack of supervision and the incident.** Since no evidence supported the theory that the school had a duty to prevent an injury at a non-school function held off the school's campus and after the end of a school year, the court held for the school. *Hayes v. Sheraton Operating Corp.*, 195 So.3d 563 (La. Ct. App. 2016).

◆ A Wyoming school district sold a building to a community group. The locks were changed, and the community group began using the building. A child attended a basketball game at the building and played with others on a stage area. He was crushed and killed instantly when a heavy lunchroom bench fell on him. The bench had been leaned against a wall in a storage room adjacent to the stage. It was not known when the bench was propped there or who did it. In a state court action, the child's estate sued the school district, town and county for wrongful death. When the district sought to be dismissed, the court held the district did not breach a duty of care and did not cause the child's death. On appeal, the Supreme Court of Wyoming found the lower court had based its decision on a finding that no school employee had placed the bench against the wall. But factual issues remained that were appropriate to present to a jury. **Pretrial dismissal in negligence cases is proper only when the facts are undisputed.**

The court agreed with the estate that nothing showed the district had ever warned the community group of the dangerous condition created by the improperly placed bench. Finding reasonable jurors could reach different conclusions on the question of whether the district breached a duty of reasonable care and caused the accident, the court reversed the judgment. *Amos v. Lincoln County School Dist. No. 2*, 2015 WY 115 (Wyo. 2015).

◆ A Florida student had been twice disciplined out of school. A week after the second incident, the student threw an eight-pound book at a male classmate's head, fracturing his eye socket. Although the teacher was standing in front of the class at the time and was only a few feet away, it was later agreed that the book-throwing was spontaneous and could not have been prevented. In a state court, the classmate sued the student's family and the school district for his injuries. Among the claims was one for negligent supervision. The student's family settled the claim with the classmate, but the negligence claim against the district was heard by a jury.

Acknowledging that the teacher did no wrong, the classmate asserted the principal had been negligent for not disseminating the student's prior disciplinary record to the teacher. **The court explained that student disciplinary records are educational records that are subject to federally protected privacy rights.** While federal law allows school officials to decide which of its employees have a "legitimate educational interest" in access to disciplinary records, the court held this did not create a legal duty to make disciplinary reports available to teachers. Federal law entrusts school officials with discretion to determine which employees may have a legitimate educational interest in protected student data. The student's prior disciplinary record did not indicate a history of assault or behavior problems. Instead, the court held the case involved an instantaneous event in which the teacher had no chance to intervene. In sum, the court found no evidence of negligent supervision. The district's legal duty was to properly supervise students, not to disseminate student disciplinary records. As a result, the court held for the board. *School Board of Miami-Dade County, Florida v. Martinez-Oller*, 167 So.3d 451 (Fla. Dist. Ct. App. 2015).

◆ New York parents filed separate federal cases in which they sought declarations that a state law and rule permitting the temporary exclusion from public schools of students from state immunization requirements violated the Constitution. After the cases were consolidated, one parent testified that she objected to the law not only due to her religion, but because she believed vaccination could kill her daughter by putting her into anaphylactic shock. When questioned, the parent could not say which Catholic tenet prohibited vaccination. She cited medical reasons for objecting, but a federal magistrate judge denied her request. The court adopted the magistrate judge's recommendation to deny the families relief.

On appeal, the U.S. Court of Appeals, Second Circuit, held any due process claim was foreclosed by *Jacobson v. Comwlth. of Massachusetts*, 197 U.S. 11 (1905). In that case, the Supreme Court held mandatory vaccination was within a state's police power. Moreover, in *Zucht v. King*, 260 U.S. 176 (1922), **the Supreme Court rejected a claim that individual constitutional liberties could overcome a state's judgment that mandatory vaccination is in the interest of the whole population**. The court explained that the right to practice religion freely did not include liberty to expose the community or a child to communicable disease, ill health or death. In fact, the court explained, a state could constitutionally require all children to be vaccinated in order to attend a public school. Since the state had the power to bar children from school altogether, the court held New York's more limited action of temporarily excluding students during an outbreak of vaccine-preventable disease was clearly constitutional. A judgment for various state government agencies was affirmed. *Phillips v. City of New York*, 775 F.3d 538 (2d Cir. 2015).

◆ A Florida student said she was attacked by a classmate with a long history of discipline, bullying, fighting and class disruption. She said the attacker was in possession of a blade prior to the attack and should have been serving an in-school suspension (ISS). In a state court action against the board, the student submitted four theories of negligence. One was the theory that the board was negligent for not placing the attacking student in ISS on the scheduled day. It was claimed this allowed the attacker to be on the playground at the time of the injury. A jury agreed and found the board negligently supervised the attacker. The board appealed to a Florida District Court of Appeal, which found the board's current argument was different from its initial defenses that it had no duty to the student and was protected by immunity. It had limited the appeal to other liability theories. **As negligent supervision was an accepted basis for school liability, and the evidence supported the verdict, the student prevailed.** *Duval County School Board v. Buchanan*, 131 So.3d 821 (Fla. Dist. Ct. App. 2014).

◆ New Jersey's Supreme Court held a school principal was not liable for injuries to a pedestrian who cut across public school grounds on a Saturday and was attacked by a dog. According to the pedestrian, the dog had previously slipped out of its leash and accosted other passersby. She said the principal had called animal protection officials at least one other time when a dog was loose while school was in session. In the pedestrian's state court action, she advanced claims against the school district, principal, dog owner and the owner of the property where the dog had been leashed. After the claims against the dog owner and property owner were dismissed for failure to prosecute them, the court rejected arguments by the pedestrian that the principal and school district had a duty to prevent future attacks. She said the dog was a known danger on school property. The court held for the school district and principal, but a state appellate division court disagreed.

On appeal, the pedestrian argued the principal was on notice of the risk of an attack because he had received a report that the dog had attacked two others nine days before her injury. He had also reported dogs to the animal control unit of the police when dogs were observed at school during school hours. According to the pedestrian, the school district should also be held liable in this case because the principal knew that a vicious dog created a dangerous condition on school grounds. The court explained that proving a negligence claim depends upon the finding of a duty of care that the party being sued owes to the party bringing the lawsuit. Once a duty is found to exist, liability follows if there is a breach of the duty that causes injury and damages. In this case, **neither the principal nor the school board had any**

control over the dog or the activities on neighboring property. Once the school day ended, the principal could not monitor school grounds. There was also no relationship between the school and the pedestrian. Finally, the court found no public interest in imposing a duty on school personnel to protect persons with no relationship to a school from attacks by neighborhood dogs. Since there was no duty of care to protect the pedestrian in this case, the court held for the principal and school district. *Robinson v. Vivirito*, 217 N.J. 199, 86 A.3d 119 (N.J. 2014).

◆ Before arriving at school to help prepare for a school prom, an Oklahoma student drank alcohol. When a staff member smelled alcohol on him, she reported it to the superintendent, who obtained the student's admission that he had consumed alcohol before coming to school. But the parents were not called, as required by state law and a school policy. Instead, the superintendent told the student to go home with two other students. At some point after leaving school, the student grew distraught. He left the other students in another vehicle and later died in a one-vehicle rollover accident. His parents sued the school district and superintendent for constitutional rights violations and negligence. A federal court found enough facts to allow the negligence claim to proceed against the school district. **The district owed the student a duty of care, as he was on school grounds and participating in a school function at the time of the superintendent's questioning.** Although the court refused to dismiss a negligence claim against the district, it found no liability under the state-created danger theory. While the superintendent may have made poor choices, the court found nothing outrageous or conscience-shocking about his conduct. As a result, the constitutional claim failed and the superintendent was dismissed from the case. *Kerns v. Independent School Dist. No. 31 of Ottawa County*, 44 F.Supp.3d 1110 (N.D. Okla. 2014).

CHAPTER FOUR

Campus Law Enforcement

Page

I. SEARCH AND SEIZURE

A. The *New Jersey v. T.L.O.* Standard

The Fourth Amendment to the U.S. Constitution protects individuals from unreasonable searches and seizures. The Fourth Amendment states:

"The right of the people to be secure in their persons, houses, papers and effects, against unreasonable searches and seizures, shall not be violated, and no Warrants shall issue, but upon probable cause, supported by Oath or affirmation, and particularly describing the place to be searched, and the persons or things to be seized." Underlying all search and seizure cases in the criminal context is the "exclusionary rule," which allows a suspect to exclude from consideration any evidence seized in violation of the Fourth Amendment. The Fourth Amendment's warrant and probable cause standard does not typically apply to school officials who search students suspected of violating a law or school rules. Instead, the courts apply a "reasonableness" standard, by which the legality of a school search depends upon its reasonableness under all the circumstances.

In *New Jersey v. T.L.O.*, this chapter, the Supreme Court held school searches are "administrative searches" as they do not result in criminal prosecution and loss of liberty. The "special need" beyond law enforcement that justifies relieving school administrators from the burden of obtaining warrants is the need to protect student safety. In *T.L.O.*, the Court held: 1) a search by school officials need only be reasonable at its inception, and 2) its scope may not exceed what is necessary under the circumstances.

For example, a teacher who smells marijuana odor wafting from a student would be reasonable in believing that there was some rules violation, satisfying the first requirement that the search be "reasonable at its inception." After the student is sent to the office, an administrator or liaison officer then asks the student if he has marijuana in his possession and asks him to turn out his pockets. This kind of search is regarded as "not intrusive" and satisfies the second *T.L.O.* consideration by "not exceeding what is necessary under the circumstances." By contrast, a highly intrusive "strip search" would go beyond what would be reasonable in this case.

◆ In the *T.L.O.* case, a teacher at a New Jersey high school found two girls smoking in a school lavatory in violation of school rules. She brought them to the assistant vice principal's office, where one of the girls admitted to smoking in the lavatory. However, the other girl denied even being a smoker. The assistant vice principal then asked the latter girl to come to his private office, where he opened her purse and found a pack of cigarettes. As he reached for them, he noticed rolling papers and decided to thoroughly search the entire purse. He found marijuana, a pipe, empty plastic bags, a substantial number of one dollar bills and a list of "people who owe me money." The matter was then turned over to the police. A juvenile court hearing was held, and the girl was adjudicated delinquent. She appealed the juvenile court's determination, contending that her constitutional rights had been violated by the search of her purse. She argued that the evidence against her should have been excluded from the juvenile court proceeding.

The U.S. Supreme Court held that the search did not violate the Fourth Amendment's prohibition on unreasonable searches and seizures. Stated the Court: "The legality of a search of a student should depend simply on the reasonableness, under all the circumstances, of the search." Two considerations are relevant in determining the reasonableness of a search. First, **the search must be justified initially by reasonable suspicion of a violation**. Second, **the scope and conduct of the search must be reasonably related to the circumstances which gave rise to the search, and school officials must take into account the student's age, sex and the nature of the offense**. The Court upheld the search of the student in this case because the initial search for cigarettes was supported by reasonable suspicion. The discovery of rolling papers then justified the further searching of the purse, since such papers are commonly used to roll marijuana cigarettes. The Court affirmed the delinquency adjudication, ruling the "reasonableness" standard was met by school officials in these circumstances, and the evidence was properly obtained. *New Jersey v. T.L.O.*, 469 U.S. 325, 105 S.Ct. 733, 83 L.Ed.2d 720 (1985).

◆ An Iowa student had a record of involvement with drugs and a weapons-related offense. He was injured during a football game, and an ambulance was called for him. As paramedics were readying the student for transport to a hospital, he repeatedly asked the district superintendent to give his equipment bag to a particular teammate. He added that nobody else should "mess with it." Upon returning to the school, the superintendent searched the bag and found a loaded handgun, marijuana and drug paraphernalia.

Law enforcement officers later charged the student with several violations. Claiming the search was unconstitutional, he sought to suppress any evidence found inside his bag. The trial court denied the request to suppress the evidence found in the student's bag. After the state court of appeals affirmed the decision, appeal reached the Supreme Court of Iowa. It held that while the student's history of prior violations did not itself support a search, the presence of other factors might make such a search reasonable under the circumstances. Under *New Jersey v. T.L.O.* and other school search cases, searches are held justified when based on "the sort of common-sense conclusion about human behavior upon which practical people – including government officials – are entitled to rely." The court found school officials had a reasonable basis for the search and seizure of the bag in this case. It held they met *T.L.O.* standards. The student acted suspiciously or furtively during the relevant time. **Combined with his history of involvement with drugs and guns, the court found the school officials acted reasonably.** The student voluntarily gave the suspicious statements, which "raised a red flag." The search was not excessively intrusive, as school authorities had sufficient reason to believe he might have drugs or a gun. There was no reason to judge the search by any different standard under the Iowa Constitution. Finding the search was reasonable, the court affirmed the judgment. *State of Iowa v. Lindsey*, 881 N.W.3d 411 (Iowa 2016).

◆ Florida students who wished to attend their prom had to sign a form describing a zero-tolerance policy on drugs, tobacco and use of profanity on school property or at school activities. The policy stated that any student or guest at school activities was subject to a breath test. Prom tickets warned that no admittance would be allowed after 10:00 p.m. About 40 students arrived at the prom at 10:15 p.m. on a rented "party bus." A school resource officer entered the bus and found an empty champagne bottle and plastic cups in plain view. The driver said these items belonged to the students, but they denied this. Students were then required to pass a breathalyzer test. But since the only administrator certified to conduct the tests had already left, the students had to wait for her to return. They remained outside the prom for nearly an hour. Some students asked if they could go home instead of being breathalyzed, but the officer and an administrator told them they had to wait outside until everyone on the bus had been breathalyzed. All of the students passed the test with 0.00 blood-alcohol level, but when the testing was finished, the prom was nearly over. They later sued the school district and others in a federal court. The court found no constitutional violations.

On appeal, the U.S. Court of Appeals, Eleventh Circuit, found the district provided definitive rules prior to the prom, stating that no student would be admitted after 10:00 p.m. Next, the court found the search of the bus was supported by reasonable suspicion. Students did not have a reasonable expectation of privacy on the bus. The fact that the testing occurred away from school made no difference. Students were on notice they could be breathalyzed. Their initial detention was reasonably justified, since the officer had sufficient cause to believe they drank alcohol on the bus. **The school had a legitimate interest in testing the students, and the breathalyzer testing was held "minimally invasive."** Although the court found it was not reasonable to detain the students after they had been tested, no prior decision put officials on notice that the detention of students after being tested for alcohol use is unreasonable. As a result, the officials had immunity in the lawsuit. *Ziegler v. Martin County School Dist.*, 831 F.3d 1309 (11th Cir. 2016).

◆ An Oregon principal learned that a student had either called or texted a classmate that he would bring a gun to school and shoot her. Upon learning this, the principal called a deputy sheriff and the student's mother. While awaiting the deputy and mother, the principal searched the student's locker. After finding no gun there, he escorted the student to the office and confiscated his backpack. When the student denied making the threats, the principal continued to question him and searched his backpack, where a .45 caliber semiautomatic handgun and ammunition were found. The deputy confiscated the gun, placed the student in handcuffs and read him his criminal rights. In a juvenile court, the student sought to exclude the handgun and ammunition from the evidence. He argued the principal lacked reasonable suspicion to believe a weapon was in the backpack. In denying the student's motion, the court held the principal had relied on specific facts indicating a threat. It also held the search was not overly intrusive.

On appeal, the Court of Appeals of Oregon held a student can be searched without a warrant or probable cause when a school official reasonably suspects, based on specific and articulable facts, that the student possesses something that poses an immediate threat. In this case, the principal reasonably suspected the backpack could hold a weapon, and he did not know whether the student had the gun on his person, in the backpack, or at another place in school. The court held that **when school officials perceive an immediate threat to school safety, they must be able to take prompt, reasonable steps to address it**. As there was a real threat to safety in this case, the court upheld the search. *State v. A.J.C.*, 254 Or. App. 717 (Or. Ct. App. 2013). On appeal, the Supreme Court of Oregon affirmed the judgment, finding the search was reasonable under the circumstances. *State v. A.J.C.*, 355 Or. 552, 326 P.3d 1195 (Or. 2014).

◆ Four California police officers learned from a high school principal that a student had told a classmate he would "shoot up" the school. He was said to be a victim of bullying and had been absent from school for two days. Concerned that the student was a threat, the police went to his house. When they arrived, they knocked on the door but received no response. Nobody answered the home telephone, and the student's mother hung up her cell phone after a police sergeant identified himself and said he was waiting outside. Soon, the student and his mother came outside and learned that the officers wanted to discuss the threats. The student responded, "I can't believe you're here for that." When the sergeant asked to come inside the house to talk, the mother refused. He asked her if there were any guns in the house, and she went inside. Fearing they were in danger, the officers entered the house. Ultimately, they concluded the report about the student was false.

Later, the family sued the officers for Fourth Amendment violations. Appeal reached the U.S. Supreme Court, which found none of its prior decisions had found a Fourth Amendment violation on facts comparable to those present in this case. The Court held **a reasonable police officer could read the Court's prior decisions as allowing their entry into a residence if there was a reasonable basis to believe there was an imminent threat of violence**. As a result, the Court found a lower court had correctly held the officers had an objectively reasonable basis for their actions. This included the mother's initial failure to answer the door or the phone, hanging up the cell phone on the sergeant, refusing to answer questions, and running into the house. *Ryburn v. Huff*, 132 S.Ct. 987, 181 L.Ed.2d 966 (U.S. 2012).

B. Electronic Devices and Social Media

◆ A Missouri school district operated a camp for fifth-graders. One teacher and a teenage assistant were assigned to every cabin. A teacher videotaped nude fifth-graders inside cabins for years. When he was arrested, he pled guilty to child-pornography charges. A victim of his misconduct sued the school district and the teacher in a federal court. Claims were asserted under the federal Child Abuse Victims Rights Act of 1986 (CAVRA). The court entered a default judgment against the teacher under the CAVRA. The victim then moved to enforce the judgment against the school district. The court held the claim was filed in an individual capacity and could not be enforced against the district. It then dismissed all claims against the district.

On appeal, the U.S. Court of Appeals, Eighth Circuit, found it is well-settled that the Fourteenth Amendment's Due Process Clause protects the liberty interest of public school students from sexual abuse. Constitutional liability may be imposed on a municipality only where an official policy or custom violates federal law or directs an employee to do so. When a party claims municipal action resulted in an injury of constitutional magnitude, courts require proof of "deliberate indifference" by officials to the rights of persons injured by public employees. In this case, the victim had to show the school district's failure to supervise and train its employees amounted to deliberate indifference to the rights of persons with whom the teacher came in contact. Further, the victim had to show a pattern of similar constitutional violations to demonstrate deliberate indifference and that the district's failure to train or supervise was the moving force behind the constitutional violation. But **the school district was unaware of the teacher's misconduct until after his arrest**. Without a finding of notice to the district, there could be no liability based on deliberate indifference. Last, the court held the victim could not hold the district liable for the default judgment against the teacher on the CAVRA claim. *Doe v. Fort Zumwalt R-II School Dist.*, 920 F.3d 1184 (8th Cir. 2019).

◆ A Washington security monitor questioned a student, took his phone and searched his car. The search yielded a bong, knives, prescription and nonprescription pills, vaping and drug paraphernalia, lighters, torches and a BB gun. While awaiting the student's parent, a school resource officer told the student he was filing charges based on the BB gun, and he read him a *Miranda* warning. Although the county prosecutor did not file any charges, the school district suspended the student for 40 days. The school board later reduced the suspension to 25 days, conditioned upon completion of a substance assessment and compliance with any recommendations.

After complying with the conditions and graduating from high school, the student sued the district, the school's assistant principal (AP), security monitor and the superintendent for constitutional rights violations. The court held the student did not show the school made an impermissible seizure by confiscating his phone. Officials acted consistently with school policy when it took the phone. Finding the policy reasonable, the court held for the district and officials on claims arising from the phone confiscation. Even if he did not consent, **the court found the search was justified at its inception and reasonably related in scope to the circumstances**. The security guard believed she had seen a bong in the car. While the student argued he was denied due process, the court found no constitutional violation. There was no evidence that the district had a policy, custom or practice that was the moving force behind a violation. Last, the court found no relevant claim for damages under the state constitution. *Rorvik v. Snohomish School Dist.*, No. C17-0946-JCC, 2018 WL 3917932 (W.D. Wash. 8/16/18; appeal dismissed 12/19/18).

◆ After a sawed-off rifle was found in a trash bin at a California high school, administrators began questioning two students they suspected of bringing it to school. While the administrators interviewed them, another student walked past the office several times and looked inside. An assistant principal (AP) began to suspect him of some involvement with the gun.

When the student was brought into to the office, he became "fidgety" and "immediately reached down into his pocket." After a struggle, the supervisor took the student's cell phone. The AP knew the student was acquainted with one of the others in custody. He believed the student might be trying to contact the person who had brought the gun to school. The AP viewed the phone's contents and found pictures of students holding the sawed-off gun that was found in the trash. The student was in some of the pictures. He became irate and told the AP "Those are my photos. You can't do that." Since the student had become belligerent and "lost control," administrators called the police and suspended him from school. In juvenile court proceedings, the student objected to the use of the photos as evidence.

After the court denied the student's motion, he appealed to the state court of appeal. First, he claimed the juvenile court should not have allowed the cell phone photos as evidence because they were not properly authenticated. But the court found no merit to his arguments. A particular image from the student's phone depicted him holding a sawed-off rifle and wearing the sweatshirt he wore on the day of his arrest. The AP and arresting officer both testified that his appearance in the photo was consistent with his appearance at the time of his arrest. Next, the court held the search was governed by *New Jersey v. T.L.O.* and was "justified at the inception." The student's odd behavior near the school office, and his later fingering of the cell phone inside the office created reasonable suspicion that he could be aware of the gun which had been found on campus. He resisted efforts by school officials to keep him from using the phone and refused to explain why. Officials knew the student was acquainted with others who were being questioned about the gun. After finding officials had reasonable grounds for a search, the court found the search was not overly intrusive under the circumstances. **There was no merit to the student's claim that the school officials needed a warrant to search data on his cell phone.** Substantial evidence supported the finding that the student had knowingly possessed an assault weapon. *In re Rafael C.*, 200 Cal.Rptr.3d 305 (Cal Ct. App. 2016).

◆ A Mississippi freshman cheerleader argued with a senior cheerleading captain while the squad visited a TV station. Later, off school grounds and without using school computers, the freshman posted threats against the captain on social media. When the captain reported this, the advisor lectured the squad and then asked all squad members for their Facebook user names and passwords so she could inspect their accounts. After checking the freshman's Facebook account, the advisor suspended her from the squad for two weeks. When the freshman was not invited to join the cheer squad the next school year, she claimed others bullied her and that she suffered anxiety and depression. In a federal court, she sued the school district, advisor, principal, superintendent and others. Appeal reached the U.S. Court of Appeals, Fifth Circuit, which held that qualified immunity shields government officials from having to pay damages unless the injured party shows a violation of a right that is clearly established at the time of the violation. The contours of the right must be sufficiently clear that every reasonable official would understand it. As for the demand for Facebook passwords and account information, the court found it was not clearly established at the time of the incident that this violated federal law.

At the time of the advisor's request for student social media information, no precedent held the Fourth Amendment proscribed her actions. Since school officials acting in 2007 had no fair warning that they could not access social network accounts upon receiving information of online threats among students concerning school activities at a school function, the lower court should not have denied qualified immunity to the school officials on the privacy violation claim. Similarly, **the court held that as of 2007, no case law placed officials on notice that punishing a student based on her Facebook messages would violate the First Amendment**. *Jackson v. Ladner*, 626 Fed.Appx. 80 (5th Cir. 2015).

◆ A 14-year-old New Mexico seventh-grader refused multiple requests by her teacher to turn over her phone. The teacher stopped class and an administrator took the student to the office. There, the student ignored repeated requests to give up her phone, even after the school resource officer (SRO) intervened. The SRO told her she was in violation of school rules and a state law by texting in class and refusing to turn over her phone. After the student ignored his repeated requests to give up her phone, he placed her under arrest, handcuffed her and brought her to a juvenile detention center. In a federal court, the student's parent sued the SRO and school district. The court found evidence that the student had ignored her teacher and refused to stop texting in class. Her refusal to follow instructions required the teacher to stop class and seek help from the administration and eventually the SRO.

Since there was evidence that the SRO had probable cause to arrest the student, he was entitled to qualified immunity for the claim of wrongful arrest. There was no evidence that he used greater force than he needed, defeating the student's excessive force claim. As for the use of handcuffs, **the court found "handcuffing is appropriate in nearly every situation where an arrest is authorized."** The fact that the student was a minor did not change this. In any event, the SRO's use of force was minimal. In the court's view, it was not unreasonable for an SRO to seize contraband from a student. Removing a phone that visibly protruded from a pocket was not unconstitutional. As it was not clear that the SRO lacked probable cause to arrest the student, or that he committed any violation of state law or used excessive force, he would have immunity from liability. *G.M. v. Casalduc*, 982 F.Supp.2d 1235 (D.N.M. 2013) (10th Cir. appeal dismissed 6/6/14).

◆ Virginia high school administrators received two reports from parents that a male student had been smoking marijuana on a school bus. Later in the day, the assistant principal brought the student to the office and told him to empty his pockets. The assistant principal patted him down and searched his backpack, shoes and pockets. The school's associate principal searched the student's belongings, including a Vaseline jar, a sandwich wrapper and cell phone. No marijuana was found, and the student was sent back to class.

Later, the student and his family sued the administrators and school board in a federal court. First, the court held the receipt of information from two parents concerning a student smoking marijuana on a bus justified a search. Patting him down and searching his belongings was held reasonable. The search took place in the privacy of an administrative office and was not intrusive. Since drugs could have been found in a Vaseline jar or a sandwich wrapper, the court found it had been reasonable to search them. But the court held the administrator's search of the cell phone was not reasonable. **The search of the cell phone was not reasonably related to the objective of finding evidence of drug use on the school bus.** In addition, the court denied the associate principal's request for qualified immunity. *Gallimore v. Henrico County School Board*, 38 F.Supp.3d 721 (E.D. Va. 2014).

◆ In separate criminal cases, two adult criminal suspects claimed their Fourth Amendment rights against unreasonable searches and seizure were violated when police officers examined the contents of their cell phones after their arrests. When their appeals reached the U.S. Supreme Court, it explained that police are typically required to obtain a warrant to meet the constitutional "reasonableness" standard. Prior case law established that police may search a detainee for weapons that may be used to resist arrest. By contrast, a leading Supreme Court case held an extensive, warrantless search of a home was unnecessary to protect the safety of the police officers or to preserve evidence of a crime. In the Court's view, the risks identified in prior detention cases were not present when officers seized cell phones from criminal detainees. Cell phones held vast quantities of personal data. Searching them did not resemble the typically brief search of a suspect.

The Court refused to allow warrantless police searches of cell phones. It issued a sharp admonition to police seeking to view the contents of a suspect's cell phone: "Our answer to the question of what police must do before searching a cell phone seized incident to an arrest is accordingly simple – get a warrant." In ruling for both suspects, the Court held a cell phone search would typically reveal more than the search of a house. It recognized that "fact-specific threats may justify a warrantless search of cell phone data" if a specific risk of exigent circumstances was present. *Riley v. California*, 573 U.S. 373, 134 S.Ct. 2473, 189 L.Ed.2d 430 (U.S. 2014).

◆ The U.S. Court of Appeals, Sixth Circuit, held "using a cell phone on school grounds does not automatically trigger an essentially unlimited right enabling a school official to search any content stored on the phone." The court stated that even if checking a student's messages on the cell phone was justified by a need to determine if he was contemplating harm to himself or others, any search was subject to the two-part analysis for all school searches. It had to be tailored to the nature of the violation and related to the objectives of the search. In the court's opinion, the viewing of the student's cell phone text messages was unreasonable. **General knowledge of drug abuse or depressive tendencies was not enough to enable such a search.** Since the school district did not show that a search of the phone would reveal evidence of criminal activity, the court found the search was not justified at its inception and violated his rights. *G.C. v. Owensboro Public Schools*, 711 F.3d 623 (6th Cir. 2013).

◆ A Pennsylvania student had his cell phone on, in violation of a school policy. When a teacher confiscated the phone, a text message appeared on its screen from another student requesting marijuana. The teacher and an assistant principal then called nine students listed in the cell phone's directory to see if their phones were turned on in violation of school policy. They accessed the student's text messages and voice mail and used the phone's instant messaging feature. The student sued the teacher, assistant principal, superintendent and school district in a federal district court. It held the superintendent could not assert absolute immunity for his statements to the press. The teacher and assistant principal also had no immunity for the invasion of privacy claims. The court agreed with the family that **accessing the phone directory, voice mail and text messages, and use of the phone to call persons listed in the directory amounted to a "search or seizure" under the Fourth Amendment**. The court found no basis for the "search," as it was not done to find evidence of wrongdoing by the student, but instead to obtain evidence of possible misconduct by others. *Klump v. Nazareth Area School Dist.*, 425 F.Supp.2d 622 (E.D. Pa. 2006).

C. Strip Searches

The leading case in this area is *Safford Unified School Dist. #1 v. Redding*, this chapter. In it, the Supreme Court disapproved of an Arizona school's decision to ask a 13-year-old student to pull down her underwear and expose her breasts and pelvic area based on another student's statement that she was distributing pills at school. Although refraining from the term "strip search," the Court found the search "categorically distinct, requiring distinct elements of justification on the part of school authorities for going beyond a search of outer clothing and belongings." Further, the Court held "the suspicion failed to match the degree of intrusion."

◆ Two parents claimed the Houston Independent School District (HISD) maintained a policy of not training personnel about student rights to be free from unreasonable searches and seizures. According to the parents, an assistant principal (AP) ordered a strip search of 22 sixth-grade students in a choir class to recover $50 in missing cash. All 22 students were female, and the AP told a female school nurse to check the waistbands of their underwear. The students were told to loosen their bras and lift their shirts. The money was not found. In a federal court, the parents claimed the HISD allows school officials to conduct invasive searches of students, but provides no training about how to conduct a legal search. After review, the court granted pretrial dismissal motions by the HISD. The case reached the Fifth Circuit Court of Appeals, which found there was an undisputed constitutional violation. As the Supreme Court held in *Safford Unified School Dist. No. 1 v. Redding*, this chapter, **a search of a student's underwear is impermissibly intrusive unless officials reasonably suspect the object of the search is dangerous or is actually likely to be found in the student's underwear**. A policy of providing no training regarding employee legal duties constitutes an "official policy" that could support municipal liability if it amounted to deliberate indifference to student constitutional rights.

The court found the facts presented by the parents, if true, would permit a reasonable inference that the risk of unconstitutional searches was a highly predictable consequence of HISD's decision not to provide any training regarding student Fourth Amendment rights. Next, the court found evidence that HISD expected, or even intended the AP to order student searches. It noted that none of the HISD employees, including the principal, AP and school police, realized the search might be unconstitutional. Finding an obvious need for training, and evidence that HISD provided none, the court held the parents could proceed with their failure-to-train claims. *Littell v. Houston Independent School Dist.*, 894 F.3d 616 (5th Cir. 2018).

◆ A Georgia student told a school resource officer that a 13-year-old seventh-grader had marijuana and was giving it to others. After a search, marijuana was found in the 13-year-old's backpack. Another seventh grader unbuttoned his pants, turned away from the officer and pulled out a bag of marijuana. When the school's assistant principal (AP) learned of the searches, he mistakenly formed the belief that both students hid marijuana in their underpants. While searching a seventh-grader, the assistant principal was told that a 12-year-old also had marijuana. He had the 12-year-old student brought to the office. In the presence of the other students and the resource officer, the AP questioned the 12-year-old and asked him to empty his backpack. When no drugs were found, the AP told the student to take off his shoes, empty his pockets and take off his pants, socks and shirt. Although the student denied having any drugs, the AP told him to remove his underwear. The student asked if the search could be continued in a lavatory, but the AP refused. The student pulled down his underpants, exposing his genitals, but no contraband was found. He sued the school district, AP, resource officer and county sheriff's department in a federal court for constitutional rights violations. The court dismissed claims against the sheriff and approved a settlement between the student and resource officer. But the AP was denied immunity in the action, and he appealed.

On appeal, the Eleventh Circuit Court of Appeals noted important distinctions between the situation facing the AP and the facts facing the administrators in *Safford Unified School Dist. #1 v. Redding*, this chapter. Marijuana had already been found on three students, and the AP believed two of them had hidden drugs in their underwear. This led the court to find the search was reasonable at its inception. Next, the court found the intrusiveness of the search matched the degree of suspicion. There is a compelling interest in keeping schools drug free. **Based on the student's version of the facts, the court found a reasonable administrator in the AP's position would not believe that requiring him to strip in front of his peers was lawful.** For this reason, the court found the AP was properly denied immunity. The case was returned to the trial court for a trial to resolve remaining factual disputes based on the accounts of the parties. *D.H. v. Clayton County School Dist.*, 830 F.3d 1306 (11th Cir. 2016).

◆ Santa Fe Public Schools contracted with a private company for security at high school proms. Four female students said security guards subjected them to intrusive pat-down searches as they tried to enter the 2011 prom. Two of them said security guards pulled their dresses up and felt their bare legs. They said the security guards (all females) touched their bras, ran fingers down their dresses and patted down their back sides. In a federal court, the students sued the security company, school district, school board, principal and others. Finding the searches were likely unconstitutional, the court issued an order prohibiting the school district from performing pat-down searches without reasonable suspicion. It also dismissed the claims against the principal. **Less intrusive searching, such as with visual inspection or the use of magnetic wands, would be allowed.** The court ordered the company's guards to undergo instruction by the federal Transportation Safety Administration. The school district was ordered to stop conducting pat-down searches of every student "as a first approach." **Security officers were to use a graduated approach similar to those used by airport security guards.** Only after such an approach, and when reasonable grounds existed, could security guards use pat-down searches.

Months later, the court issued an order finding the "highly invasive" pat-down searches were attributable to a district search protocol. The fact that a private security firm did the searches did not absolve the district from liability. In the court's view, a reasonable jury could find the school district's practice of suspicionless pat-down searches arose from training or supervision that was deliberately indifferent to student rights. But the court found the evidence was largely circumstantial. In further court activity, the school district could attack the allegations made by the students. *Herrera v. Santa Fe Public Schools*, 41 F.Supp.3d 1188 (D.N.M. 2014).

◆ A Kansas student was accused by a classmate of placing marijuana in her bra while at school. After being brought to the school office, she consented to be patted down and to have her shoes and backpack searched. After the school resource officer found nothing, an assistant principal told her she would have to search her bra based on the classmate's report. Two female school officials then instructed the student to lift up her shirt and pull her bra from her body, exposing her breasts. No drugs or paraphernalia were found. Within a few weeks, the student "disenrolled from the school" and she later sued the school district. A federal court found no evidence of an unconstitutional policy or custom that would create district liability. The court expressed concern about the failure of school administrators to corroborate the classmate's tip as well as the manner of the search. But it held **the student did not identify any prior cases discussing whether a student informant's tip created "reasonable suspicion" for a school search**. Having dismissed the federal claims, the court held the state law claims should be heard by a state court. *S.S. v. Turner Unified School Dist. #202*, No. 12-CV-0246-CM, 2012 WL 6561525 (D. Kan. 12/14/12).

◆ An Arizona assistant middle school principal questioned a 13-year-old student about knives, lighters and a cigarette found in her planner. When the student denied owning any of the contraband, the assistant principal questioned her about prescription-strength ibuprofen pills and an over-the-counter painkiller. After the student denied knowing about the pills, the assistant principal told her he had received a report from a male student that she was giving pills to others at school. She denied this and allowed the assistant principal to search her belongings. He found no contraband there but told female staff members to further search the student in the nurse's office. An administrative assistant and school nurse asked the student to remove her jacket, socks, shoes, pants and T-shirt. They then instructed her to pull her bra to the side and shake it. Finally, the two staff members told the student to pull out the elastic of her underpants. No pills were found.

The student's mother sued the school district for Fourth Amendment violations. The case reached the U.S. Supreme Court, which held the male student's report created enough suspicion to justify searching the student's backpack and outer clothes. But asking her to pull away her underwear and expose her breasts and pelvic area made the search "categorically distinct, requiring distinct elements of justification on the part of school authorities for going beyond a search of outer clothing and belongings." Further, "the suspicion failed to match the degree of intrusion." The Court stated "the *T.L.O.* concern to limit a school search to reasonable scope requires the support of reasonable suspicion of danger or of resort to underwear for hiding evidence of wrongdoing before a search can reasonably make the quantum leap from outer clothes and backpacks to exposure of intimate parts." **Despite the violation, this legal area was not so well established as to deprive school officials of immunity.** *Safford Unified School Dist. #1 v. Redding*, 557 U.S. 364, 129 S.Ct. 2633, 174 L.Ed.2d 354 (2009).

D. Search and Seizure Cases

◆ A California high school assistant principal (AP) received a text message from a student, advising that another student had a gun at school. Upon questioning, the tipster stated that she had seen a Snapchat video depicting a student at the school, displaying a gun and clip. According to the AP, he was sure of the student's identity based on the tipster's description, which included the suspect's gender, race and hairstyle. The AP pulled the suspect from his classroom and brought him to the school resource officer

(SRO) and a backup officer. After searching the suspect, the SRO found a semiautomatic gun and ammunition clip on his person. In later juvenile proceedings, the suspect claimed the SRO could not search him under the "arbitrary and capricious" standard typically applied in school detention cases, due to the presence of the municipal officer called as a backup. The court denied the suspect's arguments. On appeal, the state court of appeal noted that prior California juvenile cases have established that "detentions of minor students on school grounds do not offend the Constitution, so long as they are not arbitrary, capricious, or for the purposes of harassment."

Further, California cases have held "school officials" include police officers who are assigned to high schools as resource officers. The court rejected the student suspect's argument that the presence of a municipal officer required the application of a higher standard. The fact that a campus resource officer was assisted by a backup officer not employed by a school district did not determine the correct standard to apply. **For the purpose of its Fourth Amendment analysis, "school officials" included both SROs assigned to high schools, and backup officers called to assist them.** Applying the "arbitrary and capricious" standard for school officials, the court found the detention in this case was lawful. *In re K.J.*, 18 Cal.App.5th 1123, 227 Cal.Rptr.3d 380 (Cal. Ct. App. 2018; Cal. review den. 4/18/18)).

◆ A young Florida student saw three older students in a school lavatory "examining" a handgun. He told his teacher that the student holding the gun was a tall, thin African-American with a dark complexion and a "low afro" haircut. He wore a red shirt and "skinny jeans," and was carrying a book bag with a cartoon character or "some type of bling" on it. The teacher advised the principal and school police officer of the description, and the principal emailed teachers to be on the lookout for someone with this description. The principal and officer then walked through the hallways to locate the student with the gun. The suspect student happened to be in the first classroom checked by the officer and principal. The student admitted having a gun and was charged with three offenses. In juvenile proceedings, he moved to suppress the gun and his statements from the evidence, claiming the school officials had no reasonable suspicion for the search. After denying the motion, the court found the suspect student delinquent on all three counts.

On appeal, the state court of appeal explained that **a search may be unreasonable under the circumstances if it is based on a "generalized description" of a suspect that could apply to a large number of innocent people** in the area. But in this case, the court found the description given by the younger student was very specific. He provided details about height, weight, race and skin tone, and described the approximate age, haircut, clothing and decorations on his book bag. The court found school officials acted reasonably given the grave danger posed by an armed student on campus and the relaxed constitutional standards for school searches. *R.M. v. State of Florida*, 129 So.3d 1157 (Fla. Dist. Ct. App. 2014).

◆ Based upon an anonymous tip, a Florida assistant principal removed a student from class and brought him to a conference room. A search of the student's book bag by a school resource officer yielded a loaded, semiautomatic handgun. In a juvenile court proceeding, the student sought to exclude the gun from evidence, arguing the search violated the Fourth Amendment. After a trial, the court imposed a 15-day detention and one year of probation. Appeal reached a Florida District Court of Appeal, which held that tips from informants had to be examined for "indicia of reliability."

Generally, an anonymous tip must have sufficient detail and information that could be independently verified by police to establish a level of reliability. The U.S. Supreme Court had found some circumstances justify protective searches based on a threat of extraordinary danger. Since a person's reasonable expectation of privacy is reduced at a public school, school officials are held to a standard of reasonable suspicion. In the court's view, the search in this case was reasonable. **No reasonable person would contest the government's substantial interest in protecting students from gun violence.** Given the student's reduced expectation of privacy, the moderate intrusiveness of the search, the gravity of the threat, and the reduced level of reliability necessary to justify a protective search, the court held the search of the book bag was reasonable. *K.P. v. State of Florida*, 129 So.3d 1121 (Fla. Dist. Ct. App. 2013, Fla. review den. 11/19/14).

◆ In conjunction with law enforcement officials, a Missouri school district permitted police dogs to sniff student lockers, desks, backpacks and other items that were not in a student's possession. School personnel decided a drug detection search was necessary to address a drug problem in district schools. Searches were held in all of the district's high schools. A student claimed he fully zipped his backpack when he and others were told to leave the classroom for the search. He later said he "felt like the pockets of his backpack had been unzipped and stuff." On this basis, his parents sued the school district, along with school and sheriff's officials in a federal court.

During pretrial activity, the court held for the district and officials, finding their procedures were reasonable. On appeal, the Eighth Circuit noted that the Fourth Amendment demands that a seizure of property be reasonable. **A drug dog search was found "minimally intrusive," and the court had previously found them to be an effective means to form individualized suspicion** for further, more intrusive searches. In addition, the court found the district showed an immediate need for a drug dog search based on substantial evidence of a drug problem in the school district. *Burlison v. Springfield Public Schools*, 708 F.3d 1034 (8th Cir. 2013).

◆ A California student who was searched because he was in a school hallway without a hall pass avoided a juvenile court sentence because the campus aide who detained him could not articulate a reason for performing the search. The Court of Appeal of California held that under ordinary circumstances, a search of a student by a school official must be justified at its inception, reasonably related to the objectives of the search, and not excessively intrusive. In a prior case, *In re Lisa G.*, 125 Cal.App.4th 801 (Cal. Ct. App. 2004), the court of appeal held that disruptive behavior alone did not justify the search of a student. In that case, a teacher failed to articulate a reasonable suspicion of misconduct by a student that was sufficient to justify searching the student's purse. Similarly, in this case, the aide was unable to explain a reasonable suspicion that searching the student would reveal evidence of a crime or violation of a school rule. In the court's view, **"a suspicion that a student was tardy or truant from class, without more, provides no reasonable basis for conducting a search of any kind."** As a result, it found the evidence seized in this case was inadmissible and should have been suppressed. The judgment was reversed. *In re Diego C.*, No. B232230, 2011 WL 6740151 (Cal. Ct. App. 12/29/11).

E. State Supreme Court Cases

◆ Massachusetts school employees observed "an unknown individual" on school grounds. An administrative assistant allowed him to enter the building. Upon entering, the individual gave conflicting reasons for being at the school. He first said he needed to use the lavatory, but then said he was a student at the school. He gave a fictitious name and said he needed to go to his locker. When the assistant tried to verify the individual's identity, he asked to leave, saying he had left his car running. The school's principal and vice principal then found him in the school parking lot and noticed the smell of marijuana. They asked the individual to come back into the building. He complied and was taken into a conference room. The principal questioned the individual while the police were called. At the principal's request, he emptied his pockets. When a municipal officer arrived, she conducted a "pat frisk" of the individual, which yielded a bag of marijuana and a wad of cash. She patted down the individual's backpack and found a bottle of alcohol, more cash and a pistol. The school was placed on lockdown and some employees had to remain there for hours. A police detective arrived and read the individual his *Miranda* warnings. He then handcuffed and arrested the individual. A jury trial was held, resulting in convictions of the individual for carrying a dangerous weapon on school grounds and other crimes. During the proceedings, the court denied his request to suppress his statements and evidence seized from him during the search of his backpack.

After being convicted, the individual appealed to the Supreme Judicial Court of Massachusetts. It noted that a search by school officials is permissible so long as it is reasonable under all the circumstances. On the other hand, a police officer's conduct in a school setting is governed by the traditional Fourth Amendment standard. In this case, the Fourth Amendment standard applied, since a municipal police officer conducted the search. In the court's view, the police lacked reasonable articulable suspicion that the individual committed a crime. As a result, some of the firearm and drug convictions had to be vacated. A conviction for disturbing a school was returned to the trial court for a new trial. In explaining its decision, the court found the police had relied on an "unsubstantiated hunch" by an administrator that the individual "had something on him." This, by itself, was an insufficient basis for believing he was armed and dangerous. Significantly, the principal invited the individual to come back inside the school and told him to empty his pockets. The court commented that the school administrators were appropriately cautious and did what was expected of them by calling the police. **Its decision related to the conduct of police under the Fourth Amendment warrant and probable cause standard**, not the less exacting standard for searches by school officials. *Commonwealth v. Villagran*, 477 Mass. 711, 81 N.E.3d 310 (Mass. 2017).

◆ After arriving at his school, a Nebraska student left the building to retrieve items from his truck, which he had parked on a street off campus. When the student returned, an assistant principal told him to empty his backpack and pockets. Finding no contraband, the assistant principal told the student he would search the truck. In an off-campus search, drug pipes, papers, cigarettes and lighters were found in the truck. After a hearing and administrative appeals, the student was suspended for 19 days. A state trial court held the school board violated the Fourth Amendment and improperly charged him under a student handbook provision by searching his truck, since it had been parked off campus. Appeal reached the Supreme Court of Nebraska. Noting school districts only have the powers granted to them by the legislature, the court found the Nebraska Student Discipline Act was limited to conduct "on school property, in school vehicles, or at school-sponsored activities." The court found no right of school officials to conduct off-campus searches that were unrelated to school-sponsored activities.

Although the school board argued that driving to school is a school-sponsored activity that has a "nexus" to the school, the court found this claim of authority was too broad. Instead, the court held school authority "was not intended to overlap the authority of law enforcement officers to enforce order on the public streets." **A school district did not have implied authority to conduct an off-campus search of a student's vehicle.** In this case, school officials had all the information they needed to impose school discipline when the student returned to the building. The court commented that if they suspected there was contraband in the truck, they should have notified law enforcement authorities. *J.P. v. Millard Public Schools*, 285 Neb. 890, 830 N.W.2d 453 (Neb. 2013).

◆ A North Dakota school resource officer learned about possible drug use by students a short distance from school, and a security guard was assigned to patrol the area. Two students evaded the guard, who returned to campus and told the resource officer he had "smelled something funny." When the officer followed the students in a patrol car, they walked away. The officer told the principal of their evasive behavior and said he suspected drug activity. The principal questioned one student. He emptied his pockets, which contained a pipe and synthetic marijuana. In criminal proceedings, a state court convicted the student of felony charges. On appeal, the state supreme court held the "reasonable suspicion" standard applies when school officials initiate a search or when police involvement is minimal. **The reasonable suspicion standard applied when a school resource officer acted on his or her own initiative or at the direction of other school officials to further educational goals.** The court found the relevant factors supported applying the reasonable suspicion standard in this case. The resource officer did not initiate the investigation. He notified the principal of his observations and let him decide how to handle the situation. The officer had only a small role in the questioning and worked with and at the direction of the principal. Applying the "reasonableness standard," the court held the search was justified at its inception and not excessively intrusive. It upheld the student's conviction. *State v. Alaniz*, 815 N.W.2d 234 (N.D. 2012).

◆ A New Hampshire school parking lot monitor observed a student walking away from the school. Three school employees caught up with the student as he crossed a field about 200 yards from the building. He said he did not feel well. The employees persuaded him to return to school, where they searched him under a policy applying to any student who returned to school after leaving an assigned area. An assistant principal asked the student if he "had anything on him that he shouldn't have on school property." The student handed over a small bag of marijuana he had hidden inside a sock. In juvenile proceedings, a New Hampshire family court denied his motion to exclude the marijuana from evidence. On appeal, the Supreme Court of New Hampshire found no distinction between a "search" and the treatment of the student in this case. According to the court, **courts and schools are to consider a child's age, school record, the extent of the problem to which the search was directed, the exigencies at the time, the probative value and reliability of information justifying the search, and prior experiences with the student**. Consideration of these factors did not support the state's claim that the search was "justified at its inception." There was no record of a drug problem at the school, and no administrator had any prior disciplinary experiences with the student. Since the search was not justified at its inception, it was held unreasonable under the state constitution. *In re Anthony F.*, 163 N.H. 163, 37 A.3d 429 (N.H. 2012).

◆ A Connecticut school policy allowed police to make unannounced searches on school property with drug-sniffing dogs even without warrants or suspicion of any crime. The policy recited that its inclusion in the student and/or parent handbook was the only notice required to advertise searches. A high school student was arrested as a result of contraband found during a sweep conducted according to the policy. His parents filed a state court lawsuit against the school board. After a hearing, the court found a policy of warrantless and suspicionless drug-dog sweeps on school property without notice to parents did not violate any constitutional rights. It held **the use of drug-sniffing dogs was not a "search" under the Fourth Amendment**, since "students do not have a reasonable expectation of privacy in the odor or 'aroma' emanating from their unattended lockers" and vehicles. Arguing that the trial court should have reviewed the case under the state constitution, the parents appealed. But when the case reached the Supreme Court of Connecticut, they acknowledged their son had graduated from high school. Since he was no longer subject to the policy, **the case was held moot, and the appeal was dismissed**. *Burbank v. Board of Educ. of Town of Canton*, 299 Conn. 833, 11 A.3d 658 (Conn. 2011).

◆ An Oregon student was called to the office and told that an anonymous witness saw him trying to sell drugs. After speaking to his mother, the student agreed to turn his pockets inside out. Marijuana, plastic bags and a pipe were found, and he admitted he had tried to sell marijuana. In juvenile court proceedings, the student claimed any evidence seized by school officials should be excluded from trial because there was no probable cause for a search. Finding probable cause was unnecessary, the juvenile court held the search was lawful. It also concluded that the student was delinquent. Appeal reached the Supreme Court of Oregon. It discussed Article I, Section 9, of the state constitution, which prohibits unreasonable searches or seizures. The court held school searches are different from law enforcement searches. Only searches involving safety concerns justify a departure from the "warrant and probable cause" requirement. **School officials have wide latitude to take safety precautions when they have reasonable suspicion based on specific and articulable facts that an individual poses a threat to safety or possesses an item posing such a threat.** "Reasonable suspicion" applies to searches for drugs on school property. Since officials reasonably suspected that the student had illegal drugs at the time of the search and that he intended to sell them at school, the judgment was affirmed. *State ex rel. Juvenile Dep't of Clackamas County v. M.A.D.*, 348 Or. 381, 233 P.3d 437 (Or. 2010).

◆ A New Jersey assistant principal (AP) received a report that a high school student was under the influence of drugs. After being taken to the AP's office and interviewed, the student denied any wrongdoing. A search of his pockets yielded three white capsules. The AP searched his car and denied his request to call home. The search yielded contraband, including a bag containing what appeared to be illegal drugs. A school resource officer arrested the student, who waived his right to remain silent and admitted that the contraband was his. In juvenile court proceedings, he moved to suppress evidence seized from his car as a violation of his right to be free from unreasonable searches and seizures. Based on a finding that the AP's search of the car was reasonably related to a suspicion that the student had drugs and posed a danger to the school, the trial court denied the student's motion. Appeal reached the Supreme Court of New Jersey, which explained that under *New Jersey v. T.L.O.*, this chapter, the school setting required some easing of police search standards in view of the need to maintain school discipline and safety. The court found no reason to avoid the *T.L.O.* standard in vehicle cases, as "the school setting calls for protections geared toward the safety of students." **The court was not convinced by the student's claim to a greater expectation of privacy in his car than he might have in a locker or purse.** A "reasonable grounds" standard applied to the search of a student's car on school property by school authorities. Based on a classmate's statements, the student's apparent drug use, his statements and his possession of pills, it was reasonable for the AP to extend the search to the student's car. As a result, the court affirmed the judgment. *State v. Best*, 201 N.J. 100, 987 A.2d 605 (N.J. 2010).

◆ An Arkansas teacher confiscated a student's cell phone as he was using it in violation of a school rule. Although his parents demanded the return of the phone, it remained in the school office for two weeks, as required by a district policy. It was then returned, but the family sued the teacher and principal in a state court for trespass and taking property without due process of law. The court held for the district, and appeal reached the Supreme Court of Arkansas. On appeal, the parents claimed the Arkansas Code did not authorize the confiscation. The court explained that the section pertained only to the suspension or dismissal of students from public schools. **State law declared that school policies were to "prescribe minimum and maximum penalties, including students' suspension or dismissal from school."** Arkansas school boards have broad discretion to direct school operations, and "courts have no power to interfere with such boards in the exercise of that discretion unless there is a clear abuse of it." The court refused to interfere with the board's decision about the best way to enforce its policy. *Koch v. Adams*, 361 S.W.3d 817 (Ark. 2010).

F. Police Participation and *Miranda* Warnings

1. *Miranda* Warnings

The Fifth Amendment forbids the government from compelling a person to testify against him or herself in a criminal case. In *Miranda v. Arizona*, 384 U.S. 436 (1966), the U.S. Supreme Court announced the now familiar constitutional rights advisory known as the "*Miranda*" warning.

Under *Miranda*, a criminal suspect who is in police custody "must be warned that he has a right to remain silent, that any statement he does make may be used as evidence against him, and that he has a right to the presence of an attorney, either retained or appointed." Police must advise criminal suspects of their rights whenever there is a "custodial interrogation."

When police take a student into custody for questioning, the student must be advised of his or her Fifth and Sixth Amendment rights. The Supreme Court of Pennsylvania has held school police officers are to be considered the same as municipal police. But courts in Texas, Rhode Island, New Jersey, Massachusetts, Florida and California have held school officials need not issue *Miranda* warnings when questioning students about rules violations. In *State v. Antonio T.*, this chapter, the Supreme Court of New Mexico held that while a school official may insist that a child answer questions relating to school disciplinary proceedings, any statement elicited by the official cannot be used against the child in a delinquency proceeding, unless the child has made a knowing and voluntary waiver of rights.

◆ An Indiana school resource officer found a bomb threat scribbled in a boys' lavatory and identified two students as the suspects. He escorted one of them to a school office. Although the vice principal led the questioning, three uniformed officers were present. One officer asked the student to provide a handwriting sample to see if it matched the lavatory scrawl. Another officer urged the student to "just tell the truth." In response, the student began crying and admitted he had written the threat. The officers arrested him, and he was charged with two crimes. In juvenile court proceedings, he claimed the officers should have given him a *Miranda* warning, since he was in police custody. The court denied the student's request and found him delinquent on both counts. Appeal reached the Supreme Court of Indiana, which found Indiana law permits an unemancipated juvenile to waive *Miranda* rights only via counsel or a custodial parent or guardian. If the law is not followed, the state cannot use the juvenile's admission as evidence.

In the court's view, the student was being questioned in a custodial setting. Three uniformed officers were present. A reasonable person in the student's position would feel more vulnerable to outside pressure than an adult or older student. While the vice principal led the questioning, the court noted one officer urged him to confess and that the officers held a "tag-team probe." **This was a police interrogation because the officers should have known their conduct was reasonably likely to elicit an incriminating response from the student.** As he was in a custodial interrogation in the school office, his incriminating statements should not have been used against him. *B.A. v. State of Indiana*, 100 N.E.3d 225 (Ind. 2018).

◆ In a companion case to *B.A. v. State of Indiana*, above, the Supreme Court of Indiana upheld a student's juvenile conviction for writing graffiti in a lavatory. **An assistant principal (AP) was not required to read the student his *Miranda* rights, as there was no police involvement at the time.** In general, civilians need not issue *Miranda* warnings. When police officers are not present, a student is neither in custody nor subject to a custodial interrogation - unless school officials are "acting as agents of the police" during any questioning. In this case, the court found no resource officer was in the room when the AP questioned the student. Further, the court found no evidence suggesting the police directed or encouraged the AP to act as an agent. In fact, the court noted the AP had initiated the investigation before asking the resource officer to intervene. Since the AP was not acting as a police agent, the court found no *Miranda* warnings were necessary. *D.Z. v. State of Indiana*, 100 N.E.3d 246 (Ind. 2018).

◆ A ninth-grader was found unconscious in a Georgia school lavatory. An assistant principal (AP) reviewed surveillance video footage of the ninth-grader entering the lavatory. Soon after he entered, two other students entered together. A third student then entered alone. The principal and AP interviewed the first two students separately. One of them admitted he may have hit the ninth-grader. The first two students who followed the ninth-grader into the lavatory began texting each other, leading the principal and the AP to suspect they were trying to coordinate their stories. As a result, the school's SRO seized their cell phones and informed them she would be requesting a search warrant to see their texts. When a student's mother arrived, she told her son not to cover up for anyone and to tell what he knew about the incident. The student then stated that he had choked the ninth-grader until he was unconscious. A trial court found the SRO's seizure of the cell phones created a custodial interrogation. This triggered the requirement for the SRO to issue the student his *Miranda* warning. Because the SRO failed to inform the student of his rights before he gave his statements, the court suppressed them. Prosecutors appealed to the Court of Appeals of Georgia, which explained that law enforcement officers must give a *Miranda* warning prior to questioning when a subject is in police custody.

A *Miranda* warning is required when a suspect has been formally arrested or has been restrained to an extent associated with an arrest. In this case, the student was called to the principal's office by the school administration, not the SRO. When the SRO first arrived, she did not consider the student a suspect and did not treat him like one. The student was allowed to speak to his mother, who encouraged him to tell the truth. Under the circumstances, the court found a reasonable person in the student's position would not consider him or herself as deprived of the freedom of action. The fact that his own mother elicited his statement was an important reason for allowing the trial court to use the statement. As a result, the statement should not have been suppressed. *State v. Daniell*, 346 Ga.App. 792, 817 S.E.2d 358 (Ga. Ct. App. 2018; Ga. cert. denied 3/11/19).

◆ A Mississippi municipal police officer came to a high school to investigate damage to a security camera. Security footage captured the image of a juvenile who attended the school. The juvenile depicted on the security footage said another student was also involved in the incident. The officer then arrested the other student and charged him with malicious mischief. Neither the vice principal nor the officer called his parents. The vice principal repeatedly asked the student if he was involved in vandalizing the camera. The officer handcuffed the student and juvenile and escorted them out of school. The student was charged with a misdemeanor and ordered to pay $40 in restitution for the damage. In a federal court, the student and his parents sued the city, chief of police, arresting officer and the vice principal for civil rights violations. The court explained that an action based on an unlawful conviction or sentencing depends upon proof that a conviction or sentencing was reversed or invalidated.

In this case, a youth court had ordered the student to pay restitution and he admitted being present when the camera was vandalized. **Since the officer had probable cause to arrest the student, there was no "unlawful seizure."** Parents have no constitutional right to be notified and present during an investigation or questioning of children under *Edmonds v. Oktibbeha County, Mississippi*, 675 F.3d 911 (5th Cir. 2012). The parents said the police acted in concert with the school by routinely questioning students without probable cause. But the court held they did not show any officers were ever told to make unlawful arrests. The court held the city, police chief and officer were entitled to judgment. Although the school district and vice principal failed to join the motion for dismissal, the court held they would be granted judgment unless there was a timely objection filed by the family. *Bryant v. City of Ripley, Mississippi*, Civ. No. 3:12 CV37-B-A, 2015 WL 686032 (N.D. Miss. 2/18/15).

◆ New Mexico teachers noticed a student was acting drunk and referred him to the assistant principal (AP). She questioned him in the presence of a school resource officer (SRO). The student admitted bringing alcohol to school and then drinking it. At the AP's request, the SRO gave the student a breath test, which tested positive. Only then did the SRO advise the student of his right to remain silent. The student declined to answer the SRO's questions about his possession of alcohol. In a state court, the student was charged with a delinquent act. He asked the court to suppress statements he made to the AP because they were elicited without a knowing, intelligent and voluntary waiver of his right to remain silent. The court denied the student's motion, and appeal reached the Supreme Court of New Mexico.

The court found that under a state law, a child suspected of committing a delinquent act cannot be questioned without a constitutional rights advisory. **In order to proceed with questioning, a child had to knowingly, intelligently and voluntarily waive his or her rights.** If this right was violated, the child's statement was excluded from court proceedings. The court held that the state law was not confined to law enforcement officers. As a result of the legislature's broad language, the requirement of a knowing, intelligent and voluntary waiver of a child's constitutional rights applied to the statements elicited by the AP. There was a difference between questioning a child for school disciplinary matters and questioning based on criminal suspicion. While the AP could compel answers from the student and use them for school discipline, the court held they could not be used in court proceedings without showing compliance with the statute. *State v. Antonio T.*, 352 F.3d 1172 (N.M. 2015).

◆ A Kentucky principal investigated a report that a student had unlawfully entered school and stolen money from a classroom. He told the student to "tell the truth," and said that a police officer was in the building. The student then admitted being involved in the burglary. After the confession, the principal walked the student to his office. There, the officer read the student his *Miranda* advisory and questioned the student in the presence of the principal and a juvenile justice officer. The student repeatedly stated "I don't want to tell on myself." But he eventually admitted he was involved in the theft. In juvenile proceedings, the student sought to suppress his statements. The court held the student was not in police custody when he admitted being involved in the burglary. On appeal, the state court of appeals held that while police must issue *Miranda* warnings when they question a suspect in custody, the requirement generally does not apply to school administrators. **As principals are not trained or equipped to perform police investigations, they do not issue *Miranda* warnings.** But when a principal acted in concert with the police, a different rule applied. Because the police officer repeatedly questioned the student while he was in custody after he said he did not want to answer questions, the court held the confession could not be used as evidence. *A.K.M. v. Comwlth. of Kentucky*, No. 2012-CA-001190-DG, 2014 WL 3887910 (Ky. Ct. App. 2014).

◆ After a narcotics detector dog ran through a California school, a 15-year-old student was sent to the office. A school resource officer ordered her to sit down, but she refused. She said the officer handcuffed her and "slammed her to the ground." The student claimed the 240-pound officer kept his weight on her and refused to let her get up. When paramedics arrived, the student said she had a "swollen and blooded face, carpet burns on her arms, and a broken clavicle bone." She claimed the officer had placed a hood over her head and that her hands remained painfully handcuffed behind her. In a federal court, the student said school employees, including the assistant principal, were in the room when the officer apprehended her but did not intervene. Among her charges were use of excessive force and battery by the officer. After finding the school district had Eleventh Amendment immunity, the court held **there was no authority for a claim that failure by school officials to intercede against police or school resource officers violated clearly established federal rights**. *Tasia R. v. Grossmont Union High School Dist.*, No. 13cv2874, 2014 WL 3734475 (S.D. Cal. 7/28/14).

◆ A Minneapolis school security officer and a school resource officer (SRO) approached students in the school cafeteria in response to a report that they were out of control. A 19-year-old student with disabilities said the security officer used a racial epithet and that he told the officer "he wouldn't be doing all of that, all of that without the badge." An associate educator who was outside the office said she heard the student yelling and swearing at the officers and that he refused to follow their directions. She said "the next thing I remember is one of the officers had him in a neck restraint," and that one officer said "night, night," or "good night." The student accused the security officer of lifting him out of a chair. He said he struggled to get out of a choke hold as the SRO encouraged the officer to "put him to sleep." The student blacked out. In a federal court, he sued the city, security officer and SRO for civil rights violations. In view of the highly conflicting accounts of the incident, the court held a reasonable jury could find the officers had no basis for requiring him to meet with them. **The court also found a jury could reasonably find the SRO encouraged the security officer when using a choke hold, or at least should have intervened but did not.** In further court proceedings, the officers would not enjoy qualified immunity. *Thomas v. Barze*, 57 F.3d 1040 (D. Minn. 2014).

◆ A uniformed school resource officer removed a 13-year-old North Carolina seventh-grader from class to question him about break-ins in his neighborhood. A police investigator, an assistant principal and a school intern were also present. After the student denied any wrongdoing, an assistant principal urged him to "do the right thing." The resource officer told the student "this thing is going to court," and threatened him with juvenile detention. The student then admitted he had committed the crimes.

Only then did the officer inform him he could refuse to answer the questions and that he was free to leave the room. After offering further details, the student wrote a statement at the officer's request. After juvenile petitions were filed against the student, his public defender moved to exclude the statements and evidence obtained from the school interview. Finding the student was not "in custody" of the police at the time of the interrogation, the juvenile court found him delinquent. Appeal reached the U.S. Supreme Court, which held a duty to issue a *Miranda* warning arises if there has been such a restriction on a person's freedom as to render him or her in police "custody." According to the Supreme Court, a child's age and the school setting were relevant to the *Miranda* analysis. If the age of a child suspect was known to the officer at the time of questioning, or would have been objectively apparent to a reasonable officer, the Court held **consideration of age was consistent with the *Miranda* custody analysis**. The Court reversed the judgment and returned the case to a state court to determine if the student was in police custody at the time of the questioning. *J.D.B. v. North Carolina*, 131 S.Ct. 2394, 180 L.Ed.2d 310 (U.S. 2011).

2. Liability Issues

In *Chavez v. Martinez*, 538 U.S. 760 (2003), the Supreme Court held courts cannot award damages against police investigators who wrongly induce suspects to provide incriminating information unless it is actually used in a criminal prosecution. Until compelled statements are used in a criminal case, there is no potential violation of the Fifth Amendment.

◆ A Connecticut student communicated primarily in American Sign Language (ASL) due to his profound deafness. He became angry at a teacher and ran from the school campus. After a standoff at a construction site, school officials called the police. The officer instructed the student to put down a rock. These instructions were translated by the dean into ASL, and the teacher signed the message to the student. When the student continued to hold the rock, the officer warned him he would use a taser if he did not put it down. The message was again translated by the dean and signed by the teacher. Believing the student had again ignored him, the officer tased him. A second tasing was performed in order to allow handcuffing of the student.

In the student's federal court action for constitutional rights violations, the officer was denied qualified immunity. On appeal, the Second Circuit Court of Appeals explained that qualified immunity protects officials from liability for damages as long as their conduct does not violate clearly established rights of which a reasonable person would have known. Prior case law clearly established that police officers cannot use a taser on a compliant or non-threatening suspect. **In this case, the court held the officer had a reasonable belief that the student presented a risk of harm to himself and others.** The officer had to consider the risk that the student would flee. Under the circumstances, the court refused to find the officer acted unreasonably. It instructed the trial court to award him qualified immunity. *Muschette v. Gionfriddo*, 910 F.3d 65 (2d Cir. 2018).

◆ The Ninth Circuit Court of Appeals held two California school resource officers (SROs) who arrested and handcuffed a group of middle school girls to teach them a lesson and command their respect clearly violated their Fourth Amendment rights. In the court's view, the actual motivation of the arresting SRO was clear. He told the students he was arresting them to prove a point and to teach them a lesson. **The court held the arrest, handcuffing and transportation of the students was a disproportionate response to the school's needs.** The SROs faced a room of seven seated, mostly quiet middle school girls, and only generalized allegations of fighting and conflict amongst them. The court explained that qualified immunity insulates an officer from liability unless precedent places a legal issue beyond debate. At the time of the arrests, it was clearly established that a police seizure at the request of a school official must be reasonably related to its purposes, and not excessively intrusive under the circumstances. **The court held no officer could have reasonably believed the law authorized the arrest of middle school students in order to prove a point.** Last, the court rejected the officers' claims that probable cause existed to arrest the students under a state law. *Scott v. County of San Bernardino*, 903 F.3d 943 (9th Cir. 2018).

◆ Despite finding a Maryland school resource officer (SRO) used excessive force by handcuffing a calm and compliant 10-year-old student, the Fourth Circuit Court of Appeals held the SRO should have immunity in the student's lawsuit because no case law clearly defined her conduct as a constitutional violation. The case involved a calm, compliant 10-year-old who was handcuffed several days after hitting another child. She had no prior behavior incidents or involvement with law enforcement. The court found the use of force intruded upon the student's Fourth Amendment rights. In finding a constitutional violation, the court commented that even a child with a history of attacking school officials should not be handcuffed if, at the time of the handcuffing, she did not present a danger. As the student presented no such risk, the court held the handcuffing was unjustified. Next, the court commented that officers should use restraint when dealing with student misconduct. Handcuffing is counterproductive to the mission of the schools. But the court found no case law put the SRO on notice that she was violating the student's rights by handcuffing her. The SRO was thus entitled to qualified immunity in the case. **The court's holding made it clear that in future cases handcuffing a student under similar circumstances would give rise to a violation.** *E.W. v. Dolgos*, 884 F.3d 172 (4th Cir. 2018).

◆ A Kentucky school resource officer (SRO) arrested a high school student who was accused of harassing a classmate. He made the arrest based on an investigation by an assistant principal (AP), concluding that the student broke several laws relating to terroristic threats, harassment and menacing. The SRO read the student her *Miranda* warnings, arrested and handcuffed her, and transported her to the county youth center. A juvenile court later dismissed the charges against the student, and she sued the AP, SRO, school district and county entities for civil rights violations. In addition, she brought state-law claims against the AP and SRO for assault, false imprisonment and malicious prosecution. A federal court held that in order to conduct a legal search or seizure, a school official must show "a reasonable basis for believing that the pupil has violated the law or a school rule." What constitutes a "reasonable basis" depends on the circumstances.

In this case, the student was detained in the course of an investigation. A report stated he was threatening and harassing the classmate to the point that she skipped a class. According to the court, **"courts have consistently held that information from informants can provide a basis for reasonable suspicion" in a school search/seizure case**. The court found the AP had a reasonable basis for detaining the student. He did not violate her Fourth Amendment right to be free from unreasonable search and seizure. Similarly, the court found the SRO had probable cause to place the student under arrest based on his review of the AP's investigation, video footage and written statements from other students. *Boyd v. Jefferson County Public Schools*, No. 3:16-CV-00023-CRS, 2017 WL 4685737 (W.D. Ky. 10/18/17).

◆ Missouri school officials, including an elementary principal and a school resource officer (SRO), were required to defend a federal civil rights lawsuit challenging the handcuffing of a seven-year-old student during a behavior incident at his school. In refusing to award pretrial judgment to the district, SRO and principal, the court observed that there were conflicting accounts about whether the student tried to flee from the SRO and whether he was screaming in the hallway and presented a safety threat. The parties disagreed about the amount of time from the SRO's arrival at the classroom until he used the handcuffs and whether anyone else was in the hallway and at risk due to the student's conduct. Since the court could not determine whether the SRO deprived the student of his constitutional rights when he handcuffed the student, the court denied pretrial judgment on that claim. Since many facts remained in dispute, it refused to determine whether the SRO was entitled to qualified immunity against the claim. **As the court found the principal's role in the incident was unclear, she was granted qualified immunity at this stage.** *K.W.P. v. Kansas City Public Schools*, 296 F.Supp.3d 1121 (W.D. Mo. 2017).

◆ A seven-year-old New Mexico child with autism weighed 50 pounds and stood just over four feet tall. He had a behavior intervention plan (BIP), but it did not include a physical restraint strategy. For two hours, the child disrupted his class and did not respond to interventions. Calls were made to the parents, but the father refused to come to school because he was busy at work. After locking himself in the school nurse's lavatory, the child ran out and into the cafeteria. A security officer reached the child's mother by phone, and she agreed to come to the school. She consented to the restraint of her child. After kicking the officer, the child sat on the floor with his legs crossed. But while waiting for his mother, he started playing with a rubber band and disregarded the officer's instructions to put it down. The child shot the officer with the rubber band twice. She then stepped on the rubber band, and he started to kick her. After the child disregarded the officer's further instructions, she placed him in handcuffs. When the mother arrived, she demanded removal of the handcuffs and took pictures with her cell phone.

The parents sued the school district in a federal court for violating the Americans with Disabilities Act. Finding no discrimination or denial of a reasonable accommodation, the court held for the school district. On appeal, the U.S. Court of Appeals, Tenth Circuit, found no evidence that the district or its staff took action against the child based on a disability. No authority suggested a 15-minute interruption of a disabled child's school day was a denial of benefits. Nothing convinced the court that the district knew any lack of training was likely to harm the child's rights. **The court noted the mother had given the officer permission to restrain her child without mentioning particular limits on the type of restraint.** Finding all the claims failed, the court held for the school district. *J.V. v. Albuquerque Public Schools*, 813 F.3d 1289 (10th Cir. 2016).

◆ A nine-year-old Utah student stole an iPad from his school. The principal saw him with it and tried to take it away. The student struggled with the principal and he hit, bit and head-butted other school employees. After the student's grandmother arrived at the school, he began to calm down, and the employees released him. When a police officer arrived at the school, the student was seated in a hallway. The officer told him "we can do this the easy way by you talking to me, or we can do this the difficult way or hard way by you not talking to me." The officer then grabbed the student by the arm and pulled him up. Witnesses stated that the student grabbed the officer's arm. She responded by putting the student in a "twist-lock," which involved twisting his hand to place tension on his arm. The officer then pushed him against the wall and handcuffed him. The officer escorted the student to the office and cited him for theft. Later, the grandmother sued the city and police officer in a federal court for constitutional rights violations.

During pretrial activity, the court found no evidence that the officer immediately placed the student in a twist-lock. It was found that the student grabbed the officer first. Under the circumstances, the court held the use of a twist-lock restraint was objectively reasonable. Appeal went before the U.S. Court of Appeals, Tenth Circuit, which found the grandmother herself had made a statement that the student grabbed at the officer before she applied a twist-lock. Every other witness to the event stated the child had grabbed the officer first. During pretrial activity, the officer denied using excessive force and said the student had grabbed her gun. In finding a twist-lock was not a constitutional violation under these circumstances, the court commented that **the Fourth Amendment does not require the police to use the least intrusive means of detention**. It was reasonable for the officer to try to de-escalate the situation and command the student's compliance with a twist-lock. As the lower court held, there was no constitutional violation. *Hawker v. Sandy City Corp.*, 591 Fed.Appx. 669 (10th Cir. 2014).

◆ A Delaware school resource officer (SRO) interrogated an eight-year-old student in a room with a classmate who was accused of bullying. The SRO used the student to elicit a confession of school misconduct from the classmate. The SRO carried a gun, handcuffs and other police equipment. After the incident, the student's parents sued the SRO and other officials.

When the case reached the Supreme Court of Delaware, it held a reasonable eight-year-old in the student's position would not have felt free to leave the room. Next, the court noted the SRO had said he was 99% sure the student was not involved in the reported bullying incident. According to the court, **the fact that the SRO "shamed" the bully into confessing supported a finding that his seizure of the student was unreasonable**. There was evidence that the student was so upset that he could not return to school for the rest of the year. The court held he could proceed with a claim for infliction of emotional distress. It returned the case to the lower court for further review of the Fourth Amendment, emotional distress and false imprisonment claims. *Hunt v. State of Delaware*, 69 A.3d 360 (Del. 2013).

◆ An 11-year-old California student forgot his medication for attention deficit hyperactivity disorder. He became unresponsive on the school playground. Due to fears that he would try to leave campus, a teacher called the police. When the officers arrived, she told them that the student was a "runner" who had forgotten his medication. The officers handcuffed the student and put him in a squad car. As his parents were out of town, the officers brought him to his uncle's business. In a federal court, the student's parent alleged state and federal civil rights claims. The family settled its claims against the teacher and school district. A jury found the city and officers were not liable for excessive force and unlawful seizure. The judge found the verdict "inconsistent and incomplete." Further instructions to the jury failed to clarify the inconsistency, and appeal reached the Ninth Circuit.

The Ninth Circuit found no violation of clearly established law and held the officers had qualified immunity regarding both federal claims. But since the judge's instructions to the jury and later attempts at clarification were potentially misleading, the court found there had to be a new trial. Months later, the majority of judges of the Ninth Circuit decided to reconsider the decision. It then issued a new decision finding the chief and the police officer were entitled to qualified immunity on the unlawful seizure claim. But the court held **the officers did not have immunity for an excessive force claim based on keeping the student in handcuffs for 40 minutes**. In denying immunity for the excessive force claim, the court found the student "was doing nothing more than sitting quietly and resolutely in the school playground." *C.B. v. City of Sonora*, 769 F.3d 1005 (9th Cir. 2014).

◆ An Oregon state child protective services worker and a deputy sheriff interviewed an elementary student at her school without a warrant or the consent of her parents, based on suspicion that her father had sexually abused her. At some point, the student said she had been abused, and her father was charged criminally. Years later, the student's mother sued the social worker and deputy sheriff. The court held the officials violated the Constitution, but granted their request for qualified immunity. When the case reached the U.S. Supreme Court, it held **public officials had a right to appeal decisions that found their conduct violated the Constitution**. This was true even if they were entitled to immunity and would not have to pay monetary damages. An official who was entitled to immunity still had an interest in appealing from an adverse decision in order to "gain clearance to engage in the conduct in the future." Fear of constitutional liability should not unduly inhibit officials in the discharge of their duties. But the student was now nearly 18. As she would never again be interviewed by child protection officials, the Court held the case was now moot. *Camreta v. Greene*, 563 U.S. 692, 131 S.Ct. 2020, 179 L.Ed.2d 1118 (2011).

II. DISCIPLINE ISSUES

A. Weapons Possession

For downloadable forms related to this topic, log on to our website at *www.SchoolSafetyAndSecurityAlert.com* and search "Sample Parent Letter Following Weapons Incident" and "Student Knife Contract."

◆ A Minnesota school district suspended a student for 10 days for possessing and brandishing a BB gun on school grounds. While he was suspended, many teachers met with him to discuss and provide him schoolwork. The school district assigned an intervention specialist to help the student. After his expulsion hearing, the board voted to adopt a recommendation for expulsion. The student sued the school district in a federal court, arguing it failed to provide him proper alternative education services. The court declined to hear the case, since the student had a state administrative forum and could then seek judicial review. *B.L. v. Mahtomedi School Dist.*, No. 17-1193, 2017 WL 1497855 (D. Minn. 4/26/17).

In the student's administrative case, the commissioner of the department of education found substantial evidence that the student willfully violated a reasonable school board regulation. But she held the student should only have been expelled for the current semester, as the board did not provide him due process and did not provide a full written explanation of its action. Appeal reached the Court of Appeals of Minnesota, which rejected the student's claim that no substantial evidence supported his expulsion for violating the school's zero-tolerance weapons policy. The court further rejected the student's argument that he was not aware of the policy because it was not "clear and definite to provide notice to students that they must conform their conduct to its requirements." In the court's view, **the school's annual distribution of a student handbook summarizing its weapons and disciplinary policies was sufficient to notify the student that he was not allowed to possess a gun or look-alike on school property**. Further, the student's concealment of the gun indicated awareness that he was violating a school rule. But the court affirmed the commissioner's decision to reduce his expulsion to one semester. *In re Expulsion of B.L. from Independent School Dist. No 832, Mahtomedi Public Schools*, No. A17-1174, A17-1228, 2018 WL 2090615 (Minn. Ct. App. 5/7/18).

◆ A West Virginia teacher smelled smoke and suspected that someone in the classroom was using a vape device. She asked the user to come forward and when nobody did, she announced a search. The teacher and five students observed a student walking with his backpack to another part of the room. He stopped and placed something into a classmate's backpack and then returned to his seat. The classmate showed the teacher the contents of her backpack, revealing a pistol. The classmate denied that the pistol belonged to her, and the student claimed he was looking for some lotion in her backpack. Police investigated the incident and collected statements from students who reported seeing the student place something in the classmate's backpack. A notice to the student's attorney from the district superintendent advised that the possession of a handgun on school property is a Level 4 violation of state and local policies. She further advised the attorney that she would recommend an expulsion from school for up to 12 consecutive months. At the hearing, the student's attorney called a police sergeant as a witness. The sergeant admitted no physical evidence directly linked the student to the pistol. But on cross-examination, he stated that circumstantial evidence indicated the student was in possession of the pistol on school property. After the hearing, the board voted to expel the student.

The family appealed to a state circuit court, which affirmed the expulsion decision. On appeal, the Supreme Court of Appeals of West Virginia found no error in the board's conclusion that the evidence supported a finding that the student possessed a handgun at his school. The teacher and five students observed the student putting something into the classmate's backpack. **While evidence of his gun possession at school was circumstantial, the court found it was sufficient to support the expulsion.** *E.R. v. Jefferson County Board of Educ.*, No. 16-0836, 2017 WL 2608440 (W. Va. 6/16/17).

◆ At 14-year-old Pennsylvania student stabbed a classmate in the neck with a pencil multiple times. The school board voted to expel him under a school rule pertaining to the possession of a weapon on school property. A state trial court reversed the board's decision, finding the pencil could not be a "weapon" as defined in the district policy. Appeal reached the Commonwealth Court of Pennsylvania, which noted the rule was based on a state-law provision. The rule stated "a student shall not possess, handle or transmit a weapon while on any school property, while at any school-sponsored or approved activity or while walking or being transported in any manner to or from a school or school-sponsored or approved activity." The rule defined "weapon" to include "any knife, cutting instrument, cutting tool, explosive, mace, nunchaku, firearm, shotgun, rifle and any other tool, instrument or implement capable of inflicting serious bodily injury." The court found that when deciding whether an object was a "weapon," the inquiry focused on an object in isolation and considered its inherent capabilities. It found the district rule prohibited the mere possession of a weapon, providing a definition of "weapon." A pencil was not an object similar or comparable to the weapons listed in the rule. **While finding the student's conduct reprehensible, the court upheld the decision finding she did not possess a weapon as defined in the school rule.** *S.A. v. Pittsburgh Public School Dist.*, 160 A.3d 940 (Pa. Commw. Ct. 2017).

◆ Minnesota school officials conducted a random search of a high school with a drug-sniffing dog. After the dog alerted on a student's locker, a school liaison officer searched the locker and found a purse containing a three-inch hunting knife. The student said she put the knife in her purse after helping with chores on a friend's farm but later forgot about it. At a school board hearing, witnesses testified that the student was an outstanding scholar who participated in sports and mentoring programs. But the board voted to expel her for the last six weeks of the school year. The state commissioner of education affirmed the decision, and the student appealed to the state court of appeals. It found the state Pupil Fair Dismissal Act (PFDA) permits expulsions for willful conduct by a student. The court agreed with the student that she did not commit a willful violation of the board's weapons policy. It held the PFDA requires not just a violation of a school policy, but awareness by the student of the policy and a deliberate, conscious, intentional choice to violate the policy. She did not willfully violate the school policy by bringing the knife to school and not disclosing that the knife was in her locker after the lockdown and search began.

Appeal reached the Supreme Court of Minnesota. It held the PFDA requires a student to know of a school policy and make a deliberate, intentional decision to violate that policy before the student may be dismissed from school under the "willful violation" provision of the act. **In sum, the court found the school board did not explain how the student's accidental bringing of the knife to school constituted a willful violation of the school district's weapons policy.** As a result, the court found the school board's decision was not supported by substantial evidence. Last, the court affirmed the lower court's decision that the record lacked substantial evidence that the student had exposed anyone to actual or probable harm. *In re Expulsion of A.D. From United South Cent. Public Schools No. 2134*, 883 N.W.2d 251 (Minn. 2016).

◆ A California campus safety officer entered a classroom to ask a student about a stolen iPod. After the suspect denied knowing anything, the officer searched the bags of all students present. A small folding knife was found in a student's handbag, and it was turned over to the police. School administrators suspended the student pending an expulsion. In a federal court, she sued the security officer, principal, an assistant principal and the school district. In pretrial activity, the court found **there was reasonable suspicion that the stolen iPod was in the possession of a student in the classroom**. After the officer determined the original suspect did not have the item, the court held it was reasonable for him to conduct a limited search of other students in the classroom. The search was not intrusive, as the officer did not touch the student. Since case law did not put him on notice that the search for the iPod was prohibited, the court held he had qualified immunity. Among the student's many civil rights claims was that retaliation and reprisals by school administrators precluded her from gaining higher education financing, leading to economic damages in excess of $1 million. But the court found her assertions conclusory and without sufficient factual detail. **School officials did not violate the Constitution by giving the knife to the police.** A review of the complaint indicated only that her grades had fallen, and an administrator ordered her to pick up some trash. As a result, the court held the case should be dismissed. *Gallardo v. Hanford Joint Union School Dist.*, No. 1:12-cv-01612 GSA, 2015 WL 641657 (E.D. Cal. 2/13/15, 9th Cir. appeal dismissed, 3/1/16).

◆ A Michigan high school freshman had conflicts with a classmate. On a school day, she tweeted "stab stab stab. Going to stab stab stab you today to see your insides, ya ya ya." The classmate told an assistant vice principal (AVP) about the tweets. After investigating, the AVP obtained a written statement from another student who said the student had told her she planned to stab the classmate with a knife she had in a binder. The AVP called the student's mother. The next day, the AVP met with the student and her family. She told them of the charges without revealing the statements. The AVP suspended the student, and the board later met to consider expulsion. The student requested a closed session where she answered questions and submitted a statement from her psychologist. The board then voted for expulsion. The student sued the school district, board members and administrators. The case reached the U.S. Court of Appeals, Sixth Circuit, where the parent argued the suspension exceeded 10 days because the AVP made the suspension during their phone conversation.

The court found that even if the AVP had suspended the student by phone, there was no due process violation. **Students who are a continuing danger may be immediately removed from school.** The court found there had been no due process violation, regardless of whether the student had received witness statements. She received an adequate explanation of their contents to prepare her defense. All told, the student had received three opportunities to tell her story, hear the charges against her and present evidence. Rejecting all her arguments, the court held for the school district. *C.Y. v. Lakeview Public Schools*, 557 Fed.Appx. 426 (6th Cir. 2014).

◆ A 14-year-old California charter school student with attention deficit hyperactivity disorder (ADHD) brought a knife to his charter school and threatened others with it. He was dismissed from the school. In a state superior court, the student sought a special order (called a writ) declaring that the board did not provide him with a hearing as required by state Code of Civil Procedure Section 1094.5. He also said his knife did not meet applicable state education code definitions. The court denied the student's petition, finding the dismissal was proper based on his conduct. On appeal, the Court of Appeal of California rejected an argument that the knife was too short to meet a definition under state Education Code Section 48915.

According to the student, a "knife" had to meet each of the various descriptions in Section 48915. In the court's opinion, the characteristics described in Section 48915 were listed in the alternative. Proof of the court's interpretation could be found in the listing of both folding and fixed blades in the law. As the knife met Section 48915 definitions, the court held the student could not rely on the section to claim he was not in possession of a knife. Next, the court rejected the student's argument that the board order had to be set aside since it did not include any findings. Significantly, the court held the student was not entitled to an evidentiary hearing. There was a difference between a dismissal by a charter school and an expulsion under the education code. As charter schools were generally exempt from the laws governing school districts, **the court held state Education Code Section 48918 hearing requirements were inapplicable**. A dismissed charter school student could immediately enroll in another school. In fact, a letter to the parent from the charter school had advised her to enroll him in another school and had attached his transcripts to facilitate this effort. As the student was not entitled to a hearing, the court affirmed the judgment. *Scott B. v. Board of Trustees of Orange County High School of Arts*, 217 Cal.App.4th 117, 158 Cal.Rptr.3d 173 (Cal. Ct. App. 2013).

B. Possession of Drugs and Alcohol

◆ Mississippi's Supreme Court held the parent of a middle school student who was disciplined for a drug offense could not challenge hearing procedures that she claimed were in violation of his constitutional rights. The court found the parent did not raise her constitutional theory until after the lower court entered its judgment. She also did not provide notice to the state attorney general of her constitutional challenge. **The court stated that a party is not entitled to relief simply because he or she is unhappy with the judgment.** In prior cases, the court had barred constitutional challenges where a party failed to provide proper notice to the state attorney general. In this case, the notice was untimely. Further, the lower court did not mistakenly or accidentally omit an analysis of the constitutional issue. Instead, the issue was not properly before the lower court, as the parent's motion came after the court entered its final judgment. Declining to review the lower court's order, the court affirmed this part of the judgment. Since other aspects of the case were not properly before the supreme court, the lower court's order returning the case to the disciplinary hearing committee for a new hearing was affirmed. *Harbour v. Tupelo Public School Dist.*, No. 2018-CA-00219-SCT, 2019 WL 2461250 (Miss. 6/13/19).

◆ A District of Columbia student did not convince a court that charter school officials had to re-enroll him after he was expelled for a marijuana offense. Because the student had learning and emotional disabilities, the charter school had to provide him with an interim alternative placement for the remainder of the school year. But the charter school complied with this requirement. If the student had no access to services from the local educational agency (LEA), the school would still be responsible for providing him with a free appropriate public education. The school was not obligated to assist the student with his current placement efforts. Federal regulations referred to an LEA's obligation to provide access to education during the same school year in which discipline occurs. The court found that by implication, this indicated that **a school's obligation to a student in a particular academic year following discipline does not automatically extend to a subsequent school year**. Next, the court disposed of the student's Fifth Amendment argument. Since the student did not identify an individual or government entity that was a policymaker, he could not pursue his constitutional rights claims. Last, the court found the student was unable to demonstrate any bad faith or gross misjudgment by the school officials that might create Section 504 liability. As a result, the court dismissed the case. *D.P. v. Washington Leadership Academy Public Charter School*, No. CV 18-2868, 2019 WL 1317235 (D.D.C. 3/22/19).

◆ Indiana school officials accused a student of using a high school computer to sell marijuana. After he was suspended pending an expulsion, his parent requested a formal hearing. She noted a student handbook provision declaring that students may be represented at hearings by parents and/or counsel. At a hearing, the school excluded the student's attorney. A hearing examiner decided to expel the student for several months. When the board held another hearing, the student's attorney was again excluded.

Following the board's decision to expel the student, the family petitioned a state court for review. The court upheld the board's decision and the student appealed to the state court of appeals. On appeal, the court noted that Indiana Code § 20-33-8-21 limits judicial review of school board expulsion cases to the issue of whether the board acted without following state-law procedures. In this case, **the student did not raise any issue of compliance with relevant provisions of state law**. He did not argue that the minimum statutory requirements included a right to have an attorney present at a hearing. The court commented that schools should comply with their own handbooks. It found the policy's "unartfully bare reference to counsel opens itself to interpretation." But it refused to find the school board's interpretation inconsistent with the handbook provision, and upheld the judgment for the board. *S.B. v. Randolph Eastern School Corp.*, No. 18A-MI-1575, 2018 WL 6441623 (Ind. Ct. App. 12/10/18).

◆ A group of Illinois parochial school students said the school had a random drug-testing policy that resulted in many false positive results. One of the students was white, while the other six were African-American. Several years prior to the events leading to the lawsuit, the school received a federal grant of $149,831 for its drug testing program. The school contracted with a private laboratory to conduct drug tests. Student admission contracts stated that students agreed to participate in the drug-testing program. When selected for testing, students provided hair samples, which were sent to the laboratory. Each of the students in the lawsuit claimed to have had hair testing that yielded a positive result for use of cocaine. In almost every case, the students said later testing (usually conducted by a clinic of the student's choice) yielded negative results for cocaine use. Some of these tests were done by urinalysis while some tested hair. When the students filed a federal action against the school, they charged the school guidance counselor who administered the drug-testing program with accusing some of the parents of being drug dealers. It was also claimed that she stood by the private testing contractor used by the school, despite disputed test results.

In some cases, students were required to submit to additional testing. In at least two cases, students were required to withdraw from the school in lieu of expulsion. The court held for the school, finding no support for the claims. On appeal, the U.S. Court of Appeals, Seventh Circuit, noted the lower court's findings that nothing supported a plausible case for race discrimination. There was no claim that the testing of hair (as opposed to blood or urine) had a racially disproportionate impact. Nor was it claimed that the school's contractor even knew the race of persons whose hair was being tested for drug use. Nothing indicated the school guidance counselor should be liable for constitutional violations, as the families did not show she was "a state actor." Further, the court found claims arising under Title VI of the Civil Rights Act and 42 U.S.C. § 1981 could not succeed since there was no claim of intentional race discrimination. There was no claim by the families that students were systematically disadvantaged based on race. One of the students who had been expelled was white. The court found the guidance counselor and her supervisors were faced with conflicting test results. **It found no racial motive, but only "confidence" in the testing program and the authenticity of the contractor's testing procedures.** *L.P. v. Marian Catholic High School*, 852 F.3d 690 (7th Cir. 2017).

◆ A Louisiana student said school officials interrogated him and forced him to unlock his parent's cell phone without notice to the parent. His parent filed a federal court complaint against the school board. In pretrial activity, the court held punitive damages were unavailable in a case arising under 42 U.S.C. § 1983. A government entity such as a school board is not subject to Section 1983 liability unless there is a violation of a federally protected right that can be attributable to the enforcement of a municipal policy, practice or decision of a final municipal policymaker. In this case, the court found the student did not identify a specific board policy. Although he attempted to bring a state law claim against the board for violation of the state's pupil discipline law, the court found he did not identify which provision of law the board was charged with violating. **Based on the student's failure to make specific charges against the school officials, the court dismissed all the claims.** *Decossas v. St. Tammany Parish School Board*, No. 16-3786, 2017 WL 1133114 (E.D. La. 3/27/17).

◆ A North Carolina student was arrested for charges of possessing a knife on school grounds, theft, possession of less than an ounce of marijuana and possession of drug paraphernalia. According to the student's parent, school officials did not provide any kind of hearing, but he served a 10-day out-of-school suspension for the incident. Almost three months later, he was searched on consecutive school days by a school official. A small amount of marijuana was found during the second search. Another 10-day suspension was imposed on the student and he was placed in an alternative learning program (ALP) for the rest of the academic year. Although the parent tried to appeal the discipline, a district administrator informed her that there was no right of appeal. A hearing was later granted but the student did not attend it because the board sought to limit the proceeding to 15 minutes. The family filed a federal court complaint against the board. After weeding out many of the student's 17 claims, the court focused on his due process claims. It noted that the first suspension was for 10 days. Under North Carolina law, a student is not entitled to appeal a principal's decision to impose a short-term suspension. However, the student correctly argued that he was entitled to discuss the short-term suspension with a school administrator under *Goss v. Lopez*, 419 U.S. 565 (1975). There was evidence that school officials did not provide the student with the opportunity to tell his side of the story when being arrested and removed from the school by the police. While he was not entitled to a hearing before the school board or superintendent, the court found it was plausible that he was not told of the school discipline when being taken into police custody. **As a result, the court held the student was now entitled to an opportunity for an informal hearing to present his side of the story.** On the other hand, neither state law nor *Goss* provided him with a right to a hearing to consider an ALP assignment. The court found the student received all the process he was due concerning the second incident. A North Carolina law eliminates any right to appeal to a local board regarding a disciplinary ALP placement, so long as the student can make timely progress toward graduation and grade promotion. *Clodfelter v. Alexander County Board of Educ.*, No. 5:16-CV-00021-RLV-DCK, 2016 WL 7365183 (W.D.N.C. 12/19/16).

◆ A California high school student was sent to detention at least 14 times for tardiness and other offenses. At a disciplinary meeting, he admitted smoking marijuana before coming to school. A school administrator found he was a danger to persons or property or threatened to disrupt the instructional process. She ordered his transfer to a continuation school for the rest of the school year. The student's appeal later reached the Court of Appeal of California. It held state law provided for involuntary transfers to continuation schools "only when other means fail to bring about pupil improvement." But the word "only" was not synonymous with "all," and the court rejected the argument that "all" other means of correction had to be exhausted before an involuntary student transfer. While the student had a fundamental interest in a public school education, the court found this interest was not at stake in an involuntary transfer case.

In contrast to an expulsion or suspension, the court found involuntary transfer to a continuation school did not deny access to public education. The court held the disciplinary meeting complied with state law requirements by offering the student and his parents a chance to inspect and challenge documentary evidence, question witnesses and present evidence. *Nathan G. v. Clovis Unified School Dist.*, 224 Cal.App.4th 1393, 169 Cal.Rptr.3d 588 (Cal. Ct. App. 2014).

◆ A California school administrator suggested a "sting operation" to trap a 14-year-old student suspected of selling drugs at school. Administrators agreed to a plan that involved arranging for a 12-year-old student to buy drugs from the 14-year-old. But they did not contact the student's parents or law enforcement officials. A school administrator gave the 12-year-old a marked $5 bill and after several attempts, the student was able to buy some marijuana from the older student. Later, the 12-year-old student's parents sued the school district and officials in a state court. A trial was held at which testimony revealed the 12-year-old was still in fear of retaliation by the seller. A jury found he had severe emotional distress due to the conduct of administrators. The jury awarded him $1 million for past and future noneconomic losses, plus $15,250 for tutoring and other economic losses.

On appeal, the Court of Appeal of California rejected the school district's argument that misconduct by the family's lawyer justified a new trial. Even if the lawyer's statements had been improper, the court found they were unlikely to have any effect on the verdict. **In the court's view, there was sufficient evidence to support the damage award.** A psychologist who examined the student found he had post-traumatic stress disorder. The court explained that the standard for reversing a jury award required a showing that the jury was inflamed by passion or prejudice so as to "shock the conscience." There was no such showing of this here. A comparison of awards from other cases was of no value, and the court upheld the jury verdict for the student. *Roe v. Los Angeles Unified School Dist.*, No. B240654, 2013 WL 6451773 (Cal. Ct. App. 12/9/13).

C. Employees

In *Metz v. Bethlehem Area School Dist.*, this page, the court relied on *New Jersey v. T.L.O.*, 469 U.S. 325 (1985), the leading Supreme Court case on student searches, in the drug testing case of a Pennsylvania teacher.

◆ An Ohio teacher began exchanging text messages and Snapchats with a high school senior a few weeks before she was scheduled to graduate. They eventually began meeting in isolated locations, where the student later said they "made out." When their relationship was reported to the school administration, the teacher was suspended. An investigation uncovered text messages indicating the student and teacher had kissed in isolated locations "many times" prior to her graduation. The state board of education approved the school district's recommendation to terminate all contracts with the teacher based on insubordination, conduct unbecoming a professional and pressuring the student to be dishonest with law enforcement officers.

Following a hearing, a state hearing officer found the teacher engaged in conduct unbecoming an educator. The state board declared him permanently ineligible to apply for any license it issued. Later, an Ohio court approved the state board's decision. On appeal, the Court of Appeals of Ohio found the teacher admitted exchanging many flirtatious texts with the student prior to her graduation. Substantial evidence supported the state board's findings. Although the teacher raised other arguments, the court rejected them. **Finding his first text message to the student indicated he had crossed appropriate student-teacher boundaries, the court upheld the board's decision.** *Bollinger v. State of Ohio, Dep't of Educ.*, No. 9-18-07, 2018 -Ohio- 3714 (Ohio Ct. App. 9/17/18; appeal not allowed, 154 Ohio St.3d 1481, 1/23/19).

◆ Finding Texas law did not permit the full expunction (erasure) of all the arrest and prosecution records of a teacher for online solicitation of a former student, a state court held parts of an order describing her underlying conduct were not subject to expunction. After reviewing the relevant Texas law, the court found a person placed under arrest is entitled to have all records and files relating to the arrest expunged. The court held this language plainly limited the scope of expunction to "the arrest." The court held the expunction statute is not intended to eradicate all evidence of wrongful conduct, but only to prevent the record of a wrongful arrest from clouding a person's reputation for life. In this case, **the Texas Education Agency (TEA) had records pertaining to conduct taking place almost five years before by the teacher's arrest for online solicitation**. In the court's view, the lower court had correctly held the TEA could retain the records with certain information redacted. The parts of the records describing the teacher's underlying conduct were not subject to expunction as they were not "records and files relating to the arrest." *Texas Educ. Agency v. H.C.V.*, 575 S.W.3d 30 (Tex. Ct. App. 2019).

◆ Charges of misconduct were brought against a New York teacher for operating a motor vehicle while intoxicated and in possession of a loaded pistol for which he did not have a license. A hearing officer found the misconduct was incompatible with the standards required to be seen as a positive role model for students. After the school district complied with an order to terminate the teacher's employment, he appealed to a New York trial court. The court denied the petition and dismissed the case. On appeal before the New York Supreme Court, Appellate Division, the teacher argued he was subjected to an added stigma under the circumstances of the case that required the hearing officer to require the district to prove its case by a preponderance of the evidence. When reviewing compulsory arbitration proceedings in education, the court was required to accept the credibility determinations of the hearing officer, even if there was conflicting evidence and room for choice. In this case, the court found the hearing officer's decision had evidentiary support and was not arbitrary and capricious.

Further, the teacher received adequate due process. He received notice of the charges that was reasonably specific in light of all the circumstances and allowed him to prepare an adequate defense. Last, **the court found the penalty of employment termination was not irrational or shocking to one's sense of fairness in view of the facts in this case**. As the teacher's remaining arguments lacked merit, the court affirmed the decision terminating his employment. *Johnson II v. Riverhead Cent. School Dist.*, 166 A.D.3d 880, 88 N.Y.S.3d 434 (N.Y. App. Div. 2018).

◆ A Pennsylvania teacher was involved in a child custody dispute. His school district received a copy of a letter from the opposing counsel in the dispute which indicated the teacher had tested positive for cocaine use. A district human resources director met with the teacher and a union representative and stated that the teacher had to submit to a drug test. If he failed to take a drug test, his job would be in jeopardy. The teacher refused to take a drug test and again refused when the district sent him a letter requiring him to do so based upon reasonable suspicion of drug use. Five days after refusing the first test, the teacher submitted to urinalysis drug testing, which confirmed the presence of cocaine. The district notified him of a hearing and informed him he would be discharged for willful neglect of duties and immoral conduct. At a school board hearing, the director testified that the teacher had shown hostility toward him during their meeting and indifference to his offense. During his hearing, the teacher admitted that after refusing to take the first test, he used cocaine at a Super Bowl party. This was one day after the letter instructing him to undergo drug testing.

The board terminated the teacher's employment. Arguing that the drug test was unconstitutional, he appealed to a state court. After the court affirmed the judgment, the teacher appealed to the Commonwealth Court of Pennsylvania. **The court found public school teachers hold safety-sensitive jobs and can be compelled to submit to drug testing based on "reasonable suspicion."** This standard is less demanding than the probable cause standard but requires more than a "hunch" of criminal activity. Information from an informant may supply reasonable suspicion if certain factors are satisfied. The court found the district had reasonable suspicion to require the drug testing in this case, as it proved the information from the attorney's letter was reliable. Moreover, the teacher's "cavalier attitude" at his meeting with a district official supported the suspicion that he used cocaine. Finding reasonable suspicion to conduct the drug test, the court held the teacher's constitutional challenge failed. *Metz v. Bethlehem Area School Dist.*, 177 A.3d 384 (Pa. Commw. Ct. 2018).

◆ An Alabama band teacher was fired for leaving a pistol in his locked office while he accompanied the band to a competition in Georgia. At a board hearing, the teacher argued his excellent record justified a lesser penalty. But the board voted for termination based on violation of its weapons policy. A hearing officer later found the teacher violated the board's policy and that the board had authority to discharge him. While finding the teacher's exemplary service record justified a lesser, the hearing officer declined to reduce the sanction. He felt the state Students First Act of 2011 did not authorize him to modify a school board's decision.

After the state court of civil appeals upheld the decision, the case reached the Supreme Court of Alabama. The court held a deferential arbitrary-and-capricious standard of review applied to termination challenges under the Students First Act. Unlike the appeals court, the supreme court held the arbitrary-and-capricious standard permitted a hearing officer to impose a lesser penalty than a board of education, if the officer found the sanction imposed by the board was arbitrary and capricious. In 2015, **the court returned the case to the hearing officer with instructions to review the sanction that had been imposed by the board of education under the arbitrary-and-capricious standard of review**. *Lambert v. Escambia County Board of Educ.*, 199 So.3d 761 (Ala. 2015).

When the case returned to the hearing officer, he found the board did not sufficiently consider the evidence in deciding to dismiss the teacher instead of suspending him. The board appealed to the court of civil appeals. It found the supreme court has held that review of a board's decision must be extremely deferential. **The Students First Act expressed an intent to restore the primary authority and responsibility for maintaining a competent educational workforce with school boards.** If a board has examined the relevant data and stated a satisfactory explanation, the court found its decision not arbitrary. It rejected the teacher's argument that the board failed to articulate a reason for dismissing him instead of suspending him. There was evidence that the board considered the unintentional nature of the violation, the lack of harm to students, the teacher's excellent record and other factors. Finding the hearing officer did not properly defer to the board under the arbitrary and capricious standard, the court upheld its decision. *Lambert v. Escambia County Board of Educ.*, No. 2150548, 2016 WL 5338669 (Ala. Civ. App. 9/23/16; Ala. cert. denied, 11/18/16).

◆ Nevada police arrested a teacher at his home for marijuana possession. He maintained the substance was for medical purposes, but he pleaded guilty to an offense and was placed on probation. His employing school district began dismissal proceedings based on immorality, conviction of a felony involving moral turpitude, and any cause that constituted grounds for license revocation. The teacher's application for unemployment benefits was denied by the state employment security division (ESD) based on his guilty plea. The ESD found the school district had discharged him for "workplace misconduct," which disqualified him from eligibility for benefits. After an unsuccessful petition to a trial court, the teacher appealed to the Supreme Court of Nevada. The court found the teacher had not been convicted in his criminal proceedings. Instead, the proceedings were put on hold to allow him to complete his probationary period and avoid the entry of a conviction. Section 453.3363(4) of the state code specified that a discharge and dismissal of this type was not a conviction for purposes of employment, civil rights or any statute or license, or for any other purpose.

When the ESD denied benefits to the teacher, he was midway through his probationary period, so a dismissal and discharge of the criminal case had yet to occur. Moreover, the court held an employer could not use a guilty plea to establish misconduct-based grounds for termination for the purpose of denying unemployment compensation during a probationary period. The school district had relied on the guilty plea as grounds for both terminating his employment and establishing that it was misconduct-based, making him ineligible for benefits. In addition, the school district had changed its stated grounds for termination upon the teacher's entry of a guilty plea. Its amended notice of termination recited that he had been actually convicted for possession of a controlled substance in violation of state law. **The school district had improperly equated the teacher's guilty plea with a felony conviction, and the court found further review by the ESD was necessary.** An employee's termination, even if based on misconduct, did not necessarily require disqualification under the Nevada unemployment compensation law. The court held the ESD would have to determine whether the school district proved the teacher had committed disqualifying misconduct. In doing so, it would not be able to consider the guilty plea. *Hohenstein v. Nevada Employment Security Division*, 346 P.3d 365 (Nev. 2015).

◆ A Massachusetts court affirmed the denial of unemployment benefits to a cook who was fired for repeatedly refusing to submit to a drug/alcohol test. Although the cook denied being under the influence of alcohol or drugs, two school officials observed evidence of slurred speech, inability to control her limbs and incoherent rambling. In addition, the cook had a prior record of poor attendance and threatening behavior toward students. The court rejected the cook's arguments that she was undergoing a "stress attack" and that she did not understand her contract required her to undergo drug and alcohol testing. *Dottin v. City of Cambridge*, 87 Mass.App.Ct. 1103, 24 N.E.3d 1060 (Table), 2015 WL 264108 (Mass. App. Ct. 1/22/15).

D. Fighting and Violence

In *Boyd v. Jefferson County Public Schools*, this chapter, a Kentucky court held school officials did not violate a student's rights by detaining her and investigating charges that she harassed and threated a classmate, then provoked a fight with her. The court held school officials acted reasonably.

◆ A Delaware charter school student claimed a classmate assaulted, battered and head-butted him while they were at school, causing permanent injuries. According to a state-court complaint, the school acted with reckless indifference to the student's rights and engaged in willful, wanton and reckless conduct in allowing the assault. In pretrial activity, the school claimed the student did not plead enough facts to avoid immunity under the Delaware State Torts Claims Act. The court explained that the duty to supervise students is "ministerial" and thus unprotected by immunity. On the other hand, the manner and methods of student supervision are "discretionary" and are entitled to immunity. As the school argued, the complaint did not assert enough facts to overcome state-law discretionary immunity. In fact, the student did not even identify the classmate he accused of the assault. The court held that in negligence cases, parties cannot rely on conclusory statements and must assert enough facts to overcome sovereign immunity. In this case, **the complaint did not assert that the school had prior knowledge that the student or others had been attacked by the classmate or failed to take reasonable efforts to prevent the incident**.

The court held the complaint did not indicate reckless indifference or a malicious intent by the school. It found no facts showing that the school failed to supervise students or did not exercise due care to protect them or provide for their safety. Next, the court found the student did not plead sufficient facts to show gross and wanton negligence by the school, as he did not show an extreme departure from the ordinary standard of care, or conscious indifference toward his rights. Wanton negligence has been defined as conduct so unreasonable and dangerous that a person should know that imminent harm is likely. Next, **the court held the student did not show the school acted with reckless indifference to his rights regarding the incident**. Although he asked for permission to continue seeking information that might lend support to his claims, the court declined this request. It noted that the pretrial information gathering process known as discovery should not be used as a substitute for matters that should have been included in the complaint. Finding the school was entitled to immunity, the court dismissed the case. *Ward v. Gateway Charter School*, No. N17C-08-355 RRC, 2018 WL 3655864 (Del. Super. Ct. 7/18/18).

◆ A Georgia student was disciplined for fighting with a classmate on school grounds. A school secretary who saw the fight said the classmate "was definitely the aggressor." The student's mother (who worked at the school) stated that the student tried to get away from the classmate. But she said the classmate insisted upon fighting her. Surveillance video corroborated statements that the classmate insisted on fighting and lunged at the student after she tried to retreat. Despite this evidence, a hearing officer found the student violated a school rule by "being involved in a fight on the school grounds." The student appealed from a school board order requiring her expulsion (or an alternative school placement).

A state court reversed the board's decision. On appeal, the court of Appeals of Georgia affirmed the judgment. It applied a criminal law on self-defense in finding the student was not guilty of the school disciplinary charges. When the case reached the state supreme court, it found the burden of proof from the criminal self-defense law cited by the lower court did not apply in a civil action. In failing to apply a civil law standard, the lower courts committed error. **The civil standard of "a preponderance of the evidence" applies in school discipline cases, not the criminal law standard of "beyond a reasonable doubt."** As the lower courts found, the record did not show that the board considered the student's self-defense arguments. Instead, it merely found her "guilty for being involved in a fight." The court could not tell from the record whether the board had actually considered the self-defense argument. In the court's view, "simply being involved in a fight is insufficient to constitute a disciplinary infraction" if a student acts in self-defense. *Henry County Board of Educ. v. S.G.*, 301 Ga. 794, 804 S.E.2d 427 (Ga. 2017).

III. TRUANCY, JUVENILE JUSTICE AND CHILD PROTECTION

A. Truancy

Students have argued that failure by school officials to enforce truancy policies should result in school liability for off-campus injuries. But in *Collette v. Tolleson Unified School Dist. No. 214*, 203 Ariz. 359, 54 P.3d 828 (Ariz. Ct. App. 2002), the court held a school district had no duty to prevent students from leaving campus. Similarly, the Supreme Court of Florida has held that a school's general duty to supervise students does not create a duty to supervise the movements of all students at all times.

◆ After an Arkansas parent repeatedly failed to get her children to school and refused to follow through with assistance offered to help her obtain housing and services for her children, a family court terminated her parental rights. Following a series of hearings, the court found the parent had no housing, income or transportation and had made no progress on her case plan in the prior 16 months. Significantly, the court found she did not remedy the cause of removal of the children from her custody. In the court's view, the school district had gone above and beyond expectations by providing curbside pickup for the students. But the parent did not accept this service. **Termination of her rights was found in the best interest of the children, who were in a stable placement with a foster mother.**

On appeal, the Court of Appeals of Arkansas held the Arkansas Department of Human Services (DHS) showed termination of the parent's rights was in the best interests of the children. DHS witnesses testified that she declined housing and bus transportation for the children and kept up her relationship with a boyfriend in violation of court orders restraining him from contact with the family. As the evidence indicated the DHS sought protections for the children and terminated the parent's rights only after it became clear that services were not helping her, the court affirmed the judgment terminating her parental rights. *Lopez v. Arkansas Dep't of Human Services*, 2018 Ark. App. 532 (Ark. Ct. App. 2018).

◆ During the 2014-15 school year, a Kentucky student accumulated 13 unexcused absences. Rather than face a petition for educational neglect, the parents withdrew him from school and placed him in a private school. The next school year, the parents re-enrolled their child in the public school system, where he resumed his pattern of unexcused absences and tardies. After the student reached seven unexcused absences or tardies, the county board of education petitioned a family court for a finding of educational neglect. In family court proceedings, the parents explained that most of their son's absences and tardies were due to sleeping in and/or behavior issues. They noted the proceeding was actually brought under the compulsory attendance laws to adjudicate their child's status, and for that reason was not truly a neglect petition. Under the parents' theory, the compulsory attendance law did not authorize a finding of educational neglect. The family court held the petition supported a finding of educational neglect.

Although the court expressed concern about "the parents' failure to allow [the] Child to face the consequences of his action," it did not order his removal from his parents' custody. Instead, the court ordered that he have no more unexcused absences, and that his school only accept a doctor's statement for excused absences. The parents appealed to the Court of Appeals of Kentucky, which found "one of the legislative purposes of the dependency, neglect and abuse statutes is to protect a child's fundamental right to educational instruction." Finding the dependency, neglect and abuse statutes permit a petition for educational neglect, the court held the family court was authorized to consider the case. While the compulsory attendance law was not directly applicable in a petition for educational neglect, the dependency, neglect and abuse statutes incorporated a "habitual truant" definition. In this case, the court found the evidence showed the student had a pattern of unexcused school absences and tardies, which the parents failed to justify. **As a result, the court held the family court was authorized to consider the petition and to find the parents neglected their child's educational needs.** *M.B. and K.B. v. Warren County Board of Educ.*, No. 2016-CA-001761-ME, 2018 WL 1773515 (Ky. Ct. App. 4/13/18).

◆ A 15-year-old Massachusetts' student with autism and a severe bladder condition had anxiety disorder, obsessive-compulsive disorder (OCD) and post-traumatic stress disorder. Because of her bladder condition, the student had a great deal of trouble toileting, and she needed to use the restroom frequently, often for hours at a time. Her bladder condition was compounded by her cognitive and emotional disorders. Due to her autism and OCD, the student had "obsessive rituals," was intolerant of public settings and could not use public lavatories. Even with a shortened school day and home-based services, the student accumulated enough absences to trigger the habitual truancy provisions of the state Children Requiring Assistance Statute (CRA) statute. A few months after she enrolled, the school district filed a CRA petition. After a hearing, a judge adjudicated her a child requiring assistance. According to the judge, the student's many absences were "actions taken by the child not to attend school."

On appeal, the Supreme Judicial Court of Massachusetts explained that a CRA proceeding may be initiated when a student "willfully fails to attend school for more than eight school days in a quarter." **A child may only be proven to be habitually truant when a petition is proven "beyond a reasonable doubt."** Next, the court found the CRA statute's habitual truancy provision requires "purposeful conduct by the child." When a child's repeated failure to attend school arises from reasons indicating delinquent behavior, it is considered "willful" under the CRA statute. In this case, the court held the evidence did not show beyond a reasonable doubt that the student willfully failed to attend school. Since the record did not support a finding that the student willfully failed to attend school, the court returned the case to the juvenile court for an order dismissing the CRA petition. *Millis Public Schools v. M.P.*, 478 Mass. 767 (Mass. 2018).

◆ Alabama's Juvenile Justice Act required the Alabama State Board of Education (ASBE) to publish a definition of the term "truancy." The term was one of several for which a juvenile court could declare a child in need of supervision. An ASBE rule declared that a student with seven unexcused absences within a school year was "truant" for the purposes of a juvenile petition. However, a provision of the ASBE rule allowed any local education agency to adopt a policy more rigorous than the state policy. Two local boards of education established policies that permitted the filing of a truancy petition if a student had only five instances of truancy. After attendance officers for the local boards filed truancy petitions against two students for habitual truancy, the students challenged the ability of the boards to create policies defining truancy to include a child with less than seven unexcused absences in a school year. Although the students had only six unexcused absences each, the court found both had committed truancy and were in need of state supervision, treatment, rehabilitation, care and protection. The students were placed on probation for six months and ordered to perform 25 hours each of community services. They appealed to the Court of Civil Appeals of Alabama, which consolidated the cases.

The court found no evidence that either student had been absent without an excuse for seven days, and thus no support for finding them habitually truant. In the court's view, the legislature delegated the task of defining the term "habitually truant from school" to the ASBE. **No statutory language authorized the ASBE to delegate the duty of defining "habitually truant from school" to local education boards.** As there was no evidence that the students violated state law, they could not be found in need of supervision. *K.L.M. v. State of Alabama*, 168 So.3d 1264 (Ala. Ct. App. 2015).

◆ Massachusetts high school officials assigned a student to Saturday school for repeated tardiness. He was then suspended for failing to attend Saturday school. In a state court, the student claimed his due process rights were violated by this detention. The court held for the school officials, and appeal reached the Court of Appeals of Massachusetts. It found no violation of his state or federal due process rights. Instead, the court described the Saturday school assignment as "relatively minor punishment" for violation of school disciplinary rules set forth in the student handbook.

The punishment was held "directly, clearly and rationally related to the offense." Next, **the court found no merit to a claim that the discipline violated fundamental family rights to personal privacy and illegally interfered with parental rights and prerogatives**. A claim that punishment invaded privacy rights by demanding a "specific" reason for tardiness was held "specious." It was sufficient that the student handbook required a reason for the tardiness. There was no due process violation, as the Saturday assignments complied with the student handbook. The student received a thorough explanation of the charges and an opportunity to be heard. As the disciplinary process had been conducted with basic fairness, the court held for the town. *Doe v. Town of Weston*, 85 Mass.App.Ct. 1102, 3 N.E.3d 616 (Table), 2014 WL 695743 (Mass. Ct. App. 2/6/14).

◆ A Wyoming student missed 36 days of school over four months. Thirty of the absences were unexcused and he was failing his classes. The student's mother did not respond to letters and personal visits from a state department of family services (DFS) social worker, and the county filed a juvenile petition alleging the student was a neglected child. At an initial hearing, the mother appeared and denied the charges. The court ordered the student to remain in her custody under DFS supervision and to complete a summer education program. At a later hearing, the court charged the mother with a misdemeanor for neglecting the student by failing to provide an adequate education. On appeal, the mother argued the juvenile court had improperly applied child protection laws instead of the state compulsory attendance laws. Under this theory, the mother argued the school had to give her notice and counseling before the case could be referred to a prosecutor.

The Supreme Court of Wyoming held the compulsory education laws did not apply in this case. Instead, the case arose under state child protective services statutes. As the state argued, **the DFS and prosecuting attorney fully complied with the child protective services statutes in this juvenile neglect proceeding**. State compulsory attendance laws addressed the duties and did not govern DFS cases. In this case, the mother received proper notice and an opportunity to be heard under the child protection statutes. Since the mandatory requirements of the state compulsory attendance laws did not depend on school district counseling or written notices to a parent concerning unexcused absences, the court held for the state. *In re JM*, 2014 WY 114, 334 P.3d 568 (Wyo. 2014).

◆ A Nebraska student missed 48.14 school days during a school year. A school guidance director sent her family letters explaining that state law banned more than five absences per quarter or 20 days in a school year for any reason. The school requested medical records to assess whether the absences were excused by a serious illness. Records showed the student had been sick, but two statements indicated she was to return to school. No meeting was ever held among the parents and school officials to discuss an attendance plan. But the school referred the case to the county attorney, who filed a petition for habitual truancy from school. A juvenile court found the student was habitually truant. On appeal, the Supreme Court of Nebraska noted that state law permitted a school attendance officer to make a report to the county attorney if a child was absent more than 20 days per year, even if the absences were excused. **Noncompliance with the compulsory education statutes without first being excused by a school established truancy and created juvenile court jurisdiction.**

The student's noncompliance with the compulsory education statutes had been proven. The court found evidence to overcome the student's claim that her due process rights had been violated. The school sent her family many letters before taking action, and the county attorney's office also wrote to the family regarding possible prosecution. Like the trial court, the supreme court rejected the student's argument that the school had to provide the services described in the compulsory education statutes before she could be found truant. **The court rejected the student's claim that juvenile court authority was premised on school compliance with Nebraska compulsory attendance statutes.** Since compulsory attendance laws imposed no preconditions on juvenile court jurisdiction, the district did not have to comply with the services described in the laws before the proceeding was initiated. As a result, the court held for the state. *In re Interest of Samantha C.*, 287 Neb. 644, 843 N.W.3d 665 (Neb. App. 2014).

B. Special Education Students

A federal regulation at 34 C.F.R. Part 300.535(a) explains that special education protections do not shield students who commit crimes or juvenile offenses from law enforcement efforts. No federal law prohibits an agency from reporting a crime committed by a child with a disability to appropriate authorities or prevents state law enforcement and judicial authorities from exercising their responsibilities with regard to the application of federal and state law to crimes committed by a child with a disability.

◆ Delaware school officials violated a student's due process rights during expulsion proceedings for fighting a classmate. In reaching this decision, a state court focused on the school's failure to make witnesses available for cross-examination at his expulsion hearing. A state superior court noted that courts do not overturn school board decisions unless they are contrary to law, not supported by substantial evidence or are arbitrary or capricious. Moreover, **a board's disciplinary decision will be upheld unless the punishment was so disproportionate to the offense as to be shocking to one's sense of fairness**. Although the expulsion report included statements from the principal and two witnesses, these persons did not testify at the hearing and were not made available for cross-examination. The court held this was "fundamentally unfair and a violation of due process." Next, the court held the decision to expel the student was arbitrary and capricious.

The school board relied on a code provision that applied to out-of-school criminal conduct. As the incident took place in school, the court held the expulsion was not supported by the evidence. It held the expulsion was so disproportionate to the offense as to be shocking to one's sense of fairness. Finding the board's decision-making process was not rational, the court held for the student. *Board of Educ. of Smyrna School Dist. v. E.D.*, No. N18A-03-001 ALR, 2018 WL 6566754 (Del. Super. Ct. 12/11/18).

◆ Pennsylvania school officials violated federal special education laws by expelling a student with Crohn's disease for misconduct and not finding him eligible for an IEP, according to the Third Circuit Court of Appeals. At age six, the student was diagnosed with Crohn's disease, which causes abdominal pain, diarrhea, fatigue, weight loss and malnutrition. His school performance was generally strong through grade six, but his behavior and academics worsened significantly in grade seven. The school district created a Section 504 plan allowing the student accommodations including an "any time pass" for access to a lavatory or the nurse's office. In grade ten, the student was disciplined for trying to leave school grounds during school hours. When he was threatened with expulsion, his parents filed a due process complaint. The court found he needed specially designed instruction and that homebound instruction was insufficient for him. For this reason, **the school district should have investigated whether his problems stemmed from his debilitating disease**. In sum, the court held for the student, holding that the district violated its federal special education child-find duty and Section 504 of the Rehabilitation Act. *Culley v. Cumberland Valley School Dist.*, 758 Fed.Appx. 301 (3d Cir. 2018).

◆ A California student pleaded guilty to misdemeanor theft and marijuana charges and was placed on probation. Within four months, he was charged with five sexual offenses against his nine-year-old niece. The student's probation was revoked, and he admitted to one count of lewd conduct. The next year, he was found unsupervised in the presence of children under 13. After admitting failure to enter a treatment program, the student was ordered to juvenile detention for 77 days and then to his mother's custody under supervision. But his probation was revoked due to absences or tardiness at school and other counts. Following revocation of his probation, the student was ordered into a "level A" placement. On appeal, the Court of Appeal of California held the student had forfeited his claim that he had special needs because he failed to show he had an IEP.

While a report regarding his sexual crimes stated he had once had an IEP, his mother said he received passing grades and was "not a special education student." Despite evidence that the student had a specific learning disability, a later study reported his only identified educational need was English as a Second Language. At his juvenile disposition, the court found no IEP had been established. As a result, **the court had found the student was not an individual with special needs**. But the student correctly argued that the juvenile court should not have ordered him to pay $20 for each drug test. The costs of required testing cannot be made a condition of probation. *In re Jose G.*, No. C076503, 2015 WL 3814292 (Cal. Ct. App. 6/19/15).

◆ A sixth-grade Philadelphia student died from an asthma attack. According to a complaint against her school district, her teacher, principal and other staff knew of her chronic asthma. On the morning of the student's death, she told her teacher she was having trouble breathing. The teacher responded that no nurse was on duty and that she "should be calm." Although her condition worsened, the complaint alleged nobody contacted emergency medical aid or took her to the hospital. It was asserted that she was kept at school despite having reported that she could not breathe. Later in the day, the student was driven home and then taken to a hospital. On the way, she suffered a respiratory arrest. Emergency workers and hospital staff were unable to revive the student. A medical examiner declared her cause of death to be acute exacerbation of asthma. In pretrial activity, the court refused to dismiss claims against the school district. **There was evidence that the student was kept at school and denied medical care or permission to take medication.** As an intentional violation of rights was asserted, the court denied the district's request for a pretrial ruling. A claim for deprivation of life and liberty was not dismissed, as facts were alleged to support a state-created danger claim. Since willful misconduct was alleged, the court denied the district's request for state law immunity. *Estate of Massey v. City of Philadelphia*, 118 F.Supp.3d 679 (E.D. Pa. 2015).

C. Child Protection

In *Dole v. Huntington Union Free School Dist.*, 699 Fed.Appx. 85 (2d Cir. 2017), the court held that where school officials have a sufficient basis to suspect potential abuse of a child, they are owed "unusual deference" by the courts. In *Heotis v. Colorado State Board of Educ.*, No. 18CA0057, 2019 COA 35 (Colo. Ct. App. 3/7/19), **the court found teachers are required to report any known or suspected child abuse or neglect without regard to whether the knowledge or suspicion occurs in a professional capacity**.

◆ Finding Colorado's mandatory reporting law does not limit the reporting duty of teachers to their professional capacities, the state court of appeals upheld an administrative decision denying the license renewal application of a teacher who did not report her then-husband's abuse of their child. The court rejected all the teacher's arguments, holding the mandatory reporting duty is not limited to the circumstances under which a reporter learns of suspected abuse or neglect. Further, **the court found the law did not limit a teacher's reporting duty to knowledge of abuse or neglect that was learned about or first suspected during employment**. While the teacher claimed she should be excused from making a report based on her battered woman syndrome, the court noted this was not her reason for failing to make a report. Evidence indicated she was trying to keep her family intact.

Although the teacher claimed cases from Georgia, Washington and Delaware were instructive, the court found Colorado legislators intended a broader application of the reporting duty than is required in those states. In sum, **the court found Colorado public school teachers are required to report any known or suspected child abuse or neglect without regard to whether the knowledge or suspicion occurs in a professional capacity**. It held substantial evidence supported the denial of the teacher's license renewal application. *Heotis v. Colorado State Board of Educ.*, No. 18CA0057, 2019 COA 35 (Colo. Ct. App. 3/7/19).

◆ Based on evidence that a Washington principal discouraged abuse reports to child protection and law enforcement agencies, the Ninth Circuit Court of Appeals permitted the grandparent of a deceased child to pursue a civil rights case. Prior to the student's death, school staff, including his teachers, observed numerous signs of abuse and neglect but did not report them to the state department of social and health services or a law enforcement agency. A burn was observed on the student, and he said his "mother" (his custodian/aunt) hurt him. There was evidence that a school counselor who made an abuse report during the year was told to have no contact with the student or his family after she made the report. She said that instead of reporting abuse to appropriate authorities, the principal made calls "to first attempt to 'work it out' with parents." Shortly before his death, the student told teachers "my mom punched me in the head." But staff did not immediately report this to child protection or law enforcement, and he was beaten to death by his aunt.

In a federal court, the grandparent filed claims against school officials including the principal and the district superintendent. She also sued the school district and the state department of social and health services. **The court found evidence of a school practice or policy of delaying abuse/neglect reports to child protection authorities.** Among the court's findings was that school employees observed numerous signs of abuse and neglect, including bruising and scratches on the student's face and head, burns, aggressive behavior and excessive absences. The counselor testified that the superintendent and principal did not report child abuse in order to avoid confrontations with hostile parents. When the case reached the Ninth Circuit, it held the grandparent could pursue her theory that there was an official school policy requiring staff to report suspected abuse only to the principal. The court held a reasonable jury could find an official school policy affirmatively placed the student in danger. Evidence indicated the counselor was directed to have no contact with the student and that his primary teacher was not told of her abuse report. *Davis v. Washington State Dep't of Social and Health Services*, 773 Fed.Appx. 367 (9th Cir. 2019).

◆ Tennessee parents claimed school staff retaliated against them for advocating for their child by making three child abuse reports. After the reports were investigated and closed, they removed him from school and sued the board of education. A federal court dismissed the case, and they appealed to the Sixth Circuit Court of Appeals. Although the parents argued the board violated federal disability laws and the First Amendment, the court found they produced no direct evidence of retaliation based on advocacy for their child. Further, the court found no evidence of a causal connection between the reports and any protected activity. The court found no merit to the parents' claim that there was insufficient evidence to report abuse because their child had problems interacting with peers. During the student's second-grade year, a manifestation determination review was held because he hit a classmate. While the parents argued the reported conduct was a result of his disabilities, **the court found the manifestation determination did not indicate that all his future misconduct resulted from his disability**. Last, the court found the parents did not claim the board had a policy of retaliation for protected speech. *M.G. v. Williamson County Board of Educ.*, 772 Fed.Appx. 287 (6th Cir. 2019).

◆ A New York teacher learned that a parent struck a second-grade student with her hand and a belt. When the school social worker was advised of the incident, she stated that a report should be made to Child Protection Services (CPS). A CPS social worker interviewed the parents and the principal. Following the investigation, the CPS closed the case as unfounded. The parent later sued the school district, principal and social worker in a federal court for violation of her rights to intimate association, infliction of emotional distress and municipal liability. Prior to a trial, the court dismissed the claims for privacy violations and emotional distress.

Nothing indicated the parent called CPS to retaliate against the parent for voicing complaints. The court held the parent could not rely on an incident taking place ten months earlier as evidence of a retaliatory motive. Because no federal claims remained, the court declined to hear the state-law defamation claim, which could be heard in state court. The parent appealed to the U.S. Court of Appeals, Second Circuit. As the lower court found, **school administrators are mandated reporters who are owed "unusual deference." Where an administrator has a sufficient basis for reporting potential abuse, a report is not retaliatory.** In this case, the student told the principal that her mother had hit her with a belt after checking her out of school. The court found this created a sufficient basis to suspect potential abuse of the student. There was no evidence that the parent's complaints some 10 months prior to the abuse report played a role in the decision to make the mandated report. The court held for the district and officials. *Maco v. Baldwin Union Free School Dist.*, 726 Fed.Appx. 37 (2d Cir. 2018).

◆ An Oregon student told a school counselor "a little more than a year ago my brother molested me." When the counselor asked what she meant by "molested," the student gestured to her upper torso, making a circular motion from her neck to her stomach. Based on her familiarity with the student, her experience and training, the counselor concluded the touching had not been sexual in nature. The brother would have been 11 or 12 years old at the time and the student did not seem distressed about it. Later in the day, the counselor told her supervisor she planned to contact the parent. She stated that she did not call child protection authorities or law enforcement because "there was nothing sexual about what was going on or no abuse of any kind." Nothing was filed under the school district's sexual incident response process. But the counselor called the student's mother and told her the student had used the word "molested" to describe her brother's actions. She said the mother told her she doubted the student's account but would talk to her about it. The counselor also called the mother later to follow up. Over six months later, the student told her non-custodial father and stepmother about the incident. The father reported the brother had molested and sexually abused the student. Based on the father's report, the superintendent placed the counselor on leave and began an investigation. Her dismissal was recommended and the board of education voted in favor of the recommendation on grounds of neglect of duty and insubordination.

A panel of the Oregon Fair Dismissal Appeals Board (FDAB) reversed the dismissal decision and the school district appealed to the state court of appeals. The court found the case involved an evaluation of the extent to which a mandatory reporter is permitted to exercise independent judgment in determining whether there is "reasonable cause" to conclude there was abuse of a child. **"Reasonable cause" is not defined in law, but the court found the term is equivalent to "reasonable suspicion," which it deemed a "very low evidentiary threshold for deciding that a complaint is founded."** Under the "reasonable suspicion" standard, the court rejected the school district's argument that the counselor could not make any inquiry of the student or exercise any independent judgment concerning her statements. While a mandatory reporter's obligation to report does not depend upon an investigation of the truth of a claim or suspicion of abuse, the court commented this does not mean there is no role for the exercise of judgment. As the counselor found any touching was "just horseplay, not sexually motivated," the court affirmed the FDAB's decision. *Meier v. Salem-Keizer School Dist.*, 284 Or.App. 497 (Or. Ct. App. 2017).

◆ A New York mother complained to her child's school about pervasive bullying. The child then told his teacher and a school psychologist that his father would break his toys and hit him with a back scratcher, and that he had grabbed his mother's wrists. Apparently feeling they should confirm his report with further evidence of abuse, the employees tried to pull his pants down. They then reported the parents to Child Protective Services (CPS). Later, the parents sued the school district and board of education in a federal court. The court found a sufficient basis existed to suspect abuse, and it held for the school district and board. The parents appealed to the U.S. Court of Appeals, Second Circuit. **The court found school officials, including teachers, are required to report to the CPS when they have a reasonable cause to suspect a child has been abused or mistreated.**

In a prior case, the court found New York's interest in encouraging teachers to protect students is so strong that state law confers immunity from civil and criminal liability when they report suspected abuse in good faith. By contrast, state law exposes teachers to liability for willful failure to report suspected abuse. State law creates a presumption that a school official acting in the scope of his/her employment is acting in good faith, so long as he/she did not engage in willful misconduct or gross negligence. As the lower court found, the school officials had a sufficient basis to suspect potential abuse. There was no clear showing of any retaliatory or punitive intent. Finding none of the parents' arguments had any merit, the court affirmed the judgment for the school district and board. *Dole v. Huntington Union Free School Dist.*, 699 Fed.Appx. 85 (2d Cir. 2017).

◆ A teacher at the preschool of a three-year-old Ohio child observed that his eye was bloodshot. When she asked what happened, he said "nothing." He later said he fell. Under better light, the teacher noticed red marks on the child's face. A lead teacher lifted the child's shirt and saw more injuries. After further questioning, the child identified his mother's boyfriend as the perpetrator. The next day, a social worker took the child and his 18-month-old sister from their grandparents' home. A physician discovered other bruises and injuries suggesting child abuse. The sister had black eyes, a swollen hand, and a large burn on her face. Two of her pigtails had been ripped out of her hair at the roots. A grand jury later indicted the boyfriend on five counts of felonious assault. At his trial, the prosecution introduced some of the child's statements to teachers as evidence of guilt. The court found the child incompetent to testify. But it allowed his statements to the teachers to come into evidence, finding they were sufficiently trustworthy.

A jury found the boyfriend guilty on all but one of the counts, and he was sentenced to 28 years in prison. He obtained reversal by higher courts in the state court system. On appeal, the U.S. Supreme Court found the case implicated the Confrontation Clause of the Sixth Amendment to the U.S. Constitution. The clause excludes testimonial statements of witnesses who do not testify at a criminal trial, unless the witness is unavailable at trial and the accused had a prior opportunity for cross-examination. According to the state of Ohio, the child's statements were not testimonial and should be allowed as evidence. The Court agreed, ruling that in an ongoing emergency, the primary purpose of questioning was not to create a record for trial. In such cases, statements were outside the scope of the Sixth Amendment. In this case, **the child's statements were not made with the primary purpose of creating evidence for the prosecution**. Instead, the Court held the child's statements took place during an ongoing emergency investigation. Finding the teachers' objective was to protect the child, the Court found no constitutional violation and held his statements had been properly used as evidence. *Ohio v. Clark*, 135 S.Ct. 2173 (U.S. 2015).

IV. GANGS AND CAMPUS INTRUDERS

A. Civil Cases

◆ A Massachusetts high school principal suspended a student for a reported off-campus gun theft, citing a school district policy calling for the suspension of students charged with a felony. Although the student's mother told the school superintendent no criminal charges had been issued, he refused to lift the suspension. In a letter, he acknowledged that charges might not have been filed. Later, a county juvenile authority charged the student with a misdemeanor for receiving stolen property under $250. An agreement was reached with the school district to lift the suspension. But the district refused to let the student attend her class graduation ceremony. Instead of appealing and returning to school, she took online classes and received tutoring. She graduated one year after the rest of her class. In a state court, the student sued the school district for damages based on her grief and stigmatization caused by not being permitted to participate in her senior year and being excluded from her graduation ceremony.

Appeal reached the Supreme Judicial Court of Massachusetts. It noted an 1845 state law allows students to sue their districts for improperly excluding them from school. A 1994 state law allows school principals to suspend students for felony charges, but the student was not charged with a felony. The 1994 law appeared to be the only state law permitting suspension from school for an act occurring off school grounds. **The court found the student produced facts that satisfied the 1845 law allowing her to sue the school district for being unlawfully excluded from her school.** In ruling for the student, the court held students have an immediate opportunity to have their suspensions lifted or shortened, or to receive an alternative placement. *Goodwin v. Lee Public Schools*, 475 Mass. 280, 56 N.E.3d 777 (Mass. 2016).

◆ A Georgia school resource officer (SRO) confronted three students who were loitering in a school hallway and told them to come with him to the school office. A student became defiant and profane and shoved the SRO when he tried to handcuff him. Another SRO then arrived, and the officers took the student to the floor and handcuffed him. After being brought to the school office, the student continued his combative, loud, and profane behavior. He disparaged and threatened an SRO before being taken to a youth detention center for three days. A school administrator later advised the parents that the student was not suspended and could return to school after his release from juvenile detention. After the student returned to school, the board held an expulsion hearing. At his hearing, the student said he hit the SRO in self-defense. But the hearing officer found he violated the student code. Before the board of education, the student asserted violation of a state code provision requiring a school disciplinary hearing within 10 days of a suspension. Adopting the hearing officer's findings, the board modified the discipline by finding the disciplinary action "complete" as of the date of its decision. Appeal reached the Court of Appeals of Georgia.

The court noted that at the school disciplinary hearing, the student said he acted in self-defense. But he was not suspended before his disciplinary hearing. He was instead told he could return to school upon release from detention. **According to the court, law enforcement and juvenile officers could not cause a school "suspension."** This defeated the claim that his school hearing was not held within 10 days of a "suspension" and was untimely. There was "more than sufficient evidence" in this case that the student had cursed and repeatedly refused to follow the SRO's directions. As the evidence justified a suspension, the court held for the board. **State law permitted school administrators to report student criminal action to a law enforcement agency or officer for investigation.** *Fulton County Board of Educ. v. D.R.H.*, 325 Ga.App. 53, 752 S.E.2d 103 (Ga. 2013).

◆ A Minnesota kindergartner said that he did not want to go outside with his class for recess. He stayed in a supervised detention room in the school office, but an aide instructed him to use a lavatory down the hallway instead of the one in the detention area. While in the lavatory, the kindergartner was sexually assaulted by a recent high school graduate who had been inside the school several times in the days before the assault. He entered the school through a side door without signing in and obtaining a visitor badge. The kindergartner's mother sued the school district for negligent supervision and failure to have and enforce a specific policy on school security. A court denied pretrial judgment on the negligent supervision claim, and the Court of Appeals of Minnesota agreed that a trial was required on that issue. The aide had let the kindergartner go unaccompanied to a restroom outside a detention room equipped with its own lavatory, and the graduate somehow got in the school building without signing in and wearing a badge. But the school district was entitled to immunity for not having a specific policy to protect elementary children from intruders. **These decisions took place at the planning level and involved the evaluation of financial, political, economic and social factors.** *Doe v. Independent School Dist. No. 2154*, No. A09-2235, 2010 WL 3545585 (Minn. Ct. App. 9/14/10).

◆ Gang activities at a West Virginia high school escalated when a gang leader was arrested for shooting a police officer. Gang members verbally assaulted the faculty and staff at school, and fights and disturbances became prevalent. The principal advised staff members that the slogan "Free A-Train" was banned. A student wrote "Free A-Train" on his hands several times and was suspended for 10 days. He sued the school board in a federal district court for speech rights violations. The court held schools may ban gang-related clothing if evidence indicates a potentially disruptive gang presence and gang-related disturbances. Recent federal cases suggest schools may regulate expression if they can reasonably forecast material and substantial disruption at school. This defeated the student's claim that speech must lead to an actual disruption before school administrators may suppress it. As students and parents had expressed fear over the use of the slogan, administrators could reasonably forecast that allowing the student to keep displaying it may have exacerbated the tensions and increased these fears. **The court held the "distraction from classes or intimidation from passive displays of support may serve as the basis of a disruption,"** and found no speech rights violation. *Brown v. Cabell County Board of Educ.*, 714 F.Supp.2d 587 (S.D. W.Va. 2010).

B. Criminal Proceedings

In *Edmonds v. Oktibbeha County, Mississippi*, 675 F.3d 911 (5th Cir. 2012), the U.S. Court of Appeals, Fifth Circuit, held **parents have no constitutional right to be notified and present during an investigation or questioning of their children by police officers**.

Michigan's Comprehensive School Safety Plan Act calls for the development and evaluation of model practices for school safety in public and nonpublic schools and public school academies. Among other things, the school safety measures must address the development and evaluation of school safety model practices. They must address statewide school safety information policy and emergency operation plans, the role of school safety liaisons, emerging trends in school safety technology requirements, and baseline safety requirements for schools. Ninety-Ninth Michigan Legislature, Regular Session, P.A. 548, H.B. 5828, Michigan Statutes §§ 28.801, 28.805, 28.807, 28.809.

Michigan's Student Safety Act provides for confidential reports of potential harm or criminal acts directed at students, school employees and schools. The act establishes a hotline for filing reports, creates a student safety fund and provides for procedures on the handling of confidential information related to the act. Ninety-Ninth Michigan Legislature, Regular Session, P.A. 670, S.B. 991, Michigan Statutes § 752.913.

Another Michigan law prohibits school districts and public school academies from commencing construction of new school buildings or major renovations of existing buildings unless the district or academy consults with the law enforcement agency that will be the first responder for the building regarding school safety issues. Ninety-Ninth Michigan Legislature, Regular Session, P.A. 437, S.B. 990, Michigan Statutes § 380.1264.

Michigan law requires each school board or nonpublic school to designate a liaison to work with the state school safety commission and the office of school safety to identify model practices for school safety measures. Ninety-Ninth Michigan Legislature, Regular Session, P.A. 549, H.B. 5829, Michigan Statutes § 380.1241.

◆ A California man stole the keys to a public elementary school and then placed a jar containing sodium and cyanide near a play area that was easily accessible to children. He then left black envelopes containing notes for teachers throughout the school. The notes read: "[T]his is a game to test your ability of how far each and every one of you is willing to go in order to secure the safety of your children." The notes stated that in order to assure the safety of students, teachers would have to unlock padlocks at access points to the school by 8:00 a.m. on that day. The notes warned of a solution that releases "a very poisonous cyanide gas," and "a relatively strong acid." The notes threatened that if teachers did not perform the tasks, "there will be consequences to follow, possibly affecting the children. Make your choice."

In later criminal proceedings, the man stated that "he wanted the teachers to feel fear." At a restitution hearing, school officials testified about the consequences of the incident to the district and the community. They stated that the incident had a "direct impact on the financial solvency" of the district. Students and staff were transported to other schools, and the district lost $94,669 in state funding based on average daily attendance (ADA). Although the probation department recommended $456,163.09 in restitution for the school district, the court ordered the man to pay the district a total amount of $235,341.17. After pleading no contest to certain criminal charges and being placed on probation, the man appealed to the state court of appeal, where he argued the restitution award included items that were not directly related to the incident. After noting that courts have broad discretion to impose probationary conditions to foster rehabilitation and protect the public, the court explained that **restitution orders need not be limited to the exact amount of a loss for which a criminal defendant is found culpable**. The man's careful planning indicated he did not simply commit a harmless prank. He terrorized the district on the anniversary of the September 11, 2001 attacks and administrators feared the school district was the target of another terrorist attack. The elementary school had to be closed for two weeks. Further, the court found the district incurred substantial costs consistent with its duty to protect students and staff. In sum, the court held restitution of $235,341.17 was reasonable. This included $ 2,778.88 to re-key classrooms at the elementary school, $21,728.22 for security costs, $11,933.87 for relocation expenses, $23,810.23 for construction costs due to security concerns and $19,044.14 for administrative costs. Also upheld was the trial court's order in include $32,585.75 for chemical testing, $8,245.16 for classroom lockdown kits distributed across the district and $20,545.92 for a visitor software system. However, the court found the trial court had improperly failed to deduct $68,722.56 from the restitution award to reflect the amount of partial reimbursement by the state for the loss of ADA funding. While otherwise affirming the award of restitution, the court ordered the man to pay the state $68,722.56 for the portion of ADA reimbursement already paid by the state to the school district. *People v. Landen*, 243 Cal.Rptr.3d 487 (Cal. Ct. App. 2019).

◆ A Louisiana security guard wanded a student at her school with a metal detector. The search revealed a concealed knife, razor blade and can of mace on her person. Police were summoned, and they arrested the student and confiscated the items. In a juvenile court, charges were filed against the student for illegally carrying a weapon. The court found the student guilty of the charges. She was placed on probation with special conditions for six months. On appeal to the Court of Appeal of Louisiana, the student claimed she could not be convicted under a state law prohibiting the carrying of a firearm or dangerous weapon onto school property. She said the law required possession of a firearm or a dangerous weapon and so did not apply to the carrying of a knife, razor blade or a can of mace to school.

The court found that while pocket knives and utility blades had innocent uses, these items could not be dismissed as "standard school supplies." **The court found the concealment of items on the student's person suggested that she foresaw using them as weapons.** As a result, the evidence was sufficient to support the juvenile delinquency charges. *State of Louisiana In the Interest of R.D.*, 158 So.3d 936 (La. Ct. App. 2015).

◆ A Kansas municipal police officer confronted a jogger whose dog was running loose on school grounds. The jogger was placing items from the trunk of her parked car into an athletic bag on the ground next to her car at the time. When the officer looked down, he saw a handgun case in the athletic bag. After questioning the jogger, the officer recovered a 9 mm handgun from her and informed her that it was illegal to have a firearm on school property. The gun was not loaded, and the magazine clip was empty.

The jogger stated she did not have any ammunition in her possession. A state court considered a criminal charge of possessing a firearm on school property in violation of Kansas law. The court held that since school was not in session at the time of the offense, the jogger should be acquitted of the charge. The state appealed to the Court of Appeals of Kansas, which noted that trial courts are not permitted to inquire into legislative intent, unless there is ambiguity or lack of clarity. In this case, state law declared that possession of a firearm by any person (other than a law enforcement officer) on any school property or grounds was a criminal offense. No exception applied to this case. **The court held that whether school was in session was irrelevant to the outcome of this case.** If the jogger's argument was correct, a sniper arriving on school grounds would not violate state law until a student actually arrived on school property or if classes were in session. As a result, the court reversed the judgment. *State of Kansas v. Toler,* 41 Kan. App.2d 986, 206 P.3d 548 (Kan. Ct. App. 2009).

CHAPTER FIVE

Employment

Page

I. HIRING

Having trustworthy staff is vital for school safety – and getting staff you trust starts with good hiring practices.

The U.S. Department of Education's 2017 guide, "Addressing Adult Sexual Misconduct in the School Setting," highlights **one major safety issue that responsible hiring practices can help keep out of your school: sexual abuse of students**.

Available at *rems.ed.gov/ASMTrainingGuide.aspx*, the guide cautions educators not to put all their reliance on background checks.

Background checks are important – and failure to run them likely breaches your state's law and could lead to negligent hiring claims. But one limitation with criminal background checks is that some serial abusers haven't faced criminal consequences. If they aren't in the database, they won't show up in a search of it – and the database also may not include older or out-of-state convictions.

While background checks are necessary – but may not be perfect – the guide says the info applicants provide on your employment form may give you a better heads-up of a potentially risky hire. But you have to know the red flags to spot – such as job-hopping, frequent moves and any break in professional licensure.

Other good advice includes asking applicants during interviews what they do to make sure they maintain professional boundaries with students.

You may also want to emphasize the policies your school has in place to protect student and how strictly you enforce them.

A. Negligence and Constitutional Claims

◆ A high school basketball player at a preK-12 Christian school reported her coach texted: "I want to be in you" and that he loved her, wanted to marry her and didn't want her to be with her boyfriend. She'd deleted the texts, but phone records showed he'd sent her more than 3,200 texts in three months. A former student also said he'd kept contacting her online to ask about her sex life. The head asked him to resign – but didn't report suspected sexual abuse to state authorities.

The coach later passed background and criminal-history checks to get a coaching job at a public school. There, he sent personal texts to a girl on his team and went on to have sex with her. Caught, he pleaded guilty to child pornography and the sexual abuse of a minor.

The public-school student sued the private school and its headmaster, alleging the failure to report the earlier misconduct there caused her later abuse. The case went up to the Third Circuit, which found her negligence *per se* claim required further proceedings as she'd validly alleged the private school defendants breached a law designed to prevent public harm; here, the state's Child Protective Services Law. The Third Circuit also found a jury could find the sheer volume of texts, allegations of inappropriate messages, and rumors of misconduct were enough to require the private school to report suspected sexual abuse or exploitation under the law in effect at the time. It sent the case back to the federal trial court. *Nace v. Pennridge School Dist.*, 744 Fed.Appx. 58 (3d Cir. 2018).

On remand, the trial court refused to grant the private school defendants judgment without a trial. A jury could find that **if the private school had reported the coach to child protective services, the school district would have known the risk he posed and wouldn't have hired him**. *Nace v. Pennridge School Dist.*, No. 15-333, 2019 WL 1429575 (E.D. Pa. 3/29/19).

◆ A school district told a woman **she had to be fingerprinted for a full background check and also pass a drug test to be hired** as a substitute teacher. She refused to submit to the drug test and sued the school board, alleging its suspicionless drug test violated the Fourth Amendment. As a matter of first impression, the Eleventh Circuit held it didn't. Generally, urinalysis tests of public employees must be supported by individualized suspicion of wrongdoing – but a narrow exception to the rule allows suspicionless searches that serve special government needs. The court found one here. "As we see it, ensuring the safety of millions of schoolchildren in the mandatory supervision and care of the state, and ensuring and impressing a drug-free environment in our classrooms, are compelling concerns." It affirmed the lower court's decision not to grant her request for a court order that would have put the district's suspicionless drug testing of substitute teachers on hold. *Friedenberg v. School Board of Palm Beach County*, 911 F.3d 1084 (11th Cir. 2018).

◆ A high school student said a male teacher she met in an extracurricular program as a sophomore groomed her. They started having sex in her junior year. A year later, a teacher and a student told administrators they'd seen her parking her car at a nearby school and getting into the teacher's car. This triggered an investigation, but the student said she was treated like the wrongdoer and it didn't stop the abuse, which continued for two more years. She sued school defendants on multiple charges, including claims against the principal and the superintendent under the Massachusetts Tort Claims Act (MTCA). The MTCA distinguished between a public employee's failure to alleviate or respond to a private harm (not actionable) and creating the injury-causing circumstance in the first place (actionable). The court refused to dismiss those claims because **negligently hiring the abusive teacher – and giving him the authority to remove her from other teachers' classes – may have created the injury-causing circumstances**. *Doe v. Town of Stoughton*, No. 17-cv-12337-IT, 2018 WL 1951180 (D. Mass. 4/25/18).

◆ A mother sued New York City for, among other things, negligent hiring and retention of a school janitor, who the mother said called her daughter "retarded" and a "bitch" in front of other middle school students. The city's department of education asked the court for judgment without a trial, arguing the janitor was the employee of an independent contractor that provided janitorial services to the middle school. The court **refused to grant it judgment on the negligent hiring and retention charges because the defendants didn't provide evidence to prove the janitor wasn't their employee** or that he was the employee of a company when he allegedly insulted the student. On appeal, the appellate court affirmed. *Gadson v. City of New York*, 156 A.D.3d 685 (N.Y. Sup. Ct. App. Div. 2017).

◆ Student "John Doe's" freshman English teacher was arrested after having inappropriate physical and phone contact with him, including sexting and phone sex. After other students saw the school district's police questioning John, they decided he was the student behind her arrest. They harassed him about it. He went on to attempt suicide and ultimately graduated from an out-of-state private school. John and his family sued the district and district officials, and they included a charge that the principal violated John's substantive due process rights by hiring the teacher. To state a valid constitutional violation, John had to show the principal was deliberately indifferent to his rights – a much higher standard than negligence. **He claimed the teacher told him she was hired even though the principal knew of her flirtatious or inappropriate relationship with a different male student.** A Nevada federal judge found the claim failed. John hadn't established that the principal made the hiring decision or that the teacher's behavior toward the other student demonstrated a high degree of risk that she would go on to sexually abuse a different student – so the court found John didn't plausibly allege the principal acted with deliberate indifference to his rights. *Doe v. Clark County School Dist.*, No. 2:15-cv-00793-APG-GWF, 2017 WL 1483428 (D. Nev. 4/21/17).

B. Background Checks

◆ A school district offered a "public services" class to expose students to careers in fields like firefighting and policing. An applicant to teach the class had the required credentials. The district ran a fingerprint search on him and found no felony convictions.

His paperwork said he'd been a security guard and a city's "Special Enforcement Officer" for parking. He told a high school principal and two vice principals he was a former police officer. No one at the high school called the police to confirm this. If they had, they would have learned he'd never been a police officer. They later admitted they wouldn't have hired him if they'd discovered this. His former supervisor at the police department said he also would have told them the man was fired from his parking job for "making sexual innuendos" to women.

Hired by the school, he sexually molested a student. The school then discovered he had a history of domestic violence. The molested student sued the district, alleging it negligently failed to screen him and protect her.

The trial court dismissed the district from her lawsuit but an appeals court reversed the decision, writing that "a reasonable factfinder could conclude that **had the district's employees conducted a basic background check" for more than only the felonies the state code says disqualify teachers from hire, they would have "uncovered a past" that would have stopped them from hiring him**. "Had he not been hired, he would not have had the opportunity to sexually abuse" the student. And as his criminal and employment background was "knowable" from a background check, the district couldn't show its supervision of the student was reasonable. The decision to dismiss the district from her lawsuit was reversed. *C.G. v. Glendale Unified School Dist.*, No. B277157, 2019 WL 990178 (Cal. Ct. App. 3/1/19).

◆ A school bus driver had religious objections to having her fingerprints taken. **After a new state law required a background check that included being fingerprinted, she told her employer that "the book of Revelations prohibits the 'mark of the devil,' which she believes includes fingerprinting**, and that she will not get into heaven if she submits to fingerprinting." She asked her employer for the religious accommodation of being allowed to submit to a background check that didn't include fingerprinting. It allowed an alternative background test for an employee with "unreadable" fingerprints – but not for her. She sued for religious discrimination under Title VII and the state's human rights act. The employer asked the court to dismiss the suit. It refused, finding she'd stated a valid claim, given that the employer had provided another employee the accommodation she requested – and hadn't shown that providing it to her would subject the employer to an undue hardship. *Kaite v. Altoona Student Transportation, Inc.*, 296 F.Supp.3d 736 (W.D. Pa. 2017).

◆ In the summer of 2015, three Pennsylvania school **districts required construction companies to produce criminal background checks for all construction workers** assigned to school projects. After at least 14 workers were disqualified on that basis, their union sued the districts. The trial court issued a preliminary injunction that prohibited the districts from requiring the background checks – but an appeals court reversed it. The trial court based its order on the fact that the school code exempted contractors who had "no direct contact with children" from its background check requirement. But the appellate court reversed it because it found the order went beyond the scope of a preliminary injunction. A preliminary injunction is supposed to return the parties to the status quo before the act occurred that's being sued over. The appeals court said that would be a return to the district's practice of requiring background checks for independent contractors – not the preliminary injunction's order to districts to let disqualified workers work at schools and not insist on background checks for contractors who wouldn't have direct contact with children. *United Union of Roofers, Waterproofers, and Allied Workers, Local Union No. 37 v. North Allegheny School Dist.*, Nos. 2392, 2477 & 2493 C.D. 2015, 2017 WL 1382227 (Pa. Commw. Ct. 4/18/17).

◆ After child porn was found on a special-needs teaching aide's computer, the principal identified a "non-verbal and almost non-communicative" student in one image. The aide was convicted of offenses related to secretly viewing or recording another person without consent, and the child's parents sued the district for negligence. The principal testified she'd contacted his previous employers. Under Arizona law, **a public employer had immunity for claims based on an employee's felony unless it knew about the employee's propensity to commit the crime**. After the parents discovered a prior employer had fired him for touching a patient's vagina and telling her "she felt moist[,]" they claimed the propensity exception applied. They argued the principal should be deemed to know why the previous employer fired the aide, thus informed of his criminal propensity. But the trial court granted the district summary judgment, and an appeals court affirmed, finding the exception only applied if the district actually knew of his criminal propensity. The parents didn't show it did. *Gallagher v. Tucson Unified School Dist.*, 349 P.3d 228 (Ariz. Ct. App. 2015).

◆ A man lost his job after the New York City Department of Education (DOE) refused to certify him as a school bus driver. His application disclosed he'd been convicted of two drug-related felonies 16 years prior and three misdemeanor thefts – the most recent 13 years ago when he was 41. He explained the crimes were related to a drug addiction he'd since overcome. DOE denied his application, deciding **the seriousness of his crimes and the mature age when he committed them made him unsuitable to have authority over children in the largely "unsupervised environment of a school bus."** He sued, alleging the district violated a state law banning unfair discrimination based on past criminal convictions. The trial court found in his favor, but an appeals court reversed – and the state's highest court affirmed. The law didn't create an entitlement to licensure or employment, and it included a safety exception. To overturn the denial, the bus driver had to show the district's decision was arbitrary or capricious. He couldn't. *Dempsey v. New York City Dep't of Educ.*, 33 N.E.3d 485 (N.Y. 2015).

◆ Just after his January hire, a new assistant principal pulled a 16- or 17-year-old special ed student out of class to talk to her about a bullying problem she'd reported. A few days later, they exchanged phone numbers. He texted her. That night, he picked her up and took her to a hotel, where they had sex. He went on to sometimes pull her out of class, prompting classmates to roll their eyes and call her a "home-wrecker." In April, teachers told the principal they suspected an improper relationship, but the purported victim and other students denied it. After a different student went to a school resource officer, the police investigated and arrested the assistant principal. The student and her mother then sued the superintendent and principal for negligent hiring in violation of Pennsylvania law. They alleged the school officials' background check should have discovered he'd pleaded guilty to a disorderly conduct offense of inducing a minor to buy alcohol. While **that was a different offense, the court found "it does indicate a history of targeting minors"** and so suggested the school defendants negligently hired him. However, the court dismissed the claim, finding the student and her mother didn't allege the malice or willful misconduct required to strip the defendants of their state-law immunity from negligence claims. *M.S. ex rel. Hall v. Susquehanna Township School Dist.*, 43 F.Supp.3d 412 (M.D. Pa. 2014).

◆ The mother of an eight-year-old Louisiana student dropped her daughter off at around 7:20 a.m. for the school breakfast, which was to be served at 7:30. A janitor stopped the student on the way in and told her that a teacher wanted to see her. He led her to an upstairs classroom, put a towel over her head, told her to bare one foot and touched her with a part of his body that wasn't his hand. She reported the incident despite his warning not to, and her mother sued the school board for vicarious liability and negligence in its retention/supervision of the janitor. A court granted pretrial judgment to the school board, but the court of appeal reversed, finding issues of fact that required a trial. However, the court did state that **the board could not be liable for negligent hiring of the janitor because it performed a background check on him and found no criminal record**. *Booth v. Orleans Parish School Board*, 49 So.3d 919 (La. Ct. App. 2010).

◆ An Indiana high school teacher had a sexual relationship with a student during her freshman and sophomore years. When the school discovered this two years after the fact, it promptly suspended the teacher, who later pleaded guilty to sexual battery and resigned. The student's parents sued the district for negligent hiring. A federal court ruled against them, and the Seventh Circuit affirmed. Although the parents asserted he'd assaulted two former students prior to his hire – marrying one of them – the school never learned of those relationships. It received positive references from the teacher's previous employer and interviewed him several times. He also possessed a valid teaching license and was not on a list of known sex offenders. And there was no indication that the former student he married had been in a sexual relationship with him while he was her teacher. Thus, **the school's thorough hiring procedures protected it from the claim of negligent hiring**. *Hansen v. Board of Trustees of Hamilton Southeastern School Corp.*, 551 F.3d 599 (7th Cir. 2008).

II. EMPLOYEES, GENERALLY

Under most state laws, employers can be held liable for negligent supervision or retention if the employer knew or should have known of an employee's unfitness and didn't act – such as by investigating, discharging or reassigning the employee.

Public employers, like school districts, can often be held liable for an employee's negligence while acting within the scope of his or her employment. But if an employee is exercising discretion with respect to school safety and not acting in bad faith, maliciously or with a conscious indifference to the rights of others, the employee will probably be entitled to state-law immunity from suit.

That said, state laws vary – and some provide much broader immunity for negligence claims.

As for federal law, government employees are entitled to qualified immunity on claims under federal laws or the Constitution if the law was not clearly established at the time of the alleged violation.

A. Immunity

◆ An assistant principal found contraband, including knives and a cigarette, in an Arizona middle school student's day planner. The student denied that the contraband was hers and also denied distributing drugs to fellow students, but agreed to let him search her belongings. He searched her backpack and found nothing. He then had an administrative assistant take her to the nurse's office, where the nurse and administrative assistant made her strip to her underwear, then asked her to pull her bra out and shake it, and to pull out the elastic on her underpants, exposing her breasts and pelvic area to some degree. They found nothing. She and her mother sued for Fourth Amendment violations, and the case reached the U.S. Supreme

Court. The Court held that the strip search violated the Fourth Amendment because the assistant principal did not have sufficient suspicion to justify its extent. However, **the law was not clearly established at the time of the search**. Thus, the assistant principal, the administrative assistant and the nurse were entitled to qualified immunity. Only the district could be liable for the Fourth Amendment violation. *Safford Unified School Dist. No. 1 v. Redding*, 557 U.S. 364, 129 S.Ct. 2633, 174 L.Ed.2d 354 (2009).

◆ A former student in Utah claimed a teacher groomed him and then took him to her home during school hours for sex. He said they had sex on other occasions on campus. He sued the school district for negligent hiring, retention and supervision, but the trial court dismissed the case, finding state law made the district immune to this suit. The appeals court affirmed, writing, "It might seem counterintuitive that our law provides no civil remedy against a school district that is alleged to have negligently hired and retained a teacher who has illegal sexual contact with her minor students." The court added that in the state supreme court's 1993 decision in *Ledfors v. Emery County School Dist.*, the state's high court suggested that the state legislature might want to change the law as it was "unfortunate that any parent who is required by law to send his or her child to school" can't sue "negligent school personnel who fail to assure the child's safety at school." The appeals court noted the legislature had failed to do so – so "the District is entirely immune from suit for the acts alleged here." *Larsen v. Davis County School Dist.*, 409 P.3d 114 (Utah Ct. App. 2017)

◆ High school administrators heard rumors a 16-year-old special ed student with a disciplinary record of sexually harassing girls was asking girl students to have sex with him in a school bathroom. They investigated but couldn't substantiate the rumors. When a 14-year-old girl told a teacher's aide he'd just asked her to have sex with him in a bathroom, the aide suggested she go along with it just long enough for them to catch him in the act and end the harassment. The two say they ran the plan by an assistant principal. She seemed "disinterested" and didn't OK the plan or tell them not to do it. The girl went into the bathroom with the boy. By the time the aide got teachers to check on the bathroom, he'd raped her. The girl's guardian sued the school board and school staff for claims that included negligent/wanton hiring, training and supervision. An Alabama federal judge granted most of the defendants judgment without a trial, finding them protected by state law immunity. But the Eleventh Circuit affirmed the judge's decision that the assistant principal was not entitled to immunity. Alabama public employees were not entitled to immunity if they acted beyond their authority. Based on the student's story, the assistant principal ratified the plan by not stopping it. Under regulations adopted by the board of education for dealing with students' sexual harassment complaints, **using one student as bait to catch another student committing sexual harassment went beyond an assistant principal's authority**. The Eleventh Circuit reversed the judge's decision that the aide was entitled to immunity on the student's tort of outrage claim. Using the girl as bait was likely to – and did – cause her emotional distress, and carrying out the plan was extreme and outrageous conduct. *Hill v. Cundiff*, 797 F.3d 948 (11th Cir. 2015).

◆ After a Delaware fourth-grade class watched a movie on a 32-inch screen TV perched atop a four-to-five-foot-tall rolling cart, the teacher told a student to move the cart to the back of the room. As she was pushing it, the TV's cord got tangled in the cart's wheels. The TV fell, striking the student's head and knocking her down. The student's mother sued district defendants, including the teacher, for personal injury. The trial court found the suit blocked by the state's immunity statute. The Delaware State Tort Claims Act provides all state political subdivisions, including school districts and their employees, immunity for discretionary acts performed in good faith and without gross negligence. The student's mother claimed the teacher was grossly negligent to have a student move the TV cart. Instead, the court found that allowing a student to assist in a classroom task does not constitute gross negligence: "a gross deviation from the standard of conduct that a reasonable person would observe." At most, the teacher was negligent. As **gross negligence was required to overcome the teacher's immunity to a personal injury claim**, the trial court granted the district's request to dismiss the case. *Morales v. Family Foundations Academy, Inc. School,* No. N12C-03-176 JRJ, 2013 WL 3337798 (Del. Super. Ct. 6/11/13).

◆ A North Carolina teacher was accused of allowing a teacher's aide to regularly force-feed and abuse a severely disabled student in her classroom. The aide allegedly yelled at the student, force-fed him to the point of choking, used abusive language, violently jerked his head and pulled his hair, and intimidated him with a stuffed toy because she knew it terrified him. After the student was hospitalized, his parents sued the teacher, the district and various officials. The teacher sought immunity, which a trial court denied. Subsequently, the North Carolina Court of Appeals affirmed that decision, noting that the teacher did not meet the test for public official immunity because her position was not "created by statute." Further, the complaint alleged that the teacher knew of and might have witnessed the abuse, and yet never intervened on the student's behalf. And the abuse violated clearly established constitutional rights of which the teacher should have known. *Farrell v. Transylvania County Board of Educ.*, 682 S.E.2d 224 (N.C. Ct. App. 2009).

◆ A Tennessee high school principal decided to temporarily deny a female student access to a weightlifting class in the last semester before graduation. The class was scheduled to include about 30 males and one other female. Students were required to "spot" one another, requiring some physical contact. **The principal consulted with the weightlifting teacher and decided to remove the girls from the class for "safety and liability**

reasons," fearing a possible sexual assault. A school official confirmed that the school would not permit enrollment of one or two girls in a class with all male students and a male teacher. After a state attorney notified the director of schools about a possible Title IX violation and informed the principal that the students could not be removed from class because of their gender, the principal allowed the students to return to class. The other student chose not to return, and the student who did return missed only three days of class and earned an A. However, she claimed that the incident caused her great stress and sued for constitutional rights violations.

A federal court granted the board's motion to dismiss the case, and the Sixth Circuit affirmed. Here, the principal was not executing an official board policy at the time he ordered the student's removal, and he was not acting as a board policymaker. The board had no role in the decision to remove the student from class, and it took immediate corrective action as soon as the director of schools learned about the incident. *Phillips v. Anderson County Board of Educ.*, 259 Fed.Appx. 842 (6th Cir. 2008).

◆ An Ohio student attacked another student after gym class. The victim's parents sued the school district, claiming it knew of the attacker's history of assaulting students, yet did not take the necessary precautions to protect other students from him. **A trial court held that the district was immune, noting that it did not act with malice, in bad faith or recklessly.** It also found that **the teacher's supervision at the time of the attack was not even negligent**. The Ohio Court of Appeals affirmed. Although the student aggressor was disruptive at times, there were no indications that he was terrorizing other students. The fact that he had been in a juvenile detention center several times was not enough to put the school on notice that he was likely to attack another student. *Aratari v. Leetonia Exempt Village School Dist.*, No. 06 CO 11, 2007 WL 969402 (Ohio Ct. App. 3/26/07).

B. Safety Policies

◆ A young woman claimed years of abuse by a middle-school gym teacher began when she, in eighth grade, asked if she could attend his class. He made the 14-year-old his special helper, letting her take roll and count the laps other students ran. He also had her help him outside class. The head of the PE department made a few disgruntled comments but didn't report the situation or try to stop it. Meanwhile, the gym teacher was approaching her sexually. He molested her in a hotel that summer and went on to stalk her throughout high school, raping her at least twice. She concealed her whereabouts from him when she was in college. She sued the district for negligence. The trial court granted the district judgment without a trial, but an appeals court reversed, finding a trial was needed on her negligent supervision claim. **District employees testified that a teacher taking a student from another teacher's class without administrators' approval violated school policy.** The court found that, especially because the teacher who failed to report this was the department head, the failure could support a finding of negligence. *C.A. v Los Angeles Unified School Dist.*, No. B281333, 2019 WL 1649637 (Cal. Ct. App. 4/17/19).

◆ A vocational agriculture teacher had a 15 feet by 20 feet classroom that opened onto a 40 feet by 60 feet workshop that had tools and heavy machinery. He was teaching younger students in the classroom when three seniors unexpectedly ask to take their final early. The teacher left the younger students unattended while he set up laptops in the workshop for the seniors' exam. It took longer than expected, but **he was only gone six minutes. That was still long enough for a student to put a "sleeper hold" on two students, choking them.** One, a special needs student, briefly lost consciousness. The teacher was unaware of the misbehavior. Students later reported it out of concern for the special needs student. The principal reviewed surveillance video from the classroom, and then the superintendent initiated termination proceedings. The board fired the teacher for good and just cause, but a trial court overturned the dismissal. An appeals court affirmed. **The board alleged the teacher had a pattern of willfully ignoring district policy, but admitted they'd never warned him about it.** The courts found the evidence suggested other things – like the layout of his class space – were responsible for his purported misbehavior. Also, the student who misbehaved took "advantage of a small window of opportunity" to "engage in serious misconduct" while the teacher attended "to other tasks directly related to his teaching responsibilities[.]" None of this added up to good and just cause to fire him. *Badertscher v. Liberty-Benton School Dist. Board of Educ.*, 29 N.E.3d 1034 (Ohio Ct. App. 2015).

◆ For more than two years, teachers picketed in front of a middle school at morning drop-off. They were protesting the district's failure to reach a contract with their union. When rain was forecast for a planned protest, teachers voted to park in front of the school that morning and display their picket signs in the car windows. They left room for dropped-off students to reach the sidewalk but not for parents to pull up to the curb as usual. Parents had to let children out in the middle of the street in the rain, and traffic backed up in both directions. Parents called the school about the traffic jam, and the principal called the police. The traffic snarl also made at least 16 teachers late that day. The picketing teachers were charged with misconduct. Two – one fined $500 and the other fined $1,000 – appealed to a court. Participating in a peaceful union protest is protected from retaliation under the First Amendment. The teachers alleged a violation of their speech rights. A trial court found the discipline was legal. The teachers appealed, and an appeals court reversed. The district appealed, and New York's highest court reversed again, upholding the discipline because the way the teachers engaged in their protected speech rights, "interfered with the safety of students[.]" The court found **the teachers' speech rights "were**

outweighed by the District's interests in maintaining an orderly, safe school[.]" *Santer v. Board of Educ. of East Meadow Union Free School Dist.,* 13 N.E.3d 1028 (N.Y. 2014).

◆ A fired New Jersey school bus driver filed a bias charge with the state civil rights agency to allege his termination was discriminatory. The board of education agreed to settle his claim. As part of the settlement, the board agreed to reinstate him. He went back to work. Two months later, **the supervisor of security rode along on an afternoon run and heard a school bus full of students "shriek in fear"** because a railroad crossing gate had come down on top of the bus while its back end was still on the tracks. The driver ignored it when the vehicle ahead of him pulled up to give him room to clear the tracks. The bus remained on one set of tracks while a commuter train sped past on the next set, so close it made the bus rock. Something similar happened on the morning run five days later. Meanwhile, the board was getting calls and letters from parents complaining about the driver and worried about their children's safety. The board fired the bus driver for unsatisfactory performance, and the driver sued the board for breaching their settlement agreement. The court granted the board judgment. The bus driver appealed, but the appeals court affirmed, finding: **"[T]he Board's first responsibility was the safety and welfare of the children in the district,"** and it had reasonable grounds to question the driver's safety – including "uncontradicted evidence of two life-endangering incidents." The board didn't breach the settlement agreement by firing the bus driver under these circumstances. *Valos v. Garfield Board of Educ.*, No. A-3313-12T2, 2014 WL 4355637 (N.J. Super. Ct. App. Div. 4/9/14).

◆ A front office employee at a Georgia high school was approached by a man who claimed to be a student's uncle. She failed to ask for identification or verify that the man was allowed to check out the student. In fact, only the student's parents were allowed to check her out of class early. When the student arrived at the office, the man told her that her mother had sent him to pick her up. He then took her to his daughter's house and molested her. The student's parents sued the principal and the employee in their individual capacities. The defendants sought immunity, but the Georgia Court of Appeals granted it only to the principal. **The employee had a mandatory duty to verify that the man had the right to sign the student out of school and failed to do so.** As a result, the lawsuit against her could proceed. A jury would have to decide whether the molestation was a reasonably foreseeable consequence of her failure to follow the rules. *Cotton v. Smith*, 714 S.E.2d 55 (Ga. Ct. App. 2011).

◆ A Pennsylvania student was sexually assaulted by a driver's education teacher during a solo lesson. When she complained, the district suspended the teacher, but the principal sent out letters asking people to contribute to the teacher's defense and stating that he thought the student was lying.

After the teacher was reinstated, the student left school and sued the district, claiming that it ignored the teacher's misbehavior for years before the incident, making it possible for him to assault her. She asserted that the teacher hadn't even been disciplined after asking a student if he could see her pierced nipple. The district sought to have the case dismissed, but a federal court allowed parts of the lawsuit to continue. The student had alleged a custom of inadequate training for employees who are likely to respond to incidents of sexual harassment. The district also allegedly had a custom of ignoring or downplaying reports of harassment, and had a custom of suppressing specific complaints of harassment against the teacher. Finally, **the school district had a custom of allowing the teacher to take students out for driving lessons alone, in violation of official school district policy**. As a result, the student's lawsuit against the district could proceed with respect to those claims. *E.N. v. Susquehanna Township School Dist.*, No. 1:09-CV-1727, 2010 WL 4853700 (M.D. Pa. 11/23/10).

◆ A Louisiana special education teacher noted that a student began making a sound he typically made before self-injurious episodes. When he starting hitting himself on the head, she called the PE coach, two paraprofessionals and the principal. She was pushed into a wall while trying to keep a mat under the 185-pound student to prevent injury. During the 45-minute struggle, she was twisting and sliding the entire time. However, she was not hit, knocked down or bitten by the student. When she sustained injuries to her hand, she nevertheless sought "assault pay" from the board. A court granted pretrial judgment to the board, but the court of appeal reversed, noting that there was a question of fact as to whether the teacher's injuries were a result of an assault by the student. **If the student intended to harm her during the episode, she would be entitled to assault pay.** The case required a trial. *Miller v. St. Tammany Parish School Board*, No. 2008 CA 2582, 2009 WL 3135208 (La. Ct. App. 9/11/09).

◆ In 2005, an Oregon school district adopted a policy that any employee having a firearm in school or at a school event would face discipline up to and including termination. A teacher in one of the district's schools had an ex-husband whom she feared might turn violent. She sought to bring a handgun to school, asserting that she was licensed to carry a concealed weapon and that she needed it for self-defense. The district's human resources department warned her that she could be fired for bringing the gun to school, and she sued. She claimed that the policy was illegal because Oregon law states that only the legislature can "regulate" firearms or pass ordinances concerning them. A court dismissed her claim, holding that the law didn't apply to workplace policies, and the Oregon Court of Appeals affirmed that decision. It noted that the state law was only intended to prevent cities and counties from creating a patchwork of conflicting laws concerning firearms, and that it wasn't intended to reach as far as internal employment policies. *Doe v. Medford School Dist. 549C*, 221 P.3d 787 (Or. Ct. App. 2009).

◆ A West Virginia county board of education implemented a random drug testing policy for all safety-sensitive employees, which included teachers. Three teachers and their union sued to block the new provisions from taking effect, claiming that the random testing would violate their Fourth Amendment right to be free of unreasonable search and seizure. A federal court granted a preliminary injunction prohibiting the board from enforcing the policy. **The board failed to show that there was a special need for the suspicionless searches.** In addition, the teachers did not hold safety-sensitive positions as that term has been defined by the Supreme Court. Thus, they did not have a reduced expectation of privacy. Finally, the risk of harm from not testing was more speculative than real. *American Federation of Teachers-West Virginia, AFL-CIO v. Kanawha County Board of Educ.*, 592 F.Supp.2d 883 (S.D. W. Va. 2009).

C. Fitness for Duty

◆ A school custodian in Ohio told the superintendent the first-grade teacher was his "best friend" and he wanted to leave her children money in his will – but she'd given him the wrong address for her house. He then said the teacher had been "rubbing her hair against his face and whispering in his ear that she wanted to give him alcohol." Alarmed, the superintendent put him on paid leave while she investigated. Among other things, **his union rep told her that the custodian's erratic behavior made the rep worry he posed a danger to the teacher, students and the custodian himself.** The teacher said he'd been making her feel uncomfortable and she'd already asked for a court order of protection. It was granted later that month. Meanwhile, a district mental-health specialist had determined he should not return to the school because he posed a safety threat. The custodian went on to tell a doctor that he heard voices and saw visions, including of the teacher's husband raping her. Told he had to obtain a "Fit for Duty" slip from a mental health professional before returning to work, he instead retired and sued the district, alleging disability bias, retaliation for reporting the teacher had sexually harassed him, First Amendment retaliation and a deprivation of his due process rights. But the court found all his claims failed – and that the district had placed him on leave not for an illegal reason but because of genuine concerns about his mental condition and the risk it might pose to the school community. *Carnes v. Lima City Schools*, No. 3:16CV1860, 2018 WL 2045783 (N.D. Ohio 5/2/18).

◆ A five-year-old's foster mother's job meant she couldn't pick him up when kindergarten ended. She arranged for his older cousins – students at the same school – to sign him out. On a day when no one signed him out, his kindergarten teacher, a 38-year educator, followed school policy by bringing him to the school office to let staff know. She then brought him to the after-school program she taught. At some point she realized he was gone. She assumed someone had picked him up. Meanwhile, his foster mother had arrived. As he wasn't in the office, she drove around until she found him. He was several blocks from school, trying to cross a busy street. **Confronted by the principal, the teacher argued she wasn't responsible for a child not enrolled in her after-school program.** Interviewed by the department of family services, she blamed the foster mother for not picking him up on time. The board of education found the teacher had engaged in conduct unbecoming her profession under Ohio law. It revoked her educator license and held her ineligible to apply for any license issued by the board. She appealed, but both a trial court and an appeals court affirmed. Among other things, it found there was sufficient evidence to support the unbecoming conduct finding and to permanently revoke her teaching certificate. *McClendon v. Ohio Dep't of Educ.*, 77 N.E.3d 523 (Ohio Ct. App. 2017).

◆ A new principal at a Chicago school implemented the CHAMPS positive behavior support program to help teachers manage their classrooms and to put safety procedures in place. The staff handbook said CHAMPS protocols were required schoolwide and reminded teachers corporal punishment wasn't tolerated. Parents went on to complain a male teacher had physically disciplined their children. The Chicago Board of Education issued five charges, including conduct unbecoming a Chicago public school employee. At his dismissal hearing, one student testified the teacher hit him and another student in the back of the head after one of them stepped on a milk carton, causing it to burst. Another **said the teacher threw him out of the classroom by his hair and neck for misbehaving and then slammed his head against a bulletin board**. A third said the teacher grabbed him and another student by their necks and pushed them against the front board for misconduct. He also said the teacher hit him for not having his homework. Parents presented evidence that included photos of bruises and scratches and a recording of the teacher admitting he'd forcibly removed a child from his classroom. Among other things, the board concluded he'd administered corporal punishment, which was grounds for dismissal without the opportunity for remediation. The teacher appealed, but the court confirmed the decision to fire him, finding no breach of his due process rights. It also rejected his claim that the decision to fire him was arbitrary and capricious, finding **his use of force was unreasonable and unnecessary to maintain student safety and discipline**. *Booker v. Board of Educ. of City of Chicago*, 65 N.E.3d 380 (Ill. App. Ct. 2016).

◆ A 36-year-old high school English teacher in New York began buying guns around the same time he had online conversations with a friend who worked as a psychic medium. The teacher told her he thought the government was controlling the weather and said he wanted to shoot down one of the planes "that sprays chemicals through the sky[.]" A "female friend" of his then anonymously called the FBI, which alerted local law enforcement. They began to monitor him online and at school. Soon after, **he instant-messaged the psychic medium that he believed the government had**

controlled the mind of the Newtown Elementary School shooter, but a bigger problem was the "entities that came to this planet in order to try to control us … I'm working on deprogramming myself … that has been the nightmare of my life."

After he intimated he might have a secret mission to remove evil people from power during "a civil war in America," the police stopped him on his way home from a trip to the gun store and involuntarily committed him. His refusal to cooperate with the psych evaluation the district required prompted a charge of misconduct/conduct unbecoming a teacher. The district also charged him with incompetence to work as a teacher due to mental illness. After an eight-day hearing, the district discharged him.

He sued the district, the police and other local officials, claiming they conspired to retaliate against him for his exercise of constitutionally protected speech. The court dismissed the claim, finding **his speech wasn't protected as it constituted true threats** and didn't address matters of public concern. Also, the district could reasonably predict it would cause a disruption at work that potentially outweighed the value of his speech, and he was fired because of the potential disruption, not in retaliation for his speech. The court found that if his speech had become known while he was still a teacher, it "would have caused substantial (and well-justified) disruption that far exceeded the value of plaintiff's delusional, paranoid and far-fetched conspiracy theories." It dismissed the suit. *Heller v. Bedford Cent. School Dist.*, 144 F.Supp.3d 596 (S.D.N.Y. 2015).

◆ A tenured second-grade teacher in New Jersey used a motorized wheelchair and crutches. He was put on administrative leave based on allegations of conduct unbecoming a teacher. Among other offenses, **he allegedly urinated into a bottle in front of students and had them take the bottle to the bathroom to empty it**. He was also accused of urinating in and around the trash can in his classroom with students nearby. An administrative law judge (ALJ) found the district proved 14 of 17 charges brought against him. The commissioner of education adopted the ALJ's recommendation to revoke his tenure and remove him as a teacher. He appealed, but a court affirmed. Under New Jersey law, a tenured teacher could only be dismissed for "inefficiency, incapacity, unbecoming conduct, or other just cause." **Unbecoming conduct was defined as conduct that tended to destroy respect for government employees and confidence in the operation of public services.** The court found the commissioner had a more than sufficient reason to remove the teacher. As the ALJ found, even if he couldn't make it to a bathroom – which wasn't credibly proved – he didn't report what he'd done and make sure the trash can in his classroom was cleaned. *In re Tuitt*, Dep't of Educ. No. 307-10/11, 2014 WL 10208983 (N.J. Super. Ct. App. Div. 8/10/15).

◆ While an elementary school custodian was telling the principal about her problems with the head custodian, she mentioned she'd previously considered suicide. The principal called the school resource officer, who called the police. Officers arrived and took the custodian to a crisis center. She was placed on unpaid leave and told she couldn't return to work until she'd completed a fitness-for-duty evaluation with a psychiatrist. After the doctor decided she was disabled by disorders that included depression, she was placed on an extended leave. Though her own psychiatrist cleared her to return to work about four months later, the district required her to be cleared by its psychiatrist – but then waived the requirement and let her come back to work at a different elementary school. She sued the district, **alleging it violated the Americans with Disabilities Act by requiring a fitness-for-duty evaluation before she returned to work**. A Florida federal judge found it didn't, writing, "Employers may require a medical evaluation to assess an employee's fitness to return to work after a health-related absence." *Rodriguez v. School Board of Hillsborough County, Florida*, 60 F.Supp.3d 1273 (M.D. Fla. 2014).

◆ A high school physics teacher taught a math and physics class for struggling students. Many had behavioral issues or were diagnosed with attention deficit disorder or other learning-related conditions. To engage them, the teacher developed a less authoritarian, more collaborative teaching style. That meant students were more familiar with him than with other teachers. One day in class, a 17-year-old girl said she wasn't happy with her grade and asked if she could pay for a better grade. A male student responded, "You mean short of sexual favors?" The teacher joked, "Yes, that is the only thing that would be accepted." The students laughed. He added, "Don't be ridiculous," and said the only thing that would improve her grade was better work. He offered her extra help after school. When she arrived to take him up on the offer, he was helping another female student. **The student again asked to pay for a better grade. He replied she already knew "the only thing that I would accept is a sexual favor."** She laughed, but the other student reported the teacher's remark. He was put on administrative leave, investigated for sexual harassment, and ultimately fired for conduct unbecoming a teacher. The teacher appealed, and the matter went to arbitration. The arbitrator found that despite the teacher's intent, the remarks were objectively inappropriate and made a student uncomfortable enough to complain – so violated the school's sexual harassment policy and created a hostile educational environment. Even so, the arbitrator reinstated him, finding that was in the best interest of district students, given 11 years of strong performance weighed against a comparatively minor isolated incident. A court affirmed the arbitration award, but Massachusetts' highest court vacated it, finding the arbitrator didn't have the authority under the state's teacher's statute to reinstate the teacher. That law required the arbitrator to assess conduct that jeopardized students' safety or self-esteem primarily in light of the pupils' interest in a safe learning environment. **The arbitrator's error was in letting "pupils' interest in the academic success of their school to override their interest in a safe, supportive**

classroom environment.” The court found that ran contrary to the law’s stated purpose “and the high standards of behavior the public expects from its teachers.” *School Committee of Lexington v. Zagaeski*, 12 N.E.3d 384 (Mass. 2014).

◆ A Kentucky high school’s SRO took two boys to the principal after classmates overheard them talking about a bomb and saw they had a map. The principal determined they had been discussing a video game. A few days later, on the same day as the school shooting in Newtown, Connecticut, the Spanish teacher dictated a letter to a student and told the student to sign his own name. It claimed a student had twice brought weapons to school and had “plotted a map of bomb and gun attack sites around the school area” but wasn’t disciplined. **The letter asked if the superintendent was “afraid to enforce school rules[.]”** The superintendent met with police and then closed the high school and middle school to search for weapons. None were found. Final exams scheduled for that day were postponed. The lost day was made up on a day the rest of the district had off. After police discovered the Spanish teacher wrote the letter, **the superintendent fired her for insubordination and conduct unbecoming a teacher**. The teacher sued, alleging violation of her free speech rights. She asked for a court order to reinstate her employment pending the resolution of her lawsuit. The court refused, finding she wasn’t likely to win her suit. Assuming the teacher was speaking as a private citizen on a matter of public concern, the district’s interest in promoting the efficiency of its educational services outweighed any speech rights she had in the letter. She mailed the letter the day after Newtown shooting, and the day the school reopened, attendance was down by 10%. Also, closing the schools affected around 900 students and their families. This, plus the rescheduled exams and make-up day, meant she significantly impeded school operations. As the court found her speech wasn’t protected, she wasn’t likely to win her case. *Pacheco v. Waldrop*, No. 5:13-cv-00044-TBR, 2013 WL 2581016 (W.D. Ky. 6/11/13).

◆ A tenured high school teacher in New York received several unsatisfactory evaluations and claimed that he was also denied certain benefits and opportunities. He sought an accommodation for dust and pollen allergies, which the school claimed it provided. He then sent letters to the assistant principal, calling her “*Mein Fuhrer*,” and referring to her as a “snooperviser.” He also referred to himself as “an indentured subject of her sick experiment.” Fearing he represented a threat to the safety of staff and students, the school reassigned him to administrative work at another high school and required a psychological evaluation. Pending the results, his photograph was given to school safety officers and custodial staff who worked in his old high school building during evenings and weekends to ensure that he would not enter the building. He was determined to be fit for duty and was returned to the classroom without any loss of pay or benefits. He then sued for discrimination under state and federal law. A federal court granted pretrial judgment to the defendants. Here, the school provided an accommodation that met the requirements listed in the Board of Education Accommodation. He merely found them unsatisfactory. Further, **the reassignment was a temporary measure taken to ensure the safety of students and staff, and he was transferred back to a teaching position once the evaluation found him fit for duty**. *Krinsky v. Abrams*, No. 01 CV 5052(SLT)(LB), 2007 WL 1541369 (E.D.N.Y. 5/25/07).

D. Failure to Train

◆ After a college student said she'd had a sexual relationship with her high school band director, he pleaded guilty to one count of corruption of minors. She sued the district, **alleging it violated her Fourteenth Amendment substantive due process rights by not training staff to recognize a teacher's "grooming" of a student and report it**. But to hold a government employer liable for this under Section 1983, the former student had to show the district was on notice of a need to provide such training. Instead, she failed to show the district was aware of the band director's misconduct or any other violation of students' rights that put it on notice of the need to provide this training for staff. The Third Circuit found a Pennsylvania federal trial court was right to grant the district judgment without a trial on this claim. *Kobrick v. Stevens*, 763 Fed.Appx. 216 (3d Cir. 2019).

◆ A Texas teacher reported another teacher for hugging a student. This triggered an investigation by the principal into whether the teacher's relationship with the student was improper. Two days later, the student committed suicide. His adoptive parents sued the district to allege, among other things, that the district violated his constitutional rights by failing to properly train and supervise its employees. **To succeed, the parents had to show the teacher's supervisor acted with deliberate indifference.** As there was undisputed evidence that the district prohibited teacher-student relationships, required staff to report sexual harassment and regularly held training sessions on these policies there was no inference that this was the case. And as the principal not only personally observed the student for unusual behavior but had a security guard talk to him to make sure he was OK (the guard assured the student he'd done nothing wrong) there was also no evidence "from which a reasonable jury could conclude that [district] officials were deliberately indifferent to [the student's] plight." *Ramos v. Webb Consolidated Independent School Dist.*, 724 Fed.Appx. 338 (5th Cir. 2018).

◆ A freshman boy in Nevada kept missing his sixth-period class. In May, he had sexual relations with his English teacher. Police at the school found out about it the next day and took him to an office to question him – and left a window open. Other students overheard. When the teacher was arrested later that day, students put two and two together. The following year, he claimed another teacher gave him a hard time and accused him of putting her friend out of work. He tried to kill himself. His parents placed him in a private school in another state and sued the school district. Although other claims were allowed to continue against the district, a Nevada federal judge dismissed the parents' claim that the district negligently failed to train the teacher that abused him. Under Nevada law, the district didn't have immunity for negligent acts committed in bad faith – but **the parents failed to provide any facts to back up their claims** that the teacher had a reputation of flirting with male students, the district knew about it but failed to stop her or that it knew the student was spending his sixth periods with the teacher and turned a blind eye. Without such facts, their claim couldn't stand, so the court dismissed it. *Doe v. Clark County School Dist.*, No. 2:15-cv-00793-APG-GWF, 2016 WL 4432683 (D. Nev. 8/18/16).

◆ Special ed aides went to elementary school administrators to complain about the teacher of a class of multi-handicapped students. The teacher allegedly screamed at children (sometimes, "I hate you!"); ignored their basic needs; and incited escalating behaviors by throwing their property in the trash, walling them off behind dividers, and taking their food. She made a child who used a walker crawl to the bathroom, made another child stand in front of the class for extended periods, and knocked a table into another child's mouth. A principal responded to the aides' concerns by saying that "she went to college for this; she knows what she's doing[.]" Finally, the school librarian – who also complained with no result – called the police. After investigating, they decided not to prosecute the teacher or the school district. She was allowed to resign with severance pay and a positive reference. No school administrator was reprimanded for not reporting the abuse. Parents only discovered the complaints about the teacher after a citizen activist's work got the records of the investigation released. Five of her former students and their parents brought a Section 1983 claim to allege the district was liable for violating the children's substantive due process and equal protection rights as well as their rights to be free of unreasonable seizures. The district objected it couldn't be sued under this section, but the court decided it could be based on an allegation that **the district failed to train administrators to identify potential abuse of students, appropriately report it and inform parents of the allegations**. *H.M. v. Board of Educ. of the Kings Local School Dist.*, 117 F.Supp.3d 992 (S.D. Ohio 2015).

◆ A woman that a kindergarten teacher had never met announced she was there to take a child out of school. The teacher asked for the woman's ID and verification that the woman was allowed to do so. The woman refused to provide any documentation, but the teacher released the child to her anyway. The woman went on to brutally sexually abuse the child, severely injuring her, before abandoning her in a playground, where the child was found by a sanitation worker before dawn on a January morning. Among other claims, the child's mother brought a Section 1983 *Monell* claim against Philadelphia's school district and its school reform commission. The mother alleged their failure to train the teacher on policies about releasing students amounted to deliberate indifference to the kindergartner's rights. The court refused to dismiss the claim, finding the mother alleged the district defendants were **aware of the risk of child abduction yet didn't train and supervise staff on its policy that preK-8 students were never to be released to adults who weren't properly identified** and checked against school records – and that this was what caused the alleged violation of the child's Fourteenth Amendment due process right to bodily integrity. *L.R. v. School Dist. of Philadelphia*, 60 F.Supp.3d 584 (E.D. Pa. 2014).

III. SCHOOL SECURITY STAFF

A. School Resource Officers

◆ A police officer served as a school resource officer (SRO) at the school his son attended. He told the school district's director of security that students upset with him were threatening to hurt his son. The SRO said his boss didn't take the right protective measures and the other students attacked and injured the boy. The district went on to 1) deny the SRO's request to pay to transfer his son to another school district's school, and 2) decide not to re-employ the SRO, saying it was because his son attended the school. The officer sued the district, alleging it violated his First Amendment rights, but the court dismissed the case. To validly claim the district violated his right to petition the government or retaliated against him for exercising his speech rights as a citizen, **the officer had to show his speech was on a matter of public concern. While bullying qualifies as such, the officer wasn't speaking about bullying as a matter of interest to the public at large.** Instead, he was speaking privately to his employer in emails or conversations about a purely personal grievance: the treatment of his son at school. As such, his speech wasn't protected by the First Amendment, and his claims failed. *Kimble v. Kingston City School Dist.*, No. 1:18-CV-575 (N.D.N.Y. 3/19/19).

◆ Soon after a Pennsylvania school district hired its school resource officer to also be its chief security officer, a sporting goods store called the police to report its video surveillance showed an adolescent boy stealing a crossbow. A detective called the SRO, who identified the boy as a student at the middle school. While the SRO and school administrators investigated at school, a local **TV reporter called the district's public relations (PR) officer to say the station was sending a news van to school based on the tip that there was a child with weapons and ammunition, creating a possible active shooter situation**. The PR officer said his info was wrong, but the reporter refused to call off his team, saying his source was "excellent." There was also a news van parked near the police station. A detective called the SRO, wanting his help to call off the reporters so police could process the student without revealing his identity. The SRO called the reporter to say the tip he'd received was unfounded. The reporter believed him. This made the superintendent suspect the SRO had leaked the story to the press in the first place. The district canceled the SRO's contract. The SRO then sued it and the superintendent for violating his First Amendment right to free speech. Both sides asked for judgment without a trial, but the court found further proceedings are needed as a jury could decide either way on key issues. Was the SRO acting within his official duties when he called the reporter? (If yes, his speech wasn't protected.) Did his speech involved a matter of public concern? (It had to in order to be protected speech.) Was his public employer justified in firing him for the speech – even if it was protected – because it impaired the proper performance of the job they were there to do? (The jury could find, for example, that he called the media without his employer's authority to do so.) Finally, **to find the district fired him in retaliation for First Amendment-protected speech, the jury would have to find the SRO's speech was a substantial or motivating factor in the decision to fire him**. The facts were not so decisive that a reasonable jury could only decide this case one way, so the judge refused to decide the case without a trial. *LaTorre v. Downington Area School Dist.*, 253 F.Supp.3d 812 (E.D. Pa. 2017).

◆ An Ohio school resource officer's employment contract specified that he had to "maintain a cooperative working relationship" with the county sheriff's department and be a "commissioned law enforcement officer" of Ohio. Two years after he was hired by the school, a citizen's complaint against him as a deputy led the county sheriff to revoke his commission. Learning of this, the school superintendent informed him he'd be fired if he didn't resign. He provided a letter that said he was resigning "due to the fact that I am no longer affiliated with" the sheriff's office. He then applied for unemployment compensation benefits. His request was denied on the basis that **he was fired for just cause – he'd been told at hire that he was responsible for maintaining his license**. He appealed, saying the sheriff had revoked his commission without having all the facts and the school had laid him off to give him "the opportunity to draw unemployment "until the matter was resolved and his commission was reinstated. His request for unemployment benefits was again denied, this time because he "quit without just cause." He appealed to a court, which reversed the decision to deny him benefits. But on further appeal, an appeals court affirmed the unemployment compensation review commission's decision to deny him benefits. The commission's decision stood because it wasn't unlawful, unreasonable or against the manifest weight of the evidence. *Parrett v. Administrator, Unemployment Compensation Review Comm'n*, 90 N.E.3d 50 (Ohio Ct. App. 2017).

◆ When Shawn Logan was in the sixth grade at a Pennsylvania middle school, school police officer Robert Lellock took Logan out of class on several occasions to sexually abuse him in a janitor's closet. In 1999, the principal discovered the two alone together in a room at school. In 2013, Lellock was convicted in state court for crimes against Logan, including indecent assault and endangering the welfare of children. Logan went on to repeatedly try to bring a successful claim against the district to allege it breached his constitutional rights. The court twice dismissed his claim, but allowed him to try again. On his third attempt, it dismissed his claim for good. Logan alleged the district violated his substantive due process rights by not properly train staff on: 1) the proper circumstances for school police officers to remove a student from class, and 2) detecting and reporting the sexual abuse of students. Though calling it "tragic and deplorable that Logan was sexually abused by a person who was supposed to protect him[,]" a federal judge found Logan's third try hadn't met the constitutional standard of showing school defendants were deliberately indifferent to his rights. To do so, he **had to allege facts that showed his abuse was a highly predictable consequence of the district failing to train staff on the proper circumstances for school police officers to remove a child from class** and on detecting and reporting sexual abuse. He didn't, and this time the court decided the dismissal would stand. *Logan v. Board of Educ. of School Dist. of Pittsburgh*, No. 15-499, 2017 WL 1001602 (W.D. Pa. 3/15/17).

◆ A part-time school resource officer brought his personal laptop to work, wanting the district technology officer (DTO) to help him with his problem uploading images to Craigslist. While she was helping him, there was a knock on her door. They ignored it. Not long after, there was another knock. When the person began to unlock the door, the DTO opened it to find a staff member needing help in the computer lab. The DTO went to the lab to provide it. When she came back 15 to 20 minutes later, the SRO was still in her office. He then went back to his duties. Later that day, after he'd clocked out but she hadn't, he showed her self-defense moves she wanted help with. Two days later, both were called in to answer questions to help administrators determine "why people were not where they should be when they're on the job." Ultimately, the DTO was suspended from work for one day and the SRO was fired after he refused to resign. The superintendent later explained the DTO's supervisor felt she could be effectively monitored, but **the director of safety and security felt he could no longer trust the SRO because he'd changed his story several times**. The safety director said he needed to be able to trust his officers "because of their role and responsibilities." The SRO sued the district for sex discrimination in violation of state law, saying he was fired while a female employee who committed the same infraction only got a one-day suspension. The trial court granted the district judgment without a trial, finding the SRO couldn't state a *prima facie* case of discrimination. An appeals court affirmed. To allege discrimination by comparing his discipline to another employee's, the employees had to be similarly situated. The court found the DTO and the SRO weren't. They didn't have the same supervisor and "were not subject to the same standards by virtue of their job duties." Importantly, unlike her, the SRO's job duties included patrolling and being a highly visible presence on campus. Agreeing he failed to state a *prima facie* case of gender discrimination, the appellate court affirmed the trial court's decision to grant the district judgment without a trial. *Hanson v. Bell-Chatham Community Unit School District #5*, No. 4-16-0406, 2017 WL 462543 (Ill. App. Ct. 2/2/17).

B. Other Safety Personnel

◆ A security guard applied to be a high school's director of safety and security. He didn't get the job. He claimed the board of education then cut his hours from full-time to part-time and reduced his salary. He resigned and sued the board of education and two individual defendants. He claimed one man convinced the board to give the superintendent a raise in return for creating the job specifically for a second man – and that the job was "so particularized" that only the second man could qualify for it. He never told the school or the board his suspicions but later sued, bringing a state-law whistleblower's claim and a common law wrongful-discharge claim. Both claims were dismissed, and an appeals court affirmed the dismissals. Whistleblowing typically involves a report of something that is believed to be illegal. Here, the employee reported nothing, and **simply filing a job application didn't qualify as a whistle-blowing activity**. To state a valid wrongful discharge claim, he had to show his firing was contrary to a clear mandate of public policy. But instead of identifying a clear public policy, the former security guard only made broad allegations of corruption without providing the facts to back it up. Both claims were properly dismissed. *Daniels v. High Point Board of Educ.*, No. A-1112-17T1, 2019 WL 166578 (N.J. Super. Ct. App. Div. 1/11/19).

◆ Around 1,600 New York City school crossing guards, all women, joined a class action lawsuit to allege illegally unequal pay on the basis of sex in violation of the federal Equal Pay Act and New York City's and New York State's human rights laws. The New York City Police Department employs the school crossing guards as well as police officers. The crossing guards claimed the NYPD illegally paid them less than male "Traffic Enforcement Agents Level II," even though the guards alleged both groups of employees did substantially the same work. The court granted the city judgment without a trial, finding they didn't. **The difference in pay was justified by "stark differences in training, job requirements, and job responsibilities[.]"** Among other things, the agents, unlike the crossing guards, were required to have a high school diploma and pass a civil service exam. They were also full-time employees who could be required to work nights, weekends and overtime – unlike the crossing guards, who didn't work more than five hours a day, usually during school hours. Finally, agents could issue summonses, testified in court and worked under more dangerous conditions – often in busy intersections and at night. As the jobs were not similar enough to merit the same pay, the women's claims failed. *Miller v. City of New York*, No. 15cv7563, 2018 WL 2059841 (S.D.N.Y. 5/1/18).

◆ An African-American security officer at a New Jersey high school had an unblemished work record when the school board hired its first districtwide director of security. The new director assigned him to work outside in harsh winter weather, disciplined him for a dress code violation, overly monitored him, reprimanded him for being away from his post and finally transferred him to a less prestigious middle school. He sued the district for racial discrimination under Title VII, but the court found he failed to state a valid claim. The Third Circuit agreed. He didn't show he suffered an adverse employment action: a significant change in employment status like not being hired, being fired or passed over for promotion, being reassigned with significantly different responsibilities or suffering a significant drop in benefits. While he did make much less in overtime in his new position, there were changes to overtime that impacted all the officers. Also, he couldn't show racial bias. The director explained he transferred an Hispanic officer to the high school because of the growing number of Spanish speakers there and sent the officer to the middle school because **he was needed to accommodate the physical demands of the disabled students and because he was an "excellent de-escalator."** *Stewart v. Union County Board of Educ.*, 655 Fed.Appx. 151 (3d Cir. 2016).

◆ The security department at a California high school received a call regarding vandalism on campus. Three campus security officers responded, while a peace officer with the unified school district drove his patrol car around the perimeter of the campus. The three campus security officers encountered a group of students, and one officer ordered a student with whom he'd had many conversations in the past to stop running. The student instead continued to flee, stopping only when the peace officer encountered him after he exited the campus. After the student was convicted of willfully resisting a public officer in the discharge of his duties, he appealed, asserting that campus security officers were not "public officers" under the law. A state court ruled that campus security officers are public officers, but the California Court of Appeal reversed the conviction, holding that campus security officers are not public officers. On further appeal, the California Supreme Court reversed the court of appeal, holding that **school security officers are "public officers."** A public officer is understood to include a variety of public officials and employees who perform law enforcement related duties in connection with their employment. *In re M.M.*, 278 P.3d 1221 (Cal. 2012).

◆ **A school security officer in Tennessee used gory photos in a scared-straight presentation to highlight the dangers of drunk driving.** He tried to ensure that none of the students would see pictures of dead relatives by checking names, asking teachers about students with potential issues, telling students they didn't have to look at the photos (which were placed in an envelope with the victims' names on the outside), and warning them about the nature of the accident and the names of the victims. Despite these precautions, a student saw a picture of her father. She didn't use her father's last name and knew him by his nickname rather than his given name. She and her mother sued the city for negligent infliction of emotional distress, and a judge awarded them nearly $67,000. However, the Tennessee Court of Appeals reversed, holding that the security officer didn't breach his duty to the students and that he'd taken reasonable steps to prevent such traumatic harm. *Marla H. v. Knox County*, 361 S.W.3d 518 (Tenn. Ct. App. 2011).

◆ A security guard with a private company worked at a junior high school in New York. When a student fight broke out on campus, he intervened and ended up sustaining injuries. He brought a lawsuit against the school district, claiming negligent supervision, but a court ruled in favor of the district. An appellate division court affirmed, noting that **the district owed no legal duty of protection to the security guard**. The duty to supervise students was intended to prevent injuries to other students, not to adult security guards. *Stinson v. Roosevelt U.F.S.D.*, 877 N.Y.S.2d 400 (N.Y. App. Div. 2009).

◆ A high school safety officer's daughter, who attended the school where she worked, got into an altercation with another student outside the school. The altercation resulted in the filing of charges against the safety officer's daughter. A day later, the safety officer called the other student's mother, claiming that she did so at the direction of the assistant principal for security. She asked the mother to come to the school to participate in a mediation. **The mother alleged that the safety officer threatened her on the phone, telling her that if she cared about her daughter's safety, she would drop the charges.** Based on the alleged threat, the safety officer was charged with aggravated harassment. After she was convicted, she appealed. A New York appellate division court upheld the conviction, noting that the lower court permissibly discredited her testimony that she never made the threat. *People v. Wilson*, 872 N.Y.S.2d 124 (N.Y. App. Div. 2009).

◆ A New York school security officer became involved in an altercation with an honors student who entered the school before the start of scheduled classes. When the security officer asked the student to leave the building, the student refused to do so. The incident escalated, and the officer arrested the student. As the officer prepared to escort the student from the building, the principal asked the officer to take the student through a back entrance to save her the embarrassment of passing through the front entrance, where hundreds of students were waiting to enter. After the officer denied the principal's repeated requests to take the student out the back door, the principal physically blocked the main entrance to the school. **The security officer then attempted to arrest the principal, who flailed his**

arms and kicked the officer to avoid being handcuffed. Eventually, the principal was charged with one count of resisting arrest and one count of obstruction of governmental administration. The principal asked to have the charges dismissed, and a court agreed to do so. The principal had a solid performance history, and his conduct did not threaten the safety of the officer or the school community. His request to take the student out the back entrance was reasonable. *People v. Federman*, 852 N.Y.S.2d 748 (N.Y. City Crim. Ct. 2008).

IV. EMPLOYEE PREPAREDNESS AND RESPONSE

Coordinating employee responsibilities with respect to crisis prevention and response is critical. One way to aid in forming an effective team among school employees is to conduct a staff skills inventory that matches individual employees with particular areas of experience and/or expertise. For a form to give staff to help you stay on top of this, search for "Staff Skills Inventory" in the Forms Library at *www.SchoolSafetyAndSecurityAlert.com.*

◆ A divorced couple's parenting plan required the father to tell the school when the mother had his permission to pick their son. He hadn't notified the school on a day the mother and her new husband arrived to pick him up. Forced to wait while the school secretary repeatedly tried to contact the father, the stepfather got impatient. The secretary overheard him tell the boy that if the doctor confirmed the stepfather had cancer at his appointment "next Tuesday ... **I'm going to come back in here with an AK-47 ... kill everybody in here and then kill myself."** The secretary asked the principal if they should call 911. She said no, concerned about "causing a scene" that would upset children at a science club meeting. But a police-officer friend of a teacher later took a statement from the principal and got a warrant for the stepfather's arrest. A jury later convicted him of disorderly conduct and attempted terrorism, but the attempted terrorism conviction was reversed on appeal. The state's law required the fear of bodily injury to be "imminent." The stepfather's threat about "next Tuesday" didn't meet that standard. So the appeals court returned the case to the lower court for sentencing only on the disorderly conduct conviction. *State v. Watts*, No. M2013-02750-CCA-R3-CD, 2015 WL 3863242 (Tenn. Crim. App. 6/23/15).

◆ A Pennsylvania teacher confiscated a student's knife. He informed the principal and his program's director, but he didn't think their response went far enough. He emailed them three days later to complain about their response. Shortly thereafter, he confiscated brass knuckles from a student. After he became irate at a staff meeting and swore at another teacher, he was suspended for eight days, but a union arbitrator later overturned the discipline. He wrote to the state's school safety center to report unsafe classroom conditions, and later sued the principal and the program director for **violating his free speech rights by retaliating against him for speaking out about school safety**. A federal court granted pretrial judgment against him. Here, it was one of his duties to ensure school safety, so he wasn't speaking as a citizen when he complained, but rather as an employee. *Ankney v. Wakefield*, 2012 WL 2339683 (W.D. Pa. 6/19/12).

◆ An Alabama special education teacher sustained injuries when a student whom she had repeatedly reported as violent attacked the principal in the office and while doing so bit her, knocked her down and kicked her in the head. She sued the school district for violating her Fourteenth Amendment rights by failing to remove the student from school and by **failing to train her to handle him, despite knowing of his propensity for violence**. She claimed that this amounted to deliberate indifference to her safety. The district sought to have the case dismissed, and a federal court agreed that the case ought to be dismissed. The teacher failed to show that the district's policies amounted to deliberate indifference so as to reach the level of a constitutional violation. And this was not a case of a state actor inflicting injury on the teacher, but rather a private individual. As a result, the court dismissed the case. *May v. Mobile County Public School System*, No. 09-00625-NS-C, 2010 WL 3039181 (S.D. Ala. 7/13/10).

◆ On September 15, 1999, New Jersey's governor declared a state of emergency due to the approach of Hurricane Floyd. However, in Rutherford, New Jersey, less than an inch of rain fell that day, and school officials didn't cancel after-school football practice. After the practice, a 16-year-old student got a ride home from a teammate's sister. About a half-mile from the field, the driver lost control of the car on a curve and struck a tree. The student, who was sitting unrestrained in the rear passenger seat, suffered severe head injuries and sued the school district for negligence, asserting that it should have canceled the practice because of the hurricane warnings and that it shouldn't have let him go home with the teammate's sister, given the weather. A court ruled for the district, and the Superior Court of New Jersey, Appellate Division, affirmed. Here, most of the severe weather from the hurricane arrived the following day rather than the day in question. Because of the absence of extraordinary weather conditions, **the district's employees did not breach a duty of care to the student by not canceling the practice due to the impending hurricane**; nor did they breach a duty of care by allowing the teammate's sister to drive him home. *Pluchino v. Borough of Rutherford*, 2010 WL 335041 (N.J. Super. Ct. App. Div. 2/1/10).

◆ A custodian in Washington received a call from her supervisor asking her to report to work early to replace a distraught co-worker. The supervisor offered no further explanation. When the custodian arrived at school, the district superintendent repeatedly directed her to clean up the scene of a student's suicide. However, a law enforcement officer told her not to touch anything. She also learned of the possibility that the deceased student had left a bomb in the building. She was ordered to accompany the principal on a search for the bomb and was later given permission to clean up the suicide site. However, when she picked up a book bag, she was told to drop it. The book bag apparently contained a pipe bomb, which was detonated on a school field. The superintendent told her to make it look as though nothing had happened at the site. She finished her work at 4:15 a.m., at which point she was distraught and physically ill.

She had to return to the school by 8:00 a.m. to hand out cookies and coffee as counselors assisted students and staff. For the next several days, she had to clean up candles and cards left by students at the scene of the suicide. Later, she sued the school district and superintendent for infliction of emotional distress. A state court held that workers' compensation was her exclusive remedy, but the Washington Court of Appeals reversed. It held that **her post-traumatic stress disorder resulted from the performance of her duties over several days**. Thus, her injury was excluded from the workers' compensation act's definition of an occupational disease. Her lawsuit could continue. *Rothwell v. Nine Mile Falls School Dist.*, 206 P.3d 347 (Wash. Ct. App. 2009).

◆ An Ohio high school principal convened a meeting with senior staff members to discuss the subject of testing during a week when state educational tests were being administered at the school. While the meeting was in progress, the principal was informed that a female student had been assaulted and forced to perform sex acts on a number of male students. She was also told that another male student had videotaped part of the assault. She did not call the police or the department of children services. Instead, she set up a meeting for the following morning to discuss the assault. She also failed to report the sexual assault as her supervisor instructed her to do. She left at 4 p.m. to take care of some personal business without leaving anyone in charge. Nor did she assign anyone to meet with the police officers who had been summoned to the school by the victim's father. The board of education fired her, and she challenged the termination.

The Ohio Court of Appeals upheld the decision to fire her, noting that she violated state law by failing to report the sexual assault. Further, her failure to follow her supervisor's order to report the assault also justified her discharge. **She was not relieved of her duty to contact law enforcement just because the victim's father had called the police.** And her failure to handle the situation immediately was further evidence that she had been properly fired. *Crenshaw v. Columbus City School Dist. Board of Educ.*, No. 07AP-883, 2008 WL 802708 (Ohio Ct. App. 3/27/08).

CHAPTER SIX

Extracurricular Activities

Page

I. AFTER-SCHOOL/SUMMER SCHOOL PROGRAMS

Schools can no longer throw open their doors so that neighborhood children can use their facilities after the school day ends. Nor can they rely on minimal supervision for after-school programs. Threats to security and student safety mean they must now devise plans for how to safely engage students after the school day ends.

Some well-recognized means of decreasing risk are:

- reducing the number of open doors
- concentrating after-school activities in limited areas

- assigning trained personnel to supervise activities rather than relying on custodians
- developing emergency/crisis preparedness training, and
- if contracting with an outside entity to run a program, building into the contract security requirements that must be followed.

A. Negligent Supervision

◆ While the drowning of an autistic student was tragic, a county educational service center wasn't liable for his death, an Ohio appeals court held. The seven-year-old attended a summer enrichment program for students with disabilities at his school. The boy – like many children with autism – had a tendency to wander. As such, he was assigned an aide. The day he died, the boy was taken to the gym by his aide. Once inside, the aide let go of the boy's hand. He wandered off. A janitor found him in the pool and jumped in to save him. Resuscitation efforts failed, and the boy died. His parents filed a negligence claim. They said the latch on the pool door was defective – and that is what allowed their son to get in the pool area and ultimately caused his death. To state a valid negligence claim, the parents had to show that the door was the proximate cause of their son's death. That wasn't the case here – as **he was not hit or trapped by the door**, the court explained. The court held for the county. *Kinderdine v. Mahoning County Board of Developmental Disabilities*, 69 N.E.3d 49 (Ohio Ct. App. 2016).

◆ Two ninth-graders slipped into a locker room during football practice and urinated all over a tenth-grader's gym locker. His father sued the school board, alleging negligent supervision. The Louisiana Court of Appeal upheld a judgment in favor of the school board, noting that there was no evidence that the coaches weren't properly supervising students at the time of the incident. **No one at the school had any notice that misbehavior might occur in the locker room because such an incident had never occurred before.** *Creekbaum v. Livingston Parish School Board*, 80 So.3d 771 (La. Ct. App. 2011).

◆ A California school district created an unstructured "open playground" for students who couldn't be picked up right away after school. Allegedly as few as two adults were responsible for overseeing up to 300 students. One seven-year-old student who stayed after school in the program was asked by another student to join a "kissing club" in an unlocked shed. She went to the shed, where a boy stuck his tongue in her mouth, which upset her so much that she left. Two days later, the student who had recruited her informed her that she had to come back to the club, which she did out of fear. At this meeting, the recruiter forced her to pull down her pants and the same boy then took off his pants and rubbed against her from behind. She later told a fifth-grader, who told the playground supervisor, who called the student's mother, who brought in the police. In the lawsuit that followed, the school asserted that it didn't have a duty of care to children who participated in voluntary after-school programs. A court agreed, but the California Court of Appeal reversed, holding that a trial was needed to determine if the lack of supervision was responsible for the student's injury and if the injury was foreseeable. Here, **the after-school program, despite its voluntary nature, created a special relationship between the school district and the program participants**. And the student had a right to reasonable protection while in the program. *J.H. v. Los Angeles Unified School Dist.*, 107 Cal.Rptr.3d 182 (Cal. Ct. App. 2010).

◆ A Connecticut elementary student participated in an after-school program run by the town of New Milford. While hanging on a basketball rim installed seven feet above the ground, he fell onto the concrete surface below and sustained injuries. He sued the town and the employees who had been supervising the program for negligence. After examining the "imminent harm" exception to discretionary act immunity, the Superior Court of Connecticut ruled in favor of the town. The imminent harm exception test requires three things: (1) an imminent harm; (2) an identifiable victim; and (3) a public official to whom it is apparent that his or her conduct is likely to subject that victim to that harm. Here, the supervisors testified that no one else had ever been hurt after dropping from the rim. Nor was hanging on the rim a prohibited activity. **Since there was no apparent risk of injury to the student, the town and employees were entitled to immunity.** *Zaborowski v. Town of New Milford*, No. LL1CV054002368S, 2007 WL 1413911 (Conn. Super. Ct. 4/24/07).

B. Duty to Protect Students

◆ A 14-year-old student injured his hand while playing basketball during an after-school program. **His hand hit a metal cage a foot away from the backboard, and the tip of a finger stuck there.** He sued the school to recover for his injuries. A court awarded him over $1 million in past and future damages (for the next 40 years). The Supreme Court, Appellate Division, upheld the finding of liability, noting that the student had not assumed the risk of such an injury. However, the damage award was excessive. The court offered the student $300,000 in damages or a new trial limited to determining an appropriate amount. *Robinson v. New York City Dep't of Educ.*, 94 A.D.3d 428 (N.Y. App. Div. 2012).

◆ A New York middle school student disobeyed his mother's instructions to attend an after-school program. Instead, he went to a park after school and fell from a swing, breaking his leg. He sued the after-school program, claiming a failure to adequately supervise. A trial court ruled against him, and the New York Supreme Court, Appellate Division, affirmed. A school's duty to supervise students is coextensive with its custody and control over them. Here, **the student got hurt while he was beyond the after-school program's authority**. Neither the program nor the school was responsible for his injuries. Even though the program failed to notify the student's mother that the boy didn't show up that day, that failure did not cause the child's injuries. *Fotiadis v. City of New York*, 853 N.Y.S.2d 591 (N.Y. App. Div. 2008).

◆ A California school opened its campus at 7:00 a.m., but trouble spots, such as restrooms, were unsupervised before 7:45 a.m. School administrators knew that one eighth-grade special education student was usually dropped off at 7:15 a.m. A classmate who also had disabilities teased and ridiculed the student daily before classes began. The student sometimes went to the office to escape this, and he complained to the staff. He was told to stay away from the classmate, even after he told the vice principal this did not work. The classmate twice isolated the student and sexually assaulted him. The district learned of the incidents and expelled the classmate, who was also arrested. The student was hospitalized with depression, and he attempted suicide. He sued the school district and the classmate's family. A jury trial resulted in a verdict of over $2.5 million for the student, and the district appealed.

The Court of Appeal of California observed that **school districts have a well-established duty to supervise students at all times while on school grounds. This duty included supervision during recess and before or after school.** The district was liable for injuries resulting from the failure of school staff to use ordinary care to protect students. The district unlocked its gates at 7:00 a.m. each day, but did not provide supervision until 7:45 a.m. It could have simply precluded students from arriving early or kept them in particular areas of the school. The district's claim to immunity failed because there was no exercise of discretion by the principal, and evidence that he knew of the classmate's violent behavior. The damage award was not excessive, and the court affirmed the judgment. *M.W. v. Panama Buena Union School Dist.*, 1 Cal. Rptr. 3d 673 (Cal. Ct. App. 2003).

◆ The family of a New York student brought a lawsuit against the board of education, seeking to recover damages for injuries the student allegedly sustained when, upon being pushed by a schoolmate, he fell down a staircase at a public school during an after-school program run by the YMCA of Greater New York. There was no handrail on the right side of the staircase where the student was walking. The supreme court denied the board's motion for pretrial judgment and the Supreme Court, Appellate Division, affirmed. The testimony of the student at a hearing and at his deposition demonstrated that he tried to grab the handrail on the opposite side of the stairs to stop his fall, but could not reach it. The unchallenged statement of the family's expert **engineer demonstrated that the absence of a handrail on the right side of the staircase was a violation of the applicable building code**. Thus, there were triable issues of fact as to whether the absence of the handrail was a proximate cause of the student's injuries and whether the fact that he was pushed by a fellow student severed any nexus (connection) between the city's alleged negligence in the design of the staircase and his injuries. The case required a trial. *Ocasio v. Board of Educ. of City of New York*, 35 A.D.3d 825, 827 N.Y.S.2d 265 (N.Y. App. Div. 2006).

II. FIELD TRIPS AND OFF-CAMPUS ACTIVITIES

Field trips provide a dual challenge to schools. First, they must ensure the safety of their students off school grounds, in settings where outside influences are not as easily controllable.

Second, they must ensure the safety of the general public from reasonably foreseeable acts of violence or horseplay by students. This latter concern, while slight for many schools (especially elementary schools), can be a real problem for others.

Increased supervision presents the single easiest solution, especially the usage of parent volunteers to assist with oversight. But this also presents a problem: how to verify that parent volunteers are not a threat. Background checks are the best insurance policy against threats to students.

Some schools charge parents to conduct background checks; others impose a fee for all students for field trips, a part of which can be used to conduct the background checks.

A. Negligent Supervision

1. Duty of Care

◆ A Louisiana mother couldn't show teachers acted with gross negligence in connection with a student's alleged injury, so a state appeals court dismissed her claim. In 2010, an autistic student went on a field trip to a movie theater. As everyone got off the bus, the student started running around. His teachers grabbed his hands and escorted him across the street. The boy fought them and became physically violent, so the teachers placed him in a two-person restraint. They gave him his medicine, and he settled down. He was able to watch the movie without incident. His mom sued, alleging her son got hurt when the teachers restrained him. The court dismissed the claim, and the appellate court affirmed. The real issue, the court explained, was whether the teachers' actions during the field trip constituted gross negligence or intent to harm. That wasn't the case here, the court found. Both teachers testified that they'd put the boy in the restraint only after he attempted to run into the street and fought to get away from them. Two paraprofessionals testified that the boy attacked the teachers by kicking, head-butting and biting them. **The evidence didn't support the allegations that the teachers intended to harm the child, and it didn't show their actions amounted to gross negligence**, the appeals court found. The ruling to dismiss was affirmed. *Baheth v. LaFayette Parish School System,* No. 17-821, 2018 WL 1936980 (La. Ct. App. 4/25/18).

◆ Connecticut's highest court upheld a $41.5 million verdict for a student who suffered permanent brain damage on a school field trip. In the summer of 2007, the student went on an educational field trip to China with her private boarding school. There, she was bitten by a tick while she was hiking. She contracted tick-borne encephalitis, a viral infectious disease that attacks the central nervous system. She suffered permanent brain damage. Her parents sued, claiming negligent planning before the trip and careless supervision during the trip caused life-changing harm. A jury awarded the family more than $41 million. The school appealed the jury award, and the long legal battle went all the way to the state supreme court. The school said the award was excessive. The court noted the student's condition rapidly deteriorated after hiking. Further, she had to be transferred to a Beijing hospital before her parents arrived. Further, by the time they arrived from New York to Beijing, their daughter was partially paralyzed. That meant the parents had to arrange for their daughter to be airlifted to a New York hospital. **The loss of life's enjoyments was compensable, but it was hard to measure, the court said, so those "damages [were] best left to jury."** It upheld the award. *Munn v. The Hotchkiss School,* SC 19525, 2017 WL 3473811 (Conn. 8/11/17).

◆ A California federal court refused to dismiss the negligence claim of a student who suffered serious injuries while on a mandatory field trip. The student had several disabilities, and the school was aware of her health issues. The district required students to participate in a nearby camp activity. The student's mother worked with the defendants to craft a care plan to ensure the child stayed safe during the trip. Specifically, she showed the teacher how to use her daughter's breathing machine and shared a written doctor's order, which stated that the child could not be exposed to direct sunlight. **While on the trip, she was left in the sun – despite her crying and complaints that she didn't feel well.** She was given Tylenol and told to lie down. A nurse wasn't provided. The student suffered injuries, including second-degree burns, heatstroke, health exhaustion and permanent damage to internal organs, including kidney failure. Her mom filed a negligence lawsuit. To state a valid claim, the mother had to show that the school breached its duty to protect the student, which caused her to suffer damages. The case had to go before a jury. *J.M. v. Pleasant Ridge Union School Dist.*, No. 2:16-00897 WBS CKD, 2016 WL 5930636 (E.D. Cal. 10/11/16).

◆ Staff at a private high school in Florida intercepted end-of-year party invitations with a faintly visible liquor bottle in the background. The principal announced that he intended to stop by the party and also talked with the host's parents to ensure that they would be home to chaperone. He arrived at the party around 4:00 p.m., confirmed that the host's mother was there, and left. About forty-five minutes later, two students who had gotten someone else to obtain alcohol for them left the party. They were drunk and crashed their car into a tree. One student died; the other became a quadriplegic. He and his parents sued the school and its archdiocese for negligence, **asserting that the principal, by undertaking to check on**

the party, had a duty to act with reasonable care, and that he breached that duty. A jury found the school defendants 25% at fault, but the Florida District Court of Appeal reversed. First, the private school's contract with students clearly stated that the school wasn't liable for events not officially sanctioned. Second, the accident occurred outside school hours at a non-school activity. The court refused to punish the school for the principal's good deed of checking up on the students. *Archbishop Coleman F. Carroll High School, Inc. v. Maynoldi*, 30 So.3d 533 (Fla. Dist. Ct. App. 2010).

◆ After being released from school on a rainy day, a 12-year-old New York student used a cell phone to call his mother, who was parked across the street. Although there was a stop sign, crosswalk and crossing guard at one intersection, and a stop light and crosswalk at the other, the student crossed in the middle of the street at his mother's direction. He was hit by a car and sustained injuries. His mother sued the school district for negligence in dismissing the student in an area it knew was hazardous. The New York Supreme Court, Appellate Division, dismissed the case, noting that schools are not insurers of student safety. **Schools' custodial duty of care for students ends when the students pass out of their "orbit of authority."** Here, the student was hurt while off school property and under the control of his mother, and there was no indication that the school had created a special hazard. *Vernali v. Harrison Cent. School Dist.*, 857 N.Y.S.2d 699 (N.Y. App. Div. 2008).

◆ Approximately 200 eighth-grade students from a middle school in Texas went on a field trip to an athletic club, where the activities included swimming. No lifeguards were hired. Sometime during the day, an eighth-grader drowned in the swimming pool. His family sued the district and various employees under 42 U.S.C. § 1983. The district employees sought pretrial judgment, asserting that they were entitled to immunity for their actions. The trial court disagreed, and the employees appealed to the Texas Court of Appeals. The claims here included allegations that the school district employees committed constitutional violations because they failed to properly supervise and/or discipline the student on the field trip. The court held that the school district employees were acting within the scope of their discretionary authority at the time of the incident. Further, **there was no special relationship to create a constitutional duty on the part of the employees to safeguard the student against potential harm during the field trip**. The employees should have been granted pretrial judgment. The appellate court reversed the lower court's decision. *Leo v. Trevino*, 285 S.W.3d 470 (Tex. Ct. App. 2006).

2. Harmful Acts of Others

◆ A student on a field trip to the National Zoo in Washington claimed that he was assaulted, kicked, and beaten by five male students who were on a school field trip with their private, non-profit school chartered under

District of Columbia law for at-risk youths. **He alleged that at the time of the attack, the students were unsupervised.** He also alleged that he suffered a concussion and injuries to multiple areas of his body. He sued the school, alleging negligent supervision. The school sought to dismiss the case, arguing that it owed the victimized student no duty to provide a constant watch over its students during a school field trip in order to prevent an unforeseeable act of violence. The injured student argued that the school did owe him a duty of care and cited to the Restatement of Torts (2d) § 319:

> One who takes charge of a third person whom he knows or should know to be likely to cause bodily harm to others if not controlled is under a duty to exercise reasonable care to control the third person to prevent him from doing such harm.

The court permitted the injured student to maintain his negligence claim on the ground that the school had a duty to make reasonable efforts to protect members of the public from its students during the field trip. **A school's duty to supervise its students to guard against foreseeable harm does not disappear on field trips.** So if the injured student could show that the school should have known his attackers had a propensity for violence, the school could be liable. *Thomas v. City Lights School,* 124 F.Supp.2d 707 (D.D.C. 2000).

◆ A New York student's sixth-grade class, along with five other fifth- and sixth-grade classes, attended a drug awareness fair at a park near their school. Sponsored by the board of education and the police department, the fair permitted students to walk through the park on their own and participate in program activities that interested them. Seven teachers and four or five aides supervised the group. A student received permission to get lunch at a nearby pizzeria, but she did not return from lunch by the time her teacher decided to return to school. The teacher looked for her but did not inform any teachers or police officers providing security at the fair that he could not locate her. The student had left the park to walk home after she failed to find her classmates. On the way home, she was raped by a junior high school student and his friend. She sued the board of education for her injuries.

A jury ruled in her favor and awarded her $2,250,000 in damages, but the Supreme Court, Appellate Division, reversed. The case then reached the Court of Appeals, New York's highest court, which held that a rational jury could have determined, as the jury in this case did, that the foreseeable result of the danger created by the school's alleged lack of supervision was an injury such as occurred here. The jury permissibly determined that **the rape was the foreseeable result of a danger created by the school's failure to adequately supervise the student**. Thus, the board was liable for the student's injuries. *Bell v. Board of Educ. of the City of New York*, 687 N.E.2d 1325 (N.Y. 1997).

◆ A Washington high school sponsored a "Workday" event, in which community members donated $15 for three hours of student work to raise funds for a student association. A student's mother agreed to let her daughter split and stack firewood with a classmate's father. She learned on the day of the event that the classmate's father planned to have the students split logs with a hydraulic log splitter. The mother cautioned the student, but apparently did not turn in a parental permission slip to perform the work. While the students were operating the log splitter, they were distracted by a car, and the student lost three fingers.

The student sued the school district and classmate's father for negligence. The court found the student's mother had consented to the activity and awarded judgment to the school district. The student appealed. The Court of Appeals of Washington stated that schools are not insurers of student safety, but are liable for foreseeable wrongful acts of third parties. **Liability may result if a school supervises and exercises control over extracurricular activities.** As the student was in the district's custody, it owed her a duty of reasonable care. A jury could have found the district should have taken appropriate steps to find out what was planned for each workday location and identify any obvious safety problems. The student had presented enough evidence to receive a jury trial to decide whether her mother's consent superseded the district's duty. The court reversed and remanded the case for a trial. *Travis v. Bohannon*, 115 P.3d 342 (Wash. Ct. App. 2005).

B. School Policies – Permission

◆ Kansas' highest court determined an injured student's travel was authorized, so he was entitled to reimbursement from the school's insurance company. Several soccer players traveled to an away game in a teammate's car. They were in an accident. One teen suffered injuries that required round-the-clock care. The school purchased an insurance policy to cover injuries sustained by athletes, as well as "covered travel" to and from sanctioned events. But the claim was denied. The student's mom sued the school and its insurance company. The school said the ride to the game wasn't "authorized travel" by the school as the student chose to forgo the team bus and ride with a teammate. The school pointed to a permission slip signed by the injured boy's dad that allowed him, among other things, to "ride with other players to games." The case reached the state supreme court, which rejected the school's argument. The court held that **by "employing permission slips from parents," the school "created and sanctioned" this system of informal transportation**. The court found the student was injured during authorized travel and could be reimbursed, so the case was remanded. *Rodriguez v. Unified School Dist. No. 500*, 351 P.3d 1243 (Kan. 2015).

◆ The summer before her senior year, an Illinois student went on two school-sponsored trips to China. She was told repeatedly that alcohol was forbidden, and she signed a contract to that effect. She and other students were caught drinking during the second trip. When she returned home, her principal suspended her for 10 days. She sought a preliminary injunction to stop the suspension and only served three days because she graduated before the case came to trial. When her lawsuit challenging the suspension came before a judge, the court ruled that her procedural due process rights had been met because **she had been informed of the charges and given an opportunity to respond to them**. *Sabol v. Walter Payton College Preparatory High School*, 804 F.Supp.2d 747 (N.D. Ill. 2011).

◆ A sixth-grade student with asthma went on a field trip to a district-operated science camp. When she suffered an attack, camp counselors gave the student her inhaler and performed CPR on her until paramedics arrived. However, she died as she was being airlifted to a hospital. Her parents sued the district that operated the science camp for negligently failing to provide adequate medical staff and for misrepresenting the level of medical staffing that would be available. The case reached the California Court of Appeal, which held that the district was entitled to immunity under the state education code. **Any person on a school field trip or excursion is deemed to have waived all claims against the school district**, charter school or the state for injury, accident, illness or death occurring "during or by reason of the field trip or excursion." The parents' lawsuit failed. *Sanchez v. San Diego County Office of Educ.*, 182 Cal.App.4th 1580, 106 Cal.Rptr.3d 750 (Cal. Ct. App. 2010).

◆ A teacher employed by the Kansas State School for the Deaf (KSSD) asked an assistant football coach to recruit players to help him improve property he owned. The project involved moving discarded railroad ties that weighed 150 pounds. The school's head teacher turned down a written request for a field trip to the property, but later signed the request form. Two students and the assistant football coach accompanied the teacher to the property. When the teacher left to prepare lunch, one of the students was struck and killed by a train. KSSD's board ruled the teacher's conduct did not reflect high standards of professional conduct, especially for the safety needs of deaf students. A KSSD investigation committee adopted a motion terminating the teacher's employment for jeopardizing the health and safety of students, failing to exercise appropriate professional judgment, failing to comply with school policies, and failing to conduct himself "in a manner reflecting positively on the school." However, a KSSD hearing committee held for the teacher, finding the board did not prove he displayed a lack of professional judgment.

The case reached the Kansas Supreme Court, which **upheld the hearing committee's finding that no school policy or student safety regulations applied to the case. The board showed no evidence of a loss of confidence in the teacher**, as the testimony of members of the deaf community was "all to the contrary." While the teacher did not inform parents about the nature of the field trip, this was the head teacher's duty. There was evidence that the practice of taking railroad ties from railroad property was common and not inappropriate. The court refused to reweigh the evidence or substitute its judgment for that of the committee. *Kansas State Board of Educ. v. Marsh*, 50 P.3d 9 (Kan. 2002).

C. Other Off-Campus Issues

◆ Despite a teacher's terrible conduct, the Eighth Circuit affirmed a ruling that backed a district's training and supervision of its employees. A Missouri district sponsored an overnight camp for fifth-graders that was staffed by district employees. In 2013, a teacher pleaded guilty to child pornography charges, admitting he'd used a hidden camera to record students in the nude inside the camp cabins from 2007 to 2011. John Doe filed suit on behalf of himself and other students the teacher recorded. He filed a Section 1983 due process claim, alleging the district failed to train and supervise its staff. To hold the district liable under Section 1983, Doe had to provide evidence showing the district's failure to supervise and train its employees "amount[ed] to deliberate indifference to the rights of [students that the teacher] came into contact with." Or he could've stated a valid claim by showing the need for training was "so obvious" that district policymakers could reasonably be said to have been "deliberately indifferent to the need." But Doe failed to provide any evidence showing the district had reason to believe its training and supervision were inadequate. He also failed to show the district had notice of the teacher's inappropriate conduct. He argued that a 2004 Department of Education report, estimating 4.5 million K-12 students experienced sexual misconduct by a school employee, provided notice. But the court disagreed, saying the report addresses "sexual misconduct generally, not child pornography." **The report was "insufficient to give the district notice of [the teacher's] particular misconduct or of the risk that he would videotape students in the nude."** Without notice, the school district was not deliberately indifferent, so the ruling for the school was affirmed. *Doe v. Fort Zumwalt R-II School Dist.*, 920 F.3d 1184 (8th Cir. 2019).

◆ A Maine federal court dismissed a due process claim filed by a grieving father. In 2018, 111 seventh-graders went on a field trip to a lake in a state park. Eleven chaperones went along, and one lifeguard was on duty. Midmorning, a student reported his friend, R.I., was missing. The lifeguard and chaperones searched the lake. Emergency crews found R.I.'s body but couldn't resuscitate him. R.I.'s dad filed a due process claim. He said the school "created a danger" that led to the "unknown circumstances" of R.I.'s death. He claimed the school's egregious actions "shocked the conscience." But **he didn't allege anyone took any deliberate course of action – or inaction – to end R.I.'s life**. Acknowledging R.I.'s tragic death, the court said the facts didn't show any conscience-shocking conduct by the defendants. The complaint "[didn't] come close" to stating a valid claim, the court explained, so the case was dismissed with prejudice – meaning it's closed for good. *Abdisamad v. City of Lewiston,* No. 2:19-CV-00175-LEW, 2019 WL 3307039 (D. Me. 7/23/19).

III. ATHLETIC EVENTS

Student-athletes assume the risks incidental to sports participation and, absent a showing of gross negligence or intentional conduct by a coach, league or school, may not recover damages for their injuries.

A. Participants

1. Duty of Care

State laws require a showing that the school or its staff acted recklessly or intentionally to overcome the defense of governmental immunity.

◆ An Illinois appeals court affirmed the dismissal of a student-athlete's negligence claim. At a middle school wrestling meet, the coaches placed several wrestling mats on the gym floor. The mats were spread out to create "walking lanes" for wrestlers and coaches. The student suffered a head injury when his head hit the gym floor in a walking lane between two mats. His father filed a negligence lawsuit, alleging the decision to separate the mats to create walking lanes amounted to "willful and wanton" misconduct. The court dismissed the claim, and the appeals court affirmed the ruling for the school. Illinois case law has established that educators who take "some precautions" to protect students from injury cannot be guilty of willful and wanton misconduct – even when the precautions are insufficient. The father argued the coaches essentially removed a necessary safety device when they spaced out the mats to create the walking lanes. That was a red herring, the court said. **It reasoned that if only one mat was used, the gym floor would be exposed on all four sides.** The father couldn't cite any safety standard that required connected mats at meets. The ruling was affirmed. *Trapp v. Valleyview School Dist. No. 365-U*, 2018 IL App (3d) 170722-U (Ill. App. Ct. 6/28/18).

◆ An Iowa jury decided a school fumbled its response to a football player's head injuries, so the former athlete was awarded nearly $1 million. The student played football on his school's team. He had a pre-existing medical condition: abnormally formed blood vessels in his brain. He suffered a head injury but was allowed to keep playing and practicing, which caused internal bleeding in his brain. Then he needed surgery to remove a blood clot near the brainstem. His permanent injuries resulted in a mobility impairment. A negligence suit alleged the district and the school nurse failed to notify the football coaches about the student's potential concussion or brain injury and follow up with the student's grandmother, his guardian, to make sure he was seen by a doctor.

The student received $140,000 for past medical expenses and $850,000 in additional damages for pain, suffering, loss of future earnings and loss of mind and body. But **the jury stopped short of awarding punitive damages,**

saying the evidence didn't show "willful and wanton" disregard. *K.R.S. v. Beford Community School Dist.*, No. 4:13CV00147, 2015 WL 3745161 (S.D. Iowa 5/11/15).

◆ In New York, a cheerleader was injured while attempting a stunt at practice. The move required the girl to stand on another cheerleader's shoulders. But she fell during the stunt. She sued the district, claiming the school was negligent because it did not provide proper supervision while she attempted the stunt. The trial court refused to grant the school judgment without a trial, but on appeal, the appellate court reversed. Under New York law, **a student assumes the inherent risks of an extracurricular activity by participating**. And because falling is an obvious risk associated with cheerleading, the claim failed. *Kristina D. v. Nesaquake Middle School*, 98 A.D.3d 600 (N.Y. App. Div. 2012).

◆ An Iowa high school basketball player elbowed an opposing player in the head during a game and was immediately ejected. The other player went to the bench briefly, but then returned to the game, though he played poorly from that point on. His family sued the school district and the player, seeking damages of more than $1.5 million. The case reached the Iowa Supreme Court, which dismissed the claim against the district, noting that **the battery by the player was not reasonably foreseeable, as was required for the district to be held liable for breaching a duty of care**. The student's prior conduct, although aggressive, did not put the district on notice that he was a dangerous person. The court did uphold, however, a damage award against the student for $23,000. *Brokaw v. Winfield-Mt. Union Community School Dist.*, 788 N.W.2d 386 (Iowa 2010).

◆ A 13-year-old student on his junior high school basketball team blacked out at a Monday practice. His mother told the coach that he was only allowed to walk through plays – and could not do anything strenuous. But at the Wednesday practice, the coach made the whole team, including the student, perform a running drill. After the student collapsed and died, his parents sued the school district for wrongful death. The district asserted that the student knew better than to perform a running drill in his condition; thus, his contributory negligence prevented the parents from recovering money damages. However, the Supreme Court of Indiana disagreed. It noted that **children 7 to 14 years old are generally too young to be held responsible for their own injuries** because they lack the maturity to foresee harm and take steps to prevent it. The only way to rebut the presumption that a 7- to 14-year-old is not responsible for his injuries is to show that the child had the "mental capacity, intelligence and experience" to be accountable for himself. Since that was not the case here, the parents were entitled to recover from the district. *Clay City Consolidated School Dist. v. Timberman*, 918 N.E.2d 292 (Ind. 2009).

◆ A Louisiana cheerleader – the "flyer" on her squad – suffered injuries when she was lifted up by an untrained recruit who held onto her feet tightly even though he should have left her feet free in case she needed to jump. When she fell, she landed on her back and sustained herniated discs that left her with chronic pain. She sued the school district for her injuries, and **a jury found the district negligent for allowing the untrained recruit to participate in the difficult stunt**. It awarded her more than $274,000. However, the judge reduced the amount by one-fourth, ruling that she was a quarter to blame because she didn't fall the right way. The Louisiana Court of Appeal reversed the judge's decision and gave her the full jury award. She did not breach a duty to fall a certain way when the stunt went bad. *Comeaux v. Acadia Parish School Board*, 13 So.3d 252 (La. Ct. App. 2009).

◆ A member of a high school track team in Pennsylvania sustained injuries when a teammate hit her in the leg with a javelin during practice. She sued the district and the coaches for negligence, and she also asserted that her due process rights had been violated. The defendants sought to have the case dismissed, and a federal court agreed to do so. First, it found no due process violation because **the district had proper policies in place to deal with injuries**. And even if the district failed to comply with those policies, that was not sufficient to support a due process claim. Further, the district did not have a special relationship with her such that it owed her an increased duty of care. Finally, the district did not create the danger that resulted in her injuries. It was the teammate's decision to throw the javelin that caused the harm. *Leonard v. Owen J. Roberts School Dist.*, No. 08-2016, 2009 WL 603160 (E.D. Pa. 3/5/09).

◆ A Louisiana freshman football player injured his back in a weight training session. His physician diagnosed him with a lumbar strain and dehydrated disc, and gave him a medical excuse excluding him from football for one week with instructions for "no weightlifting, squats or power cleans." The coaching staff interpreted the weightlifting limitation to be for only one week, and a coach instructed the student to do a particular lift. He did the lift and suffered severe back pain. The student was diagnosed with a disc protrusion and a herniated disc. He lost interest in school, failed classes and transferred to an alternative school. The student sued the school board for personal injury. A state trial court awarded him less than $7,500 for medical expenses, but awarded him $275,500 for pain and suffering, future medical expenses and loss of enjoyment of life.

The school board appealed to a Louisiana Circuit Court of Appeal, which reviewed testimony that the student continued to experience severe back pain and often could not sleep. **The evidence supported the trial court's finding that he had been severely injured and would experience recurring pain that would limit his daily activities indefinitely.** The trial court did not commit error in awarding the student damages for pain and suffering. The court affirmed the damage award for loss of enjoyment of life, based on evidence that the student lost the opportunity to play varsity baseball and football. There was further evidence he suffered depression and emotional anguish. *Day v. Ouachita Parish School Board*, 823 So.2d 1039 (La. Ct. App. 2002).

◆ A Maryland high school junior was the first female football player in her county's history. She participated in weightlifting, strength-training exercises and contact drills. In the first scrimmage with another team, the student was tackled while carrying the football and suffered multiple internal injuries. Three years later, the student and her mother sued the school board, claiming it had a duty to warn them of the risk of serious, disabling and catastrophic injuries.

A Maryland trial court granted the board's motion for summary judgment, finding no such duty to warn of the risk of varsity football participation. The student and her mother appealed to the Court of Special Appeals of Maryland. There they argued the lower court had erroneously held the board had no duty to warn of catastrophic risks and that the student had assumed the risk of injury by participating. **The court found no case from any jurisdiction holding that a school board had a duty to warn varsity high school football players that severe injuries might result.** The dangers of varsity football participation were self-evident, and there was no duty to warn of such an obvious danger. The court, therefore, affirmed the order for summary judgment in favor of the school board. *Hammond v. Board of Educ. of Carroll County*, 639 A.2d 223 (Md. Ct. Spec. App. 1994).

2. Governmental Immunity

The doctrine of governmental immunity precludes school or individual liability when employees are performing "discretionary duties" within the scope of their employment. By contrast, employees performing "ministerial duties" are not entitled to immunity, as are those who do not act in the scope of their employment. "Discretionary duties" means educators have the authority to make judgment calls while "ministerial duties" means an established school policy outlines procedures that must be followed in a specific situation.

◆ Wrestling coaches in Pennsylvania were entitled to immunity in a case involving a homeschooled teen. The teen participated as a member of the district's wrestling team. At a practice, the head coach and his assistant told the team that they wouldn't be wrestling that day. In the place of their usual practice drills, they'd be playing tackle football, the coaches said. Team members played in the gym without any protective equipment. Many boys were "violently tackled to the ground in ways that it was obvious that injury would occur if the activity was permitted to continue." About 20 minutes in, a teammate tackled the homeschooled student. His femur snapped in half. The injury required surgery and extensive physical therapy. The homeschooled student filed suit, alleging the coaches created the danger that caused his injury.

The court said a reasonable jury could find that the coaches' decision to have wrestlers play tackle football without proper protective equipment could amount to conscience-shocking behavior – so it refused to dismiss the case on that prong of the analysis. Valid state-created danger claims must allege the harm was caused by the defendants' affirmative actions – not their failure to act, the court explained. Here, the boy alleged the coaches "forced" the team to "play tackle football while at wrestling practice" without proper protective equipment, which caused his injuries. That met the affirmative-action element of the claim, the court held.

Public school officials are generally entitled to immunity in personal injury cases – meaning the charges can't stick unless they violated a clearly established federal legal right. In determining whether a legal right was clearly established, the court explained, the relevant question was: **Would it be clear to a reasonable school official that his conduct was unlawful in his current situation?** But the student didn't present any similar cases showing a coach created a danger by requiring students to play tackle football on a gym floor without proper equipment. The court's own search found no such cases either. The coaches were entitled to immunity. *Cuvo v. Pocono Mountain School Dist.*, No. 3:18-cv-01210, 2019 WL 1424524 (M.D. Pa. 3/29/19).

◆ Immunity was appropriate, so Connecticut school defendants couldn't be held liable for a soccer player's leg injury, a state appeals court decided. While playing soccer in PE, the class wasn't wearing shin guards. One student kicked another, and the victim suffered a fractured left tibia and fibula. His mom filed a negligence suit against the town, the board, the principal and the substitute teacher. The court held the defendants were entitled to immunity. On appeal, the mother said school policy required shin guards for soccer, so the court made the wrong call. Generally, educators are immune from personal injury suits – unless they failed to follow an established school policy. Here, the mother pointed to the school district's sports curriculum, which included a section titled, "Safety Guidelines." Under the section for soccer, it included a bulleted list: "No metal and/or molded cleats. Wear suitable footwear and clothing. Wear shin guards for additional protection. Wear sun protection. No jewelry." After looking at the documents, the court backed the school for two reasons. First, the word "guidelines" is generally understood to mean "best practices" – not mandatory rules, the court explained. And second, **the phrase, "for additional protection" after "wear shin guards" suggested that was a discretionary call to be made if extra protection was deemed necessary**. Furthermore, the guideline followed the more direct bullet point that specifically prohibited cleats, which "logically render[ed] the use of shin guards relatively less important as a safety concern," the court held. The policy wasn't violated, so the school defendants were entitled to immunity. The court affirmed the ruling for the school. *Washburne v. Town of Madison*, 175 Conn.App. 613 (Conn. App. Ct. 2017).

◆ An Oklahoma court refused to grant immunity on the negligence claim of a student who broke his neck during a pep rally practice. A student volunteered to participate in a pep rally cheer. At a practice supervised by school staffers, he and a friend attempted a two-man somersault. But the stunt went wrong. The teen suffered a broken neck that required hospitalization and surgeries. He sued, claiming negligence. When the court dismissed the claim, the student appealed, saying the district was liable under the theory of *respondeat superior*. In other words, he said the district was responsible for its employees' negligent conduct. To determine if the district could be held liable under this theory, the court had to decide whether immunity applied. It looked at whether the district had adopted a policy to allow the pep rally and practice, whether the employees who supervised the practice had the authority to make discretionary judgment calls, and if not, whether questions existed about how their duties were carried out during the pep rally practice. The court said the first prong was met for immunity. **But it couldn't determine whether the staffers were given discretion to make judgment calls – or whether a policy outlined how coaches must make decisions for the pep rallies and practices.** Questions existed, so immunity wasn't appropriate, the court explained. The ruling was reversed, and the case was remanded for further proceedings. *Hasenfratz v. Ponca City Independent School Dist.*, 358 P.3d 964 (Okla. Ct. App. 2015).

◆ The Third Circuit excused a Pennsylvania cheerleading coach from a lawsuit, finding she was entitled to immunity. After the squad saw the "twist down cradle" stunt at a competition, they wanted to learn it. The stunt called for four "base" cheerleaders to launch a "flyer" into the air, where she does a twist before landing in the bases' waiting arms. The coach waited seven months until she thought the squad was ready. Then she had another high school's cheerleader – an assistant coach for a middle school squad – demonstrate and help teach the stunt. The squad used a large room with a concrete floor for practice. Its carpeting had little, if any, padding. The day the squad started to learn the stunt, six to eight spotters plus four base cheerleaders were ready to catch the flyer. She overshot all of them. Landing badly, she struck her head on the floor and suffered a severe injury. The injured cheerleader sued the district and the coach, alleging they violated her substantive due process right to bodily integrity. A federal judge granted the district judgment without a trial. But it ruled the coach had to stand trial, as she wasn't immune to the claim. The coach appealed, and the Third Circuit reversed. School officials have qualified immunity if sued for violation of a constitutional right that wasn't clearly established at the time. The cheerleader argued that national cheering organizations' safety standards require padded floor mats, so the coach's "deliberate indifference" constituted a violation of her right to bodily integrity. But the Third Circuit found this wasn't clearly established, as **no court decisions would've informed "a reasonable person in [the coach's] position that failure to take certain precautions in a high school cheerleading practice** would amount to a constitutional violation" – so the court ruled the claim couldn't proceed. *Hinterberger v. Iroquois School Dist.*, 548 Fed. Appx. 50 (3d Cir. 2013).

◆ While lifting weights, two football teammates quarreled over the music they were listening to over the weight room's sound system. They started pushing each other, and teammates intervened to separate them. One began walking away, while teammates held the other one back. The coach then asked them if they wanted to settle it. The student being held back said he did, and the coach said, "OK." At that point, the formerly restrained student violently attacked the other one, causing injuries. When the student sued the coach for his injuries, the Michigan Court of Appeals ruled that **the coach was not the proximate cause of the injuries**, and thus he was entitled to immunity. He did not commit gross negligence, and the other student's assault was the most direct cause of the harm. *Gray v. Cry*, No. 07-717218-NO, 2011 WL 4375074 (Mich. Ct. App. 9/20/11).

◆ Two years after a highly publicized hazing incident involving football players at a New Mexico high school, a football player at another New Mexico high school was subjected to hazing by seniors. The seniors threw him to the floor, then physically and sexually battered him. He and his mother sued various officials, including the coaching staff, the principal and the superintendent, for negligence. The officials sought to have the case dismissed on immunity grounds, but a federal court allowed the lawsuit to proceed. Here, **they knew about the hazing at the other school and yet took no action to prevent hazing at the student's school**. *C.H. v. Los Lunas Schools Board of Educ.*, 852 F.Supp.2d 1344 (D.N.M. 2012).

◆ An Illinois school district operated a summer football camp. Coaches instructed camp participants to run from a locker room to the practice field. One student tripped over a grass-concealed shot-put bumper along the route and sustained injuries. His mother sued the school district for negligence, seeking $50,000. A state court granted recreational immunity to the district, but the Appellate Court of Illinois reversed. There was a question as to whether the camp was educational in nature, which would nullify the recreational immunity provisions of state law. The case required a trial. *Peters v. Herrin Community School Dist. No. 4*, 928 N.E.2d 1258 (Ill. App. Ct. 2010).

◆ A 17-year-old student suffered heatstroke during football practice at his Mississippi high school on a hot August day. After he collapsed, emergency responders were unable to revive him. Upon his death, his family sued the school district for negligence, and the case reached the Supreme Court of Mississippi, which ruled that **the district was entitled to immunity**. The Mississippi Tort Claims Act provides immunity to state and political subdivisions whose employees act in the course and scope of their employment and exercise discretion. Here, the coaches were exercising discretion in the way they conducted their practices. *Covington County School Dist. v. Magee*, 29 So.3d 1 (Miss. 2010).

◆ A Delaware school district agreed to let its facilities be used by a charitable organization that wanted to conduct a cheerleading competition. During the event, a man fell off the bleachers, which did not have guard rails installed. He sued the organization and the district for his injuries, and the school district asserted that it was entitled to immunity. The Superior Court of Delaware noted that the organization had agreed to indemnify the district for any damages resulting from a judgment against it. **The court then found some evidence that school employees, without justification, deliberately chose not to install safety devices** and thus created a known risk. As a result, an issue of fact remained that required a trial. If the district was grossly negligent in electing not to install guard rails, the organization would have to pay the man for his injuries. But the district would not have to pay. *Boyle v. Christiana School Dist. Board of Educ.*, No. 07C-07-248 JAP, 2009 WL 4653832 (Del. Super. Ct. 11/30/09).

◆ A Georgia high school student participated in a voluntary workout session for the football team. The next morning, he collapsed and died. His parents sued the school system, school officials and several coaches, asserting that their son had been subjected to an "intense and unreasonable practice." They claimed the coaches failed to give their son enough to drink and ignored signs that he was becoming dehydrated. They also stated that the coaches failed to attend to their son until after a team meeting, even though he had collapsed during drills. They maintained that the coaches violated their son's substantive due process rights. A federal court dismissed all the defendants except three coaches, who appealed. The Eleventh Circuit held that **the coaches were entitled to qualified immunity because their conduct did not rise to a "conscience-shocking" level**. The parents made no allegation that the coaches intended to harm their son. Thus, they failed to prove a constitutional violation. *Davis v. Carter*, 555 F.3d 979 (11th Cir. 2009).

◆ A 14-year-old Minnesota student participated in a community education gymnastics program sponsored by a local school district. She performed a difficult vault known as a Tsukahara vault, which she had performed many times previously. This time she under-rotated and landed on her knees. She told a coach she would try it again, but that she would need assistance. However, when she attempted it a second time, no assistance was provided. The second time, she also under-rotated and landed on her head. She sued the school district for negligence. The district sought to have the lawsuit dismissed on grounds of immunity, but a trial court refused to do so. The Minnesota Court of Appeals reversed the lower court and granted immunity to the district. **The state's recreational use statute generally bars claims based on injuries sustained on government property that is intended for recreational use.** And no exception applied to the statute in this case. *Goetz v. Independent School Dist. No. 625*, No. A08-0254, 2009 WL 22270 (Minn. Ct. App. 1/6/09).

◆ In an effort to improve security, a Tennessee school board approved the installation of video surveillance equipment throughout one of its middle schools. The assistant principal decided to place cameras in the boys' and girls' locker rooms. Images were displayed on a computer in the assistant principal's office. They could also be accessed through a remote Internet connection. **When the assistant principal learned that the cameras were videotaping areas where students routinely dressed, he recommended to the principal that the cameras be moved, but no changes were made.** After a visiting girls' basketball team noticed the camera and complained, the principal assured the coach that the camera was not operational, although in fact it was. The next day, the locker room cameras were removed. Thirty-four students then sued for a violation of their privacy rights. The principal, assistant principal, director of schools and school board members claimed immunity. The Sixth Circuit Court of Appeals held that the board members and the director were entitled to immunity because their roles in placing the cameras were too indirect to make them liable. However, the principal and assistant principal were not immune. They violated a clearly established constitutional right to privacy at the time of the videotaping. *Brannum v. Overton County School Board*, 516 F.3d 489 (6th Cir. 2008).

◆ An Ohio student injured his forehead and wrist during a pole vault at a high school track meet. He landed on improper padding near the landing pad. The padding was later identified as in violation of National Federation of State High School Associations rules. The student sued the school district, coach and other officials for negligence. The court awarded pretrial judgment to the district and school officials, but the Court of Appeals of Ohio held that the trial court had improperly granted immunity under the state recreational user statute. The student was not a "recreational user." The student did not assume the risk of being provided inadequate safety equipment for pole vaulting. The sponsor of a sporting event has a duty not to increase the risk of harm over and above any inherent risks of the sport.

While the Ohio Political Subdivision Tort Liability Act generally grants immunity to government entities, an exception applies when an injury was caused by employee negligence occurring on school grounds in connection with a governmental function. The court rejected the district's claim to immunity. The Tort Liability Act protects employees unless they act with a malicious purpose, in bad faith, or in a wanton or reckless manner. **The**

track coach was entitled to immunity, because there was no evidence he acted with malice, bad faith or reckless or wanton conduct. The court affirmed the judgment in the coach's favor, but held the action could proceed against the school district. *Henney v. Shelby City School Dist.*, No. 2005 CA 0064, 2006 WL 747475 (Ohio Ct. App. 3/23/06).

◆ A Maine high school wrestling team ran timed drills in school hallways as part of its warm-up routine. A wrestler was seriously injured after being bumped into a window by a teammate during a drill. The school had no policy prohibiting athletic training in school hallways at the time. The student sued the school district in a state court for personal injury, asserting officials negligently allowed the team to competitively race through the hallways. The court held the district and officials were protected by discretionary immunity. The student appealed to the Maine Supreme Judicial Court, which stated that **governmental entities are generally entitled to absolute immunity from suit for any tort action for damages**. One of four state law exceptions to this rule imposes liability on government entities for the negligent operation of a public building.

The court held that allowing relay races in the school hallway was not the "operation of a public building." The focus of this case was the manner in which the team was required to run through the halls, not the operation of a high school building. To impose liability under the "public building" exception to immunity, the claim must implicate the physical structure of the building. Decisions, such as wrestling team rules, focused on the supervision of students, not the maintenance or operation of the building. **Since the failure to prohibit racing in the halls was not related to the operation of a public building, the district and officials were protected by discretionary immunity.** *Lightfoot v. School Administrative Dist. No. 35*, 816 A.2d 63 (Me. 2003).

3. Assumption of Risk and Waiver

Many courts have determined that when a participant has assumed the risks of playing sports, a school district should not be held liable for injuries.

◆ A New York appeals court affirmed a decision to dismiss an injured student's tort claim. In 2012, a student was hurt during a basketball game in PE when he was kicked in the leg by a classmate. The student filed a tort claim, seeking damages. When the court dismissed the claim, the student appealed, but the appellate court affirmed the ruling. The school said the claim was barred by "the doctrine of primary assumption of risk." The gist is, it's the common-sense idea acknowledging that "by engaging in a sport ... a participant consents to those commonly appreciated risks" inherent in the nature of the sport, which means **it wouldn't be fair to hold a school liable for injuries that are likely to occur**. However, if an injury is caused due to reckless or intentional misconduct, then the participant does not assume the risk of injury. Here, the school said the student voluntarily engaged in the basketball game and was aware of the obvious risks of the activity, including the possibility of having contact with or colliding into another player. The student didn't allege conduct showing the school was reckless, so the claim was dismissed. *Hanson v. Sewanhaka Cent. High School Dist.*, No. 07711, 2017 WL 5163149 (N.Y. App. Ct. 11/8/17).

◆ A New York appeals court refused to dismiss the negligence claim of a student-athlete who was injured before football coaches arrived for practice. The football players' horseplay got out of hand when they used a blocking sled to hurl each other through the air. A 15-year-old fractured both wrists as he landed. He and his mother filed a negligence claim, but the court dismissed the case, saying the football player "assumed the risk of injury." On appeal, the boy's mom argued **this wasn't a typical sports injury, where her son assumed the risk by participating, because "using the blocking sled to catapult each other into the air" wasn't part of the game**. And the coach wasn't on the field at the time, the mother pointed out, which she said showed the students weren't properly supervised. The court said more info was needed to determine whether the level of supervision was appropriate, so the case had to move forward. *Duffy v. Long Beach City School Dist.*, 22 N.Y.S.3d 88 (N.Y. App. Div. 2015).

◆ **A New York wrestler contracted herpes simplex I and believed he caught it from a wrestler at another school.** He sued his school, the other school and the other student for personal injury. A state court refused to dismiss the case, but the Supreme Court, Appellate Division, threw the case out. It noted that communicable diseases are an inherent danger of the sport and that students' participation is seen as an agreement to accept the obvious risks associated with wrestling. Even the student's own expert witness acknowledged that the possibility of contracting herpes and other communicable diseases from wrestling was well known. *Farrell v. Hochhauser*, 65 A.D.3d 663 (N.Y. 2009).

◆ Indiana parents received a new trial in a lawsuit based on the death of their son from heatstroke after a school football practice. The release forms they signed did not specifically waive claims based on negligence. The student, who weighed over 250 pounds, had "dry heaves" early in a morning practice session. He stopped his activity for a minute, then told two coaches he felt better. The student ate lunch during a team rest period and kept it down. He spent time lying on the locker room floor. The head coach asked the student how he felt, and the student again said he was OK. Near the end of the afternoon session, the student told a coach he did not feel well. The coach told him to get water, but he soon collapsed. The coaches took him to the locker room and placed him in a cool shower. The student lost consciousness, and the coaches called for an ambulance. He died at a hospital the following day.

The student's parents sued the school district for negligence. A jury returned a verdict for the school district. The parents appealed to the Court of Appeals of Indiana, which noted that **the release forms signed by the parents and students did not refer to "negligence."** Thus, the district was not effectively released from negligence claims. The trial court should have granted the parents' request for a jury instruction stating they had not released the district from negligence. The court reversed and remanded the case for a new trial. *Stowers v. Clinton Cent. School Corp.*, 855 N.E.2d 739 (Ind. Ct. App. 2006).

◆ A Massachusetts school district required a signed parental release for all students seeking to participate in extracurricular activities. For four years, the father of a high school cheerleader signed a release form before each season. During her fourth year, she was injured during a practice. When the cheerleader reached age 18, she sued the city in a state superior court for negligence and negligent hiring, and retention of the cheerleading coach. The court awarded summary judgment to the city on the basis of the parental release, agreeing that **the father had forever released the city from any and all actions and claims**.

The cheerleader appealed to the Massachusetts Supreme Judicial Court, asserting the release was invalid. The court held the trial court properly allowed the city to amend its answer by asserting release. **Enforcement of a parental release was consistent with Massachusetts law and public policy.** There was undisputed evidence that the father read and understood the release before signing it, and that the form was not misleading, since it required two signatures and clearly ensured parental permission was granted. It was not contrary to public policy to require parents to sign releases as a condition for student participation in extracurricular activities. The father had signed the release because he wanted the student to benefit from cheerleading. The court found that to hold the release unenforceable would expose public schools to financial costs and risks that would lead to the reduction of extracurricular activities. *Sharon v. City of Newton*, 437 Mass. 99, 769 N.E.2d 738 (Mass. 2002).

◆ A New York student participated on his high school wrestling team and was instructed before a match to wrestle an opponent in the next higher weight class. The student agreed to do so and was injured when the opponent hit his jaw during a take-down maneuver. The student voluntarily continued participating in the match after a medical time-out. He later filed a personal injury lawsuit against the school district in a New York trial court, which denied the district's dismissal motion. On appeal, the New York Supreme Court, Appellate Division, stated that **the student had assumed the risk of incurring a blow to the jaw and the injury was reasonably foreseeable in a wrestling match**. There was evidence that the size of the opponent had not caused the injury and that the student was aware of the risks involved in wrestling. The district's duty of care was limited to protecting the student from unassumed, concealed or unreasonable risks. The trial court judgment was reversed. *Edelson v. Uniondale Union Free School Dist.*, 631 N.Y.S.2d 391 (N.Y. App. Div. 1995).

B. Spectators, Employees and Parents

◆ A New York appeals court affirmed a ruling that dismissed a personal injury claim involving a dog on school grounds. A visitor brought a dog to a high school lacrosse practice. It broke loose and started chasing a student. While running from the dog, that student collided with another student who allegedly suffered injuries. That student and her mother sued to recover damages, claiming the school's inadequate supervision was the proximate cause of the injuries. To state a valid claim, the girl and her mother had to show the school authorities had "notice of the dangerous conduct which caused [the] injury." This was important, the court explained, because the school couldn't "reasonably be expected to guard against all of the sudden, spontaneous acts that take place among students daily." Here, no evidence suggested the school had notice of the danger, as there were no prior instances of dogs being brought to school fields during sports practices. **Moreover, two students colliding was a "spontaneous, impulsive and intervening act that could not have been anticipated," the court held.** The alleged lack of supervision wasn't the proximate cause of the girl's injuries, so the ruling for the school was affirmed. *B.J. v. Board of Educ. of the City of New York*, No. 7470/14, 2019 WL 1925963 (N.Y. App. Div. 5/1/19).

◆ A Pennsylvania appeals court affirmed the dismissal of a personal injury claim against a school district. In 2017, a woman went to a high school to watch her granddaughter's cheerleading competition. When she left, she tripped over a concrete parking spot bumper that was removed from the parking lot and was left sitting across a walkway. She suffered a fractured tibia. The grandmother filed a personal injury suit, and the court tossed her claim, saying the district was entitled to immunity. She filed an appeal, arguing that the court made the wrong call. She said it should've found the bumpers were "real property" under an exception provided by state law. But the court wasn't swayed by the argument. It said the state supreme court established that items not attached to real estate are not "realty," so the exception didn't apply. The parking spot bumpers weren't attached to parking spot surfaces. They were designed to be removable so snow plows could clear parking lots without damaging property. **The bumper wasn't attached, so it wasn't real property.** Here, the injury resulted from an item placed on real property, the court explained. The exception didn't apply, so the ruling for the school was affirmed. *Camacho v. West Chester Area School Dist.*, No. 390 C.D. 2017, 2017 WL 6598593 (Pa. Commw. Ct. 12/27/17).

◆ A New York appeals court dismissed the claim of a man who was injured while playing flag football on a school campus. The man and his local league played their games on the grounds of a high school. Prior to the games, he and his teammates signed a "Waiver and Release of Liability." The man said that during a game in 2015, he hurt his left foot when he jumped to catch a pass and landed on a concealed sprinkler head. He filed a negligence claim against the school and the league. Pointing to the signed waiver and release, the defendants asked the court to dismiss the claim. It did, and the man appealed. In New York, defendants establish a *prima facie* right to dismissal by producing the waiver and release the plaintiff signed. As a general rule, courts won't set aside a waiver and release "without a showing of duress, illegality, fraud or mutual mistake." Here, the court held **the language used was "clear and unambiguous" so it was "valid, enforceable and binding."** Case dismissed. *Marc v. Middle Country School Dist.,* No. 3015-2016, 2017 WL 6329846 (N.Y. App. Div. 12/11/17).

◆ Having decided a federal claim could not proceed, a Georgia federal court refused to hear a coach's state-law claims and dismissed his suit. Georgia high schools Warren County and Hancock Central were football rivals. Early in the 2011 football season, Warren fired its head coach and Hancock hired the coach as an assistant. The coach said his new team saw that year's game against Warren as a chance to "get even" for the way he was treated by his former team. A week before the game, football players from both teams got into such a heated altercation that police put one boy in handcuffs. Over the next week, the players and other students exchanged taunting text messages. The matchup was Hancock's homecoming game. Twelve officers were scheduled for security, but only four officers were at the game. Hancock lost 21-2. After their loss, Hancock players taunted the Warren team. A fight broke out. Cops rushed forward with pepper spray, and the coach tried to stop a Hancock athlete from hitting a Warren player. The Hancock athlete turned and attacked, hitting the coach in the face and head with a helmet. He suffered a "blow out" of the bones around one eye, requiring multiple surgeries and metal plates. He also needed extensive treatment in a brain injury rehabilitation program. The injuries have permanently impaired his ability to work. He sued Hancock's school district in federal court. Along with state-law claims, the coach alleged a breach of his substantive Fourteenth Amendment right to bodily integrity by failing to protect him. He said the district hired only four off-duty deputy sheriffs and knew they had no crowd-control experience. The court dismissed the claim, finding **the acts didn't "shock the conscience" in the constitutional sense**. With no federal claims remaining, the federal court dismissed the suit. *Daniel v. Hancock County School Dist.*, No. 5:13-CV-390 (CAR), 2014 WL 1813712 (M.D. Ga. 5/7/14).

◆ A New York school hosted a charity football game played by two other schools. A student who was a member of the hosting school's football team attended the charity event as a spectator. During halftime, the student went into the locker room to get gear from his locker. The locker room was being used by one of the visiting teams playing in the charity game. There, the student got into an argument with the visiting team's coach and head-butted him. Defending their coach, the team jumped the student. He suffered injuries he claimed were permanent. The student sued multiple parties for personal injury, including the city of New York and its department of education. He claimed the defendants breached their duty to provide for students' safety. But the court ruled that the defendants have no duty to protect students from injuries by a third party unless the school had a special relationship with the student. **The school wasn't liable because it had no reasonable warning the attack might occur and the attack happened "in a matter of seconds" – too fast for an onlooker to step in.** So the claim failed. *Chavis v. City of New York*, No. 101909/11, 2013 WL 3388643 (N.Y. Sup. Ct. 6/28/13).

◆ An Illinois man took his son to the local high school's batting cage to throw batting practice for him. He sat on a bucket behind a screen to throw pitches. One ball hit back by his son struck the screen, passed through the mesh, and struck him in the face, causing injury. He sued the school, alleging that it was willful and wanton in providing defective equipment. However, the Appellate Court of Illinois ruled against him, noting that **no one had seen the defect in the screen, including the man himself.** Therefore, the school couldn't have been willful and wanton in providing defective equipment because no one saw a defect. *Vilardo v. Barrington Community School Dist. 220*, 941 N.E.2d 257 (Ill. App. Ct. 2010).

◆ A Louisiana child sustained injuries when she fell while on the bleachers at a high school football game. Her parents claimed the fall was caused by a lack of adequate traction guards on the bleachers, and they sued the school board. A school custodial supervisor, however, testified that he saw the child being chased just before she fell. He also testified that the girl's family did nothing to stop her while she ran along the bleachers. A court ruled for the school board, and the Louisiana Court of Appeal affirmed. **It found no evidence that the bleachers were defective** or that there had been prior similar incidents in the area where the fall had occurred. *Mason v. Monroe City School Board*, 996 So.2d 377 (La. Ct. App. 2008).

◆ A physical education teacher at a New York high school adjusted a volleyball net that had been set up improperly by another teacher. As she stepped back from the base that supported the net, the teacher fell and twisted her ankle. She sued the board of education to recover for her injuries, and the board sought pretrial judgment. The New York Supreme Court, Appellate Division, granted the motion. It noted that **the duty to provide a safe workplace does not obligate an employer to remove hazards that typically come with the job**. Nor are employers required to protect employees from conditions or defects that are open and obvious. The teacher was hurt while performing a task that was inherent in her employment. In addition, the condition that caused the fall was open and obvious. Accordingly, the teacher could not recover damages for her injuries. *Monahan v. New York City Dep't of Educ.*, 851 N.Y.S. 2d 586 (N.Y. App. Div. 2008).

◆ A West Virginia spectator slipped and fell on ice and snow on school grounds while going to a high school basketball game. On the day of the injury, the superintendent of schools canceled all classes in county schools because of a major snow storm. But the high school principal and athletic director decided not to cancel the game. The spectator sued the board, arguing it was negligent to hold the basketball game on a day when the entire school system was closed. The school board claimed immunity under the state Governmental Tort Claims and Insurance Reform Act. The Supreme Court of Appeals of West Virginia ruled that the school board was entitled to immunity. **The court rejected the spectator's argument that the decision to hold the basketball game was an affirmative act that was not immunized.** While the act of holding the game may have encouraged her to venture out into the snow, it did not cause the conditions at the school. The Tort Claims and Insurance Reform Act provided immunity for losses or claims resulting from snow or ice on public ways caused by the weather. *Porter v. Grant County Board of Educ.*, 633 S.E.2d 38 (W.Va. 2006).

◆ A spectator at a high school football game in New York was stabbed during a fight that occurred on school grounds following the game. The spectator sued the school district and school officials in a New York trial court. The court held for the spectator, and the school appealed to a New York appellate division court. The spectator claimed the school was negligent when it failed to properly supervise the crowd. The court disagreed, holding **the district could not be found negligent because it did not have a duty to supervise non-student spectators at the game**. The court reversed the judgment and held for the district. *Jerideau v. Huntingdon Union Free School Dist.*, 21 A.D.3d 992, 801 N.Y.S.2d 394 (N.Y. App. Div. 2005).

IV. OTHER SCHOOL ACTIVITIES

Courts have held schools liable for injuries during school-sponsored events that resulted from the failure to provide a reasonably safe environment, failure to warn participants of known hazards (or to remove known dangers), failure to properly instruct participants in the activity, and failure to provide supervision adequate during age-appropriate school events, such as plays, dances, musicals and more. For a sample behavior contract at school dances, go to *www.SchoolSafetyAndSecurityAlert.com* and search "Behavior Contract/Prom Permission Slip."

A. Physical Education Class Accidents

1. Duty of Care

Courts have held that schools and staff members are not liable for injuries that are unforeseeable. It has long been recognized that schools are not the insurers of student safety. The fact that each student is not personally supervised at all times does not itself constitute grounds for liability.

◆ An Illinois judge threw out a $272,285 verdict that stemmed from a student fight as PE ended. In 2016, a fight broke out at the end of the line as students came out of the locker room. The fight occurred in an area known as "the pool hallway." At the time, one teacher was at the front of the line, leading students back to their regular class. The other was in the gym. A student was injured in the fight. He filed suit, alleging gross negligence. A jury found for the student, but the court overturned the award. **"The mere act of leaving children unsupervised" for a short time (seven minutes in this case) could not "establish willful and wanton misconduct,"** the court said. To prove "willful and wanton negligence in supervision," the boy had to show the teachers "knew or should've known that a lack of supervision posed a high probability of serious harm." Here, there was no evidence that the teachers were aware of a credible threat to the student. The verdict was overturned. *Rogers v. McConnaughay*, No. 3-17-0690, 2018 IL App (3d) 170690-U (Ill. App. Ct. 9/24/18).

◆ A New York appeals court refused to dismiss a negligence claim filed in connection with a playground accident. In 2012, a student was injured when he fell from monkey bars on a school playground. He and his mother filed a negligence lawsuit. The student said he climbed to the top of the monkey bars, where he did a cartwheel into a handstand followed by a swinging dismount. The first time, he succeeded. On his second attempt, he lost his balance during the handstand and fell to the ground. Video surveillance captured part of the second attempt. School aides were supervising the kids, but they didn't stop the student, the suit claimed. At deposition, an aide testified that if she'd seen what the boy was doing, she "absolutely would have stopped him" and "probably" would've sent him to the principal's office. She further testified the boy was a known trickster who'd been reprimanded for improper use of playground equipment. The school asked the court to dismiss the case, but it refused because **there were questions as to whether the student's prior conduct and alleged reputation warranted heightened supervision – and if so, whether that extra supervision would've prevented his injury**. The claim had to proceed. *SM v. Plainedge Union Free School Dist.*, No. 14550/13, 2018 WL 2945403 (N.Y. App. Ct. 6/13/18).

◆ An Illinois federal court rejected a negligence claim in a suit involving an injured 10-year-old, but it held a due process claim could move forward. While climbing on monkey bars, a girl fell on a seesaw located underneath them. Her teacher took her to the office. No nurse was on duty. No school administrators called 911. Within an hour, the teacher called the girl's mother. When the mother arrived, she found her daughter sitting in the hallway alone, crying and covered in blood. The mother called 911. At the hospital, the girl required two surgeries to repair a sub-clitoral laceration and drain a hematoma that developed on her labia minora. The mother sued. The court held a due process claim had to go to trial under the state-created danger theory. **A jury could find the decision to "place a crying and bleeding 10-year-old in excruciating pain in the school hallway, with no adult supervision and no attempt to address her medical needs" amounted to behavior that "shocked the conscience," the court said.** So a trial was needed. *Fonza v. Chicago Public Schools Dist. #299*, No. 17-CV-3571, 2018 WL 337811 (N.D. Ill. 1/9/18).

◆ A school wasn't liable for injuries to a student with disabilities who collided with a classmate while playing a schoolyard game, a New York appeals court held. A third-grader had an IEP and a 1:1 aide. During recess, he was playing a game of "wall ball." While chasing after the ball, the boy and a classmate ran into each other. At the time, the boy's aide was about 10 feet away, and a PE teacher was also nearby. The boy's father sued, alleging negligence. The court dismissed the case, and the father appealed. Schools have a duty to supervise students, but they aren't the insurers of student safety and "can't be held liable for every thoughtless or careless act by which one pupil may injure another," the court explained. Here, the court found **"the accident was caused by a sudden and spontaneous collision which could not have been prevented by more intense supervision"** so the alleged inadequate supervision was not the proximate cause of the injury, the court held. The ruling to dismiss was affirmed. *Tzimopoulos v. Plainview-Old Bethpage Cent. School Dist.*, 155 A.D.3d 987 (N.Y. App. Div. 2017).

◆ An Idaho federal judge refused to dismiss claims filed on behalf of a student who lost sight in his right eye after being stabbed with a stick. On April 14, 2015, an elementary school was shorthanded. Two staffers – rather than the usual four – manned the playground, as per the principal's instruction. A student with a long history of disciplinary issues stabbed a classmate in the eye with a stick while they were at recess. The injury required two surgeries and caused permanent blindness in the victim's right eye. His parents sued, alleging the principal provided negligent supervision by letting a known violent student use an understaffed playground during recess, and the district was negligent because it failed to train the principal on best practices to comply with its anti-bullying policy. The defendants asked the court to dismiss the claims without a trial. Given the attacker's history of violence, **a reasonable jury could find the principal's conduct was "reckless, willful and wanton,"** the court said. As for the claim against the district, the court noted that an established anti-bullying policy outlined general disciplinary instructions and reporting guidelines. But the principal testified that she'd never received training on administering student discipline or documenting incidents of bullying. As such, a reasonable jury could conclude that the district failed to train the principal to comply with its policy. The court refused to dismiss the claim against the principal and the district. *Wilson v. Salmon School Dist.*, No. 4:16-cv-00117-BLW, 2017 WL 3723640 (D. Idaho 8/29/17).

◆ Illinois' highest court rejected the personal injury claim of a student who was hurt while playing floor hockey. In PE class, students were allowed to choose a cardio activity. The plaintiff and 11 classmates opted to play floor hockey – as they'd done many times before. In this version of floor hockey, students used plastic rather than wooden sticks. And they used a "squishy" ball instead of a puck. Students also had other safety rules, such as no high sticks and no checking. One day, the plaintiff was injured when the ball bounced off his stick and hit him in the eye, causing injury. He filed a tort claim, saying the teacher should've made students wear available protective eyewear while playing. The long legal battle continued to the state supreme court. **The gist of the case was whether the teacher's decision not to require students to wear protective eyewear amounted to "willful and wanton" conduct, the court said.** While negligence conveys a degree of inadvertence, "willful and wanton misconduct" conveys an intent to cause harm or utter indifference to the risk of harm, the court explained. Here, the opposite was true: The evidence showed the teacher "consciously considered student safety" when she imposed several rules to help make the game safer for students. Thus, the teacher's conduct was not "willful or wanton," so she could not be held liable. *Barr v. Cunningham*, 2017 IL 120751 (Ill. 3/23/17).

◆ Wyoming's supreme court rejected the negligence claim of a student who slipped and fell in a school locker room. The student took a swimming class for her PE course. When she fell in the locker room, she injured her back. She needed three surgeries. She sued the school for negligence, claiming it failed to maintain the shower facilities in a reasonably safe condition. Her suit alleged the shower drains were backed up and flooded into the dressing area. After a trial, the court granted judgment for the school. The student appealed to the state supreme court, which upheld the ruling. **The plumber – a 16-year veteran of the district – testified that he'd only needed to "snake" the drain on one occasion, and the head custodian testified about the daily, monthly and yearly cleaning routines.** The evidence didn't support the claim that the area was not properly maintained. So her claim failed. *Halvorson v. Sweetwater County School Dist.*, 342 P.3d 395 (Wyo. 2015).

◆ A New York appeals court reversed a ruling to dismiss the suit of a student who was injured in gym class. The PE teacher told the class to walk backward fast. One girl asked to be excused from the exercise, saying her ankle hurt and felt unstable. The teacher denied her request to be excused. So the girl obeyed, but she fell while walking backward and was seriously hurt. Her family sued New York City's school district for personal injury, claiming the girl had been negligently supervised. The district asked the court to grant it judgment without a trial. It did and dismissed the lawsuit. But the family appealed, and the appeals court reversed. New York **schools have a duty to supervise students with the same degree of care as a "reasonably prudent parent."** Schools can be held liable for injuries that are foreseeably caused by their failure to do so. The appeals court decided a trial was needed to determine whether this school was negligent – as it's arguably foreseeable that a child with a weak and painful ankle could suffer a fall and an injury if forced to walk backward fast. The appeals court decided the trial court was wrong to dismiss the suit, so it sent the case back to the lower court for further proceedings. *Anastasiya M. v. New York City Board of Educ.*, 976 N.Y.S.2d 202 (N.Y. App. Div. 2013).

◆ A New York fourth-grader fell off the balance bar during a physical education class. She climbed back on the bar, fell off again, climbed up again and fell a third time, injuring her ankle. A fellow student then ran over to the teacher to tell him about it. The student's parents sued the district for negligent supervision, and the district sought pretrial judgment. Both a trial court and the Supreme Court, Appellate Division, held that a trial was required. Here, the teacher admitted that both the balance beam station and the rope climbing station required extra supervision. Therefore, a question of fact existed as to whether the district was negligent in supervising the student and whether its alleged negligence caused the student's injury. **The student's three falls, plus the fact that a student had to run to get the teacher, suggested that the teacher failed to provide the extra supervision he knew was needed.** *Talyanna S. v. Mount Vernon City School Dist.*, 948 N.Y.S. 2d 103 (N.Y. App. Div. 2012).

◆ New York high school students were playing floor hockey in a PE class when one student accidentally hurt another with his stick. The injured student sued the school district, alleging negligent supervision, and the district sought pretrial judgment. Although the trial court denied the motion, an appellate division court ruled that the district needn't go to trial on the student's claims. Here, **the injury wasn't foreseeable and it happened so fast that there was no way to avert it by closer supervision**. *Odekirk v. Bellmore-Merrick Cent. School Dist.*, 70 A.D.3d 910 (N.Y. 2010).

◆ A New Jersey PE student sustained injuries to her nose when a classmate hit her with a hockey stick during a floor hockey game. She required surgery, then sued the district, the gym teacher and the classmate to recover for her injuries. A court dismissed her claims, and the appellate division affirmed. It noted that even though gym class was mandatory and not voluntary, **she had to prove more than simple negligence by the classmate**; she had to show that he acted recklessly or intentionally when he hurt her. This she failed to do. Further, since she suffered no permanent injury, she could not pursue a claim for non-economic damages against the district. *Saracino v. Toms River Regional High School East*, 2009 WL 3460680 (N.J. Super. Ct. App. Div. 10/20/09).

◆ While playing freeze tag during a physical education class, a New York fourth-grader was knocked to the ground by a classmate. As he tried to get up, another classmate tripped over him and he fell, hitting his face on the floor. He suffered serious injuries to two permanent teeth. His father sued the school district for negligent supervision, claiming that the teacher and the teacher's aide were talking to each other when the accident happened. He asserted that the teachers should have intervened sooner and prevented the second child from tripping over his son. The New York Supreme Court, Appellate Division, ruled against him, noting that **school districts are not insurers of student safety**. The fact that the teacher and the aide did not see the accident happen failed to establish negligent supervision. The father could not show that more supervision would have prevented the injury, which appeared to result from a spontaneous and accidental collision. There was also no prior history of rough play, and the teacher-student ratio was adequate. *Doyle v. Binghamton City School Dist.*, 874 N.Y.S.2d 607 (N.Y. App. Div. 2009).

◆ A New York student, while participating in a game of dodgeball during gym class, stepped backward and tripped over a schoolmate's foot. The student and her mother sued the school district for her injuries, claiming the teacher failed to adequately supervise the class. The district sought pretrial judgment, which a trial court denied. An appellate division court, however, found for the district. **The accident happened so quickly that it could not have been avoided by even the most intense supervision.** Accordingly, the district was not liable. *Knightner v. William Floyd Union Free School Dist.*, 857 N.Y.S.2d 726 (N.Y. App. Div. 2008).

◆ A New York student was injured in PE while participating in a game of "tape ball." The game was played in the school gymnasium and involved the use of bases that were placed on the floor. One of the bases slipped when the child stepped on it. He fell and sustained injuries. His mother sued the school district, claiming the student was hurt because it failed to adequately supervise the class and failed to provide proper equipment. A trial court denied the school district's motion for pretrial judgment, and the district appealed. The Supreme Court, Appellate Division, reversed. The parent failed to prove that the district was aware of a danger and breached its duty of care in a way that caused the injury. **The PE teacher was present during the entire class period, and closer supervision would not have prevented the fall.** The school district only had to exercise the same degree of care "as a parent of ordinary prudence" in comparable circumstances, and it did so. *Milbrand v. Kenmore-Town of Tonawanda Union Free School Dist.*, 853 N.Y.S.2d 809 (N.Y. App. Div. 2008).

◆ A New York student hurt his ankle during a soccer game in gym class when another student kicked him. He and his father sued the board of education and the city to recover for his injuries. They alleged that the injuries resulted from negligent supervision. A trial court refused to dismiss the case, but the New York Supreme Court, Appellate Division, did so. It explained that **the school could be held liable only if the injury was foreseeable and was caused by a lack of supervision**. Here, the student had admitted that the kick was an accident, and it happened so suddenly that it could not have been prevented by closer or increased supervision. Therefore, the school was not liable. *Paca v. City of New York*, 858 N.Y.S.2d 772 (N.Y. App. Div. 2008).

◆ A 16-year-old Louisiana student who weighed 327 pounds collapsed and began having seizures during PE. The class was conducted by a substitute art teacher in a gym that was not air-conditioned. The temperature was at least 90 degrees. The student collapsed after playing basketball for 20 minutes and died at a hospital. The substitute teacher had played in the game instead of monitoring students. The student's parent sued the board and its insurer in a state court for wrongful death, and the court awarded her $500,000. The Court of Appeal of Louisiana found no error in trial court findings that the board breached its duty to exercise reasonable care and supervision. The lower court was also entitled to hear the testimony of a physical education professor and allow medical testimony as reliable. The court held teachers have a duty to exercise reasonable care and supervision over students in their custody, and to avoid exposing them to an unreasonable risk of injury. **As physical education classes may involve dangerous activities, due care must be used in them to minimize the risk of student injury.** *James v. Jackson*, 898 So.2d 596 (La. Ct. App. 2005). The state supreme court denied the board's appeal. *James v. Jackson*, 902 So.2d 1005 (La. 2005).

◆ A New York student was playing football in PE when a classmate threw a football tee that hit her in the eye. A state trial court denied the school district's motion for summary judgment, and the district appealed. A state appellate division court held school districts have a duty to adequately supervise and instruct students, and are liable for foreseeable injuries proximately caused by their negligence. However, **school districts are not insurers of student safety and will not be held liable for every spontaneous, thoughtless or careless act by which one student injures another**. The degree of care required is what a reasonably prudent parent would exercise under similar circumstances. The court found the teacher had not instructed students on how to properly handle the tee and never told them not to throw it. The evidence differed as to whether the students had previously thrown the tee or had seen the teacher throw it. In affirming the judgment for the student, the court held a trial court must determine if the injury causing conduct was reasonably foreseeable and preventable. *Oakes v. Massena Cent. School Dist.*, 19 A.D.3d 981, 797 N.Y.S.2d 640 (N.Y. App. Div. 2005).

◆ Three Louisiana students assaulted a classmate in their locker room after a PE class, causing serious injuries. The classmate sued the school board, the parents of the students and their insurers in a Louisiana court for personal injuries. A jury found the students were not at fault, and the court found the board 100% at fault. It held the coach caused the injuries by failing to supervise the students. According to the court, an atmosphere of roughhousing and lack of supervision invited the attack, and the board failed to conform to the required standard of care. On appeal, the court apportioned 70% of the fault to the board and 30% to one of the students.

The state supreme court held school boards have a duty of reasonable supervision over students. Boards are not insurers of student safety, and constant supervision of all students is not required. **To hold a school board liable for negligence, it must be shown that a risk of unreasonable injury was foreseeable and could have been prevented with the required degree of supervision.** In this case, the attack happened suddenly and without warning. Because it was unforeseeable to the classmate himself, there was no way for the coach to foresee and prevent it. The trial court had erroneously imposed liability on the board independent of the students. As the incident could not have been prevented with a reasonable degree of supervision, the court reversed the judgment. *Wallmuth v. Rapides Parish School Board*, 813 So.2d 341 (La. 2002).

2. Governmental Immunity

◆ Pennsylvania's highest court held a school district was not entitled to immunity in a negligence case. In 2012, a nine-year-old was hurt as he participated in a relay race during PE at his Philadelphia elementary school. As he ran, he tripped and fell, "causing him to propel into the wall at the end of the gym." No padding covered the gym's concrete wall. The boy hit his head, cut it open and lost consciousness. He suffered a concussion and missed school for more than a month. He suffered headaches and memory problems for years after the incident. The boy's mother filed a negligence claim. The school filed a motion for summary judgment without a trial, saying it was entitled to immunity. The long legal battle went all the way to the state supreme court. School defendants said no evidence showed the school was negligent in maintaining the wall or that the wall had a defect that created a dangerous condition. They said "the wall did what it was intended to do, 'stand and be a wall.'" But the state's highest court said the mother sufficiently pleaded the school was negligent "regarding the 'care' of the wall," alleging it negligently failed to apply protective padding to concrete gym walls. **The court said the "unpadded wall directly caused [the boy's] injuries, and that wall constitute[d] real property."** The state's high court held the real property exception applied, and the defendants were not entitled to immunity. The case had to proceed. *Brewington v. City of Philadelphia*, 199 A.3d 348 (Pa. 2018).

◆ A zip line that was properly constructed and maintained on a school playground could not be considered a "dangerous condition," Colorado's highest court held. In 2008, a 9-year-old was playing on her school playground when she fell from a zip line and broke her wrist. Her parents filed a tort claim. Generally, public schools are entitled to immunity from personal injury suits. But there are exceptions. In this case, the parents said a "recreation-area waiver" applied. The legal battle went all the way to the state's highest court, which held the exception didn't apply so immunity was appropriate. To show the exception applied, the parents had to establish their child suffered injuries due to a "dangerous condition of any … public facility located in any park or recreation area maintained by a public entity." Here, there was no question that the injury occurred at a public facility located in recreation area that was maintained by the state. **The crux of the case, the court said, was whether the zip line was a "dangerous condition" caused by "some negligent act or omission of the public entity in constructing or maintaining the facility."** That wasn't the case because the zip line was properly installed and maintained. Next, the parents said the zip line was a dangerous condition because it was inherently dangerous, which meant the district never should have put it on the playground to start with. The court rejected the argument, explaining that the recreation-area waiver specifically precludes blanket claims of danger based on the design of a public facility. The exception didn't apply, so immunity was appropriate. The case was remanded with instructions to dismiss the claim. *St. Vrain Valley School Dist. RE-1J v. Loveland*, 395 P.3d 751 (Colo. 2017).

◆ An 11-year-old Missouri student, while skipping rope during PE class, fell and hit her head against a cinder block wall. She was taken to the nurse's office. The nurse gave her an ice pack for her head and made sure her pupils were dilating, then called her mother to pick her up and wrote a note explaining that she had suffered a minor head injury. The note instructed her mother to wake her at midnight, which the mother did. The next morning, the student stayed in bed. At 10:30, she was unresponsive. Paramedics failed to revive her. Her mother sued the district, the superintendent, the principal, the nurse and the teachers involved. A court dismissed the defendants, but the court of appeals reversed in part, finding that **the nurse was not entitled to official immunity, nor were the teachers**. Only if they had discretion in treating head injuries would they be entitled to immunity. A trial was required on that issue. *Nguyen v. Grain Valley R-5 School Dist.*, 353 S.W.3d 725 (Mo. Ct. App. 2011).

◆ An Alabama purchasing foreman drafted bid specifications and made recommendations to his school board on bids for movable bleachers for a high school. After the board contracted for the bleachers, the foreman's office issued purchase orders, and the bleachers were installed. A student was severely injured when the bleachers collapsed on him as he and a classmate tried to close them at their teacher's request. The student sued the district and school officials, including the purchasing foreman, for negligent inspection and maintenance of the bleachers. The trial court entered pretrial judgment for all the officials except the foreman, and he appealed.

The Alabama Supreme Court considered the foreman's claim to state-agent immunity based on the discretionary nature of his activities. The student argued the foreman did not deserve immunity, as he was not engaged in discretionary functions. The court held the question of immunity was not properly addressed in the framework of discretionary or ministerial functions. Instead, it had devised an analysis based on categories of state-agent functions under which government employees are immune from liability in the exercise of judgment. One category was the negotiation of contracts, so the foreman was entitled to summary judgment for the claims that he had failed to properly evaluate bids for the bleachers and inspect them after installation. However, the court found **the act of passing along a maintenance brochure to other employees did not require judgment. The foreman was not entitled to state agent immunity** with respect to this claim, and the case was remanded for further proceedings. *Ex Parte Hudson*, 866 So.2d 1115 (Ala. 2003).

◆ Students in an Illinois PE class had to run laps or rollerblade around a wooden gym floor. Rollerbladers paid a $7 fee to use rollerblades with "experimental" toe brakes, and they were not furnished with helmets, gloves or shin, elbow and knee guards. A student who chose to rollerblade fell and broke two bones in his right leg. He sued the school district in a state court for negligence, and willful and wanton failure to provide safety equipment. The court held the district was entitled to immunity under Sections 2-201 and 3-108(a) of the state governmental tort immunity act, which affords immunity to government entities and their employees for failing to supervise students except in cases of willful and wanton misconduct. The state appellate court reversed the judgment, and the district appealed to the Supreme Court of Illinois.

The supreme court observed that the immunity act did not create duties for government entities, but accorded them certain immunities based on specific government functions. The district's failure to provide necessary equipment did not involve supervision. The tort immunity act shielded any decision by district employees that involved a determination of policy or the exercise of discretion. **"Policy decisions" were those requiring the balancing of competing interests so that a government entity had to make a "judgment call." The court agreed with the school district that its decision not to provide safety equipment was discretionary and thus entitled to immunity.** *Arteman v. Clinton Community Unit School Dist. No. 15*, 763 N.E.2d 756 (Ill. 2002).

B. Plays, Dances, Music and More

◆ A California school district wasn't liable for injuries sustained at a carnival on school grounds, a state appeals court decided. In 2012, the school's booster club submitted a request to hold a carnival fundraiser for an elementary school on campus. The district approved the request, and because the booster club was a nonprofit organization, no fee was charged for using school grounds. The president of the booster club organized the event. She contracted with a local company to rent an inflatable slide. The school didn't provide any safety instructions for the event. It also didn't advise the booster club president to do any safety checks. The school let the organizers promote the carnival with banners on school property. Teachers distributed fliers and volunteered at the event. A father took his three-year-old son to the carnival. He purchased tickets so his son could climb a 27-foot-inflatable slide. When the child reached the top of the slide, he got scared. The father asked the volunteer what to do. She told him to go on up and get his son. When the man reached his son, part of the slide suddenly deflated. The father grabbed his son and another small child as they fell to the concrete below. The father took the brunt of the fall. He suffered injuries to his left foot, his left knee and his back. After the accident, the slide was placed back upright. The father noticed the slide wasn't anchored to the ground. He sued the district and the booster club, alleging negligence. The district filed a motion for summary judgment. It was granted, and the father appealed.

Under a California law, public school districts must let nonprofit organizations that "promote youth and school activities" use school facilities under its control. Because of the requirement, the law also "apportions liability between the school district and the [nonprofit] using the school facilities," the court explained. **Specifically, the district would be liable only if the injury was caused by the school's negligence in maintaining the grounds or facilities. The nonprofit would be liable if the injury resulted from its negligence during the use of the school's facilities.** Further, the law stipulates that each party would have to "bear the cost of insuring against its respective risks and … the costs of defending itself against claims arising from those risks." The father claimed the school district was negligent because the slide was set up on grass next to concrete and the rope tethers weren't staked to the ground. But the court wasn't swayed, as the district didn't "plan, set up, operate, inspect or supervise the carnival attractions, including the inflatable slide." The court pointed out that the booster club president selected the location, and the rental company installed the slide the day of the event. The court reminded the father that the law specifically outlined that the district could not be held liable for alleged negligence of the booster club. So the appeals court affirmed the ruling for the district. *Grossman v. Santa Monica-Malibu Unified School Dist.*, 33 Cal.App.5th 458 (Cal. Ct. App. 2019).

◆ A Pennsylvania student suffered second-degree burns when a teacher demonstrated a chemistry reaction involving the ignition of methanol. The mixture exploded, and flaming liquid spilled onto the student's leg. She filed a Section 1983 state-created danger claim. She said "igniting methanol create[d] an obvious risk of explosion that could cause burn injuries to those in the immediate vicinity." But she cited no case law to support her argument. **To succeed on her claim, the student had to show the teacher's behavior "shocked the conscience" by alleging the teacher acted with "deliberate indifference."** She didn't, so the claim failed. *Green v. Mount Carmel Area School Dist.,* No. 4:18-CV-02218, 2019 WL 1787592 (M.D. Pa. 4/24/19).

◆ A fourth-grader was hurt during a hands-on math lesson at his Delaware elementary school. The assignment required students to measure items in the classroom, including a flag hanging overhead near the closed classroom door. The student was measuring the flag when a classmate returned from the restroom and opened the door. When it closed again, it shut on the boy's right pinky finger, severing the tip. His parents filed suit, alleging the teacher was negligent. The school said the teacher was entitled to qualified immunity because no school policy dictated how the teacher should've supervised her class. It's well established that the "manner in which a teacher actually supervises [students] is discretionary," the court explained, which meant the teacher was entitled to immunity. The parents argued the teacher's decision to tell kids to measure items by the door and then permit one child to leave the classroom through that door amounted to gross negligence. The court acknowledged the boy's injury was unfortunate. Even so, **having students "take measurements near a fully operational door [didn't] constitute gross negligence,"** it held. Immunity was appropriate, so the claim was dismissed. *Thompson v. Cape Henlopen School Dist.,* No. N17C-09-052RRC, 2019 WL 1308309 (Del. Super. Ct. 4/2/19).

◆ A Mississippi appeals court rejected an expelled student's claims. A group of teens rented a party bus for prom. On the way, several drank alcohol from Gatorade bottles. Suspecting underage drinking, school officials and police questioned the students. The plaintiff's written statement admitted alcohol was on the bus and he drank "less than three sips," although other students drank a lot more than "the legal amount." The plaintiff in this case was suspended for 10 days and was later expelled to an alternative school for 45 days. After an unsuccessful appeal, he filed a lawsuit. A school policy separated students' due process rights into two categories. Class I involved students accused of violating the drug policy, weapon policy or committing violence on school property. They had the right to appeal to the school board. Class II involved students who were suspended or expelled for any reason not listed in Class I. Those students had the right to first appeal to the "District Discipline Committee" and then again to the school board. Although the plaintiff was a Class II violator, the school treated him as a Class I violator, as he wasn't allowed to first appeal to the committee before appealing to the board. He said this violated his right to due process. When the court dismissed his claim, he appealed. In *Hinds County School Board v. R.B.*, the state supreme court rejected the argument that **if school policy "created a right to more than a minimal amount of process, [the failure] to provide such additional procedures results in a due process violation."** That's essentially what this student argued, the court held. He received notice and a meaningful opportunity to be heard, which was all that was required. *Keeton v. Ocean Springs School Board,* No. 2017-CA-01166-COA, 2019 WL 396979 (Miss. Ct. App. 1/31/19).

◆ An Ohio federal court rejected a Title IX claim against a coach who had a reputation for being tough on players, often using profanity and calling them names. During practices, the coach frequently insulted the student in this case, calling him "a pussy," "a spoiled rich pretty boy," and "soft." The coach taunted the student about "being afraid to take a hit" and "throwing the ball away too quickly." Soon, the rest of the team followed the coach's lead and began calling him the same names. The student and his parents complained, but nothing was resolved. He transferred to another school and filed a Title IX suit. When the school said the student didn't suffer harassment based on his sex, the student argued that the coach harassed him because he didn't conform to male stereotypes. To succeed on a stereotyping theory, the student had to show he "did not conform to traditional gender stereotypes in an observable way and that … was the basis of his harassment," the court explained. But this student didn't provide any evidence showing that he exhibited "gender non-conforming characteristics," the court noted. **Calling players offensive names wasn't a good idea, but it didn't amount to sexual harassment, the court held.** Case dismissed. *Lininger v. St. Mary's School Dist. Board of Educ.,* No. 3:16CV2853, 2019 WL 188050 (N.D. Ohio 1/14/19).

◆ The Seventh Circuit affirmed a ruling that dismissed an Indiana mother's disability bias claims. An elementary school had a choir as an extracurricular activity. In 2014, the choir was invited to participate in a local museum's Christmas concert – a three-day event featuring a variety of holiday performances. The museum wasn't affiliated with the school. Built in 1901, the building had no ramp access or elevator. A mother tried to attend the concert. But she was in a wheelchair – and couldn't access the upper floor where the concert was held. After the show, she vented to school officials about missing the show. The next year, the choir got another invite to the museum's show. Remembering the upset mother, the choral director expressed concern about the lack of an elevator. The museum's director said they were in the process of installing an elevator in the building. She said she could "safely say the elevators [would] be available" for the concert. The school informed the mother about the museum's renovation and assured her she'd be able to see the Christmas show. But installation fell behind schedule, and the elevator wasn't operational for the concert. The mother missed the show for the second year in a row. She sued the school, alleging discrimination claims under Title II of the ADA and Section 504 of the Rehabilitation Act.

The court tossed the suit, and on appeal, the Seventh Circuit affirmed. There was no question the mother missed the show due to her disability, the court said. That was unfortunate, but it didn't mean the school was at fault, the court said, as the concert was held at an off-campus building unaffiliated with the school. So it had to decide whether the concert a "service, program or activity" of the school. Because the issue was tricky, the Seventh Circuit asked the DOJ (a federal agency charged with sorting out ADA issues) to weigh in. The DOJ noted that the concert wasn't a joint venture between the school and the museum. Here, the school participated in the museum's event, the DOJ said. The museum's festival was a three-day event involving 50 school choirs, and this school was merely one participant. "No choir would be required to ensure that the entire festival [was] accessible to the entire public," the DOJ asserted. The DOJ's guidance provided framework for the Seventh Circuit, which also noted that **the school's responsibility for the event was limited to arranging for the students' attendance and musical numbers. All other matters, including planning, advertising and providing refreshments, were handled by the museum – the host of the event.** The concert wasn't a "service, program or activity" of the school, so the ruling for the school was affirmed. *Ashby v. Warrick County School Corp.*, No. 18-1371, 2018 WL 5784478 (7th Cir. 12/5/18).

◆ A New Mexico federal court refused to dismiss a student's Title IX retaliation claim. A junior participated in school sports and the theater program. In April 2016, the theater teacher started keeping the student after school, claiming he needed to stay late for the theater program. The teacher gave signed excuses to the student to explain his whereabouts when he missed other activities. That lasted about five months. The student said the teacher groomed him for sex and seemingly innocent things escalated to more problematic conduct. Eventually, the teacher took the student to his house – during school hours – and sexually assaulted him. The student's grades dropped so much that he didn't meet the school's grades eligibility requirement to participate in sports. So he was removed from the teams. The student confided to his parents that he was struggling with his grades – as well as other areas of his life – because he was sexually assaulted by the teacher. They reported the abuse to the superintendent, who notified the proper authorities. But he refused to exempt the boy from the grade requirement so he could return to sports.

The teacher was charged with two counts of criminal sexual penetration of a minor. The day before the teacher's first court appearance, a school secretary sent a text message to the junior class president, asking him to gather as many students as possible to make signs in support of the teacher. In the text message, the secretary referred to the victim as a "butt head."

She also provided info on how to get an excuse from school to attend the preliminary hearing. The class president posted the secretary's text message on Instagram and Snapchat. Dozens of students showed up to protest. They were so disruptive that the judge had to close the hearing to the public.

The student transferred to another school and filed a Title IX retaliation claim against the district. The district asked the court to dismiss the claim, but it refused. The court said **the superintendent's refusal to exempt the student from the grade requirement to play sports "in spite of the possibility that his grades suffered because of the sex abuse could be a materially adverse school action."** The court also said the student established a "causal connection" between the student's report of sex abuse and the secretary's text message to the junior class president supporting the accused teacher. When a protected act is closely followed by an adverse action, such circumstances "justify an inference of a retaliatory motive," the court explained. The claim had to proceed. *I.G. v. Board of Educ. of the Aztec Municipal School Dist.*, No. 18-124 KK/KBM, 2018 WL 4700233 (D.N.M. 9/30/18).

◆ A Utah federal judge refused to order a school to reinstate a cheerleader who was kicked off the squad after she ignored her coach's instructions regarding social media. The cheerleader signed a "Cheer Constitution," which warned squad members would be dismissed for inappropriate social media use. At the first meeting, cheerleaders received their squad T-shirts. The coach spoke to the girls about social media and specifically discussed problems with cheerleaders bullying others online. The coach told the girls not to post anything about making the squad that night – as the announcement on who made the squad would be made public the following day. The coach reminded the squad that girls who weren't selected might be upset. After the meeting ended, a group of girls – wearing their squad T-shirts – went out to dinner. On the way in a private vehicle, they sang a song that included profanity, with lyrics that depicted a conflict between girls. One cheerleader recorded a video and posted it on Snapchat. A former cheerleader who didn't make the squad that year saw it and was upset by the post. The next day, she showed it to the coach. The cheerleader who posted the video was kicked off the squad. After some negotiations, the coach agreed to let the girl rejoin the squad if she apologized and completed 50 hours of community service. But she rejected the terms. Instead, she filed a speech suit and asked the court to order the school to reinstate her without the coach's stipulations. But she couldn't show she was likely to suffer irreparable harm without the order. **It's "well-settled that a preliminary injunction movant does not satisfy the irreparable harm criterion when the alleged harm [was] self-inflicted," the court noted.** That was the case here, as the girl would've been back on the squad if she accepted the coach's compromise. The court refused to grant the order she sought. *Johnson v. Cache County School Dist.,* No. 1:18CV57DAK, 2018 WL 3242298 (D. Utah 7/3/18).

◆ An Illinois school was entitled to immunity after a young child got hurt during a classroom kitchen activity, a state appeals court affirmed. In Spanish class, the teacher baked plantain chips as part of a cultural activity. A student suffered burn injuries when he bumped into a hot aluminum baking sheet. His parents filed a negligence suit. The school filed a motion for summary judgment, saying it was entitled to immunity. The court granted the motion, and on appeal, the ruling was affirmed. **The parents didn't allege conduct that rose to the level of willful or wanton conduct.** Nor did they allege the teacher deliberately intended to harm the child or showed "an utter indifference or conscious disregard" for the student's safety. The school was entitled to immunity, so the ruling was affirmed. *Gamble v. Alcuin Montessori School*, 2017 IL App (1st) 11611738-U (Ill. App. Ct. 7/21/17).

◆ A Michigan appeals court refused to dismiss negligence claims against a shop class teacher who removed a blade guard from a table saw and then let students use it. A student suffered serious injuries to her hand while operating a table saw in a shop class. The suit claimed the teacher removed the guard from the saw, encouraged students to use the table saw without the guard and said the blade guard was only put on the table saw during inspections to appease the insurance company. The student filed a tort claim against the teacher, who did not dispute that she removed the blade guard and instructed students that the blade guard was not required for safe operation of the saw. The student stated a valid claim of gross negligence, as the shop teacher "did far more than fail to take precautions." The court noted **she took active steps to remove and discourage the use of the safety guard**. Further, a jury could conclude that the lack of the safety guard was the proximate cause of the injury, the court held. So a trial was needed. *Bellinger v. Kram*, No. 331199, 2017 WL 2302589 (Mich. Ct. App. 5/25/17).

◆ A New York appeals court refused to dismiss a personal injury claim filed by the mother of a child who was injured during recess. An eight-year-old fell from the monkey bars during recess at her elementary school. She suffered unspecified injuries. Her mom sued to recover for personal injuries, and the district asked the court to dismiss the claim. The court refused to toss the case, and the district appealed. On appeal, the court explained **the district could've gotten the case dismissed – if it had provided conclusive evidence that showed the child had been adequately supervised by a teacher or other staffer at the time of her fall, or the ground cover underneath the monkey bars was maintained in a reasonably safe condition**. But the school didn't make either showing, so a trial was needed, the court held. *Pochat v. Monroe Woodbury Cent. School Dist.*, 23 N.Y.S.3d 301 (N.Y. App. Div. 2016).

◆ A California appeals court revived the negligence claim of a student who was injured at a break-dancing practice for a talent show. A group of students practiced the routine in the mornings before school. A teacher agreed to let the group practice in his classroom. He frequently left the classroom for short periods during the practices to make copies, use the restroom and make phone calls. While the teacher was out of the classroom, a 14-year-old was seriously injured after classmates urged him to try to flip. He filed a personal injury suit. The court found the district did not have a duty to protect the boy from the inherent risks of break-dancing. It granted judgment to the school. But the appellate court said **the real issue was whether the teacher's decision – allowing middle school students to engage in a potentially risky activity, break-dancing, in his classroom without supervision – created legal liability, especially since the assistant principal had testified that he'd instituted a "no flip" policy**. The court pointed out the teacher broke school rules, as he left the room without getting another teacher to supervise or telling the group to stop dancing until he returned, and he never told the students they couldn't do flips. The court said a reasonable jury "could find this lack of supervision proximately caused [the boy's] injuries." Or, the court added, it could find the district didn't take adequate steps to enforce the "no flip" policy the assistant principal said was in place. Summary judgment wasn't appropriate. The ruling was reversed, and the case was remanded. *Jimenez v. Roseville City School Dist.*, 247 Cal.App.4th 594 (Cal. Ct. App. 2016).

◆ A New York appeals court affirmed a ruling that a school was not liable for a playground injury during recess. The plaintiff in this case was knocked to the ground by a fellow student who was running backward while attempting to catch a football. Afterward, the angry mom filed a negligence claim. The court granted judgment to the school, and the mother appealed. The appellate court affirmed the ruling for the school, as **it showed teachers were present to monitor the students, the children who were playing football had been told to stay on their side of the yard and the unanticipated spontaneous act of another child – colliding into the victim – was the proximate cause of the incident**. The ruling for the school was affirmed. *Chung v. New York City Board of Educ.*, 136 A.D.3d 608 (N.Y. App. Div. 2016).

◆ An Iowa appeals court refused to grant a new trial for a student who was injured in shop class. He was operating a table saw in his woodworking class when a piece of wood kicked back from the blade and hit him in the stomach. As he leaned forward, his left hand came in contact with the blade. It severed two fingers and severely injured two more. He sued for negligence. As part of pretrial activity, he had to list all of the damages he claimed as a result of the injury. After a four-day trial, the jury awarded the boy $28,578 for past medical expenses and $31,421 for future medical expenses. But the jury stopped short of awarding damages for loss of earning capacity. It also found the boy was 45% responsible for the injury. He appealed the verdict and asked for a new trial, claiming the jury was wrong to find "zero value for his loss of earning capacity." He insisted a reasonable juror should've concluded that the loss of one hand would have an effect on his earning potential in some manner. He pointed to an expert that testified he'd lose – over the course of his work life – around $500,000. The court rejected the argument, explaining that **a jury "is free to accept or reject any testimony."** The court affirmed the jury's decision. *T.D. II v. Des Moines Independent Community School Dist.*, No. 14-2166, 2016 WL 351516 (Iowa Ct. App. 1/27/16).

◆ School officials did not have a duty to protect a student who was hit by a car as he crossed an off-campus street as he left an after-school event, an Illinois appellate court held. The student attended an event on campus. As he was leaving, he crossed a six-lane highway. He was struck by a car and suffered injuries. His mother sued for damages, alleging negligence based on willful and wanton conduct. The court granted judgment to the school. On appeal, the mother said the school violated its duty to protect her son. To recover damages based on willful and wanton conduct, she had to show the school had a duty to protect her son, it breached that duty and the breach was the proximate cause of the injuries. She argued the school voluntarily assumed a duty to supervise students because it had provided crossing guards for prior unnamed after-school events. The court rejected her argument, as **she did not include facts about which intersections around the school had previously been assigned crossing guards, the history or frequency of using crossing guards during after-school events and whether the intersection where her son's accident occurred had ever been one of the locations that had crossing guards during prior events**. The mother failed to establish the school had a duty to protect her son, so the court affirmed the decision to dismiss her negligence claim. *Renkiewicz v. Township High School Dist. 211,* No. 1-15-0989, 2016 WL 363193 (Ill. App. Ct. 1/22/16).

◆ The Eleventh Circuit affirmed a Florida ruling that held a pre-prom breathalyzer did not violate students' constitutional rights. Students who purchased tickets to the prom had to sign a contract that stated the district's zero-tolerance policy for drugs and alcohol. It also warned students that they may be subject to a breath test. Approximately 37 students arrived at the prom on a rented party bus between 10:15 and 10:30 p.m. The dean told the students they couldn't enter the prom until the bus had been inspected. The driver gave consent for police to search the bus. He did and found an empty champagne bottle. The bus driver told the officer it belonged to the students. The entire group had to take and pass a breathalyzer test before they could attend the prom. By the time all the tests were administered, the prom had ended. Several students sued, claiming the search was illegal. They also said being detained for the breath test amounted to an illegal seizure. First, the court rejected the illegal search claim, explaining that the U.S. Supreme Court has established that "a third-party's consent is valid if he has mutual use of the property." **The driver gave consent, so the search wasn't**

illegal. Examining the illegal seizure claim, the court held the time frame was reasonable – as administering 37 breath tests took time. The students failed to state valid claims, so the ruling to dismiss was affirmed. *Ziegler v. Martin County School Dist.*, 831 F.3d 1309 (11th Cir. 2016).

◆ The Fifth Circuit refused to find a school constitutionally liable for a student's drowning death on campus. A physics class went to the school pool to conduct buoyancy experiments. They made boats out of cardboard and duct tape and then sailed them in the shallow end of the pool. The teacher told them to stay out of the water when not testing their boats. But after the experiment, some kids jumped in and swam a lap. Minutes later, one student was spotted lying at the bottom of the pool. They pulled him out and called paramedics, but he died. His parents sued his principal and physics teacher, alleging they violated their son's Fourteenth Amendment right to life. A Texas federal judge granted the school defendants judgment without a trial. The parents appealed to the Fifth Circuit, but it affirmed. Public school officials have "qualified immunity" to such suits, meaning there is no liability unless they violated a clearly established federal legal right. The U.S. Supreme Court has explained that **the purpose of the immunity rule is to give government employees "breathing room to make reasonable but mistaken judgments about open legal questions."** The parents didn't show the school defendants violated a clearly established constitutional right. To do so, they would've had to show "reasonable teachers and school officials were on notice that designing and executing a high school science experiment involving a pool violated the constitutional right to life of any student that may drown." That wasn't the case, so school officials were immune to this suit – and the federal judge was right to dismiss it. *Estate of C.A. v. Castro*, 547 Fed.Appx. 621 (5th Cir. 2013).

◆ A 15-year-old North Dakota student got badly hurt practicing a bike stunt in the auditorium for a "Sixties day" event scheduled as part of a history class. He sued the district and the teacher to recover for his injuries, and a jury decided that **the district was 30% at fault, while the student was 70% at fault**. As a result, the student was not entitled to receive anything. On appeal, the Supreme Court of North Dakota upheld that determination. Neither the student nor his parents could recover 30% of his costs from the district. *M.M. v. Fargo Public School Dist. No. 1*, 815 N.W.2d 273 (N.D. 2012).

◆ During recess, a New York third-grader passed by a fire pole that students were sliding down while another student slid down the pole. The other student barreled into him and he sustained injuries. His father sued the district for negligent supervision, and the district sought pretrial judgment, asserting that it wasn't negligent and, even if it was, any negligence was incidental to the injury and not a cause. The Supreme Court, Appellate division, held that **there were questions about whether the district properly instructed students on how to use the playground equipment** and whether it provided a proper surface. Also, there was a question as to whether the student sliding down the pole was playing tag at the time in violation of school rules. A trial was required. *Dworzanski v. Niagara-Wheatfield Cent. School Dist.*, 89 A.D.3d 1378 (N.Y. Sup. Ct. A.D. 2011).

◆ A New York second-grader sustained injuries when he was pushed down a slide by a fellow student during lunch recess, who then slid down on top of him. He sued the school district for money damages, alleging negligent supervision. The case reached the Supreme Court, Appellate Division, which ruled against him. Here, **the school provided adequate playground supervision**, and that level of supervision had not caused the student's injuries. *Benavides v. Uniondale Union Free School Dist.*, 95 A.D.3d 809 (N.Y. Sup. Ct. App. Div. 2012).

◆ A Utah high school decided to perform the play "Oklahoma." The school's drama teacher wanted to enhance the sound effects during the performance by using a gun that would fire blanks. A vice principal approved the request provided that an adult brought the weapon, kept it under control at all times and was the only person to fire it. However, the drama teacher did not ensure that the rules were followed, and a student fired the gun during rehearsals and the play's performances. The drama teacher apparently knew that the student was doing so. One day, prior to a performance, the student shot himself with a blank and died. His parents sued, alleging violations of the student's substantive and procedural due process rights. The school, the vice principal and the drama teacher sought to have the case dismissed, but a federal court dismissed only the school and the vice principal from the lawsuit. **The drama teacher may have acted in conscious disregard for the serious risks to the student, so the lawsuit against him was allowed to continue.** *Thayer v. Washington County School Dist.*, 781 F.Supp.2d 1264 (D. Utah 2011).

◆ A Connecticut student attended an eighth-grade graduation dance at a private facility. During the evening, a glass goblet fell to the floor and broke, leaving pieces of glass on the floor. A student shed her shoes while walking from her table to the dance floor and severely cut her foot on a shard of glass. She sued the school board and two teachers who chaperoned the event, alleging negligent supervision. A state court ruled that the school board was entitled to immunity, and the Supreme Court of Connecticut agreed. Here, **the school board's decision to sponsor the graduation dance was a discretionary decision that entitled it to immunity**. Further, the dance wasn't held at the school, attendance wasn't mandatory, and the student voluntarily took off her shoes. Thus, no extra duty of care was imposed on the school board to offset its claim to immunity. *Coe v. Board of Educ. of Town of Watertown*, 19 A.3d 640 (Conn. 2011).

◆ An Ohio student played in the marching band. One day, while they were practicing in a parking lot, a school maintenance employee asked the marching band director if he could mow the lawn in an area near where the marching band was practicing. School policy dictated that employees were not to mow in the vicinity of students, and when they mowed without a bag, they were supposed to use the manufacturer's discharge chute. The director told the maintenance employee he could mow near the marching band. However, the employee took the bag off the mower and did not install the discharge chute. A piece of metal ejected by the lawn mower struck a student in the head and cut an artery, causing him to lose consciousness and suffer some paralysis to his face. His family sued the school district, which sought immunity. The Ohio Court of Appeals noted that school districts are generally entitled to immunity unless employees act in a "wanton or reckless" way. Here, the family alleged that the band director and the employee acted recklessly so as to disallow immunity. The court agreed that **the maintenance employee might have acted recklessly by failing to use the discharge chute**. However, the family failed to show that the band director acted recklessly or wantonly by allowing the employee to mow near the parking lot. Thus, the director was entitled to immunity, but the maintenance employee was not. *DeMartino v. Poland Local School Dist.*, No. 10 MA 19, 2011 WL 1118480 (Ohio Ct. App. 3/24/11).

V. TEACHER BEHAVIOR OUTSIDE OF SCHOOL

Although teachers have the freedom to do as they like off school grounds while not on duty, they cannot break the law or engage in behavior that could be construed as harmful to students.

A. Inappropriate Relations With Students

◆ The Third Circuit revived the Title IX suit of a former student who fathered a teacher's aide's child. Pennsylvania administrators got reports about a possible romantic relationship between a teacher's aide and a student. School officials held a meeting, suspended the aide with pay, and then transferred her out of the student's class. But the inappropriate relationship didn't end after the meeting. The aide later had a child; the student was the father. The student filed a Title IX suit. The court tossed the claim, but the Third Circuit remanded the case, finding **a reasonable jury could find the school knew the teacher posed a threat, as administrators attended a meeting to discuss a possible affair between a teacher and a student – and that person should've done more to ensure the inappropriate conduct ended**. On the other hand, the court said some evidence – such as suspending the aide and removing her from the student's class – might support the school's position. Questions remained, so summary judgment wasn't appropriate, the court explained. It remanded the case for further proceedings. *C.K. v. Wrye,* No. 17-3541, 2018 WL 4635690 (3d Cir. 9/26/18).

◆ An Alabama court upheld the conviction of a teacher who was found guilty on child porn charges. A science teacher and cheerleading coach at a middle school regularly discussed non-school topics with students via text and social media. In 2016, a boy told the teacher that some girls on the cheerleading squad were sending nude photos to their classmates. Then the student showed the teacher a photo stored on his phone. It depicted a nude male classmate. The teacher initially told the student to get rid of the photo, but later told the student to forward the photo to him so he could investigate. Three hours later, he asked the student to send more nude photos, texting, "I wanna see peeps I know." The student sent more photos of male classmates, and the two talked about the size of the boys' genitals. Within a month, the teacher was using Snapchat to have similar chats – including asking for nude pics of teens he knew – with a different student. School policy required teachers to report "all material from students involving sexual acts," but the teacher never reported the pictures to administrators, parents or police. For reasons the decision doesn't address, the sheriff's office executed a search warrant of the teacher's home, seizing his phone and computer. Records of the conversations were found. The teacher also visited pornography websites "involving teenagers, young boys and really young boys," police reports said. The teacher was indicted by a grand jury on charges of knowingly receiving child pornography. He testified that he asked for the pictures to investigate the "sexting ring," and he discussed "how big various students were in order to determine if the photos were real." But the jury didn't buy it. He was sentenced to 120 months in prison. On appeal, he said the photos didn't fit the statutory definition of child pornography. The Eleventh Circuit disagreed, noting that **the focal point in many of the photos were of the students' genitalia**. Further, in most of the photos, the students were fully nude and fully aroused. The photos were child pornography, the court said, so it upheld the conviction. *U.S. v. Hunter,* No. 16-17205, 2017 WL 6616633 (11th Cir. 12/29/17).

◆ Rejecting the appeal of a former band director who was found guilty of enticing a child for indecent purposes, a Georgia appeals court upheld the conviction. In December of 2010, the band director called a 14-year-old student to the band room saying he needed help fixing some bass clarinets. When she arrived, she was the only student there. The band director pulled her onto his lap, stripped her and touched her before he had her perform oral sex on him. Later that day, he texted, "Thanks for the early Christmas present." Afterward, **the band director told the girl not to tell anyone or it would "ruin his job and his life."** The girl said she was shocked at what happened. This behavior continued for two years, until the girl confided in a social worker at the school. The teacher was arrested. A police investigation found the teacher exchanged 5,231 texts with the girl as well as nearly 3,000 additional texts with two other middle school students. He was found guilty on charges of enticing a child. On appeal, the teacher argued that the text messages shouldn't have been admitted into evidence. The court was not swayed, and the conviction stood. *Blevins v. The State,* A17AO639, 2017 WL 4875585 (Ga. Ct. App. 10/30/17).

◆ A teacher/coach failed to convince a Maryland appeals court to throw out his criminal conviction. In 2010, an investigation found teacher/coach had sex with a female student in the football team's locker room. The principal called the police and child protective services. The teacher was arrested. During her testimony against the teacher, the student mentioned her birthday, but not her age at the time of the attack. The teacher was convicted of sexual abuse of a minor and sentenced to 10 years in prison. On appeal, the teacher argued the state didn't prove the student was a minor at the time they had sex. **"A rational trier of fact could reasonably infer" the girl's age by doing simple math, the court said.** The conviction stood. *Brown v. State of Maryland*, No. 2616, 2016 WL 7106458 (Md. Ct. Spec. App. 12/6/16).

◆ The West Virginia Supreme Court of Appeals upheld the conviction of a teacher who engaged in sex acts with a 15-year-old girl. At trial **the victim testified she went to a male teacher's classroom early nearly every morning for five months** in 2013. There, they engaged in sex acts. She provided copies of Facebook messages and Skype conversations that substantiated her testimony. The teacher was convicted on one count of sex abuse by a person in position of trust. He was sentenced to 10-20 years confinement but ordered to serve it on house arrest with electronic monitoring. He appealed to the state's highest court, which upheld the conviction. *State of West Virginia v. Erin S.T.*, No. 15-1195, 2016 WL 6819049 (W. Va. 11/18/16).

◆ An Arkansas high school girls basketball coach sent inappropriate text messages to a number of students, including "are you drunk yet?" to a student who had obtained a public intoxication ticket, and "OMG you look good today" to another student. A school investigation found no other problems, but the school prepared to non-renew his contract at the end of the school year. Later, the coach entered into a sexual relationship with a ninth-grader. He was sentenced to 10 years in prison, with six years suspended. The ninth-grader's parents sued the principal and school officials under Title IX and 42 U.S.C. § 1983, asserting constitutional violations. The case reached the Eighth Circuit, which held that the principal and school officials were entitled to immunity because **the inappropriate text messages by the coach did not alert them to the sexual abuse that followed**. The principal and school officials had investigated following the text messages and found no evidence of improper physical contact. *Doe v. Flaherty*, 623 F.3d 577 (8th Cir. 2010).

◆ A Delaware elementary school teacher encountered a 17-year-old former student when she came to the school to pick up a younger sibling. The teacher later called her and offered to help her with her homework. After a time, **he became romantically involved, eventually engaging in a sexual relationship with the student**. The student told a friend, who told her parent, who reported it to the state police. The teacher was charged with fourth degree sexual rape because of the student's age and his position of trust, authority or supervision over her. However, the charge was later dropped. Shortly thereafter, the school board notified the teacher that it intended to fire him based on immorality and/or misconduct. After he was fired, the teacher appealed, asserting that he had not been criminally convicted, that the student no longer attended district schools, and that his positive employment evaluations indicated he was still able to teach. The Supreme Court of Delaware ruled against him, noting that he could be fired for immorality and that he had compromised his position of trust and his status as a role model. *Lehto v. Board of Educ. of Caesar Rodney School Dist.*, 962 A.2d 222 (Del. 2008).

◆ An Oklahoma student claimed that she was subjected to sexual harassment, advances and molestation by her music teacher when she was 15 years old. She claimed that he first kissed her in the school bus barn, and then began touching her inappropriately at least once a week, although the two never had sexual intercourse. When her parents learned of the inappropriate relationship, they contacted the school, which immediately suspended the teacher. He resigned shortly thereafter. The student sued the school district and the teacher under 42 U.S.C. § 1983 and Title IX. She asserted that the district had knowledge of the teacher's inappropriate behavior based on statements her boyfriend made to an assistant principal about the teacher and another student. The district moved for pretrial judgment, **claiming it never had actual notice that the teacher was acting inappropriately**. It showed that the boyfriend had admitted lying about the teacher having an inappropriate relationship with the other student. The court ruled for the school district, finding no evidence that it was deliberately indifferent to the inappropriate relationship between the teacher and the student. However, the student's lawsuit against the teacher under 42 U.S.C. § 1983 could proceed. *S.R. v. Hilldale Independent School Dist. No. I-29 of Muskogee County, Oklahoma*, No. CIV-07-335-RAW, 2008 WL 2185420 (E.D. Okla. 5/23/08).

◆ An 18-year-old Idaho student began flirting with a teacher. She confessed her feelings for him to another staff member, and the school conducted an investigation. Both the student and the teacher denied any impropriety. A month later, the teacher and student had sexual intercourse. She did not admit this until the end of the school year. The teacher resigned, and the student sued not only him but also the school district and various school officials, asserting claims of negligent supervision and violations of Title IX. Before a jury, the student presented evidence of post-traumatic stress disorder (PTSD) and other psychological harm. However, she offered no medical records, cost estimates or other statistics on damages. The school district offered testimony from a psychologist who stated that her emotional problems were triggered by the lawsuit itself and not by the sexual relationship. The jury found that the school district was liable for negligent supervision, but that the student failed to prove she was entitled to damages. It, therefore, awarded her none. On appeal, the Supreme Court of Idaho held that a reasonable jury could have found **the student proved no damages. Even her own experts disagreed as to her condition**, with one finding she did not have PTSD. It seemed that the litigation brought about the psychological difficulties by focusing the student on her experience, memories and trauma. The district's expert also believed the student pursued the lawsuit to comply with her family's request. The district did not have to pay for the negligent supervision of the teacher. *Hei v. Holzer*, 181 P.3d 489 (Idaho 2008).

◆ A Maryland high school teacher gave a 14-year-old student who had a crush on him a ride home. On the way, he took her to his house to play pool and allegedly had consensual sexual intercourse with her. After he was convicted of child abuse and sexual offenses, he appealed. The Court of Special Appeals of Maryland ruled that consensual sexual intercourse could constitute child abuse under Maryland law. The court stated that because a parent impliedly consents to a teacher taking all reasonable measures to assure the safe return of his or her child from school, including personally driving that child home; because the teacher assumed that responsibility when he agreed to drive the child home; because the events leading up to this unfortunate occurrence were set in motion on school property; and because, at the time of the offense, there had been no temporal break in the teacher and student relationship that existed between the teacher and the victim, the court upheld his conviction.

The Court of Appeals of Maryland affirmed. It rejected the teacher's argument that once he was with a student off school grounds, for a non-school-related activity, the implied consent rationale was inapplicable and that once he was no longer acting as a teacher, he did not have a responsibility to supervise the student, so could not be convicted of child abuse.

It was uncontested that the act of sexual intercourse by an adult with a 14-year-old girl qualified as "abuse" under the statute. **Although the teacher was neither a parent nor household or family member of the victim, he had "responsibility for the supervision" of the victim at the time of the alleged misconduct.** The evidence was sufficient to support the conviction. *Anderson v. State*, 372 Md. 285, 812 A.2d 1016 (Md. 2002).

◆ A 14-year-old Illinois student gave birth to a child in 1986. Blood tests indicated a 99.99% probability that the assistant principal of her junior high school was the child's father. The school district dismissed him under Section 24-12 of the Illinois School Code. Almost two years later, the assistant principal was acquitted of aggravated criminal sexual assault. The student's paternity action was closed shortly after the acquittal based on "lack of activity." A hearing officer reversed the school board's action dismissing the assistant principal in 1991, finding the district did not prove he had sexual contact with the student. A state court affirmed the assistant principal's reinstatement, as did the Appellate Court of Illinois. In 1997, the paternity case was reopened and a court ordered him to pay child support. The state superintendent of education notified the assistant principal of an action to suspend his teaching and administrative certificates for immoral conduct. A hearing officer upheld the action under Section 21-23 of the state school code. The case reached the Appellate Court of Illinois, which held that the action to suspend the assistant principal's certificates was not barred by the district's effort to dismiss him years earlier. The Section 24-12 employment dismissal and Section 21-23 certificate suspension proceedings were distinct and were brought by different entities. **The assistant principal's acquittal from criminal charges did not prevent the state superintendent from suspending his certificates. The code required the superintendent to suspend a holder's certificate for conviction of specified sex or narcotics offenses.** *Hayes v. State Teacher Certification Board*, 359 Ill.App.3d 1153, 835 N.E.2d 146 (Ill. App. Ct. 2005). The Supreme Court of Illinois denied further appeal.

B. Drugs and Alcohol

◆ Two convictions for driving under the influence (DUI) provided grounds to terminate a principal, a Pennsylvania court held. In 2010, the principal was arrested and charged with his first DUI. The charge was dropped when he agreed to go to a rehabilitative program. Four years later, he was arrested on another DUI charge. He pleaded guilty, lost his license for 12 months and spent 90 days on house arrest. The district put the principal on leave and held a hearing. Multiple district administrators, colleagues and parents testified that the principal was a bad example to his students and could not effectively lead the school. He was fired. On appeal, the termination was upheld. He sought judicial review, arguing the district lacked substantial evidence to show his conduct offended the morals of the community. But the court said it had to give weight to the evidence presented – **co-workers and parents alike testified that they believed the principal set a bad example to students**. The termination was affirmed. *Moffitt v. Tunkhannock Area School Dist.*, 192 A.3d 1214 (Pa. Commw. Ct. 2018).

◆ A Tennessee county school board decided to conduct random drug screens after a second teacher in seven years was arrested on drug charges. The board hired a private company to perform the drug screens. Four teachers and their union sued, asserting that the random drug testing violated the Fourth Amendment, and a federal court agreed. **Although teachers are highly responsible for the safety of others, making random drug screening generally permissible, the way the policy was implemented violated the law.** First, the policy didn't give teachers enough information about which drugs were being tested. It gave scientific names, but not brand names. And second, the way the policy was implemented allowed a company employee to separate out a sample into two containers (in case retesting was necessary) in front of other employees. This violated employees' privacy rights. *Smith County Educ. Ass'n v. Smith County Board of Educ.*, 781 F.Supp.2d 604 (M.D. Tenn. 2011).

◆ A California teacher received her third DUI and was placed on home detention for 30 days, but she was also allowed to teach her class during that time while wearing an ankle bracelet. Two years later, the state commission on teacher credentialing suspended her credential for 60 days. She challenged the suspension, but the state court of appeal upheld it, finding that **her drinking and driving, while off school grounds and away from children, provided enough evidence of her unfitness to teach** so as to justify the suspension. *Broney v. California Comm'n on Teacher Credentialing*, 108 Cal.Rptr.3d 832 (Cal. Ct. App. 2010).

◆ An Oregon teacher was dismissed by her school district for "immorality" and "neglect of duty" after a police search and ensuing events brought to light evidence that her husband had been using their jointly owned home to grow and sell marijuana and that the teacher was aware of that. The teacher appealed to the Fair Dismissal Appeals Board, which reversed the dismissal and ordered her reinstated. The district sought review before the Oregon Court of Appeals. It noted that the teacher's job responsibilities included instruction and extracurricular participation in the district's anti-drug program. Here, the teacher did essentially nothing to deter her husband's use of their home for illegal drug activities. Her workshop training gave clear notice that off-duty personal drug involvement was contrary to a teacher's role in connection with the anti-drug instructional program. **She had a duty to prevent her home from being used for marijuana sales regardless of how that act might upset her occasionally violent husband.** The appeals board should have focused on the propriety of her conduct in the light of her responsibilities to the district and her students. The court reversed and remanded the case to the appeals board for reconsideration. *Jefferson County School Dist. No. 509-J v. Fair Dismissal Appeals Board*, 102 Or. App. 83, 793 P.2d 888 (Or. Ct. App. 1990).

◆ A Texas teacher checked out a district vehicle to drive to a soccer clinic. Before picking up a colleague who was going to the clinic, the teacher stopped at a dry cleaner and then a grocery store, where he purchased beer and other items. A witness reported seeing him leaving the store with beer and getting into the vehicle. The teacher admitted buying beer while using the vehicle when the school principal confronted him about it. He submitted his resignation after being formally reprimanded, but he later changed his mind and rescinded it. The superintendent recommended not renewing his contract, and the school board voted for non-renewal after a hearing. The state education commissioner affirmed the decision, finding substantial evidence that the teacher was "in the course and scope of his employment while he was in possession of alcohol." A Texas district court affirmed the decision, and the teacher appealed, arguing he was on a personal side trip to run errands when he bought beer. The court held the commissioner's decision had to be affirmed unless it was arbitrary and capricious. **A court could not substitute its judgment for the commissioner's and could only review it to determine if it was supported by substantial evidence.** The teacher had admitted his error and stated buying beer "was a dumb thing to do." He also stated to the board he was acting within the scope of his duties to attend the soccer clinic. The teacher agreed it was reasonable to assume he was acting for the school when the school day began. As the commissioner's decision was supported by substantial evidence, the court affirmed it. *Simpson v. Alanis*, No. 08-03-00110-CV, 2004 WL 309297 (Tex. Ct. App. 2/19/04).

C. Assault

◆ After an Iowa student gave his football coach the finger, the coach put his hands on the student to escort him off the bus. The student said he was "thrown down the aisle." Seeing bruises on their son, his parents called the police, who charged the coach with assault. Then the state licensing board charged the coach with "student abuse." **At the hearing, the coach's previous written reprimands were examined. They included instances of the coach duct-taping droopy trousers to one student and grabbing another and ripping his shirt for calling the coach an "idiot."** The board revoked his teaching license for 90 days and his PE and coaching endorsements for good. The coach appealed to the state supreme court, which found the decision was supported by the evidence. *Christiansen v. Iowa Board of Educ. Examiners*, 831 N.W.2d 179 (Iowa 2013).

◆ A Pennsylvania school district IT employee also served as an assistant coach for the girls' softball teams. He became friends with a student's family, but the mother grew suspicious when she noticed calls from her daughter to the employee at odd hours. She went to the head coach, who went to the principal who, along with the head coach, met with the parents and the student's sister. The family told the coach and principal that they suspected an inappropriate sexual relationship. **The principal told the employee to stay away from team members and that same day, the superintendent gave the employee the option of being fired or resigning.** He resigned. Ten months later, he was charged with sexual offenses against the student. The family then sued the district under 42 U.S.C. § 1983, alleging violations of the student's Fourteenth Amendment rights, but a federal court found no evidence that district officials knew about the sexual abuse or were deliberately indifferent to it. Here, the district conducted a background check on the employee before hiring him, had a written sexual harassment policy in place, and acted promptly to force the employee's resignation when confronted with evidence that he was behaving inappropriately with the student. *Maier v. Canon McMillan School Dist.*, No. 08-0154, 2009 WL 2591098 (W.D. Pa. 8/20/09).

◆ An Oregon teacher served a school district for 19 years with no disciplinary problems. Her husband left her, moved in with his girlfriend, and sought a divorce. The teacher drove to the girlfriend's house and had an argument with her husband. She attempted suicide by taking prescription medications, then rammed her vehicle into her husband's vehicle and damaged the house. She voluntarily committed herself for psychiatric treatment. The incident was reported in local newspapers. Law officials charged her with four crimes, three of which were dropped via plea bargain. She pleaded no contest to a criminal mischief charge, which provided for dismissal with no charges if she completed her term of probation. The school board voted to dismiss the teacher after a hearing, and she appealed to the Oregon Fair Dismissal Appeals Board (FDAB).

An FDAB hearing panel heard testimony from a psychologist who said the teacher's conduct was isolated and unlikely to reoccur. The board had previously let two teachers return to work after suicide attempts, and another had returned after entering into a diversion agreement for domestic violence charges. The FDAB panel found the dismissal had been "unreasonable" under ORS § 342.905. The board overreacted to an isolated incident and had to reinstate the teacher. The Court of Appeals of Oregon reversed the panel's decision, and the teacher appealed. **The Supreme Court of Oregon stated that contract teachers may be dismissed only for immorality or neglect of duty.** The FDAB was authorized to determine whether actions by school boards were "unreasonable" or "clearly an excessive remedy." In the context of the statute, "unreasonable" meant "acting without rational or logical justification" for an action. The FDAB panel failed to apply this interpretation, and its decision did not provide a rational connection between the facts and the conclusion. The court returned the case to the panel for further action. *Bergerson v. Salem-Keizer School Dist.*, 341 Or. 401, 144 P.3d 918 (Or. 2006).

D. Other Off-Duty Conduct

◆ A state appeals court affirmed the Colorado State Board of Education's decision to deny a teacher's renewal of her teaching certificate. The teacher's then-husband sexually assaulted their daughter for several years. When the teacher found out about the abuse, she didn't report it – but a neighbor did. The state refused to renew the educator's teaching certificate, citing "unethical behavior" for failing to report the abuse. She filed a lawsuit. The teacher argued that parents aren't listed as "individuals who have a statutory duty to report child abuse." She said she had no duty to report the abuse because she learned about it at home. The court wasn't swayed. It said her job as a teacher made her a mandated reporter and her duty to report applied regardless of how she learned about the abuse. The law didn't include any limiting language, such as "during his or her professional duties" or "in their official capacity," the court said. **Moreover, the law listed two express exceptions to the reporting duty and neither applied here.** The court said it "presume[d] that express exceptions in a statute exclude all other exceptions," so it found there was no exception to reporting duties of a mandated reporter who learns about child abuse or neglect in the home. It affirmed the board's ruling. *Heotis v. Colorado State Board of Educ.*, No. 18CA0057, 2019 WL 1087027 (Colo. Ct. App. 3/7/19).

◆ A Georgia state court rejected a free speech claim filed by a teacher who was disciplined for a Facebook post. After attending a Christmas parade, the teacher weighed in on a local radio station's Facebook discussion regarding the event. Specifically, the deejays wanted to know if the community thought a Black Lives Matter float in the parade was an appropriate holiday display. In part, the teacher's comment read, "It's turned into a race matter. … The signs should read, TAKE THE HOOD OFF YOUR HEAD, AND PULL UP YOUR PANTS AND QUIT IMPREGNATING EVERYBODY. I'm tired of paying for these sorry *ss thugs." Nearly a third of the student body was black. District administrators received a lot of complaints. A county commissioner expressed concern on behalf of his constituents. Parents demanded their children be moved to another teacher's classroom, and a colleague reported that it would be very difficult to work with the teacher. After an investigation, the teacher was suspended for five days and ordered to attend diversity training. She sued, alleging a violation of her speech rights under the First Amendment. The case reached a state appeals court, which held the board president and superintendent were entitled to immunity, as they didn't violate a clearly established law. In *Pickering v. Board of Educ.*, the U.S. Supreme Court held that a public school employee's speech rights are limited by the state's need to preserve efficient governmental functions. That means the school has the authority to limit the teacher's speech if it interferes with the operations of the school. Here, the evidence showed **the teacher's post interfered with normal school operations** in many ways. District administrators didn't violate a clearly established law, so they were entitled to immunity. *Atwater v. Tucker*, No. A17A0722, 2017 WL 4784397 (Ga. Ct. App. 10/24/17).

◆ A Michigan teacher attended a bachelor/bachelorette party and engaged in a simulated act of oral sex on a mannequin. Someone photographed her without her knowledge and posted the photos on a website without her consent. Two years later, students at her school accessed the photos until they were removed. The school board suspended and then fired the teacher for engaging in lewd behavior contrary to the moral values of the educational and school community. She appealed, and the state tenure commission found no professional misconduct and ordered her reinstatement. The Court of Appeals of Michigan upheld that decision, noting that **her conduct was not only off-duty, but lawful and not involving children**. And it did not have an adverse effect on the educational process. *Land v. L'Anse Creuse Public School Board of Educ.*, No. 288612, 2010 WL 2135356 (Mich. Ct. App. 5/27/10).

CHAPTER SEVEN

Health Issues

I. ALLERGIES

A. Food Allergies

1. Generally

All foods have the potential to cause an allergic reaction, and sometimes even a very small amount is all that is needed. Seven foods – peanuts, tree nuts, milk, egg, soy, wheat and fish – account for the vast majority of all food allergies. Of these, peanuts, tree nuts, eggs and milk most commonly cause problems for children, and the majority of severe and fatal reactions involve peanuts and tree nuts. Food allergies can be managed, but they are not curable.

Millions of Americans have food allergies, and food allergies in American children have increased significantly since 1997, according to a study by the Centers for Disease Control (CDC). In addition, the CDC reported a drastic increase in the number of hospital admissions related to children's food allergies, which indicates children's reactions to the allergens are becoming more severe.

Allergies are diseases that cause the immune systems of affected individuals to overreact to substances known as allergens. In people with food allergies, the immune system identifies a specific protein in a food as a potentially harmful substance. The immune system responds to the perceived threat by producing an allergic antibody to the food. This response triggers the release of what are known as chemical mediators, such as histamine. The release of the mediators can cause inflammatory reactions in the skin, the respiratory system, the gastrointestinal system, and the cardiovascular system. A potentially life-threatening condition called anaphylaxis occurs when these inflammatory reactions occur in more than one of these systems. Approximately 30,000 episodes of anaphylactic shock and an average of 200 deaths caused by the episodes occur in the U.S. each year – primarily in children, according to the National Institute of Allergy and Infectious Disease. Common symptoms of anaphylaxis include hives, vomiting, itching, swelling, coughing, dizziness, and difficulty swallowing.

Students who have food allergies should have an action plan to indicate how school officials should manage an allergic reaction that may progress to anaphylaxis. The action plan should indicate whether emergency treatment with an EpiPen or EpiPen Junior is required. EpiPen is an auto-injector that administers adrenaline and is available by prescription only. EpiPens should be stored properly and securely, but they should also be readily available. EpiPens should be accessible to school officials. Decisions regarding whether students should be allowed to carry their own EpiPens should be made on a case-by-case basis and according to the district's policies.

EpiPens should be stored in temperatures ranging from 68 degrees to 77 degrees. They should not be refrigerated, and they should not be exposed to light or extreme heat.

Two red flags indicate that an EpiPen should be replaced, even if it has not reached its expiration date. Specifically, an EpiPen should be discarded if it has solid particles in it or if it has a pink or brown tint.

In 2016, the Food and Drug Administration (FDA) issued new instructions for proper use of the EpiPen and other epinephrine devices. In a nutshell, you should:

- Hold the leg firmly in place. Reports of lacerations and embedded needles prompted this change. Many kids kick when receiving an injection, and holding the leg steady reduces the chances of injury.
- Hold the injector firmly in place for a count of three seconds. Count slowly. This is down from the previous 10-second guideline.
- See a doctor for signs of infection at the injection site, like persistent redness, warmth, swelling and tenderness. Avoid injecting a child in the behind – as it is more likely to get infected. Always inject in the outer thigh – through clothing if necessary.

The School Access to Emergency Epinephrine Act encourages states to adopt laws that require schools to keep epinephrine auto-injectors on hand.

The law gives more grant preference to schools in states that:

- require schools to stock the auto-injectors
- allow students to self-administer medication for anaphylactic reactions (and asthmatic reactions), and
- submit a statement providing that the state's "Good Samaritan" laws adequately protect staffers who administer epinephrine to a student who is reasonably believed to be having an anaphylactic reaction.

Legislative action taken in Michigan was likely a response to the passage of this federal legislation. Effective on the first day of the 2014-15 school year, state law required all schools in the state to have at least two EpiPens in every school – and two staffers who know how to use them.

Children with food allergies present difficult challenges for school administrators and parents. Once a student is identified as having a food allergy, steps must be taken to ensure that the student can completely avoid the food while at school. Families, schools and students all have responsibilities when it comes to managing food allergies.

- It is the **family's** responsibility to notify the school of the existence of the student's food allergies and to work with the school to develop an effective management plan. It is also the responsibility of the family to teach the child to self-manage the food allergy to the maximum extent possible and to provide any required medications.
- **Schools** should form teams, consisting of the student's teacher,

the school's principal, the school's nurse, food service personnel and other key personnel to work with the student and the family to develop an effective management plan. It is advisable to adopt and enforce a policy barring eating on school buses, except to accommodate legitimate special needs. Schools would also benefit by providing training and education to staff regarding food allergies and practicing emergency drill responses to food allergy reactions.

- **Students** with allergies should be instructed not to exchange food with others and not to eat anything with unknown ingredients. In addition, allergic students should be instructed to notify an adult immediately if they ingest something they believe might cause an allergic reaction.

Constant monitoring is crucial, as problems can arise in unforeseeable ways. Here's an example: High school student Joshua Hickson was charged with assault after he smeared peanut butter on the forehead of a student with a peanut allergy. Hickson was suspended from school and charged with misdemeanor assault, which is punishable by up to a year in jail and a $5,000 fine.

2. Legal Decisions

◆ The Sixth Circuit affirmed an Ohio court ruling that rejected a mother's IDEA claim. The student had a peanut allergy and a medical care plan for preventing and responding to allergic reactions. In 2014, a school employee accidentally included sealed containers of peanut butter on breakfast carts taken into the boy's classroom. He didn't suffer an allergic reaction. Even so, his mom sued after the close call, alleging a violation of the IDEA. She claimed the school should've addressed her son's peanut allergy. **The court noted the school did address the allergy in his IEP under the heading "Other Information."** Further, it had a separate medical plan that addressed the allergy. The Sixth Circuit affirmed the ruling for the school. *Barney v. Akron Board of Educ.*, No. 17-4116, 2019 WL 919839 (6th Cir. 2/25/19).

◆ A North Carolina court rejected the intentional infliction of emotional distress claims (IIED) filed by the parents of a child who is allergic to – and was threatened with – nuts.

The child had a severe nut allergy. Learning this, a classmate identified as Student 1 told the child to "watch out" because he was going to bring nuts to school the following day. The child's parents met with school officials regarding the threat. At the meeting, school officials said the bully would be dealt with and came up with a plan for medical treatment should the child be exposed to nuts at school. Over the next several months, Student 1 continued to bully the child. So the school transferred Student 1 to another class and rearranged the lunch and recess schedules to ensure they didn't interact during those times. As time went on, Student 1 started sneaking into activities during his old recess time. Finally, when the classes of the child and Student 1 started combining, the child was diagnosed with PTSD.

His parents withdrew him and filed IIED claims against the school board and faculty members. The claim against the board was dismissed, as it was entitled to immunity. Then the court looked at the claim against the individuals. It takes a lot to state a valid IIED claim. The parents had to show that the school officials' actions were so extreme and outrageous that they went "beyond all possible bounds of decency … and [were] utterly intolerable in a civilized community."

That wasn't the case here, the court pointed out. **The school took steps to resolve the problem, including holding several meetings to address the issue, altering Student 1's schedule and developing a safety plan for the child.** The child's parents failed to meet the high bar required to state a valid IIED claim, so it had to be dismissed, the court held. *R.M. v. Charlotte-Mecklenburg County Board of Educ.*, No. 3:16-CV-00528-GCM, 2017 WL 2115108 (W.D.N.C. 5/15/17).

◆ An IEP effectively addressed a student's allergies, so she was not denied a FAPE, a New York federal held. An 8-year-old nonverbal student had several food allergies. As such, an IEP was drafted for her. It placed her in a 6:1:1 classroom, scheduled speech services and assigned a separate table in the lunchroom. But her parents weren't happy with the IEP. They rejected it and enrolled their daughter in a private school. The parents sought judicial review, claiming – among other things – that the IEP failed to properly address their daughter's allergies because it didn't list her allergy-related hospitalizations during the previous three years. They wanted tuition reimbursement. The court looked at the IEP, which said the student was "not currently on any medications … and has food allergies to eggs, dairy, fish and peanuts." The IEP further noted that the student should sit at a separate table in the cafeteria as an accommodation. **The court surmised that, at the time the IEP was crafted, nothing indicated the hospitalizations needed to be listed.** Because no evidence backed the parents' claim, the court held the IEP adequately addressed the girl's allergies. The parents were not entitled to tuition reimbursement. *NB v. New York City Dept. of Educ.*, No. 15 Civ. 4948 (AT) 2016 WL 5816925 (S.D.N.Y. 9/29/16).

◆ The IDEA does not entitle a student with severe food allergies to be accompanied throughout the school day by an individual trained in CPR and the Heimlich maneuver, so the Fourth Circuit affirmed a Maryland court ruling to dismiss the claim. A first-grade student suffered several disabilities – including severe food allergies. A one-to-one aide was assigned to the boy. The school implemented an IEP for the student, which stipulated in the event that the student choked, the assigned aide should call 911 and have trained staff perform the Heimlich maneuver. The parents weren't happy with that section of the IEP. They wanted an assigned aide who was trained in CPR and the Heimlich maneuver by their son's side at all times throughout the school day. The parents filed a due process complaint, saying the school failed to provide their son with a FAPE as required by the IDEA. The ALJ found the school satisfied the requirements of the IDEA, and the parents sued. A Maryland court upheld the ALJ's ruling, explaining "reasonableness is something less than perfection, and as found by [the ALJ], the measures that defendant has put in place provide adequate protection." The Fourth Circuit affirmed the dismissal, noting **the ALJ didn't have to consider what the school "could have done; rather, it is required to look at whether the [school's] actions were appropriate" under the law**. *SE.H. v. Board of Educ. of Anne Arundel Co. Public Schools*, 647 Fed.Appx. 242 (4th Cir. 2016).

◆ A Tennessee federal judge refused to dismiss retaliation claims filed by the parents of a girl with allergies. The child suffered from severe peanut allergies. The school teamed up with the girl's allergist and pediatrician and created a plan to address her allergies. Later, her parents raised concerns about how the plan was implemented. Afterward, they claimed the principal became angry, as if their child's health and safety was a "nuisance." Then the principal allegedly retaliated against them by reporting to child protective services they emotionally abused their daughter and by requiring the mother to "check in" at the office because she passed out flyers in her daughter's class. The parents sued, alleging retaliation in violation of the ADA, Section 504 of the Rehabilitation Act and the First Amendment. The court refused to grant judgment without a trial. **Many facts, specifically those regarding the principal's motives behind his actions, were in dispute.** More info was needed, so summary judgment wasn't appropriate. *C.G. v. Cheatham County Board of Educ.,* No. 3-14-2309, 2016 WL 1366671 (M.D. Tenn. 4/6/16).

◆ Virginia's highest court held that school officials' statements to the media were misleading and aimed at the mother of a student who died at school from an anaphylactic reaction. The mother sued, alleging six school officials made malicious statements about her to divert public anger about the school's failure to follow the student's allergy plan. She sought damages for defamation. In 2012, the student died at school as a result of an allergic reaction to peanuts. Prior to the student's death:

- her mother had informed the school of the girl's allergy
- the school was given a copy of the anaphylaxis plan signed by the student's pediatrician, and
- her mother brought an EpiPen to school for an emergency. The nurse told her to take it home, as the school stocked EpiPens.

After the student ate the peanut, she reported "bumps" and "scratching" in her throat. But she was not given medication as the plan directed. Her death received widespread attention from local, national and international media. Both mother and child were named in the articles, and several school officials were quoted. The complaint showed a common theme in 13 public statements: School officials implied the mother failed to work with the school to prevent her daughter's death.

Virginia law recognizes a claim for defamation by inference, implication or insinuation. The long legal battle went all the way to the state supreme court, which held implication was present. **The school officials' statements were clearly "aimed directly [at the mother] and no other person," the state's highest court held.** It remanded the case. *Pendleton v. Newsome*, 772 S.E.2d 759 (Va. 2015).

◆ A nine-year-old student with allergies to many foods and substances began to have trouble breathing after finishing lunch at school. A school nurse injected the student with EpiPens, but he died two days later. His parents suspected that the student's reaction was triggered by his exposure to blueberries during a classroom lesson on the morning of the event. They sued the student's school, the city department of education and the school nurse, among others. They alleged that the defendants negligently allowed the student to be exposed to a substance to which he was allergic and then failed to properly respond to his symptoms. The court held that the department of education met its obligations by formulating a proper individualized education program for the student. In addition, the school provided adequate supervision; typically there were about 10 children in the student's class and four supervising adults. Further, **the nurse did not depart from good and accepted nursing and professional practice**, especially since blueberries were not included on the list of known allergens for the child and the parents never proved what triggered the student's reaction. *Begley v. City of New York*, 111 A.D.3d 5 (N.Y. App. Div. 2013).

◆ A school proposed to accommodate a student with a nut allergy by providing that he would eat only food brought from home and would sit at a nut-free table in the cafeteria. His parents objected because the student would be eating alone. The child's doctor asked the school to seat the child at a rectangular table with a two-foot buffer between him and classmates who also had nut-free lunches. However, the school only had round lunch tables. The parents withdrew the student from school and asked for a due process hearing. A hearing officer determined that the school met its obligation to accommodate the student, and a federal court agreed. **The proposed accommodations were reasonable**, and the parents did not show that the school officials were deliberately indifferent to the student's rights. *T.F. v. Fox Chapel Area School Dist.*, No. 12cv1666, 2013 WL 5936411 (W.D. Pa. 11/5/13).

◆ The parents of a child with an allergy to nuts sued an elementary school principal and others, claiming the defendants failed to consider the possibility of excluding nut products from the school and forced the child to eat his lunch in an office away from all the other children. The lawsuit accused the defendants of failing to make any reasonable accommodations for the child. **It also claimed the child's school served peanut butter cookies to all students and caused the child to suffer an allergic reaction, even though it knew he was allergic to peanuts.** The court dismissed the parents' claim for negligent infliction of emotional distress because they did not respond to the defendants' motion to dismiss it. The court also dismissed a claim for violation of 42 U.S.C. § 1983, a conspiracy claim under 42 U.S.C. § 1985, a claim under 42 U.S.C. § 1986, a claim of intentional infliction of emotional distress, and a state civil rights claim with leave to amend. Finally, it denied a defense motion to dismiss a slander claim, which was based on the allegation that district defendants distributed false statements about the child to his classmates. *McCue v. South Fork Union School Dist.*, No. CV-F-10-233 OWW/DLB, 2010 WL 2089524 (E.D. Cal. 5/21/10).

◆ Residents of New York enrolled their child in a New Jersey nonprofit school that catered to developmentally atypical children. The child had severe food allergies and was accompanied by a private nurse at all times. He was instructed to eat only food that was supplied by his parents. The child died, allegedly after he was exposed to substances at the school and suffered an allergic reaction. The parents sued the school in a New York court, seeking monetary damages for personal injuries and wrongful death. The parents claimed that the school failed to exercise reasonable care of the child while the child was under its direction and control. The school filed a motion for summary judgment, arguing that it was immune from liability under a New Jersey statute that generally barred claims for damages against nonprofit corporations. The parents opposed the motion on the grounds that New York law did not recognize the principle of charitable immunity. The court held that the New Jersey law of charitable immunity did not apply because it offended the public policy of New York. The parents showed that sufficient contacts existed between them, the injury and New York, and they also showed that **application of the New Jersey charitable immunity statute would violate a "fundamental principle of justice."** The parents lived in New York, and the child's tuition at the New Jersey school was paid by the New York City Board of Education. Further, New York had an interest in protecting its citizens from "unfair and anachronistic foreign statutes," and the state of New York had first rejected the concept of charitable immunity nearly 50 years earlier. The school's motion for summary judgment was denied. *Begley v. City of New York*, 836 N.Y.S.2d 496 (N.Y. Sup. Ct. 2007).

◆ A child broke out in splotches and hives while at a daycare facility. Following the incident, the child's doctor determined the child was allergic to peanuts and peanut derivatives. The child then suffered a second allergic reaction at the daycare facility, after which the facility refused to provide further daycare services to her. The child's mother then sued the facility under the Americans with Disabilities Act (ADA) and state law, claiming discrimination on the basis of disability. A district court granted summary judgment in favor of the daycare facility, and the parent appealed. The appeals court upheld the district court's determination on the basis that the child did not have a "disability" as that term is defined in the ADA. Although the child's allergy was a physical impairment, it did not substantially limit her ability to eat or breathe. **The child's doctor stated that the child's allergy impacted her life only "a little bit," and the record did not show she was restricted from eating any other kind of food.** Nor did the parent show that the child was disabled under the ADA because she had a record of a disability or was regarded by the school as disabled. Finally, the court rejected the state-law claim because the child was not disabled under the state law. *Land v. Baptist Medical Center*, 164 F.3d 423 (8th Cir. 1999).

◆ A student with an allergy to peanuts went on a field trip with his elementary school class. The district's food staff, the boy's teacher, two school nurses and several parent volunteers all were aware that the child was allergic to peanuts. Nonetheless, the child was given a snack lunch that included peanut-based foods. The child reported feeling sick after he ate a peanut-based cookie. Trip chaperones did not want to curtail the activities of the other children on the trip, so they placed the student on the school bus to wait. His condition worsened, and he later died after being taken to a hospital by car. After the student's parents entered into a settlement agreement with the school district regarding the incident, a newspaper sought the release under a public disclosure act of an investigator's notes, an investigator's hand-drawn map, conference notes by counsel for the district, and counsel's report to an insurer. A trial court ruled that the records were not subject to disclosure because they were attorney work product and attorney-client privileged material. The newspaper appealed. The appeal court affirmed the determination that the records were not subject to disclosure. **The documents were attorney work product and were further protected by attorney-client privilege.** The public disclosure act's provisions relating to open government did not outweigh the countervailing interest in insulating confidential pretrial communications from public inspection. Finally, the district did not waive its privilege to keep the information private when it made selected disclosures of information to the public and the student's family. The trial court's decision was affirmed. *Soter v. Cowles Publishing Co.*, 130 P.3d 840 (Wash. Ct. App. 2006). On appeal, the Supreme Court of Washington affirmed the appeals court's decision. *Soter v. Cowles Publishing Co.*, 174 P.3d 60 (Wash. 2007).

B. Other Allergies

1. Generally

School officials need to be aware that a range of allergies other than food-related allergies may affect the school environment.

2. Legal Decisions

◆ A student with allergies to certain body sprays, perfumes, colognes, laundry detergents, fabric softeners and scented lotions alleged that his high school violated Title II of the Americans with Disabilities Act by refusing to implement a written policy against spraying perfumes at school. The student did not know which specific scents triggered reactions, how much of a particular fragrance was needed to trigger a reaction, or what the severity of any given reaction would be. The school offered several accommodations, including allowing the student to park in a different area and enter the school through a different door, allowing the student to leave class early, allowing the student to arrive at a different time, and exploring whether the student could wear a mask. **The court ruled for the school, finding it took sufficient steps to accommodate the student's condition.** Moreover, the student did not show that the written policy he sought would have been effective. *Zandi v. JVB Fort Wayne Community Schools*, No. 1:10-CV-395-JVB, 2012 WL 4472006 (N.D. Ind. 9/27/12).

◆ The parent of a two-year-old enrolled the child at a nursery school where teachers used powdered latex gloves to change children's diapers. The parent, who had an allergy to latex, asked the teachers at the school to use non-powdered latex gloves. She also asked her son's teacher to use non-latex gloves, and she offered to provide them. When the parent spoke to the head administrator at the school about switching to non-powdered gloves, the administrator initially told the parent he would look into it. The parent also had her physician send the administrator a letter explaining her allergy. Despite the request and the letter, the administrator allegedly later told the parent he was not willing to switch to another type of gloves. However, he did tell staff members not to use latex gloves when changing the diaper of the parent's child. After the parent provided the administrator with a letter discussing her rights under the law, the administrator asked the parent to withdraw the child from the school. The parent removed the child from the school and later sued it, claiming it violated a county human rights code by discriminating against her based on her latex allergy. A jury found in her favor and awarded $1,683 in economic damages and $5,000 in non-economic damages. It also awarded $22,800 in attorneys' fees. The trial court entered judgment on the verdict, and the school appealed. The appeals court reversed the lower court's judgment in favor of the parent because she did not show that her latex allergy was a disability under the law. However, the state's highest court reversed the appeals court's decision and held that **it was for a jury to decide whether the parent's latex allergy was a "handicap" within the meaning of the law** at issue. Since the evidence was sufficient for the jury to conclude the parent had a "handicap," the judgment favoring her was restored. *Meade v. Shangri-La Limited Partnership*, 36 A.3d 483 (Md. 2012).

◆ A parent of two students sued a city, a board of education and several individual defendants, claiming the defendants' failure to properly maintain public school buildings caused the students to become disabled. The parent asserted that the defendants' failure to properly maintain a middle school caused it to sustain water damage that led to mold and bacterial growth and high levels of moisture in the indoor air. She also claimed that the defendants' failure to properly maintain a high school resulted in asbestos problems, leaks and poor ventilation. **The parent said that conditions at the schools caused one of the students to suffer irreversible lung disease and the other to suffer allergies and asthma.** She claimed that the students were eligible for special education services and that the defendants wrongfully failed to provide them. The parent's suit against the defendants raised several claims, including federal claims under the Individuals with Disabilities Education Act, Section 504 of the Rehabilitation Act and the Americans with Disabilities Act. The parent also filed several state law claims. The defendants filed a motion to dismiss the case, and the parent filed a motion to remand the case to state court. The court granted the motion to dismiss several of the claims raised by the parent because the parent failed to exhaust her administrative remedies under the Individuals with Disabilities Education Act. It also declined to exercise supplemental jurisdiction over some remaining state law claims. The court remanded remaining state law claims to a state court. *Avoletta v. City of Torrington*, No. 3:07CV841 (AHN), 2008 WL 905882 (D. Conn. 3/31/08).

◆ A student with a latex allergy broke out in hives after he was given a latex ball to play with at school. His representatives sued the school district, accusing it of failing to prevent him from sustaining injury by failing to convey his special needs to teachers and aides. The representatives also raised claims under the Individuals with Disabilities Education Act and the Americans with Disabilities Act. After the school district removed the case to federal court, the representatives filed a motion to remand it back to state court. The court granted the motion to remand. **The theories of relief advanced by the student's representatives were based solely on state tort law.** Because no claim in the case arose under federal law, the court granted the motion to remand the case. *Reuther v. Shiloh School Dist. No. 85*, No. 07-cv-689-JPG, 2008 WL 191195 (S.D. Ill. 1/18/08).

◆ A village resident installed an outdoor wood-burning furnace adjacent to his garage and approximately 50 feet from the elementary wing of a local school. The resident used the furnace to provide heat for his home. Teachers, school employees and parents of students complained about the smell of smoke in the school cafeteria and some classrooms. After a school official advised the county department of health that teachers and students had allergies to wood smoke and were becoming ill from it, the health department ordered the resident to stop using the furnace. The resident sued the school district, the county and others, claiming they violated the Constitution by depriving him the right to use his property without due process of law. He also claimed an equal protection violation, alleging no enforcement actions were taken against others whose use of wood-burning furnaces caused smoke to enter the school. The court granted summary judgment against the resident. The resident failed to prove an equal protection violation because he did not identify any other resident who used wood for heating fuel. Even if he had, the equal protection claim would fail because the smoke created a respiratory hazard. The resident's due process claim failed as well, because **he did not have a constitutionally protected property interest in heating his home with wood**. The defendants' motions for summary judgment were granted. *Tallman v. County of Chautauqua*, No. 05-CV-02769A(Sr), 2007 WL 4276825 (W.D.N.Y. 12/3/07).

◆ The parents of a sixth-grade student sued the student's school principal and others under the Americans with Disabilities Act, the Rehabilitation Act and state law, claiming they failed to accommodate the student's allergic reactions to environmental factors at her school. The parents claimed the student was hypersensitive to phenol, which can be present in vapors emitted by cleaning agents or paints. The defendants filed a motion to exclude the expert testimony of the student's primary treating physician, who concluded the student was hypersensitive to environmental phenol even though the student was unable to complete a test to determine whether the hypersensitivity existed. The court granted the motion to exclude the expert's testimony. **The expert's conclusion that the student was hypersensitive to phenol was an inference that was not based on adequate scientific data, testing or methodology.** As a result, it was unreliable and was not a proper subject for expert testimony. *Kropp v. Maine School Administrative Union #44*, 471 F.Supp.2d 175 (D. Me. 2007).

◆ The parents of an eighth-grade student with multiple chemical sensitivities protested a school board's plan to use pesticides on school playing fields. The board approved the plan, and the parents asked the student's gym teacher to keep her inside while fields were sprayed. The student was assigned to begin ninth grade at a high school that was located across the street from a working farm. During the summer before the student's ninth-grade year, the student's parents asked the school district for a Section 504 Service Agreement that would permit the student to fulfill her gym requirement at a location away from the school. In addition, **they asked that the school not be sprayed with pesticides, and they asked for a transfer to a school that was located in a more urban area**. The school proposed a service agreement that excused the student from participating in outdoor PE activities and offered a transfer to the urban high school. The parents objected to the proposed agreement for several reasons. Among other things, they wanted to substitute gym class with dance, and they stated there was no guarantee that balls used indoors had no pesticides on them. After the school proposed modified agreements, the parents withdrew their request for a service agreement but continued to seek accommodations for the student. The school district submitted the matter for a due process hearing, and the hearing officer found the district offered a reasonable agreement. The school reversed the transfer offer. The parents withdrew the student and sued the district under the Rehabilitation Act, the

Americans with Disabilities Act, and 42 U.S.C. § 1983. **They claimed that the district's attempt to enter into a service agreement was an abuse of process and violated their due process rights.** The court granted the defendants' motion for summary judgment. There was no evidence that the district used process in any way not intended as proper use when it sought a due process hearing. The court also rejected the claim that the parents' civil rights were violated because they were forced into a Section 504 service agreement. To prove that the plan violated their due process rights, the parents were required to show actions on the part of the school district that "shocked the conscience." They failed to do so. The parents also failed to show that the district retaliated against them for exercising their First Amendment rights by intensifying the use of pesticides, forcing them into a service agreement or stigmatizing the student as disabled, and that claim was also time-barred. Finally, the court rejected claims of emotional distress and conspiracy. *Sutton v. West Chester Area School Dist.*, No. Civ.A. 03-3061, 2004 WL 999144 (E.D. Pa. 5/4/04).

II. DIABETES

A. Symptoms and Management

Diabetes is an incurable, chronic disease that is characterized by an inability to properly produce or use insulin, which is a hormone that converts food into energy. Lack of insulin causes blood glucose to rise to an abnormally high level, resulting in a condition called hyperglycemia. When this happens, the body may excrete blood glucose in the urine, causing it to lose its main fuel source.

There are two main types of diabetes. Individuals with Type 1 diabetes, which often afflicts school-age children, are unable to produce insulin and must receive insulin on a daily basis. Type 2 diabetes involves an inability to utilize insulin that the body produces. It can be controlled with insulin, oral medications or both.

Management of diabetes involves maintaining proper blood glucose control, a task which requires constant vigilance. Careful monitoring is imperative, and administration of insulin therapy is often required.

Controlling blood glucose levels is often a difficult balancing act. If not enough insulin is given, the individual's blood glucose level will rise to an unacceptable level. But administration of too much insulin can cause a dangerous condition called hypoglycemia, or low blood glucose. According to the U.S. Department of Health and Human Services, hypoglycemia presents a greater danger to school-age students than hyperglycemia. Some of the symptoms of hypoglycemia, include:

- shakiness
- sweating
- hunger
- pale appearance

- blurred vision
- sleepiness
- dizziness
- confusion
- disorientation
- lack of coordination
- irritability or nervousness
- change in personality
- inability to concentrate
- weakness
- lethargy
- changes in behavior

B. Legal Decisions

◆ The Sixth Circuit rejected the attempts of a Kentucky family to collect damages based on alleged disability discrimination. The student was diagnosed with Type-1 diabetes when he was four. He had to take insulin injections and needed to monitor his sugar throughout the day. During kindergarten enrollment, his parents explained his medical needs. After several meetings, the district determined he needed to be enrolled at an elementary school with a full-time nurse on staff. His parents disagreed with the placement – they wanted him to be enrolled in a school closer to home. By the time he reached the second grade, he was independently using an insulin pump, so the district agreed to transfer the boy to the school of the parent's choosing. But in the middle of the transfer, the parents moved out of the district and filed a disability discrimination suit that sought damages. To win damages, the parents had to show that the school was "deliberately indifferent" to their son's federally protected rights. But that wasn't the case, the court explained, as the school didn't ignore the boy's request for help. "Rather, **the parents simply disagreed … as to whether a nurse was necessary to provide" medical care**, the court held. So the child wasn't entitled to damages. *R.K. v. Board of Educ. of Scott County, Kentucky*, 637 Fed.Appx. 922 (6th Cir. 2016).

◆ A Washington federal judge refused to dismiss discrimination claims of a student with diabetes. A student had a severe case of diabetes, and her blood sugar had to be monitored every two hours. Her mother asked for an accommodation – a qualified school nurse – to monitor the student's blood level throughout the day. Her mom said the accommodation would help the child learn to become more independent – a goal listed in her IEP – as she entered first grade. Instead of granting the accommodation, the school said the child would be transferred to a nearby school that could handle the accommodation – but the transfer had to take place in two days. The mother rejected the district's accommodation offer, citing concerns about the abrupt change. She sued, seeking damages for alleged violations of the ADA and

Section 504 of the Rehabilitation Act. The school asked the court to dismiss the claims. It refused. The girl's mother had to show the school intentionally discriminated against the child on the basis of her disability. She did, as email documentation showed the school knew about the disability and failed to provide accommodations. The court said a reasonable jury could find the school was deliberately indifferent because it didn't act to address the child's needs. **The court pointed out the transfer accommodation could've been a reasonable one – if the school had allotted more than two days for the transition.** It didn't, so the claim had to proceed. *Snell v. North Thurston School Dist.*, No. C13-5786RBL, 2015 WL 6396092 (W.D. Wash. 10/21/15).

◆ The parent of a seventh-grade student with Type I diabetes sued a city, city agencies and city officials. In the lawsuit, the parent accused the defendants of violating the Rehabilitation Act and the Americans with Disabilities Act by denying her request to heat the child's food at school. The parent claimed that the school was required to heat the child's food because the child would skip lunch if his food was not heated. The court rejected her claim, finding that **the child's school provided adequate accommodations by offering lunch menu options and monitoring the child's blood glucose level**. Heating the student's food may have helped him adjust to his disability, but the school was required to provide only meaningful access and not preferred arrangements. The laws relied upon by the parent did not require optimal accommodations, and it was undisputed that hot food is not essential to effective management of diabetes. *Moody v. NYC Dep't of Educ.*, 513 Fed. Appx. 95 (2d Cir. 2013).

◆ The Americans Nurses' Association and other trade organizations representing registered and school nurses sued to challenge a state department of education's decision to authorize public school employees other than nurses to administer insulin to students with diabetes. The plaintiffs in the case sought declaratory relief and a writ of mandate. A lower court ruled in favor of the associations, finding that state law did not authorize unlicensed school personnel to administer insulin. On appeal, the state's highest court reversed the lower court's decision. The appeals court determined that **state law did not ban school personnel other than licensed health care providers from administering insulin to students with diabetes**. In addition, it decided that advisory statements recommending administration only by licensed professionals were not entitled to deference. *American Nurses Ass'n v. Torlakson*, 304 P.3d 1038 (Cal. 2013).

◆ The mother of a second-grade student became dissatisfied with the way her daughter's school was handling her diabetes. The mother informed the school nurse that she wanted the nurse to give the student insulin shots whenever her blood sugar tested higher than a specified level. The nurse told the mother that written authorization from a physician was required, but the mother never provided the authorization. The nurse later asked the student what she ate at home every day. She also called the student's doctor to ask what she should do if the student's blood sugar level showed a shot was needed and she could not reach the mother. Then, an anonymous caller filed a complaint against the mother with a governmental department of job and family services for medically neglecting the child. The mother later sued the school district and others, alleging that the district violated her right to privacy by asking the student what she ate at home and allegedly filing the anonymous complaint of alleged medical neglect. She also filed a retaliation claim against the school superintendent based on the superintendent's alleged role in filing the neglect complaint against her. The court granted summary judgment against the motion. It rejected her privacy claim because **she did not present authority to support the proposition that she had a fundamental liberty interest in information relating to her management of her child's diabetes**. In addition, the mother failed to produce evidence showing that the district or any of the other defendants had ever revealed the student's medical records to anyone. *Jenkins v. Board of Educ.*, 463 F.Supp.2d 747 (S.D. Ohio 2006). On appeal, the Sixth Circuit reversed the lower court's ruling with respect to the retaliation claim because factual issues existed as to that claim. *Jenkins v. Rock Hill Local School Dist.*, 513 F.3d 580 (6th Cir. 2008).

◆ A child with Type I diabetes was accepted for admission into a preschool program. The child's status as a diabetic was disclosed at the time of the initial interview. A month before the child was to start attending the preschool, his mother informed the preschool's owner that the child had been fitted with an insulin pump. The mother showed two teachers at the preschool how the pump operated. The mother claimed that the owner withdrew the child's acceptance on the day of the meeting. She sued, claiming discrimination. A trial court found that the school was a place of public accommodation under the state law and that the claim was not preempted by the Individuals with Disabilities Education Act. However, it ruled for the school because the law did not obligate the school to provide reasonable accommodations in connection with the child's care. Both sides appealed, and the appeals court affirmed in part and reversed in part. It affirmed the conclusions that the school was a place of public accommodation under the state law and that the claim was not preempted by the Individuals with Disabilities Education Act. **However, it held that the lower court erred when it concluded that the state law against discrimination did not obligate places of public accommodations to provide reasonable accommodations to individuals with disabilities.** Regulations implementing the statute indicated that the provision of reasonable accommodations was required, and the law was to be construed broadly. In addition, federal precedent under the Americans with Disabilities Act, which requires places of public accommodation to provide reasonable accommodations, was relevant. The court was unable to determine whether the school had breached its duty to provide a reasonable accommodation. So further proceedings were needed. *Ellison v. Creative Learning Center*, 893 A.2d 12 (N.J. Super. Ct. App. Div. 2006).

◆ A board of education posted a job opening for a classroom aide. State law defined the position as an aide who had completed a state-approved training program, held a high school diploma, or received a general educational development certificate. It did not include additional requirements. When the board posted the opening, it added the requirement that the successful candidate must be licensed as a practical nurse. The board added this requirement because the successful applicant would serve the needs of two diabetic students. Both students were considered "brittle" diabetics. One received insulin through an insulin pump, and the other received insulin injections. The board hired an individual who was licensed as a practical nurse. Two unsuccessful applicants, who were not licensed as practical nurses, filed grievances with a state grievance board. **They claimed that the board wrongfully expanded the statutory qualifications of the aide position by requiring the successful candidate to be licensed as a practical nurse.** The grievance board granted the grievances, finding that only a school nurse could administer the required care based on the students' specialized health needs. A lower court affirmed, and the board appealed. The appeals court held that the board of education permissibly added practical nurse licensure as a qualification for the position. It was within the discretion of the school board to hire an applicant who possessed the additional qualification of licensure as a practical nurse. The decision of the lower court was reversed. *Board of Educ. of the County of Randolph v. Scott*, 617 S.E.2d 478 (W. Va. 2005).

◆ While a high school pep band was returning to school after a basketball game, a student asked the band instructor if the bus could stop so he could use a restroom. The student claimed the instructor failed to respond three times. Other students began to tease the student, and the bus driver deliberately pumped the brakes to jar the bus and aid in the teasing of the student. The student used a profanity while demanding that the instructor let him off the bus. Before he was able to get off, the student wet himself. The next day, the instructor told the student he would not be allowed to participate in the pep band for the next game and that he might be removed from the pep band. The student was given a one-day out-of-school suspension for using profanity on the bus, and the principal later ordered him to serve three days of detention. A short time later, the student was diagnosed as having diabetes and post-traumatic stress disorder (PTSD). His parents sued the instructor, the principal and the school district, claiming that they triggered or accelerated the student's development of diabetes and caused his PTSD. After the student's physician testified that the added stress created by the bus incident "could have" contributed to the student's development of diabetes, a trial court granted summary judgment against the parents on the ground that the harm to the student was not foreseeable. The parents appealed. **The appeals court affirmed the trial court's decision because the parents failed to present enough evidence of a causal connection between the actions of the defendants and the student's injuries.** The physician's testimony was admissible only if it was based on an opinion that it was more likely than not that the defendants' conduct caused the student's injuries. The physician's testimony that the stress of the bus incident could have caused the student's injuries did not meet this standard. The trial court's decision was affirmed. *Hinkle v. Shepherd School Dist. #37*, 93 P.3d 1239 (Mont. 2004).

III. ASTHMA

A. Symptoms and Management

Asthma is a chronic inflammation of the airways. It can leave students or teachers who suffer from it feeling tired, wheezing, suffering a persistent cough or even struggling to breathe.

Without asthma, our bodies do a very good job of filtering out things like smoke, dust and mold. They get stopped before they reach our lungs by getting trapped in phlegm so they can be coughed or sneezed away.

In people with asthma, the bronchial airways become inflamed by an over-reaction to irritants. The airways swell or become blocked, making it difficult for air to reach the lungs. This over-reaction could have several causes, but the overwhelming number of children with asthma – as many as 80% – also suffer from allergies. Other causes of asthma attacks include viruses and airborne irritants.

According to the Asthma and Allergy Foundation of America, 36,000 students miss school because of asthma *every day*.

The American Lung Association says asthma comes first on the list of chronic illnesses that keep children out of school.

Most serious of all, students occasionally die from asthma attacks – and the condition is affecting more students than ever.

The Centers for Disease Control and Prevention (CDC) has estimated 7 million children have asthma. When it comes to treatment, the news is mixed. We're doing a good job of treating childhood asthma – when there's access to medicine. On the plus side, the CDC report, *The State of Childhood Asthma, United States, 1980 – 2005*, showed a direct correlation between the drop in death rates from juvenile asthma and increased medical treatment. But it also found a disproportionate number of African-American children dying from asthma. Experts say many of these deaths were avoidable. They were apparently caused by under-medication.

Which brings us to the most basic point about your school and asthma: Asthma can't be cured, but it can be controlled. And there are many things schools can do to help.

The American Lung Association defines controlling asthma as taking steps to reduce its frequency and severity in order to lessen its interference with asthmatics' everyday life. From your perspective, you not only want to keep all your students physically safe, you also want to do everything you can to make sure they're learning. A student who is worrying if the chest-tightness she's feeling is the first sign of an attack, or a student who is finding it hard to breathe, is too distracted to pay attention in class or concentrate on homework.

One crucial step in controlling asthma is to eliminate the common triggers for asthma attacks. In its publication *Asthma & Physical Activity in the School*, the National Heart, Lung and Blood Institute has identified the following as common triggers:

- exercise, especially in cold weather
- upper respiratory infections, such as head colds or the flu
- laughing or crying hard
- allergens, such as mold, dust and animal dander, and
- irritants, such as tobacco smoke, chemical fumes and chalk dust.

B. Controlling Asthma's Impact at School

There are many ways to make your school environment a place where asthmatics can breathe freely. These include:

- eliminating dust, dust mites and other allergens by keeping rugs, padded furniture, stuffed animals and cushions out of classrooms
- making sure classroom surfaces are kept clear so that janitors can wipe and mop them
- impressing on staff that using highly scented personal products – including laundry detergents and fabric softeners – could make it harder for some students to breathe
- keeping animals out of school
- maintaining a smoke-free environment, and
- having the right air filters – and keeping them clean.

There also are several things that staff should be on the alert for when it comes to students and asthma. For example:

- Persistent coughing. The American Lung Association has stated that coughing is the most common symptom of asthma. Coughing can be a sign that an asthmatic child may be in distress. In children not diagnosed with asthma, it could be a sign that they should be evaluated for it.
- Children who experience lots of respiratory infections also should be evaluated.
- Since exercise can be a trigger, gym teachers and playground monitors need to be especially vigilant – particularly when the air is cold.
- Emotion also can play a role in the onset and severity of asthma attacks. Adults can help by staying calm, themselves.

In the CDC's *Strategies for Addressing Asthma Within a Coordinated*

School Health Program, a six-part plan of attack is suggested:

1. **Establish management and support systems for asthma-friendly schools.** These include identifying asthmatic students, setting up effective home-school-health provider communication, and assigning a person to coordinate asthma-control efforts.
2. **Provide appropriate school health and mental health services for students with asthma.** For example: following students' own asthma action plans or else a standard emergency protocol for students without individualized plans.
3. **Provide asthma education and awareness programs for students and school staff.** This could include teaching everyone asthma-control basics as well as providing quit-smoking support programs for staff.
4. **Provide a safe and healthy school environment to reduce asthma triggers.** In addition to strategies similar to those discussed above, the CDC encourages schools to use integrated pest management techniques.
5. **Provide safe, enjoyable physical education and activity opportunities for students with asthma.** Students should be encouraged to participate fully when well, but some asthmatics need preventative medication before participation. Immediate emergency access to medication also should be available.
6. **Coordinate school, family, and community efforts to better manage asthma symptoms and reduce school absences among students with asthma.** One thing schools can do is ask for parents' permission for the school health staff and the student's doctor to share health information. They also can get involved with asthma-control initiatives in the wider community.

Schools have been rising to the challenge to help control the impact of asthma on their students in other ways.

Some schools have obtained special equipment to make sure children can get necessary treatment at school.

One piece of equipment some schools consider vital is a peak-flow meter. This is a handheld device that measures how well people can move air out of their lungs.

Another piece of equipment is a nebulizer, a device that turns asthma medication into a fine mist that can be breathed in to penetrate deeply into the lungs. Some states have laws requiring nebulizers in schools.

Schools have also been educating themselves on the subject to better help their students. One excellent free resource you might want to check out is the American Lung Association's *Back to School with Asthma Toolkit*, available at *lung.org*.

In addition to learning about asthma, reducing triggers, training staff and having the right equipment, the following cases illustrate that a quick and appropriate response to a student asthma attack is absolutely necessary.

C. Legal Decisions

1. Asthma-Related Deaths

◆ A Maryland federal court refused to dismiss Section 1983 negligence claims filed against two PE teachers by the estate of a student who suffered a fatal asthma attack. The girl suffered from asthma and used an inhaler to control her symptoms. Her teachers knew she had asthma. They were given a copy of her emergency treatment plan and knew that her asthma could be life-threatening. In mid-Oct. 2015, the student had an asthma attack in PE in front of her teachers. She used her inhaler, which helped her recover.

About six weeks later, the student had another asthma attack in PE. She told her teacher that she was having trouble breathing and asked permission to get her inhaler from the locker room. This time, the PE teacher denied the request. A short time later, the student again asked the teacher if she could go to the locker room to get her inhaler because as she was still having trouble breathing. Again, the teacher said no. After a while, the student returned to her teacher, who was standing with the boys' PE teacher. The girl informed them that she couldn't breathe and she was going to the locker room to get her inhaler.

Both teachers watched the girl leave the gym. Neither went to help her or sent a classmate to help her. She never made it to locker room. A short time later, the student was found unconsciousness on the floor just outside the gymnasium. The school nurse administered artificial respiration to the girl while another employee called 911. The girl died at a nearby hospital. Her estate filed Section 1983 negligence claims against the PE teachers in their individual capacities.

Gross negligence is "more than simple negligence, and likely more akin to reckless conduct," the court explained. To state a valid claim of gross negligence, the estate had to show the teachers intentionally "fail[ed] to perform a manifest duty in reckless disregard of the consequences as affecting the life or property" of the student. Here, the estate alleged the PE teachers knew the student had asthma and knew how to treat her symptoms. Despite this, **the one teacher repeatedly refused to let the girl get her inhaler and both teachers failed to assist the student in what they knew could be a life-threatening situation**. That was enough to state a valid claim, so the case moved forward. *Grant-Walton v. Montgomery County Board of Educ.*, No. TDC-17-2339, 2018 WL 2451204 (D. Md. 5/30/18).

◆ The Illinois Supreme Court refused to review a district's appeal from lower court decisions upholding a $2.5 million verdict for the estate of a student who died from an asthma attack at school. In 2008, the boy collapsed during his English class. The school and teacher knew the student had asthma and took meds to help control the symptoms. The teacher ran to the boy's side and sent two classmates to the nurse's office. But the teacher didn't call 911, and he failed to tell anyone else to do so for approximately seven to 20 minutes. This violated school policy. When paramedics arrived, they were unable to revive the boy. An autopsy determined the cause of death was asthma. The boy's mother filed a tort claim, and a jury found the teacher's failure to follow school policy by immediately calling 911 amounted to "willful and wanton conduct." It returned a $2.5 million verdict for the estate. The district appealed. **On appeal, the court decided it was reasonable to find the teacher's inaction "was so out of balance with the danger posed" to the student that it rose to the level of "willful and wanton conduct."** The district appealed to the state's highest court, which declined to hear the case without opinion. *In re Estate of Jeffrey Stewart*, No. 121335, 2017 WL 603354 (Ill. petition for leave to appeal denied 1/25/17).

◆ A Pennsylvania federal judge refused to dismiss claims filed by the estate of a student who died from an asthma attack at school. School officials knew the sixth-grader had asthma and took medicine to treat her symptoms. One day, the student complained to her teacher about breathing problems. No nurse was on duty, so the teacher told the student to "be calm." School policy prohibited the use of medicine "without the supervision of a nurse." The girl's condition worsened, but no medical attention was sought. After school ended, the girl's mother drove her to a hospital. There, she died from "an acute exacerbation of asthma," doctors said. The girl's estate sued, alleging constitutional violations. **The court said a reasonable jury could find the school violated the girl's rights – as school defendants may have "acted affirmatively to [the girl's] detriment by maintaining a policy ... of not permitting students to use prescription medication without a nurse on duty."** The court refused to grant qualified immunity to the principal and district. *Estate of Massey v. City of Philadelphia*, 118 F.Supp.3d 679 (E.D. Pa. 2015).

◆ Because the evidence supported the jury's verdict that a district's negligence did not cause an asthmatic student's death, a Washington Appeals court affirmed the verdict for the school. A student had both asthma and life-threatening allergies. The school had a doctor-prescribed inhaler on the premises for her in case of an asthma attack. It also had her doctor-prescribed EpiPen for an allergic emergency. One day she had trouble breathing and said she felt sick. The staff at the school's health room were familiar with her medical conditions. They decided she was having an asthma attack, so treated her with the inhaler. They tried it again when she didn't get better and then called 911. The school nurse had prepared an emergency health care plan for the student, but staff didn't look at it that morning. They also didn't call the school nurse. The student lost consciousness before the ambulance arrived. Staff didn't perform CPR, and the girl died. An autopsy attributed the death to asthma. The family sued the school district, its school health clerk, and the school nurse for wrongful death. The family claimed the district defendants were responsible for her death because they didn't administer the EpiPen or give her CPR. At trial, expert testimony established the girl probably would have survived if staff had administered the EpiPen before she lost consciousness or administered CPR after she did. The epinephrine posed no real threat of side effects, and an asthma attack could qualify as a medical emergency. The jury decided the school defendants were negligent but their negligence didn't cause the girl's death. The family appealed, but the appeals court affirmed. To find against the school defendants, the jury had to decide their negligence proximately caused the student's death. It didn't. And because the jury could have found staff might not have administered the EpiPen or performed CPR even if they consulted the emergency plan or contacted a school nurse, the verdict didn't go against the evidence – so the appeals court affirmed it. *Mears v. Bethel School Dist.*, No. 403, No. 43121-1-II, 2014 WL 3933555 (Wash. Ct. App. 8/12/14).

◆ A California appeals court found the state's field-trip immunity law meant neither district could be sued over the death of one district's asthmatic student at another district's outdoor "camp."

The school district San Diego County Office of Education (SDCOE) owned and operated "Camp Fox" at the base of Palomar Mountain. The camp provided science-related programs to students. Its staff were all SDCOE employees.

Sixth-grader Virginia Sanchez from the McCabe Union School District went to Camp Fox for a voluntary five-day field trip with her class. While there, she had an asthma attack. Staff gave Virginia her inhaler and performed CPR until paramedics arrived, but she died.

Virginia's parents sued SDCOE for negligence. The trial court awarded SDCOE summary judgment, finding it immune under state law. The parents appealed, but the appellate court affirmed.

State law provided immunity to "the district, a charter school, or the State of California" for a student's "injury, accident, illness or death" while on a field trip. The parents claimed this immunity was only for the school district the student attended, so it could sue SDCOE. The court disagreed, finding the statute covered both districts – so blocked the parents' lawsuit entirely. *Sanchez v. San Diego County Office of Educ.*, 182 Cal.App.4th 1580 (Cal. Ct. App. 2010).

◆ At the start of an academic year, the mother of a five-year-old kindergarten student with asthma gave the school nurse asthma medication and an inhaler. She also provided an authorization and a pediatrician's directive regarding use of the inhaler, and she gave the nurse a separate authorization for an allergy medication.

The child began coughing in class, and the nurse gave him inhaler medication and determined he was breathing, alert and not in distress. The child's mother was notified, and she picked him up from the school. The nurse suggested the mother take the child to his pediatrician. But when the child became ill during the ride, she drove home and went inside to dial 911. The child died shortly after emergency personnel took him to the hospital.

The mother sued the school district and others, claiming the nurse was negligently hired and committed malpractice. The trial court denied a summary judgment motion filed by the district and nurse. They appealed. The appeals court reversed. **The child's mother did not show the defendants breached a legal duty owed to her or the child.** The mother removed the control of district employees. Also, she decided to take him home rather than to the doctor, as the nurse had suggested. *Williams v. Hempstead School Dist.*, 850 N.Y.S.2d 459 (N.Y. App. Div. 2007).

◆ An appeals court affirmed a verdict for a school district in a wrongful death suit brought by parents of a student found dead in a locker room shortly after his teacher gave him permission to go there to use his inhaler.

During gym class, a 14-year-old with a history of mild asthma asked his gym teacher for permission to go get his prescription inhaler from the locker room. The teacher said he could. Between five and 15 minutes later, the teacher found the student lying on the locker room floor with the inhaler in hand. The boy wasn't breathing and was later pronounced dead.

The boy's parents sued the school district for wrongful death. **The main issue at trial was if the school was negligent not to supervise the boy when he went to the locker room to get his inhaler.** If the court found it foreseeable the student was likely to die without supervision while he retrieved and used his inhaler, it would have found the school negligent.

But the Ohio trial court did not find the lack of supervision likely to lead to the student's death. First, the father testified it was normal for the boy to get and use his inhaler without adult supervision. Second, there was expert testimony the likelihood of this kind of death from only mild asthma was "one in a million." The parents appealed, but the appellate court affirmed the verdict for the school. *Spencer v. Lakeview School Dist.*, No. 2005-T-0083, 2006 WL 1816452 (Ohio App. Ct. 6/30/06).

◆ The New Mexico Supreme Court decided parents could sue a school district for wrongful death after a substitute gym teacher ignored an asthmatic student's request to stop exercising and then administrators responded inadequately to her ensuing asthma attack.

A 14-year-old special ed student's IEP said she was asthmatic. Her parents gave the school permission to get her emergency medical help without contacting them first. They also told her gym teacher exercise could trigger an attack. The gym teacher agreed to let her rest instead of participating if she felt an attack coming on. The day the gym class had a substitute teacher, the student asked for permission to rest, but the sub said no. The student began to have trouble breathing. Others saw her face was red, and she was crying as she struggled to keep up with the class. The student used her inhaler after gym, but collapsed at her desk as her next class began. The teacher called the front office and then tried to administer the student's inhaler. A school secretary with some nursing training arrived, checked the student's vital signs and asked the office to call 911 – but the call wasn't made. Instead, staff put the student in a wheelchair and wheeled her into the hall. Seeing her there, a school police officer called 911. By that time, it was 15 minutes after the start of her asthma attack. When medical personnel arrived, the student had stopped breathing and couldn't be revived. Her parents sued the school district for wrongful death, but a trial court and then an appeals court found the district was immune to the suit. The parents appealed to the New Mexico Supreme Court. It reversed, allowing the parents' wrongful death suit to go forward. An exception to the state's immunity law OK'd school districts to be sued for negligence in operating or maintaining a building. The supreme court found **the school's failure to follow its safety procedures for a special needs student was similar to failing to follow procedures for a fire drill**. It failed to follow its procedures by ignoring the student's IEP, not administering CPR and not calling 911 immediately. Immunity also wasn't proper here because the school knew the student was asthmatic, but an employee forced her to keep exercising in spite of her visible distress – so the school actively participated in causing the asthma attack. *Upton v. Clovis Municipal School Dist.*, 141 P.3d 1259 (N.M. 2006).

2. Other Asthma Cases

◆ A teacher who alleged school construction caused her asthma could bring disability bias claims against the school board, but not a claim of negligent failure to provide her a safe working environment.

A school board divided an elementary school art classroom in half by putting in a new wall. This left the room with poor ventilation, as there were no operable windows, exterior doors or air conditioning.

The art teacher complained about water damage to the ceiling tiles as well as strong construction odors from paints, sealants and adhesives. Ultimately, the students' art classes were moved elsewhere, but the teacher had to be in the room twice a day to load and unload art supplies. **She said the exposure to construction odors, dust and mold left her with asthma.**

The teacher went on medical leave in October. She filed a workers' comp claim in December – and says a school-board-requested medical exam confirmed conditions in the classroom caused her asthma.

The board installed an air filter, and she returned to work in January – but had a severe asthma attack after workers removed the skylight in the room while she was teaching, releasing dust and particles.

The teacher's doctor removed her from work for the rest of the year. She returned for the following school year, but discovered the air filter in her classroom had been recycled from a school since demolished due to mold problems. She says it was replaced by a poor-quality filter.

Her doctor removed her from work for the next school year, and she was diagnosed with multiple myeloma, an environmentally induced disease.

The teacher sued the board of education and others, alleging multiple claims. The school defendants asked the judge to dismiss her suit.

The judge found the defendants had state-law immunity with respect to the teacher's claim that the town and board negligently failed to provide her a safe working environment – so dismissed it.

But the judge found her claims under the Rehabilitation Act could go forward. They alleged the board discriminated against her and retaliated against her by failing to accommodate her disability. *Gallagher v. Town of Fairfield*, No. 3:10-cv-1270 (CFD), 2011 WL 3563160 (D. Conn. 8/15/11).

◆ A school board was ordered to pay $130,000 to a disabled student who was hospitalized for six months after an asthma attack that could have been prevented if the school had followed its policies.

Under a middle school's policy, critical student health information was supposed to be collected from enrollment forms, entered into computer records, red-flagged and copied to the student's teachers. The policy also required setting up individualized education program (IEP) meetings for transferring special ed students as soon as possible – preferably within two weeks. The student had mental retardation and qualified for special education, but a school social worker didn't come to his home to get his IEP information until mid-October.

The mother told the social worker the student had severe breathing problems and said the school should call 911 if he had trouble breathing at school. The student's enrollment forms clearly stated he had asthma, and his mother gave the school a doctor's note to allow him to use his inhaler at school. But the mother didn't include this information on the student's PE health form or write any response to the form's request to list any reason the student should sit out PE or have a modified gym program.

In late October, a classmate saw the student stop while doing laps in PE class. When he clutched his chest, she asked if he needed his inhaler. He nodded. She ran to tell the PE teacher, but the teacher told both children to keep running. The teacher later said he hadn't been told the student had asthma and mental retardation. Later that day, the mother picked up the student because he was ill.

When the breathing treatments his mother tried at home didn't work, she called an ambulance. The student spent the next six months in the hospital. A doctor stated his health crisis was caused by overexertion in PE class and failure to use his inhaler.

The student's mother sued the school board under the Tennessee Governmental Tort Liability Act. The court held for the student. The school board appealed, but the appellate court affirmed.

Under the act, governmental entities could be held liable for student injuries caused by staff members' "operational" acts – but not by their "discretionary" acts. Generally, "operational acts" are actions taken pursuant to an established order or policy, while "discretionary acts" are acts involving planning or policy-making.

The court noted the board already had policies in place to notify teachers about a student's health problems. **But the policy wasn't followed, so the**

judge found the board negligent for not following its own policies. The appellate court also upheld the apportionment of the blame and its damages award. The lower court judge decided the mother was 20% at fault because she didn't provide information on the PE health form. The rest of the fault was apportioned to the school board. It was ordered to pay the student $130,000, the highest amount allowed under the act. *Small v. Shelby County Schools*, No. W2007-00045-COA-R3-CV, 2008 WL 360925 (Tenn. Ct. App. 2/12/08).

IV. AUTISM

A. Safety Risks Associated With Autism

Approximately 50% of students diagnosed with autism have a tendency to wander away from home and school, according to a study published in *Pediatrics*. Researchers interviewed more than 1,200 families who have an autistic child between the ages of 4 and 17. The participants shared how wandering affected their families:

- About 50% said their child had wandered at least once
- Half said their child stayed away long enough to worry them
- 65% admitted wandering put their child in a dangerous situation involving traffic, and
- Almost a quarter (24%) said their child was at risk of drowning while wandering.

Autistic students' tendency to wander doesn't disappear just because they're at school. If wandering is a potential issue, it should be addressed in students' IEPs. To keep autistic students safe, the Autism Wandering Awareness Alerts Response and Education (AWAARE) Collaboration recommends ensuring:

- teachers and school staff know if a student has a tendency to wander
- proper architectural barriers around school property are maintained to prevent wandering
- teachers communicate with parents and school officials communicate about all wandering incidents, even if they appear to be small or minor occurrences
- that wandering triggers, such as loud noises, are limited as much as possible, and
- all staff know they should never wait to call 911.

B. Legal Decisions

1. Autism-Related Deaths

◆ School officials weren't entitled to immunity in a case involving a student death, so a Pennsylvania federal court denied a motion to dismiss the claim. A seventh-grade, autistic student lived close to his school, so he was considered a "walker." Most days, his older sister walked to and from school with him. One day in 2015, she had to stay after school, and the boy tried to walk home alone. He was struck and killed by a car while crossing a busy street. No crossing guard was on duty. The boy's parents filed a Section 1983 substantive due process claim, alleging the school created the danger that led to their son's death. Here, the court decided **a reasonable jury could find the school put the boy "in a dangerous position by requiring him to walk to and from school along a dangerous road, knowing of his disabilities and the fact that he would have to cross the road in question."** The right to substantive due process is clearly established, the court said, so the case had to proceed. *Weiser v. Elizabethtown Area School Dist.*, No. 147-625, 2018 WL 1071939 (E.D. Pa. 2/27/18).

2. Other Autism Cases

◆ A California federal court approved a $530,000 settlement to resolve claims filed by the parents of an autistic student. The parents claimed the school failed to provide their son with Applied Behavioral Analysis therapy. Instead, they said school staff used "restraint, seclusion and other ineffective aversive responses." The parents said classroom aides injured the student over a period of two years, causing physical harm and emotional trauma. They said this conduct reinforced and escalated the boy's behavioral issues. They also claimed the district also failed to provide "necessary academic instruction." They sued, alleging violations of Section 504 of the Rehabilitation Act, the ADA and other claims. Under the settlement, the district agreed to pay an amount "not to exceed $430,000" for the student's educational expenses, such as tuition, therapeutic services, speech, language and occupational therapy, behavior services, tutoring, etc. It also agreed to pay $100,000 for damages and/or attorneys' fees. **The court found the settlement was "fair and reasonable."** The agreement was approved. *F.E. v. Moreland Unified School Dist.*, No. 16-CV-03983-BLF, 2019 WL 1411235 (N.D. Cal. 3/28/19).

◆ The Third Circuit affirmed a ruling in favor of a Pennsylvania school. As a student with autism finished his fourth-grade year, his parents asked school officials to hold him back rather than promote him to the fifth grade. The school refused. The parents filed a due process complaint, and through mediation, the parties reached an agreement. The parents agreed that their son would advance to fifth grade. In exchange, the school agreed to hold another IEP meeting to discuss the student's learning goals, share his standardized test scores with parents and pay for an independent educational evaluation. After the IEP meeting, the school updated the student's IEP to reflect the parents' input.

The parents filed a second due process complaint, saying the IEP "failed to address the deficiencies" in year-end assessments. A hearing officer ruled for the parents, and the school appealed. The court reversed, finding the hearing officer "improperly considered whether [the student] made sufficient progress under the IEP [and] exaggerated the importance of minor shortcomings in the IEP." The parents appealed.

The Third Circuit affirmed the ruling for the school, explaining that the U.S. Supreme Court has held IEPs weren't "guaranteed to produce any particular outcome." **Because the IDEA's intent was "more to open the door of public education to handicapped children on appropriate terms than to guarantee any particular level of education once inside," an IEP's adequacy "can only be determined as of the time it is offered to the student, and not at some later date," the court said.** The hearing officer erred by relying on post-IEP performance to evaluate the IEP. Further, he erred by finding the student "did not make progress … on certain goals in the IEP." But any review of an IEP must consider "whether the IEP [was] reasonable, not whether the court regard[ed] it as ideal." The court affirmed the ruling for the school. *Colonial School Dist. v. G.K.*, No. 18-2190, 2019 WL 588781 (3d Cir. 2/13/19).

◆ Parents of an autistic student failed to convince a federal court that Maryland school officials violated the IDEA. When the team put the student's IEP together, the boy's parents were OK with most of it. But they weren't happy that it included "lunch and recess in the general education setting, which offered no educational benefit to [the student] and present[ed] safety concerns," like his tendency to run – a common safety risk associated with autism. They filed a complaint. **A school official testified about strategies in the IEP that addressed running, such as "runners" being placed at a table far from the cafeteria door**, and the lunch staff had training and experience working with autistic students. She also testified that social interaction during lunch gave the boy opportunities to address social skills goals in the IEP. The ALJ said the parents' claims about safety risks were speculative and not enough to find the student was denied a FAPE. The mother sought judicial review, but the court affirmed the ALJ's ruling, finding no error in the decision for the school. *A.H. v. Jack R. Smith*, No. PWG-18-243, 2019 WL 528212 (D. Md. 2/8/19).

◆ An Arkansas federal court rejected a mother's claim that her son's school district violated the IDEA. In 2007, a student showed signs of autism and was put on an IEP. He regularly acted out, including climbing cabinets and taking off his shoes when he got frustrated. He couldn't make it through a full day of school. By the time he reached middle school, the IEP team determined he would attend school for 360 minutes per week, with a goal of working up to half-days of school. The team developed a behavior plan to handle his non-compliant behavior, including ignoring inappropriate behavior. When he lost control, the staff were instructed to "get assistance, block and move [and] assess environment for safety."

In 2016, his violent behavior escalated. In one incident, he yelled curse words and called classmates "retarded" and "autistic," and he announced to everyone that he was going to destroy the classroom. The next day, he threw classroom chairs while yelling, "[F-bomb] this class." When he was told he'd have a day of in-school suspension, he was furious and walked outside. The assistant principal followed him outside to try to calm him down, but the student said, "Don't talk to me or I'll cut your throat."

The school met with the boy's mom to let her know he was suspended for 10 days. At that meeting, she said if her son threatened to hurt someone, he would do it, so the school needed to leave him alone and let him do what he wanted. After the suspension, communication broke down. The mother refused to show up for meetings or answer phone calls. She filed a complaint, and a hearing officer found the school violated the IDEA. It appealed. The boy's mother argued the assistant principal didn't follow the IEP procedures. She said he should've given her son time to cool off when he lost his temper and walked out. But the court disagreed, saying the IEP strategy directed school staff to "block and move and assess the environment for safety" when the boy was out of control, as leaving campus would've been "a potential safety hazard." **Further, nothing in the IEP required school staff to let the boy leave school property, the court held. "Each strategy in a behavior plan must be flexible, and schools must have some leeway."** The court overturned the hearing officer's ruling. *Bentonville School Dist. v. Smith,* No. 5:17-CV-05134, 2019 WL 291641 (W.D. Ark. 1/23/19).

◆ A Connecticut federal court dismissed an intentional infliction of emotional distress claim filed by an autistic student's father. In March 2014, a father dropped his son off at school. A short time later, he was called back to the school due to safety concerns, including that his son said he was going to bring a weapon to school, and he had a hit list of names including classmates and teachers that was labeled "Subjects for Weapon X." School administrators decided the boy needed to have an emergency evaluation at a nearby psych ward. An ambulance and the police had been called – which upset the student a great deal due to lights and sirens. The father explained to the special education coordinator that "Weapon X" was a cartoon character, "like Spiderman." The father said he'd take his son to the hospital because the ambulance would upset him even more than he already was agitated. The special education coordinator didn't like that idea, but after a talk with police officers, the father was allowed to take the boy home. The father filed an intentional infliction of emotional distress claim against the special ed coordinator. To state a valid claim, the father had to show the coordinator's conduct was extreme and outrageous. That wasn't the case here, the court said. Under district's policy, administrators with knowledge of a threat were required to take proper steps to report the incident to the principal, the student's family and appropriate resources. **While the coordinator might've found a less stressful way to handle the situation, her conduct was not "beyond all possible bounds to decency," the court held.** The claim failed. *Suraci v. Hamden Board of Educ.*, No. 3:17-cv-152(JBA), 2019 WL 161501 (D. Conn. 1/10/19).

◆ The Ninth Circuit revived a sexual abuse claim under an exception to California's Government Claim Act. A teacher and her aides played a "game" with a nonverbal autistic student who was three years old at the time the abuse was discovered. According to the boy's father, he walked into the classroom and found the teacher and several aides sitting in a circle, holding their bare feet in the child's face. The boy was laying on the floor, clutching his genitals. When the father confronted the teacher, she reportedly laughed and said the child was "becoming a little man." Teachers liked to wear different color nail polishes on their toes to see which "colors aroused him the most." The family said the boy continued to be aroused by toes, which caused them embarrassment and prevented them from going out in public. Several years later, they filed a lawsuit, alleging – among other things – that the teacher's conduct amounted to abuse. The court dismissed the claim, noting that it was time-barred. It further pointed out that the parents never reported the "game" to police or child protective services. On appeal, the Ninth Circuit reversed, saying the sexual abuse claim gets special consideration under the state's Government Claim Act. Under that law, the "alleged conduct would have constituted a lewd or lascivious act," the court explained. It further noted that the adults could've violated the law without touching the victim if the "requisite specific intent" of the adults was to arouse or gratify "the lust of the child or the accused." **It didn't even matter that the adults themselves were not sexually aroused, the court said. What mattered was that "they intended to arouse [the child] for their humor."** That was enough evidence to allow the claim to proceed, the court held. *Garedakis v. Brentwood Union School Dist.,* No. 16-16332, 2018 WL 2996661 (9th Cir. 6/15/18).

◆ A Louisiana mother couldn't show teachers acted with gross negligence in connection with a student's alleged injury, so a state appeals court dismissed her claim. In 2010, an autistic student went on a field trip to a movie theater. As everyone got off the bus, the student started running around. His teachers grabbed his hands and escorted him across the street. The boy fought them and became physically violent, so the teachers placed him in a two-person restraint. They gave him his medicine, and he settled down. He was able to watch the movie without incident. His mom sued, alleging her son got hurt when the teachers restrained him. The court dismissed the claim, and the appellate court affirmed.

The real issue, the court explained, was whether the teachers' actions during the field trip constituted gross negligence or intent to harm. That wasn't the case here, the court found. Both teachers testified that they'd put the boy in the restraint only after he attempted to run into the street and fought to get away from them. Two paraprofessionals testified that the boy attacked the teachers by kicking, head-butting and biting them. They further testified that the child wasn't injured during the incident. Finally, the court pointed out that, although the mother claimed the child suffered a head injury, the medical billing record showed he was treated for "chronic rhinitis" – but it didn't mention treatment for a head injury. **The evidence didn't support the allegations that the teachers intended to harm the child, and it didn't show their actions amounted to gross negligence**, the appeals court found. The ruling to dismiss was affirmed. *Baheth v. LaFayette Parish School System*, No. 17-821, 2018 WL 1936980 (La. Ct. App. 4/25/18).

◆ A New Hampshire federal judge refused to dismiss a claim filed on behalf of an eight-year-old who was force-fed by his special ed teacher. The child was diagnosed as being on the autism spectrum. His IEP outlined that he had trouble chewing and swallowing, so he was at risk of choking and aspiration. The special ed teacher used so-called "tough love" to get the boy to eat, including force-feeding him, taking his chair away at mealtimes, pinching his mouth open and shoving food into it, covering his mouth with her hand until he swallowed and yelling at him. Many co-workers complained about the teacher. She ended up resigning. The mother sued, alleging a substantive due process claim. She said the district was deliberately indifferent in the need to train and supervise its workers. There was evidence that co-workers complained about the special ed teacher's conduct, so **a reasonable jury could conclude that the district failed to provide proper training**. A trial was needed, so the case had to move forward. *B.A. v. Manchester School Dist. SAU 37*, No. 15-cv-433-JD, 2017 WL 3049424 (D.N.H. 7/18/17).

◆ A school did not violate the IDEA by holding an IEP meeting while an autistic student's father was on vacation, so a Hawaii federal judge ordered the clerk to close the case. The student has autism, so the boy was entitled to services. The school set up an IEP meeting to determine an appropriate plan for the child. The boy's father canceled and postponed the meeting several times. School officials continued to postpone the meetings and reached out to the father for potential dates to reschedule. He ignored or failed to respond to the school's attempts to reschedule at least three times. This pattern continued for more than six months. Eventually, school officials held the IEP meeting without the father, citing the need to comply with the IDEA. The child's father filed a due process hearing request. The hearing officer held for the school. The father sought judicial review, challenging the hearing officer's decision. If schools hold an IEP meeting without a parent, then educators must document their attempts to schedule the IEP meetings with parents. In this case, the school's records showed the father had canceled or postponed a scheduled meeting on four occasions and ignored or failed to respond to the school's attempts to reschedule on three occasions. **The Ninth Circuit – which this court follows – has repeatedly held that when parents fail to respond to schools' attempts to schedule IEP meetings, then the meeting can go on without the parent.** As such, the school did not violate the father's rights by "excluding him from his son's IEP meeting," the court held. It affirmed the hearing officer's ruling for the school and ordered the clerk to close the case. *P.M. v. Dept. of Education*, No. 15-00437-LEK-RLP, 2016 WL 6434072 (D. Haw. 10/31/16).

◆ The search of an autistic student may have crossed a line, so the Third Circuit refused to dismiss a lawsuit. Pennsylvania school officials knew an autistic student got extremely agitated when people touched him and/or invaded his personal space. In 2015, he was searched as part of an investigation prompted by rumors that he brought a knife to school to stab a classmate. First the principal searched the student's locker. No knife was found. The boy emptied his pockets and lifted his T-shirt to show he didn't have a weapon. But at some point during the search, the principal allegedly touched and crowded the student, and he reacted. He suffered a fractured kneecap, bruises and cuts. He sued, claiming the search was illegal. The suit alleged the principal "touched" and "hit" the student during the search and "slammed him to the ground." The lawsuit included state tort claims against the principal and sought damages for his injuries. The case reached the Third Circuit, which refused to dismiss the claims. The student stated a plausible claim that the search might've gone too far, the court explained. Even though the principal knew the boy had autism and was sensitive to touch, **something triggered the boy during the search – so much so that he suffered serious injuries**. That needed to be examined by a jury, the court explained. Likewise, the court refused to dismiss the tort claims because questions remained. A trial was needed. *Salyer v. Hollidaysburg Area School Dist.*, No. 3:16-57, 2016 WL 5376218 (3d Cir. 9/26/16).

V. MENTAL HEALTH

A. Emotional Problems vs. Mental Illness

In "Mental Health Surveillance Among Children – United States, 2005-2011," the data provides information on mental disorders, including:

- ADHD
- disruptive behavioral disorders (such as oppositional defiant disorder and conduct disorder)
- autism spectrum disorders, and
- mood and anxiety disorders (including depression, substance abuse disorders and Tourette syndrome).

The study found children between the ages of three and 17 had:

- ADHD (6.8%)
- Behavioral or conduct problems (3.5%)
- Anxiety (3%)
- Depression (2.1%)
- Autism spectrum disorders (1.1%), and
- Tourette syndrome (.02%)

The study also found:

- ADHD was the most prevalent current diagnosis among children between the ages of three and 17.
- Boys were more likely than girls to have ADHD, behavioral or conduct problems, autism spectrum disorders, Tourette syndrome and cigarette dependence.
- Adolescent boys between the ages of 12 and 17 are more likely than girls in the same age bracket to die from suicide.
- Adolescent girls between the ages of 12 and 17 are more likely than boys in the same age bracket to suffer from depression and/or abuse alcohol.

Although most people associate student mental illness with school violence, this connection is not always present. As pointed out in the June 2007 Report to the President on Issues Raised by the Virginia Tech Tragedy, most people who are violent do not have a mental illness, and most people with a mental illness are not violent.

Apart from the fact that the stereotypical connection between violence and mental illness is often absent, mental illness should be de-linked from school violence also because mental illness already bears enough of a social stigma – and too many students don't seek help for that reason.

B. Violent Students and Privacy Laws

While most people with mental illness aren't violent, the university student who committed the deadliest school shooting in U.S. history was. The young man who killed 32 people at Virginia Tech in April 2006 suffered from depression and an anxiety disorder called selective mutism.

In middle and high school, he received help under a special education plan. When his middle school teachers noticed he was writing about killing himself and other people in 1999 after the Columbine shootings, he was treated by a psychiatrist.

The fact that the student's university wasn't alerted to these red flags by his records led the governor-appointed Virginia Tech Review Panel to conclude that the state's mental health laws were flawed. Complicating the issue, the panel also found there was widespread confusion about sharing records among schools. Even when it came to students likely to harm themselves or others, schools weren't sure what information they could release to other schools without violating state and federal privacy laws.

Similarly, the Report to the President on Issues Raised by the Virginia Tech Tragedy found that schools were so worried about violating student privacy – or being sued for doing so – that they were likely to share less information about serious potential problems than the law actually allowed.

It is important to be aware of the fact that some state laws and regulations have stricter privacy requirements for student records than the federal Family Educational Rights and Privacy Act (FERPA) and the privacy rule of the Health Insurance Portability and Accountability Act. That said, one result of the Report to the President was the creation of new guides to help schools and parents better understand FERPA's requirements. They are available at *ed.gov/policy/gen/guid/fpco/ferpa/safeschools*.

This FERPA guidance for elementary and secondary schools specifies that:

- Schools don't need permission in an emergency to release "education records" to parties like law enforcement, public health officials or medical personnel if the release will protect anyone's health or safety.
- Guidance posted at *rems.ed.gov* also reminds administrators who release info under this FERPA exception to make a note of the disclosure in the student's education records. The note should include: the info that was disclosed, the parties who received it and the threat that prompted the disclosure. The note should be made as soon as reasonably possible.
- The *ed.gov* guidance also spells it out that school officials don't need permission to pass along their personal observations about a student to the proper authorities. For example, if a teacher overhears a student making a threat, she can report it to the police.
- The school employees who serve as the school's "law enforcement unit" – responsible for calling the police when the school suspects a crime – might keep its own records, such as investigation logs. These are not "education records" subject to FERPA, so no permission is needed to disclose them. But the Department of Education suggests avoiding any confusion by keeping these documents separate from "education records."
- Tapes of students recorded by security cameras maintained by the "law enforcement unit" are also not "education records" subject to FERPA. Because of this, the Department of Education suggests schools that haven't designated a "law enforcement unit" should do so and assign the unit this responsibility.
- Schools have to notify parents every year about FERPA rights. In this notification, the school has to let parents know which office or school official serves as its "law enforcement unit." The Department of Education has suggested one way to go about this, which you can see if you turn to its Model Notification of FERPA Rights.
- In your notification to parents, you should list "law enforcement unit" personnel employed by the school as "school officials" with a "legitimate educational interest." This will mean they can access protected student records – but also that they are bound by the same FERPA restrictions as other school officials concerning "education records."
- You can send all "education records" to a transfer school or postsecondary institution a student plans to attend without parents' permission – so long as you have stated on your notification to parents that you make these disclosures to other schools. If you haven't stated this, you have to make a reasonable attempt to notify

the parent of the disclosure (unless the parent asked you to send the records, of course). Also, if asked, you have to provide the parents a copy of the information you disclosed as well as provide them the opportunity for a hearing on the matter.

Finally, although the responsibility for any judgment call remains yours, you can email the Department of Education's Family Policy Compliance Office at *FERPA@Ed.Gov* for a fast reply on a routine question. You can write to them for "a more formal response" at:

Family Policy Compliance Office
U.S. Department of Education
400 Maryland Avenue, SW
Washington, DC 20202-8520

Many perpetrators of school shootings, including the one whose attack prompted the FERPA guidance above, have ended the rampage by killing themselves. But while a violent death *at school* is a relatively rare occurrence, the numbers are much higher when it comes to off-campus suicides among those ages 10 to 24 – and this is of increasing concern not only to school officials but also to lawmakers because the evidence increasingly links student suicides to things that have happened at school.

C. Self-Injury

Self-injury habits start younger than most people might think, according to a study published in *Pediatrics*. Researchers at the University of Denver and Rutgers University teamed up to conduct the study in Colorado and New Jersey. Participating students in both locations shared similar reports about their behavior. Of the third-grader participants:

- 8% admitted they'd intentionally hurt themselves by cutting, burning or poking their skin with sharp objects.
- Nearly two-thirds of those students said they'd intentionally hurt themselves more than once.

Other findings include:

- 4% of sixth-graders self-injured their bodies, and
- about 13% of ninth-graders developed the habit.

Some students claim self-injuring helps them cope with emotional stressors, such as family issues, bullying and difficulty in school.

To reduce physical pain, the body releases endorphins, which are basically "feel-good hormones." Some researchers believe this naturally occurring endorphin release may explain why students "feel better" after hurting themselves. Self-injury is often difficult to spot because most students keep wounds hidden, according to the Mayo Clinic. Warning signs that may indicate self-injury include students who:

- have fresh wounds or scars, such as from burns or cuts
- keep sharp objects on hand

- spend a lot of time alone
- wear long sleeves and pants – even in hot weather, and
- claim to have frequent accidents or mishaps.

The full study is available at *bit.ly/cutting555.*

D. Suicide Prevention

In 2010, the CDC reported a study by its scientists (published in the online edition of the *Journal of Pediatrics*) showed a connection between kids getting bullied and an increase in their suicidal thoughts and behaviors.

The CDC also reported suicide is the third leading cause of death for 10- to 24-year-olds, with boys overwhelmingly more at risk than girls. Boys account for 83% of the suicides for that age group.

But it was a girl's suicide after bullying that grabbed the most press attention in 2010 – partly because of the community's unusually legalistic response to the tragedy. First, in a highly unusual move, the district attorney filed criminal charges against the students who allegedly bullied Massachusetts student-suicide Phoebe Prince. Second, the state quickly enacted an anti-bullying law in response to two student suicides (one of them Prince's).

Many states have also decided they need to do more to prevent such tragedies. Colorado, Georgia, Mississippi and New Hampshire passed anti-bullying legislation in 2010, and Kentucky law began to require middle schools and high schools to provide suicide prevention information to students – and training on suicide prevention techniques to educators.

The suicide of college student Tyler Clementi prompted New Jersey to enact "The Anti-Bullying Bill of Rights" in 2011, amending its existing anti-bullying law. Now considered the toughest law in the country, it also contains a suicide-prevention component.

The federal government also provided some extra help to schools trying to put the pieces together after student suicides.

Grants awarded by the U.S. Department of Education's Office of Safe and Drug-Free Schools include Project School Emergency Response to Violence (SERV) awards. The funds they provide are intended to pay for resources districts need to recover from traumatic events and make affected schools safe places for students again.

If you're looking for ideas for suicide-prevention at your school, you might want to check out "The Youth Suicide Prevention School-Based Guide" at: *theguide.fmhi.usf.edu.*

Student suicides highlight the need for schools to help students with transitory emotional problems. Many students who consider suicide (or actually commit it) are suffering an "unbearable" problem that could be made bearable with the right kind of help from an adult.

Suicide risks for depressed students can start earlier than expected, according to a study published in the *Journal of Adolescent Health.* Collecting data on suicide attempts from 883 students who suffered from depression, researchers found:

- more than 40% of students who attempted to commit suicide first tried before high school, and
- the rate of suicide attempts rose sharply around the age of 12, or sixth grade, and continued to increase through the ninth grade.

Researchers concluded that mental health programs may need to start in elementary and middle school.

A student suicide is a traumatic event not only for the student's family but for his school community as well. When a student does commit suicide, grieving parents may try to make sense of the tragedy by blaming the school for things the school did or did not do to prevent it.

E. Legal Decisions

1. Liability for Student Suicide

a. Federal Law

◆ An Illinois federal court rejected claims that a school created a danger that caused a student suicide. An honor student with no history of behavior or mental health issues was accused of showing a sex tape of himself and a girl to his hockey teammates. The girl was upset, and the incident was reported. The dean and the SRO called the boy to the office and questioned him for 20 minutes. They searched his phone. No video was found, but an audio recording was. The SRO said it "concerned child pornography, which [was] obviously illegal." The dean called the boy's mom and then told him to wait at the student-services office until she arrived.

The student didn't seem to be upset as he chatted with the secretary. But then, he slipped out of the office and left school. He walked to a parking deck a mile away and jumped from the ledge of the fifth floor. A passerby called 911 and started CPR, but the teen died at a nearby hospital. His parents sued, alleging school officials created the boy's emotional distress and caused his death. The Seventh Circuit addressed a similar claim in 2002. In *Martin v. Shawano-Gresham School Dist.*, a student was suspended from school, which distressed her. The school decided to let her go home alone, where she committed suicide. **The Seventh Circuit concluded the school didn't "create or increase a risk to [the student] by suspending her from school, even if that action caused severe emotional distress."** It further noted the state didn't "create or increase the risk of suicide by arresting or detaining an individual, even when the arrest cause[d] severe emotional distress." Applying *Martin* to this case, the court held the school did not create or increase a risk to the boy. Finally, the court said even if the school's affirmative act of leaving the boy in the office without strict supervision may have been ill-advised, it was not conscience-shocking behavior. The claims failed. *Walgreen v. Heun*, No. 17-cv-04036, 2019 WL 265094 (N.D. Ill. 1/17/19).

◆ A student's estate stated a *prima facie* Title IX claim, so an Ohio federal court said a trial was needed. In 2014, the student killed herself.

Her parents say their daughter's suicide was the result of severe bullying she endured at school and online. They raised Title IX and other claims. To prevail on a Title IX claim, the estate had to show the student-on-student harassment was so severe that it deprived her of educational benefits and the school knew about the harassment but was deliberately indifferent to it. Court documents list 18 examples of bullying. One example was that bullies created a fake Instagram account entitled "[Girl's name] is Gay" and included comments like, "I love to [F-bomb] random people in the woods." The girl and the creators of the account ended up fighting at school. **The girl and her parents reported the account to school officials, but they did not investigate, the suit alleged.** It also claimed the school took no disciplinary action against the classmates who created the Instagram account and didn't do anything to help get the page taken down. Further, the suit claimed the school didn't make any effort to keep the bullies away from the student. That was enough to state a valid claim, so the claim had to proceed. *Estate of Olson v. Fairfield City School Dist. Board of Educ.*, No. 1:15cv787, 2018 WL 4539440 (S.D. Ohio 9/21/18).

◆ The Fifth Circuit affirmed a Texas court ruling that dismissed a lawsuit involving a student suicide. A teacher saw a colleague and a student engaged in questionable conduct and reported the incident to the principal that same day. He launched an investigation, put the accused teacher on administrative leave and talked to the student, who denied having an inappropriate relationship with the teacher. The principal assured the boy he'd done nothing wrong. At his home that night, the boy committed suicide. His parents filed a Title IX suit. The court dismissed the claim, and on appeal, the Fifth Circuit affirmed the ruling. To win a Title IX claim, the parents had to show the school acted with deliberate indifference. A reasonable jury couldn't come to that conclusion, the court said, as **the evidence showed the teacher quickly reported her concerns and the principal immediately launched an investigation and removed the accused teacher from the building**. The school wasn't deliberately indifferent, so the court affirmed the ruling for the school. *Ramos v. Webb Consolidated Independent School Dist.,* 724 Fed.Appx. 338 (MEM) (5th Cir. 2018).

◆ A California federal judge refused to dismiss due process claims filed against four school administrators in their individual capacities. A student committed suicide. She left a note indicating that she thought her life was over because she was kicked out of school. The girl had gotten into an argument that escalated into a physical fight with a classmate. The girl's mother said the principal and vice principal didn't give her daughter the chance to tell her side of the story. They allegedly told the mother that the girl couldn't return to school and purportedly pressured her to transfer her child to another school in the district to avoid having to go to an alternative school. The student was transferred to the second school, where she got into a fight and was suspended. Her mother said the principal and vice principal at the second school refused to allow her daughter to respond to the charge before the suspension. After the girl committed suicide, her mom filed a lawsuit against the principals and vice principals of both schools in their individual capacities, **alleging they violated her daughter's right to due process by disciplining her without listening to her account of what happened**. The administrators asked the court to toss the suit, but it refused, saying the mother stated valid claims. The case had to proceed. *Neil v. Modesto City School Dist.*, No. 1:17-cv-0256-LJO-SKO, 2017 WL 2911578 (E.D. Ca. 7/7/17).

◆ A California boy who had mental health issues and made at least three suicide attempts was entitled to special education services, so the Ninth Circuit remanded the case for an appropriate remedy. A second-grader was diagnosed with bipolar disorder, oppositional defiant disorder and attention deficit disorder. In spite of this, he maintained good grades. As such, he could not be classified as a student with a disability, school officials decided. They didn't create an IEP for him, but they did provide 1:1 direction with a paraeducator and mental health services. Between the second and fifth grade, the student behavior problems at school, attempted suicide at least three times and was twice hospitalized for mental health treatment. After a long battle with the school, his mom ended up suing, and the case reached the Ninth Circuit. **It surmised, "it is hard to imagine how an emotional disturbance so severe that it resulted in repeated suicide attempts would not interfere with his school performance."** The court remanded the case and ordered the lower court to tell the school to formulate an IEP for the student. *L.J. v. Pittsburg Unified School Dist.*, 850 F.3d 996 (9th Cir. 2017).

◆ A junior violated a freshman's right to privacy in a restroom by posting a video on Snapchat, so a California appeals court refused to overturn his criminal conviction. The junior went into a school restroom. In one of the stalls, the freshman was fake moaning loudly while pretending to masturbate. The junior recorded a video and posted it on Snapchat with a caption that read: "I think this dude is jacking off." The footage didn't show the freshman's face, but he was easily identifiable as his unique tennis shoes were visible between the stall door and the bathroom floor. The video circulated through the school, and students made fun of the freshman. Two weeks later, he committed suicide, leaving a note that read, "I can't handle school anymore." One of the freshman's friends told school officials about the video, and they called the police. The junior admitted he'd made the video and posted it on Snapchat. He was arrested and found guilty of unauthorized invasion of privacy by means of a cell phone camera. He appealed the conviction, arguing he didn't violate the freshman's privacy because he only recorded what was "exposed to public view – feet through the gap between the stall wall and the floor." The court didn't buy that excuse, noting that **"the bathroom, including a public bathroom stall, is perhaps the epitome of a private place."** Further, the court said "over 50 years of California case law has ensured that persons in a public toilet may reasonably expect that they are not being secretly recorded." The junior violated the freshman's right to privacy, so the conviction stood. *People v. M.H.,* No. D067616 (Cal. Ct. App. 6/21/16).

◆ A school could not be held liable for the suicide attempt of a student who was bullied about her eating disorders, a New York federal judge held. The student suffered from anorexia and bulimia. She was allegedly bullied by classmates about her weight and eating disorders for approximately 18 months. She and her parents said they complained to school officials many times, but they failed to take steps to stop the bullying. The girl attempted to commit suicide by drug overdose. Her parents transferred her to a different school and filed a lawsuit, alleging a violation of the Equal Protection Clause. The court dismissed the claim, as **weight and disability are not vulnerable classes under the Equal Protection Clause** – and since the complaint didn't allege a class-of-one claim, the plaintiffs failed to state a valid claim. *Terrill v. Windham-Ashland-Jewett Cent. School Dist.,* No. 1:15-CV-0615 (GTS/DJS), 2016 WL 1275048 (N.D.N.Y. 3/31/16).

◆ After a high school student with Asperger's Syndrome killed himself, his parents sued, alleging the district and principal violated his "liberty right to be free from psychological and bodily abuse" by not training staff to protect him from bullying – but a Georgia federal judge dismissed the case.

Seventeen-year-old Tyler Long hanged himself at home, leaving a note saying "This World [*sic*] will be a better place without me." He had Asperger's syndrome, and Tyler's friends and parents said he'd been bullied at school because of it.

After his death, students wrote "we will not miss you" and "it was your own fault" on school walls – and some wore nooses at school.

Tyler's parents sued his principal and the district, alleging they breached Tyler's substantive due process right to be free from abuse.

The judge dismissed the case, finding **school defendants didn't have a constitutional duty to protect Tyler from other students**.

The Due Process Clause protects citizens from government officials' abuse of power. Apart from a few narrow exceptions, it *doesn't* require the government to protect citizens from each other.

Under Eleventh Circuit law binding on this Georgia federal court, the government had a duty to protect a citizen from other citizens if it had the victim in custody. Courts had found jail constituted custody, but not school.

A narrow exception existed when a government official caused harm by conduct that was "arbitrary or conscience shocking in a constitutional sense." That standard could be met by excessive corporal punishment at school. The parents claimed it was met by school defendants' failure to train staff to protect the student despite knowing he had a disability and was being bullied – but that was negligence or deliberate indifference at most.

As the parents' substantive due process claim didn't meet the required legal standard, the judge dismissed it. *Long v. Murray County School Dist.*, No. 4:10-CV-00015-HLM, 2012 WL 2277836 (N.D. Ga. 5/21/12).

◆ Texas parents said their 13-year-old son committed suicide after being repeatedly bullied at school. They said much of the misconduct took place in the school locker room. Among their claims was that members of the football team stripped the student, tied him up and put him in a trash can. Students called him "fag," "queer" and "homo," and one student videotaped the attack. The parents said the video was then put on YouTube. Shortly after this incident, the student committed suicide. According to the parents, school officials knew of the bullying but were deliberately indifferent to it.

In a federal court, the parents asserted the school had policies against bullying, but officials ignored them. The court dismissed the case. On appeal, the Fifth Circuit Court of Appeals held the complaint asserted widespread harassment by peers. In addition to the videotaped incident, it was alleged that football players accosted the student in the locker room many times. There were charges that boys took off his underwear while a teacher observed them. As a result, the court reversed the judgment on a Title IX claim and returned it to the district court. **The court held the removal of a person's underwear without consent on numerous occasions would constitute pervasive sexual harassment.** But the parents could not pursue their equal protection claim, which had been properly dismissed. *Carmichael v. Galbraith*, 574 Fed.Appx. 286 (5th Cir. 2014).

◆ A California federal judge refused to dismiss equal protection claims based on a principal's and assistant principal's failure to investigate and discipline the bullying of an openly gay student.

After Seth Walsh came out as gay in the sixth grade, classmates called him "pansy" and "sissy," pushed him into lockers and suggested he kill himself. His mother reported this. **The principal said classmates "in a perfect world" wouldn't harass Seth**, but these students were at a difficult age and the principal couldn't change attitudes they learned at home.

When Seth was in the seventh grade, the bullying became more widespread, sexually explicit and confrontational. The principal and vice principal saw it, and Seth's mother reported it, but the administrators took no steps to stop it. At some point, the vice principal suggested the solution to the problem was for Seth to leave school.

In September of Seth's eighth-grade year, the day after other students threatened and assaulted him, Seth hanged himself at home. Seth's mother sued the district and district officials, alleging multiple claims. The school defendants asked the judge to dismiss her suit. The judge dismissed some claims, but not her equal protection claim against the principal and vice principal. They argued the mother couldn't make this claim as she hadn't shown they responded differently to harassment claims made by non-homosexuals. The judge found she didn't have to at this stage of the case. To make her equal protection claim at this stage, Seth's mother only had to show Seth was discriminated against due to his membership in an identifiable class. She did by showing Walsh suffered pervasive harassment as a homosexual and that neither administrator took disciplinary action – instead only saying he wouldn't be discriminated against in a perfect world or that the solution to a student being harassed at school was for the student to leave the school. *Walsh v. Tehachapi Unified School Dist.*, 827 F.Supp.2d 1107 (E.D. Cal. 2011).

◆ An Ohio federal judge found that "however tragic and unfair [it] may seem," a school had no constitutional duty to protect a student from student-on-student bullying – or from killing himself because of it.

Eric Mohat committed suicide at age 17. His parents claimed he was driven to it by constant bullying and harassment that school officials were aware of but did nothing about. His parents sued the school district, alleging they were deprived of their substantive due process rights to familial association, a liberty interest under the Fourteenth Amendment's Due Process Clause. Generally, the Constitution doesn't require public school officials to protect a citizen's life, liberty or property interests against "the invasions of private actors" – such as the students who harassed Eric.

One exception to this rule is the state-created danger exception, but the court found the exception didn't apply in this case because school officials didn't take *affirmative action* that increased the danger to the student.

The parents alleged the school's failure to step in when other students bullied Eric contributed to or caused his suicide. But this was an alleged failure to act rather than an affirmative act.

The court wrote that "although parents should be able to expect that their children will be kept reasonably safe when under the school's supervision, the school had no constitutional duty to take affirmative action to protect Eric from harm imposed by other students through bullying[.]" *Mohat v. Mentor Exempted Village School Dist. Board of Educ.*, No. 1:09 CV 688, 2011 WL 2174671 (N.D. Ohio 6/1/11).

◆ A Texas federal judge dismissed a suit that claimed a school district violated a student's rights by not doing more to prevent her suicide attempt.

High school staff confiscated a note from the student that prompted the principal to call her mother to advise she get counseling for the girl. A year later, the student spent a week at a psychiatric treatment facility. Not long after her release, she was arrested for shoplifting. The day after her arrest, her mother went to school. She told the school secretary about the arrest and asked to be called if "anything happened[.]" **In English class, the student told a friend she was going to kill herself.** The friend told the teacher, and the teacher sent the student to a counselor. The mother later claimed the counselor was so busy she simply sent the student to her next class without telling anyone else about her suicide threat.

The student was excused from her next class to go to the bathroom. There, she tried to kill herself. The attempt was unsuccessful but allegedly left her with a permanent injury. Her mother sued the district and several individuals under Section 1983 of the U.S. Code. She alleged they violated the student's rights by not adopting a suicide prevention program and not taking steps to prevent her suicide attempt. The school defendants asked the judge to dismiss the suit. He did. To violate Section 1983, either a school official must commit "deliberate conduct" that makes the official "the 'moving force' behind the injury" or else the district must create a "special relationship" with the student – such as by making a specific promise to keep him or her safe. Unlike most jurisdictions, the Fifth Circuit doesn't recognize a "state-created danger" ground for liability – which can make a district liable if it increased the danger to the student. The court found **this suit only alleged negligence** – not a valid claim of a constitutional violation under Section 1983. So the court dismissed it. *Hejny v. Grand Saline Independent School Dist.*, No. 2-10-cv-50-TJW, 2010 WL 2521007 (E.D. Tex. 6/17/10).

◆ A school did not have the responsibility to protect a student from committing suicide even though the student could be considered emotionally fragile and there had been a rash of suicides at the school in previous months.

A female student was raped when she was 13 years old and then had the trauma of testifying against her rapist in court. Less than a year later, the student was out on the school softball field with her gym class when several of her classmates began harassing her about the rape and her decision to testify. The student became upset. She shouted obscenities and threatened to hurt them. The gym teacher broke this up and told the student to go back to the locker room. There, the student tried to hang herself.

Classmates found her and called for emergency help. The student did not die, but she went into a coma. She ultimately emerged from the coma but was left with permanent impairments.

In the three months before this incident, seven students at that middle school had attempted suicide. Several of the attempts had happened at school or school events, and the student knew at least two of the students.

The student's parents sued the board of education and the gym teacher, alleging they violated the student's right to substantive due process. The trial court dismissed the case. The parents appealed, but the First U.S. Circuit Court of Appeals affirmed.

The parents argued the school had a duty to protect the student because it knew she'd been raped the year before and other students had attempted suicide. But this was not enough for the school to recognize her as part of an identifiable group of students at risk for committing suicide. Also, the gym teacher's actions were not bad enough to shock the conscience, another prerequisite to a finding of a constitutional violation. He only reprimanded a 14-year-old for misbehavior and sent her out of class. *Hasenfus v. LaJeunesse*, 175 F.3d 68 (1st Cir. 1999).

b. Negligence Issues

◆ Vermont's highest court rejected claims filed by the estate of a student who committed suicide after he was assaulted by teammates on his high school football team. In 2009, school officials learned kids, including football players, played "no homo," a game where a student complimented a same-sex classmate, and then immediately said, "no homo" to signify that he wasn't gay. The athletic director instructed athletes to stop playing the game, wrote letters to parents about the game and began investigating whether additional verbal harassment or other inappropriate behaviors were taking place. Football players were put on probation for the 2010 season. There were no other reports about students playing the game.

Two years later, a student transferred to the school. He joined the football and lacrosse teams. He attended a team dinner on campus. There, one teammate held the student down while another assaulted him with a broomstick. The victim did not report the incident or tell his parents. He quit the football team the following year and then died by suicide.

In the spring of 2013, a teacher's son told him about the assault on the student at the team dinner in 2011. The teacher reported it to the school. This was the first time the school was notified about the incident.

Police investigators interviewed members of the football team. Several described some team members' behaviors, including exposing their genitals, pretending to "hump teammates" and shoving their exposed genitals onto other players. One told investigators that he'd quit the team because he didn't want to be associated with such behaviors.

The mother of the student who committed suicide filed a negligence suit against the district and the board. The case continued to the state's highest court. The mother argued the "no homo" game put the school on notice that a broomstick assault was foreseeable. But the court didn't buy that logic for a couple of reasons. First, it said there was a big difference in a nonphysical game and a physical attack. Next, it pointed out that the "no homo" game had been discontinued two years before the student's transfer to the school. Further, it was undisputed that the school was unaware of the attack on the student until the police investigation after his death, the court pointed out. In addition, the school had no knowledge of the team's locker room antics until the police investigation.

Bottom line: **Knowing that students made homophobic comments to each other, with no accompanying physical contact, did not put the school on notice that two students would forcibly assault a teammate.** *Stopford v. Milton Town School Dist.*, No. 2017-398, 2018 WL 6005260 (Vt. 11/16/18).

◆ A New York district and board of education could not be held liable in a wrongful death suit filed by a grieving family, a state appeals court affirmed. After an investigation, a middle school principal determined a student had engaged in misconduct. As such, the boy was suspended. That evening, he killed himself. The boy's parents filed suit to recover damages for wrongful death against the principal, the district and the board of education. The suit claimed that the boy's suicide was caused by the defendants' negligent investigation into the misconduct allegation. The court dismissed the family's claim because the complaint failed to state a cause of action. On appeal, the ruling was affirmed. Under New York law, school officials cannot be held liable for acts that are discretionary in nature. Here, the investigation qualified because state law recognizes that discretionary acts "involve the exercise of reasoned judgment, which could typically produce different acceptable results," the appellate court explained. **Generally, a discretionary act is anything where an educator has the authority to make a judgment call.** Bottom line: The claim wasn't actionable under state law, so the ruling to dismiss was affirmed. *Juerss v. Millbrook Cent. School Dist.,* 161 A.D.3d 967 (N.Y. App. Ct. 2018).

◆ A Connecticut school board was not entitled to immunity in a case involving a bullied student's suicide, so a state superior court denied a motion to dismiss the claim. A student was bullied throughout middle school. Administrators had documented incidents of name-calling, teasing, property theft and physical violence. As the boy transitioned into high school, the middle school counselor informed the high school about the bullying the boy had endured. The bullying problem continued in high school, and the boy committed suicide at the start of his sophomore year. His parents sued the district, the board and the town, alleging the defendants' conduct was "gross, reckless, willful or wanton." The board filed a motion to dismiss, saying it was entitled to sovereign immunity. The court pointed out that a state statute clearly limited sovereign immunity in instances involving bullying. No protection was available in instances where the school did not act in good faith, the court explained. **The complaint alleged gross negligence – a heightened form of negligence.** At this early stage in the case, that was enough to establish the court needed more info to determine whether the board's conduct amounted to gross negligence. The claim had to proceed. *Palosz v. Town of Greenwich*, No. FSTCV156026131S, 2017 WL 1334286 (Conn. Super. Ct. 3/21/17).

◆ The Sixth Circuit rejected a suit that alleged a Tennessee school's negligence led to a teen's suicide. When the student was a freshman, his mother said he was bullied by three classmates who said he was gay, call him the F-word slur, beat him with belts in a "game" known as "Belt Wars" on several occasions, and told him to "go home and kill himself." In February 2014, he took his own life after he came home from school. His mom filed a negligence claim. When the district court tossed the suit, his mother appealed. To state a valid negligence claim, she had to show – among other things – that the school's actions or omissions were the proximate cause of the student's death. She didn't make that connection because she failed to provide evidence that showed the school knew about the alleged bullying. **"A school with no knowledge of bullying has no reason to believe the**

anti-bullying policy needs enforcement, let alone that failure to enforce the policy may result in a student's death," the court explained. The ruling to dismiss was affirmed. *Tumminello v. Father Ryan High School, Inc.*, No. 16-5165, 2017 WL 395106 (6th Cir. 1/30/17).

◆ An Illinois district wasn't liable for the death of a student in an elementary school restroom, a state appellate court held. The student and his class lined up in a third-floor hallway to go to PE. The teacher realized the student wasn't in line but took the class downstairs to the gym. Then the teacher checked his mail and went to look for the boy. By the time the teacher returned to the third floor, the student had been found in a restroom. He was hanging by his collar on the hook of a stall door. He died the next day, and his death was ruled a suicide. His mother filed a wrongful death suit, claiming the district was negligent and its actions amounted to "willful and wanton" misconduct. The claim was tossed. The state's tort law doesn't allow negligence-based claims for failure to supervise an activity on public property. The court let his mother refile. In the amended complaint, the mom added information about her son's mental health issues, dating back to 2007. Her complaint alleged the school knew but failed to provide proper IEP and Section 504 plans to help keep her son safe. The school asked the court to dismiss that claim, saying the suicide wasn't foreseeable. The court did – noting the mother didn't show the school owed the boy a special duty. A second amended complaint alleged the school knew about a "hanging game" that students played in the bathroom. This claim was also dismissed, as it failed to show the school was the proximate cause of the suicide.

His mother appealed to the state appellate court, which held **the evidence didn't support her allegations**. So the ruling for the school was proper. *Marshall v. Evanston Skokie School Dist. 65*, No. 1–13–1654, 2015 WL 1442040 (Ill. App. Ct. 3/2/15).

◆ The Fifth Circuit reversed a Texas federal judge's decision that parents of a bullied student who committed suicide didn't provide evidence of the severe, pervasive sexual harassment needed for a valid Title IX claim. The student's parents said other boys bullied their son in the locker room in front of a teacher several times – including forcibly pulling off his underwear. Days before the student committed suicide, football team members attacked him in the locker room. They called him "fag," "queer" and "homo" as they stripped him, tied him up and put him in a trash can. Other students watched. One uploaded a video of the attack to YouTube. To sue the district under Title IX for deliberate indifference to student-on-student sexual harassment, the boy's parents had to show the harassment was severe and pervasive. The federal judge dismissed the claim. But **the Fifth Circuit reversed, as "[t]he removal of a person's underwear without consent on numerous occasions plausibly constitutes pervasive harassment of a sexual character."** It reversed the dismissal of the parents' Title IX claim. *Carmichael v. Galbraith*, 574 Fed.Appx. 286 (5th Cir. 2014).

◆ A New York court refused to dismiss the personal injury claim of a mother whose son committed suicide after being bullied. The student and his mother made multiple reports to school officials about the bullying. But the bullies were never disciplined. In 2010, the student came home from school and killed himself. His mother sued the city and the district for negligence. She asked the court to award her damages for her son's personal injuries as well as for the emotional injuries and financial expenses his suicide caused her. The court dismissed her suit against the city, as it's well established that New York City isn't liable for its school district's negligence. The court also dismissed the claims for the injuries caused by the suicide. Under New York law, the district can't be held liable for the suicide because the student wasn't in school custody at the time.

But the court held a trial was needed on the district's liability for the personal injuries the student allegedly suffered at school before his death because he was on school premises when the alleged bullying took place. While the school took steps to combat bullying – talking to classes about misusing the word "gay," putting up posters and passing out brochures on harassment and how to report it – **the school didn't discipline the students who allegedly harassed the alleged victim in this case**. So the court refused to dismiss the mother's negligent supervision claim. *Elissa v. City of New York*, 990 N.Y.S.2d 780 (N.Y. Sup. Ct. 2014).

◆ Montana's highest court affirmed a ruling that a school wasn't liable for a student-athlete's suicide. The 17-year-old senior had racked up a long disciplinary record for things like talking back, theft, fighting and skipping school. After a school counselor saw him "putting a can of chew in his pocket," the principal, superintendent, and athletic director explained to the teen that having tobacco at school had triggered a school suspension – plus a 60-day suspension from sports under the athletic department's policy. The student was on the varsity wrestling team. He became very upset when he realized the sports suspension meant he would miss the state tournament. Later that day, he committed suicide while at home. His mother sued the town, the school and the superintendent, saying her son died due to their negligence. The trial court granted the school defendants judgment without a trial. His mother appealed to the state supreme court, but it affirmed. The rule in Montana is: No one but the suicide victim is responsible for his or her death. The court was willing to consider an exception based on foreseeability, but it found the exception didn't apply. In this case, **the student didn't tell anyone he felt suicidal or reacted to prior disciplinary punishments by threatening or attempting suicide**. The court said that if a student responds to discipline by getting suicidal – but the school has no reason to know about it – the school is not liable for an ensuing tragedy. *Gourneau v. Hamill*, No. DA 13-0210, 2013 WL 5634125 (Mont. 10/15/13).

◆ Delaware's highest court found school officials may be liable for failing to warn a suicidal student's family – even though the student killed himself at home. The court held that the school's inaction could be "negligence per se" – a legal doctrine that deems conduct negligent because it violated a law or regulation. The doctrine was relevant in this case because a state regulation requires schools to try to contact parents or guardians immediately if students are "clearly dangerous to themselves." A student told his school's behavior interventionist (BI) that his friend had tried to kill himself. The BI called the suicidal student into her office, where the boy admitted he had tried to take his own life. They talked for about four hours before the BI felt the student was OK. Then the boy was sent to class. The BI was a contract employee, so she emailed school staff to explain how she'd handled the incident and asked if she needed to do anything else. No one called the boy's family. That night, the student hanged himself at home. **The boy's family sued, claiming the school was negligent.** The court granted the school judgment without a trial. But the high court reversed, finding more info was needed with respect to the negligence per se claim. It wrote the family can base this claim on "violations of the State Department of Education and the School District's mandatory requirements to notify a parent or guardian" if a student is suicidal. So the case was sent back to the trial court for further development. *Rogers v. Christina School Dist.*, No. 45, 2013 WL 3722554 (Del. 7/16/13).

◆ A Connecticut judge found school staff's alleged failure to follow a suicide-prevention policy may have made a student's suicide foreseeable – so he refused to dismiss negligence claims against them.

The school system was required by state law to have a suicide-prevention policy. The policy required any "school employee who may have knowledge of a suicide threat" to report it to the principal. It also required them to immediately refer an at-risk student to emergency medical personnel, a school psychologist or a school social worker. The policy specifically said the student was not to be left alone or allowed to go home alone. Instead, he could only be released to a responsible adult.

Student Michael Girard was allegedly despondent over a breakup.

His mother and stepfather – the Caseys – alleged high school staff heard Michael say he was going to hurt or kill himself. They also said a counselor knew Michael was suicidal, but let him go home alone one morning.

He died at home that day of a methadone overdose at around 10:30 a.m.

The Caseys brought a negligence suit against the board of education plus the superintendent, the principal and the counselor in their official capacities. The school defendants asked the judge to strike the negligence claims against them. He refused.

The general rule in Connecticut is that only the person who commits suicide can be held legally responsible for it. This is partly based on the theory that the act can't be predicted. The court found that rule may not apply in this case because Michael's suicide may have been foreseeable.

The judge concluded "a student's suicide could be a foreseeable

result of school staff's failure to follow the suicide prevention policy" – so he refused to dismiss the negligence claims. *Girard v. Putnam*, No. CV085002754-S, 2011 WL 783599 (Conn. Super. Ct. 1/28/11).

◆ The Ninth Circuit affirmed parents couldn't hold a school responsible for their son's suicide because they couldn't show a harsh lecture he got at school was the proximate cause of his decision to shoot himself.

Three California students left their middle school without permission to attend public protests against a law that would have made it illegal to help undocumented immigrants. One of them was on juvenile court probation for bringing a knife to school. His mother later said he could have been sent to prison for three years for violating probation.

Back at school, the students were called to a vice principal's office. According to one of them, he pointed to the students, saying, "You guys are all dumb, dumb, and dumber." He lectured them about the possible consequences of truancy – including police involvement, a $250 fine and a juvenile hall sentence. He also said they couldn't participate in a year-end trip to Disneyland.

After school, the boy on probation told a classmate he was afraid his mother would be mad at him and worried about the fine and juvenile hall.

The mother was running errands that day, but called home. The boy told her what had happened, but not in a way that made her fear for his safety. When she got home, however, she found he'd shot himself.

The student left a suicide note telling his family he loved them and saying: "Tell my teachers [they're] the best" and tell the vice principal "he is a motherf#@ker."

The boy's parents sued the school district, the principal and the vice principal, arguing they'd negligently caused the boy's death. A California federal court found they hadn't. The parents appealed to the Ninth U.S. Circuit Court of Appeals, but it affirmed the judgment.

To make their case, **the parents had to show the vice principal's harsh lecture was the proximate cause of the boy's suicide**. They couldn't.

Between hearing the lecture and killing himself, the boy went to classes and then spoke with a classmate and his mother. He also wrote a detailed suicide note. The court said: "The record seems to show he had the opportunity to appreciate the nature of his actions."

Because the parents couldn't show a reasonably close connection between the harsh lecture and the boy's suicide, judgment for the school defendants was proper. *Corales v. Bennett*, 567 F.3d 554 (9th Cir. 2009).

◆ A student's bereaved family failed to establish that a teacher's negative remarks to the student, apparently echoed in his suicide note, were a substantial factor in causing his death – because there wasn't reliable evidence the teacher actually said them. A 13-year-old eighth-grade boy struggled with his grades. His family made it a rule he couldn't go hunting if he didn't pass his classes. When the boy got his fall mid-term grades, he saw he had failed every class except gym. He complained to his science teacher that this meant he wouldn't be able to go deer hunting. The teacher said he told the boy he wouldn't be going anywhere – meaning he wouldn't be going hunting. But according to the family, another student later told them the teacher actually said, "Your life is going nowhere" and called the student one of the dumbest people he had ever taught. But the family couldn't identify the student they said told them this.

The next day, the boy shot himself after the rest of his family left the house. He left a note saying, "I relize (*sic*) my life is going noware (*sic*) fast so I decided that I don't need to live anymore." A trustee acting on behalf of the boy's family brought a wrongful death suit against the school, arguing school staff had caused the boy's suicide. The court held **the school didn't have a legal duty to prevent the suicide because the school could not have foreseen it**. The trustee also argued the boy used the same words in his note that his science teacher allegedly spoke to him, which meant these spoken words were a substantial factor in causing the suicide. However, the evidence that the teacher actually said those words wasn't reliable. The trustee appealed, but the appellate court affirmed. *Jasperson v. Anoka-Hennepin Independent School Dist. No. 11*, 2007 WL 3153456 (Minn. Ct. App. 10/30/07).

◆ An English teacher didn't violate a state duty to report a student was suicidal – even though the student killed himself six months after turning in an essay about overcoming suicidal tendencies – because the essay discussed past (not present) suicidal ideation. For the student's junior-year high school English class, he wrote an essay in April called "My Most Difficult Decision." In it, he stated he had overcome the urge to kill himself and that the trigger for that urge was gone, and he could enjoy life now. His teacher wrote him a note on the essay saying he was glad he was no longer suicidal, but to come talk to him if the urge to kill himself ever came back.

The student's family moved to another state for the student's senior year. That November, his mother told police the student was missing, she'd found a note in his room saying "I'm sorry," and he'd written "Goodbye" on his calendar over the day he'd disappeared. The family was also missing a rifle, but the student's mother told police she had no reason to believe he was suicidal. Not long after, his body was found in the state his family had moved from. The deceased student's family sued the district and his former English teacher, arguing they had failed to comply with their state law duty to warn if a teacher had direct knowledge a student had suicidal tendencies. The case reached the state supreme court, which found **there was no violation of the duty to warn because a student's suicidal tendencies had to be present rather than past in order to trigger it – and the student's essay discussed overcoming an urge to kill himself in the past**. *Carrier v. Lake Pend Oreille School Dist. No. 84*, 134 P.3d 655 (Idaho 2006).

c. Sexting-Related Cases

◆ An Ohio federal judge refused to dismiss Title IX and equal protection claims brought against a school board based on its response to students circulating a nude photo of a student who later killed herself. In May of Jessica Logan's senior year, a counselor sent her to the school resource officer (SRO) after she reported her nude photo was being texted around the school. (A proceeding dismissing a claim against the SRO in this suit is reported later in this section.) Jessica went on to appear on a TV show about sexting. Her identity was disguised, but her parents claimed people saw through the disguise. On the show, Jessica cried over harassment she was experiencing at school – which her parents say got even worse after the TV appearance. She killed herself that summer.

Her parents sued the school board and several school officials. The school defendants asked the court to grant them summary judgment. **The judge could decide the case without a trial only if the parties agreed on all the facts that could affect the legal outcome.** They didn't when it came to the Title IX and equal protection claims.

To make their Title IX sexual harassment claim, the parents had to show the harassment was severe enough to deprive Jessica of access to educational benefits or opportunities, district officials knew about the harassment, and the officials were deliberately indifferent to the harassment. The parties disagreed about whether the school defendants knew the nude image of Jessica was circulating and students were harassing her because of it.

To win their equal protection challenge, the parents had to show a key policymaker for implementing the school's sexual harassment policy, such as the principal, treated Jessica's report of harassment differently than other students' reports of harassment. Again, the parties disagreed whether administrators knew Jessica was being harassed. As the parents and school defendants disagreed about key facts that could change the legal outcome of these claims, the judge refused to grant school defendants judgment without a trial. *Logan v. Sycamore Community School Board of Educ.*, No. 1:09-cv-00885, 2012 WL 2011037 (S.D. Ohio 6/5/12).

◆ A Florida federal judge held a school board wasn't constitutionally liable for a 13-year-old's suicide following a sexting incident. Though tragic, an isolated incident of a staff member failing to follow the suicide-prevention policy didn't rise to a constitutional offense.

The student texted a suggestive photo of herself to a boy, and other students were harassing her about it. A teacher noticed shallow cuts on the girl's thigh and sent her to the office to talk to a counselor.

The school board had a written policy on suicide prevention. It required staff members to notify a student's parents if the student appeared to be at risk of suicide. In the office, a school social worker counseled the student and then signed a "no-harm contract" with her. In it, the student agreed not to "attempt suicide or die by suicide" and to call the social worker if she had suicidal thoughts again. **The counselor didn't notify the student's parents that their child was at risk of suicide.** The next day, the student killed herself at home. Her parents found the no-harm contract their daughter had signed with the social worker. They sued the school board, alleging it had violated their and their daughter's Fourteenth Amendment substantive due process rights by failing to train the social worker in the suicide prevention policy.

A municipality could be liable for a constitutional violations if it failed to properly train staff and knew the failure to train amounted to a deliberate indifference to constitutional rights. However, a single incident of a breached right wasn't enough to support this claim.

The court found the parents couldn't hold the school board liable, while noting that the parents had alleged "an admittedly tragic but isolated incident in which a social worker failed to follow established protocol." *Witsell v. School Board of Hillsborough County*, No. 8:11-cv-781-T-23AEP, 2011 WL 2457877 (M.D. Fla. 6/20/11).

◆ A Kentucky federal judge dismissed a claim against a principal, finding she couldn't have prevented a student's suicide attempt. The male student attempted suicide after his girlfriend discovered he'd texted nude photos of himself to a male teacher.

A high school student sent nude photos to a math teacher who'd been tutoring him – and giving him backrubs, touching his legs, and exposing himself to the student at a YMCA. One Saturday morning, **the student's girlfriend found the nude photos and texts on the student's phone**. They quarreled. He went home around 11:00 a.m. and attempted suicide.

Meanwhile, the girlfriend called a different teacher to report what she'd discovered. The teacher passed the information along to the principal via a voicemail he left on her home phone. She got the message late Saturday or early Sunday. On Monday morning, the principal spoke to the girlfriend and then suspended the math teacher and called the police. The math teacher was later arrested and fired.

The student sued the principal. Among his charges, he alleged the principal committed the tort of outrage by not investigating and calling the police as soon as she got the voicemail. He said a call to his mother could have prevented his suicide attempt. The judge dismissed this claim. The principal got the voicemail hours after the student's suicide attempt, so an immediate investigation couldn't have prevented it.

In addition, Kentucky cases didn't allow an outrage claim alongside a negligence claim based on the same allegations – unless the allegedly outrageous conduct was intended "to cause extreme emotional distress in the victim[.]" The student had brought negligence claims against the principal based on the same allegations and didn't show she was trying to cause him extreme emotional distress. *Cole v. Shadoan*, 782 F.Supp.2d 428 (E.D. Ky. 2011).

◆ Parents of a girl who committed suicide didn't convince an Ohio federal judge that an SRO increased the risk to their daughter's life by mishandling a sexting incident. The judge dismissed the SRO from the lawsuit.

High school senior Jessica Logan texted a nude photo of herself to a male classmate. It wound up on several classmates' phones. They harassed her, and she went to the SRO.

The SRO confronted Logan's classmates, telling them to delete the photo and stop harassing her. He also asked a prosecutor if Logan could take legal action, but was told she had no case as she wasn't a minor.

The SRO told Logan a television reporter had contacted him, hoping to create awareness about the consequences of sexting by telling students' stories. With her parents' approval, Logan agreed to a televised interview, hoping to influence other girls not to sext. It aired with her appearance and identity concealed and her voice altered.

Logan's parents said she was subjected to increased harassment at school after the interview. Logan then killed herself.

Her parents sued the SRO, saying he increased the risk to Logan's life by encouraging her to be interviewed. The judge disagreed and dismissed the SRO from their lawsuit.

Government officials like police officers are immune from federal claims unless they violate clearly established rights a reasonable person could be expected to know about.

The SRO had no general constitutional duty to protect Logan's life. But her parents argued the state-created danger exception applied, saying he had a duty to protect her because he'd increased the risk to her life.

The judge disagreed, finding the claims weren't credible. The parents alleged the SRO encouraged Logan to be interviewed on TV – but the court found he only gave her the reporter's phone number. They also claimed the interview intensified her harassment at school – but no evidence supported that allegation. Though they claimed the SRO was deliberately indifferent to the danger he'd caused Logan, **the judge found the SRO acted in good faith to try to help the student**. Finding the SRO was entitled to qualified immunity, the judge dismissed him from the case. *Logan v. Sycamore Community School Board of Educ.*, 780 F.Supp.2d 594 (S.D. Ohio 2011).

2. Other Mental Health Issues

◆ A Massachusetts federal judge refused to dismiss discrimination claims against a city and a district in a proposed class action lawsuit. The district operated a public day school separately from its neighborhood schools. About 230 K-12 students – all of whom have mental health disabilities – were enrolled in the day school. It offered limited extracurricular activities – especially compared to the neighborhood schools in the district. But students who attend the day school couldn't participate in programs at the neighborhood schools. One parent filed suit on behalf of his child and other students at the day school, alleging disability bias in violation of the ADA. **The suit claimed the children could be educated alongside their non-**

disabled peers in neighborhood schools if reasonable accommodations were made. The father stated a valid *prima facie* claim, as the boy's disability was undisputed, and "since only students with mental health disabilities are enrolled at [the day school]," the father "adequately pled that the exclusion of [his son] from the neighborhood schools was by reason of his disability," the court held. So the claim had to proceed. *S.S. v. City of Springfield, Massachusetts*, 146 F.Supp.3d 414 (D. Mass. 2015).

◆ A New Jersey federal judge refused to dismiss claims that a school violated the ADA, Section 504 of the Rehabilitation Act and the First Amendment. A student had attention deficit disorder, and his IEP outlined that he frequently doodled in class and carried a sketchbook. Days after the shooting at Sandy Hook Elementary School, a teacher noticed a drawing in the notebook. It featured a glove with a flame coming out if it. Concerned, the teacher notified the vice principal. The principal simultaneously called the boy's mother and police, who arrived at the family home with fire officials, crisis responders and a bomb squad. They searched and found wires, chemicals and switches – materials that could be used to make a bomb. Turns out, it was later explained the boy had the items to complete an engineering homework assignment. Nonetheless, he was criminally charged and spent 17 days in a juvenile facility. Upon release, he was ordered to four months of house arrest with an ankle bracelet. The boy received home instruction – and the district began proceedings to expel him. After two days of criminal proceedings, a judge found the child was not guilty. Even so, the district refused to allow him to return to school for 16 months. He sued, alleging a laundry list of claims. The court held three claims could move forward. It refused to dismiss claims that the school violated the ADA, Section 504 of the Rehabilitation Act and the First Amendment. **More info was needed to determine whether the school's response to the drawing was reasonable**, the court held. So the claims had to proceed. *K.J. v. Greater Egg Harbor Regional High School Dist. Board of Educ.*, No. 14-145(RBK/JS), 2015 WL 5039460 (D.N.J. 8/26/15).

◆ A North Carolina court ruled against a student who was sentenced to life without parole following a shooting. The student unsuccessfully argued that the jury wasn't properly instructed on the insanity defense.

On August 30, 2006, high school student Rafael Castillo shot and killed his father at home. He then drove to school, where he set off smoke bombs and shot two students.

When Castillo's gun jammed, **the school's resource officer (SRO) and a teacher told Castillo to put down his weapons**. He did, and the SRO arrested him. Charges against Castillo included first-degree murder, discharging a gun on school property, and assault with a deadly weapon with intent to kill. At trial, the jury considered whether he was not guilty by reason of insanity. Under North Carolina law, a jury could reach this conclusion if it determined Castillo had a "disease or deficiency of the mind" that so impaired him that he didn't know "the nature or quality of his act" or wasn't capable of knowing if it was right or wrong. Castillo's defense attorney argued the boy believed God wanted him to "sacrifice" his father. He'd also written in his diary, "I might save some children from sin" – and told officers immediately after the shootings that he'd tried "to save those kids from sex, drugs, pornography, and abusive people" like his father. When his mother later visited him at a mental institution, he told her that he "did the right thing." But there was also evidence Castillo had idolized the Columbine shooters. He'd visited Columbine with his mother and bought himself a black trench coat during the trip. He'd also tried to kill himself on the anniversary of the Columbine shootings.

Several experts testified Castillo couldn't tell right from wrong and that he thought he was getting messages from God. But a hospital psychiatrist testified Castillo was severely mentally ill but could tell right from wrong. **She testified that he'd idolized the Columbine shooters and wanted to share their notoriety.**

The jury found Castillo didn't qualify for the insanity defense. He was sentenced to life without possibility of parole. Castillo appealed, arguing he was entitled to the defense. He claimed the judge had improperly instructed the jury. But the appeals court found no error. The judge's instructions tracked the language in the state's Pattern Jury Instructions. Also, if the judge had agreed to use the instructions requested by Castillo's attorney, it wouldn't have affected the outcome because it wouldn't have changed the question the jury had to answer: whether Castillo was "under a delusion that God commanded him to kill his father and carry out a school shooting[.]" *State v. Castillo*, 713 S.E.2d 190 (N.C. Ct. App. 2011).

◆ Parents couldn't simply sue a district over its refusal to decide a student with depression and anxiety qualified for special education. Before suing, they first had to "exhaust administrative remedies" via hearings.

An Ohio elementary school student's academic performance deteriorated. He began to have anger issues and exhibit "demonstrated explosive behavior." He also began to refuse to go to school and to make comments about committing suicide. In March, his mother asked the district to conduct a Multi-Factored Evaluation (MFE) to assess the student for special education eligibility. She said the principal told her it was too late in the year to conduct an MFE. Two months later, his mother gave the school guidance counselor a copy of a psychiatrist's report diagnosing the student with ADHD, Asperger's Disorder, anxiety disorder and severe depression. She again asked for an MFE. Administrators again denied her request. The parents and the district continued to discuss the matter over the summer. **Less than a week before the start of the new school year, the school district refused to concede the student had a disability.**

The parents sued the district under the Individuals with Disabilities Education Act (IDEA), Section 504 of the Rehabilitation Act and the Americans with Disabilities Act. The district asked the federal judge to dismiss the suit because the parents couldn't sue over an IDEA issue under any law without first exhausting administrative remedies, as required under the IDEA, by completing every hearing and appeal required by the state's special education law. The judge agreed with the district that the parents had to exhaust administrative remedies before going to court. He dismissed the case. *Doe v. Dublin City School Dist.*, No. 2:09-cv-738, 2010 WL 1434318 (S.D. Ohio 2010).

◆ A school custodian diagnosed with post-traumatic stress syndrome caused by events surrounding a student's gruesome suicide at school was allowed to sue the school district for damages – her remedy wasn't limited to workers' comp.

A school custodian was called in to work early because a student had shot himself in the head in the main entrance of the high school. After the school superintendent ordered her to clean up the site, she overheard a police detective say the dead student's name. She'd known the boy and was so upset she had to take half an hour to compose herself.

When she returned, the police told her not to touch the site. Instead, the principal told her to go through the classrooms where the boy had attended classes that day to look for any bombs he might have left. She found none.

When she returned, she got the OK to clean the site. She found a book bag in the corner and was carrying it away when she was told to leave it, so she dropped it. Later, she found out a robot had carried it out of the building and watched as a bomb squad detonated a pipe bomb that had been in the book bag. This shocked and frightened her, as no one had warned her the bag had belonged to the suicide victim – and she'd dropped it, not suspecting it might contain a bomb.

The superintendent told her to make it look like the suicide hadn't happened. **She was there cleaning – including soot from the bomb detonation as well as brain matter, bone bits and blood – until after 4:00 a.m.** She was told to come back by 8:00 a.m. She spent the day handing out cookies and coffee to students, staff and parents there for grief counseling as well as guarding the school gates. The custodian was also ordered to clean up the suicide site every night because other people left candles and cards there to honor the boy who'd died. She found removing these items extremely upsetting. Over the next few weeks, she experienced anxiety, sleeplessness, recurring nightmares and frequent crying. She was diagnosed with post-traumatic stress syndrome.

The custodian sued the school district alleging intentional and negligent infliction of emotional distress. The trial court dismissed the suit, deciding her only remedy was to file a claim under the state's worker's comp statute. She appealed, and the appellate court reversed.

Washington's Industrial Insurance Act provided the exclusive remedy for workers injured in the course of their employment – but the appellate court found it didn't apply here because the custodian's injuries didn't fit the act's definition for "injury." The act defined an "injury" as "a sudden and tangible happening, of a traumatic nature, producing an immediate or prompt result[.]" That wasn't the case here, as the emotionally traumatic events the custodian suffered did not occur suddenly or have an immediate result. Also, her mental injury wasn't the result of any one or identifiable task ordered by the district. Since her injury didn't fall under the definition of the state's worker's comp statute, she wasn't limited to that remedy. The appellate court found her emotional distress suit could go forward. *Rothwell v. Nine Mile Falls School Dist.*, 206 P.3d 347 (Wash. Ct. App. 2009).

◆ A student wasn't eligible for special education on the basis of emotional disturbance because his depression wasn't pervasive and didn't adversely impact his academic performance. The student made two suicide attempts as a high school freshman and was admitted twice to a facility that provided psychiatric treatment. As a sophomore, he turned in homework to his teacher Mr. Kieffer in which he wrote that he was planning to take over the world and then "kill ... or something that won't get me in trouble ... all the teachers that gave me F's," adding: "fair warning, Mr. Keefer [*sic*]."

The district expelled the student for threatening a teacher and paid for him to attend an alternative school for students with behavioral problems.

The student's mother asked the district to assess him for special ed. At a meeting to discuss this, she said the school should have determined the student had a mental illness disability based on his suicide attempts and psychiatric treatments as a freshman.

But after evaluating him, the school determined he wasn't eligible for special ed. The mother asked for a due process hearing. The hearing centered on whether the student's condition was an emotional disturbance that adversely affected his academic performance as defined by the IDEA's regulations. The hearing officer decided it was and that the school had to provide him services.

The district appealed in federal court. By this time, the student was a junior, not receiving special ed, successfully carrying a full class load, no longer depressed and enjoying playing on a football team. The district asked for summary judgment, and the court granted it.

The evidence showed the student didn't have an "emotional disturbance" under the IDEA. His inappropriate behavior and emotional responses were isolated incidents, not exhibited over a long period of time and to a marked degree. Also, the fact that he'd received passing grades – two As, a B and a C – at the end of his freshman year indicated his problems hadn't adversely impacted his academic performance to the degree required for him to be eligible to receive services under the IDEA. *St. Joseph-Ogden Community High School Dist. No. 305 v. Janet W.*, No. 07-CV-2079, 2008 WL 170693 (C.D. Ill. 1/17/08).

VI. WEIGHT-RELATED ISSUES

A. Weight Management

The body mass index (BMI) method is a typical way to screen children and adolescents for excess weight and obesity. BMI assesses weight in relation to height. More information about BMI – plus charts – is available at *www.cdc.gov/growthcharts*.

One touted advantage of using BMI to determine whether students are at a healthy weight is that the method is minimally invasive – which is important when dealing with a vulnerable population such as children. But while asking for students' weights or having them get on a scale does not physically invade their bodies, it might trigger a big emotional reaction.

School officials might want to remember how touchy the subject of personal body weight is in this culture. Because of the possibility of an overwhelming emotional reaction (which can be closely followed by hurtful teasing and/or bullying as other students pick up on it) some sensitivity on the school's part might be called for when personal body weight is discussed. Schools – and state legislatures – are getting more involved in health initiatives to combat the problem. This is because an unhealthy body weight poses serious health issues.

1. Obesity

"Obesity" means a person's body weight is much higher than considered healthy for a person of that height. Children whose weight is above what is deemed a healthy range have been shown to be at greater risk of developing – or suffering more from – certain diseases and other health problems. These include:

- diabetes
- asthma
- liver problems
- gall stones
- acid reflux
- sleep apnea
- hypertension
- high blood pressure
- high cholesterol levels, and
- depression linked to self-esteem.

In addition to health problems, students who are overweight or consider themselves to be overweight are more likely to attempt suicide, according to a survey conducted by the *Journal of Adolescent Health*. More than 14,000 high school students participated in the study, which examined the links between teen suicide attempts and body mass indexes. With results equal in boys and girls, the study determined suicide risk is higher for students who are obese, are overweight, and/or have perceived notions of being too heavy.

The number of overweight students between the ages of 12 and 19 has tripled in the previous two decades, according to the CDC. The percentage of overweight children jumped from between 5% and 6% to its current percentage of around 17% – more than one obese child among every six.

The leap is even greater in some individual groups. In the early 1970s, 4% of 6- to 11-year-old children were overweight. By the early 2000s, that percentage had more than quadrupled to 18%.

Schools officials are coming up with their own strategies, too. For example, more and more elementary schools are deciding to eliminate birthday "treats" – if the treat is food. There are lots of creative ways to celebrate a child's birthday at school that have nothing to do with cupcakes, such as letting the student pick a story to read to the class.

A big concern is using food as a reward, according to a report, *Bridging the Gap*. In it, school administrators were asked, "Are teachers allowed to use food as a reward for good behavior?" They answered:

- Yes (30%)
- Yes, but it is discouraged (31%)
- No (39%).

Nearly one-third of teachers are free to use food as a reward without any resistance from school administrators, according to this survey. Physical activity, such as extra recess or a game, would be a better reward for good behavior, according to former First Lady Michelle Obama's "Let's Move!" plan. A disturbing trend reported by the CDC is that Type II diabetes – formerly called "adult onset diabetes," because that was typically when it started – has begun showing up in children and adolescents.

When onset occurs this early, the complications that go with the disease (such as kidney failure and cardiovascular disease) also set in much earlier.

Schools can help students lower this risk, according to a 2010 HEALTHY national study. More than 4,600 middle school students who were overweight participated in the study and took Type II diabetes "intervention" steps at school, such as:

- going to longer gym classes
- eating more nutritious lunches
- getting classroom education on signs and symptoms, and
- engaging in other school activities that promote a healthy lifestyle.

By the end of the study, the group had a 21% lower obesity rate than their non-participating counterparts.

And according to a 2008 *New York Times* investigation, children are also increasingly being prescribed medications for other obesity-related conditions – such as acid reflux, high blood pressure, high cholesterol – that, like Type II diabetes, were virtually unseen in children 20 years ago.

Another worrying finding is that, according to 2009 research, obese adolescents have the arteries you'd expect to find in people in their forties.

Even when obesity is not linked to a serious illness, overweight children are missing more days of school, according to a study published in a 2007 issue of the journal *Obesity*. Among the 1,000 fourth- and fifth-graders the study followed, the overweight children missed two days more of school a year than the average-weight students.

Another problem related to overweight students that virtually every school has to deal with is teasing and bullying. A 2004 study showed that overweight children are more likely to be bullied than normal-weight children. There is a huge social stigma attached to obesity in this country.

State legislatures are well aware of the problems. Recent laws include policies to make sure schools provide healthier food options for students – and restrict or keep trans fat out of school food.

Published in *Pediatrics*, a 2012 study found that laws restricting the sale of sugary snacks and drinks at school help students avoid excessive weight gain. Conducted over a three-year period, the study tracked weight changes of 6,300 students. It found that students living in states with laws restricting the availability of sugar gained 2.25 fewer pounds than their peers who were able to purchase sugary snacks and drinks at school.

When it comes to wider social problems that drive up the incidence of obesity – and over which schools obviously have no control – the Department of Agriculture offers help through the National School Lunch Program and the School Breakfast Program.

There is a direct correlation between poverty and obesity. Fresh fruits and vegetables cost a lot more than fast food and are not nearly as filling. The original reason behind the South's tradition of fried foods was that adding fat was a way the poor could make a limited amount of food go farther. Deep frying makes food more filling so it can feed more people.

Where children live can also have a huge impact on their weight. It is almost universally true that poor areas of towns are short on two health basics: stores that stock affordable fresh food, and safe outdoor places where children can ride bikes or run around and play.

Schools cannot be expected to solve the problem of poverty, but they can help to fight off its nutritional impact on their students by making sure children participate in PE classes and by making sure eligible students take advantage of the U.S. Department of Agriculture's School Breakfast Program and National School Lunch Program.

But due to the social stigma associated with poverty, the very students who most need it may not want to be seen getting a free-or-reduced meal. Depending on how things are set up at your school – or ways you can change them – it may be possible to protect students' dignity *and* get healthy food into their bodies.

2. Eating Disorders

The National Eating Disorders Screening Program (NDESP) coordinated the first nationwide screening initiative for U.S. high school students in 2000. With more than 35,000 participants, the study revealed that 25% of girls and 11% of boys reported "disordered eating and weight control symptoms severe enough to warrant clinical evaluation," according to researchers. The study concluded that screening high school students for potential eating disorders may identify at-risk students. These students may benefit from early intervention, which would help prevent long-term health complications associated with anorexia and other eating disorders.

Students who have eating disorders usually have unrealistic fears about gaining weight and distorted perceptions about their bodies. They also tend to deny the seriousness of their illness.

Eating disorders are commonly divided into two categories: anorexia nervosa and bulimia nervosa. Many individuals exhibit symptoms from both anorexia and bulimia. The disorders can be overcome, but doing so is extremely difficult for students for two reasons:

1. Anorexia and bulimia aren't really about food. The disorders stem from a negative self-image. While onset can occur at any age, eating disorders are commonly triggered just before or during puberty. In practical terms, students are most likely to develop eating disorders during puberty because that's a time when their bodies are changing, which can lead to self-doubt. Reflecting today's extreme "societal pressure to be thin," advertising and the media only make students' self-image problems worse, according to the National Alliance on Mental Illness (NAMI).
2. In previous years, more students who suffered from anorexia and bulimia often felt alone and isolated. But technology has enabled students from around the world to interact with others who also suffer from eating disorders. The Internet has thousands of underground websites dedicated to promoting and maintaining anorexic and bulimic lifestyles. Sufferers have personified the disorders, commonly calling anorexia "Ana" and bulimia "Mia." Some students with eating disorders even refer to "Ana" or "Mia" as their best friend. Because students communicate primarily via technology, this online support system to perpetuate the disorders makes intervention and treatment more challenging than ever. On the websites, sufferers share tips on how to trick others into thinking they are eating and how to avoid giving in to hunger pains. The pro-ana/pro-mia online community glorifies anorexia and bulimia, calling them lifestyle choices rather than disorders.

In addition, anorexic females experience amenorrhea, which is the absence of three consecutive menstrual cycles due to extreme weight loss.

They also complain about feeling cold when others are comfortable. This is a sign of hypothermia, which is caused by a drop in body temperature caused by excessive weight loss. Lanugo (very fine hair, such as on newborns) may grow on the face or body. Other visible body changes include brittle nails, thin hair and dry, yellow skin.

Anorexia is potentially life-threatening. Seriously underweight students who refuse to eat have been shown to be at greater risk of developing – or suffering more from – certain diseases and other health problems, such as:

- damage to vital organs (heart, kidneys, brain)
- low heart rate

- mild anemia
- low blood pressure
- irregular heart rhythms
- heart failure
- osteoporosis, and
- death by starvation.

A study conducted by the National Alliance on Mental Illnesses (NAMI) found that anorexia nervosa has the highest mortality rate of all psychiatric illnesses. The majority who suffer from anorexia are female adolescents between the ages of 15 and 24. However, anorexia has also been diagnosed in girls as young as seven and boys. When people suffer from anorexia, they often develop eating rituals. For example, they may cut food into tiny pieces or refuse to eat in front of others. Common excuses for not eating include:

- "I already ate."
- "I had a big breakfast/lunch."
- "I just brushed my teeth."

School officials and parents can watch for warning signs that students may need help. Potential signs of an eating disorder include:

- feeling an unattainable pressure to succeed
- ongoing, unexplained weight loss, and
- going to the restroom immediately after meals.

Teachers and school officials should be aware of red flags at school that might indicate anorexia. They should watch for students who:

- have lost a significant amount of weight
- become extraordinarily reclusive
- wear very baggy clothing (to hide excessive weight loss)
- wear lots of layers (to add bulk as well as to keep warm)
- huddle around near heat vents or radiators (to keep warm)
- skip meals or bring their own low calorie food, and
- exercise during lunchtime instead of eating.

Anorexic students have specific challenges at school. Teachers and school officials can help students by:

- allowing severely malnourished students to opt out of physical activity until health improves
- remembering that lunchtime and meals are stressful for students who have eating disorders, and
- offering alternative meal locations other than the cafeteria, if the student desires.

Anorexia can be triggered by internal factors. For example, anorexic behaviors might be triggered by a personality trait. One of the most common personality traits of anorexics is perfectionism. Because of this, it may take an anorexic student longer to complete tests. Teachers can help anorexic students perform to their academic potential by allowing them to have a warm drink or a blanket to reduce chills (a common side effect), which often cause students to be distracted from their assignments.

The disorder can also be triggered by external challenges, such as peer bullying – and that can cause legal hassles for school officials.

For example, a mother in Pennsylvania filed a lawsuit against Pittsburgh Public Schools, claiming school officials failed to stop five male classmates from bullying her daughter about her weight. The victim and the bullies were sent to the guidance counselor's office and the principal's office at least three times, according to the suit. The victim alleged that the bullying was "open and apparent."

The suit claimed the ongoing bullying the girl suffered triggered an eating disorder – which eventually required her to leave school to enter an inpatient anorexia nervosa program. Filed under Title IX, the lawsuit didn't have to prove bullying *caused* the student's anorexia. Instead, the girl's mother only had to show the school failed to protect her daughter, which caused her to miss school.

School officials asked for dismissal, but the court refused to grant it because the U.S. Supreme Court has already ruled that peer-on-peer harassment violates Title IX if the school doesn't stop the abuse, and as a result, the victim loses educational opportunities. *Mary V. v. Pittsburgh Public Schools*, No. CA 9-1082, 2010 WL 562909 (W.D. Pa. 2/17/10).

The district paid $55,000 to settle the claim.

People who suffer from bulimia binge and purge. Sufferers frequently eat unusually large amounts of food and immediately try to remove the ingested calories by inducing vomiting, taking laxatives and exercising excessively. Students with bulimia often:

- feel as if they can't control their eating behavior
- refuse to eat in public, but binge in private
- eat to the point of discomfort during binges
- use or abuse laxatives, dietary supplements and herbal remedies
- exercise obsessively, and
- worry and complain they are fat.

Most students who are bulimic maintain normal body weight or are slightly overweight, which makes it harder for school officials and parents to detect the problem. This is extremely dangerous because bulimic students face health risks including:

- amenorrhea
- abnormal bowel functioning
- damaged teeth and gums
- dehydration
- gastroesophageal reflux disorder
- irregular heart rhythms
- chronically inflamed or sore throat
- kidney problems from diuretic abuse
- swollen salivary glands in the cheeks

- sores, scar or calluses on knuckles or hands (from forced vomiting)
- depression, and
- anxiety.

The majority who suffer from bulimia are female adolescents and young adults who have been subjected to "teasing" about their appearance from family members and/or peers. Binging and purging is done in secret, so many students who have bulimia successfully hide their disorder. Red flags that might indicate students are bulimic include:

- wearing very baggy clothing to hide weight fluctuation
- following erratic diets, such as eating only a certain color food
- making frequent trips to the restroom – especially after eating
- talking about food constantly
- bringing their own food in a purse or book bag, and
- avoiding the cafeteria (or other social eating environments).

Eating disorders are common among student-athletes. A recent study conducted by the ERCI found that more than one-third of female athletes reported attitudes and behaviors that put them in the "at risk" category for eating disorders. Sports that require athletes to weigh in or maintain a certain size to stay competitive further increase students' risks. Examples include gymnastics, bodybuilding, diving, wrestling, track and field, figure skating and dance.

Paying attention to warning signs is the most important thing coaches can do to help students, according to Karin Kratina of the National Eating Disorders Association. The leading causes of death for students with eating disorders are suicide and cardiac arrest. School officials and coaches can help reduce athletes' vulnerability to eating disorders by:

- adopting a positive coaching style in favor of an authoritative one
- influencing and supporting teammates by displaying health attitudes about athletes' sizes and shapes, and
- emphasizing contribution and teamwork more than a win-at-all-cost competitive mind-set.

Female student-athletes who have eating disorders have additional health risks, such as the loss of menses – which leads to calcium and bone loss. This means female athletes are more prone to stress fractures of the bones, according to a study relating to the impact of eating disorders on women's health and athletic activity conducted by the University of Minnesota Tucker Center.

The U.S. Department of Health and Human Services compiled the following list of recommendations school officials can follow to promote healthy weight control for student-athletes:

1. Nutritional needs for growth and development must be placed above athletic considerations. Fluid or food deprivation should never be allowed. There is no substitute for a healthy diet consisting of a variety of foods from all food groups with enough energy (calories)

to support growth, daily physical activities, and sports activities. Daily caloric intake for most athletes should consist of a minimum of 2000 calories. Athletes need to consume enough fluids to maintain proper hydration levels.

2. In sports for which weigh-ins are required, athletes' weights and body composition should be assessed once or twice per year. The most important assessment is obtained before the beginning of the sport season. This should include a determination of body fat and minimal allowable weight when the athlete is adequately hydrated. Weigh-ins for competition should be performed immediately before competition. Athletes should be permitted to compete in championship tournaments only at the weight class in which they have competed for most other athletic events that year.
3. Male high school athletes should not have less than 7% body fat. This minimal allowable body fat may be too low for some athletes and result in sub-optimal performance. Female athletes should consume enough energy (calories) and nutrients to meet their energy requirements and experience normal menses. There are no recommendations on body-fat percentages for female athletes.
4. A program for the purpose of gaining or losing weight should (a) be started early to permit a gradual weight gain or loss over a realistic time period, (b) permit a change of 1.5% or less of one's body weight per week, (c) permit the loss of weight to be fat loss and the gain of weight to be muscle mass, (d) be coupled with an appropriate training program (both strength and conditioning), and (e) incorporate a well-balanced diet with adequate energy (calories), carbohydrates, protein, and fat. After athletes obtain their desired weight, they should be encouraged to maintain a constant weight and avoid fluctuations. A weight-loss plan for athletic purposes should never be instituted before the ninth grade.
5. Any athlete who loses a significant amount of fluid during sports participation should weigh in before and after practices, games, meets, and competitions. Each pound of weight loss should be replaced with one pint of fluid containing carbohydrates and electrolytes before the next practice or competition. Fluids should be available, and the drinking of fluids should be encouraged at all practices and competitions.
6. Weight loss accomplished by over-exercising; using rubber suits, steam baths, or saunas; prolonged fasting; fluid reduction; vomiting; or using anorexic drugs, laxatives, diuretics, diet pills, insulin, stimulants, nutritional supplements, or other legal or illegal drugs and/or nicotine should be prohibited at all ages.
7. Athletes who need to gain weight should consult their physician for resources on healthy weight gain and referral to a registered dietitian. They should be discouraged from gaining excessive weight, which may impair performance, increase the likelihood of heat illness, and

increase the risk of developing complications from obesity.

8. Ergogenic aids and non-therapeutic use of supplements for weight management should be prohibited.
9. Young athletes should be involved in a total athletic program that includes acquisition of athletic skills and improvement in speed, flexibility, strength, and physical conditioning while maintaining good nutrition and normal hydration. This should be done under the supervision of a coach who stresses a positive attitude, character building, teamwork, and safety.

B. Nutrition

1. School Meals

The U.S. Department of Agriculture's School Breakfast Program and National School Lunch Program require schools to serve meals that are low in fat and provide a certain percentage of the Recommended Dietary Allowances of protein, Vitamin A, Vitamin C, iron, calcium and calories – one-third for school lunches and one-quarter for school breakfasts.

Poor nutrition, from which many children suffer, has a negative impact on brain development and school performance.

In 2010, former governor of California Arnold Schwarzenegger signed SB 1413 into law. The legislation requires public schools in the state to provide students with access to fresh, free drinking water in food service areas during meal times at schools. The law took effect on Jan. 1, 2011.

To meet the new legal requirement, schools:

- gave students 8-ounce bottles of water with their meals, and
- supplied 5-gallon containers of bottled water and paper cups for students in the lunchroom.

There's still room for improvement in school nutrition. For example, in 2010, the Physicians Committee for Responsible Medicine (PCRM) analyzed lunch menus from 18 schools across the country.

The result? Schools are still serving meals that are too high in saturated fat and sodium, according to PCRM nutritionist Kathryn Strong.

After the analysis was complete, PCRM identified what it called the worst lunches to serve to students. Here are the top five worst school lunches:

- Beef and cheese nachos. Topping the list, this meal has too much sodium (1,500 mg) and fat (24 g).
- Meatloaf and potatoes packs unhealthy calories (472) and cholesterol (78 mg).
- Cheeseburgers, which often have more saturated fat than students should have in an entire meal.
- Grilled cheese sandwiches and cheese quesadillas (tied) are loaded with saturated fat (7 g) and sodium (nearly 1,000 mg).
- Pepperoni pizza. The average slice contains saturated fat (6 g) and its processed meat has also been shown to increase cancer risk.

Schools can help children develop healthier eating habits by offering:

- more fruits, vegetables, lean meats and whole grains
- less fat, and
- appropriate portion sizes.

Students may balk at the options, but schools can take steps to encourage students to eat healthier foods, according to research conducted at Cornell University. Smarter Lunchroom researchers found that students are more likely to choose healthy meals when schools:

- provide healthy "grab and go" options in the lunchroom
- offer fruits and veggies as "default" sides
- make a gradual switch to whole grains, and
- sell suggestively at the register, as in "Would you like to add an apple?"

Be prepared to think creatively, too. For example, school officials in Minnesota looked for ways to get students to at least try healthy options instead of just grabbing the typical go-to favorites, such as the ones listed above. But students weren't interested, so the staff stirred up some intrigue by holding a "coolest veggie" contest.

Cafeteria staffers passed out sample cups of veggies to students who were waiting in the lunch line. Four veggies were in the running: jicama sticks, portabella mushrooms, red peppers and pickled beets. After lunch, students filled out a survey to vote for their favorite. When the votes were tallied, jicama sticks was named the coolest veggie.

Getting students' input helped the school find out which healthy options students would eat. Jicama sticks remained one of the students' favorite veggies on the lunch menu for years.

School officials can do other things to promote healthy lunch choices – and doing so doesn't have to break the budget. Smarter Lunchrooms suggested the following well-planned tweaks to the layout of school cafeterias to improve students' lunch choices:

- The cash register. Remember – convenience is key! Students stand in line waiting. What last-minute items of convenience will they add to their trays? Replace chips and other pre-packaged goodies with fresh fruit or 100% fruit juice.
- The menu. What's in a name? Turns out, plenty when it comes to food. One cafeteria reported a 28% increase in sales after "vegetable soup" was renamed "rich vegetable medley soup." Smarter Lunchrooms recommends three specific food labels: nostalgic, regional and descriptive. For example: Grandma's chicken noodle soup, real Boston baked beans and creamy corn chowder.
- Walls and tables. Get creative by adding brightly colored posters of healthy fruits and veggies – and nutritional info – on cafeteria walls. Add a "try it table" – use table tents to invite students who are waiting in line to sample healthy options.
- Display cases. Lighting affects the way students view their choices. Make sure healthy lunch options are visually appealing by using

well-lit display cases. Place the healthiest options at students' eye levels.

- The web. More and more cafeterias are putting their menus on school websites. Students who plan their meals based on online menus usually stick to healthier food choices than students who make decisions on a whim – while they're waiting in line and starving. If you haven't posted your menu on the web yet, it might be a good time to consider going online.

The Healthy School Meals Act of 2010 was one of the catalysts behind school lunch reform. The legislation required key changes to be tested in a pilot program, which was an overwhelming success in Berkeley, California schools.

2. Education

Wellness initiatives are designed to foster healthy food choices at a young age and to create habits that last a lifetime. Doing so helps students reduce health risks and increase their quality of life. Also, as opposed to going on and off reduced-calorie diets, developing good eating and exercise habits helps students maintain a healthy weight while ensuring their bodies have the nutrients to grow into healthy adults.

A key element is educating students on the benefits of healthy choices. Talk about it. Promote it at your school.

For example, remind students that being healthy is a lifestyle. Every healthy thing they do today – such as eating an apple instead of a candy bar or taking the stairs instead of the elevator – will pay off tomorrow. Getting into healthy habits has a cumulative effect.

School officials should also consider the products promoted when students participate in school fundraising efforts. Do students sell candy bars? Are other options available? Non-food items that can be sold during school fundraisers or used as rewards include:

- special school supplies
- homemade crafts
- gift certificates to local gyms or mini-golf courses, and
- discount coupons to local sporting goods stores.

C. Physical Activity

There are six national standards for physical education (PE) in U.S. schools.

1. development of motor/movement skills
2. knowledge and application of movement concepts
3. personal/social responsibility
4. regular participation in physical activity
5. development and maintenance of physical fitness, and
6. valuing physical activity.

Every student in the U.S. needs physical activity, whether it's in a formal PE program or free play at recess – and more students are getting it at school.

VII. MORE HEALTH-RELATED CASES

◆ A Texas school didn't violate the IDEA by discontinuing some special ed services in a student's IEP, the Fifth Circuit decided. Parents of a third-grader with speech impairments weren't happy with proposed changes to their daughter's IEP. Specifically, they were upset that the district planned to discontinue the assistance of a sign-language interpreter and also planned to remove the educational goal of improving the girl's ability to speak. Her parents filed a due process hearing request. **Multiple educators testified that the girl preferred and relied on her iPod Touch as her primary method of communication and that little to no progress had been made in her ability to speak.** After the hearing officer ruled in the school's favor, her parents sued. But the court found no error. On appeal, the Fifth Circuit affirmed the ruling for the school. *E.M. v. Lewisville Independent School Dist.*, No. 18-40409, 2019 WL 1466959 (5th Cir. 4/1/19).

◆ The U.S. Supreme Court clarified that the IDEA's "exhaustion requirement" can't be used as a get-out-of-jail-free card when the main issue is discrimination. The student had a severe form of cerebral palsy and a service dog to assist her with basic daily life activities. School administrators refused to admit the dog, contending that the student's IEP "rendered the dog superfluous." Her parents withdrew her from school and filed a complaint with the Office for Civil Rights (OCR). When OCR sided with the parents, the school did an about-face and invited the student and her dog to the school. Concerned about resentment from school officials, her parents declined the offer, enrolled the student in a different school, and sued, alleging disability bias under Title II if the ADA and Section 504 of the Rehabilitation Act.

The legal battle went all the way to the U.S. Supreme Court. The justices looked at the language of the legislation mentioned in this case. The IDEA establishes procedures to resolve FAPE disputes between parents and educators. "Administrative remedy" procedures give schools a chance to make things right before getting sued in court. And when parents skip the procedures and try to file suit before exhausting the remedies, courts dismiss IDEA claims. But the IDEA isn't the only federal disability law. The ADA and Section 504 ensure access to public facilities for people with disabilities of all ages.

The Court noted that there's likely to be overlap in coverage, as the same conduct may violate all three statutes. But due to the differences, some complaints brought under the ADA and Section 504 may simply seek relief for discrimination, regardless of FAPE obligations under the IDEA. For that reason, what matters is the "gravamen" – or the crux – of the complaint, the Court deduced. The Court outlined a two-point test to determine whether the IDEA's exhaustion requirement applies to disability-related complaints:

1. Could the plaintiff have brought the claim if the alleged conduct occurred at a public facility that was not a school?
2. Could an adult at the school have pressed essentially the same claim?

If "yes," then a FAPE issue isn't likely to be the crux of the complaint, so exhaustion wouldn't be required – and parents would get the greenlight to proceed with their bias lawsuits. But if the answers are "no," then the "gravamen" is likely to be a FAPE issue – which would require parents to exhaust the remedies before suing.

This ruling made it clear that parents can skip exhaustion if the case is really about disability bias – not educational services. The Court remanded the case with instructions to decide whether the parents had to exhaust the remedies. *Fry v. Napoleon Community Schools*, 137 S.Ct. 743 (U.S. 2017).

On remand, a Michigan federal court applied the Court's "gravamen" guidance and decided both answers were "yes," so exhaustion wasn't required. Here, the parents filed the action in federal court under the ADA and Section 504. Further, the court said no evidence suggested the suit sought relief for the denial of a FAPE. Their daughter no longer attended the school, so no IDEA relief was even available, the court also pointed out. The court said t**he crux of the case was discrimination – not educational services – so the parents didn't have to exhaust the remedies** under the IDEA. *E.F. v. Napolean Community Schools,* No. 12-15507, 2019 WL 1002355 (E.D. Mich. 3/1/19).

◆ A California school could place a student with Down syndrome in special ed classes, the Ninth Circuit held. Through the seventh grade, the student was in general education classes with a support specialist and a 1:1 aide. But her grades were falling, and her IEP goals weren't being met. She was also regressing, teachers said. The IEP team wanted to put her in special ed classes when she went to the eighth grade, but her parents weren't on board. They rejected the IEP and filed a complaint.

An ALJ backed the school, and the parents sought judicial review. The case reached the Ninth Circuit. It noted the evidence suggested the girl wasn't benefiting from a general education curriculum. She wasn't making academic progress, even with a modified curriculum and a 1:1 aide. **Moreover, evidence indicated she was regressing and beginning to withdraw.** Teachers testified that she frequently put her head on her desk in frustration and refused to participate in class. The ruling for the school was affirmed. *Solorio v. Clovis Unified School Dist.,* 748 Fed.Appx. 146 (9th Cir. 2019).

◆ A Virginia federal court refused to dismiss disability discrimination claims against a school district. A senior with Down syndrome had been receiving special ed services since he was in the second grade. From the start, his parents made it clear that they favored an IEP with rigorous goals, as the ultimate objective was for their son to graduate with a standard diploma – not a certificate. Problems started during the student's first year of high school. His parents said some teachers didn't agree with the goals in the IEP, so it wasn't followed. Specifically, they said their son wasn't encouraged to participate in class. Instead, he was allowed to watch videos on YouTube. His parents filed an administrative complaint alleging the school denied their son a FAPE. After the hearing officer sided with the school, the boy was removed from general ed classes without his parents' consent. The school also prevented the boy from taking state standardized tests – which were necessary tools to help him achieve the goal of receiving the standard diploma. His parents brought discrimination and retaliation claims under the ADA and Section 504 of the Rehabilitation Act. The Fourth Circuit applies the same analysis to discrimination claims for both laws. When educational services were at the center of the dispute, "gross misjudgment or bath faith must be established for both Section 504 or ADA claims," the court explained. Here, a reasonable person could find the school acted in bad faith or used gross misjudgment. So the discrimination claims had to proceed.

As to the retaliation claims, the court held the parents established a *prima facie* case, as they alleged their son was engaged in a protected activity (taking the state tests to achieve a goal in his IEP); the school took an adverse action against him, (preventing the boy from taking the tests after the hearing officer's decision); and the boy's protected activity was "causally connected" to the school's adverse action. The court refused to dismiss the claims, so a trial was needed. *B.D. v. Fairfax County School Board*, No. 1:18-cv-1425, 2019 WL 692804 (E.D. Va. 2/19/19).

◆ A California appeals court upheld a controversial state law. In 2016, the California Legislature passed SB 277, which "eliminated a parent's ability to opt out of vaccination requirements imposed on children" based on parents' personal beliefs. Specifically, the law said school administrators "shall not unconditionally admit" any child to "any private or public elementary or secondary school" unless the child has been fully immunized against 10 specific diseases. Further, the law says a student would be exempt if a doctor states in writing that the child could not be immunized due to medical circumstances. In early 2015, the state of California became the "epicenter of a measles outbreak which was the result of unvaccinated individuals." Prior to the outbreak – from 2000 to 2012, the number of Personal Belief Exemptions from vaccinations required for school entry rose 337%. In certain pockets of California, exemption rates were as high as 21%, putting communities at risk for preventable diseases. Studies showed "vaccination rates of up to 95% [were] necessary to preserve herd immunities and prevent future outbreaks," according to the state's Senate Committee on Education. Here, the plaintiffs alleged SB 277 violated their substantive due process rights because it infringed on their rights to bodily immunity and to refuse medical treatment. They said it also illegally conditioned the right to attend school on giving up the right to bodily immunity and to refuse medical treatment. Further, they alleged SB 277 negated their parental right to make decisions in the upbringing of their children. To determine whether a person's liberty interest for purposes of substantive due process has been violated, courts have to balance the rights of the individual against relevant state interests. When the state infringes on a person's rights, "strict scrutiny" applies. A law that was subjected to strict scrutiny could be upheld only when it was "narrowly tailored to promote a compelling government interest," the court explained. **It's well established that "laws mandating vaccination of school-aged children promote a compelling government interest of ensuring health and safety by preventing the spread of contagious diseases."** So SB 277 was upheld. *Love v. State Dep't of Educ.*, 240 Cal.Rptr.3d 861 (Cal. Ct. App. 2018).

◆ A Tennessee federal court decided the parents of a student with Down syndrome were entitled to tuition reimbursement. The student had an IEP. When he reached the third grade, the IEP team wanted to move him from a mainstreamed classroom to a segregated classroom solely for children with disabilities. The parents objected to the IEP. They enrolled the boy at a private school and paid for a full-time aide to assist their son. Once the boy was settled at the new school, his parents filed an IDEA complaint alleging the school denied their son a FAPE. The matter ended up in court, and it held the alternative placement didn't satisfy the IDEA so the parents weren't entitled to reimbursement.

On appeal, the Sixth Circuit said the court made the wrong call. It said regardless of whether the private school was structured in the same way the district was, "the student had a personalized curriculum and a paraprofessional aide dedicated just to him," so he could work at his own pace with frequent repetition, intense 1:1 instruction, and repeated prompting and reinforcement. He produced a daily journal, had nightly homework and received report cards, which showed he had a regular school experience, the court pointed out. As such, the alternative placement satisfied the IDEA. The Sixth Circuit remanded the case to determine appropriate tuition reimbursement.

On remand, the court determined the parents paid $7,500 annual tuition plus $9,000 to $17,128 per year for the personal paraprofessional aide for five school years (third through seventh grades). The defendants argued the parents couldn't recoup the costs of the aide's fees, but **the court rejected the argument because "the aide was a crucial component" of the private school's ability to provide a proper placement under the IDEA**. As such, the court ordered the defendants to reimburse the parents in the amount of $103,724. *L.H. v. Hamilton County Dep't of Educ.*, No. 1:14-CV-00126, 2018 WL 6069161 (E.D. Tenn. 11/20/18).

◆ New York's highest court clarified that requiring students to get flu vaccines doesn't violate state law. A city health code required children between the ages of 6 months and 59 months who attended school programs to get an annual flu shot. Some medical and religious exemptions were granted. A group of parents sued, and the case reached the Court of Appeals of New York. Parents who objected to the requirement argued the city overstepped its authority by requiring flu vaccinations. They claimed "the flu vaccine rules [were] invalid because they conflict with Public Health Law" and "the state legislature has preempted the narrower field of mandatory school vaccinations by enacting a comprehensive statutory scheme." As to the conflict preemption allegation, the court said nothing in the law suggested that the list of vaccinations was exclusive or couldn't be expanded on by local municipalities. Thus, no conflict existed, the court said. Turning to the question of field preemption, the court said **it wasn't unusual for the state to "set the floor for public health regulations while permitting localities to adopt stricter measures."** Bottom line: The flu vaccine rules didn't conflict with state law and weren't preempted, so the parents' claim failed. *Garcia v. New York City Dep't of Health and Mental Hygiene,* No. 64, 2018 WL 3147611 (N.Y. 6/28/18).

◆ The Ninth Circuit revived an IDEA claim filed by a California mother. A student had speech and hearing issues. A district said she was eligible for special education services and created an IEP that aimed to help her speech and language issues. But it went on to decide the student wasn't eligible for services for her hearing impairment because the district's evaluations didn't identify that her "permanent hearing loss impairs her ability to process [info] through her hearing aids." After internal procedures, the mother sued, and the case went to the Ninth Circuit. **It noted that the district used the definition for "deafness" not "hearing loss."** The error wasn't harmless, so the court remanded the case for further proceedings. *S.P. v. East Whittier City School Dist.,* No. 16-56549, 2018 WL 2453865 (9th Cir. 6/1/18).

◆ A Utah federal judge rejected an ADA claim filed by a non-disabled student who wanted to bring a service dog in training to school. The owner of a dog breeding business purchased a dog with the intention of training it as a service animal and donating it to a child with special needs. The owner hired her daughter – a high school student – to be the dog's full-time handler. The owner emailed her daughter's principal to explain that the dog would be attending school as a service dog in training. After reviewing school policy, the principal told the owner the dog couldn't attend school as a service dog in training. Negotiations broke down, and the matter ended up in court. The judge said Utah law didn't require schools to "allow a service animal in training accompanied by a non-disabled student into a high school classroom." Under the ADA, permitting a service animal to accompany a student with disabilities to class may be required as a reasonable accommodation. But the Utah statute doesn't extend the ADA accommodation requirement to non-disabled students, the court explained. **A plain-language reading of the statute couldn't be read to require accommodations to non-disabled individuals with service animals in training to the same extent required for disabled individuals with service animals under the ADA**, the court said. *Naegle v. Canyons School Dist.*, No. 2:17-cv-23-DB, 2018 WL 2376336 (D. Utah 5/24/18).

◆ A Massachusetts federal court tossed an ADA claim filed against a private school – but it allowed a retaliation claim to move forward. A boy had Electromagnetic Hypersensitivity Syndrome (EHS) and suffered symptoms such as headaches and nosebleeds purportedly caused by his school's Wi-Fi connection. His parents asked the school to replace the Wi-Fi with Ethernet access. The school said total Wi-Fi removal wasn't feasible. It proposed to let the boy use an Ethernet connection and have an 8-foot separation from Wi-Fi emissions sources. The parents withdrew the boy and filed suit, alleging the school failed to grant a reasonable accommodation in violation of the ADA. They also claimed the school retaliated by not allowing their son to participate in school sports while he was studying at home due to EHS health complications caused by the school's Wi-Fi connections. To state a valid ADA claim, the parents had to show the school's Wi-Fi caused their son's EHS-related health symptoms. They didn't make that showing, the court said. Medical experts showed that it was plausible that the boy suffered from EHS, but they failed to consider other environmental factors that might've contributed to the symptoms, the court explained. There was plenty of "circumstantial evidence … but it [was] impossible to conclude that the evidence on record would allow a reasonable jury to find that a causal link" existed between the school's Wi-Fi and the boy's EHS symptoms, the court said. It tossed the ADA claim. Next the court looked at the retaliation claim. The parents said the school refused to let their son participate in school sports during a medical leave for his EHS symptoms. At that time, they'd already started the interactive process of accommodation talks. They said the school's refusal to let their son participate amounted to retaliation for the ADA request. **The school offered no explanation for the exclusion, so the retaliation claim had to go to trial**, the court said. *G. v. The Fay School, Inc.*, No. 4:15-CV-40116-TSH, 2017 WL 4381668 (D. Mass. 9/29/17).

◆ A New Jersey appeals court backed a Commissioner of Education's decision not to reinstate a teacher after a fitness-for-duty exam. A special education teacher suffered repeated panic attacks. One was so severe that the school had to call 911. She was put on administrative leave pending a mental fitness examination. The doctor diagnosed the teacher with three mental health disorders and concluded she was "at a high risk for continued problems" unless specific accommodations were provided. With them, she could return to work. But the commissioner decided the teacher wasn't eligible to return to work, citing student safety concerns. So the teacher sued. But courts generally don't second-guess state agencies' decisions – unless the agency clearly botched the call. That wasn't the case here, the court said, noting that **student safety was a valid concern**. It affirmed the commissioner's ruling. *C.H. v. School Dist. of the City of Camden*, No. 122-6/15, 2017 WL 3611598 (N.J. Super. Ct. App. Div. 8/23/17).

◆ The Fourth Circuit rejected race discrimination claims of a bi-racial teacher who said she wasn't allowed to return to work with a medical restriction. The North Carolina teacher took a two-week medical leave after suffering from insomnia and having high blood pressure. A doctor cleared her to return to work with "no prolonged standing" but the board rejected the restriction as unreasonable. The teacher filed a racial discrimination suit that reached the Fourth Circuit. But **she failed to provide evidence showing she was treated differently than white colleagues**, so the court affirmed the ruling to dismiss the claim. *Swasso v. Onslow County Board of Educ.,* No. 16-2347, 2017 WL 3432388 (4th Cir. 8/11/17).

◆ A summer school teacher who was shot by a student was eligible for disability benefits, Hawaii's highest court recently held. On June 30, 1988, the teacher suffered serious injuries after being shot in the chest during a summer school session. The shooter, a student, was sentenced to life in prison. When doctors said the teacher was incapable of returning to her teaching position, she filed a disability retirement claim. It was denied, and the legal battle reached the state supreme court. The teacher was a member of the state retirement system through her regular full-time position as a public school teacher. She contributed to the fund through deductions taken from her salary paid over 12 months. In the summers, she worked as a part-time summer school teacher. That position – on its own – didn't provide eligibility for the state retirement system. Her summertime salary was paid with separate paychecks. No deductions were withheld for contributions to the state retirement fund from the summertime paychecks. The board of trustees for the state retirement system decided the teacher was not entitled to benefits because the shooting happened during the summertime – when she wasn't making contributions to the fund. The state's highest court disagreed, noting that the teacher "did in fact make contributions to [the state fund] year-round through deductions from her academic year salary, which was paid by the DOE over 12 months." Moreover, **members who contributed to the retirement system were eligible for service-connected disability retirement if they were "permanently incapacitated for duty as … the proximate result of an accident occurring while in the actual performance of duty."** That was what happened here, the court said, so the teacher was eligible for retirement benefits. *Stout v. Board of Trustees of the Employees' Retirement System, State of Hawaii,* No. SCAP-15-0000582, 2017 WL 2928787 (Haw. 7/10/17).

◆ In Illinois, a PE teacher failed to show an injury "arose out of his employment," so a state appeals court affirmed a ruling to deny workers' compensation benefits. In 2013, the teacher and a few students were waiting for the rest of the class to finish "dressing out" for PE class. As they waited, a student attempted to "run up" the gymnasium wall. The student challenged the teacher to try it. He did. Then the student goaded the teacher about not being able to make it as far up the wall as the kids could. The teacher tried again, and "felt a popping sensation" in his knee. He was out of work for three months and filed a comp claim. The state commission denied the claim, finding the injury was not "incidental to his employment" as it was not a part of the curriculum the day he was injured. On appeal, the teacher argued he'd been attempting to build rapport with students while waiting for other kids to change and class to begin. Courts don't second-guess the commission's findings unless they were obviously erroneous. And that wasn't the case here, as the evidence supported its finding that **the injury was not a result of the teacher's job duties, as it occurred before class began and outside of curriculum and was the result of his second attempt to run up the wall – after a student's goading**. Further, running up a wall was not the only way to build rapport with students, the court said. It affirmed the denial. *Thompson v. The Illinois Workers' Compensation Commission,* 2017 WL App (4th) 160531WC-U (Ill. App. Ct. 7/6/17).

◆ An Arizona federal judge rejected a mother's allegation that an IEP team's decision to continue a meeting after she left amounted to a denial of a FAPE. The student had learning disabilities and an IEP that outlined services to help her succeed in school. In late 2012, the IEP team met to formulate the student's 2013 IEP. The district scheduled a two-hour meeting. The girl's mother and her advocate (an education consultant) attended the meeting. At the beginning of the meeting, the consultant said she could only stay for the allotted two hours. After the two hours had passed, the consultant suggested reconvening at a later point to continue the discussion.

District officials agreed the IEP team would meet at a later date to make addenda and finalize the IEP. But the district also told the mother and the consultant that the IEP team would finish the IEP during the current meeting, as the current IEP was set to expire within a few days. The mother and the consultant left while the IEP team continued the meeting. Then the IEP team met with the mother and the consultant two more times – once in January and February – where changes were made to the 2013 IEP. The mother wasn't happy with the IEP. She filed a due process complaint, but the ALJ denied the majority of her requested relief. The mother thought the ALJ made the wrong call.

She sued, alleging the district denied T.P. a FAPE by "significantly imped[ing] parental participation in the IEP by continuing an IEP meeting" after she left. The court disagreed.

The mother participated in IEP in most of the meeting – with a consultant – on that specific day. Further, the court noted, **the mother and consultant participated in two follow-up meetings and helped make**

changes to the IEP. The evidence didn't support the claim that she was denied meaningful input in the IEP, so the ALJ's ruling was affirmed. *Pangerl v. Peoria Unified School Dist.*, No. CV-14-00836-PHX-JJT, 2017 WL 603834 (D. Ariz. 2/15/17).

◆ A federal court in Indiana rejected a former groundskeeper's disability discrimination claim. When school officials suspected that a groundskeeper had become a safety risk, they invoked the school's fit-for-duty policy.

It required workers to undergo fitness-for-duty exams when concerns were raised about their ability to safely perform job duties. The maintenance supervisor noticed the worker's physical condition had deteriorated so much that he had trouble performing basic – but essential – job duties, like climbing ladders and bending over to clean. The school required him to undergo a fitness-for-duty exam. It hired an independent physical therapist to observe him at work. The therapist determined the worker couldn't safely perform the essential functions of his groundskeeper job as it would put him at risk for severe back injuries. The school transferred the worker to a hall monitor position. But he never reported for the new job, and he was eventually fired. He filed a discrimination lawsuit, claiming a violation of the ADA.

The court granted the school's motion to dismiss. To win an ADA claim, he had to show he could perform the essential duties of the job with or without accommodation. He couldn't. The school offered him an accommodation in the form of the transfer, but he didn't show up for duty in his new role. Case dismissed. *McLane v. School City of Mishawaka*, No. 3:15CV119, 2017 WL 430843 (N.D. Ind. 2/1/17).

◆ New Jersey's highest court held a school board and a school nurse were entitled to immunity for a tort claim filed by the parents of a child who developed a lazy eye. The child participated in routine eye screening when she was in elementary school. The school nurse administered two visual acuity tests over two years. The child failed both tests, but the parents weren't notified until after the results of the second test came in. Then a private doctor diagnosed the child with amblyopia – more commonly known as a lazy eye. Nine years later, the parents filed a tort claim, alleging the defendants breached their duty of care by failing to timely notify them about the results of the first test. The case went all the way to the state supreme court. Under the New Jersey Tort Claims Act, public employees can be held liable for failing to make an examination — if the exam or the diagnosis is for treatment. But that wasn't the case here, the court noted, as **this visual acuity test was a routine screening — not a course of treatment**. Further, "exposing schools … to liability for failure to adequately communicate the results of a physical examination would have a chilling effect on public entities that administer public health exams," which would effectively undermine the overarching purpose of preventative exams — to foster public health and wellness, the court opined. Immunity was appropriate, so the claim failed. *Parsons v. Mullica Township Board of Educ.*, 142 A.3d 715 (N.J. 2016).

◆ An Illinois federal court determined a mother could not pursue IDEA claims because she didn't have legal custody of the child. The father had a state court order awarding him custody of the child. Per the noncustodial mother, the child had a history of behavioral issues at school and was diagnosed with ADHD. She said school staff never implemented a Section 504 plan to accommodate his ADHD and that the plan was inadequate. The mother wanted an IEP for her son. The school didn't create one. After two unsuccessful due process hearings, the mother sought judicial review, alleging she had a right to enforce her son's right to a FAPE. **The Seventh Circuit – which this court follows – has held that a biological parent's rights under the IDEA depend on the custody arrangement of the parents as defined by state law and applicable custody orders.**

Under Illinois state law, the custodial parent is the one who has the authority to make educational decisions – unless a custody order stipulates otherwise. This mother's custody order didn't.

In the Seventh Circuit's view, a noncustodial parent cannot upset choices committed to a custodial parent by state law. In this case, the father was the child's custodial parent, so the hearing officers correctly found the mother lacked educational decision-making authority and lacked standing to bring an IDEA due process complaint to challenge the district's decisions. *Smith v. Meeks*, 225 F.Supp.3d 696 (N.D. Ill. 2016).

◆ A New York federal court refused to grant an injunction allowing three Islamic children to attend public school without meeting state and local immunization requirements.

The father had four children in the district. The eldest child was properly immunized. The others were missing some – but not all – immunizations required by state and local law. The school notified the father in writing about the missing vaccinations. He submitted a request for a religious exemption.

But it was denied based on inconsistency – as the eldest child had been fully vaccinated and the younger three had been partially vaccinated. The school issued notices of exclusion that prohibited the three children from attending school until they were vaccinated. It explained the appeal process, but the father didn't file an appeal.

He sued, asking the court to order the district to let his kids attend school. He said refusing to let them violated their constitutional right to due process. But the court refused to grant the order, as the father wasn't likely to win his claim. First, he didn't appeal the decision, so he failed to exhaust the remedies. And moreover, **he claimed he needed a religious exemption for his Islamic faith, but he failed to provide evidence that showed Islam prohibited vaccinations and a logical explanation for the inconsistencies regarding his children's vaccinations**. The court denied the injunction request and ordered the clerk to close the case. *Watkins v. Dep't of Educ.*, No. 16-CV-2256 (WFK)(LB), 2016 WL 5867048 (E.D.N.Y. 10/7/16).

◆ The Eleventh Circuit affirmed a Florida ruling that held a school did not violate the IDEA by holding an IEP meeting without the parent. The student suffered a traumatic brain injury and was entitled to special ed services. For three months, the school unsuccessfully attempted to contact the student's mother to schedule an IEP meeting. Finally, it conducted the IEP meeting without the mother. She sued, alleging the school violated the IDEA by not including her in the IEP meeting. Under the IDEA, if a parent doesn't attend an IEP meeting, schools must keep records of the school's attempt to schedule the meetings, including detailed records of phone calls made and attempted – as well as the results of those calls; copies of letters and emails sent to parents – and any responses received from the parents; and detailed records of visits made to the parent's home or place of employment – and the results of those visits. The school's **documentation showed the mother either missed or refused to attend scheduled IEP meeting on four separate occasions** within three months, the court noted. No IDEA violation occurred, so the ruling to dismiss was affirmed. *A.L. v. Jackson County School Board*, 635 Fed.Appx. 774 (11th Cir. 2015).

◆ Protecting the privacy rights of a pregnant 15-year-old did not amount to insubordination, New Hampshire's highest court held. The student confessed to the guidance counselor that she wanted to get an abortion without telling her mother. **She refused to talk to her mom, saying she was worried about her safety.** Looking for advice, the counselor contacted an ACLU attorney, who said the student was entitled to privacy. The counselor urged the principal to contact the ACLU attorney. The principal refused. Two days later, the attorney reached out to the principal to discuss the issue. During that conversation, the principal disagreed with the attorney and told her that he was going to tell the student's mom. The attorney filed a petition for a temporary restraining order blocking the principal from contacting the student's mother about the pregnancy. The court granted the order.

Four months later, the counselor received a non-renewal notice due to insubordination and breach of student confidentiality. The local school board upheld the decision. The counselor sought review. Appeal reached the state board of education, which reversed the ruling and ordered the counselor to be reinstated. But it didn't address remedies like back pay.

The district appealed, and the counselor cross-appealed, saying she was entitled to remedies. The state supreme court found:

- district policy only required the counselor to discuss disagreements with the principal. She did, so she wasn't insubordinate, and
- talking to the attorney didn't violate the student's privacy rights, because a FERPA exception allows sharing info if it's necessary to "protect the health or safety of a student." The girl said she had safety concerns about telling her mom, so the exception applied.

The ruling to reinstate the guidance counselor was affirmed, and the case was remanded to determine whether she was entitled to remedies including back pay. *Appeal of Farmington School Dist.*, 138 A.3d 496 (N.H. 2016).

◆ An Ohio court refused to dismiss a claim that a middle school principal violated a student's privacy rights by contacting her healthcare provider to obtain her medical information. As the student was recovering from back surgery, the hospital prepared medical excuses and accommodation forms for the school. Her parents met with school officials to craft a Section 504 plan so the girl could return to school. After the meeting ended, the principal contacted the hospital without obtaining permission. At that time, he allegedly spoke to an administrative assistant at the hospital about the girl's medical condition and treatment, persuaded the administrative assistant to make changes to the hospital's paperwork and provided misleading information to the administrative assistant to induce the paperwork changes. The girl's parents sued the district, the board, the principal, the hospital and the administrative assistant. School defendants asked the court to dismiss the claims, saying they were entitled to immunity. The court dismissed the claims against the board and the district. But it refused to dismiss several claims against the principal, including improperly inducing the hospital employee to disclose nonpublic medical info, bad-faith conduct and invasion of privacy. The principal appealed, saying he was entitled to immunity. But **if proven true, the allegations could show the principal "may have attempted to supersede ... the protections to [the girl's] health and safety as duly advised by her own physician,"** the court explained. Further, determining whether conduct is "malicious, wanton, reckless or in bad faith are generally for jury to decide," the court held. The claims had to proceed. *Schaad v. Buckeye Valley Local School Dist. Board of Educ.*, No. 15-CAE 080063, 2016 WL 693546 (Ohio Ct. App. 2/12/16).

◆ A New Hampshire federal judge refused to order a district to provide a handler for a student's service dog. An eight-year-old nonverbal student suffered from seizures. His trained service dog alerted to seizures. The boy couldn't handle the dog for two reasons: He used a "gait belt" for balance, and he's nonverbal so he couldn't issue voice commands. Administrators told the boy's parents that they had to provide a handler for the dog. They sued and asked the court to order the school to pay an employee to handle the dog. To get an injunction, the parents had to show – among other things – that they were likely to win their claim. They didn't. The court noted that the dog needed to be handled all day long – rather than just for short intervals such as during short breaks to relieve itself. But the ADA specifically says that public schools aren't required to care for or supervise a service animal. The parents weren't likely to win their claim, so the injunction was denied. *Riley v. School Administrative Unit #23,* No. 15-cv-152-SM, 2016 WL 183525 (D.N.H. 1/14/16).

◆ School defendants were entitled to immunity in a lawsuit that claimed a search crossed the line, a New York court held. A 14-year-old girl was called to the nurse's office to meet with the nurse, the psychologist and the social worker – all employees of the district. Someone reported that the girl had been cutting herself. The nurse ordered the girl to lift her shirt to her bra and pull her pants down to her ankles. No indication of self-harm was found. Unconvinced, the social worker searched the girl's social media accounts to see if photos showed signs of cutting. None did. The girl's mom sued, alleging violations of the First Amendment. The school defendants asked the court to dismiss the claim, saying they were entitled to immunity. Not all searches are protected by the Fourth Amendment. Whether it applies depends on the nature of the search, the court said. For example, if the purpose of the search is to find evidence of a crime, then the Fourth Amendment applies. But **the law's fuzzy on whether searches for medical purposes are protected by the Fourth Amendment**. In this case, both searches were made for medical reasons – to see if the girl had injured herself, the court held. "Given the contradictory holdings from different circuits," the court concluded that it was not clearly established that a search for medical purposes would violate the student's Fourth Amendment rights. So immunity was appropriate, the court determined. *Masciotta v. Clarkson Cent. School Dist.*, 136 F.Supp.3d 527 (S.D.N.Y. 2015).

◆ A Pennsylvania federal judge refused to dismiss claims of a disabled student who was expelled. The student had ADD and Dysthymic Disorder. In 2011, he admitted he gave synthetic marijuana – known as "spice"– to a classmate. At the time, spice was still legal but considered contraband, as per school policy. He was recommended for expulsion. At the hearing, **the board found the student guilty of possessing contraband at school**. He was expelled for more than a year. His mom sued, alleging a laundry list of claims. The judge tossed the majority but allowed two to continue. His mother stated valid *prima facie* claims that the school violated:

- the student's right to due process and discriminated against him based on his disability by failing to consider it during the expulsion hearing, and
- Section 504 of the Rehabilitation Act by failing to provide the student with the same protection received by other non-disabled students because the board didn't consider his disability at the hearing.

Because questions existed, the court held the claims could proceed. *K.A. v. Abington Heights School Dist.*, 2015 WL 1812821, No. 3:12-CV-2486 (M.D. Pa. 4/20/15).

◆ A school's policies on service dogs violated Title II of the Americans with Disabilities Act (ADA), a Florida federal court held. A student had cerebral palsy and seizures. His mother got a trained service dog for him. The district said it would allow the animal at school if the mother:

- paid for liability insurance to cover the dog and listed the district as an insured party, as per district policy
- provided documentation for the dog's vaccinations as per district's policy, which exceeded state-law requirements, and
- provided a handler for the dog.

The mother sued, claiming the district's policies violated the ADA and its failure to provide reasonable accommodations was discriminatory. At trial, the court looked at the district's policy alongside the Title II regs regarding service dogs. The court found the liability insurance requirement violated the ADA because those costs were "over and above what other students" pay for school fees, the vaccination requirement was discriminatory as it "exceeded state law regarding the regulation of dogs permitted at school," and the requirement for a separate handler violated the ADA, as the regs clearly "permit tethering [to a wheel chair] as handling."

The district argued the student couldn't act as the dog's handler because he couldn't take the dog outside alone. It noted schools aren't responsible for care and supervision of service dogs. The court rejected that argument, explaining "care and supervision" entails much more – feeding, training, grooming – than just relief breaks. **A reasonable accommodation would be to have a staffer go outside with the student and the dog**, the court explained. So the school had to allow the dog – and drop the tacked-on requirements. *Alboniga v. School Board of Broward County Florida*, No. 14-CIV-60085-BLOOM/Valle, 2015 WL 541751 (S.D. Fla. 2/10/15).

◆ Indiana's highest court ruled a school might've concealed info about a student death, so her parents' suit could go forward. The student had Down syndrome and had trouble eating. Her dining plan required the school to monitor her food intake and cut up her food. In 2009, the student choked after a paraprofessional failed to cut up her food. No one attempted CPR or the Heimlich maneuver. The nurse arrived 10 minutes later but was unable to clear the student's airway. That's when 911 was called. The student died. The cafeteria supervisor told staffers they'd be fired if they spoke to anyone about the incident. Months later, a cafeteria worker told the student's parents "things were not done properly." They filed a notice of tort claim in January 2010 and filed suit six months later. The state asked for judgment, saying the parents didn't file the notice of tort claim within 180 days. The case went to the state supreme court. State law generally bars tort claims that aren't filed within 180 days. But an exception applies if the defendant:

- "has actual knowledge of a wrongful act and intentionally concealed it from the plaintiff," or
- took action that was "calculated to prevent inquiry or to mislead."

The court held **a reasonable jury could find the school covered up info about the student's death**. The exception applied, so the case was remanded. *Lyons v. Richmond Community School Corporation*, (Ind. 2014).

◆ A 13-year-old student was admitted to a hospital for treatment of a MRSA infection. Over a period of 47 days, the student received treatment that included nine surgeries. The student's mother spoke to the principal of the school and other school officials about the possibility of home-schooling for the student. The mother was told that no teacher would go to the student's home for homeschooling because the student had MRSA. School officials also told the mother that the student's sister and two cousins, who attended a different school, needed to be picked up from school at once because they had been in close contact with the infected student. The school officials further informed the mother that none of the children would be permitted to return to school until they had received a "clean bill of health from a physician." The sister and cousins did not have any symptoms of MRSA, and they did not have a doctor. The student's doctor provided his school with informational literature about MRSA, including information indicating that children should not be excluded from school due to MRSA infection. School officials continued to ban the student, his sister and his cousins from school, and they were not provided any homeschooling services. The children's mothers sued the schools' principals and the district superintendent, claiming they violated the students' constitutional rights to due process and equal protection. The court denied a defense motion to dismiss the case. **Some process is required before a child is excluded from school, and the parents alleged that school officials banned their children from school without properly investigating whether allowing them to attend would pose an unreasonable risk of harm.** As to the substantive due process claims, which were based on the allegation that the school officials abused their power by arbitrarily banning the students from school, the court said the allegations supported an inference that the officials acted arbitrarily and irrationally. The equal protection claims, which were based on the charge that other students with contagious diseases were not banned from school, were not dismissed. It was too soon in the case to conclude that the parents would be unable to show that other students with contagious diseases were allowed to stay in school and that school officials lacked a good reason to make the distinction. *King-Cowser v. School Dist. 149*, No. 07 C 6551, 2008 WL 4104354 (N.D. Ill. 8/25/08).

LIST OF ONLINE FORMS

The Center for Education & Employment Law® is committed to making smart decisions to protect the environment and manage our environmental impact responsibly. As part of our effort to go green and improve usability, we've added our entire Forms Library to our website.

Visit *www.SchoolSafetyAndSecurityAlert.com* and search any of the titles below to download a form. And using the downloaded format means it's easier than ever to customize forms to your specific needs.

Forms

1. After a Student Suicide: Crisis Response Team Leader's Checklist
2. Announcement of Student Death Due to Accident or Illness
3. Announcement of Student Suicide
4. Authorization to Release Children in Emergency
5. Behavior Contract/Prom Permission Slip
6. Bomb Threat Procedures and Checklist
7. Bus Transportation Accident Response
8. Checklist: Reunification After a Crisis
9. Checklist: Steps to Take Within 24 Hours of a Nonfatal Food Allergy Reaction
10. Checklist of Characteristics of Youth Who Have Caused School-Associated Violent Deaths
11. Concussion Quiz for Coaches, Athletes and Parents
12. Crisis Procedure Checklist
13. Crisis Team Member List
14. Dealing With Suicidal Students
15. Emergency Phone Numbers
16. FEMA's Earthquake Preparedness Checklist
17. Food Allergy Policy Checklist
18. Food Allergy Response: Documentation Checklist
19. Gas Leak Response
20. Gender Support Plan
21. Gender Transition Plan
22. Harassment/Bullying Incident Report Form
23. Hazard Assessment Checklist: Baseball, Soccer. Lacrosse, Field Hockey

24. Hazard Assessment Checklist: Kitchen/Cafeteria
25. Hazard Assessment Checklist: Science Laboratory
26. Hazardous Spill Response
27. Identifying Potential Hazards Along Evacuation Routes Checklist
28. Initial Announcement of Crisis Event
29. Intruder Response
30. Mental Health Help: When Students Face Death
31. Mentor Acceptance Letter
32. Mentor Contract
33. Mentor Contract and Release Information
34. Mentor Rejection Letter
35. Model Policy for Body Cams
36. Parent/Guardian Mentoring Contract
37. Parent Information Sheet – Post Disaster
38. Parent Letter: Unexpected Student Death
39. Parent Letter Regarding Asthma
40. Parent Letter Regarding Child with Allergy
41. Parent Letter Regarding Flu
42. Parent Letter Regarding Flu Prevention
43. Parent Letter Regarding Weapon at School
44. Parental Consent Form for Mercury Testing
45. Playground Safety Checklist
46. Playground Safety Checklist for Kids
47. Physician Letter Regarding Asthma
48. Prevention Checklist: Involving Students
49. Priorities for a Food Allergy Management and Prevention Plan Checklist
50. Protocol for Responding to Student Suicide Attempt
51. Public Information Release
52. Quiz: How Asthma-Friendly Is Your School?
53. Quiz: 10 Playground Safety Questions
54. Restraint and Seclusion: 15 Principles
55. Sample Diabetes Management Plan
56. Sample Letter: Sudden Student Death
57. Sample Letter Home Following Crisis Event
58. Sample Letter to Parents About Student Vaccinations

59. Sample Letter to Parents Regarding Sexting
60. Sample Notice to Parents Regarding Lockdown Drill
61. Sample Parent Letter: Notice of Bus Accident
62. Sample Parent Letter: Pre-Incident
63. Sample Parent Letter Following Weapons Incident
64. Sample Response to Anaphylactic Shock
65. Sample Statement to the Media: School Bus Accident
66. Sample Statement to the Media: School Violence
67. Sample Suicide Notification Letter: When Family Requests That Cause of Death Remains Undisclosed
68. School Violence Prevention and Intervention Checklist
69. Seclusion/Restraint Documentation
70. Situations Involving Severe Weather
71. Situations Involving Weapons
72. Special Assistance for Evacuation
73. Staff Development Checklist
74. Staff Skills Inventory
75. Staff Skills Survey Form
76. Student Knife Contract
77. Student Pledge for iPad Use
78. Substitute Teacher Letter Regarding Student With Allergy
79. Suicide Notification Statement for Students
80. Thank You Letter – Faculty/Staff
81. Threats and Hazards Types and Examples
82. Threat Assessment Checklist: Student Information
83. Violent Situations
84. Vulnerability Hazard Assessment Checklist: Art, Music and Dance Rooms
85. Vulnerability Hazard Assessment Checklist: Athletic Facilities
86. Vulnerability Hazard Assessment Checklist: Auditoriums, Theaters and Performing Arts Centers
87. Vulnerability Hazard Assessment Checklist: Building Interior
88. Vulnerability Hazard Assessment Checklist: Buses and Parking
89. Vulnerability Hazard Assessment Checklist: Classrooms
90. Vulnerability Hazard Assessment Checklist: Communications Systems

91. Vulnerability Hazard Assessment Checklist: Emergency Operations Plans
92. Vulnerability Hazard Assessment Checklist: Grounds and Building Exterior
93. Vulnerability Hazard Assessment Checklist: Health Practices and Health Services Centers
94. Vulnerability Hazard Assessment Checklist: Instructional Facility
95. Vulnerability Hazard Assessment Checklist: Library/Media Center
96. Vulnerability Hazard Assessment Checklist: Play and Outdoor Recreation Areas
97. Vulnerability Hazard Assessment Checklist: School Climate and Culture
98. Vulnerability Hazard Assessment Checklist: Website
99. Vulnerability Hazard Assessment Checklist: Welding, Woodworking, Agricultural and Shop Areas
100. What are "Education Records?"
101. Youth Pledge: Walking and Bicycling
102. 911 Script: Cheerleader Injury

THE JUDICIAL SYSTEM

To allow you to determine the relative importance of a judicial decision, the cases included in ***Keeping Your School Safe & Secure: A Practical Guide*** identify the particular court from which a decision has been issued. For example, a case decided by a state's highest court generally will be of greater significance than a state intermediate court case. Hence a basic knowledge of the structure of our judicial system is important to an understanding of school law.

Almost all the reports in this volume are taken from appellate court decisions. Although most education law decisions occur at trial court and administrative levels, appellate court decisions have the effect of binding lower courts and administrators so that appellate court decisions have the effect of law within their court systems.

State and federal court systems generally function independently of each other. Each court system applies its own law according to statutes and the determinations of its highest court. However, judges at all levels often consider opinions from other court systems to settle issues which are new or arise under unique fact situations. Similarly, lawyers look at the opinions of many courts to locate authority which supports their clients' cases.

Once a lawsuit is filed in a particular court system, that system generally retains the matter until its conclusion. Unsuccessful parties at the administrative or trial court level generally have the right to appeal unfavorable determinations of law to appellate courts within the system. When federal law issues or constitutional grounds are present, lawsuits may be appropriately filed in the federal court system. In those cases, the lawsuit is filed initially in the federal district court for that area.

On rare occasions, the U.S. Supreme Court considers appeals from the highest courts of the states if a distinct federal question exists and at least four justices agree on the question's importance. The federal courts occasionally send cases to state courts for application of state law. These situations are infrequent and, in general, the state and federal court systems should be considered separate from each other.

The most common system, used by nearly all states and also the federal judiciary, is as follows: a legal action is commenced in district court (sometimes called trial court, county court, common pleas court or superior court) where a decision is initially reached. The case may then be appealed to the court of appeals (or appellate court), and, in turn, this decision may be appealed to the supreme court.

Several states, however, do not have a court of appeals; lower court decisions are appealed directly to the state's supreme court. Additionally, some states have labeled their courts in a nonstandard fashion.

In Maryland, the highest state court is called the Court of Appeals. In the state of New York, the trial court is called the Supreme Court. Decisions of this court may be appealed to the Supreme Court, Appellate Division. The highest court in New York is the Court of Appeals. Pennsylvania has perhaps the most complex court system. The lowest state court is the Court of Common Pleas. Depending on the circumstances of the case, appeals may be taken to either the Commonwealth Court or the Superior Court. In certain instances the Commonwealth Court functions as a trial court as well as an appellate court. The Superior Court, however, is strictly an intermediate appellate court. The highest court in Pennsylvania is the Supreme Court.

While supreme court decisions are generally regarded as the last word in legal matters, it is important to remember that trial and appeals court decisions also create important legal precedents. For the hierarchy of typical state and federal court systems, please see the diagram below.

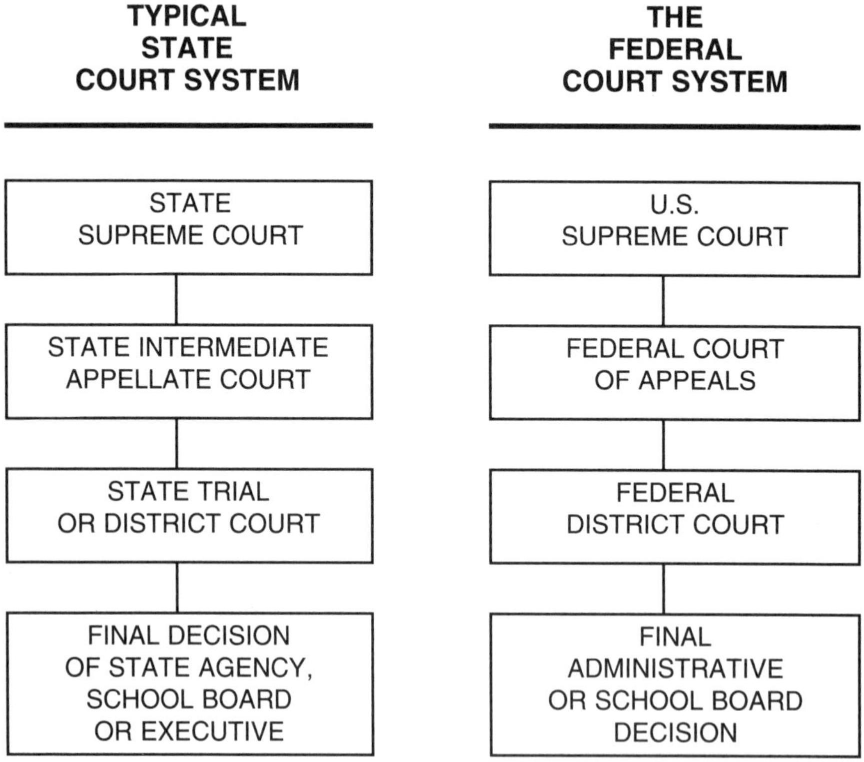

Federal courts of appeals hear appeals from the district courts which are located in their circuits. Below is a list of states matched to the federal circuits in which they are located.

First Circuit	—	Maine, Massachusetts, New Hampshire, Puerto Rico, Rhode Island
Second Circuit	—	Connecticut, New York, Vermont
Third Circuit	—	Delaware, New Jersey, Pennsylvania, Virgin Islands
Fourth Circuit	—	Maryland, North Carolina, South Carolina, Virginia, West Virginia
Fifth Circuit	—	Louisiana, Mississippi, Texas
Sixth Circuit	—	Ohio, Kentucky, Michigan, Tennessee
Seventh Circuit	—	Illinois, Indiana, Wisconsin
Eighth Circuit	—	Arkansas, Iowa, Minnesota, Missouri, Nebraska, North Dakota, South Dakota
Ninth Circuit	—	Alaska, Arizona, California, Guam, Hawaii, Idaho, Montana, Nevada, Northern Mariana Islands, Oregon, Washington
Tenth Circuit	—	Colorado, Kansas, Oklahoma, New Mexico, Utah, Wyoming
Eleventh Circuit	—	Alabama, Florida, Georgia
District of Columbia Circuit	-	Hears cases from the U.S. District Court for the District of Columbia
Federal Circuit Appeals	—	Sitting in Washington, D.C., the U.S. Court of Federal Circuit, hears patent and trade appeals and certain appeals on claims brought against the federal government and its agencies.

HOW TO READ A CASE CITATION

Generally, court decisions can be located in case reporters at law school or governmental law libraries. Some cases can also be located on the Internet through legal websites or official court websites.

Each case summary contains the citation, or legal reference, to the full text of the case. The diagram below illustrates how to read a case citation.

case name (parties) ↘ — case reporter name and series ↓ — court location ↙

Scott v. Waits, 703 S.E.2d 419 (Ga. Ct. App. 2010).

↗ volume number — ↑ first page — ↑ year of decision

Some cases may have two or three reporter names such as U.S. Supreme Court cases and cases reported in regional case reporters as well as state case reporters. For example, a U.S. Supreme Court case usually contains three case reporter citations.

first reporter — third reporter

Meritor Savings Bank v. Vinson, 477 U.S. 57, 106 S.Ct. 2399, 91 L.Ed.2d 49 (1986).

second reporter

The citations are still read in the same manner as if only one citation has been listed.

Occasionally, a case may contain a citation which does not reference a case reporter. For example, a citation may contain a reference such as:

case name ↓ — year of decision ↘ — first page ↓ — date ↓

Fenrich v. The Blake School, No. A17-0063, 2017 WL 3863849 (Minn. Ct. App. 9/5/17).

↗ court file number — ↑ WESTLAW[1] — ↑ court location

The court file number indicates the specific number assigned to a case by the particular court system deciding the case. In our example, the Minnesota Court

[1]WESTLAW® is a computerized database of court cases available for a fee.

of Appeals has assigned the case of *Fenrich v. The Blake School* the case number of "No. A17-0063" which will serve as the reference number for the case and any matter relating to the case. Locating a case on the Internet generally requires either the case name and date of the decision, and/or the court file number.

Below, we have listed the full names of the regional reporters. As mentioned previously, many states have individual state reporters. The names of those reporters may be obtained from a reference law librarian.

P. **Pacific Reporter**
Alaska, Arizona, California, Colorado, Hawaii, Idaho, Kansas, Montana, Nevada, New Mexico, Oklahoma, Oregon, Utah, Washington, Wyoming

A. **Atlantic Reporter**
Connecticut, Delaware, District of Columbia, Maine, Maryland, New Hampshire, New Jersey, Pennsylvania, Rhode Island, Vermont

N.E. **Northeastern Reporter**
Illinois, Indiana, Massachusetts, New York, Ohio

N.W. **Northwestern Reporter**
Iowa, Michigan, Minnesota, Nebraska, North Dakota, South Dakota, Wisconsin

So. **Southern Reporter**
Alabama, Florida, Louisiana, Mississippi

S.E. **Southeastern Reporter**
Georgia, North Carolina, South Carolina, Virginia, West Virginia

S.W. **Southwestern Reporter**
Arkansas, Kentucky, Missouri, Tennessee, Texas

F. **Federal Reporter**
Decisions from the thirteen federal courts of appeals.

F.Supp. **Federal Supplement**
Decisions from federal district courts within the thirteen federal judicial circuits. *See The Judicial System, p. 575* for specific circuits.

Fed.Appx. **Federal Appendix**
Contains unpublished decisions of the U.S. Circuit Courts of Appeal.

U.S. **United States Reports**
S.Ct. **Supreme Court Reporter** > U.S. Supreme Court Decisions
L.Ed. **Lawyers' Edition**

GLOSSARY

Americans with Disabilities Act (ADA) - The ADA is a federal law that bars discrimination on the basis of disability in several contexts, including employment, access to programs and services provided by public entities, and access to places of public accommodation.

Assumption of Risk - A defense to a claim of negligence, in which the defendant asserts that the injured plaintiff is barred from recovery because he knowingly and voluntarily exposed himself to the hazard that caused his injury.

Biometrics - Methods and techniques used to identify individuals on the basis of a behavioral or physical characteristic or trait.

Class Action Suit - Federal Rule of Civil Procedure 23 allows members of a class to sue as representatives on behalf of the whole class provided that the class is so large that joinder of all parties is impractical, there are questions of law or fact common to the class, the claims or defenses of the representatives are typical of the claims or defenses of the class, and the representative parties will adequately protect the interests of the class. In addition, there must be some danger of inconsistent verdicts or adjudications if the class action were prosecuted as separate actions. Most states also allow class actions under the same or similar circumstances.

Clery Act - see Jeanne Clery Disclosure of Campus Security Policy and Campus Crime Statistics Act.

Crime Prevention Through Environmental Design (CPTED) - An approach to increasing safety in a variety of contexts, including the school context, that recognizes the important role that the design of the built environment can play in reducing the risk of criminal activity.

Cyberbullying - Student bullying that is perpetrated via the Internet, mobile phone or other electronic technology.

Due Process Clause - The clauses of the Fifth and Fourteenth Amendments to the Constitution which guarantee the citizens of the United States "due process of law" (see below). The Fifth Amendment's Due Process Clause applies to the federal government, and the Fourteenth Amendment's Due Process Clause applies to the states.

Due Process of Law - The idea of "fair play" in the government's application of law to its citizens, guaranteed by the Fifth and Fourteenth Amendments. Substantive due process is just plain *fairness*, and procedural due process is accorded when the government utilizes adequate procedural safeguards for the protection of an individual's liberty or property interests.

Enjoin - see Injunction.

Equal Protection Clause - The clause of the Fourteenth Amendment which prohibits a state from denying any person within its jurisdiction equal protection of its laws. Also, the Due Process Clause of the Fifth Amendment which pertains to the federal government. This has been interpreted by the Supreme Court to grant equal protection even though there is no explicit grant in the Constitution.

Establishment Clause - The clause of the First Amendment which prohibits Congress from making "any law respecting an establishment of religion." This clause has been interpreted as creating a "wall of separation" between church and state. The test frequently used to determine whether government action violates the Establishment Clause, referred to as the *Lemon* test, asks whether the action has a secular purpose, whether its primary effect promotes or inhibits religion, and whether it requires excessive entanglement between church and state.

Exclusionary Rule - A rule that allows criminal suspects to have excluded from consideration any evidence that is seized in violation of the Fourth Amendment.

42 U.S.C. §§ 1981, 1983 - Section 1983 of the federal Civil Rights Act prohibits any person acting under color of state law from depriving any other person of rights protected by the Constitution or by federal laws. A vast majority of lawsuits claiming constitutional violations are brought under § 1983. Section 1981 provides that all persons enjoy the same right to make and enforce contracts as "white citizens." Section 1981 applies to employment contracts. Further, unlike § 1983, § 1981 applies even to private actors. It is not limited to those acting under color of state law. These sections do not apply to the federal government, though the government may be sued directly under the Constitution for any violations.

Family Educational Rights and Privacy Act (FERPA) - A federal law that protects the privacy of student education records.

Fourth Amendment - Federal constitutional amendment that protects individuals from unreasonable searches and seizures.

Free Exercise Clause - The clause of the First Amendment which prohibits Congress from interfering with citizens' rights to the free exercise of their religion. Through the Fourteenth Amendment, it has also been made applicable to the states and their sub-entities. The Supreme Court has held that laws of general applicability which have an incidental effect on persons' free exercise rights are not violative of the Free Exercise Clause.

Government Accountability Office (GAO) - A federal agency that acts as the investigative arm of Congress. The GAO examines matters relating to the receipt and payment of public funds.

H1N1 Flu - Also referred to as swine flu based on early indications that it resembled influenza viruses that normally occur in pigs, 2009 H1N1 is an influenza virus that was first detected in humans in the United States in April 2009. In June 2009, the World Health Organization (WHO) declared that a pandemic of this flu had begun. Typically, those who contracted the virus recovered without the need for specialized medical treatment. But certain people, including people age 65 or older, people younger than five, pregnant women, and people with certain preexisting medical conditions, were at high risk of developing severe complications. In August 2010, the WHO announced that the virus had "largely run its course" but also noted the likelihood of continued localized outbreaks.

Incorporation Doctrine - By its own terms, the Bill of Rights applies only to the federal government. The Incorporation Doctrine states that the Fourteenth Amendment makes the Bill of Rights applicable to the states.

Individualized Educational Program (IEP) - The IEP is designed to give children with disabilities a free, appropriate education. It is updated annually, with the participation of the child's parents or guardian.

Individuals with Disabilities Education Act (IDEA) - Also known as the Education of the Handicapped Act (EHA), the Education for All Handicapped Children Act (EAHCA), and the Handicapped Children's Protection Act (HPCA). Originally enacted as the EHA, the IDEA is the federal legislation which provides for the free, appropriate education of all children with disabilities.

Injunction - An equitable remedy (see Remedies) wherein a court orders a party to do or refrain from doing some particular action.

Jeanne Clery Disclosure of Campus Security Policy and Campus Crime Statistics Act - A federal law requiring colleges and universities to disclose information regarding crime on and around campus.

Jurisdiction - The power of a court to determine cases and controversies. The Supreme Court's jurisdiction extends to cases arising under the

Constitution and under federal law. Federal courts have the power to hear cases where there is diversity of citizenship or where a federal question is involved.

***Miranda* Warning** - Warning that police must provide to an individual in police custody before proceeding with questioning.

MRSA - MRSA, which stands for Methicillin-resistant staphylococcus aureus, is a type of staph bacteria that is resistant to certain antibiotics.

National Incident Management System (NIMS) - a system developed by the Secretary of Homeland Security to provide a national template that helps government, private, and nongovernmental organizations effectively coordinate efforts during crisis events.

Negligence per se - Negligence on its face. Usually, the violation of an ordinance or statute will be treated as negligence per se because no careful person would have been guilty of it.

Overbroad - A government action is overbroad if, in an attempt to alleviate a specific evil, it impermissibly prohibits or chills a protected action. For example, a law attempting to deal with street litter by prohibiting the distribution of leaflets or handbills could be challenged as overbroad.

Rehabilitation Act - Section 504 of the Rehabilitation Act prohibits employers who receive federal financial assistance from discriminating against otherwise qualified individuals solely on the basis of disability.

Remand - The act of an appellate court in returning a case to the court from which it came for further action.

Remedies - There are two general categories of remedies, or relief: legal remedies, which consist of money damages, and equitable remedies, which consist of a court mandate that a specific action be prohibited or required. For example, a claim for compensatory and punitive damages seeks a legal remedy; a claim for an injunction seeks an equitable remedy. Equitable remedies are generally unavailable unless legal remedies are inadequate to address the harm.

Res Judicata - The judicial notion that a claim or action may not be tried twice or re-litigated, or that all causes of action arising out of the same set of operative facts should be tried at one time. Also known as claim preclusion.

Safe and Drug-Free Schools and Communities Act - Federal law supporting programs that prevent violence in and around schools, prevent illegal alcohol, tobacco and drug use, and foster a safe and drug-free school environment.

Section 1981 & Section 1983 - see 42 U.S.C. §§ 1981, 1983.

Sheltering-in-place - A planned response to the danger presented by the possible release of environmental contaminants that calls for students and personnel to take refuge in a safe interior location.

Sovereign Immunity - The idea that the government cannot be sued without its consent. It stems from the English notion that the "King can do no wrong." This immunity from suit has been abrogated in most states and by the federal government through legislative acts known as "tort claims acts."

Special Relationship Doctrine - A legal doctrine by which a state defendant can be held liable for a person's injury if the state defendant took actions that created a legal duty to protect the person from injury.

Standing - The judicial doctrine which states that in order to maintain a lawsuit a party must have some real interest at stake in the outcome of the trial.

State-Created Danger Doctrine - A legal doctrine by which a state defendant can be held liable for a person's injury if the state's actions either created or significantly increased the danger that caused the injury.

Statute of Limitations - A statute of limitation provides the time period in which a specific cause of action may be brought.

Swine Flu - see H1N1 flu.

Summary Judgment - Also referred to as pretrial judgment. Similar to a dismissal. Where there is no genuine issue as to any material fact and all that remains is a question of law, a judge can rule in favor of one party or the other. In general, summary judgment is used to dispose of claims which do not support a legally recognized claim.

Supremacy Clause - Clause in Article VI of the Constitution which states that federal legislation is the supreme law of the land.

Title IX - Federal law barring discrimination on the basis of sex under any educational program or activity that receives federal financial assistance.

Title VI - A part of the Civil Rights Act of 1964 that prohibits discrimination based on race, color or national origin in programs or activities that receive federal financial assistance.

Title VII of the Civil Rights Act of 1964 (Title VII) - Title VII prohibits discrimination in employment based upon race, color, sex, national origin, or religion. It applies to any employer having fifteen or more employees. Under Title VII, where an employer intentionally discriminates, employees may obtain money damages unless the claim is for race discrimination. For those claims, monetary relief is available under 42 U.S.C. § 1981.

Vacate - The act of annulling the judgment of a court either by an appellate court or by the court itself. The Supreme Court will generally vacate a lower court's judgment without deciding the case itself, and remand the case to the lower court for further consideration in light of some recent controlling decision.

Writ of Certiorari - The device used by the Supreme Court to transfer cases from the appellate court's docket to its own. Since the Supreme Court's appellate jurisdiction is largely discretionary, it need only issue such a writ when it desires to rule in the case.

INDEX